Military Self-Interest in Accountability for Core International Crimes

Morten Bergsmo and SONG Tianying (editors)

Second Edition

2018
Torkel Opsahl Academic EPublisher
Brussels

This and other publications in TOAEP's *FICHL Publication Series* may be openly accessed and downloaded through the web site http://www.toaep.org/ which uses Persistent URLs for all publications it makes available (such PURLs will not be changed). This publication was first published on 29 May 2015. The Second Edition was published on 21 April 2018.

© **Torkel Opsahl Academic EPublisher, 2018**

ISBNs: 978-82-8348-098-6 (print) and 978-82-8348-099-3 (e-book).

Dedicated to those in armed forces who articulate military rationales
for accountability for core international crimes

EDITORS' PREFACE TO THE SECOND EDITION

The second edition of this anthology is expanded with a new Chapter 17 by Professor René Provost on "Accountability for International Crimes with Insurgent Groups". Our Chapter 1 has been modified.

We thank again the authors and TOAEP editors, Gareth Richards, Manek Minhas and CHAN Ho Shing Icarus, for their contributions.

Morten Bergsmo and SONG Tianying

Editors' Preface to the First Edition

This anthology contains papers linked to the conference 'The Self-Interest of Armed Forces in Accountability for their Members for Core International Crimes' held at Hoover Institution of Stanford University on 27 November 2012. The seminar was co-organized by the Centre for International Law Research and Policy ('CILRAP'), Stanford University, and UC Berkeley War Crimes Studies Center. The seminar and anthology are parts of a CILRAP research project funded by the Royal Norwegian Ministry of Foreign Affairs.

As co-editors we would like to thank the Ministry as well as Stanford University, in particular Richard Saller and Richard Sousa. We also place on record our appreciation to the authors for their work and to the editorial team of the Torkel Opsahl Academic EPublisher designated for this book: Pauline Brosch, Gareth Richards, Nikolaus Scheffel, Alf Butenschøn Skre, Moritz Thörner and Angela Tritto.

Morten Bergsmo and SONG Tianying

PREFACE

The contributions in this volume address an issue that has occupied historians since the beginning of European historiography – that is, the relation of moral values to rational self-interest in war. The classic formulation of the opposition of rational self-interest to moral principles was laid out in Thucydides's famous Melian dialogue in Book Five (chapters 85–116) of his great classic, *The History of the Peloponnesian War*.

The context for this episode was the aggressive expansion of the Athenian empire during the Peloponnesian War between coalitions led by Athens and by Sparta. In 416–15 BCE the Athenians moved to subjugate the small island of Melos as part of their tribute-paying empire. Melos had originated as a Spartan colony and tried to maintain a position of freedom and neutrality between Sparta and Athens. When the Athenians demanded submission, the Melians refused. Thucydides used this setting to imagine a debate between the Athenians and the Melians on the theme of power and justice. As the Melians realised, the stakes could not have been higher: if they resisted the Athenians and lost, they would pay with their lives by way of enslavement or slaughter.

Thucydides has the Athenians begin the debate with a brusque dismissal of "specious pretences" based on just desserts for past actions, concluding that "when these matters are discussed by practical people, the standard of justice depends on the equality of power to compel. *In fact, the strong do what they have the power to do and the weak accept what they must*". (This is perhaps the most famous sentence of the whole history). The Athenians' stark realism asserts that there is no place for a framework of justice where the powers are unequal.

Forced to make their argument on the basis of pragmatic self-interest, the Melians respond that everyone – even the powerful Athenians – have an interest in upholding the value of justice, because at some point in the future the tables will be turned and the Athenians will need to appeal to principles of justice. If the Athenians wield brutal power, the Melians predict, "your fall will be a signal for the heaviest vengeance and an example for the world to meditate upon". The Athenians brush off this argument, saying that they will deal with this contingency if it arises.

The Melians then try a different appeal to the self-interest of the Athenians with the claim that unjust behaviour on their part will drive other neutral states to become enemies. The Athenians counter that if they accede to the Melian request to maintain neutrality, they will be seen to be weak. They are better off through a show of force, intimidating others to bow to their power.

Unable to convince the Athenians on the basis of their self-interest, the Melians finally revert to the position that their honour requires them to fight for their freedom and to avoid base cowardice. As far as the Athenians are concerned, honour and shame are foolish considerations when the powers in a conflict are so uneven and self-preservation is at stake.

In the end, the Melians refused to submit to the Athenians and suffered the consequences when their Spartan allies did not come to their rescue. The Athenians besieged their city, forcing an unconditional surrender by the Melians. "The Athenians put to death all the men of military age, and sold the women and children as slaves".

Eleven years later the Spartans got the upper hand over the Athenians, besieged the city and starved them into submission. The horrific suffering of the Athenians amounted to a grim sort of poetic justice, which the Melians predicted but did not live to relish. As an ancient historian, I am heartened to see that the contributions of this volume do not accept the bleak claim of the Athenians that "might makes right irrelevant", and explore the reasons why a framework of humanitarian justice really can serve all sides, the powerful and the weak alike, as the Melians hoped.

Richard Saller
Kleinheinz Family Professor of European Studies
Vernon R. and Lysbeth Warren Anderson Dean
School of Humanities and Sciences
Stanford University

FOREWORD BY ANDREW T. CAYLEY

This year is the 20th anniversary of the tragic events which took place in and around Srebrenica and Žepa in eastern Bosnia-Herzegovina in July 1995. Following an intense military assault by Bosnian Serb Forces on the United Nations-protected areas of Srebrenica and Žepa, in July 1995, Bosnian Muslims fled Srebrenica to the nearby town of Potočari, where the women, children, and the elderly were loaded onto packed buses and transported away from their homes in Eastern Bosnia. Thousands of males were detained in horrific conditions and subsequently summarily executed by Bosnian Serb forces. In 1999 I was part of the trial team for the first international prosecution for these events at the International Criminal Tribunal for the former Yugoslavia ('ICTY'). I recall my profound shock at the systematic and cold brutality of an organised so-called "professional armed force". I had served in the armed forces of my own country, the United Kingdom, and I simply could not imagine how officers and soldiers of any armed force, in the last ten years of the 20th century, could meticulously plan and then execute the extinction of forty thousand people.

Srebrenica naturally falls at the extreme end of the spectrum of military offending. Events such as these are rare. But it should be recalled that one of the reasons the first prosecution, in respect of Srebrenica, had to take place at the ICTY was because in 1999 the Bosnian Serb authorities simply could not recognise that these events had ever taken place at all. To this day, after multiple prosecutions and convictions, the Bosnian Serb authorities, while now at least acknowledging the events in Srebrenica, still seek to minimise the scale of them.

While in the late 1990s the ICTY was struggling with the investigation and prosecution of events at Srebrenica, the work of the *ad hoc* tribunals was generally having a strong catalytic effect on the formation of a permanent international criminal court. It became clear, first through the efforts of the ICTY and the International Criminal Tribunal for Rwanda, that legal accountability for crimes committed in armed conflict was more than an idealistic aspiration. With the formation of the permanent International Criminal Court ('ICC'), those states signing and ratifying the ICC Statute were obliged to incorporate its provisions into domestic law. In the United Kingdom, for example, both military and civilian courts have jurisdiction over the crimes contained in the ICC Statute by virtue of domestic legislation.

Shocking events like those at Srebrenica and the astonishing legal developments of the last 20 years have compelled armed forces, around the globe, to re-examine their compliance with international humanitarian law and to re-educate themselves on the now much more refined and comprehensive forms of criminal culpability available for operational offending. As a result of all these developments, military operations carry far more risk then they did 20 years ago. Most modern armed forces will never engage in events like those which took place at Srebrenica in 1995. Even so, the use of lethal force, collateral damage and injury, the treatment of civilians and prisoners of war are now subject to a level of legal scrutiny not imaginable two decades ago. And Srebrenica is one of the many reasons why law is so embedded in military campaigns today. Military planners now routinely consider the legal implications of operations. Winning the hearts and minds of local populations, where troops are deployed, depends on many factors, but disciplined behaviour is certainly one of them. Counter-insurgency operations against non-state actors, who are most unlikely to comply with the laws of armed conflict, present even more challenges for armed forces signed up and bound by the laws of war. It seems the future will be dominated fighting non-state actors.

Compliance with international norms of humanitarian law and human rights law, by a state and its armed forces, is to a very great extent a measure of the civilisation of that society. Srebrenica had catastrophic consequences for the victims and their families. But the failure of the perpetrators of what happened at Srebrenica, to be judged by their own military and civilian courts, has left a terrible stain on their national reputation.

Reviews of military operations to ensure their compliance with the law can be a painful, expensive and lengthy process. But because of the interests at stake it has to be done. Where individuals have committed disciplinary or criminal offences during military operations, they are much more likely to face a court today than they were 20 years ago. Covering up military offending today is no longer an option, bearing in mind most states' domestic obligations, in respect of core international crimes, and the ever-watchful eye of the ICC, charged with encouraging member states themselves to carry out genuine investigations and prosecutions of crimes covered by the ICC Statute.

A conference was held at Stanford on 27 November 2012 to discuss in great detail the interests at stake, for armed forces, in ensuring the prosecution of core international crimes. Those discussions have now been encapsulated in this excellent publication. It will be an admirable guide for military lawyers and military commanders, shape operational and prosecution policy, and assist in the development of adequate training regimes.

A generation has almost come and gone since an army planned and executed the extermination of an entire society at Srebrenica. These events will and should never be forgotten. They will continue to send a powerful message from the past to the future and provide a bleak and grim reminder of humankind's capacity to revert to acts of brutality under the stresses of conflict. If nothing else, the long roll of the dead of Srebrenica will remain a shocking warning, to even the most well-ordered and -regulated armed forces, of the necessity for accountability for actions on operations and the strict legal requirements of adequate training and planning. I commend this book to you and the laudable goals it seeks to achieve.

Andrew T. Cayley CMG QC
Director Service Prosecutions, United Kingdom

FOREWORD BY WILLIAM K. LIETZAU

Recent decades have witnessed substantial efforts to move us from an epoch characterised by horrific crimes and impunity to one of human rights and accountability. At the very least, this book and the discussions contained herein might be viewed as building blocks in that endeavour. But it is much more than that. The worst crimes known to man have always been those associated with war. And if *inter arma enim silent legis* ('among arms, the laws fall mute') is to become the historical anomaly that we all wish it to be, then self-discipline of those most directly involved in war-fighting is likely to be far more than a building block; it is the cornerstone. Fortunately, as the ensuing chapters elucidate, the march of history continues to place an ever-increasing premium on self-discipline and self-imposed accountability with respect to core international crimes.

It does not take complex analysis to understand why looking to militaries to hold their members accountable is so fundamentally important to any real progress in protecting human rights in armed conflict and diminishing war's devastating effects. Obviously, self-discipline is always the most efficient means of restraining misbehaviour in the first instance. But that is even truer in the war-fighting context. Of all the international community's well-intended endeavours to foster accountability and end impunity, none is more important than that addressed in this book.

Soldiers are uniquely situated to be impacted by core international crimes. Criminal conduct involves individuals crossing lines that delimit society's views of appropriate, civilised behaviour. Although most professional militaries today are populated by loyal citizens committed to the rule of law, we must remember that once engaged in armed conflict, those troops – not of their own volition – have already crossed some of those lines. When soldiers are required to enter a world in which killing is lawful and even encouraged, they are forced past normal boundaries where traditional societal restraints are removed and the likelihood of war crimes is increased.

Besides the amplified vulnerability to lawlessness, the combat soldier's world is one in which the impact of traditional deterrence mechanisms is greatly reduced. Although our preference will always be that potential criminals be compelled by honourable and righteous motives, society has always depended on punitive enforcement and the concomitant deterrence it fosters to inhibit those who might otherwise be tempted to commit crimes. The ascent of international criminal law during the past two decades is testament to that fact. But the deterrent component of external criminal justice mechanisms is far less effective in war.

First, we should recognise that heightened, extreme motivations accompany the very decision to go to war. Just as the lawfulness of killing in war is a foreign concept to individuals who live most of their lives outside of armed conflict, so too war itself is largely antithetical to the ideal post-United Nations Charter world where States do not resort to the use of force against other States. When those engaged in armed conflict have determined the cause to be so great that they would risk blood and treasure to secure it, 'normal' deterrence mechanisms become less relevant.

Just as a logical decision to engage in criminal behaviour is more explicable in war, so is the probability of simple depravity undeterred by normal methods. In war, not only is killing lawful but so too is being killed more likely. When combat activities take a man to the precipice – when life-and-death situations are confronted on a daily basis – the deterrent impact of potential incarceration is unlikely to have the same gravity as it might in a peacetime scenario. This is especially true when punishment can only occur after an extensive trial process; conversely, life and death are decided with the mere pull of a trigger.

The bottom line is that we have every reason to believe externally imposed accountability has had and will have relatively minimal deterrent impact on those engaged in armed conflict. And even if extra-military prosecution were impactful, history demonstrates that the number of soldiers held to account by non-military authorities is quite small. We often look to the International Military Tribunal at Nuremberg as the genesis of individual accountability for the most egregious crimes under international law. Yet, for all its fame, only two dozen of the thousands involved in committing wartime atrocities were prosecuted there. And the International Criminal Court has spent 12 years and a billion dollars to convict only two. Throughout history, the vast majority of disciplinary measures that could predicate deterrence have come from internal military discipline. And logic tells us that will be the case in the future as well.

This is the bad news – that recent developments in external accountability mechanisms are unlikely to yield substantial influence to prevent core international crimes. But the good news is that, as this book points out, accountability for violations of international humanitarian law is absolutely a matter of self-interest for 21st-century military forces. And the trend is positive.

There are a number of traditional reasons for self-interest in accountability that have persisted for centuries. Military effectiveness has always been closely tethered to good order and discipline. And permitting serious criminal behaviour is certainly not conducive to maintaining that order. An increasing number of militaries are realising that they need to hold their own accountable simply to maintain military effectiveness.

The US military has, for decades, had its military justice system challenged by outsiders who question the need for such substantial command involvement in military prosecutions. The debate remains lively today, but the first retort has been steadfastly consistent: the military justice system requires the heavy involvement of command authorities because the court-martial system is first and foremost necessary to ensure the good order and discipline of armed forces – it is not merely a mechanism for retributive justice. Regardless of the optimum accountability structure, the interest in effectiveness and operational efficiency is undeniable.

Another reason for the interest in internal accountability is that the law of armed conflict was written to provide practical benefit to wartime missions. The underpinnings for most law of war norms are found not in deontological theories – which hold little sway in the life-and-death world of the battlefield – but in the consequentialist, utilitarian arguments regarding the positive effect of *jus in bello* adherence to the war-fighting effort. When prisoners of war are treated humanely, enemy combatants are more likely to surrender. When vanquished adversaries are treated fairly and with equanimity, counter-insurgencies are more likely to evaporate.

Finally, adherence to international humanitarian law has been justified as fostering reciprocal compliance. Sadly, however, the cogency of this argument has waned over the years. At an earlier time, US military leaders were taught that the law of war was written "by warriors, for warriors". As part of an international law regime based on reciprocity, the law of war was designed to make sense to commanding officers both by increasing the likelihood of military success and by appealing to the nobler, selfless characteristics of soldiers, thus facilitating humane conduct that would be mirrored by one's adversary. Indeed, in an even earlier day, "chivalry" was listed among the fundamental principles of the law of war. Those days have passed, and States in modern armed conflicts fight without expectation of reciprocity from guerrilla or terrorist fighters.

The demise of reciprocity as a justification for adherence to the law of war, however, does not mean that accountability for militaries is not a matter of self-interest. The other reasons that State armed forces have always sought self-disciplined forces continue and have been bolstered by experience. And today's national armed forces fight more frequently with all-volunteer forces for whom concepts of honour persist, independent of reciprocity expectations. Even more importantly, changes in the international community and the predominance of non-international armed conflict militate in favour of self-imposed accountability, not against it. The various conflicts of the past decade bear this out.

In the era that preceded the 1949 Geneva Conventions, a Westphalian world order was plagued by international armed conflicts in which State armed forces fought in extreme hostilities that fit their moniker: "world war". Although the armies of that era were equally interested in self-disciplined forces for the sake of military effectiveness, such internal self-discipline might not extend to national decisions (for example, few would argue that the primary problem with concentration camps was the undisciplined nature of Nazi troops). More recent humanitarian law clarifies norms that would prohibit soldiers from obeying the unlawful decisions of national governments. And dissemination requirements make it more difficult for national authorities to change the rules midstream. Most US forces, for example, would be unlikely to obey orders to commit offences that they know from prior training to be war crimes.

At least for well-trained armed forces that claim adherence to international humanitarian law, traditional deterrent effects are still intact. More importantly, on the modern battlefield they are heightened. For disciplined State armed forces, the danger of atrocities or mass violations of core international crimes is tethered to State interests; and this is where changes in the modern world assist us. In the Second World War some armies were fighting for the very survival of their nations. Thus, those norms that seemed ineffectual in assisting the war effort might be discarded in the interest of national existence. Conversely, in modern conflicts between State armed forces and insurgent or transnational terrorist groups, the State armed forces are not likely to be in a position where their survival is at stake. They may fight to defeat criminal elements that threaten security but, at least among major powers, the particular battlefield outcome is rarely in question. State armed forces today engage in combat to preserve peacetime society. Therefore, it is never in their broader interest to undermine the very rule of law for which they fight.

Similarly, the current global economy and international structures increase the premium on lawful conduct. The conclusion of an armed conflict today will not include complete annihilation of the opposing force. We live in a multipolar world where reputation at the end of – and indeed during – the conflict is perhaps as or more important than any particular outcome on the battlefield. Clausewitz's maxim about war being policy by another means is truer today than it was nearly two centuries ago. And we can rest assured that no State today will find benefit in a policy of having its military forces commit core international crimes.

A successful armed force in today's conflicts is one that furthers its own interests while undermining the enemy interests that run counter to it. And those interests will always include furthering (or at the very least being perceived to have furthered) the rule of law. Even if sometimes championed as a matter of hypocrisy, we happily live in a world where stature within the international community depends on allegiance to the rule of law and accountability. Therefore, if a military's forces do not embrace accountability for core international crimes, they undermine their very *raison d'être*.

By the nature of their work – killing, capturing, destroying – militaries will always operate in circumstances that are fertile for egregious violations of international humanitarian law. Sadly, recent international efforts in criminal enforcement are unlikely to significantly alter the deterrence equation for those crimes. But the coin of persuasion is self-interest. And, as is explored in this volume, military self-interest in accountability has never been higher. Let us pray that it remains so.

William K. Lietzau
Colonel, US Marine Corps (retired)
Senior Associate, Center for Strategic and International Studies
Formerly US Deputy Assistant Secretary of Defense
for Rule of Law and Detainee Policy

FOREWORD BY WILLIAM J. FENRICK

Armed conflict, inevitably and regrettably, involves death and destruction, and most of this death and destruction is caused by the armed forces of the parties to the conflict. Professional military officers regard themselves as managers of the controlled use of violence. As a general statement, the properly controlled use of violence is in compliance with international humanitarian law and an effective use of limited resources. The improperly controlled use of violence may result in both the commission of serious violations of international humanitarian law and the waste of important and limited resources which should be used elsewhere.

Military professionals do have an important self-interest in accountability for core international crimes, in part because such accountability fosters discipline which is essential to the controlled use of violence. Needless to say, there are a wide variety of other reasons for favouring accountability. Accountability and compliance are in accord with professional ethics, whether or not the other side complies with the law. Accountability will, or should, encourage compliance with international humanitarian law. Lack of accountability may hinder mission accomplishment in the field as local populations become increasingly hostile. Lack of accountability may also result in the loss of popular support at home with a resulting undermining of the war effort. One must note the gradual loss of support for the American war effort in Vietnam following the disclosure of American war crimes such as My Lai, notwithstanding the fact that forces on the other side in fact committed far more war crimes. One must also observe that Western democracies appear to have an inherent inability to keep the commission of war crimes by their own side secret and this inability is exacerbated by modern technology, as exemplified by WikiLeaks.

The core international crimes are aggression, genocide, crimes against humanity and war crimes. Except in instances where regime change has occurred, there is usually such a degree of higher-level involvement in aggression, genocide and crimes against humanity that prosecutions for such offences allegedly committed by members of the armed forces before their own military tribunals are not practicable or desirable. In such cases, trials must be held before civil courts or international tribunals where fairness and transparency may be adequately demonstrated. Military self-interest in accountability need not be demonstrated or encouraged exclusively by means of judicial proceedings within the military justice system. It can also be demonstrated by encouraging and facilitating the handling of cases outside the military justice system.

On occasion, however, it may be quite appropriate to handle war crimes cases within the military justice system as such cases would, frequently, not presume or require the involvement of higher-level military or political leaders. Indeed, as many civilian justice systems exercise jurisdiction almost exclusively on the basis of the territorial principle, it may be difficult to prosecute some war crimes cases before national civil courts. There are potential advantages to prosecutions before military tribunals. They may be held in the territory where the alleged offences occurred thereby demonstrating to the victim groups that the military forces take their legal responsibilities seriously. Such proceedings may also demonstrate to more junior members of the armed forces that it is not just remote civilian authorities, but their military superiors, too, who are concerned about compliance with the law. As a practical matter, it may be easier to prosecute some cases before military tribunals which, in substance, involve the commission of war crimes, by assimilating them to military offences with fewer elements. For example, an accused service member who is alleged to have killed a civilian or a prisoner of war may be charged before a military tribunal with murder in lieu of a war crime as such a charge may be easier to prove but still require proof of all the elements for which an accused is morally culpable.

In one area, the development and prosecution of conduct of hostilities offences, military professionals have both a great personal interest and a particularly relevant expertise. Almost all of the cases in which core crimes have been prosecuted before national or international tribunals have involved what might be regarded as 'behind the lines' offences or offences in which the victims are 'in the hands of' or under the control of the alleged perpetrators. Almost none of the cases prosecuted after the Second World War involved alleged offences committed in combat. None of them involved alleged unlawful attacks. Indeed, the only tribunal to date which has prosecuted unlawful attack charges is the 'ICTY'. This action by the ICTY is to be commended as the alternative is to regard the law concerning conduct of hostilities offences such as unlawful attacks as merely hortatory. The hortatory approach was the one practised before the ICTY came into existence. That being said, the ICTY has not always adopted approaches to unlawful attack charges that would be regarded as sensible and viable by responsible military professionals from States which engage in armed conflict and take their obligations under international humanitarian law seriously.

Neither military professionals nor international jurists should develop their analyses of combat-related legal concepts such as military necessity, proportionality, military objective, indiscriminate attack or attack directed against civilians in a vacuum. Each should be educated by the other and both must bear in mind that civilian standards should prevail, but these standards ought to take adequate account of military realities, of what can actually be done in particular circumstances.

There is no generally accepted rule of precedent in international law. Appellate chambers of individual tribunals such as the ICTY may bind their trial chambers. Outside of the individual tribunals, however, judicial decisions have a persuasive effect. Military professionals and their legal advisers have an understandable and important degree of self-interest in ensuring that individuals are held accountable for all core international crimes, particularly those related to the conduct of hostilities, as these offences set the parameters for how military forces should wage war. If the ICTY, the first tribunal to prosecute conduct of hostilities offences, is criticised for occasionally not getting things absolutely right, it is entitled to respond: Where is the case law from other tribunals, national or international, to help us get things right? There is none.

William J. Fenrick
Formerly, Commander, Canadian Armed Forces,
Member, Commission of Experts for the former Yugoslavia,
Senior Legal Adviser, ICTY Office of the Prosecutor, and
Professor, Schulich School of Law, Dalhousie University

TABLE OF CONTENTS

1

Ensuring Accountability for Core International Crimes in Armed Forces: Obligations and Self-Interest

Morten Bergsmo* and SONG Tianying**

1.1. Topic and Discourse Parameters

This anthology seeks to further an emerging discourse on 'military self-interest in accountability' for genocide, crimes against humanity, war crimes and aggression.[1] The topic was first conceptualised and introduced for a conference at Stanford University on 27 November 2012, co-organised by the University, the Centre for International Law Research and Policy ('CILRAP', through its department, the Forum for International Criminal and Humanitarian Law), and the UC Berkeley War Crimes Studies Center.[2] The location may have stimulated a confident sense of an innovative approach among conference participants. But it goes without saying that such a sentiment is not sufficient to trigger a broader, ongoing discourse on a new topic in the neighbourhood of well-established fields, such as professionalisation of armed forces, dissemination of international humanitarian law, and criminal justice for core international crimes. More is required to innovate in this borderland of sustained human endeavour over many decades. It was not difficult to find experts interested in the topic of 'military self-interest in accountability'; the response to the call

---

* **Morten Bergsmo** is the Director of the Centre for International Law Research and Policy, and Visiting Professor at Peking University Law School.

** **SONG Tianying** is a Researcher at the European University Institute in Florence. She was formerly Legal Officer at the Regional Delegation for East Asia of the International Committee of the Red Cross.

[1] These categories of crimes are referred to as 'core international crimes' for the purposes of this anthology and the research project of the Centre for International Law Research and Policy of which this book is an integral part.

[2] For information about the conference, see the persistent URL http://www.fichl.org/activ ities/the-self-interest-of-armed-forces-in-accountability-for-their-members-for-core-interna tional-crimes/.

for conference papers was very positive. But in the absence of published sources directly on the topic, the authors and editors have worked to make this anthology a catalysing discourse opener, involving perspectives from different military and legal traditions, regions, professions and generations.

With sufficiently representative and qualified participation, anthologies that come out of communitarian research projects[3] have the potential not only to serve as a coherent knowledge product, but also to generate a wider sense of ownership in the discourse and, hence, a more genuinely global process of thought-fertilisation and -development. Both are important for a topic such as 'military self-interest in accountability'. This is particularly the case in this period of time when the consensus around the international legal protection of civilians and those most vulnerable in conflict and transitions can and should be deepened.

In his foreword, William K. Lietzau – a distinguished lawyer of the United States military who also played an important role in the negotiations to set up the International Criminal Court ('ICC') – observes that of "all the international community's well-intended endeavours to foster accountability and end impunity, none is more important than that addressed in this book".[4] He goes on to say that the "coin of persuasion is self-interest. And, as is explored in this volume, military self-interest in accountability has never been higher. Let us pray that it remains so".[5] We share Lietzau's well-informed and noble aspiration, and have dedicated this volume to "those in armed forces who articulate military rationales for accountability for core international crimes". Where a culture of military self-interest in accountability has not yet taken hold, persuasion efforts require such articulation.

---

[3] CILRAP uses the terms 'communitarian scholarship' and 'communitarian research' about its research projects where, after an internal process of conceptualisation and definition of the research topic, it opens up the inquiry through a competitive, public call for papers; holds an expert conference in which anyone can register to participate without a fee; edits the conference papers and sometimes additional papers not presented at the conference; and publishes them in print and open access in a manner that treats all potential readers equally in terms of factors such as the timing of the release, format and page numbering, and other citation qualities.

[4] See William K. Lietzau, "Foreword", p. xi.

[5] *Ibid.*, p. xv.

The goal of this book is to increase our understanding of this articulation process and the contexts in which it is played out. It also provides information, reasoning and arguments that may aid the construction of military rationales for compliance and accountability, and, more widely, raises self-awareness and understanding within armed forces and governments of the existence and nature of military self-interests in accountability. These self-interests should be discussed, elaborated and made as familiar as bread-and-butter or rice in the diets of armed forces, to such an extent that they become an integral part of their decision-making, education and communication cultures. It may even be useful to generate pedagogical and work-process language around the self-interests, such as by numbering, mapping or classifying them, or by giving them popular labels or nicknames.

Section 1.3. below makes a tentative contribution by listing 26 formulations of self-interests under some initial headings. We invite further elaboration and adaptation of this taxonomy. Military professionals and training mechanisms around the world deserve and need to have access to a more comprehensive statement of these self-interests. This project can only represent a cognitive and knowledge-resource beginning of a broader effort, which should be conducted in languages additional to English, and not be limited to the Anglosphere and its usual extensions.

Neither the organisers of the Stanford conference nor the editors of this volume have imposed strict definitions on the authors and other participants in this research project. A nascent discourse should not be stifled and locked into established or hastily defined sub-categorisations. That does not mean that discourse actors were left without guidance and direction. The original concept paper of the Stanford conference[6] started by placing the topic of military self-interest in accountability in the context of the evolution of criminal justice for core international crimes since the early 1990s. Accountability for war crimes, crimes against humanity and genocide has received increasing international attention since the establishment of the International Criminal Tribunal for the former Yugoslavia in 1993. Internationalised criminal tribunals were subsequently established for Rwanda, Sierra Leone, Cambodia, Iraq and Lebanon, and we

---

[6] CILRAP's Forum for International Criminal and Humanitarian Law, "The Self Interest of Armed Forces in Accountability for the Members for Core International Crimes", Hoover Institution, Stanford University, 27 November 2012 (http://www.fichl.org/fileadmin/fichl/ activities/121127_Seminar_on_Self-Interest_of_Armed_Forces__draft_concept_and_pro gramme__121125_.pdf).

have seen high-profile war crimes cases against former leaders such as Slobodan Milošević, Saddam Hussein and Charles Taylor. During the same period, a number of States have prosecuted their own citizens or refugees from war-affected countries before national military or civilian courts. Although there have been some controversies,[7] the overall trend since the mid-1990s has been one of increased support for criminal justice accountability for flagrant violations of international criminal law.

The political and diplomatic rhetoric put forward in favour of criminal justice accountability for atrocities in the period from 1993 to 2015 frequently referred to the struggle against impunity and the argument that there can be no lasting peace without justice. But underlying this rhetoric has been an emphasis on the *obligation* to investigate and prosecute core international crimes under international law. International lawyers in government, academia and civil society have come out in considerable numbers to explain that governments must give effect to this obligation. And governments have indeed listened to the lawyers, facilitating a very high number of core international crimes trials in the period from 1993 to 2015, at a substantial cost. Needless to say, governments sometimes pursue national prosecutions in response to purely political interests or expectations. But both the language of international legal obligation and that of political expediency can act on military or civilian decisions to investigate or prosecute, as a raised 'stick': you must facilitate prosecutions because you are obliged to do so under international law; whether or not you consider criminal justice accountability to be in your interest, you have to facilitate it.

The environment often assumes that such perceptions of military self-interest or incentives are absent or weak. The lawyers in foreign ministries and military lawyers who carry the stick of legal obligation to prosecute are often the same experts who for years have trained or shaped the system of training for armed forces in international humanitarian law. The obligations to comply with and to prosecute violations of international humanitarian law easily blend together in one message from the same messenger: you must ensure criminal justice accountability for members

---

[7] Such controversies have mostly concerned the relationship between peace processes and war crimes trials, the exercise of universal jurisdiction by national criminal justice systems, the delays in and cost of internationalised criminal justice, the reach of the jurisdiction of the ICC, the quality of the case-work of the ICC Office of the Prosecutor up until the time of writing, and the controversial first ICC Prosecutor, Luis Moreno-Ocampo.

of the armed forces as a matter of international legal obligation binding on your country. Even when undertaken by the military itself, such accountability most often tends to be rationalised and imposed as a pure obligation.

This anthology and the research project of which it is part are not concerned with the stick of legal obligation, but the 'carrot' of military self-interest in accountability. Is such accountability in the self-interest of the armed forces concerned? Why do soldiers, officers and military leaders themselves often prefer such accountability, contrary to what may be assumed? Is it because accountability mechanisms distinguish them as military professionals who are uncompromised by such crimes? Or is it because of the way individual incentive structures (such as promotion) function? Are they concerned that the commission of war crimes may undermine the public's trust in the military, increasing the security risks faced, and the size and cost of deployment in the area concerned? Or are they motivated by moral, ethical or religious reasons? Does accountability ensure higher discipline and morale and therefore secure more effective chains of command? Or is it because accountability gives them a political advantage *vis-à-vis* potential opponents? Does it promote a better public image? Could such accountability be particularly crucial when the armed forces are involved in efforts to establish a new regime in a post-conflict or -oppressive situation?

Such military self-interests in *accountability* for core international crimes will frequently apply equally to *compliance* with international humanitarian and criminal law as well. Compliance with criminal law is preferable to accountability for its violation. Suffice it to say that the former gives effect to the *Rechtsgut* protected by the criminal norm in question, while the latter seeks to remedy harm caused to that legally protected interest. This anthology does not exclude military self-interest in compliance from the analysis – that would not be practically sensitive at this stage of the discourse – but the emphasis is on the narrower phenomenon of self-interest in accountability for core international crimes. That does not mean that the point of the book is to emphasise punishment for such conduct, but rather to generate awareness of accountability also as a means of prevention or to mainstream accountability as a measure to prevent to the extent warranted by available knowledge or consensus.

The anthology encompasses both *individual* military self-interests in accountability for core international crimes, and *collective* self-interests of institutions, organisations or states. Interests will often apply to both, but many will differ between individual and collective actors. In this book the term 'military self-interests' includes both categories, including the State, its government or political-military leadership. Furthermore, the word 'military' does not exclude non-state armed groups. This second edition adds Chapter 17, where René Provost maps the law and practice of 'insurgent justice', laying ground for further discussions on motivations and self-interests of non-state armed groups' administration of justice.

A further distinction could be made between *positive* and *negative* self-interests in accountability. In Chapter 10, the Indonesian scholar Kiki A. Japutra introduces this polarity, suggesting that the "expression 'positive interests' refers to the advantages that a State may acquire, and the unfavourable situations that can be avoided, by initiating prosecution. 'Negative interests', on the other hand, refer to the unavoidable responsibilities and obligations to prosecute perpetrators as stipulated in international law".[8] Used in this way, 'negative interests' could be synonymous with the term 'obligation' as used earlier in this section. We may therefore see that an emerging notion of 'negative self-interests in accountability' will take on additional meanings.

The term 'self-interest' is not intended to be juxtaposed to the values or *Rechtsgüter* on which international humanitarian and criminal law are based. It does not imply something morally inferior or less than ideal. Needless to say, the function and nature of 'self-interests' in accountability as used in this book may be entirely selfless. But the notion does also include what Christopher B. Mahony refers to in Chapter 11 as "realist self-interest": "If armed forces refrain from sitting at the prosecuting table they remain potential prey on the ICC menu",[9] he writes, soberly arguing that "the primary interest of armed forces in prosecuting core international crimes cases is realist self-interest in controlling who is prosecuted and who is not", primarily "via early engagement in domestic prosecution of core international crimes cases".[10] More often than not, however, the authors include "ethical and moral values, self-regulation and internal disci-

---

[8] See Kiki Anastasia Japutra, "The Interest of States in Accountability for Sexual Violence in Armed Conflicts: A Case Study of Comfort Women of the Second World War", Chapter 10, p. 213.

[9] See Christopher B. Mahony, "If You're Not at the Table, You're on the Menu: Complementarity and Self-Interest in Domestic Processes for Core International Crimes", Chapter 11, p. 230.

[10] *Ibid.*, p. 258.

pline of armed forces"[11] in their discussion of likely military self-interests in accountability. Chapter 8 by Marlene Mazel and Chapter 9 by Adel Maged show the promise this topic holds for meaningful contributions that also draw on religious sources as well as ethics and philosophy, in addition to more systematic work by the behavioural and social sciences that can increase our understanding of patterns of conduct in and by armed forces as regards compliance and accountability. This multidisciplinary potential should be tapped, as ownership in the discourse gradually broadens and it takes on a life of its own in different knowledge communities.

Moreover, with the expression 'accountability for core international crimes' the anthology does not distinguish between accountability in *military* or *civilian* criminal jurisdictions. Both forms of criminal justice are included, and authors discuss the topic with regards to both in the following chapters. In fact, the chapters by Elizabeth L. Hillman, Bruce Houlder, Christopher Jenks and Franklin D. Rosenblatt all primarily discuss military criminal justice, whereas the chapters by Arne Willy Dahl and Elizabeth Santalla Vargas explicitly analyse the merits of military and civilian criminal jurisdictions under the thematic shelter of military self-interest in accountability for core international crimes.

Neither is the term 'core international crimes' restricted to classifications under international criminal law proper (such as crimes against humanity or genocide). It also includes classifications under regular domestic criminal codes, whether military or civilian (such as murder or rape), as long as the underlying conduct speaks to core international crimes, and not only domestic or so-called ordinary crimes. After all, violations of law of war had been punished long before the conception of 'core international crimes' and considerations for interests of civilians or enemy soldiers.[12] Jenks's chapter considers in detail how members of US armed forces are charged with offences under the US Uniform Code of Military Justice and not the core international crimes provisions in international legal instruments. As long as the conduct in question may amount to core international crimes, it still falls within the scope of this anthology and research project.

---

[11] See Róisín Burke, "Troop Discipline, the Rule of Law and Mission Operational Effectiveness in Conflict-Affected States", Chapter 15, p. 360.

[12] See David Luban, "Human Rights Thinking and the Laws of War", in Jens David Ohlin (ed.), *Theoretical Boundaries of Human Rights and Armed Conflict*, Cambridge University Press, Cambridge, 2016, pp. 45–77.

The topic of military self-interest in accountability is intimately linked with the comprehensive practice and discourse of *professionalisation of armed forces*. In Chapter 5, Hillman shows that, in the case of the USA, "long before war crimes, crimes against humanity, genocide and aggression were acknowledged as core international crimes, the professionalisation of the army was paving the way for war crimes accountability".[13] Importantly, she claims that the "professionalisation of the US Army increased its interest in accountability. It elevated principles, encouraged discipline and led to more ways to prevent, identify and prosecute violations of law".[14] Her proposition makes comparative and in-depth knowledge of the professionalisation of armed forces not only relevant but central to the study of military self-interest.

When we refer to accountability in the form of investigative and prosecutorial action, as opposed to training and capacity development action, the point should not primarily be to stress self-interests in accountability to ensure more prosecutions, but to help increase the awareness of self-interests in accountability during capacity development. In this respect as well, this book can only start a process. It seeks to do so under the broader, existing umbrella of the professionalisation of armed forces.

Lietzau's foreword reminds us of the topicality of military self-interest in accountability as we begin to witness more clearly the stark limitations of international criminal justice as such. The former Director of the British Service Prosecuting Authority, Bruce Houlder, writes poignantly in Chapter 6 that the "United Kingdom has now entered a time of public inquiry and self-examination over the way it deals with crimes of abuse alleged against its military. It is going through a soul-searching time".[15] And the US Judge Advocate Franklin D. Rosenblatt warns in Chapter 13 that in "an Afghan society with ingrained beliefs about injustice at the hands of Western powers, perceived 'double standards' for service member crime likely fuel ambivalence or resentment about the American military mission".[16] Houlder reinforces the point that "the stra-

---

[13]   See Elizabeth L. Hillman, "Accountability in the 19th-Century US Army", Chapter 5, p. 62.

[14]   *Ibid.*, p. 81.

[15]   See Bruce Houlder, "The Self-Interest of Armed Forces in Accountability for Their Members for Core International Crimes: Carrot Is Better than Stick", Chapter 6, p. 87.

[16]   See Franklin D. Rosenblatt, "Awakening Self-Interest: American Military Justice in Afghanistan and Iraq", Chapter 13, p. 325.

tegic consequences of resentment towards the perceived 'double standards' of powerful foreign forces are highly relevant to current operations. Indeed, if there is not to be visible evidence of a country taking action against those of their own military who commit crimes against citizens of another country, that of itself would fuel the counter-insurgency".[17] The issue of accountability for core international crimes has reached the highest levels of the UK and US defence agendas following very costly wars in Afghanistan and Iraq at the outset of the twenty-first century.

But the need to strengthen the effect of military self-interest in accountability is shared by peace support operations generally. As Roberta Arnold points out in Chapter 14, the "misconduct of a few servicemen may have a boomerang effect not only on the deployed troops, who may lose the hearts and minds of the host nation's population, but also on the sending State's government, which may lose the necessary political support for the continuation or deployment of similar operations".[18] Concerns for public opinion at home and in receiving States, as well as the dizzying financial commitment – and sometimes tragic loss of human life – of troop-sending States make the issue of compliance and accountability with international humanitarian and criminal law a precondition for success of peace support operations. "A flabby force, an ill-disciplined force or a military that makes its own rules, worse still mixes its own messages, and does not respect international norms, will in the end defeat itself in operations, and in the public mind", warns Houlder.[19] Against the background of statements such as these, it is hard to question the practical relevance of the ensuing discourse on military self-interest in accountability for core international crimes. It deserves proper attention and investment of thought and creativity.

As readers will see from the summary of the individual chapters in section 1.2., the anthology brings together a variety of backgrounds, including country, thematic and historical perspectives. It is hoped that this diversity of experience, insights and advice will increase the ability of the book to trigger an ongoing discourse.

---

[17] Houlder, Chapter 6, p. 89, see *supra* note 14.

[18] See Roberta Arnold, "Prosecuting Members of the Armed Forces for Core International Crimes: A Judicial Act in the Self-Interest of the Armed Forces?", Chapter 14, p. 343.

[19] Houlder, Chapter 6, p. 94, see *supra* note 14.

1.2. Chapter Contributions

In Chapter 2, Arne Willy Dahl addresses the trend of "civilianisation" of military justice systems, a recurring theme of this anthology, and evaluates this phenomenon from the perspective of the armed forces' long-term self-interest in having an effective accountability system. For soldiers, military justice may provide not only the hope of fair trial but also guidance and confidence after their, sometimes, challenging decisions in combat. For commanders, such jurisdictions may minimise the damage to reputation caused by individual violations and avoid unnecessary friction with the local population in the area where the force operates. Dahl then discusses three elements for an effective justice system: independence, military expertise and portability.

In Chapter 3, Richard J. Goldstone takes on what may in effect be a precondition for military self-interest in accountability, namely a sense of ownership of international humanitarian and criminal law. Goldstone notices the worrisome trend that such sense of ownership has declined in the past two decades. He then traces the origin and evolution of international humanitarian law to the military, before considering the US armed forces as an example of how the sense of ownership has fluctuated historically. The case is made for increased military ownership and, in turn, the awareness of military self-interest in accountability for core international crimes.

Chapter 4 discusses accountability in the context of international humanitarian law implementation. SONG Tianying examines two conditions for international humanitarian law implementation: the material capabilities and willingness of the military. The first condition envisions international humanitarian law implementation through a professional military organisation, where effective accountability plays a crucial role. The second condition concerns the self-interest of the military in complying with international humanitarian law. In this regard, competing interests in military decision-making are also considered. In light of the international efforts to fight impunity, SONG concludes that the military's internal accountability for serious international humanitarian law violations is key to reinforcing its professionalism and retaining essential values in the modern age.

In Chapter 5, Elizabeth L. Hillman approaches the topic of military professionalisation and accountability by revisiting the historical evolution of the 19th-century US Army. Through two wars – the Mexican War and the Civil War, which respectively introduced a new type of military court and a new code of law – Hillman highlights the role of accountability in enhancing operational effectiveness and political legitimacy. Over time, the military's desire to avoid excessive interference from civilian authorities has prompted their interest in professionalisation and self-accountability.

In Chapter 6, Bruce Houlder depicts the landscape of military self-interest in accountability, reflecting on his experience as the Director of the Service Prosecuting Authority ('SPA'). He notices a change of ethos following the structural reform of the SPA, which is now led by a civilian lawyer. This change is an attempt to increase transparency and legitimacy of the armed forces facing public scrutiny. Historical and contemporary cases show that accountability helps States – as well as the armed forces – to move forward. Houlder further emphasises that accountability is an inherent requirement of national and international rule of law and a means to maintain internal discipline.

In Chapter 7, Agus Widjojo places the accountability analysis within the socio-cultural context in which the military operates. He sheds light on how contextual elements affected the Indonesian Armed Forces' establishment and evolution. Taking the example of the accountability process for the 1999 East Timor crisis, Widjojo examines a non-judicial alternative, namely the Indonesia-Timor Leste Commission of Truth and Friendship, and its contextual analysis of accountability. He then argues that clearly identified responsibilities that factor in the socio-cultural context may better assist the military in future self-development and the prevention of atrocities.

Chapter 8 offers an Israeli perspective on the self-interest of accountability. Marlene Mazel establishes that Israel's history, core values and institutional features contribute to its commitment to the law of armed conflict. In this connection, she recalls the Eichmann trial and its legacy for universal jurisdiction. Mazel then follows the current jurisprudence of the Supreme Court of Israel regarding the legality of certain military conduct and the importance of national investigations of alleged violations of the law of armed conflict, where the Court seeks to prevent violations, educate troops and uphold the rule of law. Finally, the Turkel reports are used to illustrate the point that effective accountability mechanisms may affirm the credibility and international image of the military.

In Chapter 9, Adel Maged investigates the relationship between the law of armed conflict and the Islamic *Sharīʿah* as he contemplates the latter's impact on military self-interest in accountability. He asserts that Islamic *Sharīʿah* has established sound legal and moral foundations for preventing and punishing core international crimes, through ethical principles of military engagement and norms regarding the conduct of hostilities in times of war. Religious beliefs should thus provide incentives for accountability in the Islamic world. Meanwhile, Maged cautions against extremist groups' abuses of interpretations of Islamic teachings to justify their atrocities.

Chapter 10 undertakes a case study of the practice of using 'comfort women' in Japanese-occupied territories in Asia during the Second World War and the related accountability process. After assessing the attitude of the successive Japanese governments and positions taken by international and domestic courts, Kiki A. Japutra concludes that there has been a lack of will to address the crimes relating to comfort women. She goes on to illustrate the 'positive interests' for States to ensure accountability for serious crimes, which are different from mere legal obligation. Such interests include preventing undesirable incursion on sovereignty, building judicial capacity, enhancing the State's image and credibility, promoting reconciliation processes, and relieving the burden of guilt and shame of the younger generation.

In Chapter 11, Christopher B. Mahony considers the ICC's principle of complementarity and the military self-interest in conducting domestic proceedings on core international crimes. In the ICC's practice regarding Colombia, Libya, Kenya, Uganda and Guinea, Mahony notices that where States demonstrated the requisite due diligence and intent to pursue the crimes, they have successfully disabled ICC investigations. By contrast, more belligerent opposition to the ICC has led to further proceedings before the Court. Therefore, it is in the military's self-interest to bring perpetrators of core international crimes to justice via domestic processes that could be politically controlled but still meet the complementarity threshold.

Chapters 12 and 13 offer insights into the balance of considerations in the US military's accountability practice. In Chapter 12, Christopher Jenks highlights the disparity in charges for similar violations of the laws of war committed by US service members and enemy belligerents. He explains the incentives behind such charging practice and poses the important question as to whether narrowing the accountability gap and increasing transparency may better serve the military's interest. In Chapter 13, Franklin D. Rosenblatt embarks on an empirical study of the effectiveness of the US court-martial system in Afghanistan and Iraq. He provides an overview of US court-martial practices in these two countries, drawing on numerous after-action reports, from which he concludes that the full-bore application of military justice is not viable in combat. Consequently, faulty accountability for military crimes has undermined counter-insurgency endeavours and diminished the armed forces' legitimacy. Rosenblatt suggests making military justice more portable and relevant to better serve strategic goals.

In Chapter 14, Roberta Arnold explores the possible self-interest in prosecuting serious international crimes, both for the military as an institution and for individual members of the military. From the institutional perspective, repressing serious international crimes benefits the military's image, corporate spirit and mission accomplishment. On an individual level, high-ranking officers may have an interest in the smooth exercise of command and control and in avoiding criminal charges as superiors, while ordinary soldiers may want to distance themselves from the misconduct of their comrades and work in a safe environment. Arnold also deems that prosecution will better serve the military's interest if carried out by a military judicial system that is independent, transparent and fair.

In Chapter 15, Róisín Burke provides a comprehensive overview of the interest of armed forces deployed on peace operations or other missions to ensure effective investigation and prosecution of serious international crimes committed by their members in host States. She draws lessons from past incidents and identifies a range of reasons for accountability: ethical and moral values, self-regulation and internal discipline (as cited in section 1.1. above), the image of the armed forces and their States, their relationship with host State populations and with their home public, retention of control by military justice systems, operational effectiveness and legitimacy, and the promotion of the rule of law.

Chapter 16 seeks to address the question of how the selection of jurisdictional forum for core international crimes may serve the military interest. Assisted by regional and international case law and practice, especially the Latin American experience, Elizabeth Santalla Vargas argues that civilian courts should try human rights violations, even if they are committed by military personnel. Similarly, civilian courts are generally more suitable to try war crimes, despite the controversies surrounding them in some contexts. The legitimacy and credibility of the jurisdictional forum may favour the military by minimising risks of superior responsibility and living up to the complementarity test used by the ICC.

The final Chapter 17 turns to administration of justice by non-state armed groups. René Provost explores the legitimacy of insurgent tribunals in light of the evolution in the relevant norms of international humanitarian law. He maps the law applicable to and by insurgent tribunals and views the validity of insurgent tribunal decisions *vis-à-vis* state recognition and the principle of complimentarity of the ICC. Provost notes the shift of the international legal order away from a statecentric one in favour of a polycentric one. This chapter sets the scene for an informed discussion of non-state armed groups' self-interest in accountability for international crimes.

1.3. List of Some Military Self-Interests in Accountability for Core International Crimes

The enumeration of self-interest in this section builds on the policy brief "Military Self-Interest in Accountability for Core International Crimes",[20] the concept paper for the Stanford conference, The Self-Interest of Armed Forces in Accountability for their Members for Core International Crimes,[21] and the presentation by Morten Bergsmo at that conference.[22] The list is further enriched by self-interests identified in other chapters of this book. It is not exhaustive and is evidently tentative in nature. In an attempt to maximise the knowledge base from which interested actors may make their own choice of terms, the items listed below are not necessarily mutually exclusive.

As stated in section 1.1. above, the list invites further research, and will hopefully be extended and adapted to various national and institutional contexts. It also seeks to serve as an operational tool, including in training and other professionalisation efforts, as well as in discussions within armed forces as to whether investigation or prosecution should commence.

---

[20] Morten Bergsmo, Arne Willy Dahl and Richard Sousa, "Military Self-Interest in Accountability for Core International Crimes", FICHL Policy Brief Series No. 14 (2013), Torkel Opsahl Academic EPublisher, Brussels, 2013 (https://www.legal-tools.org/doc/396da7/).

[21] See *supra* note 6.

[22] On file with the authors.

I.   The Values of Armed Forces or States

- Ensuring accountability is to uphold the value of the rule of law, as mentioned by Houlder (Chapter 6) and Burke (Chapter 15).
- Accountability may also uphold certain religious teachings, such as those of Islam, as elaborated by Maged (Chapter 9).
- Punishing core international crimes upholds historical lessons and maintains consistent practice and political stances, as in the case of Israel illustrated by Mazel (Chapter 8).
- Punishing core international crimes promotes and confirms ethics and morality.
- Military culture and core values are important in pursuing accountability, as discussed by Houlder (Chapter 6).

II.   Domestic Legitimacy of Armed Forces

- Accountability may contribute towards the credibility and reputation of armed forces, and consequently to legitimacy in relevant constituencies and the international community.
- The image of the military may affect recruitment and material support from the state, as noted by Arnold (Chapter 14).
- Acknowledging past crimes may give closure to the victims and help the state and the armed forces to move forward, as Houlder points out (Chapter 6). Conversely, denial may invite the public to extend the scrutiny to other aspects of the state and the armed forces, as Japutra warns (Chapter 11).

III. Accomplishment of Counter-Insurgency, Peace-Building and other Missions

- In counter-insurgency operations legitimacy among the local population, or 'hearts and minds' acceptance, is important to mission accomplishment.
- Unpunished serious crimes may increase security risks, undermine the army's political standing and feed into enemy propaganda. Unpunished crimes create the impression of 'double standards' and thwarts counter-insurgency efforts, as Rosenblatt warns (Chapter 13).

- If there is no accountability, there may be lower acceptance of deployed forces among the local population, requiring an increase in the number of troops deployed. This can become an argument of economy in favour of accountability.

- Accountability may be particularly crucial when armed forces are involved in efforts to establish a new regime in a post-conflict situation or a process of democratisation.

- When crimes are punished and known to be punished, it may dissuade the adversary from resorting to reprisals, and thus avoiding escalation.

IV. Military Self-Development and Professionalisation

- Analysis of the socio-cultural impact when identifying responsibility for atrocities may inform the military in future self-development and prevention programmes, as Widjojo argues (Chapter 7).

- Self-accountability is part of the professionalisation process of the military to avoid excessive civilian interference, as Hillman reveals (Chapter 5).

- Effective accountability helps define the armed forces as professionals with high standards.

V. Maintaining Internal Order and Discipline

- Effective investigation and prosecution of core international crimes have a pedagogical value which contributes to habitual compliance and the process of norm internalisation, as noted by Burke (Chapter 15).

- Order and discipline improve operational efficiency and avoid adverse effects on civilians.

VI. Pre-empting International Judicial Scrutiny

- Self-accountability may also pre-empt international scrutiny or interference, such as that of the ICC, as Japutra (Chapter 10), Mahony (Chapter 11) and Santalla Vargas (Chapter 16) note.

VII. Domestic Judicial Capacity Building

- Accountability at the national level is an opportunity to build domestic judicial capacity to try core international crimes, as Japutra sees it (Chapter 11).

VIII. Individual Military Personnel's Morale and Right to Justice

- It is in individual soldiers' interest to have a fair trial with fundamental judicial guarantees, by an effective justice system, as Dahl mentions (Chapter 2).
- Individual soldiers gain confidence and peace of mind as they may be assured, where appropriate, of the lawfulness of their combat decisions by an effective accountability system, as Dahl notes (Chapter 2).
- The morale and self-respect of the troops may be preserved. Loyal and law-abiding members of the military have a need to distance themselves from violations of core international crimes and a rightful expectation of seeing the case brought to justice.
- It is in the soldiers' interest to carry out their profession in an environment where they can rely on the proper conduct of their comrades and superiors, as Arnold contends (Chapter 14).

IX. Minimising Risks of Superior Responsibility

- Under the doctrine of superior responsibility, commanders may minimise the risks of their individual criminal responsibility for their subordinate's crimes by ensuring punishment, as noted by Arnold (Chapter 14) and Santalla Vargas (Chapter 16).
- The commission of core international crimes harms individual professional advancement and going clear of an effective criminal justice system provides protection against harmful suspicions.

1.4. Challenges Ahead

The scholar Mark Osiel has suggested that in a world where a strong International Criminal Court is not likely in the near future, more attention should be directed to "how military law can shape the professional soldier's sense of vocation and his understanding and cultivation of its intrinsic virtues, its 'inner morality'".[23] This ambitious statement points to real challenges ahead. In the context of this book, the "inner morality" of military law translates into those interests which the law has been made to serve. The "intrinsic virtues" of military law are those values or *Rechtsgüter* which the law protects. Upholding such values may indeed be virtuous. But the reasons why armed actors should comply with, and promote accountability for violations of, international humanitarian and criminal law include a broader range of military self-interests, some of which can wear the robe of morality and virtue. Cultivating the understanding among armed actors of these self-interests is as important as establishing and serving criminal justice accountability mechanisms for their violations.

To that end, the culture in armed forces is important. As Houlder observes: "The real danger is not the errant foot soldier. It lies in culture. Cultural values are set further up. Like corruption, the rot can start at the top, and develop its own self-protective carapace. That then becomes the greatest evil and is the hardest to eradicate. Seen in this way, the justification for a set of moral imperatives without which an individual simply will become unable to advance through ranks is an obvious aim". The extent of compliance with, and acceptance of accountability for violations of, international humanitarian and criminal law may provide an accurate reflection of the prevailing culture within armed forces and their constitutional-political context.

The military and political leadership of armed forces matters a great deal to their institutional culture and their ability to foster cultivation of the understanding of soldiers and officers. Hillman expresses the view that the "[o]fficers' role in the history of accountability in the US military is primarily as enforcers rather than as alleged violators of military laws or codes".[24] Hopeful as this statement is, it may not always be the case, certainly not if we consider countries in general. In his foreword, Andrew T. Cayley reminds us that the genocide-like acts in Srebrenica in Bosnia-Herzegovina in the summer of 1995 were the acts of the regular Bosnian Serb Army, led firmly by its top commanders. Leaders of armed forces

---

[23]   See Mark Osiel, "Obeying Orders: Atrocity, Military Discipline and the Law of War", in *California Law Review*, 1998, vol. 86, no. 5, p. 959.

[24]   Hillman, Chapter 5, p. 63, see *supra* note 12.

have a particular responsibility to increase the awareness of military self-interest in accountability for core international crimes.

The destructive capacity of the use of armed force is such that no stone should be left unturned to reduce its harmful consequences, in a never-ending common effort to humanise armed conflict, walking on a long bridge of decades of efforts to set standards, fine-tune institutional safeguards, develop training, and professionalise institutional culture. This book contributes to increased self-awareness of military self-interest in accountability. It cannot do more than to help open and activate a discourse space around this theme, tilting or opening the field, sowing seeds of new perspectives, ideas and concepts, through an exercise in communitarian scholarship.

2

Military Justice and
Self-Interest in Accountability

Arne Willy Dahl*

In 2001 the International Society for Military Law and the Law of War made a comparative study of military justice systems around the world and their development. The study was followed up in 2011.[1] One of the conclusions that can be drawn is that there has been a steady trend of 'civilianisation' of military justice systems over the last two or three decades. These conclusions are supported by information about reforms in various countries in recent years.

In many cases, the handling of military penal cases has been placed in the hands of fully civilian courts and prosecutors. In other cases, the reforms have been less dramatic, such as establishing standing military courts replacing courts martial convened by commanders for the individual case. Some reforms have also resulted in hybrid solutions consisting of civilian courts with a military element.

The driving force behind many of the reforms have been decisions by the European Court of Human Rights, demanding that courts which are independent of the military chain of command decide matters of penal punishment. Such decisions have had an impact not only on member states of the Council of Europe but also on states with historical or cultural affiliation to member states. Structures for investigation and prosecution have also been put under a similar pressure, requiring independence of those who might have an interest in the outcome.

In many of the decisions, the focus has been on securing the accused's right to a fair trial. In other cases, the attention has been on the

* **Arne Willy Dahl**, Judge Advocate General for the Norwegian Armed Forces until retirement in 2014. He was the President of the International Society for Military Law and the Law of War, 2006–2012.

[1] The study is documented in the Recueil of Seminar on Military Jurisdiction, 10–14 October 2001, which gives the national responses to a questionnaire, a report summing up the findings and other proceedings of the seminar. The Recueil can be obtained from the International Society for Military Law and the Law of War, Avenue de la Renaissance 30, 1000 Brussels, Belgium. E-mail: brussels@ismllw.org.

victim's right to an effective and unbiased investigation. Such considerations will be of particular importance when the issue is responsibility for core international crimes or other serious human rights violations, such as torture.

In addition to decisions by the European Court of Human Rights and other human rights bodies, one can also from time to time see eruptions of a more general distrust against military justice systems, from society at large. Such distrust can lead to fundamental changes, in some cases amounting to full dismantling of a military justice system and its replacement with fully civilian organs and procedures.

The aim of this chapter is to explore whether such developments should be resisted by the military, or whether they should be welcomed, fully or partially. The issue is whether accountability by independent organs is in the long-term self-interest of the armed forces and which factors are likely to promote the overall effectiveness of a system of accountability for real or alleged crimes.

2.1. The Natural Inclination to Resist Reforms

Military commanders and military lawyers will have a natural inclination to resist changes of military justice in the direction of civilianisation. After all, military justice has its roots in the military commander's need to control his soldiers. It is about punishing such acts as disobedience, abuse of alcohol and absence without leave, but also about securing proper behaviour towards civilians.[2] By enforcing discipline, the commander maintains his authority. If somebody else enforces discipline within his troops, it could undermine the commander's authority.[3] For these reasons, mili-

---

[2] William Shakespeare has provided an illustration in *King Henry V*, Act 3 Scene 7. The King has a conversation with Captain Fluellen about a successful encounter about a bridge. The King asks: "What men have you lost, Fluellen?". Fluellen answers: "[...] I think the duke hath lost never a man but one that is like to be executed for robbing a church; one Bardolph, if your majesty knows the man [...]". The King:

> We would have all such offenders so cut off: and we give express charge that in our marches through the country there be nothing compelled from the villages, nothing taken but paid for, none of the French upbraided or abused in disdainful language; for when lenity and cruelty play for a kingdom, the gentler gamester is the soonest winner.

[3] Disciplinary authority or authority to issue summary punishments is usually derived from command authority. As a personal observation, it can be noted that in discussions about which commander possesses this authority in a particular situation where the command

tary commanders are likely to resist reforms that are aimed at removing military justice from their hands.

It might, however, be useful to consider more closely which elements of possible reforms are harmful and which are beneficial. The perspective should be the enlightened long-term self-interest of both commanders as those responsible for the overall performance of their units, and soldiers in general as potential suspects, under investigation or on trial. It is my position that such enlightened long-term self-interest would concur with the interest of the general civilian society, which wants effective and disciplined armed forces with members than enjoy fundamental civil rights under the rule of law.

In other words, the military should consider its true long-term interest in order to contribute to solutions that secure the principles of fair trial and the rights of victims, also taking into account the needs of military effectiveness and the necessity of ensuring that the courts have a proper understanding of military affairs.

2.2. The Soldiers' Perspective

It goes without saying that it is in the interest of soldiers to have their cases heard in a fair trial. Important elements are independent courts, legal representation and the right to appeal. These aspects have been elaborated on by courts and academics, and should today be trivial. The author will therefore focus on some aspects of a different nature.

It is in the interest of soldiers to have their possible offences investigated, prosecuted and adjudicated by persons who are not only independent and impartial but also familiar with military affairs. Proper understanding of the case and the situation of the accused is also an important element in a fair trial. It will also be in the interest of soldiers to know and be able to show that someone has a certain degree of oversight of their actions, and the power to take action if something appears to go wrong. The author will illustrate with an example from personal experience.

---

structure is complex, it can be felt as an undercurrent that the commander who has the disciplinary authority is considered to have a more tangible command and therefore some form of supremacy vis-à-vis the commander who has not.

In 2006 the Norwegian Provincial Reconstruction Team ('PRT') in Meymanah in Afghanistan encountered a dangerous incident when it was beleaguered by a hostile mob claiming revenge for the publication of insulting cartoons of the Prophet Muhammad. Within the mob were particularly active persons aiming shots and throwing hand grenades over the wall of the PRT headquarters, succeeding in setting a vehicle of the PRT on fire at the main entrance gate. Some months after the incident an officer approached the author and said that at a certain critical moment, when the PRT was close to being overrun, he had considered machine-gunning the mob indiscriminately. The thought had, however, struck him: What will the Judge Advocate General ('JAG') say? He laid the machine gun down and stuck to aimed shots at those individuals who represented an imminent threat. He thereby saved his own conscience and reputation, and probably also the reputation and success of the whole Norwegian operation in Afghanistan.

On the other hand, it is sometimes the case that weapons are used with disastrous results for non-combatants in a way that could be problematic, requiring an investigation of the incident. When, for instance, a soldier at a checkpoint uses his gun against a vehicle that does not heed his warning signals and the vehicle in the event contained nothing but innocent civilians, one may ask whether he acted recklessly or whether he merely followed lawful orders. If such cases are investigated thoroughly and considered by an independent person who knows both the law and military life, and this person concludes that no wrongdoing has taken place, the soldier can continue his life with his head held high – in contrast to a situation when the case is either swept under the carpet or considered by someone with insufficient understanding of military law and military operations and procedures, and gives a superficial or wrong assessment.

War entails strain on soldiers and can put them in situations where they experience conflict of norms, making them feel guilty for their choices afterwards. I have twice been approached by persons who felt guilty about events that had never been investigated, in both cases through an intermediary. The first one goes back to the Second World War and was about a soldier who had been ordered to execute the local vicar for treason. The order had been given by his commanding officer, without any proper trial. The unit was about to be dissolved after having been gradually pushed by the invading enemy up through a valley until they were standing with their backs to the mountains. The soldier had taken the vicar and a firing squad with him in a truck, but had released the vicar instead of executing him. Now he felt guilty because of his disobedience to the commanding officer. My answer, via the intermediary – a local chief of police – was that an execution under the circumstances described would have been unlawful, and that the soldier had done the right thing.

The second soldier had been involved in a serious incident in Afghanistan and had shot a person who represented an immediate and mortal threat to the soldiers' unit. Through his gunsight he had seen the skull of the person split. Afterwards the sight had haunted him and he felt guilty about his act. I told the intermediary, who was his platoon leader, that under the circumstances described the shooting was both lawful and necessary and that the soldier had done the right thing. I hope my message gave him some relief.

Therefore, in addition to the official activity of a military prosecution service, its mere presence can contribute to giving soldiers both guidance and confidence, including peace of mind and the feeling of being a respectable person in spite of having made difficult choices on the site, and participated in warlike acts with lethal consequences for human beings.

2.3. The Commander's Perspective

As Shakespeare demonstrated, it is in the best interest of the military that units preserve goodwill and co-operation with local civilians. This is particularly important in unstable situations, where the allegiance of the local population can shift. In counter-insurgency operations it is paramount to maintaining legitimacy in competition with the insurgents.

As shown above, incidents that affect locals negatively can easily happen. These could range from mere accidents to real or alleged war crimes or other core international crimes. A commander might feel tempted to preserve the reputation of the unit by seeking to avoid unfavourable incidents becoming known publicly. If this is not possible, he may seek to downplay the gravity of the case by manipulating facts. Considerations of loyalty among colleagues may lead to a conspiracy of silence.

Such cover-ups are likely to be exposed sooner or later, and thus backfire. For the commander, even mere passivity with regard to initiating or facilitating investigation and prosecution of war crimes or other core international crimes can lead to responsibility under the rules of command responsibility. For him, and for the reputation of the military, it is much better that the case is investigated immediately and disciplinary action taken in minor cases, or that the case is submitted for prosecution if it is of sufficient gravity.

An incident involving the Norwegian Army can serve as an illustration. In 1999 rumours reached the JAG office indicating that Norwegian soldiers had subjected a young Kosovar to harsh treatment. A judge advocate was sent to the area to support the ongoing investigation conducted by the military police, although local commanders tended to downplay the seriousness of the affair and seemed not to see the need for any investigation. In the event, the case was found to be serious enough, but nothing like a war crime. A few weeks later I received a journalist from a major newspaper in my office who was able show me what the next day's front page would look like, with a rather embarrassing picture showing how the young Kosovar was being treated. Did I have any comment on the picture? Fortunately, I could tell him that we had submitted the case a few days earlier to the relevant military authorities with a recommendation for disciplinary action. Thus, the damage to the reputation of the army was kept at a minimum and unnecessary friction with the local population in Kosovo was avoided.

2.4. An Effective Justice System Best Serves Military Self-Interest

2.4.1. The Issue of Independence

Although it was of no consequence in the above-mentioned case, it has served the reputation of our armed forces well that the office of the Norwegian JAG is independent, outside the chain of command and actually receives its funds from the Ministry of Justice. This is particularly important when a high-profile case is investigated and the conclusion is that no crime has taken place, or that the case is less grave than it was assumed to be. It is much more convincing when an acquittal is given by an independent body than when the army has investigated and acquitted itself.

The conclusion, then, seems to be that it serves the long-term interest of the armed forces to have independent bodies to investigate, prosecute and adjudicate cases, in particular when they are of certain gravity. There are, however, also downsides. If independence means distance – in organisation, geography and mentality – one may find oneself in a situation where the independent bodies lack understanding of military affairs. If such lack of understanding leads to unwarranted sentences or acquittals, it is time to pull the brakes.

2.4.2. The Need for Expertise

In criminal cases, a court needs to know both the law and the factual aspects. Expert witnesses are often called upon to explain forensic details that may shed slight upon what the accused may or may not have done or intended to do. In financial cases, accountants may be called in to explain what the accounts show with regard to possible tax fraud or whatever the case is about. In some sectors, many countries have concluded that specialised courts are needed to deal effectively with particular cases.

One may ask whether this could also be relevant for military cases. In Norway, where the system is fully civilianised in peacetime, the specialised prosecutors occasionally have to explain important aspects of the case to the court – aspects that would have been known to the court if its members had some basic military experience. If the defence counsel, too, has to rely on the explanations of the prosecutor, one may ask whether the trial is really fair and balanced.

If one may doubt that the court needs expertise, one can hardly doubt that the investigators need it. During a preliminary investigation in the former Yugoslavia, a military lawyer had a discussion with a civilian investigator about the possible sources of some artillery shells that had struck a marketplace. The discussion revealed that the civilian investigator was unaware of the fact that artillery can hit targets on the other side of a mountain.[4] Had it not been for the presence of a colleague with military experience, the investigation would have risked being derailed.

This was a trivial example. In a high-tech environment such as in air and missile warfare, the demands for expertise are substantially higher. An investigator who does not understand, for example, weapons options, fusing, guidance systems, angle of attack, optimal release altitudes, command and control relationships, communications capabilities, tactical options, available intelligence options, enemy practices, pattern of life analysis, collateral damage estimate methodology, human factors in a combat

---

[4] Personal conversation with the late Judge Advocate Terje Lund.

environment, and so forth, will struggle to *effectively scrutinise* an air strike.[5]

One may, of course, ask whether any investigator, prosecutor or judge has a full understanding of all such factors. My answer is that he or she must have sufficient knowledge to know what to ask, who to ask and to understand the answers. This kind of and degree of knowledge is most likely found among persons who are familiar with the military environment, preferably also with the affected service.

2.4.3. The Need for Portability

If independence is obtained by severance of all connections with the military, one may also find oneself in practical difficulties when cases arise at units deployed overseas.

When soldiers are accused of having committed crimes against local civilians whom they are supposed to protect, it does not create a good impression to put the accused on an airplane for prosecution at home. The local affected civilians need to see that justice is done, which is best demonstrated by having deployable courts. This does not go well together with a civilian justice system. Any court that is going to sit in a combat area must do so as guests, if not members, of the armed forces. Preparations have to be made with regard to transport, billeting, security and, in many cases, vaccination. Attire suitable to the climate and general conditions may have to be issued – what the armed forces could offer might be uniforms. Such preparations should be done in advance, involving judges who are mentally prepared and willing to be deployed. In other words – close co-operation between the armed forces and the court is required.

In this connection, it can also be mentioned that status of forces agreements typically allow for exercise of jurisdiction by *military* courts of the sending state, while civilian courts exercising jurisdiction on foreign territory is an anomaly, which would require special arrangements with the host country.

---

5   Michael N. Schmitt, "Investigating Violations of International Law in Armed Conflict", in *Harvard National Security Journal*, 2011, vol. 2, no. 1, p. 31.

2.5. Jurisdiction Over Civilians

Human rights bodies have been sceptical with regard to military jurisdiction over civilians. This seems to have been out of a concern that military courts may not be impartial in cases that could be seen to have national security implications. In a report of the special rapporteur on the independence of judges and lawyers prepared for the United Nations General Assembly in 2013, it is said that military jurisdiction should be restricted to offences of a military nature committed by military personnel.[6]

Such concerns may be relevant with regard to countries where the military form a social and legal structure that is separated from the civilian sector. In other countries, where the military prosecution and/or the military courts are under the ultimate control of the civilian society, such concerns seem to have less weight. This would, for instance, be the case if the judgments of military courts can be appealed to the Supreme Court of the country and, in particular, if the military prosecution takes directions from the director of public prosecutions.

The issue of jurisdiction over civilians may look different when seen from the perspective of a unit deployed abroad, in contrast to a unit in a garrison in the home country. At home, it may not be of critical importance to the military whether a civilian person with some connection to the military has his case tried at the local district court or by a military court, particularly if the crime is not of a military nature which requires understanding of military affairs to adjudicate.

---

[6]   UN General Assembly, "Independence of judges and lawyers – Note by the Secretary-General", UN Doc. A/68/285 ('Knaul report'), para. 15:

> In the present report, the Special Rapporteur addresses these concerns and proposes a number of solutions that are premised on the view that States that establish military tribunals should ensure that such tribunals are an integral part of the general judicial system and function with competence, independence and impartiality, guaranteeing the exercise and enjoyment of human rights, in particular the right to a fair trial and the right to an effective remedy. *Also, their jurisdiction should be restricted to offences of a military nature committed by military personnel* (emphasis added).

The report gives particular attention to military and special tribunals in terrorism-related cases. In its resolution adopted on 27 March 2014 on the integrity of the judicial system (A/HRC/25/L.5) the UN Human Rights Council does not, however, reiterate this passage but focuses on the fact that military tribunals, when they exist, must be an integral part of the general justice system and operate in accordance with human rights standards, including respecting the right to a fair trial and due process of law guarantees (operative para. 2).

An important factor is, however, the increasing use of civilian contractors in conjunction with military forces. This is visible both at home and with units deployed abroad. In some cases, such contractors perform security functions that may lead to serious situations if not performed correctly.[7] Cases may have to be investigated and those responsible brought to justice. If military commanders have no summary punishment jurisdiction over such persons, and military courts that could be deployed have no penal jurisdiction over them, the end result could in practice be impunity. The potential for scandals, or at least complicated and inefficient prosecutions, is evident.

In the end, it could be an issue of the human rights of victims, as well as of the standing of the deployed military force among the local civilians, whether proper arrangements securing effective jurisdiction over civilians also exist.

2.6. Jurisdiction Over 'Civilian' Offences

If a soldier murders his wife, is this a case that ought to be handled by a military justice system? One may say that a murder is a murder and can be handled equally well, if not better, by civilian investigators, prosecutors and judges than by the military equivalents.

What if a soldier steals from his fellow soldiers? Is this a case of a military nature? It may not have been included as a provision in the military penal law, but it will certainly affect the cohesion and effectiveness of the unit involved. The commanding officer will perceive a need for having the case investigated and solved quickly, maybe with a higher priority than the civilian police (if within reach) would give to a similar offence involving two civilians.

From this it emerges that the dividing line between military and civilian offences may be fluid.[8] In Norway, as long as security regulations existed only within the military, breach of security (short of espionage) was a breach of service duties, in other words a military offence. When, in 1999, general legislation on security was enacted in Norway, breach of security became in principle a civilian offence.

---

[7]   *Ibid.*, Knaul report, paras. 89, 102, where it makes allowances for such situations.

[8]   *Ibid.* The Knaul report says in para. 32: "There is no consistency between different military legal systems with regard to what is meant by the term 'military offence'".

After the adoption of the 1998 ICC Statute of the International Criminal Court, a number of countries have enacted implementing legislation. War crimes, crimes against humanity and genocide, also known as 'core international crimes', have been defined in national law more or less based on the ICC Statute. Are such crimes of a military nature and should military courts deal with them? Some would explicitly exclude serious human rights violations from the jurisdiction of military courts.[9] The main concern, however, has been about cases where members of the armed forces are accused of serious violations such as extrajudicial executions, enforced disappearances and torture.[10] If such crimes take place within a country that is torn by civil unrest, there could be reasons to fear that the military might be tempted to shield the perpetrators and that the cases should, for this reason, be handled by the civilian justice system.

In other countries, the focus of attention would be on possible war crimes committed by members of the armed forces. In these cases the dividing line may also be fluid. For example, if a soldier intentionally shoots a civilian, it is a war crime. If he does so in the erroneous belief that the civilian was directly participating in hostilities, it may be a breach of the 1977 Additional Protocol I to the 1949 Geneva Conventions if he did not take all feasible precautions to verify that he was attacking a lawful target. This is not necessarily a war crime, at least not under the ICC Statute. It may also happen that he did not aim at the civilian at all, but used his weapon in breach of the applicable Rules of Engagement. This will turn the act into a military offence. Now, the issue of which law applies may not be apparent before the case has been investigated. It may be clear that a civilian has been shot and that the soldier most likely bears some responsibility for it, but it can be uncertain up to the point of sentencing under which law.

This said, it may be noted that cases about crimes against humanity or genocide do not necessarily have a significant military component. The perpetrators may be civilians, as they typically were in Rwanda, or the acts themselves were not part of a military operation, such as when inmates of a concentration camp are mistreated. The link to the military can be tenuous or totally absent and the arguments in favour of a military involvement in investigation, prosecution or adjudication weak. Such cases

---

[9] *Ibid.*, para. 106.
[10] *Ibid.*, para. 66.

are not the focus of this chapter, but those that have a clear connection to military activity.

My recommendation would therefore be that in cases, in particular those that arise from military operations, the jurisdiction over core international crimes and military offences should not be divided more than strictly necessary. This is particularly relevant in the investigation phase when it may be unclear whether one is facing one or the other.

2.7. Conclusions

The discussion in both national and international fora has revolved around the independence of military courts and, to some extent, also the independence of military prosecution and investigation. The 'frontline' seems to be between those who in the name of human rights want to abolish or severely restrict military prosecution, on the one hand, and those who defend it as necessary for military effectiveness, in particular under battlefield conditions, on the other. In support of the latter position, it could be added that a fully 'civilianised' system may not be able to deal effectively with military offences when it is most needed. This also goes for militarily organised justice systems if their jurisdiction is so heavily restricted that they cannot deal with cases that may be of great importance to the military as well as to potential victims of crimes.

The second report of the Turkel Commission (2013) concludes that – consistent with the Geneva Conventions and their Commentaries, decisions by tribunals and state practice – a military justice system is not necessarily inconsistent with the principle of independence. But it adds:

> In summary, in order to achieve an 'effective investigation' it must be conducted independently. The principle of independence consists of both institutional independence (for example, the prosecution is separate from the judiciary) and practical independence (for example, the investigators are in no way connected to the incident under consideration).[11]

In other words, it is not just any military justice system that will pass the test. Generally speaking, the same requirements that can be in-

---

[11] Turkel Commission, The Public Commission to Examine the Maritime Incident of 31 May 2010. Second Report: Israel's Mechanisms for Examining and Investigating Complaints and Claims of Violations of the Laws of Armed Conflict According to International Law, February 2013, paras. 73, 74.

ferred by international humanitarian law sources, as well as international human rights sources, concur with those requirements that are best suited to maintaining the standing of the armed forces in the eyes of the general public as well as its own members. One should, however, take care not to 'throw out the baby with the bathwater' by going to extremes that may prove counterproductive.

The important question that many countries struggle with is whether military commanders should give up their control of military justice in order to have a system that is perceived as fair by the general public. Equally important, however, is whether a process as indicated by current trends should run to the other extreme, separating the investigators, prosecutors and courts totally from the military structure, or whether one should seek some compromise solution, like the 'golden mean' indicated by Aristotle.

In this chapter I have tried to show that it is not necessarily in the best interest of the military to retain more or less self-contained military justice systems where military commanders have a prominent role. Important arguments include the following:

1. To retain the confidence of the general public, who are the taxpayers and elect the legislators, the military should avoid or remove any grounds for suspicion of possible cover-ups or abuse of power, in particular with regard to core international crimes.

2. To retain the confidence of its own personnel, fair trial and impartiality of courts and tribunals should be upheld. Justice must not only be done, it must also be seen to be done.

3. To retain the self-esteem of the personnel, it has to be kept under good discipline, thereby keeping up its good reputation.

4. The military should be able to show that all offences, including alleged war crimes and other core international crimes are investigated impartially and effectively and that the findings are credible. For this reason, organs for investigation, prosecution and adjudication should be independent of any person or organ that might have an interest in the outcome.

5. A good relationship with local civilians in overseas deployments is best served by disciplined troops that are kept visibly accountable by an effective and independent justice body.

6. Some countries might prefer to develop a justice system which is organised by the military, in the direction of independence. Other countries might be recommended to include certain military elements into their basically civilian systems, in order to handle military cases effectively. In both instances, military commanders should be able to provide valuable input, to the benefit of both military effectiveness and a fair and credible handling of cases.

3

Ownership of International Humanitarian Law

Richard J. Goldstone*

This anthology concerns the pertinent topic of the self-interest of armed forces in accountability for members who are responsible for core international crimes. This is an innovative and important topic. My chapter deals with what may in effect be a precondition for armed forces to experience such self-interest in accountability, namely that they possess a sense of ownership of international humanitarian and criminal law in the first place. It is my impression that this military sense of ownership has declined relatively speaking during the 20 years that have passed since the establishment of the *ad hoc* tribunals for the former Yugoslavia and Rwanda in the early 1990s. This is a worrisome trend, the reversal of which could directly affect the perception of military self-interest in accountability.

In the following sections, this chapter addresses the evolution of international humanitarian law and how it has been linked to national armed forces from the start, before considering the United States Armed Forces as an example of how a sense of ownership in international humanitarian and criminal law has fluctuated historically. The case is made for increased military ownership in this area of international law.

* **Richard J. Goldstone** is a former Justice of the Constitutional Court of South Africa and was the first Chief Prosecutor of the United Nations International Criminal Tribunals for the former Yugoslavia and Rwanda. In the recent years he has taught at several leading American universities. Justice Goldstone was appointed by the Secretary-General of the United Nations to the Independent International Committee, which investigated the Iraq Oil for Food program. In 2009 he led the UN Fact Finding Mission on Gaza. Among his other professional endeavours, Goldstone served as chairperson of the Commission of Inquiry regarding Public Violence and Intimidation that came to be known as the Goldstone Commission; and of the International Independent Inquiry on Kosovo. He was also co-chairperson of the International Task Force on Terrorism, which was established by the International Bar Association; director of the American Arbitration Association; a member of the International Group of Advisers of the International Committee of the Red Cross; and national president of the National Institute of Crime Prevention and the Rehabilitation of Offenders (NICRO). He is also a foreign member of the American Academy of Arts and Sciences and an honorary member of the Association of the Bar of the City of New York.

3.1. Recent Shift of Ownership of International Humanitarian Law

International humanitarian law or, as it was originally called, the law of war, goes back several centuries and was based on reciprocity. The theory was that the best way to ensure humane treatment for one's soldiers who fall into the hands of the enemy was to treat the enemies' soldiers under one's own power in a humane manner.

For a long time, the laws of war were not written, but based on well-recognised and accepted international custom. At times, they were also reinforced by religion and morality.

Until recent decades, those laws were owned and fashioned by the military. They did not fall within the remit of civilian authorities. That ownership appears to have become lost and it has somehow, perhaps unwittingly, been ceded to civilian government and to non-governmental organisations, both domestic and global. Today, this development appears to be taken very much for granted. This is unfortunate.

We should examine the reason for this shift and ask whether a movement back would not be timely, sensible and very much in the interests of the military establishment and, indeed, governments and their citizens. Military ownership of international humanitarian and criminal law extends to its enforcement, including accountability for individual force members who commit serious violations. Increased military ownership of international humanitarian and criminal law may raise the awareness within armed forces of their actual self-interest in such accountability for core international crimes.

3.2. The Lieber Code and International Humanitarian Law Growing Out of the Needs of Armed Forces

The first and most important codification *stricto sensu* of the customary laws of war was American – the Lieber Code of 1863. It was adopted by the Union Army at the time of the Civil War and became known as 'General Orders 100'. For over half a century the Lieber Code remained the official US army code for land warfare.

Francis Lieber was an unusual man. He was German and as a young man he had fought for the German Army against Napoleon. He came to the United States where he obtained citizenship in 1832. He was well educated and became a professor at South Carolina College. He detested slavery and moved to New York in 1857 where he became a professor at Columbia College and subsequently at the then newly established Columbia Law School. During the Civil War, Lieber's eldest son died fighting for the Confederacy while his two younger sons were fighting in the Union Army. One of them lost an arm in Tennessee. While visiting him in hospital, Lieber met General Henry W. Halleck, the commander of the Union forces in the West. When Halleck was appointed military adviser to President Lincoln, he requested Lieber to propose a "code of regulations for the government of armies in the field of battle authorised by the laws and usages of war".[1]

The resulting Lieber Code was a highly moral conception and dealt with the treatment of prisoners as well as prohibiting the use of poison in warfare. It recognised that rape as an instrument of warfare was a crime subject to death penalty.[2] In this regard the Lieber Code was more than a century ahead of its time.

The Lieber Code's historic importance lay in its recognition of the necessity of systematising the accumulated experiences and practices of the preceding decades. Its influence on all subsequent humanitarian law becomes evident in the Geneva Conventions and in the army manuals of many countries.

International humanitarian law – and especially the Geneva Conventions – were designed to guide the actions of the military during an international armed conflict. Their violation had no common criminal law consequences. They were rather matters for internal military investigation and sanction.

It was the exponential increase in the numbers of deaths and injuries of civilians, raping of women and displacement of populations that pushed civilian authorities to assume the control of humanitarian law.

Between 1864 and 1929 successive Geneva Conventions governed the treatment of sick and wounded members of armed forces in the field and at sea. They were extended to cover air war and the protection of prisoners of war, but did not govern the protection of civilians during

---

[1] See George B. Davis, "Doctor Francis Lieber's Instructions for the Government of Armies in the Field", in *American Journal of International Law*, 1907, vol. 1, no. 1, pp. 13–25.

[2] Francis Lieber, Instructions for the Government of Armies of the United States in the Field (Lieber Code), Article 44 (http://www.legal-tools.org/doc/842054/).

armed conflict.[3] That is hardly surprising given that armies fought against armies; civilians were not the intended objects of attack until well into the twentieth century.

Halfway through the twentieth century, deliberate attacks against civilians became the norm. According to Mary Kaldor, the ratio of civilian to military casualties was about 1:9 at the start of the century. This means for every civilian casualty there were about nine military casualties. In the Second World War the ratio was about 1:1. This is hardly surprising if one thinks about the intentional bombing of cities, large and small. During the past 30 years or so the ratio has risen to about 9:1, that is, for every military casualty there are nine civilian casualties. The ratio at the beginning of the century was completely reversed by the end of that most bloody 100 years.[4]

The previously unimaginable horrors of the Second World War moved humanitarian law firmly into the criminal law arena. It was at the insistence of the United States that Nazi leaders were placed on trial at Nuremberg. For the first time, there was acceptance and definition of the concept of crimes against humanity.

Those horrific crimes also led to the inclusion of the grave breach provisions in each of the four 1949 Geneva Conventions and the express language that their violation may constitute criminal conduct. For the first time in an international treaty, universal jurisdiction was conferred with respect to those offences. All 196 states party to the Conventions at the time of writing are enjoined by the Geneva Conventions to investigate and prosecute grave breaches wherever and by whoever committed. A state, unable or unwilling to do so, is under an obligation to hand the suspected war criminal to a state that is able and willing to do so.

---

[3]   They are the Convention for the Amelioration of the Condition of the Wounded in Armies in the Field, 22 August 1864; Geneva Convention for the Amelioration of the Condition of the Wounded and Sick in Armies at Sea, 6 July 1906; Geneva Convention Relative to the Treatment of Prisoners of War, 27 July 1929.

[4]   Mary Kaldor, *New and Old Wars: Organised Violence in a Global Era*, Polity Press, Cambridge, 1999, p. 100.

3.3.   The Case of the United States Armed Forces and Their Contributions to International Criminal Justice

The Nuremberg Trials were considered sufficiently successful to lead politicians and international lawyers to press for a permanent international criminal court. There is reference to such a court in Article 6 of the 1948 Genocide Convention and in Article 5 of the 1973 United Nations Convention that declared apartheid in South Africa a crime against humanity. However, it was to take almost half a century before such a court was established.

The United States was primarily responsible for moving the United Nations Security Council to establish the first truly international criminal tribunal for the former Yugoslavia. In turn, the United States strongly supported the establishment of the second *ad hoc* tribunal for Rwanda. The author knows from personal experience how crucial the support of the United States was for the work of those tribunals. The United States provided generous assistance in human resources, financial support and, perhaps most important of all, by placing political pressure on Balkan governments to comply with orders of the Yugoslavia tribunal. It was such pressure that led to the appearance in The Hague of the Serb and Croatian leaders indicted by the tribunal. It is remarkable that every single one of the persons indicted by that tribunal has ended up in The Hague. During the author's time as chief prosecutor that would have been regarded as quite impossible. The United States' support for the Rwanda and Sierra Leone tribunals was similarly generous and important. Yet again, it was the United States that pushed for the diplomatic conference in Rome that led to the establishment of the International Criminal Court ('ICC') . With regard to those developments, the United States military establishment was fully involved and supportive. Indeed, some of our finest investigators came from the ranks of the United States military.

The work of those tribunals was recognised by the United States as being quite consistent with its foreign policy. It was only shortly before the 1998 Rome Conference on the ICC that United States military leaders began to push back against accepting the prospect that its citizens might become amenable to the jurisdiction of an international criminal court. They successfully pressed President Bill Clinton to instruct the United States team at Rome to do their utmost to build in safeguards that would exclude its citizens from that jurisdiction. Their proposals included the

Security Council holding the key to investigations and thus make them subject to the veto of each of the five permanent members of the Security Council. They also attempted to ensure that the jurisdiction of the ICC would not extend to the nationals of any non-state party.

It was unsurprising that the United Sates was unable to persuade the conference to introduce sufficient safeguards to meet its concerns; consequently, it joined only six other nations in voting against the adoption of the ICC Statute.

The definitions of war crimes contained in the ICC Statute, I would suggest, are quite consistent with the laws and moral sensibilities of the American people. The objections to the ICC were based entirely upon a suspicion that the Court would likely be biased against the United States and might be used against it for political reasons.

An attempt to meet the United States' objections in Rome was the introduction of the principle of complementarity. This makes the ICC a court of last, not first, resort. If a country is able and willing to investigate crimes allegedly committed by its nationals and decides to do so, that decision effectively deprives the ICC of jurisdiction. Supporting that principle, the United States remained concerned that it would be the ICC judges who would have the last word as to whether a domestic investigation was in fact genuine and conducted in good faith, not a facade intended only to deprive the ICC of jurisdiction. As remote as such a decision might be, the United States was not willing to surrender any sovereignty at all in this regard. It is principally for this reason that there appears, at the time of writing, to be no prospect of the United States ratifying the ICC Statute in the foreseeable future.

This opposition to the ICC Statute has not prevented the United States from assisting the Office of the Prosecutor of the ICC. That co-operation began during the second term of President George W. Bush. The first word of that co-operation, to the author's knowledge, was announced during a panel discussion that the author moderated at the annual conference of the American Society of International Law in 2006. The then legal adviser at the State Department, John Bellinger, referred to that co-operation which was then already under way. That assistance has continued under the Obama administration.

3.4. Regaining Ownership of International Humanitarian Law and Military Self-Interest in Accountability

The ICC has jurisdiction to investigate and prosecute the nationals of any state for core international crimes allegedly committed in the territory of one of the 123 countries that have to date ratified the ICC Statute. As remote as it might be, I would suggest that if a United States citizen were to be charged by the Court, it would be highly embarrassing for his or her government and especially the military. Such a situation could be avoided if the United States military authorities were to regain complete ownership of the investigation of violations of international humanitarian law allegedly committed by any of its members. Such investigations would, in effect, be taken out of the political realm. The most efficient and direct way of accomplishing this would be the promulgation of legislation that incorporates into United States law all of the core international crimes defined in the ICC Statute. Regular United States military courts should be given exclusive jurisdiction to investigate and, if thought appropriate, to prosecute alleged violations. It is unlikely in the extreme that any ICC prosecutor would be able to attack, let alone establish, that such investigations and proceedings were tainted by *mala fides* or designed as a dishonest attempt to oust the jurisdiction of the ICC. These changes should go a long way to satisfy the United States military that they have little to fear from the powers and jurisdiction of the ICC.

I would suggest that nothing in the definitions of crimes in the ICC Statute would in any way be inconsistent with the United States Constitution, existing legislation or the moral imperatives that drive the United States to seek justice for, and protection of, innocent civilians and other non-belligerents.

Some of those definitions are already recognised in domestic law. I refer in this context to genocide and the grave breaches of the Geneva Conventions. However, humanitarian law has made huge strides in the past 21 years since the establishment of the Yugoslavia Tribunal. Even a cursory reading of the ICC Statute will demonstrate that. The extent to which those provisions of the ICC Statute should become part of the domestic law of the United States is a decision that ultimately Congress should make in full consultation with United States military authorities.

The effect of what the author is proposing is to bring the United States domestic law into line with the modern humanitarian law that is accepted across the democratic world and certainly by all of those countries that the United States regards as its allies, including its NATO partners. It would also protect United States citizens, especially members of the military, from any politically driven attempt to use the ICC process against them.

This chapter also suggests that it would be a useful legislative base should the United States ever, in the years to come, decide to join its many allies in ratifying the ICC Statute and regain its leadership in the enforcement of international humanitarian law.

This chapter has used the United States Armed Forces as an example of an armed force with a long history of ownership of international humanitarian and criminal law. My general argument is that such sense of ownership should now increase again in armed forces around the world. Much of international humanitarian and criminal law specifically addresses actors in armed forces. The law concerns their work processes, the risks combatants face and their ability to cause harm. But military ownership is not only based in the subject matter of the law. National armed forces have also participated extensively in the articulation of these two interrelated disciplines of international law over several decades.

Increasing a sense of ownership of international humanitarian and criminal law in new generations of soldiers and officers will bear directly on their understanding of the need to enforce that law. This includes accountability not only for violations that might be committed by members of hostile forces but also by members of their own forces. This anthology takes steps towards articulating a rationale for military self-interest in accountability for core international crimes. As such, the project has important policy implications. This chapter argues that as a new discourse opens up on military self-interest in accountability, we should pay due attention to the need to deepen the sense of ownership of international humanitarian and criminal law in armed forces.

4

The International Humanitarian Law Implementation Paradigm and the Idea of Military Self-Interest in Accountability

SONG Tianying*

It seems that the military's willingness to comply with international humanitarian law ('IHL') is, to some extent, self-explanatory. The laws of war originated from combat practice and are essentially the military's view of order in the context of war. The rules were made in part to preserve military interests by limiting the effects of war on combatants and preventing escalation. In reality, this logic remains a mystery. Throughout history, these laws made by the military have been flouted by the military. More than that, the long-standing perception of war-generated human catastrophe and the 'inspiration' of restricted war still seem to co-exist today.

Certainly, the landscape of the battlefield has been changing. The first Geneva Conventions were concluded to protect wounded and sick combatants and prisoners of war. Soldiers were at the centre of humanitarian concerns. Subsequently, rising civilian casualties in the two world wars and in armed conflicts during the 1950s to 1970s prompted rules protecting civilian populations. Today the rhetoric has become mostly civilian-centric. With the prevalence of non-international armed conflict, non-state armed groups have become significant players in the implementation of IHL rules, rules they had no part in making. At times IHL is perceived to be more imposed than desired.

This chapter looks at two conditions for IHL implementation: the material capabilities and willingness of the military. The first condition envisions IHL implementation through a professional military organisation, where effective accountability plays a crucial role. The second condition concerns the self-interest of the military – either state armed forces

---

* **SONG Tianying** is a Researcher at the European University Institute. She was formerly Legal Officer with the Regional Delegation for East Asia of the International Committee of the Red Cross ('ICRC'). All the Internet sources in this chapter were last accessed on 26 April 2015.

or non-state armed groups – in complying with IHL. In this regard, competing interests in military decision-making are also considered. It is noted that the composition of interests may vary due to the nature of armed conflicts and objectives of the military organisations. In light of the international efforts to address serious violations of fundamental norms, this chapter points to the long-term interests in ensuring compliance with IHL. It concludes that the military's internal accountability for serious IHL violations is key to reinforcing its professionalism and retaining essential values in the modern age.

4.1. Military Capability to Implement IHL

The IHL regime consistently harbours the aspiration of an efficient military structure. A capability to implement IHL reflects the military's level of professionalism. Although IHL is designed to regulate armed conflict situations, its implementation does not happen instantaneously in the battlefield. Capacity development in this respect is a top-down, long-term and repeated effort. The education and training process is easier during peacetime than in the heat of intensive operations where other priorities take precedence. In particular, implementation requires that the structures, administrative arrangements and personnel should be in place. The second aspect of military capability is that IHL violations are prevented, and punished when they do occur. Military personnel should be familiar with IHL rules and know the punitive consequences of violations.[1]

4.1.1. Effective Structure and Control

The implementation of IHL rules presupposes an effective chain of command. This element is common to all parties to an armed conflict, be they state or non-state armed forces. The 1949 Geneva Conventions and their 1977 Additional Protocols require armed forces of the parties to be organised, under responsible command and ultimately to have an internal discipline system enabling enforcement of the treaty provisions.[2] From a hier-

---

[1]   International Committee of the Red Cross, "Implementing International Humanitarian Law: From Law to Action", ICRC Advisory Service on International Humanitarian Law, available at https://www.icrc.org/eng/assets/files/other/implementing_ihl.pdf.

[2]   Article 4, Geneva Convention Relative to the Treatment of Prisoners of War of 12 August 1949 ('Geneva Convention III'); Article 43, Protocol Additional to the Geneva Conventions of 12 August 1949, and Relating to the Protection of Victims of International Armed

archical structure stems the commanders' duty to control the activities of their subordinates.[3] Subsequently, a party to the conflict "shall be responsible for all acts by persons forming part of its armed forces" under Article 3 of the Hague Convention No. IV and Article 91 of Additional Protocol I.

Certainly, the organisational element for non-state armed groups does not necessarily require a hierarchical system similar to that of regular armed forces. Yet enforcement of IHL rules is only realistic if there exists sufficient internal control, to which the applicability of IHL attaches.

4.1.2. Education and Training

Troops are expected first and foremost to obey orders issued to them. Additional Protocol I requires commanders to ensure members of the armed forces under their command are aware of their obligations. Commanders should give orders and instructions to ensure observance of IHL rules, and should supervise their execution.[4] To that end, IHL needs to form a natural and integral part of the standard principles that guide individual military personnel's actions at strategic, operational and tactical levels.[5] Thus the military must integrate IHL into its policies, procedures, codes of conduct and reference manuals, educate officers as well as the rank and file, and adapt the orders passed down through the chain of command accordingly.[6]

Theoretical knowledge of the doctrine must be combined with practical experience. It is not sufficient that members of the military go to the battlefield equipped with half-remembered IHL lessons. In the fog of war, decisions are often made in a split second, under stress and fear; rules

---

Conflicts ('Additional Protocol I'); and Article 1, Protocol Additional to the Geneva Conventions of 12 August 1949, and Relating to the Protection of Victims of Non-International Armed Conflicts ('Additional Protocol II').

3   Articles 86, 87, Additional Protocol I, see *supra* note 2.

4   *Ibid.*, Articles 80, 82, 87(2).

5   International Committee of the Red Cross, *Integrating the Law*, ICRC, Geneva, May 2007, p. 23, available at https://www.icrc.org/eng/assets/files/other/icrc_002_0900.pdf ('Integrating the Law').

6   Daniel Muñoz-Rojas and Jean-Jacques Frésard, "The Roots of Behaviour in War: Understanding and Preventing IHL Violations", in *International Review of the Red Cross*, 2004, vol. 86, no. 853, p. 204, available at https://www.icrc.org/eng/resources/documents/misc/5zbggl.htm.

---

must be built into combat instinct so as to be effective.[7] Daily training should include principles of the law, along with the measures, means and mechanisms for compliance. The training needs to be realistic and practical, as much for the success of future operations as for compliance with the law.[8] A strict organisational structure is also necessary to give effect to training at all levels. All these practices require sophisticated legal and military expertise, since IHL enforcement is a "professionalized process of norm internalization".[9]

4.1.3. Ensuring Compliance through Accountability

Knowledge of a norm is not necessarily sufficient to induce a favourable attitude or conforming behaviour. Even highly disciplined and trained armed forces have members who act against the doctrine, whether for individual or collective reasons. Sanctions are central to determining a combatant's behaviour. In light of this, education and training need to be backed up by effective punishment.[10] Sanctions offer the hierarchy a means of enforcing orders and discipline and of showing that the whole chain of command is firm in defending its fundamental values.[11] Disciplinary and penal measures must be consistent and predictable to have exemplary and deterrent effect. Even offences less serious than war crimes should be sanctioned and seen to be sanctioned. An unpunished breach could be widely seen as permitted or tacitly encouraged, which would lead to more serious violations.[12]

---

[7] For example, South Africa's *Law of Armed Conflict Manual* explains that "in the circumstances of combat, soldiers may often not have time to consider the principles of the LOAC before acting. Soldiers must therefore not only know these principles but must be trained so that the proper response to specific situations is second nature". Cited in International Committee of the Red Cross, Study on Customary International Humanitarian Law, Rule 142, "Instruction in International Humanitarian Law within Armed Forces", available at https://www.icrc.org/customary-ihl/eng/docs/v1_rul_rule142#refFn_47_9.

[8] Integrating the Law, 2007, p. 29, see *supra* note 5.

[9] Heike Krieger, *A Turn to Non-State Actors: Inducing Compliance with International Humanitarian Law in War-Torn Areas of Limited Statehood*, SFB-Governance Working Paper Series No. 62, Collaborative Research Center (SFB) 700, Berlin, 2013, p. 12, available at http://www.sfb-governance.de/publikationen/working_papers/wp62/SFB-Governance-Working-Paper-62.pdf.

[10] Muñoz-Rojas and Frésard, 2004, pp. 8, 15, see *supra* note 6.

[11] Integrating the Law, 2007, p. 35, see *supra* note 5.

[12] Muñoz-Rojas and Frésard, 2004, p. 14, see *supra* note 6.

The accompanying legal regime to ensure accountability within the military is a command responsibility. Because of their position and control, commanders have a *positive* obligation to punish violations. If they fail to intervene, they will be held accountable for the unlawful acts of their subordinates. This explains why control over subordinates is an inherent criterion for 'superiors' or 'commanders' so far as IHL implementation is concerned.[13] The US Supreme Court already stated the underlying rationale for this in the Yamashita Judgment in 1946: "[L]aw of war presupposes that its violation is to be avoided through the control of the operations of war by commanders who are to some extent responsible for their subordinates".[14]

4.2. Military Self-Interest in Complying with IHL

In reality, mere existence of law and the military's technical readiness to apply it do not automatically result in compliance. There needs to be political willingness. Non-legal factors are often considered of significance in decision-making.

4.2.1. Legitimacy and Support

Reputation affects the legitimacy and supporting resources of parties to an armed conflict. Adhering to IHL may improve the military's reputation among their constituencies, their allies and internationally. A good record may help a party gain the moral high ground while the other party may be stigmatised in the public's perception if it refuses to comply with the rules.[15]

With the proliferation of mass media, the contemporary impact of public opinion is stronger and more immediate. Knowledge of serious

---

[13] Article 86, Additional Protocol I and Commentary to Additional Protocol I, 8 June 1977, ICRC/Martinus Nijhoff Publishers, Dordrecht, 1987, p. 1013.

[14] United States Supreme Court, *United States v. Yamashita*, Judgment, 4 February 1946, 317 U.S. 1; 66 S. 340.

[15] International Committee of the Red Cross, "Improving Compliance with International Humanitarian Law", Report prepared by the International Committee of the Red Cross, Geneva, October 2003, p. 23, available at https://www.icrc.org/eng/resources/documents/report/ihl-respect-report-011003.htm. See also Michelle Mack with Jelena Pejić, *Increasing Respect for International Humanitarian Law in Non-International Armed Conflict*, ICRC, Geneva, 2008, p. 31, available at https://www.icrc.org/eng/resources/documents/publication/p0923.htm.

violations may create doubts among the state's population, which undermines the government's domestic legitimacy. Non-state armed groups who pursue long-term political goals, such as replacing the current government, also have a particular interest in cultivating a law-abiding image that is essential to winning political and material support. The United Nations ('UN') Secretary-General noted in a 2009 report that it was important to understand the need for popular support and the group's self-image when engaging non-state armed groups.[16] Territorial gains are more sustainable with popular support. Many non-state armed groups recruit, operate and acquire materials at local level. Most importantly, the local population hosts and channels information and intelligence essential for military operations.[17] Local support could be a survival issue. MAO Zedong used a fish in water metaphor when writing on guerrilla strategies: just like fish would die without water, the guerrillas' cause would fail without the people's support.[18] Uganda's president, Yoweri Museveni, when talking about his past "revolutionary war" against the former government, stated that

> a revolutionary warrior is like Jesus. You must not drink alcohol, you must not mistreat civilians, you must not take liberties with women, and, as Mao Tse-tung said, "You should never take a single needle or thread from the people without paying for it." And in case one of our soldiers commits a mistake, especially killing people, he must be punished where the mistake was committed, in front of the people. If you take him away to punish him somewhere else, you are in trouble with the population, especially a population which is not educated. Because they will not know whether you punished him or not, they will think that you have just covered him up. So that discipline is very crucial for the revolutionary cause to succeed.[19]

---

[16] Report of the Secretary-General on the Protection of Civilians in Armed Conflict, 22 May 2012, para. 42, UN Doc. S/2012/376 ('Secretary-General's Report 2012').

[17] Olivier Bangerter, "Reasons Why Armed Groups Choose to Respect International Humanitarian Law or Not", in *International Review of the Red Cross*, 2011, vol. 93, no. 882, p. 363.

[18] MAO Tse-Tung, *On Guerrilla Warfare*, translated by Samuel B. Griffith, University of Illinois Press, Champaign, IL, 2000, chapter 6 (originally published in 1937).

[19] Yoweri Kaguta Museveni, "The Strategy of Protracted People's War: Uganda", in *Military Review*, 2008, vol. 88, no. 6, p. 9.

For non-state armed groups, fighting responsibly also increases their chances of dialogue with states, including the one they are fighting against, as well as the international community. In Colombia, Liberia, Nepal, the Philippines, Sierra Leone, Sri Lanka, the Sudan and the former Yugoslavia, non-state armed groups have concluded unilateral declarations or special agreements, as envisaged under international humanitarian law,[20] to expressly commit themselves to complying with their obligations or undertake commitments that go above and beyond what are required by the law. These instruments can send a clear message to the groups' members and encourage appropriate internal disciplinary measures.[21] In the Philippines in 2009, both the government and the Moro Islamic Liberation Front ('MILF') actively supported and co-operated with the non-governmental organisation Geneva Call to facilitate an investigation of the MILF's alleged breaches of Geneva Call's Deed of Commitment banning anti-personnel mines.[22] Some non-state armed groups may even wish to be seen as more respectful of international norms than the state against which they are fighting.[23] Conversely, the 'terrorist' label, especially when it is apparently justified, has steep political costs and doors shut quickly.

State armed forces may have similar concerns, as to whether they will receive international support or be shamed and isolated for unlimited

---

[20] Common Article 3 of the 1949 Geneva Conventions provides that parties to non-international armed conflicts may bring into force other provisions of the Conventions through special agreements. Such agreements do not affect the legal status of the parties to the conflict.

[21] Report of the Secretary-General on the Protection of Civilians in Armed Conflict, 29 May 2009, para. 42, UN Doc. S/2009/277 ('Secretary-General's Report 2009'). For overview of commitments issued by non-state armed groups, see Sandesh Sivakumaran, "Lessons for the Law of Armed Conflict from Commitments of Armed Groups: Identification of Legitimate Targets and Prisoners of War", in International Review of the Red Cross, 2011, vol. 93, no. 882, pp. 463–82.

[22] Geneva Call, "Verification Mission to Investigate Allegations of Landmine Use by the Moro Islamic Liberation Front in the Philippines Conducted", 30 November 2009, available at http://www.genevacall.org/verification-mission-investigate-allegations-landmine-use-moro-islamic-liberation-front-philippines-conducted/.

[23] For example, many non-state armed groups that have signed Geneva Call's Deed of Commitment whereby they renounce the use of anti-personnel mines are operating in States not party to the 1997 Anti-Personnel Mine Ban Convention (such as India, Iran and Myanmar). See Geneva Call, "Anti-personnel Mines and Armed Non-State Actors", available at http://www.genevacall.org/how-we-work/armed-non-state-actors/.

---

violence. The recently concluded Arms Trade Treaty[24] may further illustrate the correlation between IHL compliance and military resources. Article 6 of this treaty prohibits a state party from authorising any transfer of arms if it knows the arms or items would be "used in the commission of genocide, crimes against humanity, grave breaches of the Geneva Conventions of 1949, attacks directed against civilian objects or civilians protected as such, or other war crimes as defined by international agreements to which it is a party". In relation to export decisions specifically, Article 7 prohibits arms export if there is an "overriding risk" that the arms could be used to commit or facilitate "a serious violation of international humanitarian law" or "international human rights law". As this treaty gains momentum, it is expected to curb the arms supply for states that defy fundamental international norms.

4.2.2. Military Advantages

Military efficacy and IHL implementation could be mutually reinforcing. An efficient chain of command provides material conditions for compliance, and is at the same time reinforced through eradication of the uncontrolled use of violence in war. An efficient, disciplined army has a better chance of succeeding in its undertakings, while a loose, lawless army is bound to fail, if it could qualify as an army at all. Following the rules may also make economic sense, as it could save military resources – weapons are better used against military targets than causing needless destruction to civilians and their property.[25] Also, the military may come to realise that certain violations of IHL rules are counterproductive to military operations, in addition to their humanitarian costs.[26] For example, humane treatment of captured enemies encourages surrender. A soldier who knows that mistreatment or summary execution upon surrender is the norm is more likely to fight until death.

---

[24] The Arms Trade Treaty, entered into force 24 December 2014. As of 26 April 2015, 67 states have ratified the treaty, available at http://disarmament.un.org/treaties/t/att/text.

[25] Mack and Pejic, 2008, pp. 30, 31, see *supra* note 15.

[26] *Ibid.*, p. 30. Geneva Academy of International Humanitarian Law and Human Rights, *Rules of Engagement: Protecting Civilians through Dialogue with Armed Non-State Actors*, Geneva Academy of International Humanitarian Law and Human Rights, Geneva, 2011, p. 23, available at http://www.geneva-academy.ch/docs/publications/Policy%20 studies/Rules%20of%20Engagement.pdf.

4.2.3. Reciprocal Respect

Reciprocity is by no means the basis of the parties' obligations, yet it affects behaviour in armed conflicts. Respect for norms by one party to a conflict may encourage respect by the other. Conversely, abuses and violations committed by one party may easily provoke a similar response from the other party. In his 2009 report on the protection of civilians in armed conflict, the UN Secretary-General argued that the "incentives for armed groups to comply with the law should be emphasized, including increased likelihood of reciprocal respect for the law by opposing parties".[27] It is in the parties' common interest to adhere to IHL rules, either in international or non-international armed conflicts.

For example, reciprocal thinking is prominent in the treatment of prisoners. Two world wars abounded with bitter lessons in this respect.[28] In the notorious "shackling crisis" during the Second World War, British commandos tied up German soldiers who could not be immediately treated as prisoners of war during a landing operation in Dieppe, France. Though the commandos' act was not clearly a violation of existing law, the Germans tied up all Allied prisoners of war taken at Dieppe in retaliation. As a counter-reprisal, the British government ordered an equal number of German prisoners of war to be shackled. As the combative reactions of the two sides escalated, more prisoners of war were wearing real or substitute manacles. Article 2 (3) of the 1929 Geneva Convention relative to the Treatment of Prisoners of War already forbade measures of reprisal against prisoners of war. Germany and the United Kingdom were states parties to the 1929 Geneva Convention, and had expressly reaffirmed their intention to abide by the terms of the Convention at the beginning of the war. Yet the situation quickly descended in a downward spiral. Both the United Kingdom and Germany had sought support from their respective partners in the escalation of reprisals, and failed. It became clear to both parties that there was nothing to gain through the shackling, and that only the welfare of their own prisoners of war was in

---

[27] Secretary-General's Report 2009, para. 41, see *supra* note 21.

[28] See, generally, Geneva Convention relative to the Treatment of Prisoners of War: Commentary, ICRC, 1960, Article 13(3), pp. 141–42.

jeopardy. The treatment of prisoners of war was eventually normalised through quiet, informal de-escalations.[29]

In addition, although the law of non-international armed conflict does not provide for a comparable prisoner of war regime, many armed groups have declared that they would treat captured members of state armed forces as prisoners of war. This is often done through a commitment on the part of the armed group to apply the Third Geneva Convention relative to the Treatment of Prisoners of War.[30] As a recent example, during the Libyan civil war in 2011, the National Transitional Council declared it "would like to reiterate that its policies strictly adhere to the 'Geneva Convention relative to the treatment of Prisoners of War' as well as with the ethical and moral values of the Libyan society".[31]

4.2.4. Core Values and Personal Integrity

IHL rules, as they appeal to basic conditions of human life and dignity, are not only universal but often reminiscent of the values or ethics in local cultures and traditions. Some armed forces genuinely aspire to respect human dignity. In particular, rules regarding the protection of civilian populations, including defenceless women and children, usually do not need be imported or justified from outside. For example, the Shiite spiritual leader in Iraq Grand Ayatollah Ali al-Sistani in his "Advice and Guidance to the Fighters on the Battlefields" stated that God has placed "conditions and etiquettes" on the conduct of hostilities. These limitations are "necessitated by wisdom and mandated by the primordial nature of human beings". He specifically told fighters not to "indulge in acts of extremism", among others, not to kill an elder, a child or a woman.[32]

Holding on to the core values of IHL has positive effects on the morale of the military. On an individual level, it has been observed that most

---

[29] Simon P. MacKenzie, "The Shackling Crisis: A Case-Study in the Dynamics of Prisoner-of-War Diplomacy in the Second World War", in *International History Review*, 1995, vol. 17, no. 1, pp. 78–98.

[30] For an overview of commitments and practice of armed groups regarding treatment of prisoners, see Sivakumaran, 2011, pp. 16–17, *supra* note 18.

[31] EJIL: Talk! (Blog of the *European Journal of International Law*), "Operationalising the Law of Armed Conflict for Dissident Forces in Libya", 31 August 2011, available at http://www.ejiltalk.org/2011/08/.

[32] Grand Ayatollah Ali Sistani, "Advice and Guidance to the Fighters on the Battlefields", available at http://www.sistani.org/english/archive/25036/.

people eventually feel less about themselves after killing civilians, not
more. Such violations against others are, ultimately, also a violation of
oneself. On the other hand, it could be rewarding to treat civilians well in
war. Positive encounters with civilians may, to a certain extent, relieve the
dehumanising effects of war.[33] Dražen Erdemović, a soldier in the Bosnian Serb Army who was forced to participate in the shooting and killing of
hundreds of unarmed Bosnian Muslim men from Srebrenica, came forward several months after the massacre. Later, before the International
Criminal Tribunal for the former Yugoslavia ('ICTY'), he confessed that
the killing deeply disturbed his conscience and integrity, and he felt "terribly sorry".[34]

---

[33] Hugo Slim and Deborah Mancini-Griffoli, *Interpreting Violence: Anti-Civilian Thinking
and Practice and How to Argue against it More Effectively*, Centre for Humanitarian Dialogue, Geneva, 2007, pp. 26, 28, available at http://www.hdcentre.org/uploads/tx_news/
85InterpretingViolence-Anti-civilianthinkingandpracticeandhowtoargueagainstitmore
effectively.pdf.

[34] Dražen Erdemović's guilty plea statement, dated 20 November 1996, is online at the ICTY
website, available at http://www2.icty.org/sid/212, it reads as follows:

> I wish to say that I feel sorry for all the victims, not only for the ones
> who were killed then at that farm, I feel sorry for all the victims in the
> former Bosnia and Herzegovina regardless of their nationality.
>
> I have lost many very good friends of all nationalities only because
> of that war, and I am convinced that all of them, all of my friends, were
> not in favour of a war. I am convinced of that. But simply they had no
> other choice. This war came and there was no way out. The same
> happened to me.
>
> Because of my case, because of everything that happened, I of my
> own will, without being either arrested and interrogated or put under
> pressure, admitted even before I was arrested in the Federal Republic of
> Yugoslavia, I admitted to what I did to this journalist and I told her at
> that time that I wanted to go to the International Tribunal, that I wanted
> to help the International Tribunal understand what happened to
> ordinary people like myself in Yugoslavia.
>
> As Mr. Babić has said, in the Federal Republic of Yugoslavia I
> admitted to what I did before the authorities, judicial authorities, and
> the authorities of the Ministry of the Interior, like I did here. Mr. Babić
> when he first arrived here, he told me, "Dražen, can you change your
> mind, your decision? I do not know what can happen. I do not know
> what will happen."
>
> I told him because of those victims, because of my consciousness,
> because of my life, because of my child and my wife, I cannot change
> what I said to this journalist and what I said in Novi Sad, because of the
> peace of my mind, my soul, my honesty, because of the victims and
> war and because of everything. Although I knew that my family, my

---

4.3. Competing Interests in Decisions to Comply

Effective implementation is only possible when the military has capability and willingness. Failure to comply may be the result of a lack of capability or willingness, or both. A prominent feature of contemporary armed conflicts is the proliferation and fragmentation of non-state armed groups. They comprise a kaleidoscope of identities, motivations and degrees of willingness to observe IHL. Certain non-state armed groups or even state armed forces simply do not have consistent internal control and sufficient expertise to implement the law; they risk accountability for core international crimes and ultimate military failure. The *laissez-faire* approach sometimes derives from a combination of lack of capability and willingness to comply. Meanwhile, in other situations, the military consciously adopts and pursues policies to violate the law. Violations are operationalised *because of* their professionalism. This section will focus on the military's lack of 'willingness', not 'capability', to comply, and its connection with the characteristics of the entity itself and armed conflict.[35]

4.3.1. Group Ideologies

The problem is that some militaries' fundamental beliefs contradict IHL principles. For them, violence against civilians constitutes a goal in itself. Ideologies of "political or racial purity" are formulated by leaders who determine that policies of mass killing, rape and terror are responses to the problems they face or the ambitions they have.[36] In so-called 'identity conflicts', a party may perceive all members of the enemy population as legitimate targets, regardless of their actual role in the hostilities. Such ideologies render the distinction principle under IHL meaningless.[37] His-

---

parents, my brother, my sister, would have problems because of that, I did not want to change it.

Because of everything that happened I feel terribly sorry, but I could not do anything. When I could do something, I did it. Thank you. I have nothing else to say.

[35] For overview of anti-civilian scenarios, see Alexander William Beadle, *Protection of Civilians – Military Planning Scenarios and Implications*, Norwegian Defence Research Establishment (FFI), Kjeller, 2014, available at http://www.ffi.no/no/Rapporter/14-00519.pdf.

[36] Slim and Mancini-Griffoli, 2007, pp. 9–10, see *supra* note 33.

[37] Camilla Waszink, "Protection of Civilians under International Humanitarian Law: Trends and Challenges", Norwegian Peacebuilding Resource Centre Report, August 2011, pp. 27–

---

tory has witnessed many calculated atrocities against civilians by extremist militaries, such as the genocides committed by the Nazi Army during the Second World War and by Interahamwe and Impuzamugambi, Hutu paramilitary organisations, in Rwanda. In his foreword to this book, Andrew T. Cayley highlights the example of the Srebrenica massacre executed by the Bosnian Serb Army in full efficiency, which shows values do not necessarily come with professionalism. Where values are problematic, professionalism could be a curse: the more professional the armed forces are, the further they go in the wrong direction. The above-mentioned Erdemović case shows the extent to which the military machinery can enforce genocidal plans through ruthless internal control.

At the time of the writing, extremist groups such as Islamic State ('IS') and al-Nusrah Front continue to threaten international peace and security.[38] They remain a grave concern to the international community. IS considers that assisting its enemies in any way – such as providing clothing, food, medical treatment and so on – constitutes unbelief and apostasy. By virtue of such acts, a person becomes "a target […] whose blood is licit to shed". On 21 September 2014, an IS official spokesman, Abu Muhammad al-Adnani, called on all supporters to arbitrarily kill Westerners throughout the world – Americans, Canadians, Australians and their allies, both civilians and military personnel.[39]

4.3.2. The Utility Approach

Violations can be motivated by practical gains, such as short-term military or political advantages. The utility approach is particularly appealing to armed forces that deem themselves fighting for survival, or those that have grossly inferior military strength and technical capacity compared to

---

28, available at http://www.operationspaix.net/DATA/DOCUMENT/6547~v~Protection _of_Civilians_Under_International_Humanitarian_Law__Trends_and_Challenges.pdf.

[38] See, for example, United Nations Security Council, Resolution No. 2199, Threats to International Peace and Security Caused by Terrorist Acts, S/RES/2199 (2015), 12 February 2015; United Nations Security Council, Resolution No. 2199, Threats to International Peace and Security Caused by Terrorist Acts, SC/RES/2170 (2014), 15 August 2014.

[39] Cole Bunzel, *From Paper State to Caliphate: The Ideology of the Islamic State*, The Brookings Project on US Relations with the Islamic World, Analysis Paper No. 19, The Brookings Institution, Washington, DC, 2015, pp. 36, 39, available at http://www.brookings.edu/~/media/research/files/papers/2015/03/ideology-of-islamic-state-bunzel/the-ideology-of-the-islamic-state.pdf.

---

the enemy. In such asymmetrical conflicts, the weaker party sometimes seeks to compensate for its material inferiority by resorting to tactics prohibited by IHL.[40] For example, resorting to perfidy or launching attacks from cultural properties may exploit the enemy's desire to respect protected persons or objects, and temporarily gain the upper hand in a battle. The act of looting ruins enemy societies and contributes to war supplies. Recruiting child soldiers may increase the size of the armed forces when numbers are key to territorial control and operations on multiple fronts. In this connection, a former leader of an African armed group said: "if you want to make a large fire, you need lots of wood".[41]

In the final months of the Sri Lankan civil war in 2009, the Liberation Tigers of Tamil Eelam ('LTTE') prevented civilians within its control from escaping the heavy firepower of government forces, in an attempt to render areas immune from attack and to seek military and propaganda advantage. The consequences for civilians were catastrophic. Thousands were killed and wounded while access to medical and other assistance was extremely limited.[42]

Atrocities may serve political or propaganda purposes. During the Spanish Civil War, General Emilio Mola said: "It is necessary to spread an atmosphere of terror. We have to create an impression of mastery".[43] In addition, attacks on civilians are likely to generate considerable media attention and thus create an impression that an armed group is stronger than it actually is. An extreme case is the forced amputations of civilians by the Revolutionary United Front ('RUF') , an armed group who used to operate in Sierra Leone. The RUF resorted to this practice because of "how much international coverage the amputations were getting as compared to other aspects of the war".[44]

---

[40] More on incentives for violations of IHL in 'asymmetric conflict', see Robin Geiß, "Asymmetric Conflict Structures", in *International Review of the Red Cross*, 2006, vol. 88, no. 864, pp. 757–777; Waszink, 2011, pp. 11–13, see *supra* note 37.

[41] Bangerter, 2011, pp. 354, 371, see *supra* note 17.

[42] Secretary-General's Report 2009, para. 30, see *supra* note 21; United Nations, Report of the Secretary-General's Panel of Experts on Accountability in Sri Lanka, 31 March 2011, p. iii, available at http://www.un.org/News/dh/infocus/Sri_Lanka/POE_Report_Full.pdf ('Secretary-General's Panel on Sri Lanka').

[43] Slim and Mancini-Griffoli, 2007, p. 12, see *supra* note 33.

[44] Bangerter, 2011, p. 375, see *supra* note 17.

4.4. Long-Term Effects of IHL Compliance and International Movement Towards Accountability

Violations of fundamental norms motivated by utility are ultimately self-defeating. For example, perfidy, as it exploits and undermines the minimum trust between the parties, soon stops being effective and jeopardises the safety of protected persons. Inadequately monitored anti-personnel mines are a double-edged sword as they may be triggered by both the installers and the enemy. The Fuerzas Armadas Revolucionarias de Colombia (Revolutionary Armed Forces of Colombia, FARC) risked being a victim of its own anti-personnel mines initially laid to ensure night-time security, as they failed to remove them in the morning and 'forgot' where the mines were.[45] Former child soldiers who have been extensively exposed to war may destabilise the fragile post-conflict community. The military and political advantages expected from IHL violations are simply not sustainable. Empirical research reveals the trend among non-state armed groups that the stronger a group is the more likely it will comply with the norms of IHL.[46]

Respect for IHL also has a delayed impact when it comes to the conclusion of peace. When the conflict ends, as it will, the legitimacy of a party's power – whether in government or in opposition – might be challenged by its violations during the conflict.[47] IHL violations deepen societal divisions and perpetuate resentments, which make post-conflict reconciliation more difficult.[48]

Accountability for international crimes is an inescapable reality for armed forces nowadays. Either covering up serious violations of IHL within the military or resorting to policies of deliberate violations are no longer sustainable strategies. After government forces defeated the LTTE in 2009, Sri Lanka embarked on a long and arduous process of addressing the accountability of both the state and LTTE forces during the war.[49] To

---

[45] *Ibid.*, p. 366.

[46] Krieger, 2013, pp. 20–21, see *supra* note 9.

[47] Mack and Pejic, 2008, p. 33, see *supra* note 15.

[48] See, for example, Elizabeth Salmón G., "Reflections on International Humanitarian Law and Transitional Justice: Lessons to be Learnt from the Latin American Experience", in *International Review of the Red Cross*, 2006, vol. 88, no. 862, p. 330.

[49] Secretary-General's Panel on Sri Lanka, see *supra* note 42; Sri Lanka Commission of Inquiry, Report on Lessons Learnt and Reconciliation, November 2011, available at

---

this day, the ICTY and the Balkan states continue to prosecute war crimes and crimes against humanity committed during the Balkan conflict of the 1990s.[50] Even alleged former Nazi perpetrators are still being pursued by domestic justice systems.[51]

Failing to take adequate measures to ensure compliance with IHL has direct implications of individual criminal responsibility and other serious consequences such as arms embargoes, travel bans and asset freezes. For instance, in Resolution 1970 (2011) the UN Security Council condemned violations against civilians in Libya, demanded compliance with international law, imposed a comprehensive arms embargo and targeted sanctions, and referred the situation to the International Criminal Court ('ICC') . In Resolutions 1572 (2004) and 1591 (2005) on Côte d'Ivoire and the Sudan respectively, the Security Council called upon member states to impose travel bans and asset freezes against persons responsible for human rights and humanitarian law violations. Sudan's president, Omar Hassan al-Bashir, has cancelled official visits abroad due to the ICC's arrest warrants against him on charges of genocide, war crimes and

---

http://www.slembassyusa.org/downloads/LLRC-REPORT.pdf; United Nations General Assembly, Human Rights Council, Annual Report of the United Nations High Commissioner for Human Rights Promoting Reconciliation, Accountability and Human Rights in Sri Lanka, 26 March 2014, A/HRC/25/L.1/Rev.1; United Nations, Human Rights Council, Resolution 19/2, Promoting Reconciliation and Accountability in Sri Lanka, 16 August 2012, A/HRC/19/2; United Nations General Assembly, Human Rights Council, Resolution 21/1, Promoting Reconciliation and Accountability in Sri Lanka, 9 April 2013, A/HRC/22/1, 9 April 2013; Colleen Mallick, "Sri Lanka to Initiate New War Crimes Investigation", in *Jurist*, 29 January 2015, available at http://jurist.org/paperchase/2015/01/sri-lanka-to-initiate-new-war-crimes-investigation.php.

[50]   Ashley Hogan, "Bosnia Prosecutors Indict 10 Former Soldiers for War Crimes", in *Jurist*, 15 April 2015, available at http://jurist.org/paperchase/2015/04/bosnia-prosecutors-indict-10-former-soldiers-for-war-crimes.php.

[51]   Ashley Hogan, "Accused Nazi Officer Goes on Trial, Admits Moral Guilt", in *Jurist*, 21 April 2015, available at http://jurist.org/paperchase/2015/04/accussed-nazi-officer-goes-on-trial-admits-moral-guilt.php; Jaclyn Belczyk, "US Officials Arrest Accused Nazi Guard", in *Jurist*, 18 June 2014, available at http://jurist.org/paperchase/2014/06/us-officials-arrest-accused-nazi-guard.php; Ashley Hileman, "Germany Reopens Investigations into Hundreds of Former Nazi Death Camp Guards", in *Jurist*, 5 October 2011, available at http://jurist.org/paperchase/2011/10/germany-reopens-investigations-of-hundreds-of-former-nazi-death-camp-guards.php.

---

crimes against humanity.[52] Bashir is largely isolated under the world's spotlight.

On another front, international commissions of inquiry and fact-finding missions are increasingly used to respond to serious violations of IHL and human rights law. They set out to help a society to move forward through identification of the parties' responsibilities and recommendations of domestic measures.[53] Truth commission findings have also laid the groundwork for prosecutions, including by informing Security Council decisions to refer situations to the ICC, thereby facilitating the Court's investigations.[54]

Effective command and control by the military leadership serve its interest. Ensuring compliance with IHL and, in turn, accountability for core international crimes shows the professionalism and values of the military. It was what was expected of the military when the rules were made and remains so today. With all the bloodshed spilt during the twentieth century, the international community stays vigilant concerning the military's anti-civilian ideologies and deliberate accession to lawlessness.

Also alarming is the corrosive effect of lapses of accountability in individual deviations from the norms. Even after making the bigger philosophical decision to comply with the law, the military is sometimes reluctant to move to accountability for reasons of self-preservation and image. However, it is not plausible to sanction less serious offences but deny war crimes, or dilute war crimes to mere disciplinary breaches because of the broader implications of war crimes. Selectivity and unevenness in punishment not only undermines the implementation of IHL rules but also

---

[52] *Sudan Tribune*, "Bashir cancels Indonesia trip over denial of flight permissions: sources", 20 April 2015, available at http://www.sudantribune.com/spip.php?article54679; and Reuters, "Sudan's Bashir Cancels Plan to Attend U.N. Assembly: U.N. Official", 26 September 2013, available at http://www.reuters.com/article/2013/09/26/us-sudan-protest-bashir-idUSBRE98P06B20130926.

[53] See, for example, Yasmin Sooka, "Dealing with the Past and Transitional Justice: Building Peace Through Accountability", in *International Review of the Red Cross*, 2006, vol. 88, no. 862, pp. 311–25; Salmón, 2006, see *supra* note 48. For an overview of international fact-finding mandates between 1992 and 2013, see Marina Aksenova and Morten Bergsmo, "Non-Criminal Justice Fact-Work in the Age of Accountability", Annex, in Morten Bergsmo (ed.), *Quality Control in Fact-Finding*, FICHL Publication Series no. 19, Torkel Opsahl Academic EPublisher, Florence, 2013, p. 23 (https://www.legal-tools.org/doc/5b59fd/).

[54] Secretary-General's Report 2012, para. 64, see *supra* note 16.

corrupts the overall control and command within the military. There is a thin line between delicately covered-up digressions and unthinking all-out violations. A mature, forward-looking military should be able to overcome the immediate repercussions of admitting serious international crimes, in order to maintain the right direction in the long run.

In the course of IHL implementation, it is important for the military to look at its long-term self-interest in light of the contemporary global fight against impunity for serious international crimes. Either operating in denial and isolation or a halfway implementation is no solution. It is in the military's self-interest to raise accountability and expectations of accountability within the chain of command.

5

Accountability in the 19th-Century US Army

Elizabeth L. Hillman*

5.1. Introduction: Military Effectiveness and Legitimacy through Professionalisation

The interest of the 19th-century US military in imposing accountability for war crimes derived in no small part from its desire to avoid excessive civilian interference in military operations. Early in the US Civil War, Union General Henry W. Halleck wrote a letter to George B. McClellan, his commanding general, about the efforts of his officers. Halleck complained that "the want of success on our part is attributable to the politicians rather than to the generals".[1] Halleck's frustration with civilian control of the army was far from unusual during the 19th century. As the United States Army became a professionalised force rather than a group of citizen-soldiers summoned to temporary duty, commanding officers grew more concerned with protecting the army from civilian encroachment. Interference could come from above, in the form of meddling politicians, or below, in the ill-prepared citizen-soldiers who were thrust into the ranks during times of war. Holding soldiers accountable for crimes of war was one means of protecting and sustaining the profession of arms. It is no accident that Halleck, a scholar and reformer who became a major

---

* **Elizabeth L. Hillman** is Professor of Law at the University of California Hastings College of the Law in San Francisco, USA. Her work focuses on United States military law and history since the mid-20th century and the impact of gender and sexual norms on military culture. A veteran of the US Air Force, she taught history at the Air Force Academy and at Yale University before joining the faculty at Rutgers University School of Law, Camden in 2000. She now teaches military law, constitutional law, legal history, and estates and trusts. She is the author of *Defending America: Military Culture and the Cold War Court-Martial* (Princeton University Press, 2005) and co-author of *Military Justice Cases and Materials* (with Eugene R. Fidell and Dwight H. Sullivan, LexisNexis, 2010; 1st ed., 2007). She has testified before Congress on military sexual violence and in federal district court as an expert on sexual orientation discrimination in military law and history. Her recent work includes "Front and Center: Sexual Violence in U.S. Military Law", in *Politics and Society*, 2009.

[1] Quoted in Russell F. Weigley, *History of the United States Army*, Indiana University Press, Bloomington, 1984, pp. 244–45.

proponent of articulating and enforcing the laws of war, expressed such frustration with political oversight of army operations.[2]

Tracing the historical evolution of the 19th-century US Army reveals the importance of internal military accountability, including for crimes of war, in establishing the legitimacy of the profession of arms in the United States.[3] Left unpunished, crimes committed by soldiers threatened to undermine the status and effectiveness of a professional army in a nation wary of a standing army and suspicious of a privileged class of officers. Professionalisation of military institutions occurred later in the United States than in European military institutions. Yet long before war crimes, crimes against humanity, genocide and aggression were acknowledged as core international crimes,[4] the professionalisation of the army was paving the way for war crimes accountability.

Reform in the first half of the 19th century, including the development of military educational institutions, improved organisational structures. This and rising standards for officers transformed the army into a more professional organisation.[5] Political, fiscal and operational accountability to civil authorities enhanced the army's effectiveness and reputation.[6] To protect those gains, it became more important that the army hold soldiers accountable for misconduct. During the Mexican War in 1846–1848, the army was much admired for its success, and military courts played a major role in both operations and occupation. The US Civil War that soon followed brought the brutal military tactics and strategy that had characterised the Indian wars on the frontier to centre stage, leading Francis Lieber to draft a code that became a foundation for the modern laws of war and furthering efforts to hold soldiers accountable for war crimes.

---

[2] John Fabian Witt, *Lincoln's Code: The Laws of War in American History*, The Free Press, New York, 2012.

[3] Morten Bergsmo, Arne Willy Dahl and Richard Sousa, "Military Self-Interest in Accountability for Core International Crimes", in *FICHL Policy Brief Series*, 2013, no. 14, pp. 2–3 (https://www.legal-tools.org/doc/396da7/).

[4] *Ibid.*, p. 1, fn. 2.

[5] William B. Skelton, *An American Profession of Arms: The Army Officer Corps, 1784–1861*, University of Kansas Press, Lawrence, 1992; Weigley, 1984, pp. 144–72, see *supra* note 1.

[6] Louise Barnett, *Ungentlemanly Acts: The Army's Notorious Incest Trial*, Hill and Wang, New York, 2000; Elizabeth L. Hillman, "Gentlemen Under Fire: The U.S. Military and 'Conduct Unbecoming'", in *Law and Inequality: A Journal of Theory and Practice*, vol. 26, no. 1, 2008, pp. 1–57.

The "old army" in the 19th-century United States sought to maintain discipline in its ranks to protect its reputation as well as to win wars.

Because the professionalisation of the 19th-century US Army is largely a story of the professionalisation of its officer corps, it is important to note the dearth of prosecutions of officers as compared to the rank-and-file for any serious crimes, much less crimes of war.[7] Very few officers faced either court martial or trial before civilian courts except for 'honour' trials in which high-ranking officers accused each other of wrongdoing.[8] The courts martial of officers that did occur exposed the limited extent of accountability that the army was willing to require of its officer corps.[9] The fact that nearly all officers escaped criminal prosecution is perhaps not surprising if demographic factors such as age, education, training, and access to economic and other resources, each of which distinguished officers from their less privileged enlisted brethren, are considered. Those factors made officers less likely to commit some crimes, and more capable of successfully defending against most charges, than the enlisted force.[10] Nonetheless, such statistics undercut the impression of even-handed justice and created a perception that one of the privileges of high rank was impunity. Officers' role in the history of accountability in the US military is primarily as enforcers rather than as alleged violators of military laws or codes.

The perception that officers are not held accountable for misconduct in the same way as soldiers persisted long after the army professionalised. Officers have, however, been court-martialled on rare occasions in US military history, including for acts that constitute war crimes under virtually any definition. Most well known are the courts martial of Captain Ernest Medina and Lieutenant William Laws Calley. Both were tried for their parts in the murder and rape of hundreds of civilians during the

---

[7]   Hillman, 2008, pp. 2–3, see *supra* note 6; Elizabeth Lutes Hillman, *Defending America: Military Culture and the Cold War Court-Martial*, Princeton University Press, Princeton, NJ, 2005, pp. 9–13.

[8]   Hillman, 2008, pp. 25–26, see *supra* note 6.

[9]   *Ibid.*, pp. 1–27.

[10] *Ibid.*, p. 2; Caroline Cox, *A Proper Sense of Honor: Service and Sacrifice in George Washington's Army*, University of North Carolina Press, Chapel Hill, NC, 2007, pp. 59–60.

1968 My Lai massacre in Vietnam.[11] Medina was acquitted and Calley, convicted of 22 murders and likely guilty of many more, served but a few months in military prison and a few years under house arrest.[12] The outcome of those prosecutions left much to be desired, despite the army's deep investment in pursuing justice.[13] Yet the public reaction to the army's courts martial was fiercely in favour of the accused officers, who they viewed as victims of the army's war.

The judge advocates that prosecuted the My Lai cases deserve a place in the history of international criminal prosecutors dedicated to seeking justice at great personal cost. One of those prosecutors, Captain Aubrey Daniel III, wrote a letter of protest to the *New York Times* after Calley's court martial.[14] Daniel, who went on to a brilliant legal career in Washington DC, wrote to defend the procedural regularity of the military justice system and to express outrage at the public reaction to the verdict, which ran overwhelmingly in favour of clemency for Calley.[15] Daniel also took aim at the post-trial review process, which had so precipitously reduced the sentence to life imprisonment that had been adjudged at Calley's court martial. Perhaps if the army had chosen to prosecute Calley's crimes as violations of the law of war rather than as murders and other statutory crimes, the popular and political responses to the verdict of the military justice system would have been more deferential. By the time of the Vietnam War, professionalisation had matured in the Army Judge Advocate General's corps to the point that army lawyers fought to defend the legitimacy of the military justice system as well as the army itself.

This chapter approaches the topic of US military professionalisation and accountability in three parts. It sets out a framework for understanding the process of professionalisation and then analyses two 19th-century

---

[11] Michal R. Belknap, *The Vietnam War on Trial: The My Lai Massacre and the Court-Martial of Lieutenant Calley*, University Press of Kansas, Lawrence, 2002; and Michael Bilton and Kevin Sim, *Four Hours in My Lai: A War Crime and Its Aftermath*, Viking Penguin, New York, 1992.

[12] Belknap, 2002, pp. 4 and 232, see *supra* note 11.

[13] William George Eckhardt, "My Lai: An American Tragedy," in *UMKC Law Review*, 2000, vol. 68, pp. 671–704.

[14] Aubrey Daniel, "Letter to President Nixon", in *New York Times*, 3 April 1973, p. 12, col. 1.

[15] *Ibid.*; Eckhardt, 2000, pp. 671–704, see *supra* note 13; and Norman G. Cooper, "My Lai and Military Justice – To What Effect?", in *Military Law Review*, 1973, vol. 59, pp. 93–127.

wars in which accountability for crimes of war was influenced by the army's professional aspirations. Section 5.2. explores the meaning of 'professional', and the process of professionalisation, in theory and practice. The next two parts turn to the army in war to reveal the link between professionalisation and accountability. Section 5.3. explores how the Mexican War, in which the US Army relied on a small core of regulars supplemented by volunteers, heightened the army's concern with holding its soldiers accountable. That concern triggered the development of new military courts to both prosecute war crimes during the war itself and to keep peace during the post-war occupation. Section 5.4. assesses the Union Army in the Civil War, focusing on the development of a legal code to restrain violence amidst a massive and brutal internal conflict and the impact of a professional, but split, officer corps on accountability. The introduction of a new type of military court in the Mexican War and a new code of law in the Civil War expanded the army's means of holding soldiers accountable in the professionalising army of the 19th century, highlighting the role of accountability in ensuring the operational effectiveness and political legitimacy of the US Army.

5.2. History of Professionalisation and the Rise of Military Accountability

The history of professionalisation provides a useful framework for understanding the rise of accountability in the evolution of the US Army. The notion of military service as an occupation changed alongside the shifts in other developing professions such as law and medicine. Professionalisation was appealing to many workers because it reduced competition, established and enforced standards of performance, and promoted public service.[16] Many sociologists have, however, criticised professionalisation as a self-interested attempt to secure and maintain power.[17] Others have analysed the processes of professionalisation, recasting the history of pro-

---

[16] Gerald L. Geison (ed.), *Professions and Professional Ideologies in America*, University of North Carolina Press, Chapel Hill, NC, 1983.

[17] Paul Starr, *The Social Transformation of American Medicine*, Basic Books, New York, 1982; Norman W. Spaulding, "The Discourse of Law in Time of War: Politics and Professionalism during the Civil War and Reconstruction", in *William and Mary Law Review*, 2005, vol. 46, no. 6, pp. 2024–26; and Burton J. Bledstein, *The Culture of Professionalism: The Middle Class and the Development of Higher Education in America*, W.W. Norton, New York, 1976.

fessional organisation and exploring the political, economic and social impact of the shift from job to profession.[18]

Professionalisation in the military occurred around the same time as other professionalisation processes in the US but was made more difficult by both the distrust with which US political culture viewed the army and the uneven moral terrain of war itself. In chronological terms, the processes in the military and other professions began earlier than thought by the scholars who initially studied them. The professionalisation of law, for example, began long before the American Bar Association was founded in 1878, and the army process of professionalisation likewise began not after the Civil War, but well before.[19] Securing status and autonomy in an arena as fraught as war, in which acts that would be criminal in any other context are not only lawful but heroic, was especially important for aspiring US Army professionals. They claimed authority over the activity that imposed costs on society and government that far exceeded that of any other profession.

Studies of professionalisation in the US military began in earnest with Samuel P. Huntington's *The Soldier and the State* and sustained the interest of many historians and social scientists.[20] Published in 1957, Huntington's book named expertise, social responsibility and a corporate identity as the tenets of a profession. It also set forth a thesis that laid the foundation for future study of the military profession. Huntington argued that professionalisation in the army was caused by the isolation of its officers from civil society and that the process of professionalisation took place in the late 19th century. Subsequent scholars found signs of professionalisation in the early, not late, 19th century, and realised that officers were not as separate from civil society as Huntington had suggested.[21]

---

[18] Starr, 1982, pp. 2001–2108, see *supra* note 17.

[19] Spaulding, 2005, pp. 2029–2039, see *supra* note 17; Robert W. Gordon, "The Independence of Lawyers", in *Boston University Law Review*, 1988, vol. 68, pp. 1–83.

[20] Samuel P. Huntington, *The Soldier and the State: The Theory and Politics of Civil-Military Relations*, Belknap Press, Cambridge, MA, 1957; Skelton, 1992, see *supra* note 5; and Morris Janowitz, *The Professional Soldier: A Social and Political Portrait*, The Free Press, New York, 1960.

[21] Weigley, 1984, pp. 144–72, see *supra* note 1; Matthew Moten, *The Delafield Commission and the American Military Profession*, Texas A and M University Press, College Station, 2000, pp. 7–11, 13–17; Samuel J. Watson, "The U.S. Army to 1900", in James C. Bradford (ed.), *A Companion to American Military History*, vol. 1, Wiley-Blackwell, Malden, MA, 2010, pp. 340–46; and Jennifer R. Green, "Networks of Military Educators: Middle-

William B. Skelton's 1992 *magnum opus*, *An American Profession of Arms*, synthesised previous studies into a new consensus.[22] It shifted the chronology of military professionalisation to the beginning of the 19th century and emphasised measures of professionalisation such as formal education, specialised knowledge, loyalty to high standards of performance and ethics, and trustworthiness.[23] Skelton found that the US Army had become a stable profession by the start of the Civil War, transformed by the same historical developments – described by historian Matthew Moten as "burgeoning nationalism, economic growth and democratic egalitarianism" – that shaped the rest of the growing United States.[24]

The military professionalisation that Skelton uncovered began in earnest during the early national period with the founding of national military institutions. Although he had previously resisted a national service academy, in 1802 President Thomas Jefferson signed legislation creating the United States Military Academy at West Point. Jefferson decided to support the Military Academy because the school provided a means of training engineers and scientists for the nation, as well as for war. It also enabled him to alter the political balance of the army through faculty and staff appointments.[25]

Once begun, however, the process of professionalisation was far from smooth. The War of 1812 showcased the dysfunction of a military hindered by inadequate funding, poor co-ordination and leaders with divided loyalties. That war ended, however, with an improved army and a new generation of leaders, and was followed by an era of reform and restructuring.[26] Military training and education matured, the organisational structure of the army changed and officers developed a shared identity.[27]

The shared identity of army officers was rooted in knowledge of the science and principles of war, exclusive jurisdiction over battle, and edu-

Class Stability and Professionalization in the Late Antebellum South", in *The Journal of Southern History*, 2007, vol. 73, no. 1, pp. 39–74.

[22] Skelton, 1992, see *supra* note 5.

[23] Moten, 2000, pp. 13–15, see *supra* note 21.

[24] *Ibid.*, p. 14; Skelton, 1992, pp. 110–119, see *supra* note 5.

[25] Allan R. Millett and Peter Maslowski, *For the Common Defense: A Military History of the United States of America*, The Free Press, New York, 1984, p. 104.

[26] Skelton, 1994, p. 269, see *supra* note 5.

[27] *Ibid.*, p. 196.

cation in military history, strategy and tactics. As Henry W. Halleck, an 1839 graduate of West Point and later general-in-chief of the Union Army during the Civil War (and author of the letter quoted in the introduction above), wrote in a 1846 treatise:

> War is not, as some seem to suppose, a mere game of chance. Its principles constitute one of the most intricate of modern sciences. The general who understands the art of rightly applying its rules, and possesses the means of carry-ing out its precepts, may be morally certain of success.[28]

War was predictable, precise and explicable to Halleck and other theorists.[29] Military professionals could master its nuances, construct for-tifications and plans of attack that would ensure victory, and, given suffi-cient resources, prepare for future conflict. This approach to war was deeply flawed, as both history and historians – particularly Brian McAllis-ter Linn in *The Echo of Battle* – have shown.[30] Even so, the idea that suc-cess in war was determined by technical, battlefield preparation and exe-cution proved successful in promoting the profession of arms.

The aspect of professionalisation that proved most difficult for the military to fulfil was securing the trust of the public and its leaders. In a 1964 article, the political scientist Harold Wilensky, who had served in the US Air Force during the Second World War,[31] set out four essential steps to establishing professional authority. To be recognised as profes-sionals, Wilensky explained that those working in an occupation must find "a technical basis" for authority, "assert an exclusive jurisdiction", "link both skill and jurisdiction to standards of training", and gain public confidence as "uniquely trustworthy".[32] Those steps enabled workers in a field to define an area of knowledge, articulate "normative commitments

---

[28] Russell F. Weigley, *History of the United States Army*, Indiana University Press, Bloom-ington, 1984, p. 144, quoting Henry W. Halleck, *Elements of Military Art and Science*, Greenwood Press, Westport, 1971 p. 145, first ed. 1846.

[29] Brian McAllister Linn, *The Echo of Battle: The Army's Way of War*, Harvard University Press, Cambridge, MA, 2007, pp. 23–24.

[30] *Ibid.*

[31] UC Berkeley News, "Political Scientist Harold Wilensky Dies at Age 88", in UC Berkeley News Center, 1 November 2011, available at http://newscenter.berkeley.edu/2011/11/01/political-scientist-harold-wilensky-dies-at-age-88/, last accessed on 31 March 2015.

[32] Harold L. Wilensky, "The Professionalization of Everyone?", in *American Journal of So-ciology*, 1964, vol. 70, no. 2, p. 138.

to a service ideal", and occupy a field of expertise, effectively excluding others.[33] The final step in Wilensky's sociological process was a cornerstone of Skelton's definition of a profession: that the military be perceived as "uniquely trustworthy", ethical and loyal.[34] This was a more difficult proof for the army as compared to other professional institutions because of the tension that existed between civil and military authorities and the proximity of crime and wartime violence. Suspicion of a standing army, aspirations of political independence, and constitutional requirements for civilian control and limited funding of the army and navy characterised US political culture.[35] Those characteristics created tension between civil and military authorities that was heightened in the 19th century by what Skelton termed "the army's domestic constabulary role", in which it policed borders, suppressed unrest and asserted federal authority.[36] This role placed army officers directly into regional and local conflicts where state and local governments were necessarily involved, exacerbating the potential for confusion and frustration. Earning trust in such situations, regardless of the special expertise and firepower that the military offered civilian authorities, was no easy task.

Demonstrating the accountability of the army, however, helped to overcome the distrust that many civilians had of the army and its leaders. Holding professionals accountable for their obligation to meet high standards of performance and ethics was a key aspect of professionalisation itself. In the army, this meant, at least in part, the ability to remove officers who were failing in their duties. During the War of 1812, officers remained in their billets even if accused of egregious misconduct because of their political connections and an "administrative tradition" that discour-

---

[33] Paul Starr, "Professionalization and Public Health: Historical Legacies, Continuing Dilemmas", in *Journal of Public Health Management and Practice*, 2009, vol. 15, no. 6, p. S26.

[34] Wilensky, 1964, p. 137, see *supra* note 32; Skelton, 1992, p. 88, see *supra* note 5.

[35] Richard H. Kohn, "Civil-Military Relations: Civilian Control of the Military", in John Whiteclay Chambers (ed.), *The Oxford Companion to American Military History*, Oxford University Press, 2000, pp. 123–24; and Richard H. Kohn, *Eagle and Sword: The Federalists and the Creation of the Military Establishment, 1783–1802*, The Free Press, New York, 1975.

[36] William B. Skelton, "The Commanding Generals and the Question of Civil Control in the Antebellum U.S. Army", in *American Nineteenth Century History*, 2006, vol. 7, no. 2, p. 155.

aged discharge or demotion.[37] Control over the discipline that could be imposed on officers and their troops was a frequent source of conflict between military and civilian leaders during the antebellum period. General officers like Alexander Macomb sought to improve "communication and the general trend toward professional standards" in the officer corps by emphasising discipline and accountability for misconduct.[38] Respect for international law and law of war was cultivated by the curriculum at West Point and through the publication of manuals and regulations.[39] Holding officers accountable for their control over enlisted soldiers, for their ability to organise and operate effectively and for their responsiveness to national civilian authorities was critical to the growing legitimacy of the profession of arms.[40]

5.3. The Mexican War

After the War of 1812 ended, the professionalisation of the US Army continued despite reductions in funding and opposition from those who were dubious about the value of an elite officer corps.[41] Increasingly led by graduates of West Point, the army proved essential to US territorial expansion and economic growth during the decades before the Civil War.[42] Soldiers explored, fought, policed and occupied, pushing the US border south and west and keeping the frontier relatively safe for white settlers. The army supervised the "removal" of Indians, helping with voluntary resettlement on occasion but often fighting, sometimes with terrifying brutality. Despite the indifference of the public toward military institutions during the Jacksonian era, the army's "new professionalism" had earned the loyalty of its officer corps and improved considerably since the debacle of the War of 1812.

---

[37]   William B. Skelton, "High Army Leadership in the Era of the War of 1812: The Making and Remaking of the Officer Corps", in *William and Mary Quarterly*, 1994, vol. 51, no. 2, p. 266.

[38]   Skelton, 2006, pp. 163–64, see *supra* note 36.

[39]   Witt, 2012, pp. 84–86, see *supra* note 2.

[40]   Allan Peskin, *Winfield Scott and the Profession of Arms*, Kent State University Press, Kent, OH, 2003.

[41]   Millett and Maslowski, 1994, p. 135, see *supra* note 25; and Weigley, 1984, pp. 144–72, see *supra* note 1.

[42]   Millett and Maslowski, 1994, pp. 134–44, see *supra* note 25.

When the US Army entered the Mexican War in 1846, it continued to suffer from organisational shortcomings and a small army of regulars. The war required not only a great increase in the army's size and resources but also innovation in both strategy and law. The army had neither experience nor plans for anything like the foreign invasion and occupation of a large country defended by zealous guerrillas. Military officers, seduced by European military strategists, had underestimated the threats posed by Mexico and Indian resistance. Instead, army strategists had prepared for battle with European-style forces.[43] Similarly, they had no plans to address the atrocities and brutal reprisals that became common during the Mexican War.

Because many officers chose *not* to look the other way – as they had often done in past conflicts – when atrocities occurred, the army needed a legal forum to prosecute war crimes. Councils of war were created to fill this jurisdictional gap. After hostilities ended, the US Army's occupation of Mexico City trials led to another novel military court, the military commission, on which the army relied to prosecute crime and keep the peace. A mix of individuals labelled regulars, volunteers, prisoners of war, non-combatants and criminals thus found themselves defined by the legal tools of the profession of arms and subjected to military jurisdiction. Because of the convergence of professionalisation, war crimes and accountability in the Mexican War, this short and relatively uncomplicated conflict became a landmark in the history of military accountability for war crimes.

The Mexican War began in 1846 when diplomatic attempts to resolve a dispute over the southern border of Texas failed, but the deeper cause was the United States' plans for expansion, which led to annexation of Texas in 1845.[44] The outcome was by no means certain at the start of the war.[45] The US Army's leadership was marked by petty squabbles, made worse because the army was so small – some 800 officers and fewer

---

[43] Samuel J. Watson, "Knowledge, Interest and the Limits of Military Professionalism: The Discourse on American Coastal Defence, 1815–1860", in *War in History*, 1998, vol. 5, no. 3, pp. 282–84.

[44] Thomas W. Cutrer, "The Texas War for Independence and War with Mexico", in Bradford, 2010, pp. 78–92, see *supra* note 21; and Millett and Maslowski, 1994, p. 145, see *supra* note 25.

[45] Wayne Wei-siang Hsieh, *West Pointers and the Civil War: The Old Army in War and Peace*, University of North Carolina Press, Chapel Hill, NC, 2009, pp. 54–74.

than 8,000 enlisted men – that nearly all of the officers knew each other.[46] Senior commanding officers were mostly political appointees with ambition but little skill, unlike the capable junior officers, most of whom had attended West Point.[47] To muster enough soldiers for the invasion, the US Congress mobilised volunteer militias from the states, sending units of untrained volunteers to join the regular army forces for tours of short duration.[48] Volunteers were paid for their service but did not have the training or experience of soldiers in the regular army.

Despite those obstacles to victory the US won, aided by its political and economic stability, technical and logistical expertise, and the legendary campaign of General Winfield Scott, who landed at Vera Cruz and marched to Mexico City along the same route that Hernán Cortéz had taken in the 16th century.[49] In 1848 Scott rode triumphantly into Mexico City in full dress uniform, dismounted and sat at the desk previously used by the revered Mexican General Antonio López de Santa Anna to begin a US occupation for which he had carefully prepared.[50]

The combination of US Army regulars and volunteer militiamen who fought in Scott's army highlighted the importance of accountability for the professional military. Army officers found it difficult to maintain discipline and prevent unnecessary violence among volunteers, even when mixed in with regular army troops. Volunteers, drawn from a variety of civilian occupations, could be ruthless, described as "unruly freebooters whose unbridled rapacity and undisciplined behavior disgraced the flag under which they fought".[51] Some officers were volunteers who frustrated their regular officer colleagues by failing to enforce discipline and the laws of war, standing by in the face of atrocities that shocked regular officers.[52] Regular army officers had a problem: they needed a means of punishing volunteers' violations of the laws of war if they were to main-

---

[46] *Ibid.*, p. 12.

[47] Weigley, 1984, pp. 175–88, see *supra* note 1.

[48] Millett and Maslowski, 1994, p. 149, see *supra* note 25; and Peskin, 2003, p. 61, see *supra* note 40.

[49] Hsieh, 2009, pp. 54–74, see *supra* note 45.

[50] Timothy D. Johnson, *A Gallant Little Army: The Mexico City Campaign*, University Press of Kansas, Lawrence, 2007; and Peskin, 2003, p. 193, see *supra* note 40.

[51] Peskin, 2003, p. 171, see *supra* note 40.

[52] *Ibid.*, p. 170; Marcus Cunliffe, *Soldiers and Civilians: The Martial Spirit in America, 1775–1865*, Little, Brown, Boston, 1968, p. 84; and Witt, 2012, p. 119, see *supra* note 2.

---

tain control over their troops, operate effectively and protect the legitimacy of the military profession.

Trained as a lawyer and savvy about organisation and strategy both, Scott was as likely as anyone to find a solution to the army's problem. After narrowly failing to win the Whig Party's nomination for President of the United States in 1840, Scott was appointed commanding general of the army in 1841 upon Alexander Macomb's death in that office.[53] He promoted accountability and improved efficiency throughout his long army career, writing the army's drill manual for infantry as well as many general regulations.[54] Scott was more committed to fairness, due process and innovation than virtually any other army reformer, an aspect of his legacy sometimes lost in criticism of his vain and showy "Old Fuss and Feathers" persona.

Military courts during the mid-19th century, notwithstanding the efforts of the reform-minded Scott, were hardly paragons of substantive or procedural justice. Scott knew military justice not only as a commander with authority to order courts martial, but as an officer accused of misconduct. Convicted at court martial for a dubious embezzling charge early in his career, Scott later faced a court of inquiry for his alleged failure to move quickly enough during the Creek War in Georgia and Alabama.[55] Both prosecutions were initiated by officers resentful of Scott's success, and neither hindered his rise through the army's officer corps. Being tried before a military court troubled few ambitious army officers. Like Scott, they knew that courts composed of fellow officers were more likely to protect than condemn them, regardless of the evidence or charges. In the old army of the antebellum period, military courts at which officers were prosecuted seemed more about spite than discipline.[56] One army general went so far as to label officers' practice of using courts martial for personal vendettas as equivalent to desertion among the "greatest evils of the army".[57]

---

[53] Peskin, 2003, pp. 115–17, see *supra* note 40.

[54] Hsieh, p. 64, see *supra* note 45; and Peskin, 2003, pp. 62–68, see *supra* note 40.

[55] Peskin, 2003, pp. 12–13, 99, see *supra* note 40.

[56] Cox, 2007, pp. 59–60, see *supra* note 10; Hillman, 2008, pp. 25–26, see *supra* note 6; and John D. Morris, *Sword of the Border: Major General Jacob Jennings Brown, 1775–1828*, Kent State University Press, Kent, OH, 2000, pp. 190–91.

[57] Morris, 2000, p. 246, see *supra* note 56.

Scott was not reluctant to impose strict discipline on either officers or enlisted men, but he preferred that military courts focus on punishing misconduct rather than resolving grudge matches between officers. Desertion was probably the most common type of major misconduct committed by soldiers during the Mexican War. The desertion rate was high during the two-year conflict: nearly seven per cent of the entire army deserted, some simply switching sides to join hundreds of "Irish and German Catholic immigrants who signed up to fight alongside their fellow Catholics in Mexico".[58] Volunteer militiamen deserted at rates no worse than regulars, though some officers nonetheless blamed volunteers for running away from danger and hardship more often.[59]

Scott's interest in procedural fairness might have reduced the desertion rate if so many officers had not resisted his reforms. Scott wanted a rule of law that constrained officers as well as enlistees, hoping to end officers' abuse and neglect of soldiers.[60] Enlistees endured low pay, poor conditions and brutal corporal punishment, all of which contributed to unauthorised absence.[61] Scott worked to end excessive punishments, including flogging, which he finally succeeded in abolishing in 1861.[62] Scott did not succeed, however, in convincing his officer corps to enforce the same rule of law for enlistees as for officers. When he ordered military courts to try officers for maltreatment of subordinates, the courts acquitted their peers. In one case, the court not only acquitted an officer for striking a soldier with his sword, it proceeded to issue a commendation to the officer – and then disobeyed Scott's order to reconvene and explain their verdict.[63] During his martial rule in Mexico City, Scott insisted on discipline from officers and troops alike.[64] For this general, if not his subordinates, due process was as essential for soldiers as other necessities of

---

[58] Witt, 2012, p. 125, see *supra* note 2.

[59] Peskin, 2003, p. 170, see *supra* note 40.

[60] *Ibid.*, p. 121.

[61] Skelton, 1992, pp. 267–273, see *supra* note 5; and Edward M. Coffman, *The Old Army: A Portrait of the American Army in Peacetime, 1784–1898*, Oxford University Press, New York, 1986, pp. 193–94.

[62] Peskin, 2003, p. 122, see *supra* note 40.

[63] *Ibid.*

[64] *Ibid.*, p. 194.

life like adequate housing and sanitary conditions, which Scott also carefully monitored.[65]

Scott applied similar principles of due process, not the summary discipline or outright neglect to which others resorted, to the grave problem of prosecuting war crimes. Prior to Scott's arrival in Mexico in 1847, General Zachary Taylor's troops had marched from the Rio Grande to Monterey, leaving a trail of destruction in their wake and gaining Taylor, soon to be elected president of the United States, a reputation for wanton brutality.[66] Some of the volunteer militias, such as the Louisiana contingent, were virtually uncontrollable, committing rape, murder and property crimes with abandon.[67] The guerrilla tactics employed by Santa Anna's forces, which included slaughter and torture of captives, triggered reprisals that led to even more indiscriminate violence.[68] Whereas Taylor had decided that US soldiers could not be tried in Mexico for war crimes, Scott disagreed. He reinterpreted the rules and used military commissions to prosecute more than 300 soldiers for crimes such as "assassination and murder, malicious stabbing or maiming and rape, malicious assault, battery, robbery, theft, the wanton desecration of churches, and the destruction of private or public property".[69]

Army officers who rejected Scott's efforts to restrain the abuse of officers may have supported his campaign to control excessive violence among volunteers because of their shared interest in distinguishing regulars from undisciplined volunteers.[70] Scott himself had not always been so invested in redressing this kind of crime. During the forced removal of the Cherokee from Oklahoma in 1838, for example, Scott was troubled by the Georgia militia's slaughter of the Indians but "closed his eyes to these atrocities" and did not step in.[71] During the Mexican War, however, the war crimes and reprisals of volunteers were of greater concern to Scott and others in the regular army, which was proving its mettle in battle and

---

[65]   *Ibid.*, p. 123.
[66]   Witt, 2012, p. 119, see *supra* note 2.
[67]   Millet and Maslowski, 1994, p. 149, see *supra* note 25.
[68]   Witt, 2012, p. 121, see *supra* note 2.
[69]   *Ibid.*, p. 123.
[70]   Millet and Maslowski, 1994, p. 149, see *supra* note 25.
[71]   Peskin, 2003, p. 107, see *supra* note 40.

occupation alike.[72] Scott sought to constrain the behaviour of soldiers, even imposing what one eminent historian termed "draconian punishment on soldiers who committed crimes against civilians", to limit popular resistance and enhance order and control.[73] He succeeded in supervising a military occupation that the historian Russell F. Weigley praised as "efficient and honest", a description that would have pleased the reform-minded general.[74] He realised that the army's professional reputation and ability to govern after victory could be undone by indiscipline and crime if perpetrators were not held accountable.

5.4. The Civil War

The predominance of untrained volunteers and conscripts among the three million soldiers who fought for North and South made discipline a grave problem for army officers, much as it had been during the Mexican War but on a far larger scale.[75] The US Civil War imposed unprecedented stress on the army as a profession. Its scale far exceeded any other US conflict, with some 8,700 battles compressed into four years.[76] It left 620,000 soldiers dead, more than the total US military deaths in every war through the mid-20th century combined.[77] Its breadth and intensity exposed every flaw, laid bare every weakness, in US military strategy, organisation and law.

Commanding generals and lesser officers alike were forced to adapt to new weapons, tactics and personnel. Officers who doubted the legitimacy of guerrilla warfare had to rethink their opposition after seeing it practised with such success by the Confederacy.[78] Those suspicious of the effectiveness of African-American soldiers were surprised by the valiant efforts of the United States Colored Troops in 1863, created after Presi-

---

[72] Cutrer, 2010, p. 91, see *supra* note 44; and Peskin, 2003, p. 107, see *supra* note 40.

[73] Linn, 2007, p. 75, see *supra* note 29.

[74] Weigley, 1984, p. 188, see *supra* note 1.

[75] Drew Gilpin Faust, *The Republic of Suffering: Death and the American Civil War*, Vintage Books, New York, 2009, p. 39.

[76] Millet and Maslowski, 1994, pp. 162–240, see *supra* note 25; and Brian Holden Reid, "The Civil War, 1861–5", in Bradford, 2010, pp. 99–118, see *supra* note 21.

[77] Faust, 2009, p. xi, see *supra* note 75.

[78] Millet and Maslowski, 1994, p. 179, see *supra* note 25.

dent Lincoln issued the Emancipation Proclamation.[79] African-American men who had been considered assets of the South at the start of the war instead fought bravely for the Union. Officers could not respond effectively by relying only on past military experience and training.

Despite its effort to professionalise, the regular army's preparation for the Civil War left it flat-footed, ill-prepared to manage the application of frontier-style, irregular warfare to the mass engagements of the battle between North and South. Neither law nor lawyers, nor medicine and doctors, were ready to address the carnage and crimes of the war either. The intensification of the drive toward modern professionals that occurred after the war was in part a response to the failure of expertise and science to control the war's devastation.[80] The distrust with which many regular officers viewed volunteers and conscripts, a product of the army's emphasis on professionalisation and their experience during the Mexican War, did not serve them well in commanding units forged almost entirely of non-regulars.[81] The army was also hindered by the division in its ranks after the South's secession forced officers to choose a side. A case in point: General Pierre Gustave Toutant Beauregard commanded the Confederate artillery that fired at Fort Sumter to open the war in April 1861. Major Robert Anderson, the commander of Fort Sumter who quickly raised a white flag of surrender to save his troops from being overrun, had been Beauregard's artillery instructor at West Point.[82] West Pointers served on both sides of the conflict, as did brothers; Colonel Francis Lieber, author of the code detailed below, had three sons who served during the war, two with the Union armies and one with the Confederates.[83] Volunteers as well as officers found their pre-war communities torn by differing allegiances. 160,000 men from border states Maryland, Kentucky and Missouri joined the Union Army; 85,000 from the same states volunteered for the Confederacy instead.[84] Such divided loyalties affected the regular ar-

---

[79]   Dudley Taylor Cornish, *The Sable Arm: Black Troops in the Union Army, 1861–1865*, Longmans, Green, New York, 1956.

[80]   Spaulding, 2005, p. 2010, see *supra* note 17; and Gerald W. Gawalt (ed.), *The New High Priests: Lawyers in Post-Civil War America*, Greenwood Press, Westport, CT, 1984.

[81]   Weigley, 1984, p. 244, see *supra* note 1.

[82]   Millet and Maslowski, 1994, p. 162, see *supra* note 25.

[83]   Witt, 2012, p. 180, see *supra* note 2.

[84]   Millet and Maslowski, 1994, p. 179, see *supra* note 25.

---

my's leadership and rank-and-file, exacerbating its strategic and organisational shortcomings.

When Beauregard's artillery shelled Fort Sumter into submission in the spring of 1861, Winfield Scott, 75-years-old and five decades into his army service, was still the commanding general of the army.[85] Although Scott's well thought-out Anaconda Plan foreshadowed the strategy of exhaustion and attrition with which the North eventually won the war, he was ousted in September 1861 by George B. McClellan, an ambitious 35-year-old who himself was relieved of command in March 1862 after a dismal performance.[86] McClellan's commitment to a past style of large military operations and distrust of civilian authority made him ineffective, much like many of the other generals from the army's corps of regular officers.

Disorder reigned on Civil War battlefields, the familiar fog of war made worse by commanders' inability to control troops of far greater number, deployed across far larger distances, than in the battles for which their training had prepared them. Guns with greater firepower and range extended the gap between officers and their troops, a problem far more challenging because of the sheer size of the forces that fought.[87] For example, in the Battle of Antietam (or Sharpsburg) in 1862, which pitted McClellan's 88,000 men against Lee's 50,000-man Army of Northern Virginia and left 24,000 dead, confusion prevented either side from exploiting advantages gained.[88] Even in mass battles that approximated the European engagements for which professional men-at-arms had trained, the new conditions of warfare eroded officers' command and control over troops.

Preventing excessive violence on a large scale was also more difficult during the Civil War than in the past. Acts of vengeance by individual soldiers multiplied as the war progressed and losses mounted, further limiting officers' ability to restrain their troops.[89] Retribution against African-American soldiers and civilians thought to be supporting federal troops was common and especially grisly. Mass murder and torture of

---

[85] Hsieh, 2009, p. 108, see *supra* note 45.
[86] Millet and Maslowski, 1994, p. 170, see *supra* note 25.
[87] Hsieh, 2009, pp. 112–116, see *supra* note 45; and Faust, 2009, p. 39, see *supra* note 75.
[88] Millet and Maslowski, 1994, p. 196, see *supra* note 25; and Cornish, 1956, see *supra* 79.
[89] Faust, 2009, p. 35, see *supra* note 75.

---

captives was all too common by Confederate troops who refused to treat African-American soldiers as prisoners of war, deeming them slaves, not soldiers. Most infamous was the Fort Pillow massacre in which 300 African-American soldiers were killed, most after they had surrendered, by Major General Nathan Bedford Forrest's Confederate cavalry during spring 1864 raids into Union-held West Tennessee and Kentucky.[90]

High strategy as well as individual vengeance also raised the level of wartime violence and destruction. The Union Army's ruthless methods after 1863 earned the descriptive term "hard war".[91] General William Tecumseh Sherman, West Point graduate and unremarkable army officer prior to the war, carved a path of destruction through the South that was virtually unlimited in terms of damage to property.[92] Sherman's 'March to the Sea' and Philip Sheridan's raids in the Shenandoah Valley to destroy the South's food supply were frontier-style campaigns that targeted the economy and society of the Confederacy rather than its army.[93] Confederate hero Stonewall Jackson's vicious rhetoric matched Sherman's "war is hell" exhortations.[94] Both South and North struggled to manage the strategic and moral consequences of a seemingly unbounded war.

In response to the battlefield and leadership challenges of the war, the Union Army sought to improve accountability by restoring discipline and enhancing its ability to function both during and after battle. The most important accountability measure that the army pursued was the articulation of the principles of lawful warfare in an elaborate code. Historian John Fabian Witt analyses the origins and impact of the code that Colonel Francis Lieber drafted at the army's request, released as General Orders No. 100 in May 1863. Lieber's code was a comprehensive statement of the laws of war that embraced the necessity principle, which permits any destruction or method "indispensable for securing the ends of war".[95] That principle accepted the perspective of Carl von Clausewitz, a military intel-

---

[90] *Ibid.*, pp. 44–46.

[91] Mark Grimsley, *The Hard Hand of War: Union Military Policy Toward Southern Civilians, 1861–1865*, Cambridge University Press, New York, 1995.

[92] Witt, 2012, p. 277, see *supra* note 2.

[93] Grimsley, 1995, see *supra* note 91.

[94] Charles Royster, *The Destructive War: William Tecumseh Sherman, Stonewall Jackson and the Americans*, Alfred A. Knopf, New York, 1991, p. 329.

[95] Witt, 2012, pp. 235–37, see *supra* note 2; and Spaulding, 2005, pp. 2061–71, see *supra* note 17.

lectual and "prophet of modern total war", who had nothing but contempt for efforts to limit the violence of war, but nonetheless went on to detail an elaborate set of exactly such limits.[96]

The principle of necessity threatened to consume the limits set out by other principles by authorising extreme violence, but it articulated a boundary and encouraged soldiers to consider moral limits. President Abraham Lincoln interpreted the line between moral and criminal violence as a line between violence that advanced the war effort and violence undertaken for personal gain or vengeance.[97] Upholding a higher standard of conduct was essential for Union officers for the same two reasons it had been during the Mexican War: they thought they could both win the war faster with disciplined troops and ensure public confidence in the occupation that would follow if they sought to prevent and prosecute unnecessary violence.[98]

The scale and disorder of the Civil War eroded the control of both regular and non-regular officers, leaving soldiers to make their own decisions about what was permitted, required or 'necessary' in wartime situations. For example, Sherman's strategy of moving troops quickly, without pausing to maintain supply lines, gave lesser officers wide discretion in meeting the imperative that they provide adequate provisions for their troops. This "decentralised foraging" often led to lawlessness.[99] With so many soldiers empowered to decide which acts of destruction or appropriation were crimes and which were acts of war, inconsistency made discipline very difficult.[100] The Union distributed copies of the Lieber Code, printed on pamphlets, to guide decisions made in the field. Education, like prosecution, served the Union Army's goal of encouraging disciplined behaviour despite the diffusion of control that characterised Civil War military operations.

The Union's interest in enforcing the Lieber Code also sparked the creation of a powerful group of professional military lawyers under the leadership of Joseph Holt, appointed Judge Advocate General of the Army in 1862. Many lawyers and judges fought in the war, on both sides,

---

[96] Witt, 2012, p. 4, see *supra* note 2.

[97] *Ibid.*, p. 118.

[98] Linn, 2007, p. 77, see *supra* note 29.

[99] Witt, 2012, p. 281, see *supra* note 2.

[100] *Ibid.*, p. 283.

---

including 22 per cent of generals in the Union Army and 30 per cent in the Confederate Army.[101] Holt recruited lawyers "from among the best and brightest of the northern antislavery elite", building a team that would take nearly 1,000 men to trial for a crime of war.[102] Most of those charged were non-combatants and guerrillas, not Confederate soldiers, and the charges ranged broadly, from forgery to desecrating corpses.[103] The high volume of war crimes prosecuted was an effort to reinscribe lines of acceptable behaviour that the war had erased.

The orderly manner of the war's end was superficial vindication for the profession of arms after a long, terrible conflict that pushed the boundaries of modern warfare. Robert E. Lee met Ulysses S. Grant on 9 April 1865, in Appomattox Court House, Virginia, as equals, commanding generals who retained authority and military honour to the end. After Lee surrendered for the Army of Northern Virginia, he and other Confederate soldiers ceased fighting and went home without resistance from Grant's Union Army, following the path that the laws of war set out for a vanquished army.[104] Both generals, and many other US civilian and military leaders, had tolerated and even encouraged extreme violence during the war, yet chose to treat each other as members of a celebrated profession of arms. The extent to which the US public and civilian leadership did the same was the real measure of the army's professionalisation.

5.5. Conclusion: An Incomplete Transformation

The professionalisation of the US Army increased its interest in accountability. It elevated principles, encouraged discipline and led to more ways to prevent, identify and prosecute violations of law. In operational terms, the bungling performance of the army during the War of 1812, when the US narrowly escaped defeat, was a far cry from either the field manoeuvres of the Mexican War or the mass mobilisation that the Civil War brought. In legal terms, the use of military commissions and other courts, however procedurally suspect, grew to keep pace with greater interest in due process and the prosecution of misconduct. The depth and breadth of violence that continued to characterise the US way of war led to the

---

[101] Spaulding, 2005 pp. 2012–13, see *supra* note 17.

[102] Witt, 2012, pp. 264–267, see *supra* note 2.

[103] *Ibid.*, p. 268.

[104] Hsieh, 2009, pp. 1–2, see *supra* note 45; and Witt, 2012, p. 283, see *supra* note 2.

Lieber Code and subsequent articulations of the constraints that morality required during war.

Yet the transformation of the army, and of other military organisations, was incomplete at the end of the Civil War. Reconstruction and the armed conflicts that followed posed operational and bureaucratic challenges unresolved by Grant and Lee's ritual of mutual respect at Appomattox in 1865. The limits of accountability as a neutral principle within the military were perhaps most apparent in the race-based discrimination that pervaded military justice and hierarchies well into the 20th century. The US army was "still intellectually adolescent",[105] its officers unable to secure the deference, funding and status they believed the professions of arms deserved.

After the Civil War, tension persisted among officers who tried to balance sometimes competing interests in battlefield success and political legitimacy. In 1882 Emory Upton, hero of the Civil War, influential author, and perhaps the most esteemed officer of the post-war army, shot himself to death in his room at the Presidio army post in San Francisco. Upton, a brave and innovative field commander who led wartime infantry, artillery and cavalry units, served as commandant of West Point from 1870 to 1875. Yet his efforts to remake the US Army into a professionalised force worthy of a great democratic nation had, in his mind, failed. He considered US military policy "a policy of weakness and folly" because of its reliance on the leadership of untrained civilians.[106] Control of the army belonged with military experts, according to Upton. He advocated "thoroughly professional command of a thoroughly professional regular army" to save lives, shorten war and protect national values.[107]

During the many years that have passed since Upton's tragic death, military officers have often echoed his lament when the armed forces have disappointed them or the United States. Upton's imperative that military professionals have control reflects what historian Brian McAllister Linn has described as "a deeply cherished belief among America's military personnel that, if left alone, the armed services would reform themselves, and their reforms would be vindicated on the battlefield".[108]

---

[105] Moten, 2000, p. 206, see *supra* note 21.
[106] Weigley, 1984, p. 119, see *supra* note 1.
[107] *Ibid.*, p. 124.
[108] Linn, 2007, p. 41, see *supra* note 29.

Frustrated with wartime failures and unwilling to accept that professionals themselves might be partly to blame, officers have criticised the decisions of presidents, secretaries of defence and other civilian government officials who, in the mind of military professionals, exercised too much control over military operations. For example, military critics accused President Lyndon B. Johnson of losing the Vietnam War because of his obsessive control over targeting decisions during massive aerial bombing campaigns in Southeast Asia. The outcomes of each war, of course, depends on factors that have little to do with the professional training of armed forces, and civilian leaders have likely erred as often as commanding generals in decision-making during armed conflict. Yet military leaders who assail the ignorance and inexperience of civilian government officials – especially those who did not serve in the military and are not students of war and military history – are aiming at an easy target rather than accepting the limited role of state violence in crafting political solutions.

Criticism of volunteer service members likewise appeared frequently since the complaints of regular officers about volunteers and conscripts during the Mexican War and Civil War. When commanders have been ashamed by the misconduct of their troops, they sometimes sought to shift attention away from the professional armed forces and onto the corrupt influence of a degraded civil society. The torture and abuse of detainees by US soldiers in 21st-century US conflicts in Iraq and Afghanistan, for example, have been blamed on part-time soldiers inadequately trained and insufficiently integrated into the active armed forces. So long as the officer corps can distinguish the poor performance and crime of "non-regular" troops from the conduct of career military personnel, it can preserve war and military operations as the sole province of career professionals.

It may be that no matter how thorough the professionalisation of the armed forces becomes, anything short of complete autonomy and authority for commanders will not be enough. Steeped in professional values that consider specialised expertise in war indispensable and career military service a calling above any other, the US officer corps has often wanted to be left alone to prosecute wars in the most efficient and principled manner.[109] Upton's tragic frustration rests at the heart of the military's self-

---

[109] Robert L. Goldich, "American Military Culture from Colony to Empire", in *Daedalus, the Journal of the American Academy of Arts and Sciences*, 2011, vol. 140, no. 3, pp. 58–74.

interest in accountability. Law and politics mandate that the US Army be subject to civilian control. Yet in the minds of many army professionals, only a force unmoored from civilian oversight can be trusted to wage war.

6

The Self-Interest of Armed Forces in Accountability for Their Members for Core International Crimes: Carrot Is Better than Stick

Bruce Houlder*

6.1. Ethos, Legitimacy, Transparency and Self-Examination in the United Kingdom

The thesis behind this topic is an interesting one, but not just from the point of view of our focus on the armed forces. We are discussing, from a practical perspective, what is really an aspect of behavioural science that might equally, and to some benefit, be applied to a number of other disciplines.[1] We can do this by seeking the 'carrot' that can change behaviour, rather than the threat represented by the 'stick' of discipline. Such an approach might, for example, be applied to the culture behind an education programme, to how we run some of the public services, and even the medical and legal professions. It might find a strong relevance to the issue of how some schools fail and others succeed just through a change of leadership and ethos. It might be brought to bear on our financial industries and how we might change the expectation of reward simply by dint of having access to other people's money, rather than how well they create it or use it. It might be applied to our democratic institutions to change the motivation of some to apply our taxes to work for the moral advancement of mankind.

---

* **Bruce Houlder** was head of the Service Prosecuting Authority and Director of Service Prosecutions, United Kingdom, 2008–2013. He was made a Companion of the Most Honourable Order of the Bath (CB) in 2013 for his contribution to defence and service to justice. He is a tutor at the Judicial College and Recorder of the Crown Court. He was appointed Queens's Counsel in 1994, chairman of the Criminal Bar Association of England and Wales in 2001, and bencher of Gray's Inn in 2000.

1 I am indebted to the research and compilations contained in Morten Bergsmo (ed.), *Complementarity and the Exercise of Universal Jurisdiction for Core International Crimes*, Torkel Opsahl Academic EPublisher, Oslo, 2010.

It is a thesis that has particular relevance to the military not because there is a widespread culture that leads to the commission of core international crimes, but rather because there remains a lurking problem that needs addressing constantly. This is exacerbated by ongoing changes of leadership direction. It is also necessary because the lessons of history teach us that we need constant incentives to see that we do not become less than we should be.

The Mutiny Act of 1689 first formally recognised the legality of British military courts and gave parliamentary approval to the exercise of their jurisdiction. There have been many changes since then and some dark examples of the exercise of military discipline, which also serve as examples that show why the stick of discipline is not a universal panacea. All three separate service prosecuting authorities were abolished at midnight on 31 October 2009. Members of the armed services had previously led all of them. Now they were to be joined and brought under the leadership, as it happens, of a civilian lawyer. For some, the appointment of a civilian was at the time seen as almost an act of mutiny in itself. The new Act of Parliament swept away most of what had gone before; and as a result of a new landmark piece of legislation, the Armed Forces Act 2006, the new joint Service Prosecuting Authority (SPA) was created. The author was its first Director operating under a new legal framework.

Did this new creation bring a new ethos? The author naturally perhaps thinks it did, but it was not a change that the armed services failed to recognise the need for. There was much that was perhaps wrong with what had gone before, in terms that any modern jurists would wish to see in a justice system.

In the United Kingdom, accountability of the armed forces for core international crimes, and indeed all crimes committed by persons subject to service law and civilians subject to service discipline, had been the subject of much scrutiny in the years preceding the changes wrought by the Armed Forces Act 2006. Legal bombardment was directed first at the constitution of the Court Martial and later at the perceived lack of independence of some of the component parts of the service justice system, including the old prosecuting authorities that preceded the comparatively new Service Prosecuting Authority. All of these institutions largely managed to keep one step ahead of legal challenge, but by the time the new

Act became law in 2009 the need for change was becoming an increasing imperative. That process was continued with the 2011 Act.

Before this change, everything was not entirely transparent. Although trials were held in public, it was still possible for the chain of command to hide offending from public scrutiny or even provide a cloak of impunity for offending that were beginning to look, at least to some outside observers, like serious cultural defects. There was much that needed attending to both in terms of policing and in the rigour applied to prosecutorial practice. There were opportunities to push changes in some areas that needed attention. To give a small example, there was a chance to discuss how we might change the culture that leads to offences such as rape and sexual assault. If we were not to address this, how soon might it be that we have to come to terms with such offending committed as a weapon of war?

While no reliable evidence suggested any sense of cover-up of international crimes there was a recognition that, left unaltered, this might become the perception. Indeed, if there were those with a mind to subvert or hide offending, those very standards and values that underpin military discipline, which had been trusted to promote operational effectiveness, could themselves be eroded by the ability to sweep wrongdoing under the carpet. The United Kingdom has now entered a time of public inquiry and self-examination over the way it deals with crimes of abuse alleged against its military. It is going through a soul-searching time.

As the late and much lamented Lord Bingham pointed out in his book *The Rule of Law*: "The earliest rules of international law, can [...] be attributed to the self-interest of states, the need to do as one would be done by [...] and recognition that there are some mischiefs which can only be effectively addressed, if addressed by more states than one (e.g. piracy)".[2] These days, there is an even greater need for these rules to be regulated on an international basis. That is now a given.

We should be pragmatic. The moral and legal framework that international law provides should be clear. Accountability demonstrates the health of a system in a modern civilisation. It is not a necessary evil required by international convention.

---

[2]   Tom Bingham (Lord Bingham), *The Rule of Law*, Penguin, London, 2010, p. 114.

Lord Bingham mentioned "the sin of quotation", and I should ask forgiveness for that. He made the astute observation that "the point is not infrequently made that there is no international legislature, which is of course, strictly speaking, true, and that international law, as a result, lacks the legitimacy which endorsement by a democratic legislature would give". He then made his own point: "This does not impress me as a powerful argument. The means by which an obligation becomes binding on a state in international law seems to be quite as worthy of respect, as a measure approved, perhaps in haste and without adequate inquiry, perhaps on a narrowly divided vote, by a national legislature".[3]

Two methods most often deployed to achieve accountability for core international crimes are the use of a public trial, or else some form of public inquiry where for one reason or another a public trial is not possible or no longer practical. This is a vital part of public accountability, and necessary public education. It also provides the narrative for healing.

It is surprising that a BBC reporter once suggested in a live broadcast that military trials in the United Kingdom were held in secret. Perhaps that false perception was allowed to gain currency because the press far too rarely bother to send their reporters out to see what is happening in our very public courts martial. That reporter's perception could not be further from the truth – the same openness that exists in civilian trials is not lacking in the service courts. We all recognise that secret trials also achieve little of legitimacy in terms of public perception. A good example of this comes from history, in the account of Frank D. Rosenblatt:

> An insurgent leader once wrote an anger-laced list of complaints about a powerful foreign country that was occupying his country. Upset with the criminal behavior of the occupiers, he was especially incensed by their practice of whisking soldiers accused of heinous crimes back to their home country. For all he could tell, they were then exonerated in what he described as "mock trials".[4]

That leader was not a recent enemy in a country occupied by NATO forces, but Thomas Jefferson. His complaints are honoured in the American Declaration of Independence, which declares George III of England

---

[3] *Ibid.*, p. 112.

[4] Franklin D. Rosenblatt, "Non-Deployable: The Court-Martial System in Combat from 2001 to 2009", in *The Army Lawyer*, September 2010, p. 26.

> has combined with others to subject us to a jurisdiction for-
> eign to our constitution, and unacknowledged by our laws;
> giving his Assent to their Acts of pretended Legislation: For
> quartering large bodies of armed troops among us: For pro-
> tecting them, by mock Trial, from punishment for any Mur-
> ders which they should commit on the Inhabitants of these
> States.[5]

The circumstances surrounding America's founding may be different, but the strategic consequences of resentment towards the perceived
'double standards' of powerful foreign forces are highly relevant to current operations.[6] Indeed, if there is not to be visible evidence of a country
taking action against those of their own military who commit crimes
against citizens of another country, that of itself would fuel the counter-
insurgency. The stick, the very public stick, remains important. But, as to
be demonstrated below, it is not as important as the carrot. The stick could
even be seen an example of shutting the door after the horse has bolted.

The blameworthy are often brought into the public eye, and lessons
are learnt for the future, through the means of a public inquiry, by a parliamentary committee or perhaps a Senate inquiry. Sometimes civil litigation follows or the evidence that emerges in that inquiry produces itself
the need for a public criminal trial. If not, it can serve and offer closure
through public catharsis.

Countries differ as to the extent in which they are prepared to let
dirty washing be aired in public, and some perhaps over-classify events
which could be exposed to public consideration. Few countries can claim
to be angels, but none can move forward in terms of their own values and
standards if they are overprotective about what is done in their name. Education is the first step to understanding the culture that produces the kind
of crime we wish to prevent.

In the United Kingdom there have been inquiries and inquests
which have looked at allegations, in some case involving core international crimes. Litigation has also been pursued in the administrative court.
Perhaps best known is the extensive and thorough report of the Baha

---

[5]   United States Declaration of Independence, 4 July 1776, para. 17.
[6]   Rosenblatt, 2010, p. 12, see *supra* note 4.

Mousa Inquiry[7] from which many lessons have already been learned. There was a further lengthy and expensive inquiry into allegations that, in May 2004, innocent Iraqi nationals were caught in the crossfire between British forces and insurgents, that bodies had been taken from the battlefield and mutilated, that detainees had been tortured and some detainees had been murdered. The first investigation produced positive evidence to the contrary. The new inquiry, detailed as it was, secured no markedly different result. Indeed, documents in the hands of parties, but not disclosed to the legal aid authorities, emerged at a late stage to show that contrary to claims that those killed were simple farmers, they were in fact insurgents as British troops had always maintained. While some infringements of the captive prisoners' rights were established, no justification was established to support the most serious original claims that had been trumpeted cynically to the press before any serious investigation had been allowed to take place.

The threat of future claims hangs over the courts and the reputation of British forces. The obligations of the British government under the European Convention and enshrined in our own Human Rights Act rightly require such allegations to be fully investigated in a timely and effective manner. Where a prosecution is justified both on the evidence and in the public interest it should be brought. Committed and principled investigations by the Iraq Historic Allegations Team continue. This requires research and consideration of a staggering amount of material, defying in its scale all previous British-based investigations. This is intensely time consuming, and sometimes depends on the co-operation of those not always willing to give it. I hope I am not naive to hope as well as believe, as one who has been consulted and advised in respect of them prior to 2014, that the result of these investigations, or the subsequent inquests that might flow from them, and perhaps, if the evidence is there, some prosecutions, will go a long way to restoring public confidence and demonstrating that the United Kingdom sets the highest importance on accountability for core international crimes. The challenge of course continues. It is to be hoped that what happened in Afghanistan will no longer produce the multiplicity of claims that are currently under investigation. Only time will

---

[7] William Gage (Chairman), *The Report of the Baha Musa Inquiry*, Stationery Office, London, 2011, available at https://www.gov.uk/government/publications/the-baha-mousa-public-inquiry-report, last accessed on 25 March 2015.

perhaps tell. All of us will need to rise to the challenge presented in terms of investigations and in the lessons we need to learn for the future.

There are other examples. The British government has accepted that colonial forces in Kenya tortured and abused detainees during the Mau Mau rebellion against British rule in the 1950s and 1960s. There is also the long-running Bloody Sunday Inquiry which looked at the events of 30 January 1972 in the Bogside area of Derry, Northern Ireland, in which 26 unarmed civil rights protesters and bystanders were shot by soldiers of the British Army.[8] That was only 43 years ago. That inquiry, when eventually reported, brought some closure to that issue and led to a public acceptance by the Prime Minister of the contents of the report and a full public apology after it was revealed that those who had been shot were unarmed at the time and that the killings were "unjustified and unjustifiable". This public catharsis is important, and both the process and the findings have done much to heal the wounds that will long remain in Northern Ireland.

At present a non-judicial public inquiry, under the chairmanship of Sir John Chilcot, continues which is considering the period from the summer of 2001 to the end of July 2009, embracing the run-up to the conflict in Iraq, the military action and its aftermath.[9] They have been examining the United Kingdom's involvement in Iraq, including the way decisions were made and actions taken, to establish, as accurately as possible, what happened and to identify the lessons that can be learned.

All such accountability, coming even long after the event, does provide a means for countries – as well as the armed forces – to move forward by recognising what has gone before and showing a determination to change.

The Service Prosecuting Authority in the United Kingdom is a new and re-energised independent prosecuting authority, with a deep understanding of the service context vital to consideration of such cases. The key changes made by the Armed Forces Acts of 2006 and 2011 remove any potential for influence over prosecutorial decisions by the chain of command, or even politicians, though they have been known to try. The Court Martial is now a unitary court that mirrors the civil courts in both

---

8   Lord Saville of Newdigate (Chairman), *The Report of the Bloody Sunday Inquiry* (Saville Report), 10 vols., Stationery Office, London, 2010.

9   The official UK government website for the Chilcot Inquiry into the 2003 invasion of Iraq is available at http://www.iraqinquiry.org.uk/, last accessed at 2 May 2015.

the rights afforded to accused and through the more modern procedural and evidential tools available. The Judge Advocates are all civilians, the service prosecutors are civilian led and accused are represented – if they wish – by civilian lawyers. Those who are convicted may also appeal to the Court of Appeal and have, so it happens, even greater rights to challenge evidential decisions made during the course of the trial than is available in the civilian courts. What is imported, which is of value to the armed services, and I believe the public at large, is the military board that sits in place of a jury and makes the decisions both on the facts and, if necessary, on the appropriate sentence. In this there is a sense of ownership, and a pride in seeing that standards are maintained not through some disconnected tribunal, but in the sight of those that represent the standards and values which the services aspire to.

6.2. The Rule of Law, Personal Discipline and Principle

National courts, after good example and individual discipline, are the first line of defence against war crimes. Failing this, a sufficiently distinguished forum for international criminal trials should ensure no hiding place for war criminals, however powerful. The transparency and accountability of an international forum for decisions on high crimes is what civilised nations should seek, and these institutions need to be supported by more than rhetoric. Nations should not just associate themselves, but demonstrate the fullest achievable international participation with these public places of trial. They are not courts for others; they are courts for us all. This surely is a culture to be applauded, and is in the self-interest for all of the national armed services. We might all hope that this may become a given, as we all want peace, and we all should condemn cruelty, inhumanity and torture in any of its imaginative forms. It is perhaps trite to say we would all live in a better world could this be achieved, but we would also be free from the weasel words that sometimes seek to justify such conduct. We still find apologists for torture in surprising places, even among those who will condemn this in others. There can be little legitimacy where such tensions exist.

The sophistry of justification sometimes provides the food to disguise the true effects of such crimes. We have seen it in some countries in the Middle East where the language of denial, and the justifications given for terrible and cruel reprisals against fellow countrymen, give birth to a new language that appals the informed international observer. We have seen the misuse of power become an end in itself, and forget its true purpose. As that great constitutionalist Professor A.V. Dicey noted in popularising Aristotle's famous dictum, "it is more proper that law should govern than any one of the citizens",[10] or as John Locke in 1690 put it: "Wherever law ends, Tyranny begins".[11]

We have seen too many examples of that truth in recent times, particularly in North Africa and in the Ukraine, and a failure to face it in ourselves will make such words as accountability seem empty rhetoric. We do have self-interest in preserving states which found themselves on the law of a democratically elected legislative chamber. How to reconcile those laudable aims with those of different cultural traditions, without seeming to impose our own models on others who do not want them, is a problem for all of us. The rise of Islamic State (ISIS), to name but a single modern challenge, raises the bar in requiring nations to resist the cries of those who might prefer to suspend international humanitarian norms or to abandon principle in favour of short-term solutions. Democracy and respect for law should go hand in hand.

The United Kingdom, as a democratic country, respects the value of accountability in core international crimes and has readily ratified most treaties that underpin such accountability. Such ratification and respect for rule of law also have consequences. The United Kingdom courts occasionally come into conflict with other governments when it comes to the disclosure of information that such other country might consider to be of assistance to the enemy. Such conflicts need a resolution if the comity of nations is at stake, but there is nothing unusual, and something quite healthy, if from time to time the courts come into collision with their own parliaments and with those of other states or even, in a European context, with Strasbourg, so long as the rule of law is ultimately respected.[12]

---

[10] Aristotle, *The Politics*, compiled by Trevor J. Saunders, Penguin, London, 1982, Sec. 1287a18-22; see also, A.V. Dicey, *The Law of the Constitution*, J.W.F. Allison (ed.), Oxford University Press, Oxford, 2013, Part II (originally published in 1885).

[11] John Locke, *Two Treatises of Government and A Letter Concerning Toleration*, I. Shapiro (ed.), Yale University Press, New Haven, CT, 2003, Book 2, Ch. 18, Sec. 202 (originally published in 1690).

[12] Most democratic nations have rules to protect secret information from exposure in the courts – see, for example, US Supreme Court, *United States v. Reynolds*, 345 US 1, Judgment, 9 March 1953, that first recognised the state secrets privilege; see also Carrie New-

It is not the stick of prosecutions that is spelt out in the mission statement of the Service Prosecuting Authority, which I had the privilege to lead, it is the carrot. It is clear that the purpose of the service justice system is to underpin operational effectiveness. That is at the very heart of a soldier's business.

For the United Kingdom Ministry of Defence, it is the need for a strong sense of internal discipline in the way the services conduct themselves, on and off operations, that is vital. If it were not, we might as well have the errant soldiers dealt with in the civilian system and without recourse to the many disciplinary offences that are created by service discipline statutes to ensure sound internal discipline. We may as well, if that is to be the approach, abandon a system which understands and recognises the attraction of sound discipline. A flabby force, an ill-disciplined force or a military that makes its own rules, worse still mixes its own messages, and does not respect international norms, will in the end defeat itself in operations, and in the public mind. A sound democracy needs the legitimacy of a principled force, not a repressive one. That same fighting force lends legitimacy to its conduct in that space after the conflict ends, and in the nation building that must follow.[13]

6.3. The Central Question: The Tension Between Carrot and Stick – and the Fourth Estate

This section approaches the philosophical question of why accountability in the form of investigations and prosecutions should be seen as a carrot rather than a stick, to inspire good behaviour, high discipline and morale.

As mentioned above, the link to openness itself underpins the moral argument. Next, one might say that the desire for accountability, for the

---

ton Lyons, "The State Secrets Privilege: Expanding Its Scope through Government Misuse", in *Lewis and Clark Law Review*, 2007, vol. 11, no. 1, pp. 99–132; see also Shayana Kadidal, "The State Secrets Privilege and Executive Misconduct", JURIST Forum, 30 May 2006, available at http://jurist.org/forum/2006/05/state-secrets-privilege-and-executive.php, last accessed at 27 March 2015; see also UK Court of Appeal (Civil Division), *The Queen on the application of Binyam Mohamed v. The Secretary of State for Foreign and Commonwealth Affairs*, [2010] EWCA Civ 65, Judgment, 10 February 2010, for a summary of the United Kingdom consideration of these issues when international relationships are involved.

[13] Points akin to this were made in the UK House of Commons during the debate on the Armed Forces Bill 2011, see *Hansard*, vol. 521, Part No. 95, Col. 53, 10 January 2011.

---

maintenance and enforcing of high standards, is obvious to anyone that observes how nations in conflict behave when one attacks or offends another in some way. There are reprisals – an attack will occur somewhere else at a time of the enemy's choosing; lives of innocent civilians will be lost in some far away embassy. All has cause and effect.

The trouble is that, in the public debate, we seem to move forward one step and often take two backwards. The debate takes too little account of history or human nature. Certainly, in the United Kingdom, and probably in the United States and in some other countries, the debate continues at a rather depressing level. At election time, positions sometimes polarise to an almost dangerous degree. Some sections of the press will prefer the stick, or prefer revenge to something that seeks a lasting solution. Attempts are made to hold other nations to account by taking a war-like stance against them. Moderation, example and diplomacy are sometimes seen as a sign of weakness rather than an intelligent strength.

To educate the troops to show restraint, a way of bridging the tension with public opinion has to be found. Nations will need to ensure that jingoism, sectarianism or extreme solutions do not provide the language that excuses the commission of terrible crimes. One only needs to look at what has happened in Syria, where one and then other participants in what has now become a transnational argument lose all humanity and principle. No one has an interest in such a fomentation in seeking accountability for the high crimes that have been committed, but if a winner were ever to emerge we will no doubt see it.

This absence of law makes the case for impartial international justice. Those lawyers who have practised in the courts of International Criminal Tribunal for the former Yugoslavia, International Criminal Tribunal for Rwanda or in the Special Court for Sierra Leone, or even in the International Criminal Court, would perhaps describe international courts as an imperfect process, with politics still sitting very much at the centre – but it is so much better than it was 20, 30 or 40 years ago. International accountability has made great strides since then and these international efforts should receive full support. All war crimes trials rely on cooperation with states, often the very ones that were involved in the relevant war, for production of valuable documents from state archives, and to facilitate access to witnesses. States will be obligated by membership of the United Nations to co-operate, while at the same time wanting or needing to obscure information that would make public the involvement of the state in the commission of crimes and mass atrocities. There is little perfection there, but we are perhaps on a journey with international justice.

Even with a press that takes polar opposite positions to a single story (the author has seen a few of those in his own job), it is possible to find a balance and a reason to be grateful for the press we have. They still inform whatever slant they choose. They provoke informed debate, and thus prevent ill-informed prejudice from filling the vacuum which a censored press might produce. So accountability through press exposure is ultimately an engine of positive change.

Legal firms nowadays bring actions against the Ministry of Defence for one perceived failing or another, or represent those, often foreign civilians, who claim they have been harmed in some way by offensive action. There are some who may question their motives. This is unhelpful, because they ultimately increase the self-interest in the military to seek accountability among their own for such crimes as are proved to have been committed. There is legal aid funding made available to bring such actions and to assert the absolute rights of the complainants under, in particular, Articles 2 and 3 of the European Convention.[14]

As mentioned already, the press is slow to pick up on what is actually done in the service courts. This *de facto* rather than intended lack of transparency remains a problem in the author's opinion. Action taken by prosecutors to bring to trial those who commit crimes against civilians of

---

[14] European Convention on Human Rights, Rome, 4 November 1950, Article 2:
    1. Everyone's right to life shall be protected by law. No one shall be deprived of his life intentionally save in the execution of a sentence of a court following his conviction of a crime for which this penalty is provided by law.
    2. Deprivation of life shall not be regarded as inflicted in contravention of this article when it results from the use of force which is no more than absolutely necessary:
        (a) in defence of any person from unlawful violence;
        (b) in order to effect a lawful arrest or to prevent escape of a person lawfully detained;
        (c) in action lawfully taken for the purpose of quelling a riot or insurrection.
Article 3:
      No one shall be subjected to torture or to inhuman or degrading treatment or punishment.

other nations, in particular, needs to be better known than it is. If members of the public attended the Court Martial, they would surely have more faith in the process than some commentators allow them to have, as well as in the fairness of what is being done in these places. The author rather suspects that many critics of the system, including a few journalists, have never stepped inside a court-martial building. Press reports are sometimes built on the back of a partisan account rather than impartial witness.

Not putting the courts under the public microscope might be comfortable for some short-sighted public relations adviser whose concern is to protect the reputation and thus the fighting ability of the British Army, the Royal Navy and the Royal Air Force. They can be overprotective in this area. Carefully burnishing "lines to take" with the press, should they have the effrontery to ask a probing question, is no way for us to be. An overprotective approach is more likely to lead the reader to believe nothing that a government's department of defence might say without corroboration, or, worse from their point of view, lead to further enquiry from the press about the very issue they hope would go away.

When the author was Director of Service Prosecutions no one in the Ministry of Defence suggested that the author should not talk to the press; indeed, handling the media was one of the skills required for this job. There were a few who were quite obviously concerned whether a civilian could be trusted to deal with the press as they might wish. It seemed they would rather have control of the whole pitch. I do not criticise their good motives here, but simply disagree with a few who seem to consider that serious wrongdoing by the armed forces is something that would be better if it never emerged into public view.

One example of such press exposure doing more good than harm, in an area which publicity had not been given at all by the Ministry of Defence, concerned a series of prosecutions brought by the SPA, of which the public were wholly unaware until the SPA decided to court the journalists on the *Guardian* newspaper most concerned with these kinds of stories, and whom the author trusted to tell the truth.

The result was the publication of the brief and accurate facts of quite a number of successful prosecutions that the SPA had brought in connection with abuses by British soldiers on foreign nationals. These trials had not previously been brought to press attention, because the courts, although public, tend to be sited in rather inaccessible places. None of them was in the category of war crimes with the degree of severity we are considering, but that was simply because there were at that stage no such cases at that time.

The danger of suppressing public awareness has recently been highlighted in the United Kingdom in a rather unusual way. There are now proposals to remove prosecutions for some forms of contempt. As with some other countries, there is still an old offence in the United Kingdom which is an extension of the law of contempt of "scandalising the court". In Scotland it is called rather quaintly "murmuring judges".[15] This allows prosecutions for "any act designed or writing published calculated to bring a court or a judge of the court into contempt, or lower his authority".[16] An example could be: "Philandering Judge falls asleep on the job".

In the course of the *Spycatcher* litigation, an injunction was successfully applied for to prevent the publication of proceedings.[17] The *Daily Mirror* newspaper ignored it by publishing upside-down photos of three judges from the highest court with the words "You Fools!" attached. No prosecution was in the end pursued. The reason is perhaps somewhat obvious – the carrot is usually better than the stick. First, there had been no successful prosecution since 1931. An act to revive it in March 2012 in Northern Ireland was eventually dropped – there was an attempt to prosecute Peter Hain, a Member of Parliament, for his statement in a book[18] criticising the Lord Justice's way of handling a judicial review application. Adverse consequences are not always mitigated by prosecution. Also in a case like this, prosecution these days is inclined to provoke further ridicule, and some accused would welcome the opportunity to appear in person when prosecuted for such an offence in order to use the protection of the court to continue to justify the attack on the judiciary. Lastly, such prosecutions give the impression that judges are trying to stifle criticism.[19]

---

[15] Gerald H. Gordon, *The Criminal Law of Scotland*, W. Green, Edinburgh, 2001, para. 50.03.

[16] *R. v. Gray* [1900] 2 QB 36.

[17] Bibha Tripathi, *Contempt of Court and Freedom of Speech: Exploring Gender Biases*, Readworthy Publications, New Delhi, 2010, p. 68.

[18] Peter Hain, *Outside In*, Biteback Publishing, London, 2012. For a comment, see Jennifer James, "Court in the Act", in *New Law Journal*, 2012, vol. 162.

[19] US Supreme Court, *Bridges v. California*, 314 US 252, Judgment, 8 December 1941, pp. 252, 271–72.

So the message from that, albeit in somewhat of a back to front way, is to not suppress wrongs, but give them the oxygen of some publicity. We should trust people to think right thoughts, to judge issues with intelligence once they have all the information available, and allow people to believe the wrongdoing is taken seriously and that right-thinking members of the armed forces will want the world to know that the majority are not like those who are being publicly shamed and prosecuted. That in part is why there is a service justice system. The Royal Navy for example are very keen not to see the Court Martial centre at the Portsmouth Naval Base closed down and moved to a joint centre elsewhere, because they wish to see offenders who reduce the reputation of the Royal Navy brought to book under their own flag, so others of their service will be encouraged to learn by this.

As alluded to above, there were once those that appeared less than willing to have the wrongdoings of a soldier assessed by a civilian. The parliamentary reports are impressed with anxieties from some distinguished, albeit mostly retired and ennobled, servicemen about the idea that a civilian could ever understand what it means to be a soldier and to face the decisions they have to take – sometimes making life-and-death decisions with no time at all for reflection. One noble Lord was told by another noble Lord – perhaps jokingly – that he deserved to be taken out and shot for expressing such a view on the floor of the Upper Chamber. I think it is fair to say that critics have been silenced and now see a positive added value in the accountability, increased visibility and independence represented by a civilian head in the midst of service law and justice which is no longer there for the chopping!

6.4. Officers and Those under Their Command – Cultural and Core Values

In the end, the examination we are embarked upon is not to be too neatly analysed in personal terms. The majority of defendants the author saw as a prosecutor were not officers, and they were not, nor were ever likely to become, military leaders. They were the humble infanteer, the rifle carrier who did not consider these questions daily. The motivating factor at home may not always be a consideration of their chances of promotion or the good opinion of their fellows, as much as the inspirational drive of their fourteenth pint of beer on a Friday night. On operations, where there was no beer, their motivating factor would be first and foremost the protection of their own lives and the lives of their comrades. That is as it should be. On operations, ethical, moral or courageous restraint sometimes remains a difficult concept, however much it is drilled into them as part of their training.

The factors that will drive the commission of core international crimes among otherwise quite law-abiding armies are many. Obviously, a high level of losses of one's own side, unclear orders and a high frustration level among the troops will be factors. Other things will also be just as important. The dehumanisation of the enemy by the use of derogatory names and epithets, a high turnover in the chain of command, poorly trained and inexperienced troops, the lack of a clearly defined enemy, and no clear sense of mission can all be breeding grounds for serious criminal acts.

Some say that examples of human weakness produce difficult decisions for prosecutors. However, in the end, the rule of law has to be applied consistently and in a principled manner. Ill-discipline breeds more ill-discipline, promotes reprisals and, put bluntly, can and does endanger the lives of many. Self-discipline cannot be too flexible a commodity. The argument that an insurgent who may not imbue another human life with the same dignity or respect as one might, or be so inclined to afford the protections of the Geneva Conventions law, is no justification for a soldier to lower the standards of the nation he or she represents by descending to the same level as a brutalising foe. That way he brutalises the cause for which he fights, and offers it scant legitimacy.

The real danger is not the errant foot soldier. It lies in culture. Cultural values are set further up. Like corruption, the rot can start at the top, and develop its own self-protective carapace. That then becomes the greatest evil and is the hardest to eradicate. Seen in this way, the justification for a set of moral imperatives without which an individual simply will become unable to advance through ranks is an obvious aim. The following declaration appears on the British Army website:

> The Army's standards apply to everyone, from senior commanders to soldiers on the ground in Afghanistan. These standards say that behaviour should be lawful and appropriate, and demand total professionalism at all times. By signing up to these standards, soldiers show that they won't tol-

erate bad treatment of each other or of the other people that
the Army comes into contact with.

The six core standards of the British Army, for example, are those
of courage, loyalty, discipline, respect for others, integrity and selfless
commitment. These are defined in example, but prove difficult to obey in
the heat of a war. Those who need to understand this best will be the
commanders in the field who need to see that the law of armed conflict is
complied with, without allowing the men and women under their command to be constrained in the lawful pursuit of the objective. This is a difficult tension, but one that is achievable. It is right to say that most commanders would not be where they are without having shown themselves
to be exemplars of those standards and values.

Culture is vitally important, but if some modern research is to be
believed, men are not just driven by an identification with authority. Research by Alexander Haslam and Stephen Reicher declares that an understanding of the psychology of tyranny is dominated by classic studies
from the 1960s and 1970s, in particular Stanley Milgram's research on
obedience to authority and Philip Zimbardo and colleagues' Stanford
Prison experiment. Supporting popular notions of 'the banality of evil',
this research has provided the theory that people conform passively and
unthinkingly to both the instructions and the roles that authorities provide,
however malevolent these may be. Recently, though, this consensus has
been challenged by empirical work informed by social identity theoris-
ing.[20]

The former theory was that tyranny is a natural and unavoidable
consequence of humans' inherent motivation to bend to the wishes of those
in authority – whoever they may be and whatever it is required to do. Put
slightly differently, it operationalises an apparent tragedy of the human
condition: our desire to be good subjects is stronger than our desire to be
subjects who do good.

---

[20] See Alexander Haslam and Stephen D. Reicher, "Contesting the 'Nature' of Conformity:
What Milgram and Zimbardo's Studies Really Show", in *PLoS Biol*, 2012, available at
http://journals.plos.org/plosbiology/article?id=10.1371/journal.pbio.1001426, last accessed
on 27 March 2015; Stanley Milgram, *Obedience to Authority: An Experimental View*,
Harper and Row, New York, 1974; and Craig Haney, Curtis Banks and Philip Zimbardo,
"A Study of Prisoners and Guards in a Simulated Prison", in *Naval Research Reviews*,
1973, vol. 9, pp. 1–17.

The 'banality of evil' thesis was once an almost universally acknowledged truth. It is given prominence in social psychology textbooks, and has informed the thinking of historians, political scientists, economists and neuroscientists. Indeed, via a range of social commentators, it has shaped the public consciousness much more broadly and, in this respect, can lay claim to being the most influential data-driven thesis in the science of psychology.

Yet despite the breadth of this consensus, in recent years Haslam, Reicher and others have reinterrogated its two principal underpinnings – the archival evidence pertaining to Eichmann and his ilk, and the specifics of Milgram's and Zimbardo's empirical demonstrations – in ways that tell a very different story. First, a series of thoroughgoing historical examinations have challenged the idea that Nazi bureaucrats were ever simply following orders. This may have been the defence they relied upon when seeking to minimise their culpability, but evidence suggests that functionaries like Eichmann had a very good understanding of what they were doing and took pride in the energy and application that they brought to their work. Typically, too, roles and orders were vague, and hence for those who wanted to advance the Nazi cause (and not all did) creativity and imagination were required in order to work towards the regime's assumed goals and to overcome the challenges associated with any given task. Emblematic of this, the practical details of the 'final solution' were not handed down from on high but had to be elaborated by Eichmann himself. He then felt compelled to confront and disobey his superiors – most particularly Himmler – when he believed that they were not sufficiently faithful to eliminationist Nazi principles.

Second, much the same analysis can be used to account for behaviour in the Stanford Prison experiment. While it may be true that Zimbardo gave the guards no direct orders, he certainly gave them a general sense of how he expected them to behave. During the orientation session Zimbardo told them, among other things:

> You can create in the prisoners' feelings of boredom, a sense of fear to some degree, you can create a notion of arbitrariness that their life is totally controlled by us, by the system, you, me [...]. We're going to take away their individuality in

various ways. In general what all this leads to is a sense of powerlessness.[21]

This contradicts Zimbardo's assertion that "behavioural scripts associated with the oppositional roles of prisoner and guard [were] the sole source of guidance"[22] and leads us to question the claim that conformity to these role-related scripts was the primary cause of guard brutality. But even with such guidance, not all guards acted brutally. And those who did used ingenuity and initiative in responding to Zimbardo's brief. Accordingly, after the experiment was over, one prisoner confronted his chief tormentor with the observation that "if I had been a guard I don't think it would have been such a masterpiece".[23] Contrary to the banality of evil thesis, the research found that the Zimbardo-inspired tyranny was made possible by the active engagement of enthusiasts rather than the leaden conformity of automatons.

Therefore, things could be done regarding the selection of those who carry out the tasks in war that might lead to abuse, their training and their oversight. The removal of enthusiasts from these key roles, where such abuse as opposed to basic war-fighting was made possible, might be somewhere to make a start.

War can change people, and command at every level has the difficult but essential task of remaining strong in the promotion of these values in the most difficult of circumstances. The moment there is a slippage in, for example, the standards of treatment that are applied to detained persons or the captured enemy, the reputation of the Army is on a slippery path. In a post-conflict situation, those British and international troops engaged in mentoring forces of a newly emergent nation, who have acquired for themselves a less than perfect reputation for the respect of humanity, will themselves be deprived of some measure of moral authority over those they seek to train. Claims of imperialism will be more easily made, and if then what you seek is the imposition of your own values and standards, then you may as well go home. It is now almost a cliché to say

---

[21] Philip Zimbardo, *Quiet Rage: The Stanford Prison Study* [Videotape], Stanford University, Stanford, CA, 1989.

[22] Philip Zimbardo, "A Situationist Perspective on the Psychology of Evil: Understanding How Good People are Transformed into Perpetrators", in Arthur G. Miller (ed.), *The Social Psychology of Good and Evil*, Guilford Press, New York, 2004, p. 39.

[23] Zimbardo, 1989, see *supra* note 19.

that the most difficult thing for powerful nations is not to win the war but to win the peace. If there is corruption in the values of leadership then you may not win.

Western nations may appear materialistic and bankrupt of moral values to some Middle Eastern cultures, but that will be a secondary impression to the one that a principled international military presence can create face to face. The poor Afghan farmer who was caught up in the middle of a conflict not of his own choosing; the woman who sought an education and was condemned for it; the child who wished to play but who has seen his plaything seized and burned, and his family punished; the soldier who has been forced to kill rather than face the possibility of death himself, or kills himself because he is no longer able to live with what he has seen or had to do. These are the casualties of war and are those whom justice should protect or whose memories we should honour. They are the ones that looked to the language of international obligation to have some meaning. If then those who would be victors are seen as no better than those who oppressed them formerly, what has been won and how will the *casus belli* for which so many have died be justified then? It is thoughts such as these that should provide the self-interest in accountability for core international crimes.

6.5. Conclusion

If one reads the preamble of the Charter of the United Nations or the Universal Declaration of Human Rights, if one considers the atrocities that motivated and informed those declarations, and if one then considers the European Convention on Human Rights and Fundamental Freedoms, one will find that all of them begin with expressions that recognise the inherent dignity, and the equal and inalienable rights of all members of the human family as the foundation of justice and peace in the world. These instruments identify that disregard and contempt for such rights have resulted in acts of barbarity outraging the conscience of mankind. All of them reaffirm, in one way or another, the promotion of social progress and larger freedoms. The condemnation of torture in the Convention against Torture and other Cruel, Inhuman or Degrading Treatment or Punishment harks back to the UN Charter, as well as the International Covenant on Civil and Political Rights and the Universal Declaration of Human Rights. Hardly a word of this is the language of the 'stick'. It is a recognition of the evil that we are capable of, which is much better to be honest about than not. It is a recognition expressed from a positive perspective, which is the very opposite approach of a criminal statute. It is just 'carrot' and very little 'stick'.

7

Contextual Analysis of Accountability for Core International Crimes: A Perspective From the Indonesian Armed Forces

Agus Widjojo*

> When you resort to force [...] you didn't know where you were
> going [...] if you got deeper and deeper there was just no limit
> except [...] the limitation of force itself.[1]
>
> *General Dwight D. Eisenhower*

General Eisenhower was referring to the nature of war. Similarly, according to Carl von Clausewitz, the logic of war results in "reciprocal action", a continuous escalation in which neither side is guilty even if it acts first, since every act can be called, and almost certainly is, pre-emptive.[2] Ensuring individual accountability for core international crimes is essential to restraining the act of war. The military itself may also benefit from such accountability for its members. That is precisely the topic of this important book. This chapter seeks to address the topic from the perspective of our experience in Indonesia during the past decades, which are particular but nevertheless relevant to the subject-matter at hand.

Armed forces do not exist in a vacuum. Specifically, four contextual factors should be considered: the culture of the society where the armed forces live; the history of the armed forces, especially the process of the inception and historical background of the armed forces; the political en-

---

* Lieutenant General (Retd.) **Agus Widjojo** is the former Vice Chairman of the People's Consultative Assembly ('MPR') of the Republic of Indonesia and Tentara Nasional Indonesia's ('TNI') Chief of Territorial Affairs, and is regarded as one of the TNI's leading intellectuals. During his appointment as Commandant of the Armed Force's staff college (the TNI think tank), he was responsible for restructuring the political and security doctrine of the TNI. He served as a member of the Indonesia–Timor Leste Joint Truth and Friendship Commission. He is a Senior Fellow of the Centre for Strategic and International Studies, Indonesia, and was a Visiting Senior Fellow of the Institute of Defence and Strategic Studies in Singapore. He has written numerous articles on security issues in the Asia-Pacific region.

[1] Michael Walzer, *Just and Unjust Wars: A Moral Argument with Historical Illustrations*, Basic Books, and New York, 2006.

[2] *Ibid.*

---

vironment that may influence the organisational culture of the armed forces; and the evolving strategic environment to which the armed forces must be vigilant. While armed forces need to operate a highly cohesive system to react rapidly and effectively in emergencies, they also have to work flexibly in a changing world.[3]

This chapter looks at how these four factors affect the Indonesian Armed Forces' establishment and evolution. Through the example of the accountability process linked to the 1999 East Timorese crisis, the author dwells on a non-judicial approach to accountability more broadly understood, namely the contextual analysis by the Indonesia-Timor Leste Commission of Truth and Friendship. The author shows that clearly identified responsibilities that factor in the socio-cultural context may inform the military in ways that assist future self-development. This can contribute to the prevention of atrocities and, when necessary, accountability.

7.1. Communitarian Traditional Culture

Culture can be analysed as a phenomenon that surrounds us at all times, being constantly enacted, created and influential in our daily activities. When talking about why we need to understand culture, the former *Massachusetts Institute of Technology* professor, Edgar H. Schein, who is credited with coining the term 'corporate culture', argued that the concept of culture has not only become relevant to organisational analysis but has also aided understanding of what goes on inside an organisation when a different subculture and occupational process must work with each other.[4]

Traditional Indonesian culture is communitarian in nature. It holds individuals as being part of the group. This is similar to the culture of a military organisation. Perhaps this is why the issue of seeing a soldier as an individual, separated from the traditional loyalty to superiors, is controversial. In Indonesian culture, it goes beyond that, to take on the form of a patron-client relationship. The definition describes patron-client relations as a form of politics in which ties between the leader and followers

---

[3] John C.T. Downey, *Management in the Armed Forces: An Anatomy of the Military Profession*, McGraw-Hill, New York, 1977.

[4] Edgar H. Schein, *Organizational Culture and Leadership*, Jossey-Bass, San Francisco, 1992, p. 55.

are personal.[5] Earlier theorists thought of clientelism as an asymmetric face-to-face relationship between a patron and a client supported by a normative framework. According to Gerry van Klinken, this patron-client relationship implies that, rather than building state institutions that serve the general interest, the actors concerned prefer to play a complex game of deals and counter-deals.[6] Accountability, on the contrary, operates more on an individual basis.

7.2. Establishment of Indonesian Armed Forces in a Nation-in-Arms

Patron-client relations may have advantages and disadvantages, as was demonstrated during the Indonesian struggle for independence in the late 1940s. Indonesia was a nation-in-arms. It was against this backdrop that the Indonesian National Armed Forces (Tentara Nasional Indonesia, 'TNI') was first established. Apart from former members of the Royal Netherlands East Indies Army, it integrated the former Japanese-formed units of 'Defender of Homeland' and the armed wings of various national freedom fighter units.

The adoption of the guerrilla strategy meant that a solid unity within the people was essential to victory. To mobilise national resources in support of the war effort, a guerrilla government was set up, subordinating civil servants to the local military commander. In such circumstances, the Indonesian military started to gain experience acting as a government and to extend its role well beyond traditional national defence. The military practically was the government. The military's role in a nation-in-arms in defending the state against the Dutch attempt to recolonise the country led to the self-perception of the TNI as the sole guardian of the nation, in unity with the people. This built the self-confidence of the military and its self-identification with the state.

7.3. Authoritarianism and the Advent of Democracy

The paternalistic tradition of the Indonesian culture contributed to the establishment of an authoritarian regime. After some experiments in liberal

---

[5] Frances Rothstein, "The Class Basis of Patron-Client Relations", in *Latin American Perspectives*, 1979, vol. 6, no. 2, pp. 25–35.

[6] Gerry van Klinken, "The Limits of Ethnic Clientelism in Indonesia", in *Review of Indonesian and Malaysian Affairs (RIMA)*, 2008, vol. 42, no. 2, pp. 35–65.

and parliamentary democracy in the 1950s, Indonesia was well underway towards an authoritarian political system through Guided Democracy, which made Soekarno president for life. When President Soeharto succeeded President Soekarno, he modelled the authoritarian political system in a rather different way. Soeharto developed a procedural democracy through regular elections, but based its power on the formation of a strong single majority political party supported by a political military. Checks, balances and control were conducted by legislatures composed mostly of appointed representation in a conforming political culture. This set of circumstances strengthened the power of state. For the armed forces it created a sense that, as a national instrument of power carrying out a mission of the state, it could never be wrong when acting against those who violated the law or opposed the government. This led to the weakening of the sense of accountability among members of the armed forces.

In the meantime, the demise of the Soviet Union in December 1991 resulted in the end of the Cold War. Francis Fukuyama termed the situation as the end of the ideological confrontation between capitalism and communism, in his words, the "end of history".[7] The United States became the sole superpower and was able to enforce the expansion of, among other things, democracy as the universal value of the international community. Whereas during the Cold War, Third World countries were left to deal with their own internal problems, the end of the Cold War resulted in an erosion of the borders of sovereignty, in the sense that countries, in dealing with their respective national issues, would have to consider the international implications of their decisions. With the advent of democracy also came unavoidable conditions, which are part of the concept of democracy, including transparency, respect for human rights and accountability. These developments took place in less than a decade. In the context of changing values, customs and the way of doing things, this time span was felt to be too short, especially when these changes are enforced by political pressure through the use of sanctions.

7.4. Challenges to Accountability through Judicial Proceedings

The armed forces have also questioned the fairness, balance and validity of international law in domestic conflicts. In this regard, there seems to be

---

[7] Francis Fukuyama, *The End of History and the Last Man*, Free Press, New York, 1992.

a different set of standards when human rights instruments are applied to irregular insurgent organisations, on the one hand, and to government forces, on the other. For example, Peter Rowe, in *The Impact of Human Rights Law on Armed Forces*, suggests that it is not clear that "rebel organisations" are bound by the human rights instruments entered into by the states concerned. He further states that an imbalance in the protection afforded by human rights instruments is readily apparent – the actions of a state (including its armed forces) may incur a liability regarding human rights law but not (generally) the actions of the rebels.[8] Where government forces are easy to identify and locate, it is these government forces that are mostly held accountable for adherence to human rights principles, while irregular insurgent forces can get away with it. This asymmetric enforcement of the human rights principle on two opposing sides could give an advantage to the irregular insurgent forces over government forces.

Difficulties and challenges to ensuring accountability through criminal proceedings have paved the way for the development of non-criminal justice options. Although compared to judicial proceedings these mechanisms may not provide as rigorous a determination of, or as serious punishment for, individual responsibility, in many cases they represent the best or only alternative to criminal trials, valuable precursors or complements to criminal trials, or even, under some theories of justice, the optimal forms of accountability in certain situations.[9]

These challenges of asymmetry and alternative transitional justice make it all the more important to explore the self-interest of armed forces in accountability for core international crimes. Embedding accountability-processes and -preparedness in professionalisation efforts within armed forces make criminal justice accountability more immediate and sustainable. Officers and soldiers should see it as being in their interest to have such accountability, even in criminal justice does not reach non-state actors at the time, and despite available non-criminal justice options.

---

[8] Peter Rowe, *The Impact of Human Rights Law on Armed Forces*, Cambridge University Press, Cambridge, 2005.

[9] Steven R. Ratner and Jason S. Abrams, *Accountability for Human Rights Atrocities in International Law: Beyond the Nuremberg Legacy*, 2nd ed., Oxford University Press, Oxford, 2001.

7.5. Contextual Analysis of Accountability for the 1999 East Timor Crisis

7.5.1. Unsatisfactory Judicial Proceedings

One Indonesian case in point is the various human rights violations reported to have occurred prior to and immediately after the popular consultation in East Timor. The popular consultation was a political initiative taken by President Habibie on 27 January 1999 to determine the future status of East Timor. Accountability was pursued by judicial processes as well as a number of commissions of inquiry. In Indonesia, the Commission of Inquiry into Human Rights Violations in East Timor ('KPP-HAM') and an *ad hoc* human rights tribunal were formed in September 1999. These institutions produced conclusions and decisions in accordance with their respective mandates and procedures. Neither came out with satisfactory results. The *ad hoc* human rights tribunal acquitted TNI officers. Two indigenous East Timorese, the governor of the province and a pro-Indonesia militia leader, were convicted but later received clemency.

7.5.2. Contextual Analysis of Accountability by the Commission of Truth and Friendship

It was the Indonesia-Timor Leste Commission of Truth and Friendship (the 'Commission') that first concluded that gross human rights violations in the form of crimes against humanity occurred in East Timor in 1999. While the Commission identified the institutional responsibility of both pro-autonomy militias and pro-independence groups, among others, it also concluded that the TNI's reliance on such armed groups was a structural weakness that constituted a source of their institutional responsibility for human rights violations in 1999.

In order to fulfil its mandate to inquire into the nature, scope and cause of the 1999 violence, the Commission conducted research into the historical background, political dynamic and institutional structure that shaped events before and during 1999. This allowed the Commission to inform its conclusion with a broader understanding of the way in which the 1999 violence was connected to previously established institutional structures and practices. This understanding was particularly important in arriving at recommendations aimed at preventing recurrence through institutional reform and other measures.

On 5 May 1999 Indonesia, Portugal and the United Nations reached an agreement about the East Timorese referendum at the United Nations headquarters in New York. The Tripartite Agreement of 5 May stipulated that the security of the popular consultation was the responsibility of Indonesia. The agreement demanded complete neutrality of the TNI and the sole responsibility of the Indonesian national police force ('Polri') to enforce law and order, and guarantee a safe atmosphere free from all violence or any other form of pressure.

It was only on 21 May 1998 that President Soeharto resigned. Thus we see that it had not been very long since the TNI was still operating within an authoritarian political system under the dual function doctrine (*dwi-fungsi*), which stipulated that the armed forces (at the time including the Polri) existed not only as a defence and security force but also as a sociopolitical force. Another significant factor which contributed to the role of the newly renamed Armed Forces of the Republic of Indonesia (Angkatan Bersenjata Republik Indonesia, 'ABRI') in the conflict area of East Timor was the contextual interpretation that the 'total people's defence and security system' (*sishankamrata*, abbreviation of *sistem pertahanan keamanan rakyat semesta*) was to be implemented by forming civilian militias. This idea grew out of the romanticism of the struggle for independence during the late 1940s. This legacy was seen in the formation of various militias to fight for the unity of East Timor as part of the Indonesian Republic, which led to the Truth and Friendship Commission's finding of close co-operation between the militias and the TNI.[10]

A lesson learned here – which should not be disregarded – is that although accountability should be answered within the military, relevant contextual elements are essential to understanding the attitudes and behaviour of the military.

The time span between the end of the authoritarian regime and the dual function doctrine, and the deployment of the military to support the police in providing security for the popular consultation in East Timor, was too short. The situation was more difficult for the police. This was the first time that it was assigned to a mission independently of the armed

---

[10] Commission of Truth and Friendship, *Per Memoriam Ad Spem (From Memory to Hope): Final Report of the Commission of Truth and Friendship (CTF) Indonesia-Timor-Leste*, Ministries of Foreign Affairs of Timor-Leste and Indonesia, Dili and Bali, 2008.

forces. As a law enforcement institution, it had to face a sharply divided society as well as those militias who had always operated in close co-operation with the military.

The political climate was also not in favour of the security forces (ABRI and Polri). Structural and organisational changes were carried out as required, but the security forces were not trained to face a sharply divided and conflicted society. They may not even have known that the operational environment and the expectations had changed. The political setting also did not help the security forces very much to adjust to the new environment. The efforts by the Indonesian political authorities and security forces in the aftermath of the popular consultation never improved. If we assume that policy-making concerning the military is a result of the decisions of the political authorities, then what was witnessed during the post-1999 period is that the will to ensure the military was held accountable for core international crimes never really formed. This was in part a result of the democratic transition taking place. Ironically, a policy was set under Soeharto in 1991 to enforce the accountability of the TNI through investigation and prosecution, with a view to looking into the violence and shooting at Santa Cruz cemetery in Dili, East Timor. No such policy was adopted in the post-1999 period by the new democratic regime in Indonesia.

7.6. Preventing Future Violations

The carrot approach to holding the military accountable for core international crimes – as advanced by the research project of which this anthology is a part – is largely self-explanatory. It is easy to understand that it would provide incentives a professional military would look to. Effective accountability mechanisms distinguish them as military professionals, and provide incentive structures. At the same time, to prevent future atrocities, it is not enough to only use accountability or punishment. There should be an opportunity to identify weaknesses through acknowledging responsibilities.

Core international crimes are often connected to complex socio-political problems at the macro level. In many cases, they concern states that have recently undergone democratic transition or conflict transformation. Violations therefore need to be understood in context. It is not always a black-and-white situation, where the struggle against impunity is a simple decision by design or purpose. It is more a matter of changing cultures and mind-sets through education, training and enlightenment, to replace old ways of doing things with new values. These processes do require more time, but the substantive and gradual process may give longer lasting results, and, more importantly, avoid conflicts. This is not to propose impunity. Sanctions should still be imposed on those individuals responsible for crimes. But keeping in mind that the interest of the military is to learn from lessons of the past and enhance its professionalism, sanctions should be applied as part of the learning process. Furthermore, sanctions, if used as a political instrument, would only lead to a professional deficit.

The Indonesian experience suggests that with education and training, transformation may take place over time. In term of effectiveness, Indonesia provides the example of Polri in responding to terrorism. Its capacity was sharply enhanced after the first Bali bombing in 2002, at which time it worked in close co-operation with the Australian Federal Police. Criminal proceedings are still required in extreme situations. There is room for improvement if we provide opportunities through empowerment, education and training.

8

Compliance with the Law of Armed Conflict: An Israeli Perspective

Marlene Mazel*

A myriad of historical, religious, ethical, institutional and geopolitical reasons inform the State of Israel's firm commitment to compliance with the Law of Armed Conflict. Without attempting to provide a fully comprehensive account of these factors, this chapter reflects on various features of Israel's legal history and experience that have characterised and shaped its perspective with respect to compliance with the Law of Armed Conflict.

This chapter is divided into four sections. The first section considers how the history of the Jewish people, and particularly experiences of persecution and genocide during the Holocaust, led Israel to become an early pioneer of important legal doctrines, such as universal jurisdiction, which enable perpetrators of serious international crimes to be held accountable for their actions anywhere in the world, as reflected in the famous Eichmann case. The second section discusses the role that Israel's establishment as a Jewish and democratic state has played in promoting commitment by its armed forces to a code of conduct and legal principles that emphasise compliance with the Law of Armed Conflict, notwithstanding the difficult security situation that Israel has faced since its establishment and the intense challenges posed by enemy rogue states and terrorist organisations that regularly exploit and breach those norms. The third section examines the important role played by Israel's Supreme Court and its extensive jurisprudence applying the Law of Armed Conflict to Israel's conduct on the battlefield. Finally, this chapter analyses the report of the Public Commission of Inquiry established in Israel to examine the conformity of Israel's legal mechanisms for investigating alleged violations of the Law of Armed Conflict with international standards, as the

* **Marlene Mazel** is Deputy Director of the Department of International Affairs, Ministry Justice, State of Israel. The views expressed herein are those of the author alone and do not necessarily represent the position of the government of the State of Israel.

most recent example of the state's commitment to compliance and accountability in this context.

8.1. Historical Perspective and Early Legal Measures

The personal and collective experience of the Jewish people throughout history, and in particular following the murder of over six million Jews in Europe during the Second World War,[1] has played a vital and profound role in shaping the views of Israeli society and its leaders regarding the importance of ensuring the rule of law in war, no less than in times of peace, and the need for accountability as means to punish and deter the commission of such crimes. Thus, it was only natural that less than two years after its establishment, and notwithstanding the overwhelming security, economic and social challenges that were faced by the young state during that period, the State of Israel signed the four Geneva Conventions in 1949 and ratified them in 1951.[2] Following its signature and ratification

---

[1] Though there is no precise figure for the number of Jews killed in the Holocaust, the figure commonly used is six million quoted by Adolf Eichmann in the Eichmann trial. See Yad Vashem: The Holocaust Resource Center, "How Many Murdered in the Holocaust?" available at http://www.yadvashem.org/yv/en/holocaust/resource_center/faq.asp, last accessed on 13 November 2014. It is also important to recall in this context that experiences of persecution were not limited to Jewish populations from Europe, and that in the immediate years following its establishment, the State of Israel became home to more than 850,000 Jewish refugees who were either formally expelled or otherwise forced out of Arab countries in North Africa and the Middle East. See Malka Hillel Shulewitz with Raphael Israeli, "Exchanges of Populations Worldwide: The First World War to the 1990s", in Malka Hillel Shulewitz (ed.), *The Forgotten Millions: The Modern Jewish Exodus From Arab Lands*, Continuum, London, 1999, pp. 126, 133–34, 138–39; Carole Basri, "The Jewish Refugees from Arab Countries: An Examination of Legal Rights – A Case Study of the Human Rights Violations of Iraqi Jews", in *Fordham International Law Journal*, 2002, vol. 26, no. 3, p. 656–720.

[2] Israel signed the four Geneva Conventions on 8 December 1949 and ratified them on 6 July 1951. Convention (I) for the Amelioration of the Condition of the Wounded and Sick in Armed Forces in the Field, United Nations Treaty Series ('UNTS'), 1949, vol. 75, no. 970, p. 31; Convention (II) for the Amelioration of the Condition of the Wounded, Sick and Shipwrecked Members of Armed Forces at Sea, UNTS, 1949, vol. 75, no. 971, p. 85; Convention (III) relative to the Treatment of Prisoners of War, UNTS, 1949, vol. 75, no. 972, p. 135; and Convention (IV) relative to the Protection of Civilian Persons in Time of War, UNTS, 1949, vol. 75, no. 973, p. 287. Furthermore, Israel is a party to the Convention for the Protection of Cultural Property in the Event of Armed Conflict and its First Protocol (1954), the Third Additional Protocol to the Geneva Conventions of 12 August 1949 (2005), and the Convention on Prohibitions or Restrictions on the Use of Certain Conventional Weapons which may be Deemed to be Excessively Injurious or to Have Indiscriminate Effects (1980) and three of its Protocols – Protocol I on Non-Detectable

---

of the Convention on the Prevention and Punishment of the Crime of Genocide,[3] Israel was also among the first states to codify the crime of genocide[4] in its domestic law. According to the Crime of Genocide (Prevention and Punishment) Law:

> [...] "genocide" means any of the following acts committed with intent to destroy, in whole or in part, a national, ethnical, racial or religious group (hereinafter referred to as "group"); as such: (1) killing members of the group; (2) causing serious bodily or mental harm to members of the group; (3) inflicting on the group conditions of life calculated to bring about its physical destruction, in whole or in part; (4) imposing measures intended to prevent births within the group; (5) forcibly transferring children of the group to another group.[5]

In 1961 Israel brought Adolf Eichmann to trial before its criminal courts.[6] Eichmann, an SS officer who had been centrally involved in the planning and implementation of "the final solution of the Jewish ques-

---

Fragments (1980), Amended Protocol II on Prohibitions or Restrictions on the Use of Mines, Booby-Traps and Other Devices (1996), and Protocol IV on Blinding Laser Weapons (1995).

3   Convention on the Prevention and Punishment of the Crime of Genocide, UNTS, 1948, vol. 78, no. 1021, p. 277 (Israel signed the Convention on 17 August 1949 and ratified it on 9 March 1950).

4   The term 'genocide' itself was coined in 1943 by Raphael Lemkin, a survivor whose family was killed during the Holocaust. *Axis Rule in Occupied Europe*, published in November 1944, was the first place where the word 'genocide' appeared in print. Lemkin stated:

> New conceptions require new terms. By 'genocide' we mean the destruction of a nation or of an ethnic group. This new word, coined by the author to denote an old practice in its modern development, is made from the ancient Greek word *genos* (race, tribe) and the Latin *cide* (killing), thus corresponding in its formation to such words as tyrannicide, homocide, infanticide, etc.

See Raphael Lemkin, *Axis Rule in Occupied Europe: Laws of Occupation – Analysis of Government – Proposals for Redress*, Carnegie Endowment for International Peace, Washington, DC, 1944, pp. 79–95.

5   The Law Regarding the Prevention and Punishment of the Crime of Genocide, 5710-1950, LA 137, Article 1(a).

6   The prosecution took place in Israeli domestic courts in accordance with the Nazis and Nazi Collaborators (Punishment) Law, 5710-1950, Laws of the State of Israel (LSI), vol. 4, no. 64, p. 154. The crimes stipulated in this law relate to "the period of the Nazi regime" (between 30 January 1933 and 8 May 1945) and "the period of the Second World War" (between 1 September 1939 and 14 August 1945). *Ibid.*, Article 1(a).

tion", which led to the murder of six million Jewish civilians during the Second World War,[7] was ultimately convicted of crimes against the Jewish people, crimes against humanity, war crimes and membership of a hostile organisation.[8] The trial was broadcast live on Israel's national radio, Kol Israel, making it widely accessible to the general public, including thousands of victims who survived the Holocaust and immigrated to Israel following the war.[9]

The retired Israeli Supreme Court Justice, Gabriel Bach, who served as the chief prosecutor in the Eichmann trial, stated in his autobiographical notes:

> It was clear to everyone that trying and punishing just one person would not be enough to balance the picture. No trial or subsequent punishment could bring about such a result in light of such a heinous crime and tragedy. But this was not enough to diminish the feeling that something could be done to respond, and this in the most respectful and legitimate manner available to a cultured society.[10]

In addition to its importance to victims of the Holocaust and Israeli public conscience, the Eichmann trial had significance beyond Israel's borders by contributing to the development of the principle of universal jurisdiction.[11] One of the central issues raised during the proceedings was

---

[7] District Court of Jerusalem, Israel, *Attorney-General v. Eichmann* ('Eichmann case'), Criminal Case No. 40/61, Judgment, 11 December 1961, paras. 88 ff., paras. 162 ff. and para. 241.

[8] *Ibid.*, para. 244.

[9] Yad Vashem, The Holocaust Resource Center, estimates that as many as 500,000 Jewish Holocaust survivors had immigrated to Israel by 1951. See Yad Vashem – The Holocaust Resource Center, "Reparations and Restitutions", available at http://www.yadvashem.org/odot_pdf/Microsoft%20Word%20-%205817.pdf, last accessed on 14 November 2014.

[10] Gabriel Bach, "Thoughts and Reflections 30 Years after the Eichmann Trial", in *Bi-Shvil Ha-zikaron*, vol. 41, April–May 2001, pp. 4–9 (unofficial translation from Hebrew).

[11] Various Israeli domestic laws provide for the application of jurisdiction over certain grave offences which have been recognised as crimes of universal concern, even when Israel's only jurisdictional link to the crime is the presence of the alleged offender in Israel. For example: the Crime of Genocide (Prevention and Punishment) Law, see *supra* note 5; and the Nazi and Nazi Collaborators (Punishment) Law, see *supra* note 6; in addition, Section 16(a) of the Israel's Penal Law (1977) provides for the application of Israel's penal laws to those extraterritorial offences which Israel has undertaken to punish in accordance with multilateral conventions open to accession, even if the person committing the offence is not an Israeli citizen or resident and irrespective of where the offence was committed.

---

whether a national tribunal may try a foreign national for heinous crimes committed abroad on the basis of extraterritorial jurisdiction. The Jerusalem District Court held that:

> The power of the State of Israel to enact the Law in question or Israel's "right to punish" is based, with respect to the offences in question, from the point of view of international law, rests on a dual foundation: the universal character of the crimes in question and their specific character as being designed to exterminate the Jewish People. [...] These crimes which offended the whole of mankind and shocked the conscience of nations are grave offences against the law of nations itself ('*delicta juris gentium*') [...] in the absence of an International Court, international law is in need of the judicial and legislative authorities of every country, to give effect to its penal injunctions and to bring criminals to trial. The jurisdiction to try crimes under international law is universal.[12]

The decision was a landmark in the field of international criminal justice, and is of continuing relevance to victims, courts and jurists to this day.[13]

Israel continued with efforts to prosecute Nazi war criminals in its prosecution of Ivan (John) Demjanjuk over 30 years later. Demjanjuk was initially convicted at trial, although his conviction was set aside by the Israeli Supreme Court on the basis of new evidence that the Court found raised reasonable doubt about his alleged identity.[14] A number of years

---

[12] Eichmann case, see *supra* note 7, paras. 11–12.

[13] The decision in Eichmann has been widely cited by national and international tribunals, academics and non-governmental organisations to support the principle of universal jurisdiction. See International Criminal Tribunal for the former Yugoslavia ('ICTY'), *Prosecutor v. Tadić*, Case No. IT-94-1-A, Appeals Chamber Decision, 2 October 1995, para. 57; International Criminal Tribunal for Rwanda ('ICTR'), *Prosecutor v. Akayesu*, Case No. ICTR-96-4-T-A, Judgment, 2 September 1998, paras. 503, 542–54, 568; and House of Lords, *R. v. Bow Street Metropolitan Stipendiary Magistrate, Ex parte Pinochet Ugarte (No. 3)*, [2000] 1 A.C. 147, 24 March 1999, p. 273. See also Amnesty International, *Eichmann Supreme Court Judgment: 50 Years On, Its Significance Today*, Amnesty International Publications, London, 2012, available at https://www.amnesty.org/en/documents/ior53/013/2012/en/, last accessed on 2 May 2015.

[14] See District Court of Jerusalem, *The State of Israel v. Ivan* (John) *Demjanjuk*, Criminal Case No. 373/86, Judgment, 18 April 1988; and Supreme Court of Israel, *The State of Israel v. Ivan* (John) *Demjanjuk*, Criminal Appeal No. 347/88, 29 July 1988, para. 471.

later, Demjanjuk was extradited to Germany where he was prosecuted and convicted.[15]

The process of facing what happened in the Holocaust had a profound effect on how issues of accountability for core international crimes are perceived and addressed in Israeli society and its democratic institutions.

8.2. Core Universal Values Guiding the Conduct of the IDF

Jewish values and democratic principles embedded within the constitutional fabric of the State of Israel have also played a crucial part in shaping the state's commitment to many of the core principles of the Law of Armed Conflict. As stated in its Declaration of Independence in 1948, the State of Israel

> will be based on freedom, justice and peace as envisaged by the prophets of Israel; it will ensure complete equality of social and political rights to all its inhabitants irrespective of religion, race or sex; it will guarantee freedom of religion, conscience, language, education and culture; it will safeguard the Holy Places of all religions; and it will be faithful to the principles of the Charter of the United Nations.[16]

The protection of human dignity and liberty as part of the fundamental values of Israel as a Jewish and democratic state were subsequently entrenched in Israel's Basic Laws,[17] which are also rooted in the con-

---

[15] Demjanjuk was convicted of 27,900 counts of acting as an accessory to murder, one for each person who died at Sobibor. Demjanjuk appealed his conviction, but died before the appeal was heard.

[16] Declaration of the Establishment of the State of Israel, 14 May 1948 (https://www.legal-tools.org/doc/260670/).

[17] See, for example, Basic Law: Human Dignity and Liberty, 5752-1992, Sefer Ha-Chukkim 1391, 150, Article 1(a) as amended, English translation (https://www.legal-tools.org/doc/b5e017/); Basic Law: Freedom of Occupation, 5752-1992, Sefer Ha-Chukkim 1387, repealed by Basic Law: Freedom of Occupation, 5754-1994, Sefer Ha-Chukkim 1454, Article 2 (https://www.legal-tools.org/doc/4d3ea3/). These laws respectively state that: "The purpose of this Basic Law is to protect human dignity and liberty, in order to establish in a Basic Law the values of the State of Israel as a Jewish and democratic state"; and "The purpose of this Basic Law is to protect freedom of occupation, in order to establish in a Basic Law the values of the State of Israel as a Jewish and democratic state". Since 1992 the Basic Laws have been interpreted by Israel's Supreme Court as constitutional in nature, providing courts with the power to review the constitutionality of primary legislation, to declare laws unconstitutional in appropriate cases and to interpret primary legislation in

cept referred to in Jewish law as *kevod ha-briyyot*, which mandates respect by the state for all creation and the dignity of the individual, irrespective of circumstances of armed conflict or national affiliation.[18]

As the State of Israel has faced continuous security threats from the period of its establishment onwards, which necessitated the institution of mandatory military service for all Israeli men and women,[19] the values of peace, justice and human dignity were also incorporated into Israel's perspective with regard to the use of force.[20] Thus, as Israel's first prime minister, David Ben-Gurion, noted: "[t]he army's main weapon is its moral power".[21] The Israel Defense Forces ('IDF'), which was tasked

---

accordance with the Basic Laws. A law found to be unconstitutional by the Supreme Court can no longer be implemented (unless the Court stays its ruling to enable the relevant authorities to amend the legislation).

[18] This concept was discussed by Justice Rubinstein of the Israeli Supreme Court in High Court of Justice, *Abu Rahme et al. v. Brigadier-General Avichai Mandelblit, Military Advocate General et al.* ('Abu Rahme case'), Case no. 7195/08, concurring decision of Justice Rubinstein, 1 July 2009, paras. 14–16 (https://www.legal-tools.org/doc/9287e1/). According to Justice Rubenstein: "In Jewish law, human dignity – *Kevod ha-Adam* – is perceived as the reflection of God in whose image man was created, and as the basis for the obligations between man and his fellow man".

[19] Israel Ministry of Foreign Affairs website, Netanel Lorch, "Israel's War of Independence (1947–1949)" (https://www.legal-tools.org/doc/19b65c/). The Israel Defense Forces ('IDF') was established on 31 May 1948, following a decision made by the temporary government of the State of Israel on 26 May 1948. The Ordinance stated: "In a state of emergency, compulsory enlistment for all the services of the Defence Army of Israel shall be introduced" (Defence Army of Israel Ordinance 5708–1948, Article 2). According to the Military Service Law, which was initially passed on 8 September 1949, and revised several times since, enlistment in the IDF, in general, is mandatory for all Israeli citizens who have reached the age of 18. See, the Military Service Law, 5709-1949, Article 6; and Defense Service Law Consolidated Version 5746-1986 (English translation does not include changes after 1986) (https://www.legal-tools.org/doc/9cd6cb/).

[20] For example, the following article describes the efforts by Rabbi Shlomo Goren, the first Chief Rabbi of the IDF, to apply existing Jewish principles to the new challenges of a sovereign nation and military conduct, in particular the legal and ethical aspects of war: Arye Edrei, "Divine Spirit and Physical Power: Rabbi Shlomo Goren and the Military Ethic of the Israel Defense Forces", in *Theoretical Inquiries in Law*, 2006, vol. 7, no. 1, p. 257.

[21] David Ben-Gurion, *Yichud Ve Yie'Ud* [Uniqueness and Destiny of Israel], Maarachot, Tel Aviv, 1971, p. 32 (in Hebrew). See additional examples: When Ben-Gurion spoke at the end of a platoon commander's course regarding Israel's security challenges, he noted: "How have we therefore stood until now and how will we stand in the future? It is only by our qualitative advantage, by our moral and intellectual advantage" (*ibid.*, p. 43); when Ben-Gurion spoke about the responsibility imposed on a commander, due to which he must "equip himself with all the moral and mental attributes and with all the knowledge and abilities required to perform this supreme mission, on which depends the fate of the

---

with ensuring the security of Israel's civilian population and achieving the various military objectives this mission entails, thus developed and promoted among Israel's soldiers the concept of 'purity of arms', which would later be codified in the IDF code of ethics. This guiding precept calls for self-restraint and for soldiers to resort to the use of force only in those cases in which it is necessary and justified.[22]

These moral ideas were later codified in the form of the "Spirit of the IDF", the IDF's written code of ethics, published in 1994, which reflect the same basic tenets of humanitarianism that are at the core of the Law of Armed Conflict.[23] One of these directives states that:

> The IDF servicemen and women will use their weapons and force only for the purpose of their mission, only to the necessary extent and will maintain their humanity even during combat.[24]

---

state's security, the fate of the nation's liberty and physical existence. "Only a person of highly virtuous attributes will succeed in this task" (*ibid.*, pp. 60–61).

[22] The notion of 'purity of arms' is attributed to Berl Katznelson, one of the prominent labour leaders of the early twentieth century, who advocated a policy of self-restraint (*Havlagah*). Katzelson explained in Anita Shapira, *Berl*, Am Oved, Tel Aviv, 1980, pp. 588–89:

> Self-restraint means, our weapon will be pure. We learn [our] weapon, we carry weapons, we stand up to those who attack us, but we do not want our weapons to be stained with innocent blood. [...] Self-restraint is both a political and moral approach, stemming from our history and our present reality, from our character and the conditions of the war in which we are engaged.

[23] In the Abu Rahme case, the Military Advocate General explained:

> IDF soldiers are in possession of means whose destructive potential is great, and sometimes lethal. The ideal of "purity of arms", which is one of the values of the "Spirit of the IDF" and the basic moral code of the entire IDF, is designed to restrain the use of these means and forces, and to limit it to those cases in which it is necessary and justified. Cases in which IDF soldiers make prohibited use of the force and authority at their disposal are, first and foremost, contrary to the IDF's code of values, and to the basic norms of military conduct [...]

The Military Advocate General's Reply to the Petition in the Abu Rahme case, as cited in the judgment. See Abu Rahme case, para. 74 of Justice Procaccia's judgment, *supra* note 18.

[24] Israel Defense Forces, "The IDF Spirit" (https://www.legal-tools.org/doc/16e363/). The code further states: "IDF soldiers will not use their weapons and force to harm human beings who are not combatants or prisoners of war, and will do all in their power to avoid causing harm to their lives, bodies, dignity and property".

Upon enlistment, soldiers are given a pocket-sized version of the "Spirit of the IDF", and IDF soldiers are trained in how to implement these principles in practice, including through regular teaching and discussion of difficult operational dilemmas and subsequent lessons learned (*morashot krav* – translated as 'battle legacies'), which are used in training to raise sensitivity and awareness of soldiers to the importance of protecting civilians during armed conflict.[25] This training has been expanded in recent years to address the increasingly common challenges arising in the context of asymmetric warfare against non-state armed groups operating from civilian areas.

The Israeli Military Court has also expounded on and enforced these values in its jurisprudence. Thus, in a case decided in the 1950s of IDF soldiers who were tried by the military courts for serious crimes committed in Kfar Kassem,[26] it was emphasised in the Court's judgment that:

> Jewish doctrine and the laws of the State of Israel require protection of the sanctity of all human life, and even in wartime human life is not forfeited. Each commander and soldier must know that his weapon is intended for combatting the enemy and not for murdering non-combatant civilians. The eight defendants have stained the purity of arms of the Israel Defense Forces.[27]

The Military Court's decision is an example of the important role that prosecutors and the judiciary can play in upholding the principles of the Law of Armed Conflict, and of Israel's commitment to ensuring compliance among its soldiers.

---

[25] The IDF Education and Youth corps website, "Moreshet Krav", available at www.aka.idf.il/chinuch/klali/default.asp?catId=42854&docId=44491&list=1 (in Hebrew), last accessed on 17 March 2015.

[26] District Military Court for the Central Judicial District, *Military Prosecutor v. Malinki* ('Kfar Kassem case'), Case No. 3/57, Judgment, 13 October 1958. It should be noted that some of the prison terms were commuted, an issue that remains a matter of controversy in Israeli society to this day. See also Amichai Cohen and Yuval Shany, "Beyond the Grave Breaches Regime: The Duty to Investigate Alleged Violations of International Law Governing Armed Conflicts", in *Yearbook of International Humanitarian Law*, 2011, vol. 14, p. 78, noting "an Israeli conviction in the case of *Malinki* (Kfar Kasem case, 1958) instilled in the IDF the principle of the duty to disobey a blatantly unlawful order, notwithstanding the light punishment".

[27] Kfar Kassem case, *ibid.*, p. 255 (unofficial translation from Hebrew).

These core values are reflected in Israel's Supreme Court's expansive doctrine of judicial review with regard to sensitive issues pertaining to national security and armed conflict situations. As eloquently explained by the former Supreme Court President, Justice Aharon Barak, in an extensive essay on the role of a judge in a democracy, including during times of war:

> There is a well-known saying that when the cannons speak, the Muses are silent. Cicero expressed a similar idea when he said that *"inter arma silent leges"* (in battle, the laws are silent). These statements are regrettable; I hope they do not reflect our democracies today. I know they do not reflect the way things should be. Every battle a country wages – against terrorism or any other enemy – is done according to rules and laws. There is always law – domestic or international – according to which the state must act. *And the law needs Muses, never more urgently than when the cannons speak.*[28]

International humanitarian law ('IHL') is to be followed not merely because domestic or international law requires it, but because the core values of democracies demand such compliance.

Thus, in Israel's case, the jurisprudence of its courts (military and civilian) has also contributed to the clear message that maintaining moral conduct in the military is not merely a theoretical aspiration; its practical implementation is demanded.

In the Abu Rahme case,[29] Ashraf Abu Rahme and four non-governmental organisations filed a petition to the Supreme Court of Israel, in its capacity as a High Court of Justice ('HCJ'), against the Military Advocate General ('MAG') and the Chief Military Prosecutor, with regard to an allegation that in the course of a violent demonstration near the village of Billin, an IDF lieutenant colonel told a soldier to frighten a blindfolded, handcuffed detainee and ordered him to fire a rubber bullet towards his feet. Immediately after the incident the IDF opened an investigation. The commander alleged that the detainee pretended he did not understand Hebrew, and he told the soldier to draw his weapon in a man-

---

[28] Aharon Barak, "Foreword: A Judge on Judging: The Role of a Supreme Court in a Democracy", in *Harvard Law Review*, 2002, vol. 116, no. 1, pp. 150–51 (internal citations omitted and emphasis added). See also *Almandi v. Minister of Defense*, Case No. 3451/02 56(3), para. 30 (https://www.legal-tools.org/doc/9b58f0/).

[29] Abu Rahme case, see *supra* note 18.

ner that would make the detainee believe that he was going to be shot with a rubber bullet. He stated that he was surprised to hear a gunshot and the detainee yell. The soldier, who was immediately suspended, alleged that the commander had told him, "What do you think – should we fire a rubber bullet at him?". He initially thought the commander was joking in order to frighten the detainee, though at a later stage the commander told him to shoot, and he fired a rubber bullet towards the feet of the detainee. The investigation revealed that the soldier had received an order from the lieutenant colonel to shoot a rubber bullet towards the feet of the detainee and that the detainee was not seriously physically injured by the rubber bullet. Accordingly, the MAG and the Chief Military Prosecutor decided to issue an indictment against the commander and soldier in a military court for 'unbecoming conduct' in violation of Section 130 of the Military Justice Law. The MAG also recommended that the commander be suspended immediately from his position. The commander was relieved of his position by the General Chief of Staff and reassigned.

The petitioners challenged the decision of the MAG and Chief Military Prosecutor and requested that the indictment of the commander and soldier be amended, so that the commander and soldier were charged with a more serious criminal offence, such as Abuse of a Detainee Under Aggravating Circumstances (Section 65 of the Military Justice Law), reflecting the seriousness of their actions. They further alleged the case justified judicial intervention in the prosecutorial discretion of the Chief Military Prosecutor as the indictment for a minor offense under these circumstances was not in accordance with the facts and with the values of Israeli society or of the IDF. The respondents argued that the charging of soldiers with the criminal offense of 'unbecoming conduct' was reasonable under the circumstances; that they had weighed the more serious charge proposed by the petitioner, as well as other serious charges, and decided this charge was appropriate under the circumstances and in light of the disciplinary measures previously imposed on the soldiers. In addition, respondents contended that this matter did not fall within the parameters that would justify judicial review of a decision of the Chief Military Prosecutor regarding which charges to include in an indictment.

The Supreme Court held that the decision of the MAG and the Chief Military Prosecutor to indict the commander and soldier for the criminal offense of 'unbecoming conduct' was inappropriate and unreasonable under these circumstances. The Court held that the decision of prosecutor was subject to judicial review, as the offence did not reflect the serious nature of the incident or the norms of Israeli society and IDF conduct. The Court nullified the charge for the lesser offence and suggested the commander and soldier be charged with serious offence(s) reflecting the severity of the factual allegations.

Israel's Supreme Court noted that "[t]he basic rights of enemy combatants held in custody – protection of life and limb and of their human dignity – have been recognised by the Israeli legal system for generations",[30] and held that:

> These values are meant to be translated by the army and its commanders into the language of daily operations and to be reflected, in practice, in the military's activity. [...] These values are assimilated into the ethical military education that has been imparted to commanders and soldiers in the IDF since the establishment of the state. This is the mark of the Israeli Army. This ethical education must find expression in IDF operations at all levels. Among the commanders' missions is the obligation to supervise the fulfillment of these values at all levels of military operations and in all military ranks, from the rank of private to senior commander.[31]

It further noted that:

> The military justice system, which is in charge of implementing the IDF's values of conduct, must send out a determined message of consistent and decisive defence of the basic values of the society and the army, and of uncompromising enforcement in all levels – educational, commanding authority and punitive – of the fundamental principles that are shared by the Israeli society and the Israeli army and give them their ethical and humane character.[32]

---

30   *Ibid.*, para. 40 of Justice Procaccia's decision.

31   *Ibid.*

32   *Ibid.*, para. 88. On 22 July 2009, the MAG and Chief Military Prosecutor issued an amended indictment and charged the commander with the offence of threats under Section 192 of Israel's Penal Law; the soldier was charged with the offence of illegal use of a firearm in accordance with Section 85 of the Military Justice Law. In addition, both were charged with Section 130 of the Military Justice Law with the offence of conduct unbecoming an officer. On 15 July 2010, after a full trial, a panel of three judges of the Military Court, convicted the lieutenant colonel for attempt to threaten and the soldier of illegal use of a firearm. Both were convicted of the criminal offence of conduct unbecoming an officer pursuant to Section 130 of the Military Justice Law. In its 75-page decision, the Court

It is interesting to note in this context that the Supreme Court cited a rich array of sources in its decision, including speeches and writings of Israeli leaders, a poet and sources of Jewish law, which reflect core principles that are also incorporated in the modern Law of Armed Conflict. The Court referenced these sources to stress the importance of ensuring moral and restrained conduct by soldiers.[33] Thus, the obligation of Israel's soldiers to conduct themselves with self-restraint is firmly grounded not only within Israeli domestic law and international law, but it also falls within the moral code and ethos of the IDF, which is rooted, among other things, in the basic values of Israeli society and democratic traditions.[34]

Beyond the emphasis on humanitarian principles found in the decisions of the Supreme Court, these principles are also found in the IDF's ethical code. The implementation of core rules and principles of the Law of Armed Conflict are set forth in the IDF's Military Doctrine,[35] and covered by binding military orders, including General Staff regulations requiring IDF personnel to act in accordance with the four Geneva Conventions and the 1954 Hague Convention for the Protection of Cultural Prop-

---

noted that the actions of the commander warranted the conviction of the serious criminal offence as, under these circumstances, the principles of justice and legal integrity called for such a measure. The court emphasised that the commander's actions violated the core values of human dignity and purity of arms and caused significant harm to the reputation of the IDF, its soldiers and commanders. The Court also rejected the soldier's defense that he misunderstood the order, as that even pursuant to his allegations the order was illegal *per se* and he had a duty to disobey it. See Special Military Court, *Chief Military Prosecutor v. Burbang et al.*, Case No. 5/08, 15 July 2010 (in Hebrew). An article about the decision was also published on the website of the Military Advocate General (in Hebrew) (https://www.legal-tools.org/doc/1ea930/).

33 *Ibid.*, para. 18 of Justice Rubinstein's HCJ decision:

> We have brought all these in the realm of the values of the State of Israel, and more than we have brought [is] found in the writings – and the ethos embodied therein is like a pillar of fire before the Israeli military camp, in order to fulfil "Let your camp be holy" (Deuteronomy 23:15).

34 The principles of sanctity of human life and humanity are reflected in other religions as well. On the interaction between religious principles and the development of international humanitarian law, see Carolyn Evans, "The Double-Edged Sword: Religious Influences on International Humanitarian Law", in *Melbourne Journal of International Law*, 2005, vol. 6, no. 1, pp. 1–31.

35 See Hila Adler, "Teaching the Law of War in the Israel Defense Forces", in *Israel Defense Forces Law Review*, 2007–2008, vol. 3, no. 6, p. 36.

---

erty in the Event of Armed Conflict and its additional protocol.[36] Accordingly, the IDF invests considerable resources in the training and education of its soldiers as to the requirements of the Law of Armed Conflict. These have extended, for example, to the development of educational software for training military forces in practical problem-solving exercises in accordance with the principles of the Law of Armed Conflict, helping soldiers better understand how to achieve operational objectives, while complying with legal requirements and principles.[37]

While compliance with the Law of Armed Conflict begins with education and training to ensure military personnel and security forces are well-informed and trained regarding the core principles of the Law of Armed Conflict, the IDF also strengthens compliance by employing legal officers of the IDF Military Advocate General's Corps (the 'MAG Corps') to advise on the requirements of the Law of Armed Conflict in operational planning and implementation.[38] Military discipline and accountability for conduct that breaches military laws and regulations, including the Law of Armed Conflict, also form an important component in ensuring compliance. In this context also, therefore, the MAG Corps plays an important role by overseeing investigation and, where necessary, prosecuting violations of the law.

---

[36] Israel Defense Forces, Chief of Staff Order 33.0133, "Discipline – Conduct According to International Conventions to which Israel is a Party", paras. 6, 8 (https://www.legal-tools.org/doc/faf9ae/).

[37] The manner in which Law of Armed Conflict is taught and instilled in the IDF is not the focus of this chapter. Additional information is available at: Adler, 2007–2008, see *supra* note 35; State of Israel, *The Operation in Gaza Report: Factual and Legal Aspects*, 2009, pp. 77–80 (https://www.legal-tools.org/doc/2db273/). See also Israel Defense Forces website, "Seminar Teaches IDF Officers How to Protect Gaza's Civilian Population in Combat Situation", available at http://www.idfblog.com/blog/2013/07/17/seminar-teaches-idf-officers-how-to-protect-gazas-civilian-population-in-combat-situation/, last accessed at 17 March 2015.

[38] See the Military Advocate General's report on Operation Pillar of Defense, 19 December 2012 (https://www.legal-tools.org/doc/84f408/). The report asserts that the provision of legal advice is a general function of the MAG. In relation to Operation Pillar of Defense the report states that, prior to the operation, the MAG provided advice on the formulation of the Rules of Engagement, the legal assessment of potential targets and legal review of the intended weapons. During the operation, the MAG was available to advise on target classification, the use of weaponry, provision of advance warnings to civilian population and matters relating to detainees on the battlefield.

8.3. The Contribution of Judicial Review by Israel's High Court of Justice to the Implementation of the Law of Armed Conflict

In Israel, measures to ensure lawful and ethical conduct by its armed forces are undertaken at various levels and by different bodies. With respect to ensuring compliance with national law and the Law of Armed Conflict, the Supreme Court has taken a particularly active role in its capacity as the High Court of Justice.

To understand how the HCJ has interpreted its judicial review role in this context, it should be understood that the HCJ is empowered with a broad mandate to review petitioner claims that government action or policy is *ultra vires*, unlawful or substantially unreasonable. In the landmark decision of *Ressler v. The Minister of Defense*,[39] Supreme Court Justice Barak stated:

> There is no 'legal vacuum', in which actions are undertaken without the law taking any position on them. [...] In sum, the doctrine of normative justiciability (or non-justiciability) seems to me to be a doctrine with no independent existence. *My approach is based on the view that a legal norm applies to every governmental action, and that within the framework of the applicable norm it is always possible to formulate standards to ascertain the conditions and circumstances for action within the framework of the norm.*

Thus, the Supreme Court has expanded its role as a guardian of the rule of law by enabling public petitioners who do not have a direct personal interest in a matter to challenge government actions. This reform opened the doors of the Court to non-governmental organisations and political groups seeking to initiate social and political reform, and thousands of such petitions were filed. The Court, in its jurisprudence of such petitions, has further expanded the subject matter and scope of its review over time.

When coupled with the fact that customary international law, including the customary Law of Armed Conflict, forms part of Israel's common law, the Supreme Court's expansive doctrine of judicial review ensures that even highly sensitive issues pertaining to national security and armed conflict situations are not beyond the reach of the law.

---

[39] See HCJ, *Ressler v. The Minister of Defense*, Case no. 910/86, 42(2) P.D. 441, Judgment, 12 June 1988, paras. 36 and 46 (emphasis added) (https://www.legal-tools.org/doc/5bd469/).

As referenced earlier, the importance of judicial review of sensitive matters of national security was articulated by Justice Barak in *Almandi v. The Minister of Defense*, a landmark case that established the expansive judicial review of the Court on matters that arise during military operations. A petition was filed to the HCJ during IDF operations against the terrorist infrastructure in the areas of the Palestinian Authority. When the IDF entered Bethlehem, approximately 30 to 40 wanted armed terrorists, Palestinian security personnel and some civilians (approximately 200 people) had fortified themselves in the Church of the Nativity in Bethlehem, and there were also other civilians and clergymen in the compound.[40]

The Supreme Court accepted the petition for judicial review during the military operation, and held that such review is especially important during battle.[41] The Court held a special session to determine how it could ensure that extra food – beyond the essentials – were being provided to the civilians who remained in the compound. The Court asked the respondents if it would be willing to allow civilians to leave the compound, receive extra food, and return to the compound. The respondents said it would allow it. The Court concluded that since there was a well in the compound, basic water and food were provided, and the respondents were willing to provide extra food to the civilians even if they did not leave the compound, the respondents fulfilled their obligation under international law.

In another well-known judgment of the HCJ, in which the Court determined that certain methods of interrogation employed by Israel's General Security Service (Shin Bet) were unlawful, Justice Barak stated:

> This is the destiny of a democracy – it does not see all means
> as acceptable, and the ways of its enemies are not always

---

[40] The petitioners, the Governor of Bethlehem (who was in the compound) and two members of the Israeli Knesset, alleged that the clergymen were receiving food, while Palestinian civilians were not. They requested that additional food and water be allowed into the compound. They also alleged that preventing food from entering the compound violated international law. The respondents replied that the matter was not justicable, as the IDF was in the midst of a military operation and negotiations regarding the matters alleged in the petition were underway. In addition, they explained that civilians were being encouraged to leave the compound. The petitioners responded that the armed terrorists were preventing the civilians from leaving the compound, and the respondents needed to ensure enough food was being relayed for all those inside.

[41] HCJ, *Ressler v. The Minister of Defense*, para. 9, see *supra* note 39.

open before it. A democracy must sometimes fight with one hand tied behind its back. Even so, a democracy has the upper hand. The rule of law and the liberty of an individual constitute important components in its understanding of security. At the end of the day, they strengthen its spirit and this strength allows it to overcome its difficulties.[42]

The fast and easy access to the HCJ facilitates the ability of individuals and groups to challenge decisions of the government almost instantaneously regarding issues of national security, including questions of how the military conducts itself during hostilities.[43] The Court has continued to adjudicate cases even in the midst of ongoing hostilities, and when deemed necessary by the Court, senior officers of the IDF have been

---

[42] HCJ, *Public Committee Against Torture in Israel v. The State of Israel*, Case No. 5100/94, 53(4) 817, Judgment, 6 September 1999, para. 39 of President Barak's Judgment (https://www.legal-tools.org/doc/b5d8cb/). In a similar vein, the Supreme Court stated in a ruling issued during the military Operation Defensive Shield in *Physicians for Human Rights v. The Commander of IDF Forces in the West Bank*:

> [...] we see fit to emphasize that our combat forces are required to abide by the rules of humanitarian law regarding the care of the wounded, the ill, and bodies of the deceased. [...] This stance is required, not only under the rules of international law on which the petitioners have based their arguments here, *but also in light of the values of the State of Israel as a Jewish and democratic state. The IDF shall once again instruct the combat forces, down to the level of the lone soldier in the field, of this commitment by our forces based on law and morality – and, according to the State, even on utilitarian considerations – through concrete instructions which will prevent, to the extent possible, and even in severe situations, incidents which are inconsistent with the rules of humanitarian law.*

HCJ, *Physicians for Human Rights v. The Commander of IDF Forces in the West Bank*, Case No. 2936/02, 56(3) 3, Judgment, 8 April 2002 (emphasis added) (https://www.legal-tools.org/doc/83bcff/).

[43] For example, during Operation Defensive Shield: HCJ, *Physicians for Human Rights v. The Commander of IDF Forces in the West Bank*, Case No. 2936/02, 56(3) 3, Judgment, 8 April 2002; HCJ, *MK Barake v. The Minister of Defense, Benjamin Ben-Eliezer*, Case No. 3114/02, 56(3) 11, Judgment, 14 April 2002; during Operation Cast Lead: HCJ, *Physicians for Human Rights v. Prime Minister of Israel*, Case No. 201/09, 63(1) 521, Judgment, 19 January 2009; regarding early warning procedures: HCJ, *Adalah – The Legal Center for Arab Minority Rights in Israel v. GOC Central Command*, IDF, Case No. 3799/02, 60(3) 67, Judgment, 23 June 2005; and the targeted killing policy: HCJ, *The Public Committee Against Torture in Israel v. The Government of Israel*, Case No. 769/02, 62(1) 507, Judgment, 11 December 2005.

---

pulled off the battlefield to respond to allegations raised by the complainants, so as to clarify the facts in 'real time'.[44]

In addition to determining the legality of certain military conduct, the Supreme Court has articulated and emphasised the importance of the government conducting national investigations of alleged violations, and it stated that such investigations are critical to the deterrence and to the prevention of future breaches:

> [T]ragically, during the fighting and due to the manner of the fighting conducted by the terrorist organizations, innocent people may be hurt, even when the IDF operates properly. Contending with such tragedies does not necessarily lead to – nor should it always lead to – a criminal trial. We believe that we must emphasize yet again – and the State has not disputed this – that when there is a suspected deviation from the proper norms of behavior, even if there is no reason for a criminal trial, the investigating entities must conduct an examination of the incident with the appropriate tools for that purpose, *in order to deter the same kind of harm in the future, to instill an educational message in the fighting forces, to maintain the legal and moral criteria, and to demonstrate the importance of maintaining the rule of law*.[45]

Furthermore, the Court has explained that enforcement and accountability for alleged violations of the Law of Armed Conflict are es-

---

44 For example, in HCJ, *Physicians for Human Rights v. IDF Commander in Gaza*, Case No. 4764/04, 58(5) 385, Judgment, 30 May 2004, the military's compliance with its humanitarian obligations in the course of a military operation in the Gaza Strip was challenged. The colonel, who was the Head of the District Coordination Office for the Gaza Strip, was present in Court during the hearing and provided oral explanations regarding various matters in question, at times stepping out to receive additional information from his personnel in the area of operations, which he conveyed to the justices (*ibid.*, para. 14). Similarly, two petitions were filed with the HCJ during Israel's month-long military operation in the Gaza Strip in December 2008 – January 2009 (known as Operation Cast Lead). The first concerned delays in evacuating Palestinian casualties in the Gaza Strip and claims that medical personnel and ambulances were being attacked by the IDF; the second addressed the shortage of electricity in the Gaza Strip, attributed to the IDF. The HCJ held two urgent hearings within days, and ordered the State to submit a more detailed response regarding the efforts it had undertaken to fulfil its humanitarian obligations. The Court also specifically ordered the State to submit an affidavit by the Head of the District Coordination Office for the Gaza Strip, who also appeared before the Court.

45 HCJ, *Adalah – the Legal Centre for Arab Minority Rights v. Attorney General*, Case No. 3292/07, Decision of President Beinisch, 8 December 2011, para. 19 (emphasis added).

---

sential to the principle of the rule of law.[46] As noted by the HCJ in a petition pertaining in particular to the MAG's investigation policy:

> [A] criminal investigation serves to safeguard the prospective aspect of the duty to protect life, in that it deters future perpetrators, prevents contempt for the right to life and contributes to the atmosphere of upholding the rule of law.[47]

Compliance with IHL is inherent to a democracy, as IHL reflects the balance between the rights of the collective to security and the liberty and rights of the individual. As Justice Barak eloquently stated:

> In its case law, the Court applies [...] IHL, it thus applies and reflects the character of the State of Israel as a rule of law state, in which security and human rights go hand in hand. There is no democracy without security; there is no democracy without human rights. Democracy is based upon a delicate balance between the security of the collective and the liberty of the individual. This balance is reflected in IHL. This balance is reflected in the case law of the Supreme Court employing IHL as part of customary international law. Further, not only the values of Israel as a democratic state, but also the values of a Jewish State are expressed.[48]

---

[46] Abu Rahme case, para. 90, see *supra* note 18, of Justice Procaccia's decision:

> The protection of the rule of law and the defense of individual liberties are characteristics of the democratic conception that underlies the Israeli system of government. It is also an important component of Israel's approach to security. [...] The insistence upon respect for human rights and the safeguarding of human dignity, even vis-à-vis enemy individuals, are inherent in the nature of the state as a democratic, Jewish state. *These values must also find their expression in the enforcement of criminal law upon those whose conduct has violated these principles. Law enforcement in this vein is also an important component in Israel's outlook on security,* and in the capabilities and standards of the IDF. "The strength of the IDF depends on its spirit no less than on its physical power and on the sophistication of its weapons" (HCJ 585/01 *Kelachman v. Chief of Staff*, PD 58(1) 694, 719 (2003)). The spirit and moral character of the Army depend, *inter alia*, on maintaining the purity of arms and defending the dignity of the individual, whoever he may be (emphasis added).

[47] See HCJ, *B'Tselem – Israeli Information Center for Human Rights in the Occupied Territories v. the Chief Military Prosecutor*, Case No. 9594/03, Judgment of then President Beinisch, 21 August 2011, para. 10 (https://www.legal-tools.org/doc/61279a/).

[48] Aharon Barak, "International Humanitarian Law and the Israeli Supreme Court", presented at International Committee of the Red Cross and the Minerva Center for Human Rights at

---

8.4. Establishment and Findings of the Turkel Commission

This chapter has focused thus far on certain unique foundations of Israel's principles and practice regarding compliance with the Law of Armed Conflict. Another highly relevant and recent example of Israel's commitment to compliance with the Law of Armed Conflict can be seen in the establishment and work of the Public Commission to Examine the Maritime Incident of 31 May 2010, headed by the former Supreme Court Justice Jacob Turkel ('Turkel Commission').[49] The Turkel Commission was appointed by the Israeli cabinet following the flotilla incident of 31 May 2010, in which IDF forces attempted to prevent a flotilla of six vessels heading for Gaza to breach the naval blockade imposed on the Gaza Strip. IDF forces encountered violent resistance from flotilla participants, leading to an altercation during which nine of the flotilla participants were killed[50] and dozens more injured, including nine IDF soldiers. Claims that Israel's naval blockade and actions to enforce it were not in compliance with the Law of Armed Conflict led the Israeli government to establish an independent, public commission of inquiry to examine the international law aspects of the operation. Two international observers – Lord David Trimble from the United Kingdom and Brigadier General Ken Watkin QC from Canada – also participated in the work of the Commission.[51]

---

the Hebrew University of Jerusalem Conference, Hebrew University, 3 July 2013, available at Hebrew University YouTube Channel http://www.youtube.com/watch?v=fkew ANAkJo4&feature=youtu.be at 0:47–0:48, last accessed on 19 November 2014.

[49] See Public Commission to Investigate the Maritime Incident of 31 May 2010, Report, Part I, 15–16 January 2011 (https://www.legal-tools.org/doc/f2aae4/), and Part II of the Report, February 2013 ('Second Turkel Report') (https://www.legal-tools.org/doc/e8437b/).

[50] It was reported that a tenth flotilla participant passed away from injuries incurred during the incident. See "Turk Injured in Gaza Flotilla Dies after Four-year Coma", in *Haaretz*, 24 May 2014, available at http://www.haaretz.com/news/diplomacy-defense/1.592489, last accessed 26 March 2015.

[51] Lord David Trimble, Noble Peace Prize Laureate from Northern Ireland, and Kenneth Watkin, former Judge Advocate General of the Canadian armed forces, were the first international observers to take part in the Commission. Upon Watkin's resignation following his appointment as Stockton Professor of International Law at the United States Naval War College, he was replaced by Timothy McCormack, professor of international humanitarian law at Melbourne University and Special Adviser on International Humanitarian Law to the Prosecutor of the International Criminal Court. The observers participated actively in all the sessions and deliberations and heard all testimony that was brought before the Commission. Watkin remarked that: "[i]ts work is an important reflection of the commit-

---

The Turkel Commission produced two reports. The First Turkel Report dealt specifically with the question of the legality of the naval blockade and the actions of the Israeli authorities in connection with the flotilla incident. Its hearings and findings were public and available in English translation. The Second Turkel Report engaged in a comprehensive review of the mechanisms in place in Israel for investigating alleged violations of the Law of Armed Conflict and their conformity with Israel's obligations under international law.[52] Pursuant to its broad mandate, the Commission examined not only the actions of the military investigation mechanisms, but also those of other law enforcement bodies, including the Israel Security Authority and the Israel Police.

In order to assess Israel's compliance, the Second Turkel Report outlined the normative framework that governs the examination and investigation of complaints and claims regarding violations of the Law of Armed Conflict, based on a detailed review of various sources in international law and a comparative survey examining mechanisms employed in the United States, Canada, Australia, the United Kingdom, Germany and the Netherlands. The Commission consulted with leading experts in the field, including Professor Claus Kreß, Professor Gabriella Blum and Professor Michael Schmitt.[53] While there was general consensus within the international community regarding the existence of a fundamental obligation to examine allegations of violations of the Law of Armed Conflict, there were differing views and practices on the precise nature and contours of this obligation – the situations to which it applied and the manner in which it was to be implemented in the context of armed hostilities.

The Commission and its work were noted and referenced by different international actors, reflecting the fact that Israel has a transparent, robust mechanism for reviewing the decisions and policies of high level

---

ment to the Rule of Law" (Second Turkel Report, Observer Letter – Brigadier-General (ret.) Kenneth Watkin, Q.C., p. 26, see *supra* note 49).

[52] See Israel Ministry of Foreign Affairs website, "Government Establishes Independent Public Commission", Article 5 of the Commission's Mandate (https://www.legal-tools.org/doc/f68e4c/). For details and earlier examples of the appointment of various commissions of inquiry to examine government and military action pertaining to national security, see Letter of Deputy State Attorney, Mr. Shai Nitzan, to the Coordinator of the Public Commission to Examine the Maritime Incident of 31 May 2010, 6 April 2011, pp. 6–8 (https://www.legal-tools.org/doc/609bc5/).

[53] Second Turkel Report, pp. 37–38, see *supra* note 49.

officials,[54] and as a record of the factual and legal examination of the incident itself by Israel.[55]

Israel devoted extensive resources to the Commission in order to enable it to fulfil its mandate. Ultimately, after a full review, the Commission found that Israel's mechanisms for examining and investigating complaints and claims of violations of the Law of Armed Conflict generally comply with its obligations under international law. The Commission also made recommendations with regard to various 'best practices' for Israel to consider. Recently, Israel has invested significant resources to further improve its system of national investigations.[56]

---

[54] In one of the follow up reports to the Goldstone Report, issued by Judge Mary Davis, the committee stated that it "considers that the work of the Turkel Commission is relevant to its own mandate, because it is evidence that Israel does have a mechanism for carrying out inquiries into decisions and policies adopted by high-level officials". The Committee, after an analysis of the transcripts, which included testimony by the Prime Minister, Minister of Defense, Chief of General Military Staff, the Military Advocate General and others, concluded that the Turkel Commission "thoroughly examined the controversial legal and political issues presented for their consideration". See Human Rights Council, Report of the Committee of Independent Experts in International Humanitarian law and Human Rights Law Established Pursuant to Council Resolution 13/9, paras. 38 and 39, 18 March 2011 (https://www.legal-tools.org/doc/3bd812/).

[55] Timothy McCormack noted that this report "represents the first comprehensive and systematic analysis of the international law of national investigations". See Timothy McCormack, Shabtai Rosenne Memorial Lecture (26 November 2014) at 18:45, available at https://www.youtube.com/watch?v=UMAmSltyEOE, last accessed on 17 March 2015.

[56] These steps include the creation, in July 2014, of a permanent fact-finding assessment mechanism which has the responsibility to examine exceptional incidents to assist the Military Advocate General in its determination regarding whether to open a criminal investigation and to enrich the lessons learned process so that measures can be taken to minimise the risk of such incidents in future years. The fact-finding assessment mechanism has been reviewing the exceptional incidents of Operation Protective Edge (7 July–26 August 2014). Information regarding the decisions of the MAG with regard to Operation Protective Edge is available in English. See IDF, MAG Corps, "Decisions of the IDF Military Advocate General regarding Exceptional Incidents that Occurred During Operation 'Protective Edge' – Update No. 3" (22 March 2014) (https://www.legal-tools.org/doc/0bdb39/); IDF, MAG Corps, "Decisions of the IDF Military Advocate General regarding Exceptional Incidents that Occurred During Operation 'Protective Edge' – Update No. 2" (7 December 2014) (https://www.legal-tools.org/doc/01b98a/). For an earlier report, see IDF, MAG Corps, "Operation Protective Edge: Examinations and Investigation" (10 September 2014) (https://www.legal-tools.org/doc/13b81d/). See also Ministry of Foreign Affairs, "Israel's Investigation of Alleged Violations of the Law of Armed Conflict" (https://www.legal-tools.org/doc/049fd8/).

The Commission noted: "This Report, in its five chapters, is the result of considerable efforts to derive the main principles of international law from sources that are often vague and unclear, and from a comparison of legal systems and practices in other countries".[57] The Second Turkel Report's analysis was cited favourably in the UN General Assembly, 68th Session, Report of the Special Rapporteur on the promotion and protection of human rights and fundamental freedoms while countering terrorism.[58]

The appointment of the Turkel Commission and its resulting reports are a testament to the importance Israel places on compliance with the Law of Armed Conflict and measures to ensure accountability, as well as the commitment of the Israeli government to constant self-examination and improvement. The Second Turkel Report can also be seen as a valuable contribution to the further development of investigation standards under the Law of Armed Conflict.

8.5. Conclusion

As noted at the outset of this chapter, there are various historical aspects, core values and institutional features of the State of Israel that have significantly contributed to its commitment to the Law of Armed Conflict. As a democratic state adhering to the rule of law while also, unfortunately, engaged in ongoing armed conflicts in which complex legal questions arise before its domestic courts on a regular basis, Israel makes for an interesting case study for the examination of the interplay between values and their implementation in practice. Israel's practice provides evidence of the central role that domestic legal systems can and should play in ensuring compliance with the Law of Armed Conflict and the contribution of additional mechanisms such as training, legal advice and judicial review. The Israeli experience also bears out the state and military self-interests in establishing domestic mechanisms and procedures that enable continuous review and reaffirmation of the law.

---

[57] Second Turkel Report, p. 31, see *supra* note 49.

[58] United Nations, General Assembly, "Promotion and Protection of Human Rights and Fundamental Freedoms while Countering Terrorism", Note by the Secretary-General, UN Doc. A/68/389, 18 September 2013, paras. 42–45 (https://www.legal-tools.org/doc/b7065c/).

9

The Impact of Religion on Military Self-Interest in
Accountability: An Islamic *Sharī'ah* Perspective

Adel Maged*

9.1. Introduction

In general, divine religions permit fighting against aggressors and tyran-
nies, and accordingly authorise wars for specific virtuous causes: self-
defence, humanitarian reasons (to protect the persecuted), and defending
the goodness and divine message of the religion.[1] Religion in the Muslim
world has great influence, not only on the attitude of people but also on
the approach of governments and its institutions towards many issues, including those pertaining to security, justice and law.[2] As Islamic *Sharī'ah*
remains one of the recognised legal systems of the world today,[3] and the
main source of legislation in the majority of Arab countries, it is imperative to look at the influence of *Sharī'ah* when examining issues related to
security and military.

Remarkably, while the international community has recently recognised and honoured the rules that govern the conduct of hostilities, and
formulated them as part of the law of armed conflict, many Muslim scholars argue that Islamic *Sharī'ah* established meaningful and, at the same

---

*   Judge **Adel Maged** is Vice President of the Court of Cassation (Egypt) and Honorary Pro-
     fessor of Law, Durham University, United Kingdom.

[1]   See Muhammad Abū Zahra, *Nazariyat al-Harb fi al-Islam* [The Theory of War in Islam],
     Islamic Studies Series, vol. 160, Ministry of Endowment, Supreme Council for Islamic Af-
     fairs, Cairo, 2008, pp. 15–16.
[2]   Islamic *Sharī'ah*, in general terms, also contains the rules by which the Muslim nation, in
     the broadest sense of the word, is organised, and it provides all the means necessary for re-
     solving conflicts among individuals, between individuals and the state, as well as between
     the states themselves.
[3]   See René David and John E.C. Brierly, *Major Legal Systems in the World Today: An In-
     troduction to the Comparative Study of Law*, 2nd ed., Stevens and Sons, London, 1978, p.
     421; and Mashood A. Baderin (2006), "Effective Legal Representation in '*Shari'ah*'
     Courts as a Means of Addressing Human Rights Concerns in the Islamic Criminal Justice
     System of Muslim States", in Eugene Cotran, Martin Lau and Victor Kattan (eds.), *Year-
     book of Islamic and Middle Eastern Law 2004–2005*, vol. 11, Brill, Leiden, 2004, pp. 135–
     167.

time, merciful and humanistic rules governing warfare over 14 centuries ago. Those rules were established mainly in the Holy *Qur'ān* and the *Sunna* of Prophet Muhammad (PBUH), which are expressed through his sayings and deeds.[4] Subsequently, early Islamic treatises on international law like that of Muḥammad ibn al-Ḥasan al-Shaybānī[5] covered the application of Islamic military jurisprudence to international law and focused on the justification for war and the conduct of hostilities on the battlefield. The treatise of al-Shaybānī, called *Kitāb al-Siyar al-Kabir*,[6] is an established authority for all scholars researching Islamic *Sharī'ah* and is considered "the Islamic international law on matters of war".[7] The writings of many noted Western scholars assert that the work of al-Shaybānī constitutes a principal contribution to the formulation of international law.[8] Most importantly, it provides an important source of jurisprudence on

---

[4] Both the *Qur'ān* and the *Sunna* are primary sources of Islamic *Sharī'ah*. They form the basis for relations between man and God, between all persons, whether Muslims or non-Muslims, as well as between man and all aspects of creation. Thus Islam, with its rules as contained mainly in the Holy *Qur'ān* and the Prophet's *Sunna*, is a way of life and not merely religious rituals for worship. The *Sunna*, in its broad sense, refers to both the sayings and practices of the Prophet Muhammad (PBUH). Thus, the *Sunna* constitutes the normative pattern of life established by the Prophet Muhammad (PBUH). The *Sunna* has been kept and recorded in the form of *hadith* (sayings) as well as practices and deeds attributed to the Prophet Mohammad. The *Sunna* in the form of *hadith* is supplementary to the Holy *Qur'ān* itself. It helps to explain and clarify the Holy *Qur'ān* and provides practical applications of its teachings. In this chapter, as in all our work, we only depend upon reliable *hadith* reports, which were narrated by the Prophet's companions and underwent a rigorous process of authentication.

[5] Muḥammad ibn al-Ḥasan al-Shaybānī (749–805 CE) belonged to the Hanafī school of Islamic jurisprudence.

[6] His treatise on *al-Siyar al-Kabir* is recognised as one of the most important contributions in Islamic literature in the field of international law. It covers, *inter alia*, the application of Islamic military jurisprudence and is concerned with a number of modern international law topics, including the use of force, the conduct on the battlefield and the protection of non-combatants. The title *al-Siyar al-Kabir* literally means, in Arabic, the movements of people between different territories across the nations, and is referred to as "the longer book on the laws of nations".

[7] Muhammad ibn Ahmad al-Sarakhsi, *Sharh Kitāb al-Siyar al-Kabir* [Commentary on the Longer Book on International Law], Salah al-Din Munajjid (ed.), vol. 3, Mahad al-Makhtotat, Cairo, 1971, p. 13.

[8] Mashood A. Baderin, "Muhammad al-Shaybānī (749/50–805)", in Bardo Fassbender and Peters Anne (eds.), *The Oxford Handbook of the History of International Law*, Oxford University Press, Oxford, 2012, p. 1084.

---

matters related to military ethics. Therefore, special emphasis will be given in this chapter to al-Shaybānī's treatise.[9]

There is a wealth of information in various primary and secondary sources of *Sharī'ah* on the law of armed conflict that could be crystallised in order to explore the overall approach of Islamic *Sharī'ah* towards military self-interest in accountability for serious crimes committed on the battlefield. However, due to limited space, I will tackle this issue from a pragmatic point of view that could explain the paradigm behind the atrocities committed in our times, especially by non-state armed groups.

Based on the foregoing, this chapter attempts to examine the complex and multifaceted relationship of the law of armed conflict and Islam, both as a religion and a legal order, to assess the impact of Islamic *Sharī'ah* on military self-interest in accountability. It has to be noted that the core purpose of a model military justice system is to hold accountable those members of the military who are responsible for the commission of crimes, and hence modern military justice systems rely on written codes and laws that prescribe military crimes and provide sanctions for perpetrators. As we shall see below, Islamic *Sharī'ah* rules on this subject, which are founded primarily on the Holy *Qur'ān* and the *Sunna*, establish another approach to deter the commission of (serious) offences and therefore have a multilevel impact on accountability. First, this approach provides articulated measures for the prevention of the commission of serious offences during hostilities. Second, it imposes serious sanctions in cases where those crimes have been committed. I believe that the strength of Islamic *Sharī'ah* in this regard lies in the fact that the preventative measures, enshrined in its texts, provide sufficient ethical grounds that have a great impact on Muslim behaviour. Thus, I assert that Islamic *Sharī'ah* has established a meaningful and intelligible moral foundation that provides strong grounds for preventing and punishing atrocities. However, the acts of extremist groups lead most observers to think that wars in Islam are fought without restraint. Consequently, I find it crucial to shed light on the concept of *jihād* in relation to the main theme of this anthology and to illustrate that the erroneous interpretation of those texts, as we have seen in different vicious conflicts taking place in the Arab region at the time of writing, could lead to undesirable consequences.

---

[9] For greater authenticity, I rely only on the original writings of al-Shaybānī in Arabic.

As I frequently argue, Islamic law is a discipline that requires extreme caution and accuracy in addressing its principles and rules. For example, reliance on intermediary Islamic literature could lead to inaccurate conclusions and this, in turn, could also result in incorrect interpretations and misunderstandings of the Islamic *Sharīʿah* and its rulings. One who does research in Islamic law should be aware of the tools for comprehending the *Qurʾān* and *hadith* – rules of inference, the objectives of Islamic law and its principles. Accordingly, when I examine certain issues in *Sharīʿah* I try to rely mainly on the original sources of Islamic jurisprudence.

After presenting the principles of Islamic *Sharīʿah* that govern the theme of this anthology, and examining their application during the early era of Islam in the Arab peninsula, I attempt to analyse their application in contemporary times. However, my focus is on non-state armed groups acting under the mantra of Islam (as they claim) more than on regular armed military forces. The reason behind this is obvious. Most atrocities committed in the Arab region and Africa are by such groups, who do so with absolute impunity. These entities could include, *inter alia*, insurgency, militia and terrorist groups that have developed their tactics to be able to engage in belligerent operations. In order to examine Islamic *Sharīʿah* approaches with respect to these themes, we should first address an important question: When it is justifiable for Muslims to engage in war?

9.2. *Jus ad Bellum* in Islamic *Sharīʿah*

Before Islam spread in the Arab Jazīrah, it was permissible to commit all kinds of acts against the defeated, both inside and outside the war zone, and before and after war. After Islam emerged, fighting was restricted to the war zone and only between the fighters.[10] Thus, contrary to stereotypes of Islam as a source of violence, the basic rules of *Sharīʿah* promote peace, tolerance and forgiveness. In principle, the relations between Muslims and others are based on peace. In various verses, the *Qurʾān* commands Muslims to deal peacefully with those who do not fight them. Peace is the underlying principle of relations between Muslims and non-

---

[10] Abū Zahra, 2008, p. 20, see *supra* note 1.

Muslims.[11] In *Sūrat al-'Anfāl* (The Spoils of War), for example, the *Qur'ān* explicitly promotes peace: "And if they incline to peace, then also incline to it also and rely upon Allah. Indeed, it is He who is the Hearing, the Knowing".[12] This verse does not represent an anomalous voice, but speaks to the very essence of the *Qur'ānic* discourse. The same meaning is repeated, in varying language, in different verses of the *Qur'ān*. In addition, *Sharī'ah* is based on the well-known principle, stipulated by the Prophet Muhammad (PBUH): "avoid harm and inflict no harm on others".[13]

More specifically, the *Qur'ān* stresses that every individual is entitled to safety and that only unfair aggressors should be fought. On that basis, the *Qur'ān* declares in the broadest terms: "There shall be no hostility except against the aggressors".[14] It is also stated in *Sūrat al-Mumtahanah* (The Test): "Allah does not forbid you from those who do not fight you because of religion and do not expel you from your homes – from being righteous toward them and acting justly toward them. Indeed, Allah loves those who act justly".[15] Furthermore, and as emphasised by many eminent Islamic scholars, it is equally clear that "the motive for warfare in Islam is not the difference in religion or an attempt to impose the Islamic doctrine or a racist, social class on others, nor does it stem from a nationalistic tendency or material or economic interests".[16]

Accordingly, as we will see below, the *Qur'ān* has permitted wars only against those who initiate aggression or wars against Muslims. As such, wars in Islamic *Sharī'ah* should be necessary and just.

9.2.1. Just War in Islamic *Sharī'ah*

Just war theory deals in principle with the justification of how and why wars are fought. Throughout the history of Islam, and as illustrated in the contemporary literature, *jihād*, military action and just war are different

---

[11] Among the modern scholars who view peace as the basic guiding principle of the relationship between Muslims and non-Muslims is the renowned scholar Sheikh Muhammad Abū Zahra (1898–1974).

[12] *Qur'ān, Sūrat al-'Anfāl*, 8:61.

[13] *Sunan al-Darkatly*, 3/7 hadith no. 288; 2/227 *hadith* no. 83–85.

[14] *Qur'ān, Sūrat al-Baqarah*, 2:193.

[15] *Qur'ān, Sūrat al-Mumtahanah*, 60:8.

[16] Wahbeh Al-Zuhili, "Islam and International Law", in *International Review of the Red Cross*, 2005, vol. 87, no. 858, p. 280.

notions that have come to be associated. Thus, it is unavoidable to examine those terms in order to reach a comprehensive understanding of their impact on the core themes of this anthology. At the beginning of the 21st century, if not before, the Arabic term *jihād* became widely known, particularly in association with the activities of al-Qaʻida and other radical groups.[17] It is often erroneously assumed that *jihād* is the Islamic equivalent to 'holy war' and thus has military connotations. Some contemporary scholars go further and consider *jihād* to be the Islamic *bellum justum*.[18] As we shall see below, this provides an insincere understanding of *jihād*.

Unfortunately, the concept of *jihād* has arguably been central to many ongoing international and internal conflicts in several parts of the world, in particular the Middle East, and, according to the fanatics' discourse, wars are always just if waged against infidels and enemies of the faith.[19] Paradoxically, *jihād* is a term widely used today by many, though its meaning is poorly grasped. Consequently, radical Muslims, following some ill-informed writers, have translated *jihād* as "holy war" in order to justify their violent operations. It is true that numerous provisions in the *Qurʼān* and *Sunna* urge Muslims to *jihād,* however, this should be always based on proper reasons, as we will see below. Some religiously motivated non-state armed groups use false interpretations of *Sharīʻah* that contradict core Islamic values in order to justify acts of violent terror, and to support their ideological aspirations or gain the sympathy of the general public and recruit more people. This is usually done by decontextualising the reading of the texts of the *Qurʼān* and *Sunna* to justify their criminality. Despite emphatic protestations to the contrary, their justification for violence and terrorism finds no objective basis in Islamic ethics and moral traditions. They quote extensively from selective traditional Islamic jurisprudence, without paying due attention to the historical and circumstantial settings in order to justify their violence committed against Muslims and non-Muslims alike.

According to this fanatical approach, *jihād* represents a permanent state of belligerence with all non-believers, collectively encompassed in

---

[17] John Kelsay, "Al-Shaybani and the Islamic Law of War", in *Journal of Military Ethics*, 2003, vol. 2, no. 1, pp. 63–75.

[18] See Majid Khadduri, "Islam and the Modern Law of Nations", in *American Journal of International Law*, 1956, vol. 50, no. 2, p. 359.

[19] For a similar argument, see C.J.M. Drake, "The Role of Ideology in Terrorists' Target Selection", in *Terrorism and Political Violence*, 1998, vol. 10, no. 2, pp. 53–85.

the *dār al-harb* (abode of war).[20] Muslims are under an obligation to reduce non-Muslim communities to Islamic rule in order to achieve Islam's
ultimate objective, namely the enforcement of God's law over the entire
world. They use the concept of *jihād* to provide them with the initial dynamic for their actions, as it sets out the moral framework within which
they operate. It also justifies their target selection, usually the enemies of
Allah. For them, there are two categories of enemies of Allah: "the faraway enemy" and "the nearby enemy". Through false ideological motives,
radical terrorists have succeeded in deceiving and recruiting individuals
for terrorist activities all over the world and to join them to fight all types
of enemies.

For the majority of Muslims, and informed scholars, the term *jihād*
has a different connotation, as it applies to all forms of striving in life and

---

[20] From an organisational point of view, the orthodox theory of *jihād* is mainly based on the
tripartite division of the world into: 1) *dār al-Islam*, which corresponds to territory under
Islamic sovereignty where Muslim governments rule and Muslim law prevails; 2) *dār al-
sulh* or *dār al-selm*, which is the abode of non-Muslims who have entered into peace
agreements with Muslims; and 3) *dār al-harb*, where Islamic rules are not implemented
and the land is governed by non-Muslims. In essence, classical Sunni political theory divided the world into the abode of Islam, *dār al-Islam*, and the abode of infidelity, *dār al-
harb*. Others also called the latter the abode of the infidels, *dār al-kufr*. Subsequently,
some Muslim jurists added the abode of peace (*dār al-selm*) to limit *dār al-harb* only to
those territories in which there was persecution or aggression against Muslims. And, according to this classical division of the world, the followers of divine religions, mainly
Jews and Christians, can remain in *dār al-Islam* at the cost of paying a special tax (Khadduri, 1956, p. 359, see *supra* note 18). *Dār al-harb* was considered as illegitimate and war
was permitted against those who live in it. Plausibly, *dār al-harb* consisted of all the states
and communities outside the territory of Islam. Its inhabitants were called *harbis* or people
of the territory of war. For more information, see Sobhi Mahmassani, "The Principles International Law in the Light of Islamic Doctrine", *Collected Courses of the Hague Academy of International Law*, vol. 117, Brill, Leiden, 1966, pp. 250–52, and Khadduri, 1956, p.
359, see *supra* note 18. Apparently, this division has an impact on the conduct of hostilities, as it allows *jihād* against those who live in *dār al-harb*. According to fundamental religious views, *dār al-Islam* was permanently at war with *dār al-harb*, and Muslims were
under a legal obligation to reduce *dār al-harb* to Muslim rule and ultimately enforce God's
law over the entire world. Virtually every writer on Islamic law has considered these divisions. Contemporary moderate Islamic scholars are of the opinion that a principal factor
that could categorise a territory as *dār al-harb* is when it is a source of aggression to Muslims and that a Muslim fears risks to his life and property. They also consider that the division of the world, mainly into *dār al-Islam* and *dār al-harb*, does not exist in modern
times, as this approach leads to clashes between nations. They add that this division was
made in a historical era that had already elapsed, when there were enemies of the Muslim
nation and efforts were made to fight it and defeat Islam. For more information, see Abū
Zahra, 2008, pp. 44–46, 49, see *supra* note 1.

has developed some special meanings over time.[21] Thus Muslims who speak of the duty of *jihād* are referring, in the first place, to a moral duty that is based on the *Qur'ān* and *Sunna*.[22] The *Qur'ān* has laid out the purpose of *jihād* and set the rulings and foundational bases which condition this concept and through which it can be relied upon to initiate wars. Basically, the purpose of *jihād* in Islamic *Sharī'ah* is to defend oneself from aggression and to eliminate oppression and corruption. For the first time, in the second year of the Medina period, Muslims were granted permission for "military" *jihād*. The permission was revealed through *Sūrat al-Baqarah* in the *Qur'ān*,[23] just a few months before the Battle of Badr. Although Muslims had to resort to armed struggle to secure their lives and protect the newly born state, the *Qur'ān* considered engaging in warfare as an "unwanted obligation" which has to be carried out with strict observance of particular humane and moral guidelines, and which must not be resorted to except when absolutely inevitable.[24] The *Qur'ān* discourse, in general, disapproves of wars ignited by disbelievers. In *Sūrat al-Mā'idah* God says: "Each time they kindle the fire of war, Allah extinguishes it. They rush about corrupting earth. Allah does not love corrupters".[25]

Contemporary Muslim scholars persistently contend that *jihād* should not be specifically associated with the concept of war, whether "just" or "unjust". Imam ibn al-Qayyim, for example, has divided *jihād* into 13 categories. Among these categories are one's own *jihād* against immoral personal conduct, *jihād* against Satan, *jihād* against corruption, *jihād* against oppression, *jihād* against hypocrites, and so on.

Not many people understand the circumstances requiring *jihād*, or how Islamic militants justify their violent actions within the framework of the religious tradition of Islam. How Islam, with more than one billion followers, interprets *jihād* and establishes its precepts has become a criti-

---

[21] Basically, the Arabic word *jihād* literally means to exert the most effort and is equal to the following terms: struggle, exertion or expenditure of effort. Remarkably, the word *jihād* is mentioned in the *Qur'ān* 34 times.

[22] Kelsay, 2003, p. 63, see *supra* note 17.

[23] *Qur'ān, Sūrat al-Baqarah*, 2:216.

[24] Allam Shawki, *The Ideological Battlefield: Egypt's Dar al-Iftaa Combats Radicalization*, n.d., p. 12, available at http://dar-alifta.org/BIMG/The%20Ideological%20Battle%20%282%29.pdf, last accessed on 26 April 2015.

[25] *Qur'ān, Sūrat al-Mā'idah*, 5:64.

cal issue for both Muslim and non-Muslim communities. More recently, modern Muslim scholars, such as Sheikh Yusūf al-Qaraḍāwī (who is even seen by some as belonging to a radical school of thought), have reinterpreted Islamic sources with respect to *jihād*, stressing that *jihād* is essentially "defensive warfare" aimed at protecting Muslims and Islam. In his writings, al- Qaraḍāwī denounces the approach that some Islamic groups have adopted by promulgating *jihād* against infidels in the whole world.[26] Arguing that just war in Islam provides a systematic account of how Islam's central texts interpret *jihād*, he guides us through the historical precedents and *Qur'ānic* sources upon which today's claims to doctrinal truth and legitimate authority are made. Illuminating the broad spectrum of Islam's moral considerations of *jihād* would help make sense of the possibilities for future war and peace among the Muslim nations.

9.2.1.1. Extremists' Justification of Offensive *Jihād* Leads to the Commission of Atrocities

In their approach to radicalising the concept of *jihād*, fundamentalists have added rhetoric to the squabble over the nearby enemy and the faraway enemy.[27] By reviewing the literature on offensive military *jihād* developed by radical Islamists, which terrorist groups rely on nowadays, it is evident that they depend heavily on the specific radical and revolutionary writings of Sayyid Quṭb,[28] who has had an ideological impact on the proponents of offensive *jihād* from the second half of the 20th century up to the present. This radical ideology was revisited in the 1970s and endorsed in the writings of Muhammad Abd al-Salam Faraj,[29] who was an important figure in radical groups and wrote a manifesto titled *Al-Faridah*

---

[26] Yusūf al-Qaraḍāwī, *Fiqh al-Jihad* [The Jurisprudence of Jihad], vol. 1, Wahba Bookstore, Cairo, 2009, pp. 14–15.

[27] The preference for fighting the nearby enemy is an old doctrine discussed by many Islamic jurists like al-Kortoby, specifically in his interpretation of verse 9:123 of *Sūrat at-Tawbah*, which addresses the issue of the near enemy. The concept is also discussed within various commentaries on the famous *hadith*, "A man asked Prophet Muhammad (PBUH): 'Which type of *jihād* is the best?' He answered: 'A word of truth against a tyrant ruler'".

[28] Sayyid Quṭb (1906–1966) was an Egyptian Islamic theorist and author, particularly in political Islam. He was a leading member of the Muslim Brotherhood in the 1950s and 1960s. In 1966, he was convicted of plotting the assassination of the former Egyptian president Gamal Abdel Nasser and was executed by hanging.

[29] Muhammad Abd al-Salam Faraj was a member of one of the violent Islamic movements, Tanzim al-Jihad. He was convicted and sentenced to death for his involvement in the killing of President al-Sādāt.

al-Gha'ibah (The Neglected Duty), in which he heightened the duty of *jihād*. His writing was aimed at disbelieving Muslim rulers on the basis that they do not apply the rules of Islamic *Sharī'ah*. According to Faraj, they are committing apostasy from Islam and should be fought and even killed. He used this radical interpretation of the *Sharī'ah* texts as a pretext to substantiate the killing of the former Egyptian president, Anwar al-Sādāt.

Through this analysis, Faraj crystallised the offensive *jihād* theory, contending that *jihād* is the underlying principle governing the external relations of Muslims and non-Muslims. According to Faraj, rulers who are declared apostates are not eligible to declare *jihād* as they carry no authority. Thus, ordinary men and women have every right to exercise *jihād*, which is an individual obligation on all Muslims. In this way, a tripartite theory of offensive *jihād* has been completed to trigger violence against nearby and faraway enemies located in *dār al-harb* by young *jihādis* who aspire to martyrdom.

It is worth mentioning here that Ayman al-Zawahiri, the al-Qaʻida leader, promotes fighting the faraway enemy. It was not until the mid-1990s that Osama bin Laden launched the globalist strategy of giving priority to attacking the far enemy in the West. Later, Ayman al-Zawahiri reversed his long-standing concentration on the nearby enemy, joined forces with bin Laden, and became number two in the al-Qaʻida hierarchy.

It is evident that a deviant understanding of Islamic law and its application by extremist groups gave them a false justification to kill Muslims who are not in agreement with their formula for the application of Islamic law, disregarding established Islamic traditions that totally forbid even the intimidation of Muslims.[30] As indicated above, they relied on another distorted formula based on *takfir* (declaring someone an unbeliever) of others. Leading Islamic institutions in Egypt, such as Al-Azhar and Dar al-Iftaa, call this the process of "infidelising" others. Dar al-Iftaa, referring to the Islamic State ('ISIS') methodology of recruiting people to join their groups in Iraq and Syria, states:

> Their eagerness to infidelize others betrays superficial knowledge, lack of understanding, sick hearts and an erroneous methodology in seeking and acquiring knowledge. It de-

---

[30] Al-Sarakhsi, vol. 1, 1971, p. 21, see *supra* note 7.

stroys the noble objectives of the *Shari'ah* and their sublime significance.[31]

It is noticeable that ISIS recently distributed a booklet to the citizens of Mosul declaring all Arab states, except Iraq and Syria, "non-Muslim countries". The booklet obliges all Muslims to migrate and join "the land of the Caliphate", considering it the destination of migration and *jihād*.[32] This will, evidently, lead to the commission of more atrocities against those whom they consider infidels. As M. Cherif Bassiouni states, it seems that the lack of a comprehensive understanding of the correct meaning of Islam has paved the way to unqualified self-deluding religious leaders to advance their views by propagating erroneous notions of Islam that the largely ignorant masses are ready to accept and follow, rather than true religious scholars.[33]

Such extremist groups have the audacity to clothe their insanity in legal and religious robes and to ignore 1,400 years of authentic religious scholarship in Islamic sciences which has left us with an illuminating literature advocating peaceful co-existence and co-operation among people on the basis of worshiping God, purifying one's moral character and developing the world. By disrupting the spirit of *jihād* and converting it into an offensive holy war, non-state armed groups have turned the honourable characteristics of combat recognised in Islam into wars of terrorism and mass killing. Scholars, past and present, have unanimously agreed that *jihād* actually centres on securing and optimising interests and warding off harm.

9.2.1.2. Just War Does Not Justify the Commission of Atrocities

As described above, there is a consensus among Islamic scholars, who belong to the four schools of legal thought, that the killing of civilians, especially women and children, is strictly prohibited in Islamic *Sharī'ah*. Islam, in general, abhors killings and God emphasises that killing one innocent man equals the killing of all humanity in His sight, and that justi-

---

[31] Dar al-Iftaa Al-Missriyyah, "QSIS Seeks to Recruit More Combatants and Destabilize the Arab States", available at http://eng.dar-alifta.org/foreign/ViewArticle.aspx?ID=714&CategoryID=1, last accessed on 29 April 2015.

[32] *Ibid.*

[33] M. Cherif Bassiouni, *The Shari'a and Islamic Criminal Justice in time of War and Peace*, Cambridge University Press, Cambridge, 2014, pp. 5–6.

fying the killing of people by resorting to false interpretations of just war or *jihād* runs against the rules of *Sharī'ah*.

Sheikh Abū Zahra has repeatedly stated that those scholars who contend that military *jihād* is the basic principle between Muslims and non-Muslims derive their views from the reality they experience rather than from the texts of the *Qur'ān* and *Sunna*. The rulings arrived at by the classical scholars, Abū Zahra argues, are related only to the historical period in which they lived and therefore cannot be considered as definitive and binding rulings. Instead, military *jihād* is legislated to establish justice and fend off aggression. He considers the *Qur'ānic* verses that call for peace as the basic norm in Muslim and non-Muslim external relations. For Abū Zahra, the historical context cannot be underestimated.[34]

Nevertheless, by their false interpretation of the rules of Islam, violent groups have accused Muslims of disbelief, slaughtered people, frightened and displaced non-combatants, and murdered hostages without just cause. One can only wonder that if the *Qur'ānic* verses clearly establish the principle of peace as the guiding element of the relationship between Muslims and non-Muslims, how do the extremist groups derive their perverted and twisted interpretation of the *Qur'ān*? Confronting their tactics should mainly rely on exposing the false thoughts and illicit ideology to the general public and supporting the activities (and teachings) of reliable religious institutions in addressing erroneous religious thoughts and in promoting the correct teachings of the religion. It is also essential to differentiate between a faith and the actions of some of those who are affiliated with it. We should judge faiths by their teachings and the values to which the faith is calling, and not by the perception and practices of some of its followers.

We have seen how the notion *jihād* could be abused to justify hostilities against people. Interestingly, contrary to such rhetoric, in his treatise (*Kitāb al-Siyar al-Kabīr*) al-Shaybānī, followed another line of thought. Before discussing *jihād* as an incentive to combat, he discussed the concept of *ribat* mentioned in Prophet Muhammad's (PBUH) *hadith*. According to al-Shaybānī, *ribat* is to reside in the enemy's land to prevent the infidels from attacking or harming Muslims and to defend the religion

---

[34] Abū Zahra, 2008, pp. 15–16, see *supra* note 1.

(Islam).[35] Here I will focus on the traditional grounds of war as recognised in the real teachings of Islamic *Sharī'ah*.

9.2.2. Grounds of War in Islamic *Sharī'ah*

> Do not wish to encounter with the enemy, pray to God to grant you security; but when you encounter them, exercise patience.[36]

This quotation is the Prophet Muhammad's (PBUH) advice to his followers. Muslim scholars have cited as examples of unlawful wars those conducted for the purpose of occupation, colonisation, seizure or partition of territories for the purpose of avarice, selfish glory or economic gains. Each such aggressive act of unjustified violence is considered an aggressive war and has been prohibited under *Sharī'ah*.[37] Moreover, to restrain belligerents and the conduct of hostilities, according to established jurisprudence in *Sharī'ah*, war should not be declared and fighting should not be initiated until after providing the antagonist with one of three options: 1) to accept Islam; 2) to enter into a covenant with Muslims;[38] or 3) to enter into war with Muslims.[39] This indicates that war in Islam is justified only when non-military means are refused. In his treatise *Kitāb al-Siyar al-Kabir*, al-Shaybānī narrated the many occasions when the Prophet Muhammad (PBUH) did not initiate fighting before offering Islam or a pact to the disbelievers, and ordered the troops' commanders to do so. Al-Shaybānī referred to verse 15 of *Sūrat al-Isrā* (The Night Journey) as the foundation of this conduct, which provides: "And never would We punish until We sent a messenger".[40]

The *Qur'ān* limits wars only to the defence of the religion of Islam and Muslims. In general, war is permitted in Islam in cases of aggression

---

[35] Al-Sarakhsi, vol. 1, 1971, pp. 6–10, see *supra* note 7.

[36] *Sahih al-Bukhāri*, the book of *jihad*, chapter 155/156, *hadith* no. 3024.

[37] For more details, see Adel Maged, "Arab and Islamic Shari'a Perspectives on the Current System of International Criminal Justice", in *International Criminal Law Review*, 2008, vol. 8, no. 3, p. 482.

[38] Islamic traditions show that it was a regular practice of the Prophet and his successors to invite the enemy to the religion or peace before commencing hostilities.

[39] Ahmad Abu al-Wafa, *Kitab al-I'lam bi-Qawa'id al-Qanun al-Duwli wa-al-'Alaqat al-Dawilyyah fi Shari'at al-Islam* [Treatise on International Law Rules and International Relations in Islamic *Sharī'ah*], Dar al-Nahdah al-'Arabiyyah, Cairo, vol. 10, 2001 p. 95–79; and Abū Zahra, 2008, p. 51, see *supra* note 1.

[40] Al-Sarakhsi, 1971, vol. 1, pp. 75–80, see *supra* note 7; *Qur'ān*, *Sūrat al-Isrā*, 17:15.

against Muslims, either individually or collectively, as preachers for Islam, or attempts to make Muslims apostates.[41] In these circumstances, the motive of fighting in Islam is not to impose the religion on non-Muslims, but rather to prevent aggression and to defend oneself.[42] This permission includes liberation of occupied lands of Muslims, fighting in self-defence, protection of the family, property and oppressed people, and fighting insurgency groups who commit *baghi*.[43] The early Muslims fought many battles against their enemies, for good causes, under the leadership of the Prophet Muhammad (PBUH) and his commanding leaders.[44]

9.2.2.1. Self-Defence

Jihād is permitted when war is waged against Muslims and the Islamic nation. Early battles involving Muslims occurred when the pagans of the tribe of Quraysh formed armies and launched military attacks against the Prophet Muhammad (PBUH) and his followers. The Muslims fought back to defend their faith and community. In this meaning, the *Qur'ān* stipulates: "Fight in the cause of Allah those who fight against you, but do not transgress. Lo! Allah does not like the aggressors".[45]

The same meaning is elaborated in other verses of the *Qur'ān* which state:

> To those against whom war is made, permission is given [to defend themselves], because they are wronged − and verily, Allah is Most Powerful to give them victory − [they are] those who have been expelled from their homes in defiance of right − [for no cause] except that they say, "Our Lord is Allah". And were it not that Allah checks the people, some by means of others, there would have been demolished monasteries, churches, synagogues, and mosques in which the name of Allah is much mentioned. And Allah will surely

---

[41]   Al-Zuhili, 2005, p. 281, see *supra* note 16.

[42]   Abū Zahra, 2008, p. 23, see *supra* note 1.

[43]   *Baghi* in Islamic *Sharī'ah* is the armed rebellion or uprising against legitimate ruler. The crime of *baghi* includes, for example, acts of seizing and destruction of public property.

[44]   For more details on the grounds of war in Islamic *Sharī'ah*, see Abu al-Wafa, 2001, pp. 73-80, see *supra* note 39.

[45]   *Qur'ān, Sūrat al-Baqarah*, 2:190.

> support those who support Him. Indeed, Allah is Powerful and Exalted in Might.[46]

This verse emphasises the integral component of justice in conducting defensive *jihād*. At that time, Muslims were forcibly evicted from their homes due to heavy persecution by the elite of the Quraysh tribe and most left their homes and were totally deprived of their worldly goods and lacked the means to start a new life.[47] The divine words, "they were wronged" and "those who have been expelled from their homes", illustrate the reason for the legality of war, namely that Muslims are oppressed by others (the unbelievers).[48]

9.2.2.2. Persecution

Persecution and attacking the weakest are other grounds of legitimate wars. The *Qur'ān* clearly states:

> And what is wrong with you that you fight not in the cause of Allah and for those weak, ill-treated and oppressed among men, women and children, whose prayer is "Our Lord! Rescue us from this town whose people are oppressors; and bestow on us someone you raise to support us, and bestow on us someone you raise to render us victorious".[49]

This means that Islam encourages defending those who are under oppression or subjected to aggression and lending assistance to the victims of injustice, whether individuals or groups. Indeed, Islam acknowledged centuries ago the rules that govern what we nowadays call 'humanitarian intervention'. Thus, the theory of humanitarian intervention may find a basis in the verses of the Holy *Qur'ān*, which urges believers to come to the aid of the weak and oppressed. In such cases, military *jihād* is permitted to remove aggression and religious persecution against Muslims. The use of armed forces to respond to the killing of innocent Muslims could be also regarded, from classical *Sharī'ah* theory, as a form of *qasas* (retribution) prescribed in Islamic law. In this case, war is permitted until persecution ceases.[50]

---

[46] *Qur'ān, Sūrat al-Haj*, 22:39–40.

[47] Allam, *The Ideological Battlefield*, p. 13, see *supra* note 24.

[48] Al-Zuhili, 2005, p. 279, see *supra* note 16.

[49] *Qur'ān, Sūrat al-Nisā*, 4:75.

[50] *Qur'ān, Sūrat al-Baqarah*, 2:193.

All the above cases are situations that permit the use of force under the realm of just war. As to the institutional validation of war, it is established under the rules of Islamic *Sharīʿah* that there must also be a directive from a legitimate authority to wage war. During the early era of Islam, the Prophet Muhammad (PBUH) was regarded as the head of state and commander of the army, and thus the legitimate authority to declare wars. In general, it is prohibited to launch an attack without the ruler's permission because he is responsible for making the decision of declaring war.[51] This is because he has access to all the information pertaining to the enemy. His permission is mandatory except if Muslims are taken by surprise by non-Muslim enemies and fear their threat. Only then is it allowed to fight the attackers without the ruler's permission because of the general benefit therein.[52]

9.3. *Jus in Bello* in Islamic *Sharīʿah*

If war does take place, it is subject to clear regulations under Islamic *Sharīʿah*. Inscribed centuries ago, we can infer straightforwardly from Islamic *Sharīʿah* various rules relating to the conduct of hostilities on the battlefield. The following are some rules that relate to targeting and methods of combat derived from Islamic *Sharīʿah*.

9.3.1. Protection of Civilians and Civilian Objects

As a general rule, Islamic *Sharīʿah* distinguishes between combatants and non-combatants.[53] A non-combatant who is not taking part in warfare, by action, opinion, planning or supplies, must not be attacked.[54] As mentioned earlier, the *Qurʾān* established that fighters should not transgress certain limits. The transgression of these limits refers to a myriad of forbidden crimes of war: mutilating enemy soldiers, stealing from the spoils of war, killing women, children and old men, or killing monks worshipping in monasteries. Al-Shaybānī mentions in his treatise *Kitāb al-Siyar al-Kabir* that the "killing of women and children is absolutely forbidden

---

[51] Dar al-Iftaa al Misriyyah, *fatwa* (religious verdict) no. 1637 of 2009, available at http://eng.dar-alifta.org/ViewFatwa.aspx?ID=1252&text, last accessed on 5 May 2015.

[52] Shawki, *The Ideological Battlefield*, p. 161, see *supra* note 24.

[53] Abu al-Wafa, 2001, pp. 118–121, see *supra* note 39.

[54] Al-Zuhili, 2005, p. 282, see *supra* note 16.

---

according to the divine texts".[55] The transgression further encompasses a number of other forbidden actions as well, such as killing animals for no good reason, burning trees, destroying crops, ruining or polluting water sources, destroying houses or, in a more general sense, destroying the infrastructure of enemy territory.

The *Sunna* of the Prophet Muhammad (PBUH) follows this approach. Abdullah ibn Umar said that during one of the Muslim battles a woman was found killed, and, in response, the Prophet said, "she shouldn't have been killed". He disapproved of the killing of women and children.[56] To prevent the commission of serious offences during combat, the Prophet used to command his followers on their way to battle not to perform certain acts during hostilities. Anas ibn Malik narrated that the Prophet instructed his soldiers in the following terms:

> Go in the name of Allah and on the path of his Prophet, and never kill an elderly person, or a child, or a woman. Do not kill the monks in monasteries, and do not kill those sitting in places of worship. Do not cheat or commit treachery, neither should you mutilate anyone nor kill children. Do not destroy the villages and towns, do not spoil the cultivated fields and gardens, and do not slaughter the cattle.[57]

This illustrates how the Prophet extended protection to non-combatants, especially the elderly and the weak, and to their properties.

The first Rashidun Caliph, Abū Bakr al-Siddiq (who succeeded the Prophet Muhammad (PBUH) in governing the Islamic nation), instructed his army commander who was on his way to a battle, saying:

> I give you Ten Commandments[58] which you must observe on the battlefield: Do not commit treachery or deviate from the right path. You must not mutilate dead bodies; neither kill a child, nor a woman, nor an aged man. Never cut a fruit-bearing tree, nor burn them with fire. Never destroy an in-

---

[55] Al-Sarakhsi, vol. 5, 1971, p. 1556, see *supra* note 7.

[56] *Sahih al-Bukhāri*, the book of *jihad*, chapter 147/148, *hadith* no. 3015.

[57] *Ibid.*, chapter 69, *hadith* no. 1293.

[58] For more elaboration on the ten commandments of Abū Bakr, see Al-Sarakhsi, vol. 1, 1971, pp. 39–47, see *supra* note 7.

habited place; never slaughter a sheep nor a camel except only for food; and neither be revengeful nor cowardly.[59]

As Bassiouni notes, the instructions of Abū Bakr to his troops are very
close in content to contemporary international humanitarian law.[60] The
four Rashidun Caliphs strictly followed the authentic rules of Islamic
Sharī'ah as expressed in the Holy *Qur'ān* and *Sunna*.

The foregoing provides that it is not permissible in Islam to attack
civilians or civilian properties indiscriminately, as they are not considered
legitimate targets. This Islamic concept is broadly accepted by the Islamic
legal authorities, both Sunni and Shi'a alike.[61] Furthermore, it is stated
that

fighters are required to conduct themselves with good intention, and thus to try to avoid such killing. But the enemy
cannot be allowed to take advantage of these good intentions
through measures that would circumscribe the ability of the
Muslims to carry out their legitimate goal.[62]

This means that only those who pose a tangible military threat may be
targeted for intentional killing.[63] The destruction of property is prohibited,
except when there is a military necessity to do so, for example, when the
army penetrates barricades, or the property makes a direct contribution to
war, such as castles and fortresses.[64] Regrettably, this does not deter extremists from practising a different interpretation in that respect.

9.3.2. Restrictions on Means and Methods of Combat

The prohibition of using certain methods in combat was further discussed
by the proponents of the four schools of Islamic *Sharī'ah*, such as the
Shafi'i, which puts more restriction on the conduct of war. For instance,
early *Shafi'i* scholars prohibited the use of fire as a weapon during armed
conflicts, since fire, according to their jurisprudence, was the ultimate

---

[59] Related by Imam Malik. See Jalal al-Din al-Suyuti, *Tanwir al-Hawalik: Sharh 'ala Mu-
watta' Malik*, vol. 2, al-Halabi Press, Cairo, n.d., p. 6; see also Abu al-Wafa, 2001 p. 123,
see *supra* note 39.

[60] Bassiouni, 2014, p. 160, see *supra* note 33.

[61] Maged, 2008, p. 489, see *supra* note 37.

[62] See Kelsay, 2003, p. 72, *supra note* 17.

[63] Allam, *The Ideological Battlefield*, p. 75, see *supra* note 24.

[64] Al-Zuhili, 2005, p. 282, see *supra* note 16.

weapon of the Almighty (God), who would consign the wicked to eternal burning on Judgment Day; its use as a weapon of warfare was judged a usurpation of divine prerogatives. They relied on a famous saying of the Prophet Mohammad, which states: "No one may punish with fire except the Lord of Fire".[65] Accordingly, burning people alive, something already done by ISIS, is to be considered an act against Islamic *Sharī'ah*.

Islamic *Sharī'ah* also prohibits perfidy. As stipulated in many verses of *Qur'ān*, Islam prohibits perfidy and treason in all circumstances.[66] It represents an especially serious violation of the rules of armed conflict in Islamic *Sharī'ah*. Thus, all fighters, including those in non-state armed groups, are required to comply with these rules. The traditions of the Prophet Muhammad (PBUH) show that he used to instruct his fighters going into combat not to commit perfidy. If committed, he would denounce it and relinquish any support to the individual who committed it. The Prophet's successors also followed his path. It is reported that Caliph 'Umar ibn Al-Khattāb, after learning that a Muslim fighter told a Persian soldier hiding in the mountain not to be afraid and then killed him afterwards, denounced this act and gave the perpetrator a severe punishment. This is, from my point of view, a clear example of self-initiated accountability out of religious interest.

In *Kitāb al-Siyar al-Kabir*, al-Shaybānī provided many examples of prohibited methods of combat that fall under perfidy. For example, if a Muslim group entered *dār al-harb* claiming that they came as messengers from the Caliph, or that they came for trade, then they were forbidden from attacking those who were living in *dār al-harb* (the infidels).[67]

9.4. Prohibition of the Core International Crimes in Islamic *Sharī'ah*

9.4.1. Normative Prohibition

As opposed to extremist *jihādi* ideology, indiscriminate attacks and violence against civilians are prohibited according to the *ijmā* (consensus) of Muslim jurists. The annihilation or extermination of a part or the whole of

---

[65] For more details on the inviolability of religious sites in Islamic *Sharī'ah*, see Bassiouni, 2014, pp. 181–82, *supra* note 33.

[66] See, for example, *Qur'ān, Sūrat al-Mā'idah*, 5:1; and *Qur'ān, Sūrat al-Nahl*, 16:91.

[67] Al-Sarakhsi, vol. 2, 1971, pp. 507–508, see *supra* note 7.

a group of people, or the inflicting of destructive conditions of life, would fall under the most sinful acts that the Islamic *Sharīʿah* condemns.

As stipulated above, all instructions concerning the Islamic rules of *jus ad bellum* and *jus in bello* are mandatory and should be fully respected. No Muslim is allowed to overstep these rules. Massive human rights violations committed in some Muslim countries or by some so-called 'Muslims' should not be regarded as examples illustrative of the behaviour of true Muslims. Such violations are not only at variance with international norms but even more so with the basic concepts of *Sharīʿah*.[68] As repeatedly stressed in this chapter, the prohibition of commissions of atrocities in Islamic *Sharīʿah* is mostly based on ethical grounds. Thus it has been asserted by prominent contemporary scholars that the violations of contemporary international humanitarian law have long been recognised as part of *Sharīʿah* and Islamic public law.[69]

Unquestionably, all non-state armed groups' members who carry out attacks against non-combatants are in blatant violation of the core principles of international law as well as Islamic *Sharīʿah*.[70] As far as Islamic law is concerned, if non-state armed groups prove to be guilty of committing acts of *ḥirābah* (unlawful warfare) and are to be tried before a court that solely applies Islamic law, then the punishments for *ḥirābah* apply to them.[71] Islamic states have consistently condemned all violent and terrorist acts, either perpetrated by states or non-state actors.[72] Al-Azhar has also repeatedly denounced the atrocities committed by non-state armed groups.[73]

---

[68] Maged, 2008, p. 482, see *supra* note 37.

[69] Bassiouni, 2014, p. 251, *supra* note 33.

[70] Mohamed Badar, ElSayed Amin and Noelle Higgins, "The International Criminal Court and the Nigerian Crisis: An Inquiry into the Boko Haram Ideology and Practices from an Islamic Law Perspective", in *International Human Rights Law Review*, 2014, vol. 3, no. 1, p. 54.

[71] *Ibid.*, p. 55.

[72] Maged, 2008, p. 489, see *supra* note 37.

[73] Al-Azhar is the oldest Sunni institution, one of the first universities in the world, and traditionally considered the chief centre of Arabic literature and Islamic learning in the world. It is located in Cairo, Egypt.

9.4.2. Moral and Ethical Grounds for Prohibition

It is admitted among Islamic scholars that "ethics are the container of religion, the pillar of civilization, setting the basis and standards for dealings and relations between individuals and States alike".[74] The motive force in Islamic ethics is the notion that every human being is called to "command the good and forbid the evil" in all spheres of life. Accordingly, Muslims are believed to have a moral responsibility to submit to God's will and to follow His orders, as demonstrated in the Holy *Qur'ān*. One Islamic interpretation is that individual personal peace is attained by utterly submitting to Allah. This moral responsibility should forbid any Muslim from killing another person unlawfully.

As previously noted, permission was given to Muslims to fight "in the cause of Allah". This entails that during the conduct of wars, Muslim fighters have to submit to God's orders and not to transgress the limits. Those who did so were to incur divine displeasure. Indeed, Islamic *Sharī'ah* has established an ethical framework to which a Muslim soldier must adhere in the context of battle. That ethical approach is exemplified in various verses of the Holy *Qur'ān* and articulated in the *Sunna* of the Prophet Muhammad (PBUH). In *Sūrat al-Isrā* it was avowed that the ethical grounds behind the prohibition of murder are that life is sacred to God and no one can take it unless for a legitimate and just cause. It states:

> And do not kill the soul – which Allah has made sacred –
> except for just cause. And whoever is killed unjustly – We
> have given his heir authority [to demand *qasas* or to for-
> give], but let him not exceed the limits in the matter of tak-
> ing life. Indeed, he has been supported [by the law].[75]

This approach has also been established in the *Sunna* of the Prophet Muhammad (PBUH). As narrated by Abdullah ibn Omar, the Prophet said "a believer remains within the boundary of the faith unless he kills someone unlawfully".[76] Murder in Islam is a deadly sin except in the events of *qasas* and self-defence. The Holy *Qur'ān* states that murdering an innocent human being unlawfully is equal to murdering the whole of mankind. This rule is well established in the first source of Islamic *Sharī'ah*, that is, the Holy *Qur'ān*, which states in unequivocal terms that: "if anyone mur-

---

[74] Al-Zuhili, 2005, p. 273, see *supra* note 16.

[75] *Qur'ān, Sūrat al-Isrā*, 17:33.

[76] *Sahih al-Bukhāri*, the book of *Diyat*, chapter 81, *hadith* no. 2168.

ders a human being – unless it be [in punishment] for murder or for spreading corruption on earth – it shall be as though he had murdered all humankind, whereas, if anyone saves a life, it shall be as though he had saved the lives of all humankind".[77]

After the killing of the British aid worker David Haines by ISIS, Dar al-Iftaa[78] in Egypt denounced the killing and emphasised that such extremist ideologies which give birth to such brutal acts must be fought at all costs. Ibrahim Negm, the senior adviser to the Grand Mufti said:

> We are both saddened and appalled by such horrific series of killing and our pain is doubled as we are not only disheart-ened for the killing of an innocent human being but also for the audacity of the claim of these murderers to call them-selves Muslims.[79]

In conformity with contemporary jurisprudence in the law of armed conflict, through its moral predisposition, Islamic *Sharī'ah* has laid down the moral ground to prevent the commission of serious offences during armed conflicts, so one can easily know the proscriptions of the law of war through a cursory presumption of what sounds morally right or wrong.[80]

Muslim commanders were determined to follow the *Sunna* of the Prophet wholeheartedly by being fair to their enemies, following just rules of Islamic warfare and through honouring their pacts. According to Islam-ic *Sharī'ah* teachings, a military person should possess certain qualities to make him an honourable warrior. And we can deduce from the practice of the Prophet Muhammad (PBUH) a set of disciplinary rules of self-interest in chivalry, knighthood and nobility that attach to Muslim fighters. Cer-tainly, these rules forbid them from committing atrocities on the battle-field.

As we have seen, war ethics in Islam is an all-encompassing system that includes ethics before, during and after combat. The history of the

---

[77] *Qur'ān, Sūrat al-Mā'idah*, 5:32.

[78] Dar al-Iftaa al Misriyyah is considered among the pioneering foundations for *fatwa* in the Islamic world. It was established in 1895 by the high command of Khedive 'Abbās Ḥilmī, and affiliated to the Egyptian Ministry of Justice on 21 November 1895 by Decree No. 10.

[79] Allam, *The Ideological Battlefield*, p. 156, see *supra* note 24.

[80] See Gary D. Solis, *The Law of Armed Conflict: International Humanitarian Law in War*, Cambridge University Press, Cambridge, 2010, p. xxx.

Prophet's battles shows that Muslims fighters had always met the highest standards of conduct and judgment, as promulgated by Islamic *Sharīʿah* principles, thus upholding the notion of self-regulation recognised in the modern law of armed conflict, especially among members of regularly organized military units. Accordingly, I would argue that the notion of self-regulation is recognised in the Islamic law of armed conflict and well-respected, in general, among Arab and Muslim (regular) armed forces. However, the notion is not well respected, perhaps because it is not well understood among modern violent non-state armed groups who are operating in different parts of the Arab and Muslim world. As shown before, they have drained the sacred text of *Sharīʿah* to justify their criminality and terrorist activities.

Besides the ethical aspect, Islamic *Sharīʿah* has prescribed harsh religious sanctions in case of infringement of God's orders. This should cover the commission of heinous crimes during armed conflicts. Insurgency groups which commit heinous crimes against civilians, such as intimidation and mass killing, are considered as committing the crime of *ḥirābah* prescribed in Islamic *Sharīʿah*, which many Islamic *Sharīʿah* scholars apply its rules, by analogy, to the crime of terrorism.[81]

The foregoing has established that Islamic *Sharīʿah* has provided a legal and moral framework capable of enforcing the rules prohibiting atrocities, among all equally, without discrimination and, most importantly, capable of deterring future serious crimes.

9.5. Military Self-Interest in Accountability from the Perspective of Islamic *Sharīʿah*

In its "Declaration in Support for the Arab Revolutions" (31 October 2011), al-Azhar outlined the duties and responsibilities of military forces. Al-Azhar emphasised in the third clause of the Declaration that "the organised armed forces, in all Arab and Muslims nations, should be committed to their constitutional duties to protect the homeland from external threats and should not transform into an instrument of oppression and intimidation to citizens. It should not stoop to shedding civilian blood".[82] This influential statement by the chief Sunni institution in the Arab and

---

[81] For more information on the definition of the crime of *ḥirābah*, see Maged, 2008, p. 489, *supra* note 37.

[82] Adel Maged, "Commentary on al-Azhar Declaration in Support of the Arab Revolutions", in *Amsterdam Law Forum*, 2012, vol. 4, no. 3, p. 74.

Muslim world illustrates the great interest in preventing the commission of serious crimes by the regular military apparatus and in holding the perpetrators of such crimes accountable.

As mentioned before, in general *Sharī'ah* encourages Muslims to prevent wrongdoing and to hold abusers accountable. Examples of *Sharī'ah* approaches to accountability may be found in many *hadith* of the Prophet Muhammad (PBUH). In a famous *hadith*, the Prophet stressed: "If any of you sees something evil, he should set it right with his hand; if he is unable to do so, then with his tongue, and if he is unable to do even that, then [let him denounce it] in his heart. But this is the weakest form of faith".[83]

We have also seen that *qasas* prescribed in Islamic law is used as a sanction for murder and inflicting serious bodily harm to a person. As such, *qasas* has its influence in Islamic countries to hold perpetrators of murder and mass killing accountable, regardless of the identity of the victim, whether Muslim or non-Muslim. Accordingly, *qasas* will be the sanction of Muslim combatants if they kill a non-Muslim living in *dār al-selm*, who are called *ahl al-zamah* in Islamic *Sharī'ah*. The fourth Rashidun Caliph Alī ibn Abī Ṭālib ordered *qasas* against a Muslim who unlawfully killed a man from *ahl al-zamah,* stating: "A person from *ahl al-zamah* has the same rights concerning *qasas*; his blood is protected similar to our blood and he is entitled to the same *diyya* [compensation] similar to us".[84]

It has been established in this chapter that war in Islamic *Sharī'ah* is always fought for a noble cause, and thus submitting to God's will is all the more reason to scrupulously obey all the rules regarding the proper conduct of war.

Although Khālid ibn al-Walīd was a companion of the Prophet Muhammad (PBUH) and one of the greatest commanders in Islamic history (who led various victorious military campaigns, and was called, therefore, the Drawn Sword of God), the second Rashidun Caliph 'Umar ibn Al-Khattāb did not hesitate to relieve him of high command on the basis of his mass killing of the enemies. Justifying his action, Caliph 'Umar said

---

[83] Muslim ibn Hajjaj al-Nishapuri, *Mukhtasar Sahih Muslim*, Mohamad Nasir al-Din al-Albani (ed.), 2nd ed., Dar Al-Maktab Al-Islami, Beirut, 1984, p. 16, no. 34.

[84] Ibn Abidin, *Radd al-Muhtar ala al-Dur al-Mukhtar: Sharh Tanwir al-Absar* [The Answer to the Bewildered over the Exquisite Pearl: Enlighten the Insight Elucidation], Adel Abd al-Mawjood *et al.* (eds.), vol. 10, Dar Alam al-Kotob, Riyadh, 2003, p. 170.

that "Khālid ibn al-Walīd's sword carries suffering", meaning that it killed enemies excessively.[85]

Another example of religiously motivated accountability relates to atonement which is referred in Islamic *Sharī'ah* as *diyya*.[86] Islamic *Sharī'ah* not only prohibits unnecessary killing in wars, but also provides compensation to those who are killed unjustly by Muslims in their wars and quests. This is based on God's saying:

> Nor take life – which God has made sacred – except for just cause. And if anyone is slain wrongfully, we have given his heir authority (to demand justice or to forgive): but let [the heir] not exceed bounds in the matter of taking life; for he is helped (by the Law).[87]

A well-known practice of the Prophet Muhammad (PBUH) reflects the essence of this verse. On one occasion the tribe of Bani Amer treacherously killed 70 Muslims. Only one Muslim survived this mass killing. While he was on his way back after this incident, he met two men of that tribe and killed them in revenge for his companions. He did not know that there was a covenant between them and the Prophet. Regardless of what their tribe had committed against the Prophet's followers, the Prophet denounced the killing of the two men and ordered the payment of *diyya* for their families.[88]

The foregoing suggests that the sanctions for breaches of the rules of armed conflict during early Islam were a matter for the troops' leaders. Those sanctions were enforced immediately and sometimes during hostilities. If we follow the custom of Muslim militaries in recent decades, we notice that Islamic *Sharī'ah* rules on combat have a great impact on members of Arab and Muslim armies; for this reason, they are keen to avoid acts that violate the law of armed conflict. This further suggests that

---

[85] Abū Zahra, 2008, p. 21, see *supra* note 1.

[86] Islamic *Sharī'ah* recognises the concept of reparation and compensation for victims of crimes. It provides detailed rules for compensation in lieu of any harm inflicted against the physical (and also moral) integrity of persons. In this respect, the Islamic criminal justice system is based on the principle that "no blood goes in vain in Islam". Victims of violent crimes or families of deceased victims are entitled to *diyya*, that is, compensation either from the perpetrator himself or from his family or tribe. Moreover, in cases where the perpetrator is bankrupt, impoverished or unknown, compensation would be provided by the Bayt al-Mal (state treasury).

[87] *Qur'ān, Sūrat al-Isrā*, 17:33

[88] Ibn Kathīr, *Al-Bidāyah wa al-Nehāyah* [The Beginning and the End], Ali Shiry (ed.), vol. 4, Dar Ehyaa al-Turath al-Arabi, 1988, p. 1336.

---

it is prudent to use religious beliefs expounded in Islamic *Sharī'ah* as an incentive to prosecute and try core international crimes.

The rules of Islamic *Sharī'ah* that we have examined in this chapter are general and thus apply to both organised armies and insurgent forces. The latter must comply with these same rules in armed conflict. The rules of Islamic *Sharī'ah* do not lend credence to the sub-human methods employed by non-state armed groups operating deceitfully under the tenets of Islam. Indeed, this wholesale rejection of indiscriminate violence is not a question of apologetics, but rather an objective reality rooted in centuries of Islamic *Sharī'ah* which rejects the mass killing of human beings. As such, their acts certainly violate the rules of Islamic *Sharī'ah*.[89] Unfortunately, heinous crimes have only arisen in the Arab and Muslim region where certain non-state armed groups operate. One who follows the atrocities committed by those non-state armed groups, whose ideology is based on delusionary Islamic inclinations, will never expect that they could sanction their own fighters, simply because there is no self-interest on their part to holding their followers accountable. The reason behind this is apparent; they believe or claim that Islamic *Sharī'ah* justifies their criminal acts.

9.6. Conclusion

The discussion in this chapter has revealed that the principles of Islamic *Sharī'ah* could be regarded as a valid source of jurisprudence of the law of armed conflict. It has also demonstrated that the Islamic legal tradition provides a detailed set of ethical principles of military engagement and established norms that are relevant to the conduct of hostilities in wartime and, subsequently, could be recognised as a source of international law of armed conflict in this area. Although the origins and histories of Islamic *Sharī'ah* and the contemporary law of armed conflict are different, both legal systems are compatible and can complement each other.[90] In conformity with modern international humanitarian law and international criminal law norms, Islamic *Sharī'ah* comprises the obligation to prosecute and punish persons found guilty of committing genocide, crimes

---

[89] Bassiouni, 2014, p. 242, see *supra* note 33.
[90] Niaz A. Shah, *Islamic Law and the Law of Armed Conflict: The Conflict in Pakistan*, 2011, Routledge, London, p. 5.

---

against humanity and war crimes.[91] And, in general, employing Islamic *Sharīʿah* could be used as a tool to advance the application of both international humanitarian law and international criminal law in the Muslim and Arab world.

We have also illustrated the fact that Islamic *Sharīʿah* has delineated the circumstances that yield just causes of war and prevent the commission of serious crimes during armed conflicts. Moreover, the discussion suggests that Islamic *Sharīʿah* principles could lend moral authority to troops' leaders and commanders to hold accountable those responsible for international core crimes.

Islamic rules of the conduct of warfare are mainly based on the *Qurʾān* and the *Sunna* of the Prophet Muhammad (PBUH), who gave various injunctions to his forces and adopted practices towards the conduct of war that raised self-interest in avoiding the commission of serious offences. Scrutiny of the primary sources of Islamic *Sharīʿah* against the core concepts of existing norms related to military self-interest in accountability reveals that the values and principles of Islamic *Sharīʿah* are compatible, in general, with current trends that call for accountability for the core international crimes. Thus, reliance on Islamic legal traditions should be useful in controlling warfare and alleviating the horrors of wars, and holding accountable those who are involved in the commission of serious crimes. With respect to accountability, one advantage of Islamic *Sharīʿah* rules on the law of armed conflict is that they are enshrined in the Holy book of the Muslims, from the day of its creation, and thus offer sufficient expectation of compliance and accountability in the event of violation.

There is no doubt that the correct teaching of the rules of combat in Islamic *Sharīʿah* could assist in instilling self-interest in accountability. In this regard, we have seen that *Sharīʿah* is more concerned with preventative measures that control personal ethics based in beliefs and convictions. Further, it is clear that Islamic *Sharīʿah* does not give much emphasis on which jurisdiction would address serious violations of the Islamic law of armed conflict; the emphasis is that the Almighty's orders must be respected and upheld, whether by a military or civil apparatus. Thus, Islam looks at war from its moral aspect. Islamic moral reasoning plays a great role during wartime activities. This moral argument, derived from Islamic literature and culture, may, at the end of the day, be a compelling rhetoric

---

[91] Bassiouni, 2014, p. 147, see *supra* note 33.

in increasing military self-interest in accountability. The various examples highlighted in this chapter demonstrate that this approach forms one of the very strong incentives for accountability in the Islamic world.

While the concepts enshrined in Islamic *Sharī'ah* could play a great role in increasing military self-interest in accountability for core international crimes, they do not have the same effect on *jihādi* extremists who abuse the interpretation of Islamic provisions. Unfortunately, these extremist groups use key norms of Islam as a pretext to justify their violent acts and politically manipulate the religion to serve their own goals. They attribute to the *Qur'ān* what it does not preach and take the Prophet's words out of context, thus investing them with the worst of meanings – violence and savagery – to justify their acts of violence. It will require coherent efforts to deconstruct the erroneous thought methodology of these groups.

Against their advocacy, this chapter has shown that *jihād* is never to be fought solely or recognised as unrestrained killing of the enemies and should not even imply warfare. In contrast to the views that disrupt the real teaching of Islamic *Sharī'ah*, Islamic religious beliefs could be used as an incentive to prosecute and try core international crimes. The presumption is that if Muslim states are able to see the compatibility of the law of armed conflict with Islamic *Sharī'ah*, they will come to realise that enforcing accountability also serves to uphold religious teachings. However, the discussion has also exposed a lacuna in the current international justice system, which is the failure of that system to prosecute the crimes of various insurgency groups operating, particularly in the Middle East and North Africa.

Notwithstanding this conclusion, and as Islamic *Sharī'ah* has a remarkable impact on the legal and justice systems in the Muslim and Arab nations, it is imperative to rely on these principles to increase military self-interest in accountability in those nations. Only by adhering to and raising awareness of the genuine beliefs and values of Islam could we defeat false assumptions associated with Islamic *Sharī'ah*, making sure that those responsible for war crimes and other serious crimes affecting the civilian population are held accountable and to deter the commission of further atrocities in that region.

There is an ongoing call in Egypt to renew the religious discourse. I am with this approach, which seeks to address the sources of violence advocated by extremists through clarifying the rules of Islamic *Sharī'ah*. Contemporary Muslim scholars across the political spectrum should continue the quest for a realistic ethics of war within the Islamic tradition that could apply to ongoing conflicts in the Muslim and Arab nations.

10

The Interest of States in Accountability for Sexual Violence in Armed Conflicts: A Case Study of Comfort Women of the Second World War

Kiki Anastasia Japutra*

The term 'comfort women' or *ianfu* (also *jugun ianfu* or military comfort women) refers to hundreds of thousands of women recruited to serve the Japanese military as sex workers during the Second World War.[1] An estimated 80 per cent were Koreans while the rest comprised women from China, Southeast Asia, Taiwan and the Pacific region. To facilitate this practice, military installations known as so-called comfort stations were established all over Asia, in territories where Japanese troops were deployed.

The first military comfort station was established in Shanghai in 1932, at the time of the Shanghai Incident.[2] General Okamura Yasuji, the deputy Chief of Staff of the Shanghai Expeditionary Army, described the initial objective of this station as follows:

---

*   **Kiki Anastasia Japutra** is a Research Assistant at the Norwegian Centre for Human Rights.

[1]   Some have argued that, because the term *jugun ianfu* (literally, military-accompanying comfort women) was not used prior to the end of the Second World War, the entire comfort women phenomenon is a myth. However, military documents of the time refer to *ianfu* (comfort women), *gun ianjo jugyo-fu* (women working at military comfort stations) and *gun ianjo* (military comfort stations). Therefore, it is not inaccurate to refer to women confined in comfort stations set up for Japanese troops as *jugun ianfu* or *Nihon-gun ianfu* (the Japanese military's comfort women). Center for Research and Documentation on Japan's War Responsibility, "Appeal on the Issue of Japan's Military 'Comfort Women'", 23 February 2007, p. 1.

[2]   The Shanghai Incident was triggered by the detonation of the South Manchuria Railway track in Liutiaohu in northeast China (Manchuria) on 18 September 1931, an event known as the Manchuria or Mukden Incident. The explosion was made to seem as if it were the work of Chinese dissidents, thereby providing a reason for Japan to initiate war against China. In January 1932, the Japanese Imperial Army opened hostilities in Shanghai, an assault that became known as the January 28 Incident or First Shanghai Incident. Yoshimi Yoshiaki, *Comfort Women: Sexual Slavery in Japanese Military during World War II*, Columbia University Press, New York, 2000, p. 43.

> To my shame, I am a founder of the comfort women system. In 1932 when the China incident occurred, a few rapes were reported. Then I as Vice-Chief of the Staff of the Shanghai Expeditionary Army followed the practice of the Navy and requested of the Governor of Nagasaki Prefecture to send a group of comfort women. I was pleased that no rapes were committed afterward.[3]

In a document from late 1938, entitled "In Regard to the Current State of Regulations on Private Prostitution in the Concession and the Regulation of Special Prostitutes Reserved for Japanese Citizens in Shanghai during 1938", the Consulate General of Shanghai remarked:

> With the great increase in military personnel stationed in the area due to the sudden outbreak of the Shanghai Incident, the navy established naval comfort stations as a mean to aid in supporting the comfort of those troops and those stations have continued to operate up to the present.[4]

Japanese military expansion in Asia was followed by an increasing number of soldiers deployed to different parts of the region. This sudden increase in the number of soldiers created problems as the number of sex workers taken from Japan could no longer satisfy the demands of the Japanese military which numbered some two million soldiers.[5] The comfort women initially comprised Japanese prostitutes recruited in Japan on a voluntary basis. The shortage of sex workers forced Japanese military leaders to resort to the recruitment of local women, whose participation was mostly involuntary. The method of recruitment varied from coercion and abduction to deception, through which most women were recruited on the basis they would be employed as nurses or factory workers without any knowledge that they would be forced to serve the military as comfort women.

This chapter addresses two sets of questions. First, international and domestic tribunals have been reluctant to address the issue of comfort women despite the clear evidence and testimony that have been presented.

---

[3] The Women's International War Crimes Tribunal for the Trial of Japan's Military Sexual Slavery ('Women's Tribunal'), *The Prosecutors and the Peoples of the Asia-Pacific Region v. Hirohito Emperor Showa [et al.]*, Case No. PT-2000-1-T, Judgment, 4 December 2001, para. 142.

[4] Yoshiaki, 2000, p. 44, see *supra* note 2.

[5] Women's Tribunal, 2001, para. 786, see *supra* note 3.

What are the possible reasons for the reluctance to address this issue? Second, has the Japanese government shown any indication of self-interest in conducting prosecutions? If not, why should such accountability of Japanese perpetrators be in the interest of Japan? In a broader context, why should it be in the interest of states to prosecute?

10.1. The Practice of Comfort Women in Japanese-Occupied Territories

The comfort system was established by recruiting hundreds of thousands of women to serve the Japanese military as sex slaves during the Second World War. Evidence in the form of documents, the testimony of survivors and admissions by the state of Japan makes it clear that comfort stations existed everywhere Japanese troops were present, including on the frontlines, and that the women had no ability to refuse sexual demands.[6]

The comfort stations were initially established to serve the following objectives: to suppress anti-Japanese sentiment among civilians due to rape committed by members of the Japanese Imperial Army; to prevent the spread of venereal diseases; and to prevent the infiltration of spies. It was a general trend in the Japanese Imperial forces that looting and rape, during combat operations in particular, were not only tolerated but even encouraged by many commanders as a means of arousing the fighting spirit of their men.[7] As Shannon Heit notes:

> [T]he rape of the enemy's women is considered as the conquering of the enemy's property, the rightful booty for the victor and the most humiliating symbol of defeat for the opposition.[8]

---

[6] *Ibid.*, para. 789.

[7] Until it was revised, the Japanese Imperial Army Criminal Law, Article 86(2) regarded rape as a secondary crime punishable by between seven years' and life imprisonment. However, only a small number of soldiers were convicted for rape under this code of conduct each year. On 20 February 1942, the law was revised to acknowledge rape as a single major criminal offence punishable by imprisonment of between one year and life. However, the reason for this revision was not because rape constituted a crime against humanity, but mainly because it brought "shame" to the Japanese Empire. Yuki Tanaka, *Japan's Comfort Women: Sexual Slavery and Prostitution during World War II and the US Occupation*, Routledge, London, 2002, pp. 28–29.

[8] Shannon Heit, "Waging Sexual Warfare: Case Studies of Rape Warfare Used by the Japanese Imperial Army during World War II", in *Women's Studies International Forum*, 2009, vol. 32, no. 5, p. 364.

The frequent rape of civilians provoked resistance among civilians of the occupied territories, causing Japanese military leaders to initiate the establishment of the comfort facilities. It was considered to be more convenient to have females locked up in buildings designed to sexually service large numbers of men than for men to have to take the time, energy and risks necessary to go out and locate, rape and then possibly kill women to cover up their crimes.[9] In principle, what was regarded as necessary to prevent rape was to provide physical and mental nourishment within the military that could enhance the working spirit of the soldiers and prevent undesirable conduct at the same time. But the military comfort stations failed to serve their stated purposes – widespread sexual abuses against women persisted in the occupied territories.

It was also argued that rape prevention was intended only to disguise the real objective, which was not to protect civilians but to protect soldiers from rapes of 'unknowns' who might transfer venereal diseases to soldiers and Japanese citizens.[10] Military leaders feared the spread of disease could potentially create massive public health problems back in Japan once the war ended, and the regulated system of comfort stations would prevent such a pandemic.[11] Contrary to the primary assumption, the spread of venereal diseases did not only come from the rapes, but also the failure to maintain control over the soldiers' health and hygiene. Ironically, the comfort stations caused the venereal disease rate to increase among both 'comfort women' and soldiers instead of reducing it.

The last reason given for the establishment of the comfort system was security. Japanese military leaders believed that spies could easily infiltrate private brothels and that prostitutes could be recruited as spies.[12] Contrary to this argument, documents reveal the existence of three types of facilities for sex slaves: those directly run by Japanese military authorities; those run by civilians but essentially set up and controlled by Japanese military authorities; and those that were mainly private facilities but

---

[9] Kelly Dawn Askin, *War Crimes against Women: Prosecution in International War Crimes Tribunals*, Martinus Nijhoff Publishers, The Hague, 1997, p. 81

[10] Tanaka, 2002, p. 30, see *supra* note 7; Yoshiaki, 2000, p. 47, see *supra* note 2; Askin, 1997, p. 80, see *supra* note 9; and Women's Tribunal, 2001, para. 537, see *supra* note 3.

[11] Tanaka, 2002, p. 30, see *supra* note 7.

[12] *Ibid.*

with some priority for military use.[13] The fact that military authorities did not have complete control over the comfort stations used by Japanese soldiers negated the security argument over their establishment.

At the end of war, the Japanese army abandoned the comfort stations and the comfort women were left to fend for themselves.[14] Many victims of war, such as the comfort women, are still alive though very elderly. Many live under miserable conditions due to trauma and poverty, and suffer the after-effects of continuous violence without receiving proper aid and justice.[15] Survivors have reported serious and continuing medical and psychological problems due to being treated as sex slaves; most having been unable or unwilling to marry or have children and many having no family to support them.[16] In the case histories of the comfort women, physical afflictions such as sexually transmitted diseases, uterine diseases, hysterectomies, sterility and mental illnesses (including nervous diseases, depression and speech impediments) stand out.[17]

Many of these women were not willing to report crimes due to the shame that they and their families had to bear. The guilt of rape does not belong to the perpetrators but the victims themselves. A woman who experienced rape, especially in societies (such as those in Asia) where virginity is considered as a standard of measurement of the value of a woman, is viewed as dirty and worthless by society, is blamed for her inability to protect her chastity or in some cases is accused of inviting the rapes to occur. Reporting sexual violence means degrading a woman's own dignity and exposing the entire family to shame and social prejudice. Many former comfort women were subjected to social discrimination and family isolation.[18] For these reasons, most comfort women chose to live in isolation while refusing to marry due to their traumatic years of continuous

---

[13]   Karen Parker and Jennifer F. Chew, "The *Jugun Ianfu* System", in Roy L. Brooks (ed.), *When Sorry Isn't Enough: The Controversy over Apologies and Reparations for Human Injustice*, New York University Press, New York, 1999, p. 96.

[14]   Women's Tribunal, 2001, para. 362, see *supra* note 3; and Yoshiaki, 2000, pp. 192–93, see *supra* note 2.

[15]   See generally The Executive Committee International Public Hearing (ed.), *War Victimization and Japan: International Public Hearing Report*, Toho Shuppan, Osaka, 1993.

[16]   Women's Tribunal, 2001, para. 97, see *supra* note 3; and Yoshiaki, 2000, pp. 192–97, see *supra* note 2.

[17]   Yoshiaki, 2000, p. 193, see *supra* note 2.

[18]   *Ibid.*, p. 196.

violence. Memories of being a comfort woman were left behind as a dark past that each woman wishes to forget.

10.2. The Japanese Government's Political Responses to Allegations of Systematic Practice of Comfort Women

Until the early 1990s, the Japanese government continued to deny its involvement in the establishment and management of the comfort system. The Japanese government insisted that only private operators recruited comfort women, a position maintained until documents surfaced in the early 1990s that directly implicated the role of government and military officials.[19] In June 1990 the Japanese government grudgingly acknowledged that the comfort system had indeed existed, but still maintained that they bore no imprimatur of government.[20] It was the first comfort women lawsuit that same year – soon followed by other lawsuits and redress movements demanding a formal apology and reparations from the state of Japan – that succeeded in forcing the Japanese government to take notice of the issue.

Documents related to the wartime comfort women, previously claimed to be non-existent, were successfully retrieved by Professor Yoshimi Yoshiaki of Chuo University from the Library of the National Institute for Defence Studies attached to the Defence Agency in 1992, and these implicated both government and military agencies in the comfort women scheme.[21] The discovery and publication of these documents finally forced the Japanese government to issue an apology the same year. The Prime Minister Miyazawa Kiichi expressed his regrets and repeated this apology to the South Korean President in the National Assembly on 16 January 1992, five days after the publication of Yoshimi's findings in the Japanese newspaper *Asahi Shinbun*.[22]

On 6 July 1992 the Chief Cabinet Secretary Kato Koichi made a formal statement that admitted the involvement of the Japanese govern-

---

[19] Roy L. Brooks, "What Form of Redress?", in Brooks, 1999, p. 88, see *supra* note 13.

[20] David Boling, "Mass Rape, Enforced Prostitution, and the Japanese Imperial Army: Japan Eschews International Legal Responsibility?", in *Occasional Papers/Reprints Series in Contemporary Asian Studies*, 1995, no. 3, p. 14.

[21] George Hicks, "The Comfort Women Redress Movement", in Brooks, 1999, pp. 117–18, see *supra* note 13.

[22] *Ibid.*

ment "in the establishment of the comfort stations, the control of those who recruited 'comfort women', the construction and reinforcement of comfort facilities, the management and surveillance of comfort stations, the hygiene maintenance in comfort stations and among 'comfort women', and the issuance of identification as well as other documents to those who were related to comfort stations".[23] Following Kato's statement, the Japanese government released a report of the findings of a government investigation and document survey entitled "On the Issue of Wartime Comfort Women", issued by the Cabinet Councillor's Office of External Affairs on 4 August 1993. The report focused on the following points:

1. The comfort stations were established in response to the request of the military authorities at the time.

2. The objectives for their establishment were to prevent anti-Japanese sentiments as a result of rapes and other actions against civilians, to prevent diseases and espionage.

3. The widespread nature of the comfort stations in Japanese-occupied territories over a long period of time and the existence of a great number of comfort women.

4. The direct and indirect involvement of the Japanese military in the establishment and management of the comfort stations.

5. The enforced movement, deprivation of freedom and misery that the comfort women endured.

6. The coercive method of recruitment of the comfort women against their will.

The statement of the Chief Cabinet Secretary Kono Yohei further elaborated upon this report on the same day:

> Undeniably, this was an act, with the involvement of the military authorities of the day, that severely injured the honor and dignity of many women. The Government of Japan would like to take this opportunity once again to extend its sincere apologies and remorse to all those, irrespective of

---

[23] Larry Niksch, "Japanese Military's 'Comfort Women' System", Congressional Research Service Memorandum, 3 April 2007, p. 11.

place of origin, who suffered immeasurable pain and incurable physical and psychological wounds as comfort women.[24]

Through Kono's statement, the government finally acknowledged the military's involvement in the comfort system, as well as the coercion and other forceful methods used to obtain and recruit comfort women.

In 1995 the Prime Minister Tomiichi Murayama established the Asian Women's Fund, which aimed to provide reparations for former comfort women as a form of atonement and remorse. The organisation's undertakings included:

1. To raise funds from the private sector as a means to enact the Japanese people's atonement for former comfort women.

2. To support those who conduct medical and/or welfare projects and other similar projects which are of service to former comfort women through the use of government funds and others.

3. When these projects are implemented, to express once again the nation's sentiment of sincere remorse and apology to the former comfort women.

4. To collate historical documents on 'comfort women' as a source of the lessons of history.[25]

The majority of the former comfort women refused to accept this atonement money, arguing that this was not a formal atonement since the funding came from private sources and not from government itself. Experts have noted that most of the victims in the Philippines, Taiwan, South Korea and Indonesia refused to accept money from the Asian Women's Fund. Five Filipina comfort women who accepted money re-

---

[24] Ministry of Foreign Affairs of Japan, "Statement by the Chief Cabinet Secretary Yohei Kono on the Result of the Study on the Issue of 'Comfort Women'", 4 August 1993 (https://www.legal-tools.org/doc/cb4732/).

[25] The statement of the objectives of the establishment of the Asian Women's Fund was made by Chief Cabinet Secretary Kozo Igarashi in June 1995. See "Japan's Official Responses to Reparations", in Brooks, 1999, p. 129. The amount offered to each person was ¥ 2 million (about USD 17,000) for a total 285 former comfort women in the Philippines, South Korea and Taiwan. In addition, ¥ 700 million (about USD 5.8 million) has been given to support a medical and welfare project, ¥ 255 million (about USD 2.12 million) for a project to help former comfort women in the Netherlands and ¥ 380 million (about USD 3.2 million) for social welfare services in Indonesia. See Ministry of Foreign Affairs of Japan, "Recent Policy of the Government of Japan on the Issue known as 'Comfort Women'" (https://www.legal-tools.org/doc/ddbcdb/).

---

turned a letter of apology from Prime Minister Hashimoto Ryutaro because it was not a government admission of its official accountability for the abuses committed against them by the military.[26] They said they wanted "honour and dignity, not charity money".[27]

In March 2007 another controversial statement was issued by Prime Minister Abe Shinzo, in which he in effect claimed that there was no evidence of coercion in the recruitment of comfort women. Nakagawa Shoichi, then head of the ruling Liberal Democratic Party's policy-making body in the parliamentary Diet, supported Abe's claim:

> [T]here currently is no evidence that permits us to declare the military, the strongest expression of state authority, took women away and forced them to do things against their will.[28]

Abe's statements drew both support and criticism from within Japan. Some of the statements also drew criticism from the United States and a warning from the US Ambassador to Japan, Thomas Schieffer, that attempts to alter the earlier Kono Statement and revise historical accounts of the comfort system would have a negative impact in the United States.[29] The statements on coercion were later revised, providing that "[t]here probably was not anyone [comfort women] who followed that path because they wanted to follow it. In the broad sense, there was coercion".[30] Together with the withdrawal of the denial of acts of coercion committed during military occupation, Abe affirmed that he stood for the Kono Statement and expressed heartfelt sympathy and sincere apologies to the women who suffered immeasurable pain and hardship.[31] A chro-

---

[26] Committee of Experts on the Application of Conventions and Recommendations (CEACR), "Individual Observation concerning Convention No. 29, Forced Labour, 1930 Japan (ratification: 1932)" (https://www.legal-tools.org/doc/c6283a/).

[27] Women's Tribunal, 2001, para. 986, see *supra* note 3.

[28] Niksch, 2007, p. 2, see *supra* note 23.

[29] For criticisms by the former Assistant Secretary of Defense, Kurt Campbell, and the former National Security Council Asian Affairs Director, Michael Green, see Yoichi Kato, "U.S. Experts Concerned about Prime Minister Abe's Remarks about Comfort Women Issue", in *Asahi Shimbun*, 10 March 2007. For Schieffer's remarks, see Chris Nelson, "The Nelson Report", 12 March 2007, p. 3, cited in Niksch, 2007, p. 3, *supra* note 23.

[30] Martin Fackler, "No Apology for Sex Slavery, Japan's Prime Minister Says", in *New York Times*, 6 March 2007.

[31] "Press Guidance Statement of the Japanese Ministry of Foreign Affairs", 2007, cited in Niksch, 2007, p. 5, see *supra* note 23.

---

nology of Japanese political responses regarding war crimes atrocities, including the issue of comfort women, can be found in Appendix 1.

10.3. Comfort Women as a Crime Against Humanity in International Law

To argue that a crime as egregious in nature as the comfort women system should not remain unprosecuted, it is necessary to determine the gravity of the crime involved and whether it satisfies the necessary requirements to be prosecuted under international law. The first question that should be raised is whether the crime of the comfort women system was sufficiently established as a matter of international law during the commission of the crime to satisfy the requirements of *nullum crimen sine lege*.

The Japanese government has argued in other contexts that rape during armed conflict was not prohibited by the regulations annexed to the Hague Convention No. IV of 1907 or by applicable customary international norms in force at the time the acts were committed.[32] It has also argued that the 1929 Geneva Convention is not applicable because Japan was not a signatory and that the Convention was not evidence of custom.[33] Another argument that may be raised is that the term 'crimes against humanity' had only been recognised during the Nuremberg and Tokyo Tribunals, and the definition and recognition of rape and sexual enslavement as crimes against humanity were not established until the International Criminal Tribunal for the former Yugoslavia ('ICTY') Judgment in the *Foča* case (2001). Based on these arguments, Japan has considered the actions committed during the period from 1937 to 1945 as not constituting a crime under international law based on the principle of non-retroactivity.

Despite the absence of the term 'crimes against humanity' prior to the Nuremberg and Tokyo Tribunals, the concept of crimes against humanity had existed in international legal sources before the first comfort stations were created. The first 'official' international use of the concept dates back to 24 May 1915, when the governments of France, Great Britain and Russia issued a joint declaration condemning the deportation and systematic extermination of the Armenian population of the Ottoman Em-

---

[32] Women's Tribunal, 2001, para. 52, see *supra* note 3.
[33] *Ibid.*

pire and denouncing these acts as constituting "new crimes against humanity and civilisation" for which all members of the Turkish government would be held responsible together with its agents implicated in the massacres.[34] In the 1919 report of the Commission on the Responsibility of the Authors of War and on Enforcement of Penalties, the majority of members concluded that the German Empire and its allies carried out the war "by barbarous or illegitimate methods in violation of the established laws and customs of war and the elementary laws of humanity" and "all persons belonging to enemy countries [...] who have been guilty of offences against the laws and customs of war or the laws of humanity are liable for criminal prosecution".[35] Even though the statement may neither legislatively create new crimes nor create customary international law, the aggravating nature of crimes against humanity had been acknowledged prior to the Second World War.

With regard to sexual slavery, Japan appears to have declared the prohibition of sexual slavery as early as 1872 in a case in which it convicted Peruvian traders of the crime of slavery, and, pursuant to a representative sample of states, Japan included the prohibition of slavery in its national law in 1944.[36] Among the international slavery prohibition treaties concluded prior to 1937, the only treaty found to have been ratified by Japan at the time was the International Convention for the Suppression of the Traffic in Women and Children (1921), which was ratified in 1925.[37]

---

[34] Sévane Garibian, "Crime against Humanity, Online Encyclopedia of Mass Violence", 19 June 2008, available at http://www.massviolence.org/Crime-against-Humanity, last accessed on 5 April 2015.

[35] Commission on the Responsibility of the Authors of War and on Enforcement of Penalties, "Report Presented to the Preliminary Peace Conference, March 29, 1919", in *American Journal of International* Law, 1920, vol. 14, nos. 1/2, pp. 113–14; Vincent Sautenet, "Crimes Against Humanity and the Principles of Legality: What Could the Potential Offender Expect?", in *Murdoch University Electronic Journal of Law*, 2000, vol. 7, no. 1, available at http://www.murdoch.edu.au/elaw/issues/v7n1/sautenet71_text.html, last accessed on 5 April 2015.

[36] Prior to 1944 the crime of enslavement was subsumed under applicable crimes of kidnapping and forcible confinement under Japanese criminal law. Gay J. McDougall, Special Rapporteur, "Contemporary Forms of Slavery: Systematic Rape, Sexual Slavery and Slavery-like Practices during Armed Conflict", Economic and Social Council, Commission on Human Rights, Geneva, 1998, E/CN.4/Sub.2/1998/13, paras. 13–14.

[37] Reservation, however, was made not to include Korea, Taiwan, the leased Territory of Kwantung, the Japanese portion of Saghalien Island and Japan's mandated territory in the South Seas. See M. Cherif Bassiouni, "Enslavement as an International Crime", in *New York University Journal of International Law and Politics*, 1991, vol. 23, p. 445.

Unfortunately, under Article 14 of the Convention, colonial powers could exclude their colonies from the provisions that prohibited further trafficking in women and children, for which Japan took full advantage of in its dealings with Korea (claiming that Korea was a colony).[38] The 1926 Slavery Convention, although not ratified by Japan, has been regarded as customary international law as of 1937 and the abolition of slavery amounted to *jus cogens*.[39] In other words, although Japan was not party to the 1926 Convention, there was no excuse for disregarding the prohibition, and any act amounting to slavery (such as the comfort women system) should be considered as criminal under international law even before the establishment of the comfort stations.

The prohibition of rape and forced prostitution was prominently expressed in the 1863 Lieber Code, which explicitly claimed that the act of violence committed against persons in the invaded country "are prohibited under the penalty of death, or such other severe punishment as may seem adequate for the gravity of the offense".[40] Rape and sexual slavery are also delineated as a form of attack on the society in Article 46 of the Hague Convention of 1907 regarding the protection and respect on "family honour and rights".[41] Although not explicitly mentioned in the provision, such an interpretation can be based on the Martens Clause, which stands for the proposition that even though positive law fails to prohibit certain inhumane acts, such acts can be legitimately treated as crimes if their character is accepted as criminal in nature, but the offending conduct is not necessarily explicitly named.[42] The interpretation of "family honour and rights" in the context of rape and sexual violence is strengthened by the acceptance of the Hague Convention as customary international law governing the laws of war and by other law of war sources that confirm the international prohibition on the rape of civilians during armed con-

---

[38] Joseph P. Nearey, "Seeking Reparations in the New Millennium: Will Japan Compensate the 'Comfort Women' of World War II?", in *Temple International and Comparative Law Journal*, 2001, vol. 15, no. 1, p. 130.

[39] McDougall, 1998, para. 14, see *supra* note 36.

[40] Instruction for the Government of Armies of the United States in the Field (Lieber Code), 24 April 1863, Article 44.

[41] The concept of family honour includes the rights of women in a family not to be subjected to the humiliating practice of rape. McDougall, 1998, para. 17, see *supra* note 36.

[42] Women's Tribunal, 2001, para. 520, see *supra* note 3.

flict.[43] The comfort system was, by nature, a way to dehumanise and humiliate the citizens of states colonised by Japan due to the role of women as family and community property in a patriarchal order.[44] Considering the existence of provisions referring to the elements of crime contained in the practice of the comfort system, though not explicitly mentioning 'crimes against humanity', it can be concluded that the concept existed by 1937, which is relevant when assessing the requirements of the *nullum crimen sine lege* principle.

Having established how the principle of legality may be satisfied, the next examination should focus on the requirements of 'crimes against humanity'. The Women's International War Crimes Tribunal for the Trial of Japan's Military Sexual Slavery ('Women's Tribunal'), conducted in 2001, enlisted the following threshold to determine whether particular acts constituted crimes against humanity from 1937 to 1945: the prohibited acts must be committed (1) before or during war, (2) as part of a large-scale or systematic attack committed against a civilian population, and (3) in connection with war crimes or crimes against peace.[45] The nexus to armed conflict is no longer required as a matter of customary international law today, but the Women's Tribunal accepted the assertion of this requirement as an essential condition for crimes against humanity to be justiciable in the Tokyo Tribunal, and thus be applied in this case.[46] Evidence suggest that all acts of rapes and sexual slavery committed as part of the comfort system were committed before and during the war in China and the expanded war in the Asia-Pacific region.[47] The first requirement has therefore been satisfied.

With regard to the second requirement, the practice of comfort women satisfies both the "large-scale" and "systematic" requirements, although the element is disjunctive – the fulfilment of one criterion is deemed sufficient for crimes against humanity. The exact number of comfort women, as well as other relevant facts, is impossible to determine accurately since most relevant documents were either hidden or destroyed at the end of the war. Estimates, however, were made based on evidence that still exists. According to the Japanese military plan devised in July 1941,

---

[43] McDougall, 1998, para. 28, see *supra* note 36.
[44] Heit, 2009, p. 364, see *supra* note 8.
[45] Women's Tribunal, 2001, para. 534, see *supra* note 3.
[46] *Ibid.*, para. 530.
[47] *Ibid.*, para. 535.

20,000 comfort women were required for every 800,000 Japanese soldiers, or one woman for every 40 soldiers.[48] There were 3.5 million Japanese soldiers sent to China and Southeast Asia during the war, and therefore, by this calculation, an estimated 90,000 women were mobilised.[49] Another estimate comes from the discovery of a memo in the operations journal of Setsuzo Kinbara, chief of the Medical Affairs Section in the Medical Affairs Department of the War Ministry, which mentioned "1 woman for 100 soldiers".[50] Records also suggest that comfort stations were established in every territory where Japanese soldiers were present throughout the Asia-Pacific region. The number of comfort women recruited during the Second World War, as well as the spread of comfort stations in every territory where Japanese soldiers were present, clearly indicates the large scale of the system.

It is also evident that the practice of the comfort system was methodically planned, highly regulated, and invariably sustained by the Japanese military and civilian authorities wherever the troops were stationed.[51] The number of women acquired was so enormous and the pressure to expand the system was so strong that the crimes involved had to have been known to high-level participants of the system, as well as to those who oversaw its maintenance and the continuing supply of women.[52] The evidence suggests that the comfort stations provided food supplies (however minimal), condoms, medical personnel, and often dangerous 'treatments' for sexually transmitted diseases and pregnancy.[53] The costs involved in procuring, transporting and maintaining the system had to have been substantial and required a significant allocation of resources.[54]

Substantive evidence of the pervasive responsibility for comfort station policy-making and operation at all levels of the government hierarchy was evident in the recruitment memorandum sent on 4 March 1938 by an

---

[48] Tanaka, 2002, p. 31, see *supra* note 8.

[49] *Ibid.*

[50] Digital Museum: The Comfort Women Issue and the Asian Women's Fund, "Number of Comfort Stations and 'Comfort Women'", available at http://www.awf.or.jp/e1/facts-07.html, last accessed on 15 March 2010.

[51] Women's Tribunal, 2001, para. 538, see *supra* note 3.

[52] *Ibid.*, para. 797.

[53] *Ibid.*, para. 789.

[54] *Ibid.*

adjutant general in the Japanese War Ministry to the chiefs of staff of the North China Area Army and the Central China Expeditionary Forces. The memorandum provides an insight into the military's efforts to disguise the coercive nature of the comfort system, the complicity of local authorities, and the military supervision of and involvement with private actors in the recruitment process.[55] It provides compelling evidence that the Ministry of War was aware of the coercive methods used to force women into the system. The Women's Tribunal found that the Ministry of War failed to give clear instructions ensuring that the women agreed to provide sexual services, which demonstrates that the ministry knowingly authorised forcible and coercive methods of recruitment in acquiring women for the comfort stations.[56] It is evident that the comfort system was not only approved by but conducted under the direct instruction of the state (represented by the Ministry of War) as a means to achieve its military objectives. The comfort system was, in essence, "systematic" state-sanctioned rape and enslavement.[57]

The final threshold of "connection with war crimes or crimes against peace" is satisfied by observing the main objectives of the establishment of the comfort system: to prevent rape of the locals, to prevent the spread of venereal diseases, to prevent espionage and to increase the spirit of the soldiers. It can be concluded that the basic objective of the establishment was to support Japan's war effort, and many of the crimes were connected to Japan's unlawful war of aggression. The comfort women were treated as essential supplies, as the 'booty' of war, and were considered a necessary cog in the wheel of the Japanese war machine.[58] The requirement of the connection with war crimes or crimes against peace must therefore be considered satisfied. The Japanese military committed crimes against humanity.

10.4. Legal Proceedings Regarding the Issue of Comfort Women

10.4.1. International Tribunals

The International Military Tribunal for the Far East ('IMTFE') was established in 1946 to try Japanese leaders for crimes against peace (Class A),

---

[55]   *Ibid.*, para. 92.

[56]   *Ibid.*, para. 95.

[57]   *Ibid.*, para. 798.

[58]   *Ibid.*, para. 542.

war crimes (Class B) and crimes against humanity (Class C) committed during the Second World War.[59] The Tribunal was created on similar lines to the Nuremberg Tribunal, which was empowered to prosecute international crimes. The IMTFE was distinct due to the existence of the crime of conspiracy for which Japanese military leaders were tried for the acts committed on the basis of a common plan. Statements relevant to the comfort women issue were presented a number of times, but the Tribunal failed to identify it as a distinct type of crime.[60] Despite of the gravity of the crime involved and evidence indicating systematic sexual slavery, the IMTFE failed to address this issue and the egregious crime remains unprosecuted.[61]

The only known war crimes trial which succeeded in prosecuting rape and forced prostitution was the Batavia Military Tribunal in 1948. It tried the case of 35 Dutch comfort women against 12 Japanese army officers on the grounds of having committed war crimes in defiance of the laws and customs of war in the Dutch East Indies in 1944.[62] The Batavia Tribunal succeeded in prosecuting the perpetrators, with one of the accused condemned to death and others sentenced to imprisonment ranging from two to 15 years. However, the documents that state the names of both victims and the accused have been sealed, and the archives of this proceeding are not scheduled to be opened until 2025.[63]

---

[59] University of Virginia Law Library, "The Tokyo War Crimes Tribunal: A Digital Exhibition", available at http://lib.law.virginia.edu/imtfe/tribunal, last accessed on 29 March 2015.

[60] The IMTFE Judgement notes: "[D]uring the period of Japanese occupation of Kweilin, they committed all kinds of atrocities such as rape and plunder. They recruited women labour on the pretext of establishing factories. They forced the women thus recruited into prostitution with Japanese troops". International Military Tribunal for the Far East, Judgment, Tokyo, 1 November 1948, para. 1021 (https://www.legal-tools.org/doc/28ddbd/).

[61] According to Judge B.V.A. Röling, the IMTFE did know of the comfort system and, despite the testimony at the IMTFE, the issue of comfort women was not raised when the Tribunal prosecuted war criminals. However, in the IMTFE judgment, the comfort women were mentioned briefly: "[...] forced women thus recruited into prostitution with Japanese troops". *Ibid*. See also Askin, 1997, pp. 85–86, *supra* note 9.

[62] Nina H.B. Jørgensen and Danny Friedmann, "Enforced Prostitution in International Law Through the Prism of the Dutch Temporary Courts Martial at Batavia", in Morten Bergsmo, CHEAH Wui Ling and YI Ping (eds.), *Historical Origins of International Criminal Law: Volume 2*, FICHL Publication Series no. 21, Torkel Opsahl Academic EPublisher, Brussels, 2014, pp. 331–54 (https://www.legal-tools.org/en/doc/7c217c/).

[63] Askin, 1997, pp. 85–86, see *supra* note 9.

10.4.2. Findings of the Women's International War Crimes Tribunal

With the continuous failure to address the comfort women issue, in December 2000 the Women's International War Crimes Tribunal on Japan's Military Sexual Slavery was convened through the efforts of non-governmental organisations throughout Asia to ensure some form of accountability for the aging former comfort women. The case was brought against Emperor Hirohito and the government of Japan. The Women's Tribunal found Emperor Hirohito "guilty of responsibility for rape and sexual slavery as a crime against humanity" and that the government of Japan has incurred state responsibility for the establishment and maintenance of the comfort system.[64] The judgment, however, has no legally binding effect and therefore failed to advance justice. However, the Women's Tribunal succeeded in placing enormous pressure on the Japanese government, and its findings are significant in laying a blueprint for future litigation against the Japanese government in real international tribunals or in the court system of other nations.[65]

10.4.3. Inter-State Litigation

On 18 September 2000 Hwang Geum Joo, a former comfort woman, filed the first and only lawsuit in the United States District Court of Columbia, claiming that "the actions of the Japanese government in establishing and maintaining the system of sexual slavery from 1932 until 1945 violated *jus cogens* norms of international law and are not subject to the defence of sovereign immunity".[66] The demands included: (1) to declare the Japanese government violated international treaties and customary law; (2) to declare that the Japanese government violated the Alien Tort Claims Act

---

[64] Nearey, 2001, p. 144, *supra* note 38.

[65] The judgment was appealed to the UN Sub-Commission on Human Rights and further referred in Resolution 16 (1999), which includes States' obligations, "to provide effective criminal penalties and compensation for unremedied violations", and states that such obligations cannot "be extinguished by peace treaty, peace agreement, amnesty or by any other means". See Sub-Commission on the Promotion and Protection of Human Rights, "Systematic Rape, Sexual Slavery and Slavery-like Practices", Resolution 1999/16, 33rd session, 26 August 1999, paras. 12–13.

[66] United States District Court for the District of Columbia, *Hwang Geum Joo, et al. v. Japan*, Case No. 00-CV-2233. See Memory and Reconciliation in the Asia-Pacific, "Comfort Women: U.S.: Hwang Geum Joo, et al. v. Japan", 18 September 2000 (https://www.legal-tools.org/doc/8ae55c/).

---

and prohibition against enforced prostitution and rape; (3) to direct the Japanese government to make available forthwith all documents or other records related to the operation of military rape camps and/or comfort women; (4) to award plaintiffs and the class compensatory and punitive damages arising out of the unlawful behaviour of the Japanese government; and (5) a jury trial on all issues. The plaintiff further filed a motion for declaratory judgment, arguing that Japanese conduct did not enjoy sovereign immunity, which was dismissed by the District Court.

On 27 April 2001, the US Department of Justice issued a Statement of Interest of the United States of America, which claimed that

> [t]he United States District Court for the District of Columbia had no jurisdiction over plaintiffs' claims due to Japan's sovereign immunity and by virtue of international obligations entered into by the United States and other nations with Japan at the close of World War II.[67]

The statement further argued that if individual plaintiffs were allowed to impose their interpretation of the 1951 San Francisco Peace Treaty on a piecemeal basis through litigation, this would have a potentially serious negative impact on US–Japan relations and could affect the United States' treaty relations globally by calling into question the finality of US commitments. The US government asserted that the individual interpretation of the treaty could have a serious impact on the stability of the East Asian region, especially given the tension between Japan, China and Korea. In August 2002, the plaintiffs appealed to the District Court to reverse its statement that Japan enjoys sovereign immunity for trafficking in women and slavery, and that the appellants' tort law claims are non-justiciable.[68] The appeal was again dismissed by the District Court which reclaimed that Japan is entitled to sovereign immunity and further argued that the courts of the United States are not authorised to hear the case. The case was petitioned to the US Supreme Court. On 21 February 2006, the Supreme Court denied it and closed the case.

---

[67] Memory and Reconciliation in the Asia-Pacific, "Comfort Women: U.S.", see *supra* note 66.

[68] *Ibid.*

10.4.4. Japanese Courts

In the 1990s, war crimes victims began filing lawsuits against the Japanese government. As of April 2010, there had been 10 lawsuits focusing specifically on Japanese military sexual slavery, and, among these, eight lawsuits are still pending (one at the district court level, five at the high court level and two before the Supreme Court) while two have been dismissed by the Supreme Court of Japan, thus exhausting all domestic remedies.[69] The lawsuits generally consist of Japan's violation of international treaties and the devastating situation in which comfort women were forced to live. The Japanese government denied all claims on the grounds that: (1) Japan is subject to sovereign immunity; (2) Japan has settled its war crimes compensation issues by signing the San Francisco Peace Treaty in 1951 and other bilateral treaties with the countries involved; (3) individual victims' claims for damages are not justified under international law; and (4) Japan has no legal obligation to compensate the victims due to the expiration of the 20-year statute of limitations.[70]

The first lawsuit was filed by Korean victims (including Kim Haksoon) in the Tokyo District Court on 6 December 1991, who demanded: (1) an official apology; (2) compensatory payment to survivors in lieu of full reparation (¥ 20 million for each victim or about USD 154,000); (3) a thorough investigation of their cases; (4) the revision of Japanese school textbooks identifying the comfort women issue as part of the colonial oppression of the Korean people; and (5) the building of a memorial museum.[71] The government responded to these demands by reversing the earlier claims that it had no responsibility regarding the comfort women issue, admitting its involvement in the system, and further recognised the sufferings of the victims.[72] The compensation demand, on the other hand, was

---

[69] Violence Against Women in War – Network Japan (VAWW-NET Japan), "Lawsuits against the Government of Japan Filed by the Survivors in Japanese Courts".

[70] Memory and Reconciliation in the Asia-Pacific, "Judicial Proceedings: Comfort Women", available at http://www.gwu.edu/~memory/data/judicial/comfortwomen.html, last accessed on 2 April 2015.

[71] Memory and Reconciliation in the Asia-Pacific, "Comfort Women: Japan", 6 December 1991, available at http://www.gwu.edu/~memory/data/judicial/comfortwomen_japan/haksun.html, last accessed on 2 April 2010.

[72] Ministry of Foreign Affairs of Japan, "Statement by Chief Cabinet Secretary Koichi Kato on the Issue of the so-called 'Wartime Comfort Women' from the Korean Peninsula", 6 July 1992 (https://www.legal-tools.org/doc/cb2016-1/).

dismissed on 26 March 2001 by the Tokyo District Court on the following grounds:

1. Individuals cannot exercise the rights or undertake the obligations provided by international law, and damages inflicted upon individuals are supposed to be dealt with the states they belong to.

2. Customary international law can only be established when the majority of states exercise a similar practice that becomes common practice in the international community.

3. The treaties – both ratified by Japan (including the Hague Conventions and the International Convention for the Suppression of the Traffic in Women and Children) and not ratified (but having achieved the status as customary law) did not provide any clause that can be interpreted as recognising the right of victimised individuals to make claims for compensation.

An appeal was made to the decision in March 2001 and was rejected by the Tokyo High Court on the grounds that the right to demand compensation had already expired. The plaintiff further brought the case to the Japanese Supreme Court but was again rejected on 29 November 2004.[73]

The second lawsuit was filed on 25 December 1992 with the Shimonoseki branch of the Yamaguchi District Court in Fukuoka prefecture against the Japanese government, in which 10 South Korean women demanded an official apology and a total of ¥ 564 million (USD 6.66 million) based on the State Redress Law.[74] This was the first time a Japanese court granted compensation to comfort women (¥ 300,000 or USD 2,800 to each of the three plaintiffs). The court admitted that Japan had neglected its legal duty to take measures to provide reparations for the wartime victims, and further declared the comfort women system a clear case of sexual and ethnic discrimination, as well as a violation of human rights. The court further stressed that the Japanese government had failed to enact a law to fully compensate the victims, and that Japan had a responsibility to stop the suffering of the former comfort women from intensifying. The lawsuit was appealed to the Hiroshima High Court on 1 May

---

[73] See the Japanese text of the Supreme Court's ruling upholding the Tokyo High Court (https://www.legal-tools.org/doc/fec7d9/).

[74] Memory and Reconciliation in the Asia-Pacific, "Pusan Comfort Women and Women's Labor Corps Members", 25 December 1992, available at http://www.gwu.edu/~memory/data/judicial/comfortwomen_japan/pusan.html, last accessed 2 April 2015.

1998, claiming that the amount awarded was an insult to women "who were treated lower than human beings".[75] The High Court rejected the appeal on the ground that the Japanese Constitution did not clearly state the government's obligation to introduce a law on compensation, and stated that the abduction of the comfort women was not a serious violation. An appeal was brought to the Supreme Court on 12 April 2001, but was again rejected on 25 March 2003, stating that the plaintiffs had insisted on technical matters that should not constitute an appeal to the highest court. The Court also nullified the 1998 ruling which had ordered the government to compensate the plaintiffs.

The third lawsuit was filed by 18 former comfort women from the Philippines with the Tokyo District Court on 2 April 1993, to seek ¥ 360 million and to have the comfort women issue mentioned in school textbooks.[76] The lawsuit was dismissed by the District Court on the following grounds:[77]

1. The 1907 Hague Convention only defined compensation obligations "between States, and did not provide for individual victims the right to seek compensation from a State", and no international common law existed that would support the plaintiffs' demand.

2. Even if the conduct of the Japanese military constituted a crime against humanity as the plaintiffs claimed, that fact alone did not offer a legal basis for obligating the Japanese government to compensate the victims through a civil proceeding.

3. The right to make claims had already lapsed under Japanese law since the case was brought before the court more than 20 years after the end of the Second World War, exceeding the statute of limitation.

4. Japan and the Philippines abandoned any claims for compensation from each other with Japan's payment of war reparations stipulated in the 1951 San Francisco Peace Treaty.

---

[75] Ibid.

[76] Memory and Reconciliation in the Asia-Pacific, "Filipino Comfort Women", 2 April 1993, available at http://www.gwu.edu/~memory/data/judicial/comfortwomen_japan/filipina.html, last accessed 3 April 2015.

[77] Ibid.

An appeal was made to the Tokyo High Court in December 2000, but was rejected on the same grounds. The case was finally closed after the failure to appeal to the Supreme Court of Japan.

On 3 April 1993, Song Shin-do filed a lawsuit with the Tokyo District Court against the Japanese government, seeking an official apology and ¥ 120 million (USD 1 million) in compensation.[78] The case was dismissed on the grounds that individuals had no right to seek damages for what a nation did to them, and further stated that Song's suffering could not be covered by the State Redress Law as she demanded, since the law was enacted in 1947 and thus did not cover what happened before that date.[79] An appeal was made to the Tokyo High Court but was dismissed, acknowledging Japan's legal responsibility had she sued years earlier. A further appeal made to the Supreme Court of Japan in December 2000 was also dismissed, stating that Japan had no legal obligation to pay reparations due to the expiration of the 20-year statute of limitation, which put an end to this case.

A fifth lawsuit was filed on 24 January 1994. The plaintiffs, consisting of eight Dutch citizens (seven men – one former prisoner of war and six civilians – and one former comfort women), filed a lawsuit with the Tokyo District Court demanding ¥ 2.45 million each (a total of USD 176,000) in compensation for being made into forced labour and tortured by Japanese soldiers in Indonesia, which was then under Dutch control.[80] The lawsuit stated that the Japanese Imperial Army's acts violated the Geneva Conventions of 1949, as well as other international agreements prohibiting the torture of prisoner of war ('POW') as well as women.[81] The court accepted the plaintiff's argument that they were ill-treated or driven into forced labour but rejected the demands for compensation, arguing that: (1) individuals have no right to seek reparations under international law, and (2) the issue of compensation for former Dutch POWs and

---

[78] Memory and Reconciliation in the Asia-Pacific, "Song Shin-Do", 3 April 1993, available at http://www.gwu.edu/~memory/data/judicial/comfortwomen_japan/Song_Shin-do.html, last accessed on 3 April 2015.

[79] *Ibid.*

[80] Memory and Reconciliation in the Asia-Pacific, "Dutch POWs and Civilian Detainees (including former Dutch comfort woman)", 25 January 1995, available at http://www.gwu.edu/~memory/data/judicial/comfortwomen_japan/Dutch.html, last accessed on 3 April 2015.

[81] *Ibid.*

civilian internees had been settled under the San Francisco Peace Treaty in 1951 and a bilateral protocol in 1956. The case was appealed to the Tokyo High Court in December 1998, but was dismissed in 2001 upholding the District Court's ruling. A final appeal was made in October 2001 to the Supreme Court of Japan but was dismissed in March 2004.

Two consecutive lawsuits were filed by Chinese war victims before the Tokyo District Court on 7 August 1995, demanding ¥ 220 million and official apologies for the atrocities committed during the 1937–1945 Sino-Japanese War, which included germ warfare experiments, sexual slavery and the Nanjing Massacre in 1937.[82] The claim was dismissed with no factual findings, stating that an individual had no right to sue a country for compensation and that the reparations issue was resolved by the Sino-Japanese Joint Communiqué issued on 29 September 1972. Both lawsuits were rejected by the Tokyo High Court on the grounds that the Japanese government has no responsibility and the statute of limitation had expired.[83] The appeal to the Supreme Court was also dismissed on the grounds that the 1972 Joint Communiqué bars Chinese individuals from seeking compensation.

Another lawsuit was made by Chinese plaintiffs on 23 February 1996, seeking an apology and compensation of ¥ 20 million each.[84] In March 2002, the case was dismissed on the same "individuals have no right to demand compensation from the state" argument. An appeal was made in March 2005, but the High Court upheld the ruling of the District Court. The court further asserted that the sexual assault committed against them was not systematically conducted or authorised by the Japanese government.[85] The further appeal to the Supreme Court was again rejected, suggesting that the issue of compensation could be settled outside the court.

On 30 October 1998, another lawsuit was filed before the Tokyo District Court by Chinese plaintiffs accusing the Japanese government of

---

[82] Memory and Reconciliation in the Asia-Pacific, "Chinese Comfort Women: (1st Group)", 7 August 1995, available at http://www.gwu.edu/~memory/data/judicial/comfortwomen _japan/Chinese%20%281st%20group%29.html, last accessed on 3 April 2015.

[83] *Ibid.*

[84] Memory and Reconciliation in the Asia-Pacific, "Chinese Comfort Women (2nd group)", 23 February 1996, available at http://www.gwu.edu/~memory/data/judicial/comfortwomen _japan/Chinese%20%282nd%20group%29.html, last accessed on 3 April 2015.

[85] *Ibid.*

failing to provide compensation, seeking a total of ¥ 200 million in damages.[86] Unlike other lawsuits, the claim was based on the allegation of systematic rape conducted from 1941 to 1943, in which young women were abused, raped and abducted by Japanese soldiers. The District Court dismissed the claim based on the application of the law (no legal requirement to compensate victims and the expiration of the statute of limitation). Nevertheless, it called for a legislative and administrative settlement with the plaintiffs. An appeal was made to the High Court on 31 March 2005, which was rejected by upholding the ruling of the Tokyo District Court. The final appeal to the Supreme Court was also rejected in November 2005.

On 14 July 1999, nine Taiwanese comfort women filed a lawsuit with the Tokyo District Court seeking compensation of ¥ 10 million (USD 84,000) each and an official apology from the Japanese government.[87] The claim was supported by the Ministry of Foreign Affairs in Taiwan, providing evidence of the enforced sexual labour of 766 Taiwanese comfort women. The case was dismissed with no factual findings. A further appeal was made in October 2002 to the Tokyo High Court (during which two of the nine women had died), but was rejected in February 2004, arguing that there is no legal procedure for compensation stipulated under the Japanese Constitution and that a decision to redress would go beyond the reach of existing law.[88] The appeal to the Supreme Court was rejected in 2005.

The last lawsuit was made by eight former comfort women who come from indigenous minorities in Hainan Island in China.[89] The lawsuit was filed with the Tokyo District Court on 26 July 2001, demanding a total of ¥ 24 million in compensation and an official, published apology from the Japanese government for the women's deprivation of honour and

---

[86]   Memory and Reconciliation in the Asia-Pacific, "Women from Shan-xi Province, China", 30 October 1998, available at http://www.gwu.edu/~memory/data/judicial/comfortwomen _japan/Shanxi.html, last accessed on 3 April 2015.

[87]   Memory and Reconciliation in the Asia-Pacific, "Taiwanese Comfort Women", 14 July 1999, available at http://www.gwu.edu/~memory/data/judicial/comfortwomen_japan/Tai wanese.html, last accessed on 3 April 2010.

[88]   *Ibid.*

[89]   Memory and Reconciliation in the Asia-Pacific, "Hainan Island Comfort Women", 16 July 2001, available at http://www.gwu.edu/~memory/data/judicial/comfortwomen_japan/hai nan.html, last accessed on 3 April 2015.

continuous post-traumatic stress disorder due to their experiences as comfort women. The District Court admitted the fact that these women were kidnapped and forced to work as sex slaves, but further ruled that their legal right for seeking compensation had expired.[90] An appeal to the Tokyo High Court in 2007 was dismissed based on the previous rulings that Chinese individuals had no legal right to sue the Japanese government.

10.5. Facts behind and Reasons for Failure in Accountability

10.5.1. The Tokyo Trials

During the Tokyo Trials, the major problem encountered by the IMTFE was the lack of evidence to establish guilt. When the Japanese government accepted unconditional surrender on 15 August 1945, it ordered the destruction of evidence by burning and concealment of documents in order to exempt the Emperor from responsibility and to protect state officials from incrimination for war crimes and crimes against humanity.[91] The remaining documents have been classified and few have been declassified by either the Japanese government or the Allied Powers.[92] The Women's Tribunal found that the policy of incineration, as well as the concealment of documents, represents recognition by Japan itself of its wrongful acts.[93]

It has also been argued that the reason for the neglect in addressing the issue was the failure to identify the comfort women system as a sepa-

---

[90] *Ibid.*

[91] In an affidavit prepared for the tribunal, another expert, Professor Yoshida Yutaka, referred to the 1978 statements of Hirose Toyosaku, the Finance Minister at the time of surrender, in which he declared, "Immediately after the end of the war, I also burned documents according to the government policy. This is what we decided at a Cabinet meeting". According to Yoshida, Oyama Fumio, former Army lieutenant general in charge of legal affairs, confirmed in response to the Justice Ministry's post-war survey that documents were destroyed under a government order. Yoshida's affidavit also includes a 5 December 1960 public statement by Okuno Seisuke, a Home Ministry employee during the war. Participating in a Jichi University radio programme entitled "The Talk of the Days of Home Minister Yamazaki", Okuno Seisuke said that he had been ordered to destroy official documents related to the war at the end of the Second World War. Another expert, Professor Arai Shinichi, documented that just after the declaration of surrender, the General Staff Office, the Army Military and the Navy gave notice to all units to have confidential documents burned, and that the Ministry of Home Affairs burnt public documents. Cited in Women's Tribunal, 2001, para. 945, see *supra* note 3.

[92] *Ibid.*, para. 90.

[93] *Ibid.*, para. 946.

rate type of crime, distinct from 'systematic rape'. The seriousness of rape itself was yet to be recognised. Although the crime was considered a violation of customs of war under the category of 'crimes against humanity' in the Tokyo Charter, it was only classified as a crime of 'other inhumane acts'.[94] Nevertheless, we cannot rule out the possibility that the failure was intentional. What might have caused the failure to prosecute is possible to assess by examining the practice of the IMTFE, Japan, the Allied Powers, and the politics linking them at the end of the Second World War.

The IMTFE is still considered controversial. Critics suggest that the Tribunal was merely the implementation of victor's justice, with the main objective of prosecuting high-ranking Japanese military leaders. This is evident from the fact that the Tribunal overlooked crimes committed by Allied forces, including the series of bombing of 67 Japanese cities (including Hiroshima and Nagasaki), and the rapes conducted by members of the Allied forces. Judges and prosecutors were also chosen from the nations that had suffered from Japanese military activity, not from Japan or neutral nations.[95] Judging from these circumstances, it may be assumed that the IMTFE's main ambition was to punish and execute Japanese political and military leaders *not* for the atrocities they committed against the people of Asia and the Pacific (crimes against humanity), but for waging a war against the white world, and for violating their colonial entitlements, properties and privileges in that region. The atrocities committed against the non-Allied nations were considered to be less important.[96] Among the three categories of crimes, Class A (crimes against peace) were relevant for the top Japanese leaders, while Class B (war crimes) and Class C (crimes against humanity) could be charged against Japanese at any level, and only those individuals whose charges included crimes against peace were to be tried by the Tribunal.[97] It has also been argued

---

[94] Nearey, 2001, p. 136, see *supra* note 38.

[95] Richard H. Minear, *Victors' Justice: The Tokyo War Crimes Trial*, Princeton University Press, Princeton, NJ, 1971, p. 76.

[96] Lisa Yoneyama, "Traveling Memories, Contagious Justice: Americanization of Japanese War Crimes at the End of the Post-Cold War", in *Journal of Asian American Studies*, 2003, vol. 6, no. 1, p. 65.

[97] The verdict counts include: the overall conspiracy (count 1), waging war against China (count 27), against the United States (count 29), against the British Commonwealth (count 31), against the Netherlands (count 32), against France (count 33), against the Soviet Union at Lake Khassan (count 35), against the Soviet Union at Nomonhan (count 36), ordering, authorising or permitting atrocities (count 54), and disregard of duty to secure ob-

that the anticipation of the imminent Cold War with the Soviet Union, which started soon after the Second World War, influenced the IMTFE immensely in its prosecutorial policies. The United States attempted to gain Japanese support in the Cold War by rehabilitating Japan as a robust pro-Western, anti-communist capitalist regime, and by exempting a number of central figures from the trial, including Kishi Nobusuke, a high-ranking military commander who was suspected of Class A crimes but was later released without trial.[98]

It has also been argued that the reluctance to address the issue of comfort women was caused by the fact that most victims came from non-Allied countries – some were countries whose political interests were ambiguously positioned between the enemy and the Allied Powers, such as Korea and Taiwan.[99] Furthermore, the comfort women mostly came from marginalised societies (poor, non-white, indigenous, uneducated and considered to be of lower class), which made their existence as human beings less visible and their interests not shared by the rest of the world. As Catherine MacKinnon has stated, "[w]hat happens to women is either too particular to be universal or too universal to be particular, meaning either too human to be female or too female to be human".[100]

Another possible reason is evident by observing two of the main issues that the IMTFE failed to prosecute: (1) the comfort women, and (2) Unit 731 biological experimentation. The two crimes reflected the United States' own violations of international law during the Second World War, and it was in the interests of the US to prevent the scrutiny of the image of

---

servance of and prevent breaches of Laws of War (count 55). Minear, 1971, pp. 21, 203, see *supra* note 95.

[98] Yoneyama, 2003, p. 66, see *supra* note 96.

[99] According to Utsumi Aiko, "There were twenty-three Koreans and twenty-one Taiwanese among the 984 individuals who were executed for war crimes. And of the 3,419 people sentenced to life or limited imprisonment, 125 were Korean and 147 were Taiwanese". Aiko Utsumi, "Korean 'Imperial Soldiers': Remembering Colonialism and Crimes against Allied POWs", in T. Fujitani, Geoffrey M. White and Lisa Yoneyama (eds.), *Perilous Memories: The Asia-Pacific War(s)*, Duke University Press, Durham, NC, 2001, p. 211. During the post-war occupation, the US adjudicated, imprisoned and executed more than 300 Taiwanese and Korean former POW guards. The occupation forces also continued to utilise the Chinese forced labour formerly mobilised by the Mitsubishi Mining Industry at the Miuta coalmines in Hokkaido, instead of treating them formally as POWs who needed to be protected and repatriated. Yoneyama, 2003, p. 78, see *supra* note 99.

[100] Catherine A. MacKinnon, "Crimes of War, Crimes of Peace", in *UCLA Women's Law Journal*, 1993, vol. 4, pp. 59, 65.

---

the 'good war' and 'victor's justice'. Unit 731 may be considered one of the most serious war crimes committed by the Japanese Imperial Army during the second Sino-Japanese War and Second World War.[101] Despite the silence of the IMTFE regarding Unit 731, there had been indications that by the time of the Tokyo Trials the US occupying forces knew of the existence of the Japanese biological warfare experiments. Nevertheless, by the time the Tribunal had concluded its work, not a single perpetrator from Unit 731 had been indicted.[102] On the contrary, evidence suggests that the US military had secretly granted immunity to former Unit 731 members in exchange for their research data on bacteriological warfare, including information on human experiments.[103] The US government felt the necessity to secure the data for two reasons: (1) human experimentation would be impossible to conduct inside the US, and (2) the research had to be secured from reaching the Soviet Union.[104]

US biological weapons research had been conducted since 1943 with government funding of USD 60 million.[105] The programme was expanded during the Korean War (1950–1953) following the arms race with

---

[101] Unit 731 is also known as the Japanese "Factory of Death". The victims – primarily Chinese – were infected with various pathogenic bacteria (including bubonic plague, anthrax, cholera, typhus, smallpox, tuberculosis and other diseases). Some victims had vivisections performed on them. Those who did not die from the infections were no longer "viable experimental material" and were killed, and their bodies burned in crematoria. Field trials of delivery mechanisms (bombs, aerial spraying, poisoning of water and animals) were conducted on Chinese villages and cities. In Nanjing, during the two-month slaughter and rape-fest of 1937–1938, Chinese POWs were given dumplings laced with typhus and released to spread the disease, while children were given chocolate infected with anthrax. In border skirmishes with Soviet troops, pathogens were spread to thousands of Red Army soldiers. Around 30,000 to 50,000 people are estimated to have been killed from the experiments alone in the biological warfare bases, while victims of the open-air field trials reached six figures. The human suffering was incalculable. Phil Shannon, "Why the US Let Japanese War Criminals Go Free", in Green Left Online, 28 August 2002, available at https://www.greenleft.org.au/node/26840, last accessed on 15 April 2015.

[102] Ibid.

[103] Kyodo News, "Occupation Censored Unit 731 ex-Members' Mail: Secret Paper", in The Japan Times, 10 February 2010, available at http://www.japantimes.co.jp/news/2010/02/10/national/occupation-censored-unit-731-ex-members-mail-secret-paper/#.VSZVc2a4luU, last accessed on 12 April 2015.

[104] Anita McNaught, "Unit 731: Japan's Biological Force", in BBC News, 1 February 2002, available at http://news.bbc.co.uk/2/hi/programmes/correspondent/1796044.stm, last accessed on 12 April 2015.

[105] Shannon, "Why the US let Japanese war criminals go free", see supra note 101.

---

the Soviet Union, and former members of Unit 731 (which at that time had been dissolved) were invited to join the programme. Dr. Shiro Ishii, who had led Unit 731, was invited to Maryland to advise on bio-weapon projects, while other former members were employed with the payment of somewhere between ¥ 150,000 to ¥ 200,000 (equivalent to about ¥ 20 million [USD 2.37 million] to ¥ 40 million today).[106] Some leading doctors and scientists returned to Japan, changed their identities and began new lives, and some rose once again to influential positions in the medical sciences.[107]

The same argument may be applied in the case of comfort women. Evidence suggests that even before the establishment of the IMTFE, US occupation forces had been aware of the existence of the systematic sexual slavery conducted by the Japanese military. This was evident in a report entitled "Amenities in the Japanese Armed Forces" prepared in February 1945 by the Allied Translator and Interpreter Service, which gives detailed explanations regarding the comfort women system, including the management, operation and regulations of the system.[108] Despite US knowledge of the existence of the comfort system, the fact that it was overlooked indicates that the Tokyo Tribunal had decided to ignore the issue. The reason for this may have been the fact that the US Army itself approved of and used comfort women during their occupation of Japan. Records suggest that numerous comfort stations were established for US soldiers by order of the office of Japan's Ministry of Home Affairs following Japan's official surrender on 18 August 1945, administered by the Japanese Kempeitai (which had been in charge of forced prostitution dur-

---

[106] See Richard Drayton, "An Ethical Blank Cheque" in *The Guardian*, 10 May 2005, available at http://www.theguardian.com/politics/2005/may/10/foreignpolicy.usa, last accessed on 12 April 2015; and Kyodo News, "US Paid for Japanese Human Germ Warfare Data", in *ABC News*, 15 August 2005, available at http://www.abc.net.au/news/2005-08-15/us-paid-for-japanese-human-germ-warfare-data/2080618, last accessed on 12 April 2015.

[107] Franziska Seraphim, *War Memory and Social Politics in Japan, 1945–2005*, Harvard University Press, Cambridge, MA, 2006, p. 290.

[108] A comfort women interrogation report was also made around the same period by a US psychological warfare team, entitled "Psychological Warfare: Interrogation Bulletin No. 2" under the sub-section "A Japanese Army Brothel in the Forward Area", to gather information concerning the psychological conditions of Japanese soldiers in the battlefield. The team also indicated the violation to the comfort women and the deception method of procurement by the Japanese forces in its Interrogation Report No. 49. Other reports, data and images referring to the awareness of the existence of the comfort women prior to the Tokyo Tribunal were also found at the US National Archives, the National Archives of the UK in London and the Australian War Memorial. Tanaka, 2002, pp. 84-87, see *supra* note 7.

ing the war) and the Recreation and Amusement Association ('RAA') using Japanese government funds.[109] The Japanese government argued that the establishment was necessary to protect 'good' and 'respected' Japanese women from the possibility of "mass rape" by the occupation forces (in reaction to those committed by Japanese troops during the war).[110] Based on this, a massive number of comfort women from the Philippines, Korea, China and Japan were gathered together and shipped to comfort stations even after the war had ended.[111]

Although mass rape and murder did not occur as feared, rapes and other atrocities by US soldiers were rampant from the first day of the occupation.[112] The moment the occupying forces landed, the comfort stations were flooded with soldiers, which forced the RAA to recruit new women to fill the demand.[113] The comfort system for the American forces was based on the previous Japanese comfort stations, and the only difference was the fact that post-war Japanese comfort women were paid properly.[114] Like its predecessor, abuses and violence were not uncommon in the comfort stations. Ironically, even with the establishment of the comfort stations, rape and violence by the occupying forces remained out of control.[115] The military brothels serviced the US soldiers for almost a year, and were closed in the spring of 1946 by General Douglas MacArthur as Japan began its attempt to resurrect itself from its three million dead and nine million homeless.[116] In conclusion, the cases of comfort

---

[109] Lys Anzia, "Trafficking is A Long Standing Crime", in *Women News Network*, 29 September 2007, available at http://womennewsnetwork.net/2007/09/29/trqafficking-a-long-standing-crime-us-troop-use-of-japans-trafficked-women-1945/, last accessed on 12 April 2015.

[110] Tanaka, 2002, p. 133, see *supra* note 7.

[111] Anzia, 2007, see *supra* note 109.

[112] According to reports compiled by the Police and Security Bureau of the Ministry of Home Affairs on the assaults by Allied soldiers against Japanese civilians in Kanagawa prefecture: on 30 August 1945, two rape cases were reported together with one case of kidnapping, one case of bodily harm, one act of violence and 197 cases of extortion. On 31 August 1945, one rape case and 212 cases of extortion were reported. On 1 September 1945, 12 rape cases, one case of bodily harm and 75 extortion cases were reported. Almost every day from 30 August until mid-September 1945, rape, bodily harm, extortion, burglary and murder were reported. Tanaka, 2002, p. 116, see *supra* note 7.

[113] Anzia, 2007, see *supra* note 109.

[114] Tanaka, 2002, p. 147, see *supra* note 7.

[115] *Ibid.*, pp. 116–32.

[116] Anzia, 2007, see *supra* note 109.

---

women and Unit 731 have one main similarity which arguably triggered the failure to prosecute: both cases involved Allied forces.

10.5.2. Impact of Peace Treaties and Reparations Agreements

Outside the context of the IMTFE, there seem to be two main obstacles for almost all comfort women litigation before Japanese domestic courts: (1) the peace treaties and reparations agreements which prohibited any claims of war victims for reparations, and (2) the rights of individual to raise claims under international law.

The Treaty of San Francisco signed by 48 countries on 8 September 1951 marked the formal end of the Second World War. Despite its significance in bringing peace to the entire Asia-Pacific region, analysis shows that most Asian countries victimised by Japan resisted the process and the terms of this treaty.[117] The treaty was criticised as extremely generous, as it did not exact heavy reparations nor impose any post-treaty supervision over Japan, and yet its implementation has been aggressively defended by both the US and Japanese governments.[118] The formulation of the treaty was also dominated mainly by the US government, including the clauses related to war reparations and victims' claims. The Chinese government criticised this as a violation of the Potsdam Agreement between the United States, the United Kingdom and the Soviet Union for the military occupation and reconstruction of Germany, which stated that "[t]he 'Preparatory work of the Peace Settlements' should be undertaken by those States which were signatories to the terms of surrender imposed upon the Enemy State concerned". While excluding the countries that suffered the most damage during the Japanese occupation in the Asia-Pacific, the US government monopolised the formulation of the Treaty of San Francisco and relieved Japan from full war reparations, arguing that full reparations

---

[117] Neither the People's Republic of China nor the Republic of China (Taiwan) were invited to the peace conference, and neither were North and South Korea; India and Burma refused to participate; Indonesia signed but never ratified the treaty; while Philippines, though present, neither signed nor ratified the treaty until 1956. Global Alliance for Preserving the History of WW II in Asia, "Peace Treaties and Negotiations: San Francisco Peace Treaty", 2001, available http://www.global-alliance.net/SFPT.html, last accessed on 12 April 2015.

[118] John Price, "A Just Peace? The 1951 San Francisco Peace Treaty in Historical Perspective", in *Japan Policy Research Institute Working Paper*, no. 78, June 2001, available at http://www.jpri.org/publications/workingpapers/wp78.html, last accessed on 12 April 2015.

would harm Japan's economy and create a breeding ground for communism.[119]

Article 14(a) of the Treaty of San Francisco stipulates that the Japanese economy was not "presently" capable of bearing the full responsibility for war reparations. It can be argued that the damage suffered by the Japanese economy merely delayed the imposition of complete reparations, but did not permanently waive it. In fact, Japan paid war compensation to Allied POWs of a total amount of GBP 4.5 million through the International Committee of the Red Cross, but the funds were suspected to have originated from contributions of the US, British and Dutch governments during the final year of the war and not from Japan itself.[120] The funds were claimed to be unspent Allied relief money, which, under terms of Article 16 of the Treaty of San Francisco, was turned over for redistribution to the 14 Allied nations (that were signatories to the treaty), and whose citizens had suffered in Japanese captivity.[121] In the case of POWs, each was paid GBP 76 in 1952, which was said to represent the average wage of a Japanese male for 12 months at the end of the Second World War, but it would have represented only about 11 to 12 weeks' pay for an adult British male at the time.[122]

Examples have to be derived from the case of POWs since the comfort women did not publicly exist during the payment period. The comfort women started to reveal their existence in the 1990s when all issues of compensation had been settled. It can be concluded that, unlike other war victims, comfort women were not eligible for compensation under any of the peace treaties that were mostly concluded in the 1950s. In fact, the failure of the IMTFE to recognise the comfort women system as a crime shows that the comfort women were not viewed as victims of Japanese war atrocities. The calculation of damages and reparations during the formulation of the peace treaties arguably included only the victims and their families who could be identified by the time of the settlement, and this did not include comfort women. It can therefore be argued that these

---

[119] *Ibid.*

[120] Linda Goetz Holmes, "Compensation to Allied POWs", in *The Japan Times*, Letter, 22 February 2009, available at http://www.japantimes.co.jp/opinion/2009/02/22/reader-mail/compensation-to-allied-pows/#.VUYxr5Msrnh, last accessed on 12 April 2015.

[121] *Ibid.*

[122] Royal British Legion, "Background Briefing for Parliamentarians on the Claim for a Special Gratuity for Former Far East Prisoners of War (FEPOWS)", 1999.

---

treaties are inapplicable to the comfort women, who still have the right to pursue compensation. Countering Japan's traditional argument on the execution of the peace treaties, the UN Human Rights Sub-Commission has stated that

> the rights and obligation of States and individuals with respect to the violations referred to in the present resolution cannot, as a matter of international law, be extinguished by peace treaty, peace agreement, amnesty or by any other means.[123]

The peace treaties themselves, therefore, are no obstacle for individuals and states (especially to comfort women) to exercise their rights to seek compensation. This argument should include those who have not received any compensation for their suffering, and those who have received too small an amount.

The second issue is that of individual rights to raise claims against foreign states. Most lawsuits regarding comfort women have indeed been fought only by individuals without the help of their governments, with the exception of the Taiwanese case in 1999. In lawsuits that concern Japanese war atrocities – not only comfort women – most governments refused to provide support in the litigation processes. This includes the US, British, Indonesian, Chinese and South Korean governments – the states with the biggest concentrations of Japanese war victims – specifically when the issue concerns the individual rights to raise a claim for wartime atrocities against a foreign government.

10.5.3. States' Reluctance to Support International Lawsuits

In the United States, the California Code of Civil Procedure §354.6[124] allows any forced labour victim or their heir to bring an action against the

---

[123] Sub-Commission on the Promotion and Protection of Human Rights, 1999, para. 13, see *supra* note 65.

[124] The code had originally authorised those who were formerly victimised by Nazi persecution and forced labour, as well as their descendants, to bring lawsuits to demand compensation from companies and other organisations that had benefited from such forms of labour exploitation between 1929 and 1945. The amendment expands the category of the "Second World War slave labour victim" to "any person taken from a concentration camp of ghetto or diverted from transportation to a concentration camp or from a ghetto to perform labour without pay for any period of time between 1929 and 1945, by the Nazi regime, *its allies and sympathisers, or enterprises* transacting business in any of the areas occupied by or under control of the Nazi regime or its allies and sympathizers". Yoneyama, 2003, p. 65, emphasis added, see *supra* note 96.

---

entity for whom the labour was performed. Despite this, most cases in the United States[125] regarding forced labour victims and POWs of the Second World War have been dismissed on various grounds.[126] The British government similarly shows an unwillingness in supporting any claims by former British POWs.[127]

---

[125] There were approximately 27,000 American POWs and 14,000 civilian internees captured and interned by Japan during the Second World War. Gary K. Reynolds, "U.S. Prisoners of War and Civilian American Citizens Captured and Interned by Japan in World War II: The Issue of Compensation by Japan", CRS Report for Congress, 27 July 2001, available at http://fas.org/man/crs/RL30606.pdf, last accessed on 12 April 2015.

[126] On 21 September 2000, all cases filed by former Allied POWs in US courts were dismissed on the grounds that the plaintiffs' claims were barred by the Peace Treaty of 1951. On 19 September 2001, a US court ruled that other cases of victims whose countries were not signatories to the Peace Treaty of 1951 should also be dismissed on the following grounds: (1) for the Philippine victims, victims were barred by the 1956 bilateral agreement between Japan and the Philippines; (2) for Chinese and Korean victims, the California statute was unconstitutional since it "infringes on the federal government's exclusive power over foreign affairs". One claim succeeded in reaching the Superior Court in 2001 (see *Jae Won Jeong v. Onoda Cement Co. Ltd, et al.*, Superior Court of the State of California for the County of Los Angeles, Case No. BC 217805) for which Judge Lichtman ruled that the 1951 Peace Treaty did not and does not bar the claims of the plaintiff, a naturalised Korean American, because he was not a citizen of the United States at the time that the Peace Treaty was signed. He also rejected other arguments that the claim intruded upon the foreign relations powers of the federal government that federal law pre-empted the plaintiffs' claims. (The ruling by federal court judge Walker five days later upholding these arguments does not bind state cases.) In the case of *Hwang Geum Joo, et al. v. Japan* (United States District Court for the District of Columbia, Case No. 00-CV-2233), both the US and Japanese governments argued that the government of Japan is immune from the jurisdiction of the US court (the issue of sovereign immunity). Kinue Tokudome, "POW Forced Labor Lawsuits against Japanese Companies", in *Japan Policy Research Institute Working Paper*, no. 82, November 2001, available at http://www.jpri.org/publications/workingpapers/wp82.html, last accessed on 12 April 2015.

[127] In October 2008 the British government decided not to bring charges against Japanese commanders for the massacre of around 548 British and Dutch POWs who were machine-gunned in November 1943, even though there was sufficient evidence to charge the three perpetrators of the incident. The POWs were machine-gunned when the *Suez Maru* transporting them was sunk by an American torpedo attack in the Flores Sea off Indonesia. Senior politicians in Britain had debated the issue in 1949 and concluded that it was best not to pursue any charges, considering that the German war trials were finishing and around 700 war criminals had been executed in the Tokyo Trials. See Kyodo, "Britain Covered Up Japan Massacre of POWs: BBC", in *The Japan Times*, 17 October 2008, available at http://www.japantimes.co.jp/news/2008/10/17/national/history/britain-covered-up-japan-massacre-of-pows-bbc/#.VSaFpGa4k3g, last accessed on 12 April 2015. See Jon Swaine "Japanese Massacre of British PoWs Was 'Covered Up'", in *The Telegraph*, 18 September

In 1996 the Indonesian government cited two 1958 treaties, "the adverse social effects of massive compensation windfalls to individuals, a preference for compensation that benefits the whole community and the feelings of the people", as reasons for not helping comfort women plaintiffs; there was still much appreciation for Japanese soldiers who fought alongside Indonesians in the war against the Dutch after 1945.[128] The government represented by the Minister of Social Affairs, Endang Suweno, announced on 14 November 1996:

> For the people of Indonesia, the comfort women issue represents a dark, unforgettable side of their history, and it is important that every effort be made to learn from this lesson to prevent such an occurrence from ever happening again. The Government empathizes with the endless psychological and physical trauma and pain of the women who were victims of violence. However, the Government, representing a people imbued with the Panchasila philosophy, does not intend to introduce measures or policies strongly colored by emotion, and will work hard to protect the honor of women who were victimized and their families. The Government of Indonesia is of the understanding that the question of war reparations, material restitution and the right to claim from the Japanese Government was settled by two accords signed in 1958 – the Treaty of Peace Between Japan and the Republic of Indonesia, and the Reparations Agreement Between Japan and the Republic of Indonesia. In Indonesia, the Asian Women's Fund should promote projects and assistance programs related to the comfort women issue through the Indonesian Government (primarily through the Department of Social Affairs), not through any other organization or individual.[129]

Despite intense pressure against the Japanese government, the Chinese government has also been silent regarding the issue of individual complaints, neither helping nor blocking them.[130] In the case of South Ko-

---

2008, available at http://www.telegraph.co.uk/news/uknews/2983447/Japanese-massacre-of-British-PoWs-was-covered-up.html, last accessed on 12 April 2015.

[128] Philip A. Seaton, *Japan's Contested War Memories: The 'Memory Rifts' in Historical Consciousness of World War II*, Routledge, London, 2007, p. 69.

[129] Digital Museum, "The Comfort Women Issue and the Asian Women's Fund: Projects by country or region – Indonesia", available at http://www.awf.or.jp/e3/indonesia-00.html, last accessed on 12 April 2015.

[130] Seaton, 2007, p. 69, see *supra* note 128.

---

rea, the rights of both "the State and its people" to seek additional redress were waived in 1965,[131] but since August 2005 the state has started pressing the Japanese government over "legal responsibility". Viewing the governments' standing towards the issue of individual complaints, it can be concluded that they have no interest in addressing this issue. Two possible reasons for this lack of interest are: (1) they deem they are bound by the Peace Treaty of 1951 and therefore *unable* to act, or (2) they are *unwilling* to act.

Several reasons can be presented regarding this unwillingness on the part of states. First, thousands of war victims seeking compensation individually would place tremendous burdens on global legal systems to verify the facts of each case, and to try, dispense justice and accommodate appeals procedures.[132] Compensation may be considered as more practical at the state level, but at the same time they will encounter the problem of effectiveness, as compensation may not reach each and every victim.[133] The second argument is related to the issue of human rights versus state rights. States with active militaries (such as the US, United Kingdom, Indonesia and China) have much to fear if legal precedents are set for states to be considered liable for conventional war crimes committed by their armed forces in lawsuits brought by non-national individual plaintiffs.[134] It can be assumed that states choose to take a passive stance as any success in raising individual claims for war atrocities may make liable those

---

[131] Hiroshi Tanaka, "Nihon no sengo hoshō to rekishi ninshiki", in Awaya Kentaro (ed.), *Sensō sekinin, sengo sekinin: Nihon to Doitsu wa dō chigau ka*, Asahi Shinbunsha, Tokyo, 1994, p. 59.

[132] Seaton, 2007, p. 69, see *supra* note 128.

[133] Indonesia signed a memorandum of understanding with the Asian Women's Fund on 25 25 March 1997, which handed over a total of ¥ 380 million Japanese (about USD 2.8 million) collected from donors to establish houses in the places where there were reported concentrations of former comfort women. "Indonesian Assembly Chairman Seeks Solution to Comfort Women Issue", in *People's Daily*, 14 February 2002, available at http://en.people.cn/200202/14/eng20020214_90439.shtml, last accessed on 12 April 2015. In 2002 a visiting delegation of the Japanese Parliamentary Diet found that no one in the Japan-funded facilities for the elderly seemed to have been a comfort woman. The Indonesian survivors have received neither any form of redress nor the Prime Minister's "letter of apology". See "An NGO Shadow Report to CEDAW. Japan: The 'Comfort Women' Issue", 44th Session, 2009, New York, p. 3, available at http://www2.ohchr.org/english/bodies/cedaw/docs/ngos/ComfortWomen_Japan_cedaw44.pdf, last accessed on 12 April 2015.

[134] Seaton, 2007, p. 70, see *supra* note 128.

---

states whose armed forces are more exposed to the risk of committing atrocities during armed conflict.

The last argument is related to the fact that Japan has successfully established a significant presence on the world stage through its Official Development Assistance ('ODA') projects and donations to international organisations, including the United Nations.[135] Within just three decades since the end of the war, Japan had managed to position itself side-by-side with the United States as one of the top three largest global donors. Between 1991 and 2000, Japan became the largest ODA donor with 24.8 per cent of the world share. Since Japan is frequently also one of the most important trading partners for other states, these states cannot afford to take a confrontational stance. Despite the declared objectives of promoting the economic development and welfare of recipient countries, the amount of assistance that is provided as grant aid is incomparable to the amount of loans that have to be repaid, which at some point creates a tremendous amount of debt for the recipient countries. Among the highest Japanese ODA loan recipients are China and Indonesia.

10.5.4. Japan's Lack of Will to Acknowledge Accountability

Despite a series of public apologies, the Japanese government still refuses to fully acknowledge its war responsibilities. The apologies delivered have been criticised as spoken merely on behalf of the individual and failed to represent the government as a whole.[136] The statement of guilt and apology by Kono in 1993 was also criticised by the Women's Tribunal as including unacceptable euphemisms, which failed to recognise the gravity of the crime:

> By acknowledging only that the "comfort women" lived un-
> der a "coercive atmosphere," the statement conceals the di-
> rect and utter brutality to which the Japanese military know-
> ingly and intentionally subjected the "comfort women" as an
> integral part of its war effort. Furthermore, by stating that the
> women "lived in misery" and suffered "injury to their hon-
> our and dignity," the government avoided admitting that they

---

[135] *Ibid.*, p. 69.

[136] "Japan's Mass Rape and Sexual Enslavement of Women and Girls from 1932–1945: The 'Comfort Women' System", 2 July 2001.

were raped repeatedly and subjects of a system of sexual slavery.[137]

The apologies have also been nullified by various actions that are considered offensive to the dignity and memory of the victims of atrocities, such as the visits by the heads of government to the Yasukuni and other war memorial shrines.[138] The Asian Women's Fund, which was claimed as representing the Japanese people's "feelings of apology and remorse", was also controversial due to the unofficial nature of the funding which came from Japanese public donations and not government expenditure.[139] In fact, until its termination in March 2007, there was no actual reparation, acknowledgement of legal liability nor any prosecutions that provided justice for the comfort women. Even today, the issue of war memory is still considered sensitive, both inside and outside Japan.

Japanese failures to prosecute and provide reparations are arguably due to its lack of willingness to address past atrocities. Since its formal enrolment in the UN in 1956, Japan has participated actively in its social and economic activities. By 1990 its contribution reached approximately 11 per cent of the regular UN budget, second only to the United States which contributed 25 per cent.[140] In 2006 Japan's contribution to the UN budget reached 19.5 per cent, making its presence very influential in UN decision-making, to the extent that Japan was said to deserve a permanent seat on the Security Council.[141] Additionally, Japan is the main contribu-

---

[137] Women's Tribunal, 2001, para. 964, see *supra* note 3.

[138] For a chronological record of shrine visits and political statements by members of the Japanese government up to 2005, see Appendix 1.

[139] Critics suggested that by shifting the responsibility to the public, the Japanese government has been able to maintain its position of not paying out even one yen in reparations, which also leaves the government free to emphasise in private that while it does have some "moral responsibility" to former comfort women, the brunt of that responsibility rests with private citizens. See Yoshiaki, 2000, p. 24, *supra* note 3. The Women's Tribunal argued: "Privately raised funds cannot be used in lieu of official compensation in satisfaction of the state's obligation, particularly where there has been for decades no financial barrier to the state's ability to provide the compensation from the public fisc". Women's Tribunal, 2001, para. 987, see *supra* note 3.

[140] Marjorie Ann Browne and Luisa Blanchfield, "United Nations Regular Budget Contributions: Members Compared, 1990–2010", Congressional Research Service, 15 January 2013, RL30605, p. 3, available at https://www.fas.org/sgp/crs/row/RL30605.pdf, last accessed on 10 April 2015.

[141] Philip Sherwell, "U.N. Budget Crisis Looms after Third World Veto", in *The Standard*, 1 May 2006, available at http://www.thestandard.com.hk/archive_news_detail.asp? pp_cat

---

tor to Cambodia's rehabilitation and reconstruction since the high-profile UN Transitional Authority (UNTAC) mission and election in 1993, providing some USD 1.2 billion in total ODA since 1992, and remains Cambodia's top donor.[142] Japan spent USD 4.17 million on the UN-supported Extraordinary Chambers in the Courts of Cambodia, making it the biggest donor to the tribunal.[143] Compared to the budget that has been allocated to its participation in international politics, any reasonable assessment of the amounts demanded for reparations by former victims of Japanese war crimes would not have any significant impact on the country's economy. Japan has the capacity to provide a substantial amount of reparations for former victims, as well as a functioning judicial system in which to conduct prosecutions. If so, what may have caused the reluctance to conduct prosecutions and provide reparations?

The main problem is presumably rooted in the Japanese people's perception of the Second World War, especially memories of the defeat, which contradicts those of other countries, in particular those victimised by Japan during the war. The national bias, which arguably emerged from the government's effort to create an image of a 'peace-loving nation' through the reconstruction of history, may be considered as crucial in maintaining Japanese patriotism and national pride, as well as preventing feelings of guilt and shame by the old generation of Japanese to be passed down. The complications of Japanese war narratives can be observed in three controversial issues: (1) the Yasukuni Shrine visits, (2) history textbooks, and (3) the comfort women issue.

The Yasukuni Shrine was built in 1869 for those who fought and died for Japan. The memorial currently enshrines more than 2,446,000 people who sacrificed their lives for the nation.[144] Among these are the

---

=17&art_id=17703&sid=7749159&con_type=1&archive_d_str=20060501, last accessed on 10 April 2015.

[142] Gordon Jones, "Inside Out: Business in Cambodia", in Japan Inc, 31 August 2008, available at http://www.japaninc.com/mgz_september_2008_business-in-cambodia, last accessed on 10 April 2015.

[143] Sopheng Cheang, "Japan Donates $4 million to Khmer Rouge Genocide Tribunal to Pay Cambodian Staff", in *The Gaea Times*, 1 May 2009, available at http://news.gaeatimes.com/japan-donates-4-million-to-khmer-rouge-genocide-tribunal-to-pay-cambodian-staff-47037/, last accessed on 10 April 2015.

[144] The number includes both soldiers and victims from the Sino-Japanese War, Russo-Japanese War, First World War, the Manchurian Incident, the China Incident and the Second World War. Yasukuni Shrine, "History", available at http://www.yasukuni.or.jp/english/about/index.html, last accessed on 12 April 2015.

1,068 individuals who were sentenced and executed by the IMTFE, including Prime Minister *Tōjō* Hideki and another 13 Class A war criminals.[145] For the Japanese, the shrine visits by prime ministers and members of the Japanese parliament are considered acts of commemoration, showing appreciation and paying respects. On the other hand, other nations – specifically those countries that suffered Japanese invasion – consider this as an act of glorification of the war, disrespect of the victims of atrocities and a refusal to bear responsibility for the war. This is where the first contradictory perception arguably lies. The individuals, who were labelled war criminals, are Japanese national heroes, the pride of Japan, who sacrificed themselves for the Emperor and the nation, and their executions are not considered a punishment but a sacrifice. Many Japanese today still refuse to admit past wrongs and quite a few actually believe that the executed war criminals were victimised by the Allied's 'victor's justice'. A published pamphlet of the Yasukuni Shrine notes:

> War is a really tragic thing to happen, but it was necessary in order for us to protect the independence of Japan and to prosper together with Asian neighbours. [...] Some 1,068 people, who were wrongly accused as war criminals by the Allied court, were enshrined here.[146]

The views that the IMTFE was a mere exercise of 'victor's justice' and that war responsibility is a consequence of defeat are contentious. The argument may have emerged from two anomalies: (1) the fact that the IMTFE addressed none of the Allies' war atrocities, and (2) the US itself has not delivered any apology for dropping atomic bombs on Hiroshima and Nagasaki.

The second contradiction arguably lies at the heart of the narratives of the Second World War. This is evident from observing the post-war development of Japanese history textbooks, in which many facts have been revised and war-related words have been euphemised.[147] Japanese

---

[145] Japan Guide, "Yasukuni Shrine", available at http://www.japan-guide.com/e/e2321.html, last accessed on 12 April 2015.

[146] "Where War Criminals Are Venerated", in CNN, 14 January 2003, available at http://edition.cnn.com/2001/WORLD/asiapcf/east/08/13/japan.shrine/ last accessed on 12 April 2015.

[147] The most notable history textbook controversy was the 32-year Ienaga Textbook Authorisation Suits (1965–1997) in which the plaintiff, Professor Ienaga Saburō from the Tokyo University of Education, sued the government, claiming the textbook authorisation system to be "unconstitutional and illegal". The plaintiff claimed that the screeners tried to mini-

history textbooks have emphasised the cruelty of war and a 'victim consciousness' by teaching about the tragedy experienced by Japanese war victims, centred on Hiroshima and Nagasaki. The dropping of the atomic bombs has been considered the embodiment of the victimisation of the Japanese people as the world's only atomic bomb victims.[148] The 'victim consciousness' itself may have originated from the argument that war acts were conducted by the government officials and high-ranking military leaders, and the Japanese people should not be subject to collective responsibility for acts they did not commit nor had knowledge of – Japanese people should not be guilty for merely being *Japanese*.

Records from Japanese wartime newspapers suggest that during the war period most Japanese remaining in the country were not well informed about the actual situation in the battlefield. Most domestic media reporting during the war was dedicated to creating the image of a 'good war': Japan's holy mission to liberate Asian countries, the heroic actions of the troops in the battlefield, the evil US and British armies and Japanese war victims; neither atrocities nor invasions by the Japanese military were included.[149] The only realities that the people knew and experienced were when the Allies attacked Japanese territory, which reached its climax with the use of atomic bombs on Hiroshima and Nagasaki. It should also be noted that while the Japanese defeat meant celebration for many countries, for the Japanese this marked the beginning of occupation and war devastation. The defeat caused deep frustration and embarrassment among the people as the population had exhausted all their resources to support the government's war and the deaths of their countrymen became meaningless. It can be argued that the defeat of the Imperial Army un-

---

mise the cruelty of war and the importance of anti-military demonstrations. The changes requested included the following original passage: "Okinawa prefecture became the battlefield of the ground war, and about 160,000 residents, old and young, men and women died violently in the war. Among them there were quite a few people who were killed by the Japanese Army", to be rendered as: "About 160,000 [Okinawa] residents died naturally by bombs and mass suicide. Among them there were quite a few people who were killed by the Japanese Army". Another controversy arose in 1982, when a major Japanese newspaper announced that a new high school textbook had changed Japan's "invasion" (*shinryaku*) of China during 1930s into "advance" (*shinkō*). The action triggered international attention to the Japanese textbook authorisation system and the issue of war narratives. Miki Y. Ishikida, *Toward Peace: War Responsibility, Postwar Compensation, and Peace Movements and Education in Japan*, iUniverse, Lincoln, NE, 2005.

[148] *Ibid.*

[149] David C. Earhart, *Certain Victory: Images of World War II in the Japanese Media*, M.E. Sharpe, New York, 2008, pp. 215–459.

---

dermined the people's sense of nationalism, as those who gave their utmost effort to support the war without being informed about the realities of the war were forced to bear the collective responsibility of the entire nation for the crimes committed by the government and high-ranking military officers. The reconstruction of the war narratives may therefore be considered crucial to maintaining the Japanese sense of nationalism and patriotism, and to avoiding the imposition of guilt on younger Japanese.

The third contradiction lies in the issue of the comfort women. Japanese war responsibility, which was criticised as the international bias of 'victor's justice', had arguably started to fade after nearly six decades since the end of the war.[150] The comfort women (as well as other war victims) may have been the only remaining fragments of the war memories that are still able to redirect history. It should be remembered that it was the testimonies of the comfort women in 1990 that forced Japan to admit its mistakes. Documents and evidence may have been destroyed, but the comfort women are living witnesses whose testimonies are undeniable references to Japan's past atrocities. By conducting prosecutions, delivering formal apologies and paying real reparations, Japan may consider itself as admitting its past atrocities and accepting its war responsibilities. The Japanese government may have feared that the continuous demands and pressures of the comfort women would damage the nation's sense of nationalism and pride, subjecting the country to international scrutiny, as well as challenging its desired self-image as a peace-loving nation. The comfort women's success in litigation might result in the following scenarios: a revision of all Japanese history textbooks; domestic and international media reporting of the comfort women issue and other past atrocities; further research that might reveal other long-forgotten atrocities; and a flood of war victims seeking reparations. Japan's efforts to mend its history for the sake of its future generations will also be in vain as the younger generation Japanese will continue to bear the guilt and shame of the war, and there will be no peace for national heroes.

---

[150] A survey conducted in 2001 by a leading television company regarding public opinion on the official government visits to Yasukuni Shrine revealed that 68 per cent of people who were in their twenties considered that there was nothing wrong in paying homage to the war dead, while 46 per cent of people in their sixties and above were against it. Suvendrini Kakuchi, "Japan: Worship of War Dead Rekindles Brutal Memories", in IPS News, 16 August 2004, available at http://www.ipsnews.net/2004/08/japan-worship-of-war-dead-rekindles-brutal-memories-2/, last accessed on 12 April 2015.

From this, it can be concluded that Japan has shown no interest in addressing its past atrocities, either to prosecute or to provide reparations. The self-defined interests of the state can be said to have overridden its obligations under international law.

10.6. State Self-Interest in Accountability

10.6.1. Positive and Negative Interests

A state's decision whether to initiate prosecution is influenced by the different interests revolving around it. At least two types of interests can be identified: positive and negative interests. The expression 'positive interests' refers to the advantages that a state may acquire, and the unfavourable situations that can be avoided, by initiating prosecution. 'Negative interests', on the other hand, refer to the unavoidable responsibilities and obligations to prosecute perpetrators as stipulated in international law. It should also be noted that the term 'interests' focuses on the issue of the willingness of a state to conduct prosecutions and not its ability.

Lack of interest. As described in the previous section, the failure to prosecute in the case of the comfort women was heavily influenced by the lack of interest behind both international and domestic judicial systems to prosecute. In addition to Japan's reluctance to prosecute, the international judicial institutions (such as the IMTFE) showed either an inability or unwillingness to address this issue in an adequate manner. Although international law has emphasised the duty of states to prosecute, the lack of an effective enforcement mechanism and effort to ensure respect for international law provisions can still seriously impact on a state's assumption of negative interests, which was the issue in the case of the comfort women. In other words, the case of the comfort women experiences continuous failure because it attracts neither positive nor negative interests that can initiate prosecution.

The obligation to prosecute. The arguments related to a state's interest to prosecute have focused heavily on the state's negative interests. The most common reason why it should be in the interest of a state to prosecute individual perpetrators is *because they are obliged to do so*. This argument may provide an answer to why a state *should* prosecute, but it fails to reply to the question of interest as to why a state would *want* to prosecute. The possible reason for the over-exposure of negative interests may have been the existence of international law provisions which are considered a constant variable. The duty to prosecute under international law is considered as a constant in the sense that the imposition does not depend on the interest of each state, and the significance of the obligation itself is treated as amounting to the level of *jus cogens*. The interest of international law is assumed to be the desire to achieve justice. Nevertheless, the comfort women case suggests that a state's assumption of negative interests may also be influenced by the interests of international judicial institutions, and that negative interests are not merely a duty of the state under international law.

The importance of both interests. A strong emphasis on negative interests may attract prosecution, but as an enforced act, prosecution would have to face unfavourable situations, such as the state's reluctance or even refusal to co-operate. It can therefore be argued that the assumption of both positive and negative interests is essential to end the domestic culture of impunity, and one is incomplete without the other – although either one is arguably sufficient to attract prosecution. Nevertheless, priority should be given to the enhancement of the state's positive interests in complying with the principle of complementarity as promulgated in the Statute of the International Criminal Court ('ICC'). Negative interests should be treated as a safeguard mechanism to prevent failure in conducting domestic prosecution due to a lack of positive interests.

In case the state is willing but unable to prosecute, negative interests exercised by the international community can be employed to assist the state in creating the capacity to conduct prosecution. Such a role can be carried out by international tribunals, international treaty bodies, non-governmental organisations and other institutions that have the capacity to support unable states and influence unwilling states.

Many arguments regarding prosecutorial interests have revolved around not entirely persuasive arguments such as deterrence, which are arguably insufficient to convince a state to prosecute or surrender individual perpetrators.[151] In many high-profile crimes, perpetrators are high-

---

[151] John R. Bolton (then Under Secretary of State for Arms Control and International Security of the United States) criticised the ICC's argument on the prospect of deterrence as a "hopelessly legalistic view of international life" and "a cruel joke". He further argued, "hard men like Hitler and Pol Pot are often not deterred from aggression even by cold steel, let alone by a weak and distant institution with no real enforcement powers". John R. Bolton, "Flaws Undermine Concept: World Court Would Be Ineffective, Threaten U.S. Powers", in *USA Today*, 18 January 2000.

ranking government officials and military leaders who possess a strong political interest in the perpetration of the crime, and this interest is shared among the lower-rank perpetrators as a form of political conviction. Fear of prosecution is arguably a weak incentive in preventing the commission of crimes as the value of achieving political objectives is often much higher than the risk of punishment. Unless there has been a transition, prosecuting high-profile leaders may result in self-condemnation for a state, degrading the dignity of the state, and denying political convictions. The state may feel that the price of shielding the perpetrators is much lower than the burden of the prosecutorial outcomes.

To attract prosecution, the state should be convinced that it can benefit from domestic prosecution, that it is more advantageous for both the state and the international community when prosecution is conducted. The next part of the chapter will therefore identify the positive interests that may attract prosecution instead of relying merely upon the enforcement of a state's obligation. It will also argue that the commitment to conduct effective prosecution will benefit the state by positively affecting its reputation and credibility, as well as the reputation and credibility of its armed forces and its people.

10.6.2. Positive Interests: Why It Should Be in the Interest of Japan and Other States to Prosecute Atrocities

As mentioned earlier, positive interest entails the benefits of conducting prosecution as opposed to the obligations imposed as a result of external influences.

Self-scrutiny may preserve sovereignty. By initiating prosecution, the state may secure its sovereignty while at the same time avoiding scrutiny of other aspects of its internal affairs that may rise from international intervention. The issue of sovereignty is one of the main concerns for states' (such as the US, India and China) reluctance to accept the jurisdiction of the ICC.[152] The constantly developing practice regarding the ICC

---

[152] The issue of sovereignty was one of the main concerns for the US government's (Bush administration) opposition to the legitimacy of the ICC. The US, as represented by Bolton, deemed the ICC an organisation that "runs contrary to fundamental American precepts and basic constitutional principles of sovereignty, checks and balances, and national independence". See John R. Bolton, "American Justice and the International Criminal Court", in *Remarks at the American Enterprise Institute*, Washington DC, 3 November 2003. See also Usha Ramanathan, "India and the ICC", in *Journal of International Criminal Justice*, 2005, vol. 3, no. 3, p. 628. China's arguments lie on the fact that the jurisdiction of the

has become a concern for many states, as joining the ICC means that the jurisdiction of the ICC over the state is not optional, and the referral of cases can be made based on the initiative of the prosecutor or by other states parties to the ICC Statute. States might consider ratifying the ICC Statute as allowing other states to scrutinise their internal affairs, which may put the integrity of the state at risk. Moreover, the referral by the UN Security Council under Article 13(b) expands the ICC's jurisdiction to non-states parties, thus refusal to join the ICC does not exempt a state from the jurisdiction of the ICC. For example, the Security Council referred the case of Darfur, Sudan to the ICC, despite Sudan not being party to the ICC Statute. The ICC's subsequent decision to issue an arrest warrant against President Omar Hassan al-Bashir has been criticised as "trying to affect peace talks with [the] Darfur rebels and reform in Sudan".[153] The measures taken by international agencies do not always satisfy the interest of the state in question. The initiation of domestic prosecution as an act of good faith may arguably prevent the undesirable intervention which could result in the incursions to state sovereignty.

Capacity building and judicial independence. Domestic prosecution may also improve and strengthen a state's judicial capacity to investigate and prosecute serious crimes including high-profile crimes, such as war crimes, crimes against humanity and genocide, while at the same time protecting its population from these atrocities.[154] By developing an efficient judiciary, a state may claim its legitimacy and credibility to prosecute international crimes. This may arguably be a good move to pre-empt any undesirable intervention from international agencies.

Less external influence over judicial process. Capacity building domestic prosecution also allows state agencies to manage the content of

---

ICC is not based on the principle of voluntary acceptance. The ICC Statute is claimed to impose obligations on non-state parties without their consent, which violates the principle of state sovereignty. LU Jianping and WANG Zhixiang, "China's Attitude towards the ICC", in *Journal of International Criminal Justice*, 2005, vol. 3, no. 3, p. 611.

153 Guillaume Lavallee, "Sudan: ICC Trying to Affect Darfur Peace Talks", in Middle East Online, 3 February 2010.

154 The UN General Assembly stated that the UN intends itself "as necessary and appropriate, to helping States build capacity to protect their populations from genocide, war crimes, ethnic cleansing and crimes against humanity and to assisting those which are under stress before crisis and conflicts break out". See United Nations, General Assembly, Resolution Adopted by the General Assembly: 60/1. World Summit Outcome 2005, 24 October 2005, A/RES/60/1.

---

the judicial process and ensure that the outcome will not cause excessive damage to the credibility of the state. This includes the prevention of any foreseeable substantial loss that may occur as an outcome of an international prosecution.[155] Nevertheless, it should be noted that the role magnification of positive interests as described above is a double-edged sword. Although the exercise of positive interests is desired to be of higher priority, the independence of the judicial process may be put at risk. The state may use this loophole as a quick escape from its full moral and legal responsibility, which may be detrimental to the legitimacy and credibility of the state's judicial proceedings. Taking the Indonesian *ad hoc* tribunal for East Timor as an example, it was criticised as "seriously flawed and lacked credibility".[156] Another example is the case of the Sudan, in which the three special courts established by the government as a response to the alleged Darfur crimes became a mere symbolic action to prove that the state was taking action to realise justice.[157] The reliance on the domestic judiciary may significantly reduce the administrative burden and cost of prosecuting, but it will also increase the chances that the independence of the state's judiciary is compromised by political interests. To prevent this, the international enforcement of the obligation to prosecute under international law is deemed crucial – not as a priority, but rather as a safeguard

---

[155] The ICC Statute is silent regarding the State's obligation to provide reparation. The negotiators of the ICC Statute rejected the proposals to impose any kind of responsibility (even financial) on States for their officials' actions, even if the convicted defendant was acting on behalf of the State. Linda M. Keller, "Seeking Justice at the International Criminal Court: Victims' Reparations", in *Thomas Jefferson Law Review*, 2007, vol. 29, no. 2, p. 197.

[156] The tribunal, which was conducted in Jakarta in 2003, resulted in 12 acquittals and six convictions, five of which were overturned on appeal. Only the conviction of a pro-Indonesian East Timorese militia commander was upheld, but his sentence was halved to five years and he remains free pending appeal. Ellen Nakashima, "Indonesia Attempts to Avert Tribunal to Probe East Timor Jakarta Wants Truth Commission on 1999 Abuses", in *The Washington Post*, 16 July 2005.

[157] The controversial first ICC Prosecutor, Luis Moreno Ocampo, claimed that Sudan's self-scrutiny is a "cover-up" as the courts only address cases with no importance. The appointed head of the committee on Darfur Human Rights, Ahmed Haroun (the Minister for Humanitarian Affairs), is himself the subject of an ICC arrest. See Thijs Bouwknegt, "Sudan's Self-examination Is Cover-up", in *Radio Netherlands Worldwide*, 12 February 2008. Observers to the courts claimed that the court showed a complete lack of will as the courts never tried anyone linked to the Darfur atrocities, and instead preferred to prosecute local petty thieves. Cases are also dismissed if witnesses fail to turn up. See Thijs Bouwknegt, "Sudan in Turmoil as It awaits ICC indictment", in *Radio Netherlands Worldwide*, 6 January 2009.

---

mechanism – to prevent abuse of justice by the state that may arise in its exercise of positive interests.

Adjustability and compatibility. By organising the judicial process, the state can also adjust the conduct of proceedings according to the specific needs and situations encountered. The substantive and systematic context of the proceedings may also be integrated into the state's domestic law, as well as the cultural, religious and normative needs of the population, which allows more flexibility in the conduct of proceedings. India, for example, considers the issue of judicial compatibility, namely, the amount of amendment to domestic criminal law which would be necessary in order to cohere with the jurisdiction of the ICC, as one of the main obstacles to joining the ICC.[158] Initiating and prioritising domestic prosecution may significantly lessen the burden of amendment needed in the state's domestic law and constitutions in order to be able to incorporate with the ICC. Such amendments can simply involve the importation of core crime elements, and the adjustment of punitive measures as necessary, to enable domestic courts to prosecute international crimes. The acceptance of the jurisdiction of the ICC will act as a safeguard mechanism when domestic remedies have been exhausted, and the state is no longer capable of conducting prosecution. This way, the state would be able to strengthen its capacity to determine its own status of 'unwillingness' or 'inability' instead of leaving it to the discretion of the ICC.

Prevention of public scrutiny and shame. It is also possible to avoid prolonged condemnation by victims and other parties that may lead to international scrutiny and shame, such as in the case of comfort women. The fact that Japan has refused to fully acknowledge its past atrocities and provide reparations for victims has triggered continuous criticism and long-lasting tensions in its relations with other states. Since the emergence of the issue in the 1990s, the contingency of the issue is no longer focused only on comfort women, but has broadened to scrutiny of other sectors, including politics, socio-economic life and education. It can be argued that an early initiation of prosecution can prevent the dispersal of an issue before it outgrows the state's capacity to deal with it. Effective prosecution, while returning rights and dignity to the victims of atrocities, creates substantial satisfaction for the victims. This way, the state can avoid disproportionate public commotion and over-exposure by the media which

---

[158] Ramanathan, 2005, p. 631, *supra* note 156.

can be harmful to the perceived integrity of the state. In this sense, prosecutions act as a means of enhancing the state's public image and its efforts to gain the trust of other states, such as by smoothing reconciliation processes and relationship building.

Individualisation of responsibility. Particularly when the crime is conducted by an organ of state, such as its armed forces, prosecution may prevent the crime from being attributed to the state. Armed forces, as well as other state organs, represent the state, and the conduct of armed forces during hostilities can be attributable to the state. 'Attributable' in this context refers to both moral and legal responsibility of a state for the conduct of its armed forces. The conduct of the armed forces during hostilities may be considered as the conduct of the state, and the act of each individual may be identified as an act of state, if criteria set by the Draft Articles on State Responsibility are fulfilled. The state can also be held liable for the conduct of its organs as a legal person under international law as evidenced by the ICJ Judgment on Serbia-Montenegro, for which Bosnia-Herzegovina accused Serbia-Montenegro of the crime of genocide. Individual accountability clearly identifies where and to whom the responsibility (both legal and moral) of a criminal act is attributable. Without this form of identification to determine the imposition of responsibility, there will be no clear separation between the act of the individual and the act of the state. In such a situation, responsibility will automatically be shifted to the state. By punishing individual perpetrators, the state may individualise the responsibility and argue that the crime was not in the interest of the state.

Moral enhancement and deterrence. For the armed forces as an organ of the state and individual soldiers as part of the armed forces, identification of the individual culprit may: (1) distinguish the innocent members from the guilty ones, thereby putting them in a different category to law-abiding soldiers; (2) relieve the good, innocent soldiers from the moral responsibility and shame of being a part of the same armed forces to which the guilty individuals belong; (3) be an effective means of maintaining the morale of the soldiers; and (4) nurture more rational, disciplined and professional soldiers. Strong disciplinary and justice measures, while punishing the guilty individuals, also set an example to others by illustrating the consequences of committing violations. Disciplined soldiers are, more than anything, an effective preventive measure for future violations.

The protection of younger generations. Prosecution, as a form of reparation and atonement, may also relieve the burden of guilt and shame of the younger generation. David Palmer has argued that

> [i]f the people of a country do not recognize their past – and the atrocities committed in the name of their nation – even new generations become part of the guilt. [...] In fact, it is actually better to assume responsibility and from there work towards reconciliation, than just spend time talking about guilt and endlessly moralizing. For the younger generation in particular, recognition of history is essential, while moralizing about how the younger generation is "guilty" can obstruct real understanding.[159]

In other words, the recognition of past wrongs and war responsibility may actually become the source of its people's sense of national identity, instead of continuous shame and guilt that may come from denials and ignorance.

10.7. Conclusion

As outlined in the introductory section, this chapter has focused on addressing two main issues: (1) the reasons for the reluctance of international and domestic courts to prosecute comfort women crimes, and (2) why it should be in the interests of Japan – as well as other states – to prosecute. The comfort women case is considered as the best portrayal of the two main issues, as all but one of the prosecutorial efforts (the Batavia Military Tribunal) have ended up in failure and none of the legal actions has succeeded in achieving justice. The analysis of the political response of the Japanese government, as well as the judicial response by the Japanese courts, suggests that the failures to address the comfort women issue originate in the state's lack of will. At the international level, most cases regarding the comfort women have also met a dead end due to the unwillingness of both international judicial institutions and states to address the issue.

Various arguments can be offered to explain the lack of will by both international and domestic courts to address the issue of comfort women. First, prosecutions of the types of crime that can be committed by any

---

[159] David Palmer, "What is Reconciliation in the Light of War Responsibility?", Keynote Address to Japan Australia Peace Forum, Melbourne, 23 May 2009.

participant in war – including third party participants, for example, peace-keepers, inter-governmental organisation and non-governmental organisation personnel, and volunteers – such as sexual violence, arguably attracts less interest. An armed conflict is still based on an unwritten social convention that there has to be one side in which justice is prevalent. The prosecution of crimes that tend to be committed by all parties to the conflict may distort the concept of a just war, as even a hero can be perceived as a victimiser. Moreover, states are less likely to take a confrontational stance against a high-profile state, whose role in international politics and the global economy is considered as important. It can therefore be argued that the interest in prosecution is still influenced by a state's political interests. Prosecution of issues, the outcome of which may be detrimental to the credibility and legitimacy of the state, may be assumed as less likely to be conducted.

Another reason seems to be the fact that many victims are marginalised within constituencies that are far removed from the international community. These groups of victims are often people with no access to justice, while experiencing suppression by their own governments. Unless the atrocities are committed on a large scale, it is less likely that the issue will attract prosecution. This is especially so in the case of sexual violence, the fact that many victims are often reluctant to report crimes – as they fear being subjected to discrimination and mistreatment by society – may be considered as contributing to delays and failures to prosecute. The guilt and shame of rape and sexual violence are still considered as belonging to the victims rather than the victimisers.

In many cases, the reluctance to prosecute originates from the lack of incentives – positive interests – which can motivate states to initiate prosecution. The bias of international judicial entities has been over-emphasised in the enforcement of a state's obligations under international law, and relying merely on weak arguments, such as deterrence, to encourage states to prosecute. In such cases, it is not unusual for a state to refuse to prosecute. Many states, especially those that have not yet seen regime transition, may consider prosecution as self-condemnation, a mere obligation with no positive gain. An egocentric approach to force a state to comply with its obligations may result in a stronger resistance, as the state may do anything in its power to secure its right to sovereignty and integrity. Even with the mandate of the UN Security Council, there are still obstacles to the effective implementation of international law. International law still leaves much to be desired to be able to effectively breach the 'barrier of sovereignty'. In the case of the ICC, for example, the fact that many states are not party to the ICC Statute significantly limits its jurisdiction.

It can be argued that a state should be convinced that it can benefit from initiating prosecution, and more attention should be given to the enhancement of positive interests, in other words, a soft approach should be taken. Such interests may include: (1) the state's ability to secure its right to sovereignty while preventing the scrutiny of its internal affairs by international agencies or other states; (2) the contribution to judicial capacity building which may lead to an independent, credible and impartial judicial system; (3) the ability of domestic institutions to control the process and outcome of the proceedings, thereby avoiding the uncertainty which would arise if an external mechanism were to undertake them instead; (4) the possibility of avoiding demonstrations and bad publicity caused by prolonged victims and other parties which may lead to further scrutiny and shame; (5) the clear identification of the imposition of individual guilt which may prevent the shifting of responsibility onto the state itself; and (6) the protection and enhancement of the moral quality of the state's armed forces, which may arguably prevent future misconduct. The state's initiation of domestic prosecution will arguably benefit both the state and international community. However, domestic prosecution may open the possibilities for abuse of justice by the state in question. It is therefore important that the state's act of self-scrutiny be carefully monitored, specifically on crucial aspects that may have a significant impact on the impartiality and credibility of the proceedings, such as the protection of witnesses and evidence. This is arguably where the safeguard mechanism of negative interest should be implemented. The recognition of a state's positive interest in individual accountability may well motivate states to assume their duty to prosecute, which may attract more voluntary initiation of domestic prosecution.

Appendix 1

Prime Ministerial Apologies versus Yasukuni Worship, 1972–2005[160]

Prime Minister Date of Accession to Office	Major Prime Ministerial Apology	Number of visits to Yasukuni Shrine
Tanaka Kakuei 7 July 1972	**25 September 1972**: As part of the restoration of Sino–Japanese relations, expresses remorse for the "trouble" (*meiwaku*) Japan caused. The comments cause some anger because *meiwaku* is not seen as sufficiently strong.	Five.
Miki Takeo 9 December 1974		Three. In 1975 Miki was the first prime minister to worship on 15 August. Deliberately "private" (starting the "official" versus "private" worship issue).
Fukuda Takeo 24 December 1976		Four.
Ōhira Masayoshi 7 December 1978		Three. Worships despite being a practicing Christian.
Susuki Zenko 17 July 1980		Nine. Worships with the cabinet on 15 August 1980, 1981 and 1982.
Nakasone Yasuhiro 27 November 1982	**22 August 1984:** In Korea he expresses "deep remorse" (*fukai hansei*) for the trouble and "terrible damage" (*sangai*) in the past.	Ten. First prime minister to worship at New Year, 5 January 1984. 15 August 1985: "Official" worship marks the internationalisation of the Yasukuni issue.
Takeshita Noboru	**6 March 1989**: In the Diet, says the "militaristic aggression" (*gunjishugi ni yoru*	None.

---

[160] Seaton, 2007, pp. 88–91, see *supra* note 132.

6 November 1987	*shiryaku*) of the country cannot be denied. **30 March 1989**: expresses deep remorse and "feelings of regret" (*ikan no i*) for colonial rule to North Korea, the first such statement to the North. The comments are welcomed by Kim Il-sung on 4 April.	
Uno Sōsuke **3 June 1989**		None.
Kaifu Toshiki **10 August 1989**	**28 September 1990**: A cross-party delegation led by Kanemaru Shin signs a joint declaration in North Korea saying Japan should "apologise" (*shazai*) and compensate for its colonial rule. **3 May 1991**: At the ASEAN summit in Singapore, Kaifu expresses deep remorse for the "unbearable suffering and sadness" (*taekuni kurushimi to kanashimi*) caused by "our nation's acts". **10 August 1991**: Expresses remorse on a trip to China.	None.
Miyazawa Kiichi **5 November 1991**	**17 January 1992**: Revelations in the *Asahi* newspaper force an apology (*owabi*) to the comfort women on Miyazawa's trip to Korea.	One. A secret visit in 1992.
Hosokawa Morihiro **9 August 1993**	**10 August 1993**: Comments it was "an aggressive war and a mistake" (*shinryaku sensō*). **15 August 1993**: Hosokawa becomes first prime minister to offer condolences to all Asians. Speaker of the House, Doi Takako, announces parliament is considering a Diet resolution offering an official apology (*shazai*) for aggression against Asian nations. The remarks are widely welcomed in Asia. **19 August 1993**: Secretary of State Takemura Masayoshi reiterates Hosokawa's aggressive war (*shinryaku sensō*) stance, but maintains that "all compensation claims are resolved". **23 August 1993**: Hosokawa tones down his "aggressive war" comments to "aggressive acts" (*shinryaku kōi*).	None.

	27 September 1993: Hosokawa speech at the UN: "We must not forget remorse for the past". **6 November 1993**: In Korea, Hosokawa lists specific Korean grievances (such as the comfort women issue and Koreans being forced to use Japanese names) and comments that "as the aggressor" (*kagai-sha to shite*) he expresses remorse and a "deep apology" (*fukai chinsha*). This apology is very well received. **20 March 1994**: While in China, expresses remorse and an "apology" (*owa-bi*) as well as a desire to look to the future. Participated in a wreath-laying ceremony to soldiers who fought against the Japanese.	
Hata Tsutomu **28 April 1994**		None.
Murayama Tomiichi **30 June 1994**	**24 August 1994**: In Manila, expresses remorse and proposes new initiatives for joint historical research. Meanwhile, in Singapore, Leader of the House Doi lays a wreath at a memorial to Chinese massacred during the Japanese occupation. **3 May 1994**: Expresses remorse for the unbearable suffering caused on a trip to China. LI gives a lukewarm approval: "We agree with your views". Murayama becomes the first serving prime minister to visit the Marco Polo Bridge. **15 August 1995**: The Murayama communiqué (*danwa*) supplements the widely criticised parliamentary statement (9 June). This personal "heartfelt apology" becomes the standard prime ministerial apology, but eight members of the cabinet worship at the Yasukuni Shrine. South Korean President Kim Young-sam calls for "correct views of history in Japan", which indicates that the apology has not been so well received.	None.
Hashimoto Ryutarō **11 January 1996**	**26 January 1996**: In the Diet, Hashimoto states it was aggression, and restates the Murayama communiqué, but scepticism exists because of earlier comments (24	One. Ex-head of the War Bereaved Associa-

	October 1994) when, as Minister of Trade and Industry, he said he had lingering doubts about whether it could be called a war of aggression. **23 June 1996**: Hashimoto apologises (*owabi*) to the comfort women. Korea and Japan have been made co-hosts of the 2002 FIFA World Cup, necessitating closer ties. **15 August 1996**: Hashimoto expresses remorse to Asians, but after remembering those who died fighting "for the security of their nation". He also praises the precious sacrifice (*tōtoi gisei*) of the war generation. **4 September 1997**: Hashimoto in China repeats the Murayama communiqué to British POWs via Prime Minister Blair who is in Tokyo.	tion. Worships "privately" on his birthday, 29 July 1996.
Obuchi Keizō **30 July 1998**	**15 August 1998**: Obuchi repeats the Hashimoto and Murayama position. **8 October 1998**: Expresses remorse (*hansei*) to President Kim Dae-jung as part of the Japan–Republic of Korea Joint Declaration. **5 November 1998**: President Jiang Zemin of China visits Japan. Obuchi issues a verbal apology, but there is a wrangling over a written joint declaration which only mentions remorse.	None.
Mori Yoshirō **5 April 2000**		None.
Koizumi Junichirō **26 April 2001**	**8 October 2001**: Koizumi expresses remorse and apology (*owabi*) in China and visits the Marco Polo Bridge and the Anti-Japanese War Museum. Koizumi's apologies are ignored in favour of warnings about textbooks and his Yasukuni Shrine worship. **15 October 2001**: Koizumi expresses the same remorse and apology in Korea, as well as a proposal for joint historical research. But the response is the same: warnings about textbooks and Yasukuni. **17 September 2002**: The Pyongyang Declaration includes an apology to North	Five (to October 2005). Triggers a major diplomatic row with his 13 August 2001 worship on 21 April 2002, 14 January 2003 and 1 January 2004. 17 October 2005: worships in the same way as a private citizen.

| | Korea, but the apology is lost in the Japanese preoccupation with the abduction issue (Japanese citizens abducted by North Korea, five of whom returned with Koizumi to Japan).

22 April 2005: apology at an ASEAN summit, but by now relations in Asia have dipped to a new low. | |

11

If You're Not at the Table, You're on the Menu: Complementarity and Self-Interest in Domestic Processes for Core International Crimes

Christopher B. Mahony*

11.1. Introduction

The research project of which this anthology is part of seeks to identify "which forms of justice speak most effectively"[1] to military self-interest in bringing perpetrators to justice for core international crimes. This chapter focuses on the extent to which the Statute of the International Criminal Court ('ICC') accepts politicised trials under its principle of complementarity. Does the complementarity principle, which provides primacy to states unless they are "unable or unwilling",[2] tolerate politicised domestic processes? This chapter considers the military self-interest in prosecuting core international crimes cases in order to exclude ICC jurisdiction. By examining a number of situations under ICC examination or investigation, I argue that the complementarity threshold tolerates politicised processes. I argue that it is in the long-term self-interest of armed forces to bring

---

* **Christopher B. Mahony** is a Research Fellow at the Centre for International Law Research and Policy where he is engaged in research that expands on his D.Phil. thesis examining the trajectory of international criminal justice case selection independence. He is a Visiting Fellow at Georgetown University Law Center, Washington, DC, and a Citizen Security and Criminal Justice Specialist at the World Bank. He holds a D.Phil. in Politics and an M.Sc. in African Studies from Oxford University, and a B.Com. and an LL.B. from Otago University. He was previously founding Deputy Director of the New Zealand Centre for Human Rights Law, Policy and Practice at Auckland University and Director of the Witness Evaluation Legacy Project at the Special Court for Sierra Leone where he led the design of Sierra Leone's witness protection programme. He has advised the US Department of State, the International Criminal Court, the Open Society Initiative and the International Centre for Transitional Justice.

[1] Morten Bergsmo, Arne Willy Dahl and Richard Sousa, "Military Self-Interest in Accountability for Core International Crimes", FICHL Policy Brief Series No. 14 (2013), *op. cit.* (http://www.legal-tools.org/doc/396da7/).

[2] ICC Statute of the International Criminal Court, Rome, 17 July 1998, Article 17(1) ('ICC Statute').

---

perpetrators of core international crimes to justice via domestic processes that are politically controlled but still meet the complementarity threshold.

To refrain from prosecuting those of political expediency leaves those not of political expediency exposed to ICC investigation. If armed forces refrain from sitting at the prosecuting table they remain potential prey on the ICC menu. I argue, therefore, that the primary interest of armed forces in prosecuting core international crimes cases is realist self-interest in controlling who is prosecuted and who is not. In making this argument, I consider the cases of Colombia, Libya, Kenya, Uganda and Guinea. Where these states demonstrated the requisite due diligence and intent to pursue politically controlled and expedient processes, they have disabled sensitive ICC investigations. Where more belligerent opposition to the ICC was adopted – where states refuse to sit at the table – the ICC has pursued sensitive cases.

11.2. Complementarity and Political Control of Domestic Case Selection

To consider political interaction with the complementarity principle, we must assess the extent to which realist jurisdictional and functional constraints of complementarity are affected by normative pressure to independently investigate and prosecute core international crimes. Critical to considering the interest of armed forces in prosecuting international crimes is the degree of primacy complementarity affords domestic proceedings, the independence complementarity demands of domestic proceedings, and how those variables interact with other pressures upon the ICC.

ICC Statute deference to domestic jurisdictions constitutes, along with United Nations Security Council controls over jurisdiction, the most compromising element for the ICC Office of the Prosecutor's ('OTP') independence in case selection. Complementarity provides sophisticated state actors the amnesty card instrument of manipulated investigations while enjoying the credible commitment benefits of ICC Statute participation. To understand the regulatory capture and compromise of independence afforded by complementarity, its technical elements must be considered. Article 17(1)(a)–(c) of the ICC Statute renders a case inadmissible if it has been or is being investigated or prosecuted by a state with jurisdiction over the crimes in question. However, inadmissibility is voided if the investigating or prosecuting state is unwilling or unable genuinely to carry out the investigation or prosecution.[3]

11.3. Colombia: Complementarity's Low Pre-Investigation Threshold

A determination of "unable or unwilling genuinely" was never fully explored in the ICC's first investigation in Uganda. Colombia, where formal OTP investigations have not yet opened at the time of writing, has experienced close scrutiny of domestic proceedings. The Colombian government has exploited the fact that complementarity is not definitely and finally determined at one point in time, allowing for gaming and re-gaming of the complementarity threshold. Even if an investigation is opened, complementarity may be revisited several times before the commencement of a trial.[4]

A proactive Colombian government impeded OTP investigations, with US technical support, by establishing a complementarity-compliant domestic regime that still preserves impunity for elites. The Colombian government accompanied complementarity with Article 124 prevention of OTP war crimes investigations for seven years after Colombia's ratification.[5] However, for crimes against humanity, which the OTP alleges various parties in Colombia have committed, Article 124 does not apply.[6] Complementarity, therefore, remained the sole impediment to ICC investigation of crimes against humanity in Colombia. The Colombian government established the Colombian Justice and Peace Unit ('CJPU'). The CJPU initially refrained from targeting senior actors or using seniority as a case selection criterion, despite its public pledges to pursue those most responsible.[7] US government support has been critical to enabling sophis-

---

[3]   ICC Statute, Article 17, see *supra* note 2.

[4]   Jo Stigen, *The Relationship Between the International Criminal Court and National Jurisdictions: The Principle of Complementarity*, Martinus Nijhoff Publishers, Leiden, 2008, p. 245; and International Criminal Court, *Prosecutor v. Kony et al.*, ICC-02/04-01/05, Decision on the Admissibility of the Case under Article 19(1) of the Statute, 10 March 2009, paras. 25 ff. (26, 28, 52).

[5]   OTP war crimes jurisdiction over Colombia began on 1 November 2009. International Criminal Court, Office of the Prosecutor ('ICC-OTP'), *Report on Preliminary Examination Activities*, 13 December 2011, p. 14.

[6]   *Ibid.*, p. 15.

[7]   Maria Paula Saffon, "Problematic Selection and Lack of Clear Prioritization: The Colombian Experience", in Morten Bergsmo (ed.), *Criteria for Prioritizing and Selecting Core*

tication sufficient to avoid ICC investigation and pursuit of senior Colombian government suspects. Joint US-Colombian efforts to prevent ICC investigation demonstrate the predominance of functional rather than jurisdictional constraints over ICC case selection.[8] Under the US Justice Reform Program:

> The US Department of Justice provided assistance to the Justice and Peace Unit, including training of and technical assistance for prosecutors and investigators, equipment, database development, office and hearing room development, and forensic and operational support.[9]

The Department of Justice spent USD 1.54 million in 2006 and USD 2.58 million in 2007.[10] Simultaneously, the US government provides military support to the Colombian government to fight armed opposition. Secret US assistance, including substantial National Security Agency eavesdropping, is funded through a multibillion-dollar black budget. The secret support is, since 2000, supplemented by a public USD 9 billion package of mostly military aid called Plan Colombia.[11] This support implicates US actors for aiding and abetting what the OTP has reasonable basis to believe are crimes against humanity.[12] Therefore, OTP investigations in Colombia would likely shift US ICC policy towards hostile opposition. The ICC's Colombian threat to US interests dramatically heightens US engagement in softening OTP case selection independence, particularly in relation to complementarity.

The Colombian government has sought to establish and refine complementarity compliance and political utility through its 2005 Justice and Peace Law. The German government commissioned the scholar Kai Am-

International Crimes Cases, Second Edition, Torkel Opsahl Academic EPublisher, Oslo, 2010, p. 139 (http://www.legal-tools.org/en/doc/f5abed/); and ICC-OTP, *Report on Preliminary Examination Activities*, November 2013, p. 32.

[8] Judith Goldstein, Miles Kahler, Robert O. Keohane and Anne-Marie Slaughter, "Introduction: Legalization and World Politics", in *International Organization*, 2000, vol. 54, no. 3, pp. 385–99.

[9] Committee on Foreign Affairs, House of Representatives, Subcommittee on the Western Hemisphere, *US-Colombia Relations: Hearing Before the Subcommittee on the Western Hemisphere of the Committee on Foreign Affairs*, Serial 110-39, US Government Printing Office, Washington, 24 April 2007, p. 116.

[10] *Ibid.*

[11] Dana Priest, "Covert Action in Colombia," in *Washington Post*, 21 December 2013.

[12] ICC-OTP, 2013, p. 32, see *supra* note 7.

bos to study the law's compliance.[13] The Justice and Peace Law covers crimes by both left- and right-leaning armed groups after 25 July 2005.[14] The OTP has found that the Colombian armed forces, government-aligned paramilitary groups and left-wing armed groups committed crimes against humanity and war crimes since 1 November 2009.[15] Ambos found that the law, in conjunction with a 2006 Decree and Constitutional Court support, converts ordinary sentences to alternative five-year minimum and eight-year maximum sentences.[16] The "considerable" mitigation is contingent upon accused participation in "truth, justice and reparations".[17] Ambos also found that the law satisfied the ICC Statute's Article 17(1)(d) requirement of "some" state action greater than full criminal exemption, since punishment remained through considerable sentence reduction.[18] While Ambos acknowledges Supreme Court pressure to investigate state security forces, he also cites the discriminatory exclusion of the Fuerzas Armadas Revolucionarias de Colombia ('FARC') and other left-wing groups from sentence conversion due to drug trafficking or illicit enrichment.[19] Ambos notes the special Justice and Peace Chamber's filtering of eligible cases based on demobilisation and rejection of criminality. The executive, a party to the conflict, then wields final discretion to directly impede commutation of sentence.[20] Once the individual is approved, the government prosecution ascertains criminal responsibility and the authenticity of the provided testimony before a hearing is held to determine sen-

---

[13] Kai Ambos and Florian Huber, "The Colombian Peace Process and the Principle of Complementarity of the International Criminal Court: Is There Sufficient Willingness and Ability on the Part of the Colombian Authorities or Should the Prosecutor Open an Investigation Now?", Institute for Criminal Law and Justice, Department of Foreign and International Criminal Law, Georg-August Universität Göttingen, 5 January 2011 (https://www.legal-tools.org/doc/e1b72d/).

[14] Kai Ambos, "The Colombian Peace Process (Law 975 of 2005) and the ICC's Principle of Complementarity", in Carsten Stahn and Mohamed M. El Zeidy (eds.), *The International Criminal Court and Complementarity: From Theory to Practice*, Cambridge University Press, New York, 2011, pp. 1072–3.

[15] Ambos and Huber, 2011, pp. 30–31, see *supra* note 13.

[16] Ambos, 2011, p. 1072, see *supra* note 14.

[17] Pablo Kalmanovitz, "A Law of Conditionally Reduced Penalty", in Morten Bergsmo and Pablo Kalmanovitz (eds.), *Law and Peace Negotiations*, FICHL Publication Series no. 5, Second Edition, Torkel Opsahl Academic EPublisher, Oslo, 2010, pp. 8, 13 (http://www.legal-tools.org/en/doc/ef7785/).

[18] Ambos and Huber, 2011, pp. 4–5, see *supra* note 13.

[19] *Ibid.*, p. 5; Ambos, 2011, p. 1073, see *supra* note 14.

[20] Ambos, 2011, pp. 1073–5, see *supra* note 14.

tence.[21] An OTP member described Colombia's complementarity approach, which facilitates executive assistance and discriminatory justice, as "very sophisticated".[22]

The Colombian government's sophistication can be seen in Ambos's observations. He concludes that while amnesty impedes domestic prosecution or investigation, a pardon constitutes a post-trial exemption the ICC is unlikely to interpret as shielding criminal responsibility through inaction.[23] Ambos also considers the elements of 'unwillingness', including shielding, unjustified delay, and lack of independence and impartiality, to be assessed cumulatively, not individually in determining unwillingness.[24] Unwillingness, Ambos asserts, is determined by the underlying bad faith expressed in the actions or omissions of the national justice system. That interpretation provides broad OTP discretion to determine a 'bad faith' departure from 'genuine' proceedings. Ambos concludes that a five-to-eight-year sentence does not constitute shielding and that rendering of only one judgment after four years does not constitute unjustified delay.[25] He views the Colombian judiciary as adequately independent of 'direct' executive influence, suggesting indirect influence is acceptable.[26]

Ambos also recognises the very low threshold of 'unable', which requires total collapse, a substantial collapse or the unavailability of the national judicial system, including inability to obtain the accused, necessary evidence or testimony, or otherwise to carry out its proceedings.[27] Perceived political interference in efforts to obtain accused, evidence or testimony, without making value judgments about a justice system's function, Ambos asserts, may constitute inability.[28] This threshold is particularly low in that it excludes economic and other pressures on domestic courts' capacity to conform to international law and mitigate the interests

---

21 *Ibid.*, pp. 1076–78.

22 Interview with Member of the Office of the Prosecutor, International Criminal Court, The Hague, The Netherlands, 3 December 2012.

23 Ambos, 2011, p. 1087, see *supra* note 14.

24 *Ibid.*, p. 1089.

25 *Ibid.*, pp. 1090–91.

26 *Ibid.*, p. 1092.

27 *Ibid.*; ICC Statute, Article 17.

28 Ambos, 2011, p. 1093, see *supra* note 14.

of government actors.[29] In justifying the weak 'unavailability' threshold, Ambos cites the ICC Statute's use of 'substantial' instead of 'partial' (collapse) as requiring an external observer to make quantitative, easily verifiable determinations of substantial legal or factual obstacles without engaging value (quality) judgments about a justice system's functioning.[30] Thus, a poorly functioning and qualitatively corrupt national justice system may still meet Ambos's complementarity threshold as long as the system is not, for example, quantifiably over-burdened or under-capacitated.[31] Colombia's Constitutional Court, in requiring a "clear absence of necessary objective conditions to carry out proceedings", adopts Ambos's position.[32]

The OTP also determined, most importantly, that subject to appropriate sentencing, those bearing greatest responsibility have already been subject to national proceedings in Colombia.[33] By initiating 'proceedings' of ambiguous voracity and despite convicting only 11 persons after seven years of operation, Colombia's efforts continue to satisfy OTP standards.[34] The OTP's conclusions appear to correctly apply very weak, imprecise law that severely constrains the extent to which states have delegated international crimes prosecution. The very top of the Colombian elite has been commonly cited as involved in the conflict's crimes.[35] However, the International Center for Transitional Justice ('ICTJ') found that Colombia's prosecution focused on illegal armed groups and low-

---

[29] Wolfgang Friedmann, *The Changing Structure of International Law*, London, Stevens and Sons, 1964, pp. 146–47; Eyal Benvenisti, "Judicial Misgivings Regarding the Application of International Law: An Analysis of Attitudes of National Courts", in *European Journal of International Law*, 1993, vol. 4, no. 1, pp. 159–83; Jan Paulsson, *Denial of Justice in International Law*, Cambridge University Press, Cambridge, 2005, p. 4; and André Nollkaemper, "The Independence of the Domestic Judiciary in International Law", in *The Finnish Yearbook of International Law*, 2006, vol. 17, pp. 261–305.

[30] Ambos and Huber, 2011, pp. 6–7, see *supra* note 13.

[31] *Ibid.*, p. 7.

[32] *Ibid.*

[33] ICC-OTP, *Situation in Colombia – Interim Report*, November 2012, p. 50.

[34] ICC-OTP, 2011, pp. 16–17, see *supra* note 5; International Center for Transitional Justice, "Justice and Peace: Progress and Great Challenges", 5 October 2012, available at https://www.ictj.org/news/justice-and-peace-progress-and-challenges, last accessed on 5 April 2015.

[35] An example is the use of death squads by former President Alvaro Uribe's brother alleged by a former police officer who states he was paid to turn a blind eye. See Associated Press, "Retired Colombian Police Officer Accuses Uribe's Brother of Leading 1990s Death Squad", in Fox News, 24 May 2010.

---

and mid-level combatants rather than political, military and business leaders that aid and abet, or wield command control over, state security forces.[36] It is the very impunity provided to political, military and business leaders that constitutes the primary incentive for armed groups to prosecute crimes themselves.

The ease with which complementarity was satisfied emboldened the Colombian government. In 2012 it passed the Legal Framework for Peace ('LFP') as the basis for peace talks. The LFP, approved by the Constitutional Court, provides for suspension of sentences, allowing no incarceration for those convicted.[37] The OTP, in attempting to accommodate the Colombian government, stated it would approach reduced and suspended sentences on a case-by-case basis considering whether, in the circumstances, sentences are "consistent with an intent to bring the person concerned to justice".[38] However, in a leaked private letter to Colombia's Constitutional Court,[39] the prosecutor Fatou Bensouda signalled total commutation or suspension of sentence would impede complementarity:

> [T]he duration of the term of imprisonment may be a relevant factor in cases where the penalty is so disproportionate that the intent to bring the person concerned to justice can be questioned. For example, the Informal expert paper *The principle of complementarity in practice*, advanced by the Office of the Prosecutor, considered that "amnesties, pardons, or grossly inadequate sentences issued after the proceeding, in a manner that brings into question the genuineness of the proceedings as a whole" can be indicators of "shielding" or "intent". [...] Since the suspension of a prison sentence means that the accused does not spend time incarcerated, I would like to warn you that this would be manifestly inadequate for individuals allegedly bearing the great-

---

36 ICTJ, 2012, see *supra* note 34.

37 Helen Murphy, "Colombia's High Court rules FARC Peace Talks Law Constitutional", in Reuters, 29 August 2013.

38 ICC-OTP, 2012, p. 64, see *supra* note 33.

39 Rodrigo Uprimny, "Cartas Bombas", in *El Espectador*, 24 August 2013; and "Una 'Carta Bomba'", in *Semana*, 17 August 2013.

est responsibility for the commission of war crimes and crimes against humanity.[40]

Another leaked letter also insisted those "most responsible" be pursued although the LFP appears to accommodate this demand.[41] Despite this warning from the ICC prosecutor, Colombia's Constitutional Court approved the LFP, but allowed scope for agreement via rejection only of total suspension. The prosecution responded with further accommodation in its 2013 report, citing the Constitutional Court's exclusion of total suspension of sentence for those most responsible.[42] The ICC's position suggests that anything less than a 'total' suspension of sentence may demonstrate sufficient Colombian commitment to compatibility with complementarity. The ICC position remains ambiguous as to whether, for example, a week of incarceration would be acceptable for those most responsible for core international crimes. However, it does note in its 2014 report that

> the Office has informed the Colombian authorities that a sentence that is grossly or manifestly inadequate, in light of the gravity of the crimes and the form of participation of the accused, would vitiate the genuineness of a national proceeding, even if all previous stages of the proceeding had been deemed genuine.[43]

The Colombian government's sophisticated efforts signal the importance of engagement at the prosecution table prior to ICC-OTP opening of investigations.

11.4. Post-Investigation Contestation: Raising the Bar

While the complementarity threshold is very low for situations prior to the initiation of an investigation, the bar is significantly raised once the prosecution initiates investigations. The cost of failing to 'sit at the table' via a 'Colombia-like' negotiated domestic process raises the level of independence and integrity the ICC requires of a domestic process. After the ICC prosecution begins investigations, the ICC Statute requires domestic pro-

---

40 Translated letter dated 25 July 2013, from the Prosecutor, ICC-OTP, to the Government of Colombia, received 28 October 2013 via e-mail from the translating author, an NGO worker.

41 "Una 'Carta Bomba'", in *Semana*, 17 August 2013.

42 ICC-OTP, 2013, p. 32, see *supra* note 7.

43 ICC-OTP, *Report on Preliminary Examination Activities 2014*, 2 December 2014, p. 27.

---

ceedings cover the same 'case' or conduct as that investigated by the court – a condition not required of states able to satisfy complementarity prior to ICC initiation of investigations. The Statute also requires post-ICC initiation of investigations that states are able and willing genuinely to carry out proceedings.[44] The Appeals Chamber, citing Jo Stigen's requirement of an examination of some detail reflecting a sufficient measure of thoroughness, should also include "steps directed at ascertaining whether those suspects are responsible for that conduct, for instance by interviewing witnesses or suspects, collecting documentary evidence, or carrying out forensic analyses".[45]

The burden of proving those steps are taken falls to the state, which requires "evidence of a sufficient degree of specificity and probative value that demonstrates that it is indeed investigating the case".[46] The ICC Pre-Trial Chamber found that Kenyan government "assertions" that ICC indictees were being investigated were of insufficient specificity and probative value to discharge the burden of proof.[47] However, the specific reference in Article 17(3) to inability "to obtain the accused, or the necessary evidence and testimony", or otherwise to "carry out proceedings" specifies that in order to meet the complementarity threshold, a criminal justice process must enjoy the investigative capacity to obtain evidence and to retain testimony from witnesses. The OTP demanded witness protection capacity of the Kenyan government in 2009 discussions regarding complementarity.[48]

---

[44] International Criminal Court, Pre-Trial Chamber, *Prosecutor v. Saif Al-Islam Gaddafi and Abdullah Al-Senussi*, Situation in Libya, ICC-01/11-01/11, Decision on the Admissibility of the Case against Abdullah Al-Senussi ('Admissibility of the Case against Al-Senussi'), 11 October 2013.

[45] International Criminal Court, *Prosecutor v. Francis Kirimi Muthaura, Uhuru Muigai Kenyatta and Mohammed Hussein Ali*, Situation in the Republic of Kenya ('*Prosecutor v. Francis Kirimi Muthaura*') , ICC-01/09-02/11 OA, Judgment on the Appeal of the Republic of Kenya against the Decision of Pre-Trial Chamber II of 30 May 2011 entitled "Decision on the Application by the Government of Kenya Challenging the Admissibility of the Case Pursuant to Article 19(2)(b) of the Statute", 30 August 2011, pp. 23, 15, citing Stigen, 2008, p. 203, see *supra* note 4.

[46] *Prosecutor v. Francis Kirimi Muthaura*, 30 August 2011, p. 23, see *supra* note 45.

[47] *Ibid.*, pp. 32–33.

[48] ICC-OTP, Agreed Minutes of the Meeting between Prosecutor Moreno Ocampo and the Delegation of the Kenyan Government, Press Release, The Hague, The Netherlands, 3 July 2009.

The Pre-Trial Chamber, in the *Saif Al-Islam Gaddafi* case, also expressed concern about the inability of judicial and governmental authorities to ascertain control, access witness testimony and provide adequate witness protection.[49] The Pre-Trial Chamber cites elements absent from consideration in Colombia, such as governmental failure to protect detained former regime members from torture and mistreatment.[50] Unlike the threshold for trials, the ICC lowers the bar considerably when determining state ability to investigate and prosecute "in the context of the relevant national system and procedures", meaning "in accordance with the substantive and procedural law applicable" in that state.[51] Libyan law and procedure provide for protective measures. However, the Libyan government was unable to exercise control over detention facilities, or even to access, let alone protect, witnesses.[52] Further, the Pre-Trial Chamber appeared to require independent witness protection enjoying practical capacity and independence to cater to defence and prosecution witnesses.[53] It also required that the defendant be provided counsel, but remained ambiguous as to the accused's right to counsel during interrogation, given the right's absence from the Libyan Code of Criminal Procedure.[54]

In the *Abdullah Al-Senussi* case, the ICC appeared to reconsider the bar set in the *Saif Al-Islam Gaddafi* case. In *Al-Senussi*, the Libyan government, by providing material evidence of a difficult yet ongoing investigation, secured an inadmissibility finding.[55] Despite the abduction of an accused's counsel, the failure at the time of judgment to provide legal representation to an accused and unavailable witness protection capacity, the situation in Libya did not "[…] necessarily entail 'collapse' or 'unavailability' of the Libyan judicial system such that it impeded Libya's ability to carry out the proceedings".[56]

---

[49] International Criminal Court, Pre-Trial Chamber, *Prosecutor v. Saif Al-Islam Gaddafi and Abdullah Al-Senussi*, ICC-01/11-01/11, Decision on the Admissibility of the Case against Saif Al-Islam Gaddafi, 31 May 2013, p. 86, para. 209.

[50] *Ibid.*

[51] *Ibid.*, p. 82, para. 200.

[52] *Ibid.*, p. 83, para. 201.

[53] *Ibid.*, p. 87, para. 211.

[54] *Ibid.*, p. 88, para. 214.

[55] Admissibility of the Case against Abdullah Al-Senussi, 11 October 2013, see *supra* note 44.

[56] *Ibid.*, pp. 139–140.

The key discrepancy between the *Gaddafi* and *Al-Senussi* cases, other than a demonstrated investigation, appeared to be the fact that Al-Senussi was in the hands of the government. Sceptical commentary of the decision cites Al-Senussi's potential disclosure before the ICC of security details between Gaddafi, the CIA and MI6 as potentially motivating ICC apprehension about hosting the trial.[57] Robert Fisk observes that "when lawyers for Senussi demanded to know if MI6 operatives had interrogated him during his stay in Mauritania – and before his illegal rendition to Libya – Foreign Secretary William Hague declined to reply".[58]

Unlike the Kenyan government, the Libyan government bore no political risk of self-incrimination through providing sufficient evidence to demonstrate pursuit of the same persons and conduct. By refraining from providing genuine and potentially incriminating information, Kenya failed to demonstrate concrete and progressive steps to address the same case as the individuals and conduct before the ICC.[59] Kenya and Colombia are similar in that neither the governments nor the Security Council referred the situations, yet the OTP treated them differently. A former senior OTP member viewed Colombia as "a situation that should have been engaged" where "the Court did not provide an effective threat" and was not consistent.[60] The member noted: "The Prosecutor had made it clear he wanted to assist and co-operate in Colombia rather than apply pressure to see results at the national level. The opposite approach was taken in Kenya".[61]

The OTP experienced exaggerated pressure to initiate Kenyan investigations after the UN Secretary General, Kofi Annan, employed his significant agency as a norm entrepreneur by providing a list of names and accompanying evidence to the ICC Prosecutor. The Kenyan Judge who investigated the abuses had requested Annan provide the information if Kenyan complementarity efforts were not forthcoming. While the ICC prosecution still retained discretion, it constrained itself by providing a number of deadlines for the Kenyan government to initiate "genuine judi-

---

[57] Robert Fisk, "Is The Hague Making a Mockery of Justice so the CIA and M16 Can Save Face?", in *The Independent*, 31 October 2013.

[58] *Ibid.*

[59] Admissibility of the Case against Abdullah Al-Senussi, 11 October 2013, p. 88, see *supra* note 44.

[60] Interview with Paul Seils, former Head of Situation Analysis, ICC-OTP, New York, USA, 16 December 2011.

[61] *Ibid.*

---

cial proceedings against those most responsible".[62] Kenya's failure to meet these deadlines, after parliamentary refusal to approve a special tribunal, indicated parliament's disagreement with the executive as to the political cost of delegating authority. They refused to sit at the prosecution table. The ICC prosecution proceeded with investigations and indictments. Kenyan power dynamics shifted considerably when accused members of parliament won elections and took control of the executive in April 2013.

Other governments' token steps illuminate Kenya's complementarity failure to prevent ICC investigations. Guinea, for example, sought to assert absence of culpability by hiring former Special Court for Sierra Leone Prosecutor, David Crane, and Special Court investigator, Alan White, to assess its culpability. The Crane report, in alignment with the Guinean military's view, attributes responsibility for 2009 killings to a specific army unit, excluding Guinean junta culpability.[63] The report, which contradicted UN findings, was found not to be credible by the International Center for Transitional Justice.[64] The Guinean government then adopted incremental, but not self-incriminating, domestic processes sufficient to satisfy the OTP's complementarity threshold.[65]

11.5. Ugandan Utilisation of ICC Proceedings against Adversaries

Uganda has set itself a pre-emptive seat at complementarity's prosecution table. What distinguishes Uganda from Kenya is that President Yoweri Museveni's engagement with the ICC prosecution was calculated to initiate a domestic process signalling intent to prosecute crimes while stigmatising and isolating the opposition Lord's Resistance Army ('LRA') with ICC indictments. Ugandan engagement placated the OTP inclination to investigate Ugandan People's Defence Forces' ('UPDF') crimes. Although gravity and a narrow interpretation of forced displacement had already extinguished ICC jurisdiction over UPDF crimes, the Ugandan government had also provided evidence of domestic UPDF investiga-

---

[62] Christopher B. Mahony, *The Justice Sector Afterthought: Witness Protection in Africa*, Institute for Security Studies, Pretoria, 2010, p. 132.

[63] "Guinea Conakry: Stadium Killings Inquiry Not Credible", in Radio Netherlands Worldwide, 4 March 2010.

[64] *Ibid.*

[65] ICC-OTP, 2013, pp. 42–45, see *supra* note 7.

---

tions.[66] Because Ugandan engagement prevented ICC investigation of UPDF crimes, Uganda avoided the heightened obligation to investigate the 'same cases'.

The Ugandan government's complementarity calculation is reflected in the views of its consultant, Payam Akhavan. Akhavan, citing the US State Department, concludes that Uganda's justice system is "recognized for its independence and [...] has not collapsed".[67] Museveni, shortly after he referred the Ugandan situation, suggested the Ugandan government would prosecute crimes committed by the UPDF.[68] This assertion signalled to the ICC prosecution that Uganda would employ the primacy afforded it by complementarity if the prosecutor pursued UPDF crimes. The Ugandan sovereignty cost of fully implementing domestic complementarity is apparent in previous politically sensitive prosecutions. Museveni has experienced pressure to prosecute corruption involving ministers, family members and elements within the UPDF. In the case of fictional UPDF soldiers drawing salaries, Museveni used politicised military prosecution to purge UPDF elements viewed as opponents, rather than pursue those most culpable.[69] A low 'willingness' complementarity threshold, as established in the Libyan and Colombian cases, allows politicised prosecutions. This lever of case selection control constitutes the most powerful government instrument after explicit jurisdictional exclusion. It also constitutes the primary self-interest for armed forces in contemplating prosecution of core international crimes. The normative power of complementarity was diminished by the ICC's acceptance of jurisdiction despite Uganda's ostensible willingness and ability genuinely to prosecute crimes.

OTP personnel inconsistently cite complementarity as further justification for avoiding UPDF indictments. Some OTP personnel cited

---

[66] Interview with Ugandan Official, The Hague, The Netherlands, 1 December 2012.

[67] Payam Akhavan, "The Lord's Resistance Army Case: Uganda's Submission of the First State Referral to the International Criminal Court", in *American Journal of International Law*, 2005, vol. 99, no. 2, p. 415. While the US is an ally of President Museveni's, it should be noted that State Department Human Rights Reports do incriminate the UPDF.

[68] *Ibid.*, p. 411.

[69] Mahony, 2010, p. 143, see *supra* note 62.

gravity as the sole determinant.[70] However, other OTP members, as well as Ugandan government personnel, viewed Ugandan processes at the time of investigation as satisfying complementarity.[71] The OTP compiled a complementarity assessment of the military court system, including a detailed report of the number of prosecutions comparative to the number of crimes, the processes' quality, and draft legislation enabling prosecution of ICC Statute crimes.[72] The assessment, which has not been made public, drew on information from the public prosecutor's office, the Human Rights Commission, human rights organisations and a British government White Paper on the UPDF.[73] Where elements of compliance were questionable, the OTP was willing to assist, including with Human Rights Commission complaints and process effectiveness.[74] However, complementarity considerations ceased, along with engagement, once it was determined that UPDF cases would not be pursued due to insufficient gravity.[75] While civil society observers do not commonly view current or former processes as authentic, independent or capable of holding those most responsible accountable, Uganda's meagre efforts likely met the low complementarity threshold.[76]

OTP gravity determinations excluding UPDF crimes considerably diminish the integrity of complementarity's compliance pull. However, complementarity considerations may re-emerge were the Ugandan government to apprehend LRA accused and decide to try them domestically, extinguishing sovereignty costs associated with their trial before the ICC.

---

[70] Interview with Matthew Brubacher, former Analyst, Jurisdiction, Complementarity and Cooperation Division, ICC-OTP, via telephone, 15 July 2013; and Interview with OTP Member, 2012, see *supra* note 22.

[71] Interview with Gavin Hood, former Senior Policy Adviser to the Chief Prosecutor, ICC-OTP, via telephone, 24 May 2013.

[72] Interview with Brubacher, 2013, see *supra* note 70; Interview with Duncan Laki Muhumuza, Ugandan Mission to the United Nations, New York, USA, 5 November 2012; and Barney Afako, "Country Study V: Uganda", in Max du Plessis and Jolyon Ford (eds.), *Unable or Unwilling? Case Studies on Domestic Implementation of the ICC Statute in Selected African Countries*, Institute for Security Studies, Pretoria, 2008, p. 93.

[73] Interview with Brubacher, 2013, see *supra* note 70.

[74] *Ibid.*; Interview with Hood, 2013, see *supra* note 71.

[75] Interview with Brubacher, 2013, see *supra* note 70.

[76] Interview with Nicole Zarifis, Justice Law and Order Sector Foreign Adviser, Kampala, Uganda, 18 November 2012; Interview with Adam Branch, Academic, Makerere University, Kampala, Uganda, 14 November 2012; and Interview with Lyandro Komakech, Refugee Law Project, Kampala, Uganda, 16 November 2012.

Domestic trials would diminish external pressure for accompanying ICC prosecution of UPDF cases.[77] Similarly, controlled domestic trials can avoid unforeseen consequences, including subpoenas of government personnel to testify to politically sensitive issues.[78] In early January 2015, the LRA commander, Dominic Ongwen, was taken into custody by US forces after surrendering. After negotiations between the African Union, the US, the Central African Republic and the Ugandan governments, Ongwen was provided to the ICC for prosecution.[79]

In 2004 the government, with US assistance, drafted an International Criminal Court Bill, which was finally passed in 2010.[80] The ICC Act provided Uganda requisite domestic jurisdiction over international crimes and modes of responsibility for the International Crimes Division ('ICD') of Uganda's High Court to hear cases.[81] Norm entrepreneurs have protested a combination of constraints including the Court's hearing of only a single LRA case, an absence of political will to try UPDF cases and poor donor support.[82] Norm entrepreneurs also cite the pre-existence of the Amnesty Act, providing amnesty for surrendering rebels who renounce and abandon war or armed rebellion.[83] The Act, which contravenes ICD jurisdiction, provides the Minister of Internal Affairs discretion to propose a list of names to parliament for amnesty approval.[84] In the ICD's sole

---

[77] Interview with former Member, Ugandan National Security Council, 2012; and Interview with Branch, 2012, see *supra* note 76.

[78] Interview with Komakech, 2012, see *supra* note 76.

[79] Marie Harf, Deputy Spokesperson, Daily Press Briefing, United States Department of State, Washington, DC, 13 January 2015.

[80] Afako, 2008, p. 93, see *supra* note 72; Interview with Michael Ronning, USAID, Kampala, Uganda, 16 November 2012; and International Criminal Court Act, Act 11 of 2010, Uganda Gazette, no. 39, vol., CIII, 25 June 2010 ('ICC Act').

[81] ICC Act, 2010, Sections 7–9, 11; and High Court of Uganda International Crimes Division Practice Directions, Legal Notice no. 10 of 2011, Legal Notices Supplement, Uganda Gazette, no. 38, vol. CIV, 31 May 2011.

[82] Interview with Branch, 2012, see *supra* note 76; Interview with Zarifis, 2012, see *supra* note 76; Interview with Beth Van Schaack, former Deputy to Ambassador-At-Large for War Crimes Issues, US Department of State, Washington, DC, 8 November 2012; Interview with Komakech, 2012, see *supra* note 76; and Human Rights Watch, *Justice for Serious Crimes before National Courts: Uganda's International Crimes Division*, Human Rights Watch, New York, 2012.

[83] *Ibid.*; Amnesty Act, Section 3(1), Chapter 294, 21 January 2000 ('Amnesty Act 2000').

[84] Amnesty Act 2000, Section 2, see *supra* note 83; and Human Rights Watch, 2012, p. 5, see *supra* note 82.

---

case of the LRA commander, Thomas Kowelo, the Constitutional Court upheld amnesty, ordered the Amnesty Commission and the Director of Public Prosecutions to grant Kowelo a certificate of amnesty, and cease his trial.[85] All that appears to be required for complementarity compliance is for commutation of sentence to be used, as in Colombia, instead of amnesty.

Norm entrepreneurs cite enormous demands for 'credible justice' without addressing the technical complementarity threshold. Human Rights Watch's examination of the ICD found:

> For the ICD to render credible justice, including addressing crimes committed by both the LRA and Ugandan army and overcoming the legal obstacles, the Ugandan government will have to provide uncompromised political support. Donors also have a critical role to play, including by funding key needs for the ICD and stressing the importance of accountability for crimes committed by both sides.[86]

A group of donors to Ugandan justice sector reform, the Justice Law and Order Sector ('JLOS'), make more modest complementarity-oriented ICD demands of significant revision, particularly capacity to deliver prison terms.[87] JLOS actors, particularly in the context of a scaling down of ICD capacity,[88] are not optimistic about future ICD independence.[89] Early US enthusiasm for domestic processes diminished over time, as the threat of ICC pursuit of UPDF crimes diminished.[90] In May 2013, with US government support, Uganda reinstated Amnesty Act provisions for LRA combatants.[91]

---

[85] Constitutional Court of Uganda, *Thomas Kwoyelo Alias Latoni v. Uganda*, Constitutional Petition no. 036/11, arising out of HCT-00-ICD-Case no. 02/10, 22 September 2011.

[86] Human Rights Watch, 2012, p. 2, see *supra* note 82.

[87] Interview with Zarifis, 2012, see *supra* note 76.

[88] *Ibid.*; Interview with Justice Dan Kiiza, International Crimes Division (ICD), High Court of Uganda, Kampala, 15 November 2012; and Interview with Joanne Kagezi, ICD Prosecutor, interview no. 53, Kampala, Uganda, 19 November 2012.

[89] Interview with Zarifis, 2012, see *supra* note 76.

[90] Interview with Officer, US Embassy, Kampala, Uganda, 16 November 2012; Interview with Member, USAID, Kampala, Uganda, 16 November 2012; and Interview with Kiiza, 2012, see *supra* note 88.

[91] Interview with US Embassy Officer, 2012, see *supra* note 90; and Amnesty Act (Revocation of Statutory Instrument No. 34 of 2012), Uganda Gazette, Instrument 2013, 24 May 2013.

11.6. Constraints on the ICC's Independence in Case Selection

The Ugandan government feels under insufficient pressure to use commutation of sentence rather than amnesty, despite amnesty achieving the same goal – exclusion of the threat of ICC prosecution of UPDF crimes. This section considers key sources of pressure on the ICC prosecution that constrain its case selection independence, thereby diminishing pressure on the Ugandan government to engage in authentic prosecution of core international crimes. The sources of pressure include fiscal constraints, the threat of state non-cooperation, the establishment of alternative justice institutions, and accusations that OTP case selection discriminates against Africans. These instruments advance a realist state objective that further controls ICC case selection independence – the closure of situations, of which Uganda may be the first. In this environment, norm entrepreneurs have diminished effect on ICC case selection independence, including over interpretation of complementarity. More importantly, states or armed forces engaged in prosecuting core international crimes feel more confident that the ICC will not pursue them.

11.6.1. Budgetary Constraint

The first instrument to consider is budgetary constraint. The OTP, in attempting to project efficiency, refrained from mentioning budget during its early years.[92] However, budgetary restraints have started to take effect as caseloads began to increase without proportionate budgetary expansion.[93] ICC Prosecution personnel assert that case selection will still prioritise those most grave cases despite the prosecutor's statements, since 2011, that case selection is contingent on budgetary expansion.[94] Budgetary pressure is exacerbated by state pressure to engage other incidents or situations including in the Democratic Republic of Congo, Darfur and

---

[92] Interview with OTP Member, 2012, see *supra* note 22.

[93] *Ibid.*, Interview with Pascal Turlan, Judicial Cooperation Adviser, ICC-OTP, The Hague, The Netherlands, 5 December 2012; and Interview with Cecilia Balteanu, Head of Field Strategic Coordination and Planning Unit, Registry, The Hague, The Netherlands, 4 December 2012.

[94] Interview with OTP Member, 2012, see *supra* note 22; Interview with Turlan, 2012, see *supra* note 93; and ICC-OTP, *Statement to the United Nations Security Council on the Situation in Libya, Pursuant to UNSCR 1970 (2011)*, 2 November 2011, p. 5.

Myanmar.[95] Constrained budgets would have exaggerated effects where the ICC prosecution seeks to gather evidence in relation to the UPDF or any other party to a conflict that triggered ICC jurisdiction, particularly in the situation of a state self-referral. An attempt to investigate UPDF crimes in Uganda, without a global power providing information, renders the ICC particularly vulnerable to co-operative impediments. Unlike the situations in Darfur or Libya, where Security Council powers provide evidential support, state referrals from Western allies leave the OTP dependent on a direct party to the conflict to acquire evidence. An undercapacitated court exaggerates the problem of acquiring incriminating evidence in a case such as that involving the Ugandan armed forces or forces supported by Uganda or other co-operating states.[96] Budgetary constraints, therefore, constitute an entrenchment of institutional capture and a statist safeguard against entrepreneur-like ICC prosecution behaviour.

Budgetary constraint can also trigger resource reallocation, diminishing the chance of case selection reconsideration in a given situation.[97] The OTP has come under pressure to reallocate Ugandan resources, increasing the possibility of situation exit, and Ugandan abandonment of an ostensibly reassuring complementarity system – a system without politically sensitive consequence.[98] Financial pressure is particularly useful for global powers best positioned to provide evidence incriminating adversaries or complementarity support to protect allies.[99] In 2012, for example, the United Kingdom and Germany successfully sought to cut the ICC's budget, increasing prosecution dependence on state co-operation.[100]

---

[95] Interview with OTP Member, 2012, see *supra* note 22; Interview with Turlan, 2012, see *supra* note 93; and Nzau Musau, "Kenya: ICC Threatens to Drop Cases for Lack of Funds", in *The Star*, Kenya, 31 July 2013.

[96] Interview with Turlan, 2012, see *supra* note 93.

[97] Interview with Balteanu, 2012, see *supra* note 93.

[98] *Ibid.*

[99] *Ibid.*

[100] ICC, Assembly of States Parties, 11th Session, The Hague, 14–22 November 2012, ICC-ASP/11/20, Official Records, vol. 1, p. 13; and The Greens/European Free Alliance, "10th Anniversary of ICC: Budget Cuts Send Wrong Signal", News, 13 November 2012, available at http://www.greens-efa.eu/de/10th-anniversary-of-icc-8522.html, last accessed on 6 April 2015.

11.6.2. Influence of Powerful States

To this end, US ICC policy has evolved to prefer domestic venues for dealing with crimes and, where they fail, mixed international/domestic processes like the Special Court for Sierra Leone may step in, leaving solely international processes as the last resort.[101] To that extent, the US policy generally reflects a theme the ICC itself increasingly seeks to emphasise – that the ICC is a court of 'last resort'.[102] Increasing space for powerful state influence appears to be opened by budgetary pressure. The ICC's reduced 2013 budget prompted consideration of Security Council funding, US government funding or voluntary contributions for Security Council referred situations.[103]

The threat of elevated US pressure towards the ICC, were its initial case selection in situations such as Colombia and Uganda to confront US interests, can be seen in its original policy of non-cooperation and active obstruction towards the ICC. President George W. Bush's Under Secretary for Arms Control and International Security, John Bolton, led policy towards the ICC. His position was made clear in his testimony to the Senate Foreign Relations Committee after the signing of the ICC Statute. He stated:

> Our main concern should be for the President, the cabinet officers on the National Security Council, and other senior leaders responsible for our defense and foreign policy. They are the real potential targets of the ICC's politically unaccountable prosecutor and that is the real problem of universal jurisdiction.[104]

Bolton advised that the US adopt the following policy towards the ICC:

> I call it "the Three Noes": no financial support, directly or indirectly; no collaboration; and no further negotiations with other governments to improve the statute. This approach is likely to maximize the chances that the ICC will wither and

---

[101] Interview with Clint Williamson, former US Ambassador for war crimes issues, via telephone, 20 November 2012.

[102] Tina Intelmann, "International Criminal Court – African Union", in *New Business Ethiopia*, 11 October 2013.

[103] Interview with OTP Member, 2012, see *supra* note 22.

[104] US Senate, Subcommittee on International Operations, Committee on Foreign Relations, *Is a U.N. International Criminal Court in the U.S. National Interest?*, US Government Printing Office, Washington, DC, S. Hrg. 105–724, 23 July 1998.

---

collapse, which should be our objective. The ICC is fundamentally a bad idea. It cannot be improved by technical fixes
as the years pass, and in fact it is more likely than not to
worsen.[105]

This position materialised in a number of ways. First, the US sought
Article 98 agreements with many states parties which obligated those
states to hand over US persons to US custody rather than to the ICC. Second, the US passed the American Servicemembers' Protection Act
('ASPA'). The ASPA restricts US co-operation with the ICC and with
states parties unless "in the US interest", requires US personnel impunity
for US peacekeeping support, and allows the President to use "any means
necessary" to free US citizens and allies from ICC custody.[106]

Leading actors within the Central Intelligence Agency disagreed
with Bolton, viewing the ICC as a potential instrument of pressure to be
applied to adversaries.[107] The impact of Bolton's concern on the Bush
administration is reflected by the fact that efforts to achieve Article 98
agreements were reported to the White House by the Secretary of State
two to three times per week.[108] The case of Darfur, Sudan was critical in
shifting US policy towards the ICC. In 2005 the US stated its preference
of a special, *ad hoc* or otherwise, UN/African Union hybrid tribunal.[109]
After failing to persuade the Security Council to pursue an *ad hoc* or hybrid court rather than a Security Council referral to the ICC, the US position softened. The softening took the form of policy revision that allowed
active co-operation where ICC case selection and US interests were con-
gruent. However, the threat of non-cooperation persists were the ICC to
employ case selection not viewed by the US as "responsible".[110] A prose-

---

[105] *Ibid.*

[106] American Servicemembers' Protection Act of 2002, 107th Congress, 2002, H.R.4775, Sections 2004, 2005, 2006, 2007 and 2008.

[107] Interview with former Chief of Staff to the United States Secretary of State, Colonel Larry Wilkerson, Washington, DC, 7 July 2014.

[108] *Ibid.*

[109] US Department of State, Daily Press Briefing, Richard Boucher (spokesman), Washington, DC, 1 February 2005.

[110] In 2006 the US Department of State Legal Adviser, John Bellinger, while insisting the Bush administration would never allow Americans to be tried by the ICC, stated, "we do acknowledge that it has a role to play in the overall system of international justice". In a May 2006 speech, Bellinger said "divisiveness over the ICC distracts from our ability to pursue these common goals" of fighting genocide and crimes against humanity. Jess Brav-in, "US Warms to Hague Tribunal: New Stance Reflects Desire to Use Court to Prosecute

cutor might favour US-friendly states in interpreting complementarity because of a perceived implicit threat from the US or states of essential strategic importance to other permanent members of the Security Council.

In time, the United States came to view the ICC as acceptable, on a case-by-case basis, where it acted in its interests. The Ugandan, Colombian and other governments enjoying warm relations with the US may presume that the threat of a return to the Bolton policy deters the ICC prosecution from pursuit of UPDF or other cases antithetical to US interests. This consideration, along with the knowledge of the Court's vulnerable infant status informed the Ugandan government's view that it was safe to refer the situation without concern as to government or UPDF indictments.[111]

As the global economic order has shifted, allowing China and Russia to become less acquiescent at the Security Council, the dependency of the ICC on state self-referral rather than Security Council referral has increased. Complementarity, as already discussed, makes *proprio motu* assertion of jurisdiction less probable. A less active Security Council leaves the ICC prosecution more dependent on state referrals as a trigger of jurisdiction – further empowering weak states' bargaining positions with the ICC prosecution.

Weak states' negotiating position also benefits from a shifting global economic order via increased options for economic patronage. That competition diminishes international crimes-related pressure from powerful states and international justice's compliance pull. China recently made a statement in support of the African Union's pro-Kenya ICC position and recently commenced increased security co-operation to accompany its

---

Darfur Crimes", in *The Wall Street Journal*, 14 June 2006. That same year, Republican Senator John McCain and former Senator and presidential candidate, Bob Dole, stated in an op-ed:

> US and allied intelligence assets, including satellite technology, should be dedicated to record any atrocities that occur in Darfur so that future prosecutions can take place. We should publicly remind Khartoum that the International Criminal Court has jurisdiction to prosecute war crimes in Darfur and that Sudanese leaders will be held personally accountable for attacks on civilians.

John McCain and Bob Dole, "Rescue Darfur Now", in *The Washington Post*, 10 September 2006.

[111] Interview with former Member, Ugandan National Security Council, 2012.

---

significant economic engagement.[112] The shifting global economic and military order can be seen in Figures 1 and 2 that indicate China's post-2000 economic emergence as well as US predominance in both the economic and military spheres during the 1990s.

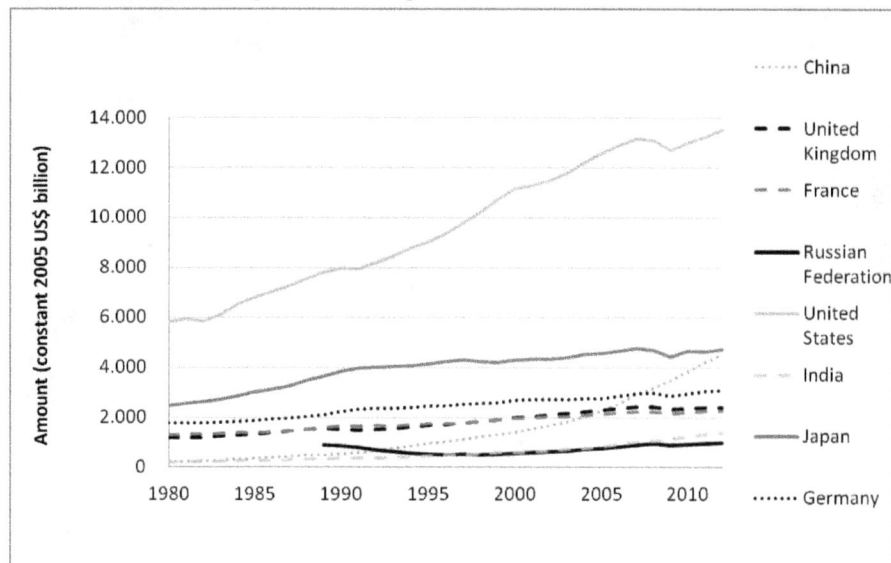

Figure 1: Country GDP, 1980–2012[113]

---

[112] Statement by Mr. MA Xinmin, Counsellor of the Department of Treaty and Law of Ministry of Foreign Affairs of the People's Republic of China, 12th Session of the Assembly of States Parties to the ICC Statute, The Hague, November 2013 ('Statement by MA Xinmin'); Simon Ndonga, "Kenya, China pact to secure borders, waters", in *Capital News*, Kenya, 3 January 2014.

[113] World Development Indicators, 1960–2014, The World Bank, available at http://data.worldbank.org/data-catalog/world-development-indicators, last accessed on 7 April 2015.

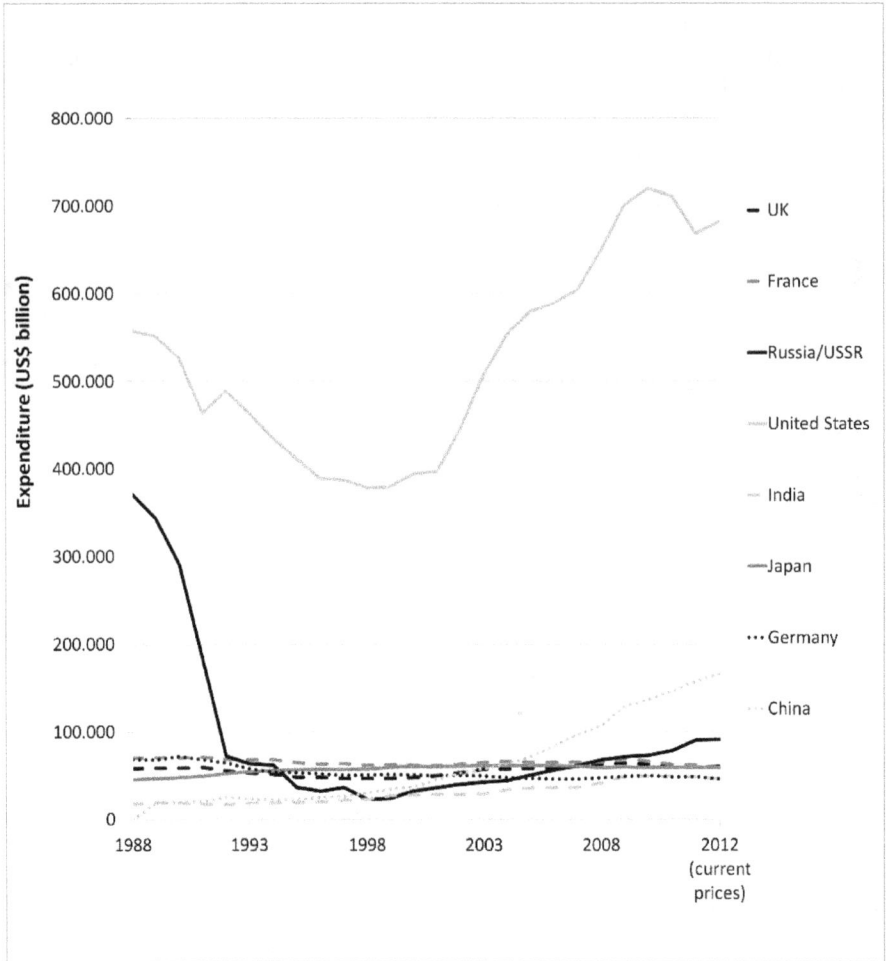

Figure 2: Military Expenditure, 1988–2012

African Union pressure perhaps provides one of the greatest deterrents to ICC prosecution pursuit of Ugandan government officials. Budgetary constraints exaggerated and have been exaggerated by co-operative leverage. The reluctance of Western powers to provide intelligence incriminating Museveni, Salim Saleh or other actors in international crimes in Uganda or the Democratic Republic of Congo is instructive to ICC prosecution inability to proceed with such cases. Goldstein *et al.*'s realist explanation of codified international institutions asserts that dominant powers bind weak members and enforce rules only where they are able to bear the enforcement costs.[114] Former senior personnel within the ICC suspected colleagues of preferring perceived Western interests, particularly those of the United Kingdom, ahead of independent application of law to fact.[115] Key actors that worked on the Luis Moreno Ocampo's campaign to become prosecutor, including Gavin Hood from the British Foreign and Commonwealth Office and Silvia Fernández de Gurmendi, were then hired into case selection decision-making roles within the Office of the Prosecutor.[116] Those individuals informed key case selection decisions as to whether to formally open investigations into situations and which cases to pursue within those situations.[117] Western powers' shaping of ICC case selection away from allies such as Museveni, Paul Kagame, Joseph Kabila, François *Bozizé*, Alassane Ouattara and their regimes, and towards adversaries, including the Sudanese and Libyan leadership, reinforces Goldstein *et al.*'s theory.[118] However, the ICC also redistributes a great degree of jurisdiction-triggering power from the Security Council to state parties. African governments' enthusiastic embrace in referring situations to direct the ICC against adversaries has been tempered by Security Council direction of the ICC against African leaders. Similarly, African leaders also bear antagonism towards the ICC prosecutor and Kofi Annan's triggering of the Kenyan situation.

11.6.3. Backlash of African States

African Union pressure perhaps provides one of the greatest deterrents to ICC prosecution pursuit of Ugandan government officials. Budgetary constraints exaggerated and have been exaggerated by co-operative leverage. African leaders clothe their attempts at case selection control in anti-colonial rhetoric that resonates among domestic constituencies by casting the ICC as racist.[119] This 'interest-based' strategy intertwines the norm of

---

[114] Goldstein *et al.*, 2000, see *supra* note 8.

[115] Interview with former Senior Member of the ICC, 28 November 2012, San Francisco, USA; and interview with former Rome Conference Delegate and former Member of the ICC Office of the Prosecutor, The Hague, The Netherlands, 4 December 2012.

[116] *Ibid.*

[117] *Ibid.*

[118] Interview with former Member, Ugandan National Security Council, 2012.

[119] *Ibid.*; Nicholas Kulish and Marlise Simons, "Setbacks Rise in Prosecuting the President of Kenya", in *New York Times*, 19 July 2013; and Justine Boulo, "Ramtane Lamamra: La CPI ignore la souveraineté de nos pays", in *Jeune Afrique*, 10 November 2013.

ICC prosecution of international crimes cases with the realist interest of protecting African governments and encroaching upon Security Council case selection control.[120] That strategy promotes self-referred situations, controlled through state co-operation, as the only cases the Court should pursue.[121] The African Union backlash, employing a number of instruments, constitutes a weak state challenge to powerful state interests reflecting powerful states' greater interest in excluding jurisdiction over aggression than in retaining sole jurisdiction-triggering discretion through *ad hoc* or hybrid courts. The African Union has requested UN Security Council deferral of proceedings against the Kenyan and Sudanese leadership and passed resolutions refusing to co-operate after the Security Council refused to comply.[122] The African Union will also provide African governments an extra complementarity filter by endowing the African Court of Human and People's Rights with jurisdiction to try international crimes. The African Union also diminished normative pressure to support ICC case selection by refusing to endorse the new prosecutor's candidacy in 2011.[123] Finally, under Kenyan and Sudanese pressure, the African Union threatened mass ICC withdrawal, a measure that would cripple the institution but jeopardise the utility of self-referred situations.[124] It reaffirmed non-cooperation on cases against the Kenyan and Sudanese leadership. The African Union resolution expressed concern as to politicised ICC indictments against African leaders, particularly in Kenya. It stressed Kenya's anti-terror leadership, the gravity of indicting Kenyan leaders, the indictments' threat to state sovereignty, and the principle of immunities for senior state officials.[125] Most importantly, the African Union decided that no charges should be commenced or continued against any person acting or entitled to act as head of state, and called for ICC suspension

---

[120] Kenneth Abbot and Duncan Snidal, "Hard and Soft Law in International Governance", in *International Organization*, 2000, vol. 54, no. 3, pp. 421–56.

[121] Interview with former Member, Ugandan National Security Council, 2012.

[122] Rick Gladstone, "African Call to Delay Kenyans Trials Fails at UN", in *New York Times*, 15 November 2013; and African Union, Decision on the Meeting of African States Parties to the ICC Statute, Assembly/AU/Dec.245 (XIII), Thirteenth Ordinary Session of the Assembly in Sirte, Great Socialist People's Libyan Arab Jamahiriya, 3 July 2009, p. 2.

[123] Interview with Member, US Mission to the UN, New York, USA, 2 November 2012.

[124] "Kenyatta Mulls Nuclear Option", in *Africa Confidential*, 2013, vol. 54, no. 21.

[125] African Union, Decision on Africa's Relationship With the International Criminal Court (ICC), Ext/Assembly/AU/Dec.1, October 2013, pp. 1–2.

of the Kenyan leadership cases.[126] The African Union also established a Security Council contact group to sensitise the Security Council to African Union concerns about case selection. Arguably the African Union's most confrontational step is to request ICC Statute amendments leading to ICC Chamber discretion to allow cases to be heard in another state, to allow accused to appear via video link and to excuse accused from attending trial.[127] In a sign of the continuing normative power of international crimes prosecution, Kenyan government attempts to revoke the prosecution's *proprio motu* power was unsuccessful.[128] The African Union's request that member states advise and consult it before referring situations demonstrates the invigorated collaborative and systematic African Union approach towards preventing even unintended ICC indictment of African leaders.[129]

The pressure upon the ICC from the African Union, Kenya, Sudan and others makes ICC prosecution inclination to reconsider UPDF investigations ever more remote, particularly given China's recent expression of support for African Union positions.[130] Observing and supporting contestations from the periphery also informs the utility of methods available to Museveni were OTP confrontation to occur. Kenyan efforts are particularly instructive. Kenya's parliament has voted to leave the ICC, it has withheld evidence and witness protection co-operation, and it threatened to cease regional terrorism co-operation with the US and other Western governments.[131] It also sought to have ICC cases transferred to the East African Court of Justice. In a critical indication of the normative power of international crimes prosecution, Western states, facing increasing competition to access Kenya's natural resources and growing economy, have adopted passive positions or have indicated support for Kenya in the face

---

[126] *Ibid.*, p. 2.

[127] ICC, Assembly of States Parties, 12th Session, Resolution ICC-ASP/12/Res.7, 27 November 2013, pp. 1, 3–4.

[128] Dann Mwangi, "Revoke Power of International Criminal Court Prosecutor to Initiate Investigations", in *Standard Media*, Kenya, 12 November 2013.

[129] African Union, 2013, p. 3, see *supra* note 125.

[130] Statement by MA Xinmin, 2013, see *supra* note 112.

[131] Nicholas Kulish, "Kenyan Lawmakers Vote to Leave International Court", in *New York Times*, 5 September 2013; "The International Criminal Court (ICC) Has Directed the Government to Officially Respond to Claims by the Prosecution that It Is Not Co-operating with the Court", in *Citizen News*, 10 December 2013.

of civil society protestation.[132] In the end, it was the "unprecedented" threats to witnesses that caused ICC suspension of the Kenyatta case after a witness admitted giving false evidence "regarding the event at the heart of the Prosecution's case".[133]

11.7. Conclusion

Like Kenya, Museveni has sought to diversify his economic patronage by engaging China.[134] The level of pressure applied to ICC case selection begs the question as to whether it would accommodate Ugandan preferences to try LRA accused domestically. To do so may only require replacing amnesty with commutation of sentence such that accused spend an ambiguously short time incarcerated, as in Colombia. ICC case selection independence has been systematically compromised by the accommodation of state self-interest in a complementarity regime that tolerates politicised prosecution – that says to governments: 'even if you take a disingenuous seat at the prosecution table, you'll remain off the menu'. This lesson may be applicable in the recent referral of the situation in the Palestinian Occupied Territories. The Israeli government has launched its own investigations of 2014 Israel Defense Force's alleged conduct in the Gaza Strip – investigations that may well meet the complementarity threshold and prevent ICC assertion of jurisdiction over Israel Defense Force conduct.[135] The Palestinian administration, on the other hand, has

---

[132] "In UN Report, ICC Urges Security Council Support to Enforce Decisions", in UN News Centre, 8 October 2013; and "Investors Don't Mind Kenya's ICC Problems", in eNews Channel Africa, 16 September 2013. See, for example, The Editorial Board, "Where Water Is Gold", in *The New York Times*, 19 September 2013; "China Steps into ICC, Kenyan Fray", in United Press International, 19 September 2013; and Geoffrey Mosoku, "France Says African Union International Criminal Court Plea Could Be Looked Into", in Standard Media, Kenya, 16 October 2013.

[133] International Criminal Court, *Prosecutor v. Uhuru Muigai Kenyatta*, Situation in the Republic of Kenya, ICC-01/09-02/11, Notification of the removal of a witness from the prosecution's witness list and application for an adjournment of the provisional trial date, 19 December 2013, p. 3; and Wambui Ndonga, "Witness 'Attrition' in Kenya Cases Alarming, Says ICC", in Capital FM, Kenya, 4 September 2013.

[134] China has secured a USD 2 billion oil concession and holds a contract to build a dam on the Nile. See "China's CNOOC wins $2bn Uganda oil field contract", in BBC News, 26 September 2013; and "Uganda Partners China's Sino-Hydro for $1.6 billion White Nile Dam", in African Globe, 21 June 2013.

[135] "Israel Opens More Criminal Investigations into Its Conduct during the Summer War in Gaza", in *Sputnik*, 7 December 2014. The United States Congress has also responded with

---

not enabled investigations of alleged conduct by Palestinians that may trigger complementarity in order to exclude the possibility of ICC prosecution of that alleged conduct.[136]

In negotiating the ICC Statute, weak states reconciled abandonment of independent exercise of jurisdiction over aggression by procuring primacy of jurisdiction under complementarity – primacy not afforded by Security Council institutions that powerful states may have pursued. Emphasising the value of encouraging domestic prosecution of international crimes has co-opted many norm entrepreneurs advocating international crimes prosecution. Failure to communicate the weakness of domestic proceedings required by complementarity undermined ICC case selection independence and the emergence of the norm of international crimes prosecution. The ICC Statute constituted a significant victory in that it expanded the territorial and personal jurisdiction of international criminal justice, particularly via provision of *proprio motu* power to the prosecutor. However, the accommodation of realist state self-interest via the principle of complementarity constituted a major regression from predecessor international courts and tribunals.

The ICC has been further constrained by pressure from weak states seeking to obtain greater control over ICC case selection while diminishing powerful state capacity to deploy the ICC against weak state governments. To this extent, contestation of case selection control between weak states and powerful states has moved from Statute negotiating in New York and Rome to the arena of functional elements such as complementarity adherence and co-operative pressure from states or regional organisations on their behalf.

The examined cases illuminate the extent to which it is now in the clear realist interest of political and military leadership of armed forces to prosecute core international crimes cases themselves. The low requirements of complementarity for domestic proceedings exclude the sovereignty cost of having to pursue politically sensitive cases. Criminal justice systems are composed of multiple interacting and interdependent entities

---

condemnation at the Palestinian decision to sign the ICC Statute and trigger investigations of IDF conduct; see Josh Ruebner, "Activists Protest One-sided Hearing on Palestine and the ICC", in *The Hill*, 6 February 2015.

[136] Oren Dorell, "Amnesty: Palestinian Groups Committed War Crimes", in *USA Today*, 26 March 2015, available at http://www.usatoday.com/story/news/world/2015/03/26/gaza-war-amnesty-palestinian-war-crimes/70492688/, last accessed on 6 April 2015.

which may be affected in subtle or overt ways to secure control of who is prosecuted and who is not.

The ICC's unwillingness to make 'value judgments' about the integrity of domestic proceedings enables not only subtle but also overt political interference to protect the realist self-interest of political or military leadership and lines of patronage. Domestic proceedings, as in the case of Colombia's domestic process, may be skewed to purge armed forces of potentially threatening elements outside the perceived patrimonial constituency of political or military leaders. As is also clear in the Colombian case, domestic proceedings may also be designed to be far more punitive towards adversaries than government or government-aligned forces. Such a design lends the government an extra instrument of pressure in negotiations – the capacity to extinguish discriminatory sentencing and provide *ad hoc* amnesty via commutation of sentence to all parties.

The Colombian case demonstrates the benefits of early engagement prior to formal opening of ICC investigation – a lower threshold. The Kenyan case demonstrates the increasing demands required of domestic civil or military prosecution of core international crimes cases when states fail to put in place even politicised 'Colombia-like' processes. While elements within the ICC believe Kenya was not treated equally to Colombia, Kenya may well have avoided formal ICC investigations were it to have launched a similar domestic process to that in Colombia. The Kenyan lesson to self-interested elements of the armed forces or political leadership is that the ICC raises the requirements to that of the same 'suspects' and 'conduct' as those investigated by the ICC when a Colombia-like process is not pursued. Domestic investigation of the same conduct and suspects poses its own costs to political and military leaders, particularly if those leaders or critical constituents must be investigated. African governments, through the African Union, now appear far more cognisant not only of the potential sovereignty costs of *proprio motu* ICC investigation, but also of the ease with which sovereignty costs can be extinguished, via early engagement in domestic prosecution of core international crimes cases.

The Ugandan case demonstrates the elevated utility of combining a domestic process that extinguishes sovereignty costs of sensitive ICC indictments while deploying ICC stigmatisation against adversaries. That scenario maximises the benefits of both excluding oneself and one's allies from the menu while placing one's adversaries squarely on it.

The examined cases demonstrate that complementarity under the ICC Statute provides armed forces and governments the greatest self-interest in prosecuting core international crimes. Many of the arguments made elsewhere in this anthology indicate that progressive and utilitarian interests are increasingly instructing state behaviour, including within the sphere of prosecution of core international crimes. The examined cases suggest the primary interest driving state behaviour remains one of realist self-interest in guarding sovereignty costs by retaining political control of core international crimes prosecutions – by taking a seat at the table, and taking yourself off the menu.

12

Self-Interest or Self-Inflicted?
How the United States Charges Its Service
Members for Violating the Laws of War

Christopher Jenks*

12.1. Introduction

In the early morning of 11 March 2012, a US service member, Staff Sergeant Robert Bales, slipped undetected from Village Stability Platform ('VSP') Belambai about 30 kilometres from Kandahar, Afghanistan. Bales was one of approximately 40 US military personnel deployed to VSP Belambai. Their mission was "to assist the Afghan government in maintaining security, reconstructing the country, training the national police and army, and providing a lawful environment for free and fair elections".[1] Sergeant Bales, however, was on a very different mission.

Bales, alone and on foot, hiked to two separate Afghan villages where he murdered 16 women and children, attempted to murder six more and assaulted others.[2] The victims ranged in age from small children to an

---

* **Christopher Jenks** is an assistant professor of law and directs the criminal justice clinic at Southern Methodist University's ('SMU') Dedman School of Law in Dallas, USA, where he has taught the law of armed conflict and criminal justice topics since 2012. Prior to joining the faculty at SMU, he served for over 20 years in the US Army, first as an Infantry officer and later as a Judge Advocate in the Republic of Korea and Iraq. In his final assignment in the US military he served as the chief of the US Army's international law branch in the Pentagon. He is the co-author of a law school textbook on the law of armed conflict and co-editor of forthcoming war crimes textbook. In 2015 he received a Fulbright grant to research emerging technologies and accountability norms in armed conflict at the Asia Pacific Centre for Military Law at Melbourne Law School, Australia. He received his undergraduate degree from the United States Military Academy at West Point, his law degree from the University of Arizona, and law masters from both the US Army Judge Advocate General's Legal Center and School and Georgetown University. A portion of this chapter was previously published and is part of his Ph.D. on the US approach to war crimes prosecutions, which he is completing at Melbourne Law School.

[1] United States Mission to NATO, "U.S. Policy Toward Afghanistan and Pakistan: A Dossier (2014)", available at http://nato.usmission.gov/afghanistan.html, last accessed on 27 March 2015.

[2] *United States v. Robert Bales*, Charge Sheet, 23 March 2012 (redacted). A copy of Bales's charge sheet is appended to this chapter as Appendix 1.

---

elderly grandmother. Bales murdered 11 members of one family, shooting most of them in front of each other, stomped to death at least one victim, and set 10 victims' bodies on fire. The US Army apprehended Bales as he attempted to return to VSB Belambai. The Army transferred Bales to the United States and prosecuted him under US military's criminal law and procedure, the Uniform Code of Military Justice ('UCMJ'). At an Army court martial held in June 2013 in the US, Bales plead guilty to 16 counts of premeditated murder, six counts of attempted murder and six counts of aggravated assault inflicting grievous bodily injury. A military panel, or jury, sentenced Bales to be dishonourably discharged and to be confined for the duration of his natural life without the possibility of parole.

In so doing, the US Army continued its long-standing policy and practice of asserting jurisdiction over its service members who commit crimes during armed conflict, and charging them with enumerated offences of the UCMJ rather than violations of the laws of war or war crimes. Yet, while not prosecuting its own service members with such crimes, the US continues to conduct military commissions at Guantanamo Bay, Cuba and to prosecute members of al-Qa'ida and the Taliban for just such offences, that is, violations of the laws of war.[3]

This chapter explores the aspects of self-interest implicated by the US military prosecuting its own service members who violate the laws of war under different criminal charges than it prosecutes enemy belligerents who commit substantially similar offences. The chapter briefly explains how the US asserts criminal jurisdiction over its service members before turning to how the US military reports violations of the laws of war. It then sets out the US methodology for charging such violations as applied to its service members, and compares this methodology to that applied to those tried by military commissions. The chapter then discusses the varied meanings of the term 'war crimes' and the way in which the 1949 Geneva Conventions can provide a benchmark against which the elements of offences, and their punishments, can be compared. While the US practice fares adequately in this comparison, the argument for a pragmatic approach to charging over the expressive value of a war crime charge is rendered untenable as a result of the disparate manner in which the US charges detainees when compared to its own service members. Ultimately,

---

[3]   A copy of charge sheet from the US military commissions is appended to this chapter as Appendix 2.

this chapter recommends adding armed conflict-related punitive articles to the UCMJ and increasing transparency in how the US holds its service members accountable for violations of the law of war.

12.2. United States Practice

12.2.1. A History of the UCMJ

The UCMJ came from the US Congress's desire, following the Second World War, to establish "a code that would apply to all branches of the military and create greater uniformity in the substantive and procedural law governing the administration of military justice".[4] While the UCMJ dates from 1951, its origins are in and with the founding of the US during the American Revolutionary War with Britain. In June 1775, the fledgling (and rebellious) Second Continental Congress enacted the Articles of War, which, somewhat ironically, were "generally a copy of the then-existing code governing England's Army".[5] Following the Revolutionary War, the US Constitution granted the US Congress the power "(1) to make Rules for the Government and Regulation of land and naval Forces"; and "(2) the power to define and punish [...] offenses against the Law of Nations".[6] Thus, beginning with the 1806 revisions to the Articles of War, US "military personnel were subject to a code that required them to obey certain laws and customs of war or face trial by court-martial or military tribunal".[7] In the century that followed, the US Congress updated the Articles of War in 1874 and 1916.[8] The articles were again amended in 1920, with lessons learned from the First World War, and in 1949 following the Second World War.[9] The 1951 UCMJ replaced the Articles of

---

[4] Mynda G. Ohman, "Integrating Title 18 War Crimes into Title 10: A Proposal to Amend the Uniform Code of Military Justice", in *Air Force Law Review*, 2005, vol. 57, p. 4.

[5] Judge Advocate General's Corps, US Army, *The Army Lawyer: A History of the Judge Advocate General's Corps, 1775–1975*, Government Printing Office, Washington, DC, 1975. The following month the Congress elected William Tudor as the first Judge Advocate General of the Army.

[6] United States Constitution, Art. 1, § 8, Cl. 14. See also Tara Lee, "American Courts-Martial for Enemy War Crimes", in *University of Baltimore Law Review*, 2003, vol. 33, pp. 52–53.

[7] Eric Talbot Jensen and James J. Teixeira Jr., "Prosecuting Members of the U.S. Military for Wartime Environmental Crimes", in *Georgetown International Environmental Law Review*, 2005, vol. 17, no. 4, p. 658.

[8] Ohman, 2005, p. 4, see *supra* note 4.

[9] *Ibid.*

War and established "a single codified system of military law, separate from the criminal justice systems of the various states and of the Article III [federal] courts".[10] The features of the UCMJ have been described as follows:

> The UCMJ permanently transformed the nature of military law. The UCMJ was more than a structural change to ensure uniformity across all branches of service. It added articles, defined new crimes, and established rules designed to protect the substantive and procedural rights of military personnel. New provisions designed to ensure a fair trial included the right against self-incrimination; equal process for the defense and prosecution to obtain witnesses and depositions; the prohibition on receiving guilty pleas in capital cases; the requirement that both prosecution and defense counsel be legally trained; the right for an enlisted accused to be tried by a panel [military jury] that included enlisted members; the requirement that the law officer (now the military judge) instruct the panel members on the record regarding the elements of the offense, presumption of innocence, and burden of proof; the provision mandating that voting on findings and sentencing be conducted by secret ballot; and an automatic review of the trial record.[11]

One of the advantages of the UCMJ is its broad jurisdictional scope:

> The UCMJ applies to all [US] service members regardless of whether the offense can be tied to military discipline and effectiveness. The UCMJ is applicable both in the United States and in foreign countries. Because the UCMJ applies worldwide, a court-martial convened under the UCMJ may be held anywhere in the world. This flexibility allows for the prosecution to take place near the situs of the crime, presumably near the location of any relevant witnesses. This makes the prosecution of a crime that occurs during the conduct of military operations, such as in Iraq [or Afghanistan], easier than it would be if the case had to be heard in a Federal Dis-

---

10   Lee, 2003, pp. 52–53, see *supra* note 6.
11   Ohman, 2005, pp. 9–10, see *supra* note 4.

trict Court or before an international body convened at the Hague or some other site distant from the court's location.[12]

For the UCMJ to exercise personal jurisdiction over US service members regardless of where in the world the service member is or whether they were on or off duty is one of the strengths of the system. But the manner in which the system charges US service members for crimes blunts the efficacy, either real or perceived, of the UCMJ as an accountability mechanism. More confusing still is that the link between jurisdiction and charging, the reporting of alleged violations by US service members is conducted using law of war terms.

12.2.2. Reporting US Service Member Violations of the Laws of War

The US Department of Defense ('DoD') issued a directive on its law of war programme in 2006.[13] The directive's stated purpose is to "update the policies and responsibilities ensuring DoD compliance with the law of war obligations of the United States".[14] The directive also clarifies investigation and reporting of "reportable incidents".[15] The directive defines the law of war as:

> That part of international law that regulates the conduct of armed hostilities. It is often called the "law of armed conflict". The law of war encompasses all international law for the conduct of hostilities binding on the United States of its individual citizens, including treaties and international agreements to which the United States is a party, and applicable customary international law.[16]

The directive then states that "[i]t is DoD policy that: [...] Members of the DoD Components comply with the law of war during all armed conflicts, however such conflicts are characterized, and in all other military opera-

---

[12] Jensen and Teixeira, 2005, p. 658, see *supra* note 7. Although one of the advantages of the UCMJ is the ability to hold courts martial in a combat theatre such as Iraq or Afghanistan, it is noteworthy that often the US military does not choose this course of action. As discussed in the introduction, Staff Sergeant Bales committed his crimes in Afghanistan and against Afghan civilians, but Bales's court martial was held in the US.

[13] US Department of Defense ('DoD') Directive 2311.01E, DoD Law of War Program, 9 May 2006.

[14] *Ibid.*, para. 1.1.

[15] *Ibid.*

[16] *Ibid.*, para. 3.1.

tions".[17] The combination of how the US defines the law of war and the policy decision to broadly apply it is, or could be, significant. It is significant because the US is claiming that its service members comply with the law governing international armed conflict, non-international armed conflict and even "applicable" customary international law in all armed conflicts, and even all other military operations, including for example, peacekeeping.

This could be the bridge over what is otherwise a significant gap stemming from the problematic inverse relationship between frequency of the type of armed conflict (international and non-international) and the applicable governing law. The vast majority of the law of armed conflict, including all four of the 1949 Geneva Conventions and their Additional Protocol I, is only triggered as a matter of law by international armed conflict. Yet there are few international armed conflicts. In contrast, non-international armed conflicts are far more prevalent,[18] but for which there is far less law. The US policy directive would avoid that problem, but only if it were clear what portions of the law of armed conflict the US is applying, which it is not. Indeed, an unprivileged belligerent the US is detaining at the time of writing at Naval Station Guantanamo Bay, Cuba has filed a legal challenge complaining of, among other things, the specific portions of the 1949 Geneva Conventions the US is not following.[19]

---

[17] *Ibid.*, para. 4.1.

[18] For example, according to the North Atlantic Treaty Organisation ('NATO'), in 2000 there were 25 armed conflicts around the world. NATO, "Statistics on armed conflicts around the world", available at http://nato.gov.si/eng/topic/threats-to-security/statistics/, last accessed on 29 March 2015. Of those, only one, the conflict between India and Pakistan, was of an international nature. See also Armed Conflict Database, available at http://acd.iiss.org, last accessed on 29 March 2015.

[19] See United States Court of Appeals, District of Columbia Circuit, *Abdullah v. Obama*, 753 F.3d 193, 4 April 2014. Abdullah claimed that his conditions of confinement violated the Third Geneva Convention governing prisoners of war because "he is not permitted to purchase personal items, family and friends are not allowed to send him food or clothing, detainees cannot choose representatives to air their grievances and copies of the Geneva Convention are not posted in prominent places" (p. 196). The United States Court of Appeals for the District of Columbia denied Abdullah's appeal on the grounds his claim was "only a bare and conclusory assertion that" the US government was in violation of certain sections of the Third Geneva Convention. Indeed, this footnote is considerably longer than Abdullah's claim, which, in toto, was "Respondents are now, and have been for a decade, violating sections 3, 25, 70–72, and 78–79".

Similarly, the policy claims that US service members will follow "applicable" customary international law, without specifying which or what law that is. As discussed later in the chapter, the US has objected to the International Committee of the Red Cross' ('ICRC') customary international humanitarian law study. It would be helpful if the US, indeed all states, were to acknowledge what they consider customary international law. In the absence of such specification, claiming to follow "applicable" customary international law is close to, if not fully, a meaningless claim.

Implementing and applying law as a matter of policy when that law would not otherwise apply should be a positive development. And it was the US practice during the Vietnam War. There, the Americans confronted a similar challenge as today, fighting one or more organised armed groups, including the Viet Cong, who, like al-Qa'ida today, do not qualify as prisoners of war under the Third Geneva Convention.[20] In contrast,

---

[20] To qualify for prisoner of war status under Geneva Convention III, an individual must fall in one of the following categories:

(1) Members of the armed forces of a party to the conflict as well as members of militia or volunteer corps forming part of such armed forces.

(2) Members of other militias and members of other volunteer corps, including those of organized resistance movements, belonging to a Party to the conflict and operating in or outside their own territory, even if this territory is occupied, provided that such militias or volunteer corps, including such organized resistance movements, fulfil the following conditions:

  (a) that of being commanded by a person responsible for his subordinates;

  (b) that of having a fixed distinctive sign recognizable at a distance;

  (c) that of carrying arms openly;

  (d) that of conducting their operations in accordance with the laws and customs of war.

(3) Members of regular armed forces who profess allegiance to a government or an authority not recognized by the Detaining Power.

(4) Persons who accompany the armed forces without actually being members thereof, such as civilian members of military aircraft crews, war correspondents, supply contractors, members of labour units or of services responsible for the welfare of the armed forces, provided that they have received authorization from the armed forces which they accompany, who shall provide them for that purpose with an identity card similar to the annexed model.

(5) Members of crews, including masters, pilots and apprentices, of the merchant marine and the crews of civil aircraft of the Parties to the conflict, who do not benefit by more favourable treatment under any other provisions of international law.

(6) Inhabitants of a non-occupied territory, who on the approach of the enemy spontaneously take up arms to resist the invading forces, without having had time to form themselves into regular armed units, provided they carry arms openly and respect the laws and customs of war.

members of the North Vietnamese Army *did* qualify for prisoner of war status. The US Military Assistance Command in Vietnam's ('MACV') response was to issue an instruction, functionally the equivalent of the current directive. Through that instruction, the US still conducted the review process to determine if a captured belligerent qualified as a matter of law for prisoner of war status. For the Viet Cong, who did not qualify as a matter of law, the instruction stated that the US, as a matter of policy, would treat them as prisoners of war. The result was two identically run prison camps, separated by a road. In one camp were members of the North Vietnamese Army, who were entitled to prisoner of war treatment as a matter of law. In the other camp were the Viet Cong, who were not entitled to prisoner of war status as a matter of law but received the same treatment as a matter of policy. The ICRC was effusive in its praise of the US policy decision, claiming that

> [t]he MACV instruction [...] is a brilliant expression of a liberal and realistic attitude. [...] This text could very well be a most important one in the history of the humanitarian law, for it is the first time [...] that a government goes far beyond the requirements of the Geneva Convention in an official instruction to its armed forces. The dreams of today are the rarities of tomorrow, and the day those definitions or similar ones will become embodied in an international treaty [...] will be a great one for man concerned about the protection of men who cannot protect themselves. [...] May it then be remembered that this light first shone in the darkness of this tragic war of Vietnam.[21]

The difference between the application of the US military's policy decisions then and now is that in Vietnam, the US was transparent about the law it was applying and thus could be monitored and inspected. The current policy directive unfortunately falls far short of its Vietnam era predecessor.

Geneva Convention Relative to the Treatment of Prisoners of War, 12 August 1949, UST. 3316, Art. 4 ('Geneva Convention III').

[21] Laurie Blank and Gregory Noone, *International Law and Armed Conflict: Fundamental Principles and Customary Challenges in the Law of War*, Aspen Publishers, Aspen, 2013, p. 232, citing George S. Prugh, *Vietnam Studies: Law at War: Vietnam 1964–1973*, Department of the Army, Washington, DC, 1975.

Having established the vague policy footing on which the current directive rests, it is surprisingly expansive and specific in what qualifies as a reportable law of war violation. The directive defines reportable incident as "[a] possible, suspected, or alleged violation of the law of war, for which there is credible information, or conduct during military operations other than war that would constitute a violation of the law of war if it occurred during an armed conflict".[22] When the low threshold of a possible, suspected or alleged violation is reached, "[a]ll reportable incidents committed by or against US personnel, enemy persons, or any other individuals are reported promptly, investigated thoroughly, and, where appropriate, remedied by corrective action".[23]

The directive speaks in terms of violations of the law of war and requires their reporting and investigation. Yet if that investigation substantiates the violation, the US military takes the next step in its self-accountability process, charging the alleged wrongdoer, but not with a violation of the law of war.

12.2.3. Charging Violations of the Laws of War

As one US Army lawyer noted in a primer for the practitioner of charging war crimes: "The first step in analyzing how to charge the servicemember is to look for any offenses specifically enumerated in the UCMJ Articles 80 through 132".[24] These articles address a wide range of criminal con-

---

[22] DoD Directive 2311.01E, DoD Law of War Program, 9 May 2006, para. 3.2.

[23] *Ibid.*, para. 4.4.

[24] Martin N. White, "Charging War Crimes: A Primer for the Practitioner", in *The Army Lawyer*, 2006, vol. 2, p. 2. As White explains, "[t]he [service lawyer prosecutor] should begin with this analysis due to the preemption doctrine. The preemption doctrine 'prohibits application of Article 134 to conduct covered in Articles 80 through 132'" (p. 2). Article 134 is for misconduct not addressed in the enumerated punitive section of the UCMJ. Article 134 of the UCMJ, among other things, allows for the incorporation of federal offences as a military charge. But under the preemption doctrine, a prosecutor may not incorporate a federal charge to address conduct an enumerated article of the UCMJ covers. For example, Article 118 of the UCMJ criminalises murder. The US Code, in Title 18 § 1111 also criminalises murder. So a military prosecutor would need to charge the murder offence under Article 118; he or she could not incorporate the federal murder offence through Article 134. However, unlike the UCMJ, the US Code specifically criminalises war crimes as such, in Title 18 § 2441. This raises the question of whether a military prosecutor could incorporate the federal statute under Article 134 and thus charge a US service member with war crimes. The answer where the underlying conduct is reflected in a punitive article is unclear. For example, if a military prosecutor incorporated the federal war crimes statute and charged a grave breach of the Geneva Conventions, the unlawful killing of a protected

duct, and include both completed and inchoate offences. The crimes listed in the UCMJ include common offences such as larceny, assault, rape and murder, and arcane offences, such as abusing a public animal and jumping from a vessel to the water. There is no enumerated offence for violating the laws of war. Yet the UCMJ itself acknowledges that "[t]o the extent permitted by the [US] Constitution, courts-martial may try any offense under the code, and in the case of a general courts-martial, the law of war".[25]

In explaining how to allege offences, the current US *Manual for Courts-Martial* provides that "[a] charge states the article of the code, law of war, or local penal law of an occupied territory which the accused is alleged to have violated".[26] Not only does this indicate the possibility of a law of war charge, the accompanying discussion details that "[i]n the case of a person subject to trial by general court-martial for violations of the law of war, the charge should be: 'Violation of the Law of War'".[27] But that discussion concludes with the guidance that "[o]rdinarily persons subject to the code [a category which includes US service members] should be charged with a specific violation of the code rather than a violation of the law of war".[28] Likewise, the Department of the Army's field manual *The Law of Land Warfare*, in a section entitled "Persons Charged With War Crimes" states that:

> The United States normally punishes war crimes as such on-
> ly if they are committed by enemy nationals or by persons

---

person, the defense would challenge such a charge under the preemption doctrine, arguing that Article 118 of the UCMJ already addresses unlawful killing. But to the extent the underlying conduct is not reflected in a punitive article of the UCMJ, charging the conduct as a war crime through Article 134 and the federal statute appears a possibility. The challenge is to identify acts which constitute a grave breach of the Geneva Conventions or violate Common Article 3 and which are not already reflected in a punitive article of the UCMJ.

25 United States Military, *Manual for Courts-Martial*, Rules for Courts-Martial r 202, 2012. See also Uniform Code of Military Justice, 10 USC § 818, Art. 18, 2010.

26 United States Military, *Manual for Courts-Martial*, Rules for Courts-Martial r 307(c)(2), 2012.

27 *Ibid.*, Discussion (D).

28 *Ibid.* The analysis of that rule, also contained in the *Manual for Courts-Martial*, adds little clarity. The appendix to the 1969 *Manual for Courts-Martial* merely states that "[i]n the case of a person subject to trial by general court-martial by the law of war [...], the Charge should be: 'Violation of the Law of War'", *Manual for Courts-Martial* (1969), Appendix 6a at 12. That same manual lists as a source of military jurisdiction, international law, which it states includes the laws of war.

> serving the interests of the enemy State. Violations of the law of war committed by persons subject to the military law of the United States will usually constitute violations of the Uniform Code of Military Justice and, if so, will be prosecuted under that law.[29]

That guidance, while not styled as an absolute requirement, has proved to be one in US practice. For example, the US charged Lieutenant William Calley with violating Article 118, murder, of the UCMJ, for his role in the My Lai massacre during the Vietnam War. There is considerable similarity between the charges against Calley and Bales. Calley was charged as follows:

> In that First Lieutenant William L. Calley, Jr. [...] did, at My Lai 4, Quang Ngai Province, Republic of South Viet-Nam, on or about 16 March 1968, with premeditation, murder an unknown number, not less than seventy, Oriental human beings, males and females of various ages, whose names are unknown, occupants of the village of My Lai 4, by means of shooting them with a rifle.[30]

Bales was charged as follows:

> In that Staff Sergeant (E-6) Robert Bales, U.S. Army, did, at or near Belambay, Afghanistan, on or about 11 March 2012, with premeditation, murder a female of apparent Afghan descent known as [redacted] by means of shooting her with a firearm.[31]

The historian for the US Army Judge Advocate Generals' Corps claims that the US has never charged a US service member with a law of war violation as such.[32] But one commentator, Professor (and former Army lawyer) Jordan Paust, claims that the US charged a service member

---

[29] US Department of the Army, *Field Manual FM 27-10, The Law of Land Warfare*, 1956, 507.

[30] *United States v. First Lieutenant William L Calley, Jr*, Charge Sheet, 5 September 1969, Specification 1. A copy of Calley's charge sheet is appended to this chapter as Appendix 3. Similar action was taken with respect to Calley's Company commander, Captain Ernest Medina. "In keeping with United States policy, Captain Medina was not charged with violations of the law of war, but rather, was charged with violations of the UCMJ". Michael L. Smidt, "Yamashita, Medina, and Beyond: Command Responsibility in Contemporary Military Operations", in *Military Law Review*, 2000, vol. 164, p. 194.

[31] *United States v. Robert Bales*, Charge Sheet, 23 March 2012 (redacted), Charge I, Specification 1.

[32] E-mail message from Fred Borch to author, 6 November 2012.

---

during the Vietnam War with "cutting off an ear from the body of an unknown dead Viet Cong soldier, which conduct was of a nature to bring discredit upon the Armed Forces of the United States as a violation of the Law of War".[33]

The legislative intent behind Rule for Court-Martial 307, or the commentary, provides no clarification.[34] Noted Army legal scholars and military justice practitioners claim that as stated in the *Manual for Courts-Martial* the US may court-martial a US service member for a violation of the law of war.[35] The US Congress has also failed to provide an answer, although it briefly discussed the issue in 1996. During the debate on the War Crimes Act, members of Congress discussed the potential for US service members to be court-martialled for violating the law of war and determined that it "was not a viable option".[36]

12.2.4. Military Commissions

The US military's internal practice stands in stark contrast to that of the military commissions, the stated purpose of which is to "try alien unprivileged enemy belligerents for violations of the law of war".[37] The Military Commissions Act of 2009 lists a host of law of war violations, including murder of a protected person, attacking civilian objects and property, pil-

---

[33] Jordan Paust, "My Lai and Vietnam: Norms, Myths and Leader Responsibility", in *Military Law Review*, 1972, vol. 57, p. 118 (referring to *United States v Passantino*, Hq. 1st Inf. Div. Special Court-Martial Order no. 11, 11 February 1968).

[34] The analysis to the subsection of Rule for Court-Martial 307 references charges under the law of war and refers to the 1969 *Manual for Courts-Martial*. Yet that version of the manual does not contain the language that "ordinarily" US service members should be charged with a violation of an enumerated punitive article of the UCMJ. The 1969 *Manual* even helpfully provides how to word a charge, saying that "[i]n the case of person subject to trial by general court-martial by the law of war [...] the Charge should be: 'Violation of the Law of War'; or 'Violation of ------, -------,' referring to the law penal law of the occupied territory". Similarly, the very first US *Manual for Courts-Martial* in 1949 included that "[t]he technical charge should be appropriate to all specifications under it, and ordinary will be written: 'Violation of the _____ Article of War,' giving the number of the article".

[35] Jan E. Aldykiewicz with Geoffrey S. Corn, "Authority to Court-Martial Non-U.S. Military Personnel for Serious Violations of International Humanitarian Law Committed during Internal Armed Conflicts", in *Military Law Review*, 2001, vol. 167, p. 76.

[36] *Ibid.*

[37] Military Commissions Act of 2009, 10 USC § 948b(a) (2009).

---

laging and the denial of quarter.[38] In its zeal to charge law of war offences in the commissions, the US added the qualifier "in violation of the law of war" to other charges, such as murder and destruction of property, when no such crimes exist, at least in the traditional, international conception of the law of armed conflict.[39]

For an example of how this disparity in charging its own service members versus its enemies plays out, consider what the specific criminal charge would be for desecrating human remains. In 2011 a US Marine scout-sniper unit permissibly engaged and killed several members of the Taliban in Afghanistan. Following the engagement, members of the unit videotaped themselves urinating on and posing with the bodies of the dead Taliban. The video was uploaded to YouTube in early 2012, went viral and drew widespread condemnation.[40] The Marine Corps prosecuted those involved, but the closest punitive UCMJ article was dereliction of duty, Article 92. The maximum punishment for wilful dereliction in the performance of duties is confinement for six months, forfeiture of all pay and allowances, and a bad conduct discharge.

While US service members have mistreated enemy remains, there is no specific charge for that misconduct, yet there is as applied to al-Qaʿida and the Taliban, despite the absence, thus far anyway, of their committing such acts. Under the Military Commissions Act of 2009 it is a crime for an unprivileged enemy belligerent to intentionally mistreat a dead body.[41] More significantly, the punishment for this offence is up to and including the death penalty. While there are stark differences in that example others

---

[38] Military Commissions Act of 2009, 10 USC § 950t(1) (2009). Given the US's opposition to the International Criminal Court ('ICC'), the similarities between criminal offences under the ICC Statute and the Military Commissions Act of 2009 are interesting. That a US citizen could not be subject to prosecution for such offences by military commission reinforces a common US stereotype: the US holds itself to a lower standard than that it claims others should meet under international law.

[39] See John C. Dehn, "The Hamdan Case and the Application of a Municipal Offence: The Common Law Origins of Murder in Violation of the Law of War", in *Journal of International Criminal Justice*, 2009, vol. 7, no. 1, p. 63.

[40] "Marine Pleads Guilty to Urinating on Corpses", in Fox News, 16 January 2013, available at www.foxnews.com/us/2013/01/16/marine-faces-court-martial-for-urinating-on-corpses-taliban-fighters-in/, last accessed at 30 March 2015.

[41] US Military Commissions Act of 2009, § 950t(20). The crime of intentionally mistreating a dead body is defined as "any person subject to this chapter [meaning non-US citizen members of al-Qaʾida and the Taliban, but not US service members] who intentionally mistreats the body of a dead person, without justification by legitimate military necessary, shall be punished as a military commission under this chapter may direct".

---

are not as clear-cut. Before the US approach can be more fully evaluated and discussed, clarifications to the terminology are warranted.

12.3. Scope of War Crimes under US Law and International Law

A common misconception is that any violation of the Geneva Conventions is a war crime.[42] First, the Conventions do not utilise the term war crimes. Instead, each of the four Conventions details violations that constitute a "grave breach" of the particular Convention. For those violations, states parties have agreed to enact legislation to provide "effective penal sanction".[43] The Conventions refer to lesser violations as "other than grave breaches" for which states parties agree to "take measures necessary for the suppression" of such acts.[44]

In its study of international humanitarian law, the ICRC attempted to identify the customary international law principles of international humanitarian law. Rule 156 of the study states that "serious violations of international humanitarian law constitute war crimes".[45] In response, the legal advisers to the US Departments of Defense and state wrote a letter to the ICRC claiming that the term war crimes "is an amorphous term used in different contexts to mean different things".[46] The US stated that:

> The national legislation cited in the commentary to Rule 157
> employs a variety of definitions of "war crimes," only a few
> of which closely parallel the definition apparently employed

---

[42] The US Army's own field manual on *The Law of Land Warfare* is, at least in part, to blame. It states, that "[t]he term 'war crime' is the technical expression for a violation of the law of war by any person or persons, military or civilian. Every violation of the law of war is a war crime"; Department of the Army, *Field Manual 27-10, The Law of Land Warfare*, Washington, DC, 1956, p. 499.

[43] Articles 49, 50, 129, 146 respectively of the Geneva Conventions I–IV; for acts constituting grave breaches, see Articles 50, 51, 130, 147 respectively of the Geneva Conventions I–IV.

[44] *Ibid.*

[45] Jean-Marie Henckaerts, "Study on Customary International Humanitarian Law: A Contribution to the Understanding and Respect for the Rule of Law in Armed Conflict", in *International Review of the Red Cross: Customary Law*, 2005, vol. 87, no. 857, p. 211, Rule 156.

[46] John B. Bellinger III and William J. Haynes II, "A US Government Response to the International Committee of the Red Cross Study *Customary International Humanitarian Law*", in *International Review of the Red Cross*, 2007, vol. 89, no. 866, p. 467. Rule 157 provides that "States have the right to vest universal jurisdiction in their national courts over war crimes".

by the Study, and none that matches it exactly. Much of the legislation cited does not precisely define "war crimes" [...]. Although the military manuals of Croatia, Hungary, and Switzerland, among others, appear to define "war crimes" as "grave breaches," the lack of specificity leaves the intended meaning ambiguous. Even among the few States that employ a definition of "war crimes" similar to that in Rule 156, no State definition mirrors the Study's definition precisely.[47]

Part of the difficulty stems from what constitutes 'serious'. This is then compounded by the definition of international humanitarian law. US federal law and the Statute of the International Criminal Court ('ICC') provide similar definitions which serve as a starting point for a comparison to their counterpart under the UCMJ.

US federal law provides that

[w]hoever, whether inside or outside the United States, commits a war crime [...] shall be fined under this title or imprisoned for life or any term of years, or both, and if death results to the victim, shall also be subject to the penalty of death.[48]

Pursuant to this approach, war crimes include grave breaches of any of the 1949 Geneva Conventions, certain articles from the 1907 Hague Convention IV, grave breaches of Article 3 common to each of the 1949 Geneva Conventions, and certain violations of Protocol II of the Convention on Certain Convention Weapons, the Protocol on Prohibitions or Restrictions on the Use of Mines, Booby-Traps and Other Devices.

---

[47] *Ibid.*

[48] War Crimes Act of 1996, 18 USC § 2441 (1996). Under the federal law, the term "war crime" means any conduct:

(1) defined as a grave breach in any of the international conventions signed at Geneva 12 August 1949, or any protocol to such convention to which the United States is a party;

(2) prohibited by Article 23, 25, 27, or 28 of the Annex to the Hague Convention IV, Respecting the Laws and Customs of War on Land, signed 18 October 1907;

(3) which constitutes a grave breach of common Article 3 (as defined in subsection (d)) when committed in the context of and in association with an armed conflict not of an international character; or

(4) of a person who, in relation to an armed conflict and contrary to the provisions of the Protocol on Prohibitions or Restrictions on the Use of Mines, Booby-Traps and Other Devices as amended at Geneva on 3 May 1996 (Protocol II as amended on 3 May 1996), when the United States is a party to such Protocol, willfully kills or causes serious injury to civilians.

The ICC Statute defines war crimes as grave breaches of the 1949 Geneva Conventions, "serious violations of the laws and customs" applicable to international and other than international armed conflict, and serious violations of Article 3 common to each of the 1949 Geneva Conventions.[49]

12.4. Comparison of Elements of War Crimes and UCMJ Crimes

How then do the elements (and punishments) of ICC Statute war crimes compare to an analogous charge under the UCMJ? This section compares the following offences: wilful killing, committing outrages against personal dignity, wilfully causing great suffering or serious injury and extensive destruction of property.

The elements for each war crime under the ICC Statute include that the conduct took place "in the context of and was associated with" an armed conflict and that the accused was aware of that conflict. Yet the introduction to the elements explains that:

> There is no requirement for a legal evaluation by the perpetrator as to the existence of an armed conflict or its character as international or non-international;

> In that context there is no requirement for awareness by the perpetrator of the facts that established the character of the conflict as international or non-international;

> There is only a requirement for the awareness of the factual circumstances that established the existence of an armed conflict that is implicit in the terms "took place in the context of and was associated with".[50]

12.4.1. Wilful Killing

Article 8(2)(a)(i) of the ICC Statute provides the following elements for the crime of wilful killing to be committed in an international armed conflict:

1. The perpetrator killed one or more persons.

---

[49] Statute of the International Criminal Court, 17 July 1998, in force 1 July 2002, 2187 UNTS 90, Art. 8 ('ICC Statute').

[50] International Criminal Court, Elements of Crimes, Doc. no. ICC-ASP/1/3 (part II-B), 9 September 2002, Art. 8.

2. Such person or persons were protected under one or more of the Geneva Conventions of 1949.

3. The perpetrator was aware of the factual circumstances that established that protected status.

4. The conduct took place in the context of and was associated with an international armed conflict.

5. The perpetrator was aware of factual circumstances that established the existence of an armed conflict.[51]

Article 118 of the UCMJ provides as follows:

1. That a certain named or described person is dead.

2. That the death resulted from the act or omission of the accused.

3. That the killing was unlawful.

4. That, at the time of the killing, the accused had a premeditated design to kill.[52]

The maximum punishment under the UCMJ is death. There is a mandatory minimum of imprisonment for life with eligibility for parole. For the ICC crimes, the maximum punishment for war crimes is "life imprisonment when justified by the extreme gravity of the crime and the individual circumstances of the convicted person".[53]

On the surface, the differences between the UCMJ and the ICC Statute are a higher *mens rea* in case of the UCMJ (premeditation) and the fact that wilful killing under the ICC requires proving both the protected status of the victim and the underlying existence of an armed conflict. Qualitatively, wilful killing is a more circumspect offence, proscribing a rule not against any wilful killing, but the wilful killing of a certain class of victims – protected persons.

Could Staff Sergeant Bales be charged with wilful killing? Even with the expansion of protected person status to include ethnicity and not just nationality,[54] the alleged victims were not protected persons for the purposes of the Geneva Conventions. They were Afghan nationals, allegedly killed in Afghanistan by a member of the US military when the US

---

[51] *Ibid.*, Art. 8(2)(a)(i).

[52] Uniform Code of Military Justice, 10 USC § 918, Art. 118, 2010.

[53] ICC Statute, Art. 77(1), see *supra* note 49.

[54] International Criminal Tribunal for the former Yugoslavia ('ICTY'), *Prosecutor v. Tihomir Blaškić*, Case No IT-95-14-T, Appeals Chamber, 3 March 2000, p. 3.

military was neither fighting against nor occupying Afghanistan, but instead aiding the government of Afghanistan in its counter-insurgency efforts. Thus, while the offence of wilful killing is uniquely tailored to armed conflict, it proves less useful in certain conflict-based settings than the more general murder charge under the UCMJ.

12.4.2. Maltreatment of Persons

Article 8(2)(c)(ii) of the Elements of Crimes outlines the elements of the crime "outrages upon personal dignity" as follows:

1. The perpetrator humiliated, degraded or otherwise violated the dignity of one or more persons.
2. The severity of the humiliation, degradation or other violation was of such degree as to be generally recognized as an outrage upon personal dignity.
3. The conduct took place in the context of and was associated with an international armed conflict.
4. The perpetrator was aware of factual circumstances that established the existence of an armed conflict.

In Article 93 of the UCMJ cruelty and maltreatment are defined as:

1. That a certain person was subject to the orders of the accused.
2. That the accused was cruel toward, or oppressed, or maltreated that person.

In the UCMJ the maximum punishment is dishonourable discharge, forfeiture of all pay and allowances, and confinement for one year. Once more the ICC Statute provides for a maximum term of 30 years or life in particularly grave circumstances. Attention is immediately drawn to the brevity of the UCMJ charge (it contains only two elements) as well as the disparity between possible punishments: one year compared to 30 years. Arguably, the UCMJ charge is not analogous to the ICC offence, or certainly not a complete equivalent. The UCMJ charge requires that the victim be subject to the orders of the accused. While being subject to orders is broadly defined, it is nonetheless a significant limitation on the application of the charge. Finally, under the UCMJ offence the victim must be alive. By comparison, an outrage against personal dignity better lends itself to the misconduct that occurs during armed conflict, particularly towards corpses.[55] For outrages against personal dignity, the Elements of Crimes provides that "'persons' can include dead persons. It is understood that the victim need not personally be aware of the existence of the humiliation or degradation or other violation. This element takes into account relevant aspects of the cultural background of the victim".[56]

12.4.3. Wilfully Causing Great Suffering or Serious Injury

ICC Article 8(2)(a)(iii) provides that the crime of wilfully causing great suffering or serious injury to body or health occurs when:

1. The perpetrator caused great physical or mental pain or suffering to, or serious injury to body or health of, one or more persons.
2. Such person or persons were protected under one or more of the Geneva Conventions of 1949.
3. The perpetrator was aware of the factual circumstances that established that protected status.
4. The conduct took place in the context of and was associated with an international armed conflict.
5. The perpetrator was aware of factual circumstances that established the existence of an armed conflict.[57]

According to Article 128 of the UCMJ aggravated assault occurs in the following circumstances:

1. That the accused attempted to do, offered to do, or did bodily harm to a certain person;
2. That the accused did so with a certain weapon, means, or force;
3. That the attempt, offer, or bodily harm was done with unlawful force or violence; and
4. That the weapon, means, or force was used in a manner likely to produce death or grievous bodily harm.[58]

---

[55] For example, some of the actions US service members have taken in recent years in Iraq could fall within this crime, notably the Abu Ghraib abuses. As the detainees were subject to the orders of the US military guards, cruelty and maltreatment could (and did) apply. In such situations, the question becomes whether a maximum sentence of one-year confinement is adequate.

[56] International Criminal Court, 2002, Art. 8(2)(c)(ii), see *supra* note 50.

[57] *Ibid.*, Article 8(2)(a)(iii).

[58] Uniform Code of Military Justice, 10 USC § 928, Art. 128, 2010.

There are a number of subsets of this offence, including when a firearm is used and when it is committed against a child under the age of 16 years. Absent one of those qualifiers, the maximum punishment is a dishonourable discharge, forfeiture of all pay and allowances, and confinement for three years.

Of the offences being compared, these two (wilfully causing great suffering and aggravated assault) may be the most similar. Interestingly, the UCMJ version applies to attempts and completed acts, while the ICC offence only applies to the completed acts. The ICC offence encompasses mental pain or suffering while the UCMJ version is limited to bodily harm. Again disparity between the possible punishment arises: the ICC crime yields a sentence range up to 30 years while the UCMJ is generally limited to three years. Even when the qualifiers are considered, the UCMJ punishment only increases to five years for a child victim and eight years when a firearm is used.

12.4.4. Destruction of Property

The crime of extensive destruction and appropriation of property is defined in the ICC Statute as occurring when:

1. The perpetrator destroyed or appropriated certain property.

2. The destruction or appropriation was not justified by military necessity.

3. The destruction or appropriation was extensive and carried out wantonly.

4. Such property was protected under one or more of the Geneva Conventions of 1949.

5. The perpetrator was aware of the factual circumstances that established that protected status.

6. The conduct took place in the context of and was associated with an international armed conflict.

7. The perpetrator was aware of factual circumstances that established the existence of an armed conflict.[59]

---

[59] ICC Statute, Art. 8(2)(a)(iv), see *supra* note 49.

Article 103 of the UCMJ provides that the crime of looting or pillaging captured or abandoned property occurs in the following circumstances:

1. That the accused engaged in looting, pillaging, or looting and pillaging by unlawfully seizing or appropriating certain public or private property;

2. That this property was located in enemy or occupied territory, or that it was on board a seized or captured vessel; and

3. That this property was:

    (i) left behind, owned by, or in the custody of the enemy, an occupied state, an inhabitant of an occupied state, or a person under the protection of the enemy or occupied state, or who, immediately prior to the occupation of the place where the act occurred, was under the protection of the enemy or occupied state; or

    (ii) part of the equipment of a seized or captured vessel; or

    (iii) owned by, or in the custody of the officers, crew, or passengers on board a seized or captured vessel.[60]

The maximum punishment is "any punishment, other than death, that a court-martial may direct".[61]

The striking feature of the UCMJ charge is that it represents a rare US military offence – one that only applies to armed conflict or during times of military occupation. Although anachronistic, this offence nonetheless demonstrates the potential for broader offences unique to armed conflict to apply to US service members.

12.5. Assessment and Proposal

The above discussion demonstrates that in some ways the crimes in the UCMJ and the ICC Statute are analogous, but in other ways they are not. The enumerated UCMJ offences are more generalised, allowing for application during both peacetime garrison settings and during armed conflict.

---

[60] Uniform Code of Military Justice, 10 USC § 903, Art. 103, 2010.

[61] *Ibid.*

But in that generalisation, it can be claimed that something is lost. Is the same offence in a garrison setting really the same as when it is committed in an armed conflict? For intra-military offences, for example, one service member assaulting another, the answer may be yes. But where the victim of the offence is not American and the armed forces are deployed in an armed conflict environment, the answer would appear to be no. The question becomes whether the various intrinsic and extrinsic values the US military justice system – designed to promote, protect and defend – operate in a domestic setting in the same manner as they do in an armed conflict.

Part of the difficulty stems from the lack of awareness of the US approach, even among legislators tasked with developing US law. In the mid-1990s, the US Congress was debating what ultimately became the War Crimes Act of 1996, which criminalised law of war violations committed by or against US nationals.[62] A report accompanying the legislation stated that "[t]he Uniform Code of Military Justice grants court-martial jurisdiction to try individuals for violations of the laws of war".[63] The report then claimed that "[t]he most famous example of a court martial for war crimes is probably that of William Calley, who was prosecuted for his part in the Mai Lai massacre during the Vietnam War".[64] Yet as discussed, the US military did not charge Calley with war crimes, it charged him with murder. But the US charges were based on substantially the same misconduct as would a charge of a crime against humanity, and the possible punishment for murder under the UCMJ – death – exceeds that of the ICC Statute.

Ultimately, there are some crimes and offences which seem to be more fully and fairly represented by enumerated punitive articles of the UCMJ than others. And the US military practice at least adequately compares with the ICC. Where the US charging practice fares poorly is the comparison between how it charges with its own service members versus members of al-Qaʻida and the Taliban for similar conducts constituting similar violations of the law of armed conflict. The US most certainly en-

---

[62] War Crimes Act of 1996. While the Act was progress, it only lessened the jurisdictional loophole in the US. Law of war violations committed by other than US nationals against anyone who is not a US national and which occur outside the US are not criminalised.

[63] US House of Representatives, House Report 104-698, 24 July 1996, p. 5.

[64] *Ibid.*

deavours to hold its service members accountable for their violations of the law of armed conflict. But that it does so differently compared to how it holds its enemies accountable is problematic.

Given the state of the United States' long history, charging its service members with law of war violations or war crimes as such, while feasible, is not likely realistic. But surely the US military can adopt some new punitive articles that reflect the armed conflict-related misconduct committed by US service members since 2001. The US could also mitigate this criticism if it were more transparent about how it meets its obligations under international humanitarian law, which the US approach to charging its service members renders even more difficult.

The Geneva Conventions require that states "provide effective penal sanctions for persons committing, or ordering to be committed, any of the grave breaches".[65] Yet the US approach to how it charges its service members hampers the ability to separate out examples of where the US has enforced its obligations (court martial of a US service member under Article 118 for killing an Iraqi civilian, for example) from other actions under the UCMJ (court-martial of a US service member under Article 118 for killing another US service member). Until 2013, none of the US military services publicly reported their court-martial results. In 2013 the United States Navy became the first to do so, which is progress but which at same time underscores the ripple effects of the US charging approach.[66] As part of a wider effort to be more transparent about prosecuting service members through the military justice system, the Navy published the results of 135 special and general courts martial which occurred between January and June 2013. For example, one entry reads as follows:

> At a Special Court-Martial in Washington, D.C., an E-3 was tried for assault consummated by a battery. The panel of members returned a verdict of not guilty to assault consum-

---

[65] Articles 49, 50, 129 and 146 respectively of the Geneva Conventions I–IV.

[66] "Document: Navy Court-Martial Summaries from Jan. to June 2013", in USNI News, 24 July 2013, available at http://news.usni.org/2013/07/24/document-navy-court-martial-summaries-from-jan-to-june-2013, last accessed at 30 March 2015. See also "Navy Releases Six Months of Court-Martial Results", in *Navy Times*, 22 July 2013, available at http://archive.navytimes.com/article/20130722/NEWS06/307220033/Navy-releases-six-months-court-martial-results, last accessed at 30 March 2015. The US Army also now releases court-martial results and in a similar fashion to the US Navy. See "Army Releases Court-Martial Verdicts for December", in *Army Times*, 23 January 2015, available at http://www.armytimes.com/story/military/crime/2015/01/23/-criminal-verdicts-discharge-results/22225147/, last accessed at 30 March 2015.

mated by a battery, but guilty to simple assault. The panel awarded a forfeiture of $1,342 per month for 2 months, reduction in rank to E-1 and 40 days confinement.

This is a significant (albeit long overdue) step and which the entire US military services should emulate. Unfortunately, it is of minimal utility in terms of demonstrating US compliance with its obligations under the Geneva Conventions. The court-martial result listed above does not reveal whether that case involved a violation of the law of war or not. We know that a court-martial panel acquitted a sailor of assault consummated by a battery and found the sailor guilty of simple assault. It is possible, though extremely unlikely, that the sailor's actions took place in Afghanistan and that the victim of the assault was a civilian, thus potentially implicating the laws of war.

How the military charges its service members generally, combined with how the Navy is reporting results, amount to a missed opportunity to demonstrate not just transparency of the UCMJ process but how the US complies with its Geneva Convention obligations.

12.6. Conclusion

One senior US military prosecutor has commented that charging decisions ultimately reflect the narrative the prosecutor wants to convey to a jury. It is difficult to envision a case where adding elements, including the existence of armed conflict or of a protected person, would render that endeavour easier. A pragmatic approach to prosecutions is not unique to the US.[67] The differences may be explained by degrees – a domestic military charge would apply to a lower-ranking individual, whereas a 'war criminal' must be an authority figure. Or, it could be argued that property destruction is appropriately addressed by the UCMJ, and that a war crime act of the same conduct would, or should, constitute a graver crime.

Yet the US approach rings hollow, maybe not in an absolute sense but certainly in a relative one. The US has been involved in armed conflict for over 10 years and is, accordingly to a commentator, in an era of

---

[67] Interview with Beth Van Schaack, Deputy Chief of the US Office of Global Criminal Justice, describing actions by ICTY prosecutors to employ charges that obviate the need for conflict classification and the use of joint criminal enterprise as a more effective modality than traditional forms of command responsibility.

"persistent conflict"[68] which will exist for "the next several decades".[69] This negates an argument that armed conflicts are not long enough to warrant unique military charges.[70] Nor is the argument that specific offences should only exist when they occur with some degree of frequency particularly persuasive, given the offences in the UCMJ such as abusing a public animal and hazarding a vessel. But fatally problematic for the US pragmatism argument is that law of war offences are detailed and employed against detainees subject to US military commissions.[71] For either reason, and certainly for both reasons, the US should modify the charges employed against its own service members.

---

[68] Pete Geren and George W. Casey Jr, *A Statement on the Posture of the United States Army 2009*, Department of the Army, Washington, DC, 2009.

[69] See also Mary L. Dudziak, *War Time: An Idea, Its History, Its Consequences*, Oxford University Press, Oxford, 2012, arguing that war is not an exceptional state but the unfortunate status quo.

[70] Moreover, as discussed above, the US military manual for courts martial has for some time contained a few conflict specific offences.

[71] This inconsistent approach to the way in which the US charges its service members versus the enemy is not new. During the Second World War, the US Army court-martialled its own service members for killing enemy prisoners of war for murder, while prosecuting Germans who committed similar acts against US POWs for violations of the laws and customs of war. See General Military Government Court at Dachau, Germany, *U.S. v. Valentin Bersin et al.*, US011 Case no. 6-24, 1945–1948.

Appendix 1: Charge Sheet of Staff Sergeant Robert Bales

CHARGE SHEET				
I. PERSONAL DATA				

<table>
<tr><td colspan="2">1. NAME OF ACCUSED (Last, First, MI)

BALES, ROBERT</td><td>2. SSN
▮</td><td>3. GRADE OR RANK
SSG</td><td>4. PAY GRADE
E-6</td></tr>
<tr><td colspan="3">5. UNIT OR ORGANIZATION

Headquarters and Headquarters Company
2d Battalion, 3d Infantry Regiment (Rear) (Provisional)
Joint Base Lewis-McChord, Washington 98433</td><td colspan="2">6. CURRENT SERVICE

a. INITIAL DATE
14 Jan 09   b. TERM 6 Years</td></tr>
</table>

7. PAY PER MONTH			8. NATURE OF RESTRAINT OF ACCUSED	9. DATE(S) IMPOSED
a. BASIC	b. SEA/FOREIGN DUTY	c. TOTAL	Pretrial Confinement	11 Mar 12 – present
$3243.30		$3243.30		

II. CHARGES AND SPECIFICATIONS

10. CHARGE: I VIOLATION OF THE UCMJ, ARTICLE 118.

SPECIFICATION 1: In that Staff Sergeant (E-6) Robert Bales, U. S. Army, did, at or near Belambay, Afghanistan, on or about 11 March 2012, with premeditation, murder a female of apparent Afghan descent known as ▮ by means of shooting her with a firearm.

SPECIFICATION 2: In that Staff Sergeant (E-6) Robert Bales, U. S. Army, did, at or near Belambay, Afghanistan, on or about 11 March 2012, with premeditation, murder a male of apparent Afghan descent known as ▮ by means of shooting him with a firearm.

SPECIFICATION 3: In that Staff Sergeant (E-6) Robert Bales, U. S. Army, did, at or near Belambay, Afghanistan, on or about 11 March 2012, with premeditation, murder a male of apparent Afghan descent known as ▮ by means of shooting him with a firearm.

SPECIFICATION 4: In that Staff Sergeant (E-6) Robert Bales, U. S. Army, did, at or near Belambay, Afghanistan, on or about 11 March 2012, with premeditation, murder a female of apparent Afghan descent by means of shooting her with a firearm.

(SEE CONTINUATION SHEET)

III. PREFERRAL

11a. NAME OF ACCUSER (Last, First, MI)	b. GRADE O-5	c. ORGANIZATION OF ACCUSER 5th Battalion, 20th Infantry Regiment
d. SIGNATURE OF ACCUSER		e. DATE 23 MAR 12

AFFIDAVIT: Before me, the undersigned, authorized by law to administer oaths in cases of this character, personally appeared the above named accuser this 23 day of MARCH , 2012, and signed the foregoing charges and specifications under oath that he/she is a person subject to the Uniform Code of Military Justice and that he/she either has personal knowledge of or has investigated the matters set forth therein and that the same are true to the best of his/her knowledge and belief.

▮	3d Brigade (SBCT), 2d Infantry Division
Typed Name of Officer	Organization of Officer
O-4	Judge Advocate
Grade	Official Capacity to Administer Oath (See R.C.M. 307(b) – must be a commissioned officer)
▮	
Signature	

DD FORM 458, MAY 2000   PREVIOUS EDITION IS OBSOLETE.

Appendix 2: Charge Sheet of the US Military Commissions

CHARGE SHEET		
I. PERSONAL DATA		

1. NAME OF ACCUSED:
ABD AL HADI AL-IRAQI

2. ALIASES OF ACCUSED:

SEE ATTACHED APPENDIX A

3. ISN NUMBER OF ACCUSED (LAST FOUR):
10026

II. CHARGES AND SPECIFICATIONS		

4. CHARGE: VIOLATION OF SECTION AND TITLE OF CRIME IN PART IV OF M.M.C.

SPECIFICATION:

SEE ATTACHED CONTINUATION SHEET OF BLOCK II. CHARGES AND SPECIFICATIONS

III. SWEARING OF CHARGES		
5a. NAME OF ACCUSER *(LAST, FIRST, MI)* TAWIL, KHALIL, M.	**5b. GRADE** CPT / O-3	**5c. ORGANIZATION OF ACCUSER** Office of the Chief Prosecutor, OMC
5d. SIGNATURE OF ACCUSER		**5e. DATE (YYYYMMDD)** 20130607

AFFIDAVIT: Before me, the undersigned, authorized by law to administer oath in cases of this character, personally appeared the above named accuser the __7th__ day of ____June____, __2013__, and signed the foregoing charges and specifications under oath that he/she is a person subject to the Uniform Code of Military Justice and that he/she has personal knowledge of or has investigated the matters set forth therein and that the same are true to the best of his/her knowledge and belief.

MARY K. KRIVDA	Office of Military Commissions
Typed Name of Officer	*Organization of Officer*
LTC / O-5	Judge Advocate, Article 136(a)(1), UCMJ
Grade	*Official Capacity to Administer Oath* *(See R.M.C. 307(b) must be commissioned officer)*
Signature	

MC FORM 458 JAN 2007

CONTINUATION SHEET – MC Form 458 (Jan 2007) – Continuation of the Charges and Specifications in the case of UNITED STATES OF AMERICA v. ABD AL HADI AL-IRAQI

CHARGE I: VIOLATION OF 10 U.S.C. § 950t(6), DENYING QUARTER

SPECIFICATION: In that Abd al Hadi al-Iraqi ("Abd al Hadi") (see Appendix A for list of aliases), a person subject to trial by military commission as an alien unprivileged enemy belligerent, did, from in or about 2003 to in or about 2004, at multiple locations in and around Afghanistan and Pakistan, in the context of and associated with hostilities, while in a position of effective command and control over subordinate forces, declare, order, and otherwise indicate to those forces that there shall be no survivors, when it was foreseeable that circumstances would be such that a practicable and reasonable ability to accept surrender would exist, with the intent to conduct hostilities such that there would be no survivors.

CONTINUATION SHEET – MC Form 458 (Jan 2007) – Continuation of the Charges and Specifications in the case of UNITED STATES OF AMERICA v. ABD AL HADI AL-IRAQI

CHARGE II: VIOLATION OF 10 U.S.C. § 950t(4), ATTACKING PROTECTED PROPERTY

SPECIFICATION: In that Abd al Hadi al-Iraqi ("Abd al Hadi") (see Appendix A for a list of aliases), a person subject to trial by military commission as an alien unprivileged enemy belligerent, did, on or about 29 September 2003, at or near Shkin, Afghanistan, in the context of and associated with hostilities, intentionally attack a military medical helicopter, which was protected property under the laws of war as a military medical aircraft bearing the emblem and distinctive sign of the Medical Service of armed forces, to wit: the red cross on a white ground, by firing at said military medical helicopter as it attempted to evacuate a United States military casualty from the battlefield, which protected property was the object of the attack and Abd al Hadi knew and should have known of the factual circumstances that established the military medical helicopter's protected status.

The Accused is liable for the above alleged offense as a principal and a co-conspirator, and as a participant in a common plan, as set forth in the section entitled "Common Allegations" which is hereby re-alleged and incorporated by reference as if set forth fully herein.

CONTINUATION SHEET – MC Form 458 (Jan 2007) – Continuation of the Charges and Specifications in the case of UNITED STATES OF AMERICA v. ABD AL HADI AL-IRAQI

CHARGE III: VIOLATION OF 10 U.S.C. § 950t(17), USING TREACHERY OR PERFIDY

SPECIFICATION 1: In that Abd al Hadi al-Iraqi ("Abd al Hadi") (see Appendix A for a list of aliases), a person subject to trial by military commission as an alien unprivileged enemy belligerent, did, on or about 7 June 2003, at or near Kabul, Afghanistan, in the context of and associated with hostilities, invite the confidence and belief of at least one person that a vehicle appearing to be civilian vehicle was entitled to protection under the law of war, and, intending to use and betray that confidence and belief, did, thereafter, make use of that confidence and belief to detonate explosives in said vehicle alongside a bus carrying German military members, resulting in death and injury to at least one person.

SPECIFICATION 2: In that Abd al Hadi al-Iraqi ("Abd al Hadi") (see Appendix A for a list of aliases), a person subject to trial by military commission as an alien unprivileged enemy belligerent, did, on or about 28 January 2004, at or near Kabul, Afghanistan, in the context of and associated with hostilities, invite the confidence and belief of at least one person that a vehicle appearing to be a civilian vehicle was entitled to protection under the law of war, and, intending to use and betray that confidence and belief, did, thereafter, make use of that confidence and belief to detonate explosives in said vehicle alongside a coalition convoy carrying British and Estonian military members, resulting in death and injury to at least one person.

The Accused is liable for the above alleged offenses as a principal and a co-conspirator, and as a participant in a common plan, as set forth in the section entitled "Common Allegations" which is hereby re-alleged and incorporated by reference as if set forth fully herein.

CONTINUATION SHEET – MC Form 458 (Jan 2007) – Continuation of the
Charges and Specifications in the case of UNITED STATES OF AMERICA v. ABD
AL HADI AL-IRAQI

CHARGE IV: VIOLATION OF 10 U.S.C. § 950t(28), ATTEMPTED USE OF
TREACHERY OR PERFIDY

SPECIFICATION: In that Abd al Hadi al-Iraqi ("Abd al Hadi") (see Appendix A for a
list of aliases), a person subject to trial by military commission as an alien unprivileged
enemy belligerent, did, on or about 29 March 2004, at or near Jalalabad, Afghanistan, in
the context of and associated with hostilities, with the specific intent to commit the
offense of Using Treachery or Perfidy (10 U.S.C. § 950t(17)), invite the confidence and
belief of at least one person that a vehicle appearing to be a civilian vehicle was entitled
to protection under the law of war, and, intending to use and betray that confidence and
belief, did, thereafter, make use of that confidence and belief to attempt to detonate
explosives in said vehicle alongside a convoy carrying United States military members
with the intent to kill and injure at least one person.

The Accused is liable for the above alleged offense as a principal and a co-conspirator,
and as a participant in a common plan, as set forth in the section entitled "Common
Allegations" which is hereby re-alleged and incorporated by reference as if set forth fully
herein.

Page 10 of 10

Appendix 3: Charge Sheet of First Lieutenant William L. Calley

Charge : Violation of the Uniform Code of Military Justice, Article **118**

Specification 1: In that First Lieutenant William L. Calley, Jr., US Army, 40th Company, The Student Brigade, US Army Infantry School, Fort Benning, Georgia (then a member of Company C, 1st Battalion, 20th Infantry) did, at My Lai 4, Quang Ngai Province, Republic of South Vietnam, on or about 16 March 1968, with premeditation, murder four Oriental human beings, occupants of the village of My Lai 4, whose names and sexes are unknown, by means of shooting them with a rifle.

Specification 2: In that First Lieutenant William L. Calley, Jr., US Army, 40th Company, The Student Brigade, US Army Infantry School, Fort Benning, Georgia (then a member of Company C, 1st Battalion, 20th Infantry) did, at My Lai 4, Quang Ngai Province, Republic of South Vietnam, on or about 16 March 1968, with premeditation, murder an unknown number, not less than 30, Oriental human beings, males and females of various ages, whose names are unknown, occupants of the village of My Lai 4, by means of shooting them with a rifle.

Specification 3: In that First Lieutenant William L. Calley, Jr., US Army, 40th Company, The Student Brigade, US Army Infantry School, Fort Benning, Georgia (then a member of Company C, 1st Battalion, 20th Infantry) did, at My Lai 4, Quang Ngai Province, Republic of South Vietnam, on or about 16 March 1968, with premeditation, murder three Oriental human beings whose names and sexes are unknown, occupants of the village of My Lai 4, by means of shooting them with a rifle.

Specification 4: In that First Lieutenant William L. Calley, Jr., US Army, 40th Company, The Student Brigade, US Army Infantry School, Fort Benning, Georgia (then a member of Company C, 1st Battalion, 20th Infantry) did, at My Lai 4, Quang Ngai Province, Republic of South Vietnam, on or about 16 March 1968, with premeditation, murder an unknown number of Oriental human beings, not less than seventy, males and females of various ages, whose names are unknown, occupants of the village of My Lai 4, by means of shooting them with a rifle.

13

Awakening Self-Interest: American Military Justice in Afghanistan and Iraq

Franklin D. Rosenblatt*

13.1. Introduction

When military forces deploy on missions beyond their own borders, should their military justice system go with them? Do courts martial convened during deployments contribute towards the operational effectiveness, and thus the self-interest, of armed forces? What are the most common impediments to implementing a system of deployed justice? A useful case study for considering these questions is found in the experience of the United States military during its missions in the 2000s in Afghanistan and Iraq. Not only were these the largest-scale military deployments of any kind in recent history but they also spanned a range of missions from peacekeeping to counter-insurgency to full combat.

Conventional wisdom holds that the American court-martial system is able to follow the military anywhere in the world and still function effectively. A group of American military law experts touted:

> In recent years, the system created and governed by the UCMJ [the Uniform Code of Military Justice, the American military justice statute] has continued to operate effectively through the increased tempo of operations and distinctive legal challenges of the ongoing wars in Iraq and Afghanistan.[1]

When speaking in platitudes rather than analysing actual practice, American military lawyers also joined this refrain: "The military justice system [...] goes wherever the troops go – to provide uniform treatment

---

* Franklin D. Rosenblatt is Judge Advocate in the United States Army. The views in this chapter are the author's, not necessarily those of the United States Army.

[1] National Institute of Military Justice, *Report of the Commission on Military Justice*, October 2009, p. 1. This document is commonly called the '2009 Cox Commission Report'.

---

regardless of locale or circumstances".[2] Another group of judge advocates concluded approvingly:

> During times of conflict, as always, military members deserve the highest protections. Judge Advocates (JAs) continue to work with commanders during contingency operations to exercise swift and sound justice in sometimes austere conditions.[3]

Surprisingly, there have been no empirical studies examining how well the court-martial system has actually performed during America's recent conflicts.[4] This chapter attempts such a study, and the findings largely contradict the conventional wisdom that the American military's deployed justice system represents an unparalleled success. Instead, after-action reports from military lawyers who deployed to Afghanistan and Iraq show a nearly unanimous recognition that the full-bore application of military justice was not a viable option in the combat zone. In practice, deployed commanders and judge advocates exercised all possible alternatives to avoid the crushing burdens of conducting courts martial while deployed, from sending cases of misconduct back to the home station, to granting leniency, to a more frequent use of administrative discharge procedures. By any measure – numbers of cases tried, kinds of cases, reckoning for service member crime, deterrence of other would-be

---

2   James B. Roan and Cynthia Buxton, "The American Military Justice System in the New Millennium", in *Air Force Law Review*, 2002, vol. 52, p. 191.

3   Center for Law and Military Operations ('CLAMO'), *Forged in the Fire: Legal Lessons Learned During Military Operations 1994–2008*, United States Army, The Judge Advocate General's Legal Center and School, Charlottesville, VA, 2008, p. 289. This statement was made by the publication's editors.

4   Some related works include Major John M. Hackel, "Planning for the 'Strategic Case': A Proposal to Align the Handling of Marine Corps War Crimes Prosecutions with Counterinsurgency Doctrine", in *Naval Law Review*, 2009, vol. 57, p. 244 (considering, "has the Marine Corps missed the mark with deployment justice, particularly with war crimes?"); Colonel Carlton L. Jackson, "Plea-Bargaining in the Military: An Unintended Consequence of the Uniform Code of Military Justice", in *Military Law Review*, 2004, vol. 179, pp. 66–67 (attributing low Army-wide court-martial numbers from 2001 to 2003 to commanders adjusting to wartime realities by increasing their use of administrative discharges to clear growing caseloads); Captain A. Jason Nef, "Getting to Court: Trial Practice in a Deployed Environment", in *The Army Lawyer*, January 2009, p. 50 (offering practitioner advice based on the author's experience and emphasising how to minimise trial delay from production of witnesses for courts martial in Iraq); and Captain Eric Hanson, "Know Your Ground: The Military Justice Terrain of Afghanistan", in *The Army Lawyer*, November 2009, p. 36 (describing the added difficulties of performing courts martial in Afghanistan).

---

offenders, contribution to good order and discipline, or the provision of a meaningful forum for those accused of crimes to assert their innocence or present a defence – it cannot be said that the American court-martial system functioned effectively in Afghanistan or Iraq. In an era of legally intensive conflicts,[5] this court martial frailty is consequential and bears directly on the success or failure of national military efforts.

The next four sections of this chapter will approach this issue from the perspectives of the reporter, attorney, military strategist and policymaker, respectively. Section 13.2. explores court-martial practices in Afghanistan and Iraq from 2001 to 2009. After an overview of courts martial conducted, the section draws on the accounts of hundreds of unit after-action reviews to investigate impediments to deployed justice. Next, the section scrutinises the types of cases tried and how misconduct in the combat zone is treated differently than misconducts elsewhere. Combined, the information in this section finds expression in the 'Burger King Theory', which holds that courts martial, much like Burger King franchises, are sometimes present in the combat zone but cannot go 'outside the wire' from the largest, most city-like bases.

Section 13.3. provides a legal analysis of two uniquely American court-martial procedures – good military character evidence and expert witness rules – that each have the potential to thwart efforts to try cases in the combat zone.[6]

---

[5] The term 'legally intensive conflicts' may also be an appropriate description of any military campaign where legal considerations are prominent, including Afghanistan and Iraq. As one observer noted: "Based on a very incomplete picture of what's happening day to day in Iraq, it appears that there's much more attention to human rights and to the laws of war than, for example, in Vietnam or Korea". See Brad Knickerbocker, "Is Military Justice in Iraq Changing for the Better?", in *Christian Science Monitor*, 7 August 2007, quoting Loren Thompson of the Lexington Institute, available at http://www.csmonitor.com/2007/0807/p01s04-usmi.html, last accessed on 20 March 2015.

[6] 'Combat zone' is not a doctrinal Army term, but is used throughout this chapter to describe the variety of conditions of the American military presence in Afghanistan from 2001 to 2009 and Iraq from 2003 to 2009. Doctrinal operational themes that have variously been applied to each of these combat zones include major combat operations, irregular warfare, peace operations and limited intervention. On the doctrinal spectrum of violence, these combat zones included unstable peace, insurgency and general war. For descriptions of these terms, see US Department of Army, *Army Doctrine Reference Publication (ADRP) 3-0: Unified Land Operations*, Headquarters, Department of the Army, Washington, DC, 16 May 2012, available at http://armypubs.army.mil/doctrine/DR_pubs/dr_a/pdf/adrp 3_0.pdf, last accessed on 20 March 2015.

Section 13.4. highlights the downstream consequences of a weak regime of criminal adjudication during overseas deployments. Although the present system's weaknesses have several troubling implications, the section is limited to two strategic consequences of combat court-martial frailty: the link between courts martial and counter-insurgency success, and diminished American legitimacy when perceptions of military impunity foment. In both Afghanistan and Iraq, the section describes how faulty accountability for military crimes set back hard-won gains on the battlefield.

Section 13.5. surveys a range of possible solutions to strengthen military justice in combat, including some that are outside the mainstream of current opinion.

13.2. The Court-Martial System Goes to War: 2001 to 2009

Wherever there are troops, there will be criminal activity.[7]

The table below shows the number of special and general courts martial conducted in Afghanistan and Iraq from 2001 to 2009.

Jurisdiction	2001	2002	2003	2004	2005	2006	2007	2008	2009
All Army	1206	1438	1343	1353	1546	1358	1446	1165	1166
Afghanistan	0	0	0	7	18	22	28	22	11
Iraq	n/a	n/a	37	117	144	79	92	63	32

Table 1: Number of special and general courts martial in Afghanistan and Iraq, 2001–2009[8]

---

[7] Major Jeff A. Bovarnick, *Notes from the Combat Zone*, Memorandum, US Army, 2002, p. 5. Major Bovarnick wrote the memorandum while serving as the Chief of Operational Law for Combined Joint Task Force 180 in Afghanistan. This document is on file at the CLAMO, see *supra* note 3.

[8] Special and general courts martial are the two kinds of court martial that resemble civilian trials. They feature a judge, formal proceedings, prosecution and defence attorneys, (often) a panel of military members for jury, and (often) verbatim transcripts of the proceedings to aid appellate review. Special courts martial are governed by Articles 19 and 23 of the Uniform Code of Military Justice ('UCMJ') and feature a sentence limit of up to one year of confinement. General courts martial are governed by Articles 18 and 22 of the UCMJ and are the traditional forum for the most serious criminal offences. Both can adjudge punitive discharges and confinement. The chart does not include the summary court martial, which "unlike a criminal trial, is not an adversarial proceeding". United States Supreme Court, *Middendorf v. Henry*, Judgment, 24 March 1976, vol. 425, p. 26. See also Article 20,

This data, when considering the large numbers of troops that were forward-deployed during the years in question, shows that courts martial were scarcer in combat zones than in the rest of the Army. In Iraq, courts martial began during the first year of operations, peaked in numbers in 2005, then settled into relatively low numbers and frequency. The military started slower in Afghanistan, with no courts martial held until the fourth year of that conflict, followed by more frequent courts martial in the middle of the decade, until plummeting numbers in 2008 and 2009. The 672 Army courts martial tried in either Afghanistan or Iraq from 2001 to 2009 were the majority of all courts martial in the combat zone among the military services.[9]

But numbers do not tell the whole story. Vietnam offers an important lesson about assuming the success of the court martial system based solely on court martial numbers. After that war, the former commanding general of US forces in Vietnam and the top Army lawyer concluded that the court-martial system did not function effectively despite the impressive number of cases tried. "In view of the developments in Vietnam, especially from 1969 on, it simply cannot be claimed that the military justice system adequately performed its intended roles in that limited war".[10] The lack of after-action reviews to document the system's deficiencies in combat was one focus of their lament:

> Many commanders found the procedures less than satisfactory because of the difficulties in performing their operational tasks and at the same time meeting the time restrictions imposed by the military justice system. Many

UCMJ; Manual for Courts-Martial, United States, Rule for Courts-Martial 1301-06, 2008 ('MCM', 'RCM'); US Army, *Pamphlet 27-7: Guide for Summary Court-Martial Trial Procedure*, 15 June 1985. The data contained in Figure 1 comes from the annual reports of the military services to the Code Committee on Military Justice. This information can be retrieved from the US Court of Appeals for the Armed Forces ('CAAF') website, http://www.armfor.uscourts.gov/newcaaf/home.htm and clicking on the link on the left of the screen for "Annual Reports".

[9] Additional research conducted by the author revealed that the numbers of courts martial conducted by other services were significantly fewer than conducted by the US Army (the focus of this chapter). For example, the Navy conducted two courts martial in Iraq, the Marine Corps conducted six general courts martial in Iraq or Afghanistan, and the Air Force did not conduct its first combat zone courts under 2006 in Iraq and 2008 in Afghanistan.

[10] General William Westmoreland and Major General George Prugh, "Judges in Command: The Judicialized Uniform Code of Military Justice in Combat", in *Harvard Journal of Law and Public Policy*, 1980, vol. 3, p. 60.

deserving cases simply were not referred to trial, with consequences on discipline impossible to calculate but obviously deleterious. The requirements for the presence of witnesses, counsel, and investigating officer to meet in an Article 32 Investigation (similar to a preliminary examination) were difficult to satisfy. Inability to obtain prompt evidence from departed witnesses, the twelve-month rotation policy, the extension of the right to civilian counsel from the United States, the total disruption of an operational unit when a major court-martial was involved – all of these are variously mentioned by knowledgeable commanders. Regrettably, these comments, observations, and complaints were rarely collected, examined, and evaluated to determine the true impact of the system, and the true impact of the system of military discipline. Statistics do not reflect these serious problems.[11]

Because the only statistics available were case totals, there was no actionable data to compel policy changes to correct combat court-martial deficiencies. The hard-learned lessons of Vietnam, they worried, might be lost without meaningful data to support what was widely known by commanders.

But times have changed, at least as far as court-martial data is concerned. Today, considerably more data on responses to misconduct from Afghanistan and Iraq is available. The US Army's Center for Law and Military Operations ('CLAMO') gathered legal lessons learned from most major units that deployed to those two countries, including insights on military justice.[12] This section draws from 276 after-action reviews

---

[11] *Ibid.*

[12] Some of the comments from these after-action reports can also be found in four publications of the CLAMO: (1) *Legal Lessons Learned from Afghanistan and Iraq, Volume I*, 2004; (2) *Lessons Learned from Afghanistan and Iraq, Volume II*, 2005; (3) *Forged in the Fire: Legal Lessons Learned During Military Operations 1994–2008*, 2008 ('Forged in the Fire'); and (4) *Tip of the Spear: After Action Reports from July 2008–August 2009*, 2009 ('Tip of the Spear'). All after-action reviews ('AAR') listed throughout this chapter are on file with CLAMO at the Army Judge Advocate General's Legal Center and School in Charlottesville, Virginia. The first three publications include some of the AAR points incorporated into the analysis by the CLAMO editors but do not include all of the military justice lessons found in the unit AARs. These three volumes are unclassified. Tip of the Spear has comprehensive coverage of AARs in place of the editorial analysis in the earlier volumes. However, since this comprehensive coverage was limited to 13 months of AARs, no combination of publications included all of the pertinent AARs, so the author still re-

('AARs') collected by the CLAMO from Iraq and Afghanistan. Few AARs were completed in the early years of the Afghanistan conflict, so the author interviewed judge advocates then present to fill in the gaps. Combined, this information helps answer questions that numbers alone do not reveal: How closely did court-martial numbers correlate to serious misconduct? What types of cases were brought to trial? What role did a unit's location play? Is crime committed on deployment treated differently than crime committed in the United States?

13.2.1. Frequently Cited Difficulties with Military Justice during Deployments

In Afghanistan and Iraq, a high operations tempo promoted good behaviour, while inactivity sowed misconduct. A judge advocate with an Army division that fought through Iraq in 2003 before settling into a base near Mosul in Iraq wrote:

> Expect MJ [military justice actions] to surge in proportion to the length of time you are stationary. As long as the Division was on the move, soldiers were too busy fighting the war to have the time to get into trouble. MJ simply exploded once we became stationary.[13]

Likewise, a judge advocate in Afghanistan in early 2002 credited his unit's lack of serious misconduct to the intensity of combat operations and the lack of downtime: "Why was the misconduct low in number and severity? A mix of really busy, tired troops, some good luck, good leaders, and good grace, I suppose".[14] As a caveat to these conclusions, the fog of major combat operations may make some misconduct more difficult to detect. A judge advocate in Iraq in 2004 initially "thought the size of the caseload was inversely proportional to the operational tempo of

---

viewed each AAR individually. Due to its unfiltered reprinting of AAR comments, Tip of the Spear is classified as "For Official Use Only", meaning that it is restricted to the public, but all excerpts from AARs in this chapter are unclassified. The CLAMO website is https://www.jagcnet.army.mil/clamo. The author obtained permission to access CLAMO's digital archives.

[13] Office of the Staff Judge Advocate, 101st Airborne Division (Air Assault), *Operation Iraqi Freedom After Action Report*, 2004, p. 51. This document is on file at the CLAMO, see *supra* note 12.

[14] E-mail message to author from Lieutenant Colonel J. Harper Cook, Deputy Staff Judge Advocate of the 21st Theater Support Command, 27 January 2010. Lieutenant Colonel Cook served with 3rd Brigade, 101st Airborne Division in Kandahar, Afghanistan from January to July 2002, a period of intense ground combat.

---

the unit. This assessment, however, was false. Crimes occur at all times during the deployment, including times of intense combat activity and during times of relative calm".[15]

Neither special nor general courts martial were conducted during initial major combat operations. The 37 special and general courts martial tried in Iraq in 2003 did not begin until later that summer, after 'active combat' ended.[16] Meanwhile, no special or general courts martial were conducted in Afghanistan until 2004, the fourth year of that conflict.

Several factors may have contributed to the absence of courts martial in Afghanistan in the first years of combat operations. In the months after 9/11, American military forces probably had higher morale and were less likely to commit serious misconduct. "A surge of patriotism has kept morale, recruiting and retention high since the attacks on New York and Washington".[17] Likewise, a senior judge advocate in Afghanistan in 2002 believed that soldiers had a clear sense of purpose and were less likely to get into trouble because the United States had just been attacked.[18]

Even if a court martial had been needed early in the Afghanistan conflict, conducting it would have been nearly impossible. The same judge advocate who described conditions in Afghanistan in 2002 recalled:

> We would have had to fly in a TC [trial counsel], TDS [trial defence services] Counsel, Judge, court-reporter, etc., and not only were flights erratic but the priority on flying in personnel were more troops and beans and bullets. There was no place to quarter any visitors – water and food were scarce, and there really was no downtime in which to pull our limited troops off of their operational duties in order to run a court.[19]

---

[15] Captain Christopher Ford, "The Practice of Law at the Brigade Combat Team (BCT)", in *The Army Lawyer*, 2004, p. 31.

[16] "Trials of soldiers in the Iraq and Kuwait areas commenced shortly after the active combat phase ended, and increased in number over the summer and fall". Annual Report Submitted to the Committees on Armed Services of the United States Senate and the United States House of Representatives, 2003, sec. 3 (Comment of the Army Trial Judiciary, within the Report of The Judge Advocate General of the Army).

[17] Thomas E. Ricks and Vernon Loeb, "Unrivaled Military Feels Strains of Unending War", in *Washington Post*, 16 February 2003.

[18] See Colonel Kathryn Stone, e-mail message to author, 29 October 2009. Colonel Stone was at the time the Staff Judge Advocate for the 10th Mountain Division.

[19] *Ibid.*

Gradually, however, the 'no resources' rationale against conducting courts martial diminished as US forces became more settled in Afghanistan. As they did so, criminal misconduct began its inevitable percolation. One judge advocate wrote in late 2002 that "some cases warrant a court-martial", but explained that the offenders in question were sent back to the United States for trial rather than tried in Afghanistan.[20] Reports by the CLAMO noted the continuation of this practice throughout the first two years of Afghanistan: "Cases involving more serious misconduct were transferred to the United States for prosecution due, in part, to the austere conditions in Afghanistan".[21]

These comments indicate that, once settled, commanders at least had the capacity for air movement (since they could fly accused, escorts and evidence back to the United States), but that they elected to use those assets to send cases away rather than convene courts martial in theatre. Why was this so? A military paralegal with an infantry unit engaged in combat in Afghanistan in 2009 explained his unit's reasons for not pursuing courts martial in country:

> Missions don't stop for courts-martial and if we have to pull a squad off the line to testify against a Soldier who is causing trouble, then someone needs to cover down for them. [...] [O]ur Brigade is already spread very thin and assets are very hard to come by. A squad who would normally be assigned to refit after spending two weeks without a shower or hot chow would be required to stay out longer depending on the duration of the court-martial. Key leaders, such as squad leaders, platoon sergeants, platoon leaders, first sergeants, and commanders end up absent from the fight and leave their units short on leadership. It's a dangerous situation and the unit is more likely to send the Soldier back to the rear

---

[20] Bovarnick, 2002, see *supra* note 7.

[21] CLAMO, *Lessons Learned, Volume I*, 2004, p. 237, see *supra* note 12; see also Office of the Clerk of Court, US Army Judiciary, Cases Charged with an Offense Committed in Iraq, Afghanistan, or Kuwait CY 2001 through CY 2009, 8 October 2009 (on file with author) (showing that 13 special and general courts martial were conducted in the United States to adjudicate crime from Afghanistan before the first court martial was conducted in Afghanistan in 2004). The report from the Office of the Clerk of Court also shows that even after courts martial began to be conducted in Afghanistan in 2004, the practice of sending offenders back to the United States for adjudication remained common. The author thanks Randall Bruns from the Army Clerk of Court office for his assistance in compiling this data.

provisional unit [at Fort Bragg, North Carolina] to be court-martialed as opposed to doing it out here.[22]

In combat operations, commanders focused their limited resources on the fight at hand. Sending serious misconduct away was considered a more effective use of resources than conducting courts martial on site.

The most common court-martial difficulty cited by deployed units was securing the live testimony of witnesses.[23] A judge advocate with a unit in Iraq in 2009 explained: "Requesting witnesses from the Continental United States (CONUS) or from Iraq and arranging travel proved to be extremely difficult".[24] Units were responsible for preparing civilian witnesses to enter a combat zone, a task that required time, effort, and interagency cooperation. A judge advocate in Afghanistan in 2009 noted some of these difficulties:

> Arranging travel for civilian witnesses and defense counsel into theater was very problematic. Civilians must have a passport, country clearance, visa, interceptor body armor (IBA), Kevlar helmet, and a DoD identification card before traveling to Afghanistan for trial. The unit learned the requirements through trial and error. In one case, a civilian witness was unable to board the aircraft leaving Kuwait because of the lack of a DoD ID card.[25]

Witness issues were often the 'make or break' factor in whether courts martial would occur at all. As a judge advocate in Iraq in 2007 explained: "The most challenging aspect of trying cases in Iraq was the specter of calling witnesses forward from outside Iraq to testify and the possibility that the need to obtain such witnesses would derail the court-

---

22 E-mail message from Sergeant James Marcum to author, 22 February 2010. Sergeant Marcum was a paralegal noncommissioned officer ('NCO') with the 4th Brigade Combat Team of the 82d Airborne Division.

23 See Section 13.3. for legal requirements to produce witnesses based on the Sixth Amendment of the US Constitution. As one judge advocate summarised: "The 6th amendment's guarantees boil down to this: the government needs to produce all its witnesses in person. Video-teleconference or telephonic testimony may not satisfy the 6th amendment". Office of the Staff Judge Advocate ('OSJA'), 101st Airborne Division (Air Assault), *Task Force Band of Brothers Operation Iraqi Freedom 05–07 After Action Report*, 2007, p. 79. This document is on file at the CLAMO, see *supra* note 12.

24 OSJA, 1st Armored Division, *After Action Review (Operation Iraqi Freedom)*, 19 February 2009, p. 36. This document is on file at the CLAMO, see *supra* note 12.

25 OSJA, 101st Airborne Division (Air Assault), *Operation Enduring Freedom After Action Review 40*, 28 August 2009. This document is on file at the CLAMO, see *supra* note 12.

martial".[26] Another judge advocate confirms that witness production demands caused derailment of deployed courts martial: "It was extremely challenging to get civilian witnesses into theater. Consequently, in some cases where calling civilian witnesses was unavoidable, the court-martial would move to Atlanta [...]".[27] Another military lawyer accurately summed up the common results from trying to compel civilian witnesses to appear at a trial in a combat zone: "Civilian witnesses would often not appear to testify at trials".[28]

Selecting and maintaining court-martial panels (a military version of juries) presented numerous difficulties during deployments.[29] In a combat zone, performing courts martial with members is logistically complex, involves dangerous travel in bringing all members to the court, and can take leaders away from their combat duties. As one legal office reported:

> The unit struggled with convening courts-martial member trials when scheduled to occur. Specifically, many members were located in remote areas of the jurisdiction. This made travel to COB [Contingency Operating Base] Speicher [near Tikrit, Iraq] for courts-martial trials difficult.[30]

Panel difficulties extended even to large, stable, garrison-style bases where the pool of potential members was co-located, presumably 'easier' to bring a panel together for court: "[Our division-level command] needed to select three or four different court-martial panels during their deployment because the units changed out so often".[31]

Perhaps anticipating these difficulties, numerous senior Army commanders decided outright to not choose panels or convene special and general courts martial. For example, in early Iraq, at least three Army divisions each decided to not try cases. The 82nd Airborne Division

[26] OSJA, 2007, p. 79, see *supra* note 23. Other witness production considerations are discussed later in this chapter.

[27] Senior Defense Counsel, Camp Arifjan, Kuwait, *After Action Report*, 13 October 2009. This document is on file at the CLAMO, see *supra* note 12.

[28] 4th Brigade, 10th Mountain Division, *Operation Iraqi Freedom After Action Review*, 2009, p. 18. This document is on file at the CLAMO, see *supra* note 12.

[29] OSJA, V Corps, *Operation Iraqi Freedom After Action Report*, May 2007, p. 13. This document is on file at the CLAMO, see *supra* note 12.

[30] OSJA, 2009, p. 37, see *supra* note 24.

[31] 10th Mountain Division, *After Action Review*, Operation Iraqi Freedom, 24–25 June 2009, p. 33. This document is on file at the CLAMO, see *supra* note 12.

declared its commander a General Court-Martial Convening Authority ('GCMCA'), but only for the purpose of appointing investigating officers for certain administrative investigations.[32] The 101st Airborne Division "made the decision not to try any general or special courts-martial in the deployed theater [...]" during its year-long deployment.[33] Likewise, the 3d Infantry Division did not select a panel and "did not try any general or special courts-martial in the deployed theater before it redeployed in August of 2003".[34]

Units also mentioned the lack of easy access to a military judge in theatre as a reason for diverting misconduct away from the court-martial track. One judge advocate wrote:

> The argument that there is insufficient work in theater to justify a full-time judge is a self-fulfilling prophecy. Units divert cases from court-martial because there is no judge in theater. This gives the impression there is not enough court-martial work in theater to justify the presence of a judge.[35]

Another judge advocate explained his unit's decision to try serious offences that would normally warrant general court martial at summary courts martial as follows: "Because a full trial at a 'general' court-martial was time-consuming – requiring a military judge to fly into Iraq – our brigade often used 'summary court-martial', a trial where the judge could

---

[32] CLAMO, 2008, p. 242, see *supra* note 3.

[33] CLAMO, *Lessons Learned, Volume I*, 2004, p. 243, see *supra* note 12.

[34] *Ibid.*, p. 242.

[35] 1st Combat Support Brigade (Maneuver Enhancement), *Task Force Warrior After Action Review*, Operation Enduring Freedom, June 2008 – September 2009, 20 October 2009, p. 14. But see interview with Colonel Stephen Henley, Chief Army Trial Judge, in Char-lottesville, Virginia, 18 February 2010. Colonel Henley corrected the notion that there was no judge in theatre, saying that the Central Command ('CENTCOM') theatre has been un-der continuous coverage of an Army judge since 2003. "We can get judges there [to courts martial in Iraq] within three days". It takes about a week to get a judge to a court martial in Afghanistan due to greater travel difficulties there. Senior commanders have afforded judges and select court-martial personnel high priority for flight manifests, which Colonel Henley believes helps get judges to courts martial faster. Colonel Henley also noted that trial dockets are posted and publicly available on the Internet, which allows units to plan ahead for trial terms. Beginning in 2010, full-time judges were assigned to serve one-year rotations in Kuwait in order to cover cases in both Iraq and Afghanistan. Before then, an activated reservist judge or judge from the Army's 5th judicial circuit in Germany served for two to three months at a time in the CENTCOM theatre; if there is not enough work in theatre, the judge returned to home station in Germany or the United States.

---

be one of our higher-ranking field grade officers".[36] Returning units frequently commented on judicial coverage and flexibility, assessing both in a broad range from poor[37] to excellent.[38]

In addition to difficulties associated with witness production, panel selection and access to judges, judge advocates faced a number of other court-martial challenges in theatre. For example, given the high operations tempo of combat, military justice was often a less immediate concern, and judge advocates who focused primarily on criminal law in the United States quickly discovered that competing priorities vied for their time and attention on deployments. "In garrison, criminal law is absolutely the number one priority. Once deployed, it became the fifth priority behind DetOps [Detainee Operations], OpLaw [Operational Law], RoL [Rule of Law], and investigations".[39]

Additionally, organisational hierarchies that were linear and easily understood in garrison tended to become confused on deployment. Modularity, a 'plug and play' concept that emphasises interchangeable units rather than organic divisions and brigades, "makes all areas of military legal practice difficult" because hierarchies and jurisdictions constantly shift as various units enter and exit theatre.[40] The jurisdictional problems associated with modularity and unit movement were not limited to the early years of the deployments. Units in Iraq and Afghanistan shifted frequently on paper and on the ground, which made determining the higher headquarters in charge of a subordinate unit difficult.[41] One

---

[36] Patrick J. Murphy with Adam Frankel, *Taking the Hill: From Philly to Baghdad to the United States Congress*, Henry Holt and Co., New York, 2008, p. 124. The former Captain Murphy served as an Army judge advocate with the 325th Airborne Infantry Regiment of the 82d Airborne Division in Baghdad, Iraq, from 2003 to 2004, before his service in Congress from Pennsylvania's 8th District, from 2007 to 2011.

[37] "If the UCMJ is intended to be expeditionary, the supporting establishment must be as well. We should either deploy judges adequately to satisfy the demand or admit that the UCMJ is a garrison tool. We cannot have it both ways". Lieutenant Colonel R.G. Bracknell, Staff Judge Advocate, Regimental Combat Team 5, US Marine Corps, *After Action Report*, Operation Iraqi Freedom, 7 August 2008, p. 11.

[38] "The judiciary provided excellent support to the BCT. The judges were available, flexible, and understanding of the challenges associated with conducting cases in a deployed environment". Brigade Judge Advocate, 3d Brigade Combat Team, 101st Airborne Division (Air Assault), *Operation Iraqi Freedom After Action Review*, 2009, p. 13.

[39] OSJA, 2009, p. 35, see *supra* note 25.

[40] CLAMO, *Tip of the Spear*, 2009, p. 371, see *supra* note 12.

[41] See, for example, *4th Infantry Division (OIF 05–07) After Action Review 30*, 2007, ("The military justice jurisdiction in theater changed constantly due to units being assigned or at-

---

brigade judge advocate noted the natural consequence of this: "The brigade commander did not always have jurisdiction over personnel assigned to his unit".[42]

Joint operations that intermixed soldiers, marines, sailors and airmen further hindered the efficient application of military justice. "Joint Justice [...] is still a challenge: it is very difficult to track AF [Air Force] and Navy misconduct actions – as well as their investigations into said misconduct".[43] Service parochialism often outweighed the combat commander's ability to seek justice: "The Navy and Marine Corps typically sent their personnel out of theater when misconduct arose".[44] Another unit wrote: "Although the Manual for Courts-Martial (MCM) permits joint justice, there was no unified service approach to military justice. Each service handled its own military justice matters".[45]

Compounding these difficulties, units usually had fewer resources to investigate crime in theatre. When back in their home stations, the military enjoyed access to military police investigators ('MPI') to investigate minor criminal offences and the professional military criminal investigators to investigate major offences. However, few of these law enforcement units deployed, and when they did deploy they were often performing duties other than law enforcement.[46] Thus, many tactical units were often forced to investigate crimes on their own without the assistance of law enforcement professionals.

---

tached to MND-B [Multi-National Division, Baghdad] either as OPCON [operational control] or TACON [tactical control]"); Memorandum from Staff Judge Advocate to Commanding General, III Corps, subject: *Operation Iraqi Freedom (OIF) After Action Report (AAR)*, 10 January 2008, p. 4.

[42] Brigade Judge Advocate, 4th Brigade Combat Team, 101st Airborne Division (Air Assault), *After Action Report*, Operation Enduring Freedom, March 2008 – March 2009, 12 May 2009.

[43] *Brigade Combat Team After Action Review*, Operation Iraqi Freedom 1, 2007. The unit and author of this AAR are not identified. For analysis of the challenges of inter-service military justice, see Lieutenant Colonel Marc L. Warren, "Operational Law – A Concept Matures", in *Military Law Review*, 1996, vol. 152, p. 66; Mark W. Holzer, "Purple Haze: Military Justice in Support of Joint Operations", in *The Army Lawyer*, July 2002, p. 1.

[44] OSJA, 2009, p. 38, see *supra* note 25.

[45] Office of the Staff Judge Advocate, Combined Security Transition Command – Afghanistan, *After Action Report*, Operation Enduring Freedom, September 2008, p. 23.

[46] CLAMO, *Lessons Learned, Volume II*, 2005, p. 200, see *supra* note 12.

13.2.2. Difficulties of Prosecuting Contested Cases

Guilty plea cases, which ease the government's burden to present evidence and witnesses to prove the elements of charged crimes, were sometimes the only cases that could be feasibly tried.[47] No deployment AAR from 2001 to 2009 described success at trying multiple contested cases. Instead, most units limited their court martial to guilty pleas. One division explained: "Because the 10th Mountain Division held only fourteen guilty pleas and no contested courts-martial, they never actually had to bring in a civilian witness from outside Iraq".[48] Another Army division in northern Iraq from 2005 to 2007 reported that it tried 22 cases, all on their main base, Contingency Operating Base Speicher.[49] Of those 22 cases tried, 20 were guilty pleas, and for each of the other two, the accused waived rights to produce witnesses and to demand a forum of panel members.[50] Another Army division sent its contested and complex cases back to the United States, where the accused "could exercise all of his or her due-process rights with minimal intrusion on the unit or danger to civilian and non-deployed DoD personnel".[51]

The heavy guilty plea practice may be rooted in past unit experiences that hotly contested cases were too difficult to perform in the combat zone. A judge advocate in Afghanistan in 2009 stated: "The expectation that you will be able to try as many contested cases to the same standard you can in garrison is unrealistic".[52] Contested cases triggered many of the difficulties described in this section, and successful defence counsel used those issues to their clients' advantage. For example, on the right to produce witnesses, a unit in Iraq wrote: "While the accused may waive their 6th amendment right of confrontation, they have no incentive to do so in a contested case".[53]

---

[47] But see Colonel Henley Interview, 2010, see *supra* note 35. Colonel Henley has personally presided over contested cases in Iraq as a trial judge.

[48] 10th Mountain Division, 2009, p. 34, see *supra* note 31.

[49] See OSJA, 2007, p. 67, see *supra* note 23.

[50] *Ibid.*

[51] 25th Infantry Division, Office of the Staff Judge Advocate (Military Justice Division), *After Action Report*, Operation Iraqi Freedom, September 2006–October 2007, 2007, pp. 2–3.

[52] OSJA, 2009, p. 35, see *supra* note 25.

[53] OSJA, 2007, p. 79, see *supra* note 23.

Because 'tough' cases are difficult on deployments, they were routinely whisked away from the combat zone. A Marine judge advocate wrote: "For Marine Corps war crimes, these decisions have universally been the same: bring the case home".[54] Another typical comment came from a Special Forces unit, whose commander "referred all serious incidents of misconduct back to the group headquarters at Fort Campbell [a US base in Kentucky]".[55] These comments, together with the frequent recourse to guilty pleas, show that cases were only prosecuted in the combat zone if an accused waived procedural rights and plead guilty in exchange for favourable treatment or a limited sentence. Hotly contested cases involving accused who vigorously asserted their rights were most often seen as too troublesome to try in the combat zone. Thus, the presence of courts martial in the combat zone was more a factor of an offender's co-operation with the prosecution than an offence's impact on the mission.

13.2.3. Combat Zone Discounting

Perhaps no other topic is as widely discussed among military justice practitioners yet never officially acknowledged as the 'combat zone discount' for deployment misconduct. The term refers to the light or nonexistent punishment deployed offenders receive for crimes that would otherwise be more heavily punished if tried in courts martial in the United States. An Army Trial Defense Services ('TDS') attorney in Afghanistan summarised combat zone discounting for criminal misconduct as follows:

> When strategizing cases, the TDS office always considered the environment. Contesting a case in theater is much more difficult on the unit than in a garrison environment and places significant limitations on the government. TDS JAs (judge advocates) should therefore strongly consider contesting cases. However, the TDS office was able, in many cases where they sought a pre-trial agreement, to get much more favorable pre-trial agreements for their clients.[56]

---

[54] Hackel, 2009, p. 248, see *supra* note 4.

[55] 1st Battalion, 5th Special Forces Group (Airborne), *Battalion Judge Advocate After Action Report*, 11 March 2010, p. 1.

[56] Trial Defense Services, Combined Joint Task Force 101, Individual Augmentee Attorney, *OEF After Action Report*, July 2008 – July 2009, 5 November 2009, p. 3.

Judge advocates frequently cited 'combat zone discounting' in their after-action reports. Admittedly, some discounting may be due to commanders showing leniency to accused who have performed well in the dangers of combat, but the comments focus on the discounting of cases the command would otherwise have taken to court martial but for court-martial difficulties. As one judge advocate explained: "Commanders did not like the logistical load brought on by trials (or the loss of Soldiers available for the fight), therefore they did not forward many cases for court-martial".[57]

The military's broad aversion to combat zone courts martial resulted in highly favourable treatment for many criminal accused who would otherwise have not received such favourable treatment. A judge advocate from a division in Afghanistan noted the need to offer unusually favourable terms in pre-trial negotiations with the defence in order to avoid the burdens of full trials: "You have to triage criminal law processing, and adjust pre-trial agreement terms to encourage more deals".[58] A military prosecutor from a brigade in Iraq described the process of 'valuation' that he encouraged his commanders to use when weighing the burdens of courts martial as follows:

> The trial counsel had to ensure commanders understood the additional cost in terms of effort and personnel to conduct judicial proceedings in country. This allowed commanders to make a reasonable calculation as to what a case was "worth".[59]

Discounting was often explicit: "[the unit's attorneys] approached defense counsel in many cases and explicitly stated that they were willing to dispose of cases more generously (to the accused) than they otherwise might".[60]

Discounting misconduct was not just an Army phenomenon; similarly situated Marine commanders also tended to shun deployed courts martial due to their difficulty. One after-action review noted: "As a result of [...] prioritization, a decline in MJ [military justice] requirements

[57] 3rd Armored Cavalry Regiment, *Operation Iraqi Freedom After Action Review*, November 2007 – January 2009, 22 April 2009, p. 11.

[58] OSJA, 2009, p. 35, see *supra* note 25.

[59] 1st Brigade, 4th Infantry Division, *After Action Report (OIF)*, March 2008–March 2009, 28 April 2009, p. 13.

[60] CLAMO, *Lessons Learned, Volume I*, 2004, p. 247, see *supra* note 12.

occurred. Alternative dispositions when available and appropriate were used".[61] Another military lawyer wrote: "As a result [of the unique deployed burdens of conducting courts martial], there were few options for case dispositions. [...] Battalion commanders should be advised prior to employment of the limitations of military justice support".[62]

A judge advocate from another brigade-sized unit away from the larger division base in northern Iraq summed up the problem well: "Trial logistics are a nightmare. [...] The risk of a trial being 'too hard' is that there will be a 'deployment discount' on disposition of charges that will badly skew the application of the UCMJ".[63]

13.2.4. The Burger King Theory of the Combat Zone Court Martial

If a deployed soldier can eat at Burger King,[64] he is also more likely to face court martial for any serious misconduct he may commit. If he is deployed somewhere without a Burger King, it is less likely that his misconduct will be addressed by court martial. This notion, which suggests that combat zone courts martial are rare except on stable, large, garrison-style bases, can be called the Burger King theory.[65]

Undergirding the Burger King theory are reports from brigade or smaller-sized units that served in remote areas, away from the large 'Burger King bases' such as Victory Base Complex in Baghdad or Bagram Air Base north of Kabul. Few such units conducted *any* courts martial. A brigade in Al Anbar province in Iraq in 2009 wrote:

---

[61] 2nd Marine Expeditionary Force, Executive Summary, Subject: OSJA, *II MEF After Action Report During OIF 06–08*, 8 July 2008, p. 10.

[62] 1st Battalion, 9th Marines, Battalion Judge Advocate, *After Action Report*, Operation Iraqi Freedom, March 2008–October 2008, 9 January 2009, p. 11.

[63] 1st Combat Support Brigade (Maneuver Enhancement), 2009, p. 15, see *supra* note 35.

[64] Burger King is a fast food chain with 7,300 independently owned franchises in the United States, including all 50 states and most large active military installations. Burger King also opened franchises for the American military in a handful of large bases in deployment locations such as Kuwait City, Kuwait; Baghdad, Iraq; Balad, Iraq; Bagram Air Base, Afghanistan; and Kandahar, Afghanistan. The Burger King slogan is 'Have It Your Way'.

[65] This rule seems opposite of the Burger King slogan, as it holds that only those who do not have access to Burger King can 'have it their way' and avoid official sanction for crime. For another theory of linkage between the presence of fast food and international affairs, see "The Golden Arches Theory of Conflict Prevention" (asserting that no two countries with McDonald's fast food franchises have gone to war with each other), in Thomas L. Friedman, *The Lexus and the Olive Tree*, Picador, New York, 1999, pp. 248–75.

RCT-8 did not conduct courts-martial while deployed. RCT-8 handled all military justice matters through NJP (non-judicial punishment), or sent the accused back to the rear. This saved RCT-8 a substantial amount of time and resources that it otherwise would have spent conducting courts-martial.[66]

A unit in southern Afghanistan in 2009 wrote:

> There is already enough strain personnel-wise on small FOBs [forward operating bases] just to meet the bare essentials for things like tower guard, entry control point teams, and basic staff functions. Pulling people for a court-martial just isn't possible sometimes. Units on larger FOBs have the people to cover down if necessary.[67]

For many small units, going to larger bases to conducts courts martial was simply too burdensome, as one judge advocate described:

> Brigade Commanders in Tallil were unable to hold SPCM/GCM [special court martial/general court martial] on Camp Adder/Ali Air Base because they were required to hold them either in Balad or Baghdad. Even a judge-alone SPCM/GCM guilty plea typically required a JA traveling to Balad/Baghdad from Tallil to be away from his/her Command for 5–7 days. In Brigades with only one JA and one 27D [Army paralegal], a SPCM/GCM in Balad/Baghdad deprived the Command of its Command Judge Advocate for the trial's duration and travel time. This deprivation often factored significantly in Commanders' misconduct disposition analysis and likely resulted in dispositions that arguably were too lenient for the misconduct (e.g., convening Summary Courts-Martial on Camp Adder for hash and valium distributors/users).[68]

For smaller units located away from the large bases, attending to the many demands of courts martial sometimes even came at the cost of shutting down the regular mission. One unit wrote:

> Witness production in Iraq is resource intensive. Even moving Soldiers in theater for a court-martial will tax line units when the Soldiers live and work off Victory Base

---

[66] Deputy Regimental Judge Advocate, Regimental Combat Team 8 (RCT-8), *OIF After Action Report*, 18 December 2009, p. 11.

[67] Marcum, 2010, see *supra* note 22.

[68] OSJA, 2007, p. 12, see *supra* note 29.

> Complex. Every witness movement requires either a seat on helicopter or convoy. A contested rape case shut down a line company for almost a week as they moved witnesses and managed the other logistics associated with trial.[69]

Even if an accused from a 'small base' were tried on a 'Burger King base', he might have grounds to challenge the legitimacy and fairness of the 'Burger King base' panel. Many large units took shortcuts with panel selection, giving "preference [...] to members located on or near a main base" in order to ease the logistical difficulties of bringing panels together for trials.[70] However, the panel member selection criteria in Article 25 of the UCMJ do not include convenience or location of the members. A defence counsel should be able to show the use of impermissible selection criteria and prejudice in having a 'Burger King base' panel decide the case of a 'small base' accused, and counsel may petition to include members from similar small bases on the panel. In this way, efforts to conduct courts martial of offences occurring on 'small bases' are further complicated.[71]

The Burger King theory helps make sense of Iraq court-martial numbers. The peak of 144 courts martial in 2005 coincides precisely with the temporary concentration of US forces onto large 'Super FOBs' that year.[72] When the Iraq Surge dispersed soldiers to smaller outposts that were closer to the Iraqi security forces and the Iraqi population, fewer courts martial were conducted (just 63 in 2008 despite the presence of an additional 30,000 soldiers).[73] In other words, large units that could

---

[69] 1st Cavalry Division, Office of the Staff Judge Advocate, *After Action Review*, Operation Iraqi Freedom, 20 November 2007, p. 12, quoted in CLAMO, *Forged in the Fire*, 2008, p. 313, see *supra* notes 3, 12.

[70] CLAMO, *Forged in the Fire*, 2008, p. 310, see *supra* notes 3, 12.

[71] This problem was observed in Afghanistan and recorded in Hanson, 2009, pp. 43–44, see *supra* note 4.

[72] Thomas E. Ricks, *The Gamble: General Petraeus and the American Military Adventure in Iraq*, Penguin Press, New York, 2009, p. 15, ("He [General George Casey, then the Commanding General of Multi-National Force-Iraq] was pulling his troops farther away from the population, closing dozens of bases in 2005 as he *consolidated his force on big, isolated bases* that the military termed 'Super FOBs'") (emphasis added).

[73] Christopher M. Schnaubelt, "Lessons of Iraq: Afghanistan at the Brink", in *International Herald Tribune*, 1 November 2008, p. 8:

> While the increase in troop strength helped enable this shift [towards protecting the population], the new strategy also played a key role by moving coalition forces that were there before the surge off large bases and in-

---

successfully prosecute guilty plea cases when all parties were within the walls of a large, city-like base had a more difficult time when those parties were scattered among several remote locations.

The Burger King theory also helps explain Afghanistan courts-martial numbers. The meagre total of 11 courts martial conducted there in 2009, despite a near doubling of the Army force, is best explained by the effort to spread out the forces to about 200 small bases and outposts.[74] Interestingly, the trend towards more spread-out forces in Afghanistan (and lower court-martial numbers) coincides with an effort to close all Burger Kings in country.[75] Thus, Burger Kings and courts martial were both relative luxuries reserved for the largest bases in Afghanistan. When the mission became more expeditionary and spread to a larger number of austere bases, both Burger Kings and courts martial dwindled in numbers.

Large bases can be reminiscent of civilian life – the atmosphere of a town or small city, civic functions, recreation opportunities, fully functioning utilities, fast-food restaurants, and courts martial whose parties and procedures resemble civilian trials in the United States. Not surprisingly, courts martial that look like civilian trials seem only able to exist in such civilianised surroundings.

13.3. Procedural Shortcomings of Combat Zone Courts Martial

> Complicating procedures which add only marginal increases in assurance of accuracy and truth-telling have no place in the combat, operational, or wartime system.[76]

---

creasing their presence among the Iraqi population through more patrols and joint security stations with Iraqi soldiers and police.

[74] See Hanson, 2009, pp. 36–37, see *supra* note 4. By 2009 the Army in Afghanistan had spread across 200 bases and outposts, and judge advocates were only present on nine of those. The Trial Defense Services office and the military courtroom are both on Bagram Air Base.

[75] Karen Jowers, "Whopper of a Decision: McChrystal Shuts Fast-Food Sellers in Afghanistan", in *Army Times*, 22 February 2010, p. 8 (describing an order by General Stanley McChrystal to limit morale and welfare programs to those tailored for an expeditionary force, a move that involved shuttering Burger King restaurants in Bagram and Kandahar). "Supplying nonessential luxuries to big bases like Bagram and Kandahar makes it harder to get essential items to combat outposts and forward operating bases" (quoting the top enlisted soldier in Afghanistan, Command Sergeant Major Michael Hall).

[76] Westmoreland and Prugh, 1980, p. 52, see *supra* note 10.

Some court-martial procedures that were developed in peacetime have dire and unintended consequences in combat. Because no 'combat zone exception' exists within American court-martial procedures,[77] the same rules apply both in and out of a combat theatre. This section analyses 'good military character' evidence and expert witness rules, two procedures with at least two characteristics in common. First, each is unique in application to the military. Second, both are broad enough that they can mandate witness travel to the combat zone for nearly any trial, thus hindering efforts to try cases.

13.3.1. The 'Good Military Character' Defence

In a civilian criminal trial, the defence may not assert that because the defendant is a good employee at work, he is therefore unlikely to have committed a crime. Evidence is only admissible in trial if it is relevant.[78] In comparison, courts martial allow a broader range of what is considered 'relevant' by allowing evidence of an accused's 'good military character' to be introduced at trial on the merits. Military appellate courts have strengthened this affirmative defence[79] to the point where an accused can

---

[77] US Army, *Operational Law Handbook*, 2009, p. 401. ("Although legal considerations may differ depending of the mission, court-martial and NJP [non-judicial punishment] procedures remain largely unchanged in a deployed setting".) Since the Afghanistan and Iraq conflicts began, one procedural change that improved the ability to conduct combat zone courts martial was the President's amendment of the *Manual for Courts-Martial* in 2007 to permit a military judge to allow any witness to testify on interlocutory questions by remote means if practical difficulties of producing the witness outweighed the need for personal appearance. See Executive Order Number 13430, 72 Federal Register 20, 213, 18 April 2007; Rule for Court-Martial 703(b)(1). On the other hand, the Army's adoption of formal rules of practice in 2004 was noted as increasing the formality and complexity of courts martial. "The Rules of Practice Before Army Courts-Martial, which were revised in May 2004, have placed an increased emphasis on formality, especially where motions practice is concerned. This change is likely to foster an increase in the complexity of future courts-martial", *Annual Report of the Code Committee on Military Justice*, 2004, p. 6 (quoting the sub-report of the Army Trial Defense Service within the Report of The Judge Advocate General of the Army).

[78] Federal Rule of Evidence 402; and Military Rule of Evidence 402.

[79] Federal Rule of Evidence 404(a)(1); and Military Rule of Evidence 404(a)(1). Although the military rule is worded exactly the same as the federal rule, military courts have broadly defined "pertinent character trait" as including good military character. The drafters of the Military Rules of Evidence in 1980 recognised a limited right to an accused offering good military character evidence. "It is the intention of the Committee, however, to allow the defense to introduce evidence of good military character when that specific trait is pertinent. Evidence of good military character would be admissible, for example, in a prose-

---

now "smother the factfinder with good soldier evidence regardless of the charges".[80]

Given this expansiveness, imagination is the only limit of what demonstrates 'good military character'; any desirable trait in a service member counts. In application, character witnesses are commonly called to testify about their willingness to deploy with an accused.[81] Other allowable 'good military character' testimony includes that an accused is "dedicated to being a good drill instructor",[82] lawful,[83] easygoing,[84] dependable,[85] and well-liked.[86] With so many traits to choose from that

---

cution for disobedience of orders", MCM, 2008, A22–33, see *supra* note 8. The extent of this rule was tested in a series of military appellate cases in the 1980s, until the Court of Military Appeals broadened the applicability of the defence to nearly any military offence. In deciding that an airman charged with stealing a television could present character evidence portraying him as an honest and trustworthy person, the court wrote,

> We do not believe that it is inconsistent with the policy of Mil. R. Evid. 404(a) to apply this definition in deciding what character traits of an accused are 'pertinent.' Thus, for purposes of Mil. R. Evid. 404(a)(1), a character trait is 'pertinent' "when it is directed to the issue or matters in dispute, and legitimately tends to prove the allegations of the party offering it".

Court of Military Appeals, *United States v. Elliott*, Judgment, 1986, vol. 23, p. 5. In sum, the court discarded the limiting guidance of the drafter's analysis and opened the door for the admissibility of "good military character" evidence in any case.

[80] Major Lawrence J. Morris, "Keystones of the Military Justice System: A Primer for Chiefs of Justice", in *The Army Lawyer*, October 1994, p. 22 (summarising recent military appellate opinions which expanded the 'good soldier' defence and allow it to be presented in any court martial). Major Morris also noted that in most cases, disingenuous use of good military character evidence can be easily rebutted by the prosecution. *Ibid.*; see also Robinson O. Everett, "Military Rules of Evidence Symposium: An Introduction", in *Military Law Review*, 1990, vol. 130, p. 3 (noting that the military appellate courts have "obliterated" the limitation of allowing only pertinent character traits by permitting the defence of good military character "in almost any conceivable trial by court-martial"). For a defence of the expanded 'good military character' defence, see Paul A. Capofari, "Military Rule of Evidence 404 and Good Military Character", in *Military Law Review*, 1990, vol. 130, p. 171, which argues that 'good soldier evidence' in some form has a long tradition in military trials.

[81] See, for example, Court of Appeals for the Armed Forces, *United States v. True*, Judgment, 1995, vol. 41, p. 427.

[82] Court of Military Appeals, *United States v. Piatt*, Judgment, 1984, vol. 17, p. 445.

[83] Court of Military Appeals, *United States v. Clemons*, Judgment, 1983, vol. 16, p. 44.

[84] Court of Appeals for the Armed Forces, *United States v. True*, Judgment, 1995, vol. 41, p. 427.

[85] Court of Military Appeals, *United States v. White*, Judgment, 1993, vol. 36, p. 307.

[86] Court of Military Appeals, *United States v. Hallum*, Judgment, 1990, vol. 31, p. 255.

are permissible and admissible, nearly anyone can qualify as a 'good soldier'.

Some troubling peacetime consequences of allowing unfettered 'good military character' evidence have already been studied, but the consequences for the combat cone also deserve consideration.[87] Military operations in Iraq and Afghanistan demonstrate the wide-reaching potential of the defence as an immunity mechanism for any accused. The peacetime trial consideration of 'Will this evidence be persuasive?' shifts in the combat zone to 'Will this evidence force the prosecution to produce witnesses, thus requiring them to drop charges or grant leniency?'

Here is how 'good military character' can change the equation. If an accused requests production of a witness at a combat zone court martial and the government does not approve the request, the military judge must decide the issue based on the materiality of the witness;[88] the judge's improper denial of a relevant merits witness risks appellate reversal. Because of the limits of military subpoenas,[89] the trial counsel may be powerless to force a witness to leave the United States, especially if the witness is a civilian or is no longer on active duty in the military. Military judges also lack the power to force witnesses to co-operate or to appear.[90]

---

[87] Elizabeth Lutes Hillman, "The 'Good Soldier' Defense: Character Evidence and Military Rank at Courts-Martial", in *Yale Law Journal*, 1999, vol. 108, no. 4, pp. 908–9. Hillman argued that the 'good military character' defence serves as an immunity shield to protect high-ranking service members from criminal convictions by masking subtle privileges of gender and race in a military society with few high-ranking women or ethnic minorities.

[88] A service member at court martial is entitled to the live production of necessary witnesses to support a defence and the right to live confrontation of witnesses offered by the government in proof of a crime. See US Constitution Amendment VI (granting a criminal accused the right to "be confronted with the witnesses against him" and "to have compulsory process for obtaining witnesses in his favor"); UCMJ Article 46, 2008 (granting the defence "equal opportunity to obtain witnesses"); MCM, 2008, RCM 703(b)(1) (implementing Article 46 of the UCMJ), see *supra* note 8; and Court of Military Appeals, *United States v. Burnette*, Judgment, 1990, 29 MJ 473, p. 475.

[89] A summary court martial or the trial counsel of a special or general court martial can issue subpoenas for the production of witnesses. MCM, 2008, RCM 703(e)(2)(C), see *supra* note 8. Subpoenas cannot compel civilians to travel outside the United States. Witnesses who are on active duty can be ordered to travel in lieu of subpoena. MCM, 2008, RCM 703(e)(1), see *supra* note 8.

[90] MCM, 2008, RCM 703(e)(2)(G), see *supra* note 8; Court of Appeals for the Armed Forces, *United States v. Quintanilla*, Judgment, 2001, vol. 56, p. 37 (noting that the military judge's powers to hold persons in contempt and to issue warrants of attachment are limited to circumstances when a subpoena was properly issued). Because a subpoena "may not be

---

Ultimately, if the government fails to provide a necessary defence merits witness,[91] the military judge may have no other choice but to abate the proceedings. The Government could propose stipulating to the witness's expected testimony in lieu of live testimony, but the defense will usually have little incentive to agree, especially if the difficulty of producing the witness could delay or entirely thwart the court martial.[92]

---

used to compel a civilian to travel outside the United States and its territories", the military judge at a combat zone court martial has no real ability to compel or sanction civilian witnesses in the United States, see MCM, 2008, RCM 703(e)(2)(A) discussion, see *supra* note 8.

[91] Prior to the judicial expansion of the 'good military character' defence, production of defence character witnesses was more limited. See Court of Military Appeals, *United States v. Belz*, Judgment, 1985, vol. 20, p. 33 (tempering the admissibility of military character evidence against the strength of the government's case, the weakness of the defence's case, the materiality of the evidence and the existence of suitable substitute evidence in the record of trial); and Court of Military Appeals, *United States v. Vandelinder*, Judgment, 1985, vol. 20, p. 45 (emphasising that affidavits could substitute for live 'good military character' testimony):

> According to the Drafters Analysis [to MRE 405(c)], this rule is required due to the world wide disposition of the armed forces which makes it difficult if not impossible to obtain witnesses – particularly when the sole testimony of a witness is to be a brief statement relating to the character of the accused. This is particularly important for offenses committed abroad or in a combat zone, in which case the only witnesses likely to be necessary from the United States are those likely to be character witnesses.

Military Rule of Evidence 405(c), however, has not yet been considered in light of newer confrontation requirements. See United States Supreme Court, *Crawford v. Washington*, Judgment, 2004, vol. 541, p. 36, and its progeny in military appellate courts. Even before *Crawford*, military courts treaded lightly when considering whether to restrict live production of defence character witnesses. The affidavit emphasis in *Vandelinder* has not since been applied in military appellate opinions, and common trial practice has emphasised the right to use affidavits *in addition to* rights to live witness testimony. See, for example, Air Force Court of Criminal Appeals, *United States v. McCommon*, Judgment, 3 September 2009, Series WL 2997036; and Air Force Court of Criminal Appeals, *United States v. Voda*, Judgment, 26 January 2004, Series WL 190265. A return to the 'binding affidavit' holding in *Vandelinder* would sensibly permit the defence to raise 'good military character' without crippling the government by requiring production of out-of-country character witnesses during deployments.

[92] A Marine judge advocate accurately noted the importance of this motivation during deployments. "In the end, defense will likely continue to require the government to produce necessary and relevant witnesses in person because it can be a successful tactic of taking away the focus of the trial counsel from preparing his presentation of the case", Major Nicole K. Hudspeth, "Remote Testimony and Executive Order 13430: A Missed Opportunity", in *Naval Law Review*, 2009, vol. 57, p. 303.

The 'good military character' defence represents a powerful tool that can be used by an accused to pressure the command to back down from a combat zone court martial. Given the prospect of the 'good military character' defence and its associated witness production problems, commanders may be reluctant to consider the court martial option when they must address criminal allegations while on deployments.

13.3.2. Expert Witnesses

Expert witness requests also have the potential to derail deployed courts martial. In general, an accused at court martial may be entitled to government-funded expert assistance. [93] When seeking an expert, the accused must submit a request to the convening authority with a complete statement of the reasons why employment of the expert is necessary, along with the estimated cost of the expert's employment. The convening authority must then decide whether to approve the request, deny the request outright, or deny the request but provide a substitute expert. If the convening authority denies the request, the military judge must decide whether the expert is relevant and necessary, and whether the government has provided an adequate substitute. As with other witnesses, the trial counsel arranges for personal production of the expert.

For the government to provide an accused with an expert witness in the combat zone, the first challenge is to find one. Local civilians in Afghanistan or Iraq may not have the desired American professional credentials or English-language ability. While the military may have some experts among its ranks in the combat zone to provide an "adequate substitute", problems remain. First, a provision restricting executive branch employees from serving as expert witnesses in cases against the

---

[93] UCMJ Article 46, see *supra* note 8; MCM, 2008, RCM 703(d), see *supra* note 8; United States Supreme Court, *United States v. Gonzalez*, Judgment, 1994, vol. 39, p. 459 (laying out the three-part *Gonzalez* test, whereby the defence must establish why the expert assistance is needed, what the expert assistance would do for the accused, and why the defence is otherwise unable to provide the evidence that the expert will provide); Lieutenant Colonel Stephen R. Henley, "Developments in Evidence III – The Final Chapter", in *The Army Lawyer*, May 1998, p. 1 (offering defence counsel additional considerations for applying the *Gonzalez* test); and Court of Appeals for the Armed Forces, *United States v. Lee*, Judgment, 2006, vol. 64, p. 213 (requiring that the accused show a reasonable probability exists that the expert would assist the defence and that denial of expert assistance would result in a fundamentally unfair trial). Indigence is not a factor for courts martial for determining an accused's eligibility for government-funded expert assistance.

United States may discourage military experts from undertaking this additional role.[94] Second, an accused may argue that the expert assistance he seeks requires independence from the military and an ability to openly criticise military practices; in that case, a military expert may appear too conflicted or restrained to be an adequate substitute.

Without access to nearby experts, the government may need to hire an expert in the United States, which presents problems for completing courts martial expeditiously. Much time, effort and expense may be needed to produce the expert; a typical description of this process came from a judge advocate who wrote that "arranging for expert witnesses to participate in courts-martial held in theater was a difficult and time-consuming process".[95] Additionally, if the expert is a civilian, the court martial must operate at the mercy of the expert's availability, since the court lacks subpoena power over experts to enforce orders and trial appearances.

Of course, these logistical concerns matter only if the expert request has merit; frivolous expert requests can be denied. For example, an accused charged with desertion will usually fare poorly in seeking a DNA expert. However, a caveat in military appellate opinions and court-martial rules seems to require a broad finding of "necessary and relevant" for at least one type of expert: those called to support a theory of partial mental responsibility.[96] In cases with specific intent elements, this theory permits the defence to present evidence that the accused did not or could not possess the mental intent to commit a crime.

---

[94] Code of Federal Regulations, 2010, section 2635.805 states: "An employee shall not serve, other than on behalf of the United States, as an expert witness, with or without compensation, in any proceeding before a court or agency of the United States in which the United States is a party or has a direct and substantial interest [...]". In the Army, the Chief of Litigation Division can authorise the expert appearance of a government employee in a case against the United States. *Ibid.* at section 2635.805(c).

[95] OSJA, 2009, p. 41, see *supra* note 25.

[96] Partial mental responsibility should not be confused with the affirmative defence of lack of mental responsibility, also known as insanity, which requires a severe mental disease or defect, a burden on the defense to prove the affirmative defense by clear and convincing evidence, and a possibility of findings of not guilty only by reason of lack of mental responsibility. See UCMJ Article 50a; MCM, 2008, RCM 916(k)(1), see *supra* note 8. Other than the defence of lack of mental responsibility, a mental disease or defect cannot be used as an affirmative defense but can be used to negate an element of specific intent such as knowledge, premeditation or intent. For an overview of the development of the theory of partial mental responsibility in the military, see Army Court of Criminal Appeals, *United States v. Axelson*, Judgment, 2007, vol. 65, pp. 513–517.

In a case decided by the highest American military appellate court, an accused who was charged with the unpremeditated murder of his 11-year-old son sought expert opinion evidence to rebut the element that he possessed the intent to kill or inflict great bodily harm at the time of the offence.[97] The defence wished to present expert testimony to show that because the accused had experienced "sleep deprivation" and "pressure", he was psychologically impaired when he committed the crime. The court agreed, and in so doing altered the landscape for expert witness production by holding that partial mental responsibility is a substantive defence that can negate the intent elements of specific intent crimes.

With such generalised hardships as "sleep deprivation" or "pressure" permitted, nearly anyone charged with a specific intent crime in the combat zone would have an invitation to seek an expert. If defence counsel can articulate how lack of sleep, pressure or some other hardship resulted in a temporary psychological impairment, the accused could qualify for expert assistance with solid backing from military case law.

As a result, in a combat zone, the procedure of requesting expert assistance could become a defence negotiating tactic designed to win dismissal of charges or the granting of favourable treatment. As one unit noticed: "Whether it was the need for expert witnesses, the command's reluctance to hold courts-martial while deployed, or the requests for transportation assets, etc., the attorneys at TDS fought to get their clients the best possible deal".[98] Ultimately, these difficulties are likely to weigh heavily in the analysis by military leaders of whether to prosecute cases on site.

---

[97] Court of Military Appeals, *Ellis v. Jacob*, Judgment, 1988, vol. 26, p. 90; Lieutenant Colonel Donna M. Wright, "'Though This Be Madness, Yet There is Method in It': A Practitioner's Guide to Mental Responsibility and Competency to Stand Trial", in *The Army Lawyer*, September 1997, pp. 18, 25–27 (concluding that partial mental responsibility can allow the defence to present evidence of the accused's mental condition for specific intent offences without having to prove lack of mental responsibility); see also Major Jeremy Ball, "Solving the Mystery of Insanity Law: Zealous Representation of Mentally Ill Servicemembers", in *The Army Lawyer*, December 2005, pp. 19–23 (cautioning that the Army court instructions for partial mental responsibility have not changed to reflect the new case law in *Ellis* and changes to RCM 916(k)).

[98] 3rd Brigade Combat Team, 82d Airborne Division, *Brigade Judge Advocate After Action Report*, Iraq, 4 February 2010, p. 25.

13.4. Operational Impacts from the Absence of Military Justice in Combat

The previous two sections described how combat zone courts martial are fraught with difficulty and are thus largely avoided in practice. The looming question now is, so what? After all, the US military continues to enjoy broad public confidence, evidenced by its repeated top standing in a poll of American public institutions, so there is little public agitation for reform to more effectively punish military crime. It may seem harsh, un-patriotic and unnecessary to emphasise shortcomings in judicial sanction against those who not only serve in the military, but who also serve in combat. This section answers the 'so what' question by exploring the strategic perils that arise from court-martial frailty on deployments.

13.4.1. Perceptions of Impunity

An insurgent leader once wrote an anger-laced list of complaints about a powerful foreign country that was occupying his country. Upset with the criminal behaviour of the occupiers, he was especially incensed by their practice of whisking soldiers accused of heinous crimes back to their home country. For all he could tell, they were then exonerated in what he described as "mock trials".

That man was Thomas Jefferson, and the grievances are memorialised in the American Declaration of Inde-pendence.[99] The circumstances surrounding America's founding may be different, but the strategic consequences of fomented resentment towards perceived "double standards" of powerful foreign forces are highly rele-vant to current operations. In recent conflicts, the United States military regularly sent cases of serious misconduct away from the combat zone rather than court-martialling on-site.[100] When this happened, affected Afghans and

---

[99] United States Declaration of Independence, 4 July 1776, para. 17 ("For protecting them [British soldiers] by mock Trial, from punishment for any Murders which they should commit on the Inhabitants of these States"). Mr. Jefferson's role in drafting this document is described at http://www.ushistory.org/Declaration/document/index.htm, last accessed on 25 March 2015.

[100] An interesting area for further study, but beyond the scope of this chapter, is an assessment of how outcomes differ for misconduct committed against foreign civilians that are tried in the United States compared to on deployment. A prominent scholar who studied the issue in 17 instances – such as the United States after My Lai in Vietnam, Argentina's 'Dirty War', and Belgian, Canadian and Italian peacekeepers in Somalia – notes a consistent re-luctance by States to fully pursue justice against their own soldiers in domestic trials. See

---

Iraqis had little chance to ever hear about the cases again. Without information, they became likely to believe in a widespread practice of criminal exoneration.

13.4.1.1. Perceptions of Impunity in Afghanistan

In Afghanistan, the common practice of sending service member misconduct back to the United States has had strategic impact. A prominent UN expert, Philip Alston, undertook a study of American responses to military misconduct in Afghanistan, and wrote that the inability of the Afghan people to learn the results of service member misconduct impaired the United States' standing in Afghanistan. "During my visit to Afghanistan, I saw first hand how the opacity of the [American] military justice system reduces confidence in the Government's commitment to public accountability for illegal conduct".[101] He elaborated: "There have been chronic and deplorable accountability failures with respect to policies, practices and conduct that resulted in alleged unlawful killings, including possible war crimes, in the international operations conducted by the United States".[102]

In speaking of both "opacity" and "accountability failures", Alston suggested a weak sense of reckoning for military crime in Afghanistan – that interested observers could not attend courts martial, read about disciplinary results in a local newspaper or talk to a commander about the status of an investigation or case. When a Western-educated, English-

---

Timothy L.H. McCormack, "Their Atrocities and Our Misdemeanours: The Reticence of States to Try Their 'Own Nationals' for International Crimes", in Mark Lattimer and Philippe Sands (eds.), *Justice for Crimes Against Humanity*, Hart Publishing, Portland, OR, 2003, p. 107, in which he writes: "Despite the rhetoric of a commitment to the principle of trying war crimes, the practice of states confirms glaring inconsistencies between those acts which are tried and those which are not – inconsistencies most readily explicable on the basis of an 'us' and 'them' mentality". McCormack adds that the "domestic trial of members of a state's own military forces for war crimes is the most politically sensitive of any domestic prosecution for international crimes". *Ibid.*, p. 134. Could it be that on-site courts martial are less susceptible to these pressures, since they are more likely to be convened for strategic military reasons, are away from domestic pressures and have local victims nearby?

[101] UN Human Rights Council, Philip Alston, "Report of the Special Rapporteur on Extrajudicial, Summary or Arbitrary Executions", Addendum: Mission to the United States of America, 28 May 2009, p. 24 ('Alston Report').

[102] *Ibid.*, p. 3.

---

speaking UN expert with a research staff cannot find out results of misconduct from cases that have been sent back to the United States, the opportunities for ordinary Afghans to learn results of military misconduct are surely slimmer. In an Afghan society with ingrained beliefs about injustice at the hands of Western powers, perceived 'double standards' for service member crime likely fuel ambivalence or resentment about the American military mission.

13.4.1.2. Perceptions of Impunity in Iraq

Based on its negotiating priorities, it appears that the Iraqi government was influenced to take action in response to perceptions that American military offenders went unpunished. During 2008 negotiations regarding the ultimate withdrawal of the American military, Iraqi jurisdiction over American service member misconduct was a top Iraqi objective.[103] Iraq even sent its top foreign minister to Japan to study terms for civilian prosecution of military crime contained in Japan's Status of Forces Agreement with the US military. In the final agreement, the United States agreed to cede limited criminal jurisdiction over American service member misconduct in Iraq.[104] At Iraq's insistence, this agreement also committed the United States to seek to hold military trials of service members in Iraq rather than sending them away; when that was not possible, the United States agreed to assist Iraqi victims to attend trial in the United States.[105] To the extent that the actions of the Iraqi government reflected the will of its people, this agreement indicated Iraqi

---

[103] "Iraq Studied SOFA When Setting Trial Criteria for U.S. Servicemen", in *Kyodo World Service*, Japan, 27 March 2009.

[104] Steven Lee Myers, "A Loosely Drawn American Victory", in *New York Times*, 28 November 2008, p. A5 (describing the US-Iraq strategic framework agreement and the American concession to cede criminal jurisdiction to the Iraqis for off-duty, off-base misconduct committed by American service members).

[105] Agreement Between the United States of America and the Republic of Iraq on the Withdrawal of United States Forces from Iraq and the Organization of Their Activities During Their Temporary Presence in Iraq, 17 November 2008, available at http://www.state.gov/documents/organization/122074.pdf, last accessed on 25 March 2015:

> As mutually agreed by the Parties, United States Forces authorities shall seek to hold the trials of such cases [involving American forces] inside Iraq. If the trial of such cases is to be conducted in the United States, efforts will be undertaken to facilitate the personal attendance of the victim at the trial.

dissatisfaction with the American military's justice practices against its service members.

The US military was often unable to keep Iraqis informed about the status of cases when those cases were sent back to the United States for adjudication. An officer from a headquarters element in Baghdad who was responsible for updating Iraqi government officials about the status of military cases in the United States wrote:

> There was no central repository cataloging this information, particularly as trials sometimes occurred at home station many months after a unit redeployed. The RoL [Rule of Law] section had difficulty in obtaining updates in some cases, usually resorting to Google searches to try to obtain information.[106]

The final result of the United States' nine-year war in Iraq taught a dramatic lesson about the link between deployable military justice and the operational effectiveness of the armed force. Towards the end of 2011, Iraq refused to grant American military members immunity for crimes committed against Iraqis as a condition for keeping US forces in country. This refusal was motivated by Iraqi public agitation about the perceived leniency and impunity shown by the military justice system to American military members who were accused of committing crimes against Iraqis.[107] This impasse between the United States and Iraq resulted in the withdrawal of all United States forces under military command by the end of 2011. In effect, the United States was forced to withdraw from Iraq not for strategic calculations of national and military self-interest, but rather for complications that arose from the performance of its regime of military justice.

13.4.2. Self-Interest in Accountability for Military Crimes – Experience of Others

The United Nations has come to recognise the importance of trying cases where misconduct occurs. In 2003 and 2004 numerous allegations

---

[106] Individual Augmentee, Multi-National Force Iraq, Office of the Staff Judge Advocate (Rule of Law Section), *After Action Report*, October 2008 – December 2008, 9 February 2009.

[107] Michael J. Schmidt, "Anger in Iraq after Plea Bargain over 2005 Massacre", in *New York Times*, 24 January 2012.

surfaced that UN peacekeepers in the Democratic Republic of the Congo ('DRC'; formerly known as Zaire) were involved in acts of sexual exploitation against local civilians.[108] When the implicated peacekeepers were sent back to their home countries rather than tried by courts martial in the DRC, civilian dissatisfaction was widespread and may have endangered the peacekeeping mission. In response, a comprehensive UN report on peacekeeping operations called for "on-site courts martial" among its top priorities:

> An on-site court martial for serious offences that are criminal in nature would afford immediate access to witnesses and evidence in the mission area. An on-site court martial would demonstrate to the local community that there is no impunity for acts of sexual exploitation and abuse by members of military contingents. [...] Therefore, all troop-contributing countries should hold on-site courts martial. Those countries which remain committed to participating in peacekeeping operations but whose legislation does not permit on-site courts martial should consider reform of the relevant legislation.[109]

Strategic concern about perceptions that the military enjoys criminal impunity abroad has grown with America's largest military ally. The United Kingdom[110] has improved military prosecutions and increased public transparency of military trials in response to lessons learned in Iraq about the strategic setbacks of shipping crime home.[111] British lawmakers[112] and military doctrine writers[113] have each emphasised that

---

[108] UN General Assembly, "A Comprehensive Strategy to Eliminate Future Sexual Exploitation and Abuse in United Nations Peacekeeping Operations", 24 March 2005, UN Doc. A/59/710, sec. 6 (prepared under the supervision of Prince Zeid Ra'ad Zeid Al-Hussein).

[109] *Ibid.*, sec. 35.

[110] The author thanks Lieutenant Colonel Nigel Heppenstall of the British Army for helpful conversations about the British military tradition.

[111] Michael Evans and Frances Gibb, "Accused Troops Will Face More Robust Courts-Martial, Says Prosecution Chief", in *The Times* (London), 2 January 2009 (describing the stance of the new top civilian in charge of British military prosecutions, at the time Mr. Bruce Houlder, in calling for tougher prosecutions after a series of court-martial acquittals that were considered a setback for the British military in Basra, Iraq. In one of those, seven soldiers from the Queen's Lancashire Regiment and Intelligence Corps were tried by court martial in England for their involvement in the death of Iraqi detainee Baha Mousa in 2003 in Basra, resulting in one conviction).

[112] House of Commons Defence Committee, *Iraq: An Initial Assessment of Post-Conflict Operations*, Volume II, Sixth Report of Session 2004–05 (UK), 23 June 2004:

---

transparent prosecutions conducted near where crime occurs help the military gain the confidence of the foreign population. In response to allegations that British soldiers beat and killed an Iraqi detainee named Baha Mousa in Basra, Iraq, the British set up a website in Arabic (the predominant language spoken in Basra), with translations of the proceedings from the public inquiry.[114]

In the United States, however, American military doctrine expresses no preference for trying wartime misconduct where it occurs.[115] This means that court-martial decisions are left to logistical questions of where it is 'easier' to conduct them. The British emphasis on this issue, and America's lack it, could be a consequence of the United Kingdom's collective understanding of the ramifications of military misbehaviour after its decades of experience in Northern Ireland.[116] It may also reflect that the British have paid greater attention to Jefferson's concern about "mock trials".

The experience of other nations and international organisations in addressing the operational consequences of military misconduct has resulted in an increasing consensus about the self-interest in holding military offenders accountable for crimes committed on deployments. A

From the point of view of justice being seen to be done and to winning the confidence of the Iraqi people, I think it would be absolutely wrong to say all our courts martial are going to be held somewhere in the South of England that I do not even know where, being a Scotsman, never mind someone from outside Basra, and I think that is the danger – that we would lose the confidence of the people.

[113] *Army Field Manual, Volume 1, Part 10, Countering Insurgency*, UK, October 2009, paras. 12–14 ("It is essential that the host nation population does not develop a perception that British service personnel are being treated with impunity").

[114] See Baha Mousa Public Inquiry, available at https://www.gov.uk/governmen publications/the-baha-mousa-public-inquiry-report (including a link to an Arabic language version of the website), last accessed on 24 March 2014.

[115] "Given the maturity of the Afghan and Iraqi theaters, commanders now have a choice of whether to conduct courts-martial in theater or at home station", CLAMO, *Forged in the Fire*, 2008, p. 311, see *supra* notes 3, 12.

[116] As a result of their involvement in Northern Ireland from 1969 to 2007, the British have achieved an admirable factual accounting of the interplay of terrorist incidents, civilian deaths, news reporting and soldier misconduct. This could serve as a useful groundwork for other studies about the operational and strategic effects of military misconduct. See David McKittrick, Seamus Kelters, Brian Feeney and Chris Thornton, *Lost Lives: The Stories of the Men, Women and Children Who Died Through the Northern Ireland Troubles*, Mainstream Publishing, Edinburgh, 2004.

---

gathering of international experts convened in California in 2012 considered this subject. Among their conclusions was: "Depending on the gravity of the case, offenses must be met with disciplinary action or criminal prosecution in order to maintain military performance and standing, thus ensuring mission accomplishment".[117]

13.4.3. How Unpunished Crime Thwarts Counterinsurgency Efforts

Counter-insurgency ('COIN') is thought of as a competition of legitimacy; the insurgent or counter-insurgent who sways and holds the support of the population wins. "Both insurgents and counterinsurgents are fighting for the support of the populace".[118] Crimes committed by combatants directly undermine that side's legitimacy. "Any human rights abuses or legal violations committed by US forces quickly become known throughout the local populace and eventually around the world. Illegitimate actions undermine both long- and short-term COIN efforts".[119] When these misdeeds are magnified, COIN success is imperilled. "Isolated misdeeds by junior soldiers or small units can adversely affect a theater of war, and undo months of hard work and honorable sacrifice".[120] As an example, Army COIN doctrine describes the consequences of French military indiscipline against Algerian insurgents from 1954 to 1962: "Illegal and immoral activities made the counterinsurgents extremely vulnerable to enemy propaganda inside Algeria among the Muslim population, as well as in the United Nations and the French media".[121] In short, COIN magnifies misconduct.

Given the strategic nature of misconduct in COIN, having a deployable justice system that allows for punishment and deterrence becomes even more important. A leading military law scholar explains the linkage of deployable justice and the promotion of good behaviour:

---

[117] Morten Bergsmo, Arne Willy Dahl and Richard Sousa, "Military Self-Interest in Accountability for Core International Crimes", in *FICHL Policy Brief Series*, 2013, no. 14, Torkel Opsahl Academic EPublisher, Stanford, p. 4 (https://www.legal-tools.org/doc/396da7/).

[118] US Department of Army, *Field Manual 3-24, Counterinsurgency*, Washington, DC, 15 December 2006, paras. 1–160.

[119] *Ibid.*, paras. 1–132.

[120] John Nagl and Paul Yingling, "New Rules for New Enemies", in *Armed Forces Journal*, October 2006, p. 25.

[121] US Department of Army, 2006, pp. 7–9, see *supra* note 118.

> By having a justice system that can travel with the forces into combat and other operations, a military encourages its forces to respect the rule of law. A military force that respects the rule of law garners respect and trust from the world community. This trust and respect can certainly carry over to world opinion about the legitimacy of the military operations.[122]

When the justice system cannot follow the force, misconduct lacks a formal deterrent. The following paragraphs describe some of the risk factors present in our force that, if left unchecked by a meaningful regime of sanction, may threaten COIN efforts.

Soldiers with criminal tendencies hurt COIN efforts, especially if they can linger without a mechanism for formal sanction. In the past decade, relaxed recruiting standards permitted large numbers of gang members[123] and prior felons[124] into the American military. An Army study showed that those who entered on 'moral waivers' were more likely to engage in misconduct than other recruits.[125] Likewise, a leading military

---

[122] Victor Hansen, "Changes in Modern Military Codes and the Role of the Military Commander: What Should the United States Learn from this Revolution?", in *Tulane Journal of International and Comparative Law*, 2008, vol. 16, no. 2, p. 425.

[123] See, for example, National Gang Intelligence Center, *Gang-Related Activity in the US Armed Forces Increasing*, 12 January 2007 (assessing the prevalence of gang members in the military as a threat to national security; noting that gang members join the military to receive military training, to access weapons and explosives, and to avoid incarceration); "Gang Warfare in the Military", CBS television broadcast, 29 July 2007, available at http://www.cbsnews.com/video/watch/?id=3107605n&tag (noting the rise of gang violence within the military; showing evidence of gang member presence among US service members in Iraq; and reporting that the Army Criminal Investigation Division increased its number of gang-related crime investigations from nine in 2004 to 61 in 2006), last accessed on 24 March 2015.

[124] See, for example, Lizette Alvarez, "Army Giving More Waivers in Recruiting", in *New York Times*, 14 February 2007 (noting that waivers granted to Army recruits with criminal backgrounds grew from 4,918 in 2003 to 8,129 in 2006, and that recruits with criminal histories made up 11.7 per cent of Army recruits in 2006); and Lizette Alvarez, "Army and Marine Corps Grant More Felony Waivers", in *New York Times*, 22 April 2008 (describing how the Army doubled the number of felony waivers granted in 2007, and how a total of 18 per cent of Army recruits received either felony or misdemeanour conduct waivers in fiscal year 2007).

[125] See C. Todd Lopez, "DOD Sets Joint Standards for Enlistee Waivers", in *Soldiers*, 2008, vol. 63, no. 10 (describing an Army study of enlistees from 2003 to 2006 that compared enlistees with moral waivers to those who did not require a waiver). The study found that those who entered on waivers had higher rates of misconduct and desertion than other en-

---

thinker asserts that this trend correlates to higher rates of military misconduct: "When enlistment qualifications go down, that means discipline rates go up".[126] One unit noted a tangible link between moral waivers and combat misconduct: "Our BCT experience was that the vast majority of downrange CMs [courts martial] were for people with moral waivers on their enlistments".[127]

Noting that COIN is a competition for the support of the civilian population, military forces must be able to deter and discipline those whose misconduct is directed at civilians. In an Army medical study conducted between 2005 and 2007, about 10 per cent of 1,844 marines and soldiers surveyed in Iraq stated that they had mistreated non-combatants and damaged civilian property when it was not necessary to do so.[128] It is admittedly difficult to extrapolate these numbers to all American forces in Iraq and Afghanistan, but even a smaller percentage represents a strategic wild card with the potential to undermine military legitimacy and sour a host population's goodwill. The need for a deterrent

---

listees. It qualified those findings by emphasising that enlistees with moral waivers re-enlisted at higher rates, scored higher on aptitude tests, and earned proportionally more valor awards and combat badges. Cf. Knickerbocker, 2007, see *supra* note 5 (providing a less positive assessment of the effects of allowing criminal waivers): "Waiving rules against recruiting men and women with criminal records is leading to a substantial rise in the number of gang members wearing uniforms and getting trained to use military weapons. Put them in a war zone where death is common and life cheap – that's a real recipe for wanton killing" (quoting retired Army Colonel Dan Smith, author and commentator on military affairs).

[126] Knickerbocker, 2007, see *supra* note 5 (quoting Gary Solis, author, frequent commentator on military affairs, and Adjunct Professor at Georgetown University Law Center).

[127] E-mail message from Captain Eric Hanson to author, 21 March 2010 (on file with author). Captain Hanson was the trial counsel of the 173rd Airborne Regiment in Afghanistan for 15 months from 2007 to 2008. Captain Hanson believes that his Regiment conducted over half of all Afghanistan courts martial during his time there.

[128] Mental Health Advisory Team (MHAT) IV Operation Iraqi Freedom 05–07, *Final Report*, Washington, DC, Office of the Surgeon, Multinational Force-Iraq and Office of the Surgeon General, United States Army Medical Command, 2006 (containing the results of interviews of 1,406 soldiers and 438 marines in Iraq on topics such as mental health, well-being, battlefield ethics and suicide prevention); Major General Gale Pollock, Transcript of News Conference, "DoD News Briefing with Assistant Secretary Casscells from the Pentagon", 4 May 2007, available at http://www.defense.gov/transcripts/transcript.aspx?transcriptid=3958 (summarising the Mental Health Advisory Team's final report), last accessed on 24 March 2015. "[A]pproximately 10 percent of soldiers and Marines report mistreating non-combatants or damaging property when it was not necessary. Only 47 percent of the soldiers and 38 percent of Marines agreed that non-combatants should be treated with dignity and respect", *ibid.*

mechanism is powerful in such circumstances, as soldiers "need to see the results of misconduct".[129]

The Burger King theory raises a thorny problem concerning the impact of soldier misconduct. When soldiers stay on large 'Burger King bases', they spend much of their time among other Americans and away from the local population. As a result, much of the crime they commit does not affect the citizens of the host nation. On the other hand, when they are stationed away from 'Burger King bases' and on smaller outposts, they spend more of their time interacting with local citizens. For soldiers who spend more time with local citizens, the criminal activity they commit will have a proportionally greater effect on the local population. However, these are the same soldiers who are the *least likely* to face court martial because they are away from large bases.

When counter-insurgent forces commit misconduct against civilians, the local commander may be able to salvage goodwill by communicating effectively with the affected civilian community. A leading thinker on modern COIN theory explains that after US forces commit misconduct, the US commander must address locals with "a clear and focused IO [information operations] campaign explaining exactly what is going on". [130] Army doctrine cites the ability to "manage information and expectations" as the top contemporary imperative of COIN.[131]

However, several impediments may hinder the commander's ability to manage information about military misconduct. First, a case that is sent back to the United States will often fall under a different commander, and the original commander cannot then attempt to influence the new commander on the disposition of the case. [132] This means that the operational imperative for prosecuting the wartime crime cannot be easily conveyed to the new deciding official who is far from the combat zone. Second, adjudicating misconduct at a court martial away from the combat

---

[129] CLAMO interview with Major Robert Resnick and Captain Charles Pritchard, 3d Infantry Division, in Charlottesville, Virginia, 20 November 2003, quoted in CLAMO, *Forged in the Fire*, 2008, p. 290, see *supra* notes 3, 12.

[130] E-mail message from Major Niel Smith to author, 7 October 2009 (on file with author). Major Smith has published four articles in *Small Wars Journal* on COIN strategy.

[131] US Department of Army, 2006, paras. 1–138, see *supra* note 118.

[132] Army Court of Criminal Appeals, *United States v. Newlove*, Judgment, 20 August 2003, vol. 59, p. 540.

zone may be neither swift nor certain. One Marine judge advocate described the delays that plagued stateside courts martial of combat zone misconduct as follows:

> From Camp Pendleton, trial counsel and defense counsel started from scratch with a very complex case in which they lacked basic familiarity with the unit's mission, enemy activities in the area, or other important aspects of the environment in which the misconduct had taken place. The eight cases ultimately required more than fourteen months to prosecute. [...] Similarly, the Haditha case still remains unresolved, more than two years since first being brought to light.[133]

Even if the commander decides that a case is important enough to try in country, he still may not be able to assuage the affected community if he cannot talk about the case. An impairment on his ability to talk about the case is the American military justice prohibition against unlawful command influence ('UCI'). "Commanders at all levels must be mindful of their role in our system of justice and be careful not to comment inappropriately on pending cases in their command".[134] This restriction may limit a commander's messages to impersonal communiqués such as, "we will investigate all allegations of misconduct", or "Article 32 is a procedure designed to...", rather than impressing his ability to control his forces and address local concerns.[135]

One example of how the UCI doctrine proved to be a strategic detriment was its role in delaying reporting of the Abu Ghraib abuse case in Iraq in 2004. A senior military lawyer who was in Iraq during that crisis later reflected: "Ironically, it was caution about unlawfully influencing the military justice system that led to the delay in senior officials' appreciating the extent of the Abu Ghraib abuse".[136] As an

---

[133] Hackel, 2009, p. 243, see *supra* note 4.

[134] Lieutenant Colonel Mark Johnson, "Unlawful Command Influence – Still with Us", in *The Army Lawyer*, June 2008, p. 107.

[135] Any suggestion that this chapter advocates unlawful command influence ought to be quickly dispelled. The UCI doctrine rightfully protects against bad-faith command interference in judicial proceedings. The prohibition on UCI protects service members, but so too do HESCO barriers, Kevlar helmets and M1A1 tanks – things that, when necessary to win the counter-insurgency fight, have been set aside or modified.

[136] Mark Martins, "Paying Tribute to Reason: Judgments on Terror, Lessons for Security, in Four Trials since 9/11", Research Manuscript, National War College, Washington, DC, 2008, p. 124. Martins draws a different conclusion than the author about the UCI lessons

aspiration, commanders should be mindful of UCI principles but should also be able to candidly discuss civilian concerns on deployments without the need to have their attorney at their side for fear of UCI violations. The proper litmus test should be whether commanders feel unduly constrained in answering the question 'What are you going to do about this?' when posed by an affected local. This fear of committing UCI appears to be a contributor to the military's poor report card on communication with affected locals about the status of military crimes in Afghanistan and Iraq:

> [T]he military justice system fails to provide ordinary people, including United States citizens and the families of Iraqi or Afghan victims, basic information on the status of investigations into civilian casualties or prosecutions resulting therefrom.[137]

13.5. Proposals to Improve Military Justice in Combat Zones

Finding that courts martial in combat zones are prohibitively difficult and that the weak system of deployed courts martial has negative strategic effects, the remaining issue is how to fix the problem. This section explores a range of possibilities.

One solution is for military and political leaders to emphasise the importance of trying cases in the combat zone whenever practicable, as the British learned in Iraq and the United Nations learned in the Congo. This emphasis ought to be reflected in national and coalition military doctrine.

Admittedly, not every court martial for combat zone misconduct can be tried in the combat zone. When cases must be tried back home, such as when crimes occur at the end of a unit's combat tour as the unit prepares to redeploy, the status of the proceedings must be effectively communicated to the affected population. The British Baha Mousa public inquiry, which used websites with the proceedings translated into the language of the affected population, should be the guiding example for American and other national reforms. The prosecution should be required to perform additional duties for stateside courts martial of combat zone

---

from Abu Ghraib, saying that the UCI doctrine should not be diminished. His research manuscript instead urges military leaders to place more emphasis on accurate investigations and timely reporting.

[137] Alston, 2009, p. 2, see *supra* note 101.

---

crimes that affect foreign civilians, such as establishing websites with trial information in the appropriate foreign language and granting a broader right for foreign persons to travel to the United States to observe trial proceedings.

Instituting this change would have a twofold effect. First, affected foreign persons would gain a meaningful way to follow cases either via the Internet or in person. Second, the added burden imposed for trying cases stateside would incentivise trying cases where misconduct occurs. Although effective communication about wartime misconduct is a strategic imperative and not a judicial one, these requirements could be most easily implemented by amending service military justice regulations. A presidential Executive Order could induce these changes not just for courts martial, but also for similar prosecutions conducted in the federal courts.

As noted earlier in this chapter, the biggest obstacle to deployed justice was the requirement to produce witnesses from outside the combat zone. The most pressing priority for military reformers is to consider the circumstances when alternatives to live witness production – including video teleconferencing and affidavits – would still ensure fair trials. Modifying confrontation requirements for units serving in combat zones is essential to the goal of revitalising deployed justice. It is unrealistic for the military to unthinkingly follow confrontation developments from civilian courts that were never intended to apply to the military. Testimony by deposition and relaxed confrontation rules were the norms for American courts martial from the time of the Revolutionary War until after the Civil War,[138] so history can help guide the task of breaking the lockstep between Sixth Amendment confrontation requirements and rights in courts martial.

Similarly, the curtailment of rights to civilian counsel should be considered for combat zone courts martial. Like the production of witnesses, the logistical challenge of bringing a private attorney in the United States to the combat zone can significantly delay a case.[139] Appropriately limiting requests for civilian counsel in theatre would decrease logistical and administrative delays, and would also put a

---

[138] Frederick B. Wiener, "Courts-Martial and the Bill of Rights: The Original Practice II", in *Harvard Law Review*, 1958, vol. 72, pp. 282–84.

[139] Major John Brooker, "Target Analysis: How to Properly Strike a Deployed Servicemember's Right to Civilian Defense Counsel", in *The Army Lawyer*, November 2010, p. 7.

positive spotlight on the professionalism and abilities of military defence attorneys. A recent proposal, which argues in favour of granting general court martial convening authorities the ability to abrogate an accused's statutory right to civilian counsel under limited circumstances, offers a useful blueprint of how to implement this.[140]

A solution to promote judicial goals in areas largely beyond current judicial reach is to strengthen the military commander's non-judicial punishment ('NJP') powers in the combat zone. This summarised justice authority is found in Article 15(a) of the UCMJ. Non-judicial punishment covers minor offences, allows for certain minor punishments short of confinement,[141] and does not result in a criminal conviction or discharge from the military. It "provides commanders with an essential and prompt means of maintaining good order and discipline and also promotes positive behavior changes in servicemembers without the stigma of a court-martial conviction".[142]

Article 15(a) permits service members to refuse NJP and instead demand trial by court martial, with one exception: when attached to or embarked in a vessel. This exception is logical; it makes little sense to allow service members to refuse NJP in places where courts martial cannot be performed, such as on a ship. Applying the same logic, another place where courts martial largely cannot be performed is in the combat zone. It makes sense that service members either embarked on a vessel or serving in a combat zone should not have the option to reject NJP and demand court martial. In such circumstances, NJP should be binding.

The Navy's approach to NJP (called 'captain's mast') emphasises its relationship to discipline, and, ultimately, the performance of military

---

[140] *Ibid.*, pp. 26–30. Major Brooker proposes "Precision-Targeted Abrogation", where a General court-martial convening authority in a combat zone can deny an accused's request for civilian counsel in certain circumstances.

[141] Maximum punishments, when imposed by a commander in the rank of major or higher, include correctional custody for 30 days, forfeiture of half pay per month for two months, reduction to the lowest or any intermediate pay grade, if the grade from which demoted is within the promotion authority of the officer imposing the reduction (more restricted for grades E5 and above), extra duty for 45 days, and restriction for 60 days. UCMJ article 15(b)(2)(H).

[142] UCMJ article 15; MCM, Part V, Non-Judicial Punishment Procedure, 2008, see *supra* note 8.

missions. A naval historian compared the Navy's approach to the Army's as follows:

> The Navy reposed special faith in its ships' captains and gave them the power to discipline their crews in order to carry out assigned missions. [...] Navy captain's mast resembled a trial. The commander called witnesses, heard evidence, and interviewed the accused at a formal hearing set aside for the purpose. When satisfied that he knew the facts, he handed down a finding and awarded a punishment. [...] Although the Army treated NJP like an administrative task, it permitted appeal from this utterly nonjudicial affair to a court-martial, which had the power to hand down a federal conviction. But one of the reasons the Navy refused to grant the right of election was that it considered mast a disciplinary matter, not a criminal one, and therefore not suitable for trial by court-martial.[143]

The idea of binding NJP may seem unusual to soldiers who have never served on ships. Marines, on the other hand, have experience with both vessel service and ground combat deployments. One Marine judge advocate from Iraq noted the advantages of applying binding NJP to the combat zone:

> A sailor deployed on the USS Arleigh Burke for local operations for two weeks off the coast of Virginia (as routine as it gets for the Navy) cannot refuse NJP, but a Marine in an infantry battalion in Al Qaim [Iraq], 150 miles from the nearest trial counsel or military judge, can refuse NJP and tie the hands of the commander to administer discipline.[144]

Deployed Army commanders similarly often have their hands tied over NJP due to court-martial frailty. One unit explained the dilemma created by the right to refuse NJP in a combat zone: "Some Soldiers requested trial by court-martial instead of accepting an Article 15.

---

[143] William T. Generous, Jr., *Swords and Scales: The Development of the Uniform Code of Military Justice*, 1973, Port Washington, NY, Kennikat Press, pp. 123–24. In the same section, Dr. Generous also describes how the Navy successfully sought to retain the 'vessel exception' when the UCMJ was enacted in 1950. The Army continued the trend identified by Generous of treating NJP as a form of judicial proceedings, going as far in 2005 as changing the NJP standard of proof to the judicial 'beyond a reasonable doubt'.

[144] Lieutenant Colonel R.G. Bracknell, Staff Judge Advocate, Regimental Combat Team 5, US Marine Corps, *Operation Iraqi Freedom After Action Report*, 7 August 2008, p. 11.

Commanders found themselves in an awkward position, i.e. prefer charges or administratively separate the soldier".[145]

Logically, service members' refusal of NJP should increase where the possibility of court-martial is remote, and two experienced TDS attorneys confirm this motivation. One said he advised clients to turn down NJP "up to ten times a month"[146] and "more than in garrison",[147] while the other wrote: "I advised turning down Art 15s all the time in Iraq. [...] It was the deployed environment that caused such recommendations".[148]

Non-judicial punishment can still thrive when away from 'Burger King bases'. Recall that in Afghanistan in 2009 American forces were spread out over 200 bases and outposts. Of those 200, only one had a courtroom and resident trial defence attorneys (Bagram Air Base), and only nine had judge advocates. On the other hand, all 200 likely either had commanders present or were regularly visited by commanders. With this broader coverage, NJP represents a realistic option for addressing routine wartime disciplinary infractions. However, it is a less useful option if any offender has the power to wholly veto it. In such circumstances, the decision to discipline should rest with military leaders, not offenders.

These reform suggestions allude to an interesting idea that a focus on crimes committed on deployment requires reversing the normal understanding of whose rights deserve protection. The study of military justice has for a long time had its core concern as protecting the rights of military members against unjust summary procedures used by the military. Advocates in the field have secured protections of the judicial rights of military members through means ranging from human rights courts to national constitutions. As the pace of military deployments around the world continues to grow, the concern in military law for the victims of military crime, as well as the self-interest of armed forces in addressing crimes, continue to grow. These concerns argue in favour of

---

[145] 4th Combat Aviation Brigade, 4th Infantry Division (Mechanized), *OIF After Action Report*, June 2008 – June 2009, 28 August 2009, p. 8.

[146] Interview with Major Isaac Sprague, US Army Trial Defense Service Attorney in Kuwait and Iraq from May 2008 to July 2009, in Charlottesville, Virginia, 18 February 2010.

[147] *Ibid.*

[148] E-mail message from Ryan Wood to author, 16 August 2010 (on file with author). Mr. Wood is a former US Army Trial Defense Service attorney who served in Iraq from January 2007 to January 2008.

summarised procedures for addressing military crime, especially in circumstances when full procedures appear to be unworkable.

13.6. Conclusion

The previous decade of the United States at war can be considered an awakening of self-interest in addressing crimes committed by military members on deployments. This realisation came the hard way, as the military experienced painful setbacks in both Afghanistan and Iraq when its regime of responding to crimes proved unable except on the largest 'Burger King bases'.

During deployments, the most important question of military justice inquiry shifts from ensuring the judicial protections of military members to the challenge of ensuring that soldiers do not enjoy impunity after committing serious crimes. Because of the outsized impact that military crime has on modern missions, it is not an exaggeration to say that military justice concerns should weigh just as heavily on military strategists as they do on attorneys.

Modifying the way military justice is managed could make courts martial more portable and relevant in combat. Changes to deployed justice should include emphasising the need for a justice system that can truly go wherever the troops go, rethinking the need for complicated procedural rules that were formed blind to their deployed consequences, and better enabling summarised procedures in circumstances when full procedures are unworkable. The American court-martial system now is quite advanced, but that means little if it cannot be used where it is needed most.

14

Prosecuting Members of the Armed Forces for Core International Crimes: A Judicial Act in the Self-Interest of the Armed Forces?

Roberta Arnold*

14.1. Introduction

With the establishment of the International Criminal Tribunals for the Former Yugoslavia ('ICTY')[1] and Rwanda ('ICTR') ,[2] after a break of over 50 years since the Nuremberg and Tokyo Trials, international civil society has found a renewed interest in the prosecution of core international crimes. Unlike their predecessors, these tribunals, along with those established in their wake, such as the Special Court for Sierra Leone ('SCSL') and the International Criminal Court ('ICC') , are civilian in character and moved by dynamics that go beyond 'victors' justice'.[3] A factor that may have motivated many states to confer jurisdiction on these civilian institutions is probably the concern of human rights scholars that

---

* **Roberta Arnold** is a researcher at the Military Academy at ETH Zurich, Switzerland, Chair of Strategic Studies. She is a former legal adviser within the International Relations Division of the Swiss Federal Department of Defence and a military investigating magistrate within the Swiss Military Justice. She holds a Ph.D. from the University of Bern and an LL.M. from the University of Nottingham. The views expressed here are the author's alone and do not necessarily represent the official position of the Swiss Federal Department of Defence.

1. United Nations ('UN') Security Council, Resolution 827, 25 May 1993, UN Doc. S/RES/827 (1993).

2. UN Security Council, Resolution 955, 8 November 1994, UN Doc. S/RES/955 (1994).

3. This is so despite the strong criticism raised by the ICTY's acquittal judgment of the Croatian Generals Gotovina and Markač. ICTY, *Prosecutor v. Ante Gotovina and Mladen Markač*, Case No. IT-06-90-A, Judgment, 16 November 2012, Dissenting Opinions of Judges Fausto Pocar and Carmel Agius (https://www.legal-tools.org/doc/03b685/); "Carla Del Ponte 'Shocked' by the Acquittal of Croatian Generals", in Dalje.com, 20 November 2012, available at http://dalje.com/en-world/carla-del-ponte-shocked-by-the-acquittal-of-croatian-generals/451145, last accessed on 21 November 2014; and Bruno Waterfield, "Croatian Hero Ante Gotovina Acquitted of War Crimes", in *The Telegraph*, 16 November 2012, available at http://www.telegraph.co.uk/news/worldnews/europe/croatia/9682855/Croatian-hero-Ante-Gotovina-acquitted-of-war-crimes.html, last accessed on 21 November 2014.

military courts may be arbitrary or biased. This change must be read in the context of a general negative attitude, particularly in Europe, towards the military,[4] which is often viewed by outsiders as a closed circle to be distrusted and strictly watched or, possibly, even eradicated. This attitude is demonstrated by the fact that in the recent years, conscription has been abolished or is highly controversial in some countries.[5] In Austria, for example, the population was called to vote on conscription on 20 January 2013, with an outcome of 40 per cent against.[6] A similar referendum was held in Switzerland on 22 September 2013 in which 27 per cent voted for the abolition of conscription.[7] Mistrust was signalled, for instance, in relation to the proposal to send the Swiss Army's Special Forces to Somalia to protect Swiss vessels from piracy in Operation Atalanta or to Libya to protect the Swiss embassy during the uprising against the Gaddafi regime.[8] Even the Swiss defence minister's political party, the Schweizer-

---

[4] See Federico Andreu-Guzmán, *Military Jurisdiction and International Law: Military Courts and Gross Human Rights Violations*, International Commission of Jurists, Geneva, 2004; Nobuo Hayashi (ed.), *National Military Manuals on the Law of Armed Conflict*, Torkel Opsahl Academic EPublisher, Oslo, 2008; and Roberta Arnold, "Military Criminal Procedures and Judicial Guarantees: The Example of Switzerland", in *Journal of International Criminal Justice*, 2005, vol. 3, no. 3, pp. 749–77.

[5] In Serbia compulsory military service was abolished on 1 January 2011, see Michael Roberts, "Serbia: Mandatory Military Service Abolished", in Balkans.com Business News, 16 December 2010; in Italy it was suspended on 1 January 2005, see Bruce Johnston, "Italy Orders a Halt to National Service", in *The Telegraph*, 25 October 2000, available at http://www.telegraph.co.uk/news/worldnews/europe/italy/1371770/Italy-orders-a-halt-to-national-service.html, last accessed on 6 March 2015. Strong discussions about the abolition of the compulsory military service are currently going on in Switzerland, Germany and Austria.

[6] AFP, "Austrians Vote to Keep Army Draft", in *The Telegraph*, 20 January 2013, available at http://www.telegraph.co.uk/news/worldnews/europe/austria/9814367/Austrians-vote-to-keep-army-draft.html, last accessed on 21 November 2014. See also "Austrians Vote to Keep Compulsory Military Service", in BBC News, 20 January 2013, at http://www.bbc.co.uk/news/world-europe-21110431, last accessed on 21 November 2014. In Germany, it was *"ausgesetzt"* on 1 July 2011, meaning it can always be reinstituted; see "Österreicher Stimmen für die Wehrpflicht", in *Zeit Online*, 20 January 2013, available at http://www.zeit.de/politik/ausland/2013-01/oesterreich-wehrpflicht-armee, last accessed on 21 November 2014.

[7] Urs Geiser, "Swiss Voters Endorse Army Conscription", in SWI, 22 September 2013, available at http://www.swissinfo.ch/eng/swiss-voters-endorse-army-conscription/369555 34, last accessed on 6 March 2015.

[8] Schweizer Fernsehen, "Bundesrat schickt Elitetruppe AAD 10 nach Tripolis", 20 December 2011; and Hubert Mooser and Simon Hehli, "SVP Will Rambo-Truppe Abschaffen",

ische Volkspartei (SVP), has been strongly critical, labelling these elite units as "Rambos".[9] Paradoxically, the main argument of those favouring conscription is the belief that a militia system can provide a better demo-cratic control mechanism of an institution that is otherwise to be mistrusted.

One way for the military to rebut this negative image is to demon-strate that it observes the rule of law. It is, therefore, in its self-interest to show that one of its priorities is to ensure servicemen suspected of serious crimes, including core international crimes, are brought to justice. This self-interest in maintaining a good image then goes hand in hand with the self-interest in successful mission accomplishment. Particularly in the framework of peace support operations ('PSO'), the misconduct of a few servicemen may have a boomerang effect not only on the deployed troops, who may lose the hearts and minds of the host nation's population, but also on the sending state's government, which may lose the necessary political support for the continuation or deployment of similar opera-tions.[10]

At the same time, not only does the military as an *institution* have a self-interest in prosecuting serious offenders, but so do its *members* as well. For example, high-ranking officers may have an interest in the smooth exercise of command and control, which facilitates mission ac-complishment, and in avoiding criminal charges as superiors. While low-er-ranking members of the armed forces may have an interest in distanc-ing themselves from the misconduct of their comrades and in operating in a safe working environment.

The aim of this chapter is to identify the various kinds of self-interest of the military in prosecuting its members for core international crimes and to discuss whether these may be used as an argument to get the military on board as a partner in the promotion of justice. Section 14.2. below examines the possible self-interests of the armed forces in

in *Blick*, 14 January 2012, available at http://www.blick.ch/news/politik/svp-will-rambo-truppe-abschaffen-id52825.html, last accessed on 21 November 2014.

[9] Mooser and Hehli, 2012, see *supra* note 8.

[10] For instance, with regard to the deployment of Swisscoy, the mandate needs to be continu-ally extended by the Parliament. See Bundesbeschluss über die Verlängerung der Schweizer Beteiligung an der multinationalen Kosovo Force (KFOR) of 8 June 2011 (BBl 2011 5511), which extended the mandate until 31 December 2014, on the basis of Article 66b (4) of the Military Law of 3 February 1995 (SR 510.10). This Federal Decision is available at http://www.admin.ch/ch/d/ff/2011/5511.pdf, last accessed on 21 November 2014.

prosecuting serious *international* crimes, taking examples from the Swiss armed forces' prosecution of serious *domestic* crimes – such as right-wing extremism or sexual abuse, which may follow the same rationale. It finds that accountability benefits both the military as an institution and individual members of the military. Section 14.3. discusses whether these may be better served by a military judicial system.

14.2. The Self-Interest of the Armed Forces in Prosecuting Serious International Crimes

14.2.1. The Self-Interest of the Military as an Institution

14.2.1.1. Good Image and Corporate Identity

Having a good image is probably the best argument to convince the military to ensure accountability for serious international crimes among its ranks. This is even truer in an era characterised by economic recession and the lack of a clear enemy that may justify criticisms of the military's high expenditure, as evidenced by calls to abolish the conscription system in several countries.

In Switzerland, for instance, the 2013 conscription referendum was the third on the matter in almost a quarter of a century.[11] It was a result of an initiative deposited on 5 January 2012 by the Society for a Switzerland without an Army (Gesellschaft für eine Schweiz ohne Armee).[12] Despite the majority vote in favour, controversy still remains. Against this background, the Swiss Army, though small and defensive in character, as some might say, could not afford to lose its good image. Although the likelihood of its members being involved in war crimes is extremely remote, serious 'ordinary' crimes (for example, sexual abuse or homicide) may have an equally negative impact. Major efforts have been undertaken to maintain a good military justice system and to promote prevention.

---

[11] Geiser, 2013, see *supra* note 7.

[12] Urs Geiser, "Les adversaires de l'armée reviennent à la charge", in SWI, 8 January 2012, Swissinfo.ch; Imogen Foulkes, "Knives out for Conscription in Switzerland", in BBC News, 11 January 2011, available at http://www.bbc.co.uk/news/world-europe-12083427, last accessed at 8 April 2015; and Silvia Steidle, "Bundesrat ist gegen die Abschaffung der Wehrpflicht", Swiss Department of Defence, 14 September 2012, available at https://www.news.admin.ch/message/index.html?lang=de&msg-id=45974, last accessed at 29 April 2015.

Since 2011, all prospective recruits and those awaiting promotion to officer or non-commissioned officer rank must undergo a personal security check. The consequences may include, beyond referral to the judicial authorities, exclusion from the armed forces or seizure of weapons.[13] More specific measures have been adopted to fight extremism and racial discrimination within the armed forces.[14] In March 2001, the chief of the armed forces introduced measures such as the exchange of information between the federal authorities and the creation of a special Extremism within the Armed Forces Unit,[15] in order to allow timely identification of the phenomenon.[16] Everybody, including civilians, may raise questions or make claims to it. Where prevention comes too late, repression will step in.

Military Tribunal 2 conducted a trial for racial discrimination on 15–16 March 2007. Three grenadiers were charged with racial discrimination for having made denigrating declarations against Jews, black people and foreigners and for having mimicked Hitler's salute in public.[17] Disciplinary complaints were filed by 11 comrades of the accused, following which the school commander ordered the opening of a preliminary investigation by the Military Justice authorities. All of them were condemned.[18]

---

[13] More information is available at Armée Suisse, "Lutte contre l'extrémisme au sein de l'armée", available at http://www.vtg.admin.ch/internet/vtg/fr/home/themen/extremis mus.html, last accessed on 21 November 2014. See in particular Swiss Military Law, Articles 22, 22a and 24, LAAM, RS 510.10 (https://www.legal-tools.org/doc/97ab32/).

[14] "Militärische Führungspositionen – Neonazis in der Schweizer Armee", in *Blick*, 7 October 2012, available at http://www.blick.ch/news/schweiz/neonazis-in-der-schweizer-armee-id2059739.html, last accessed on 21 November 2014; and Fabian Eberhard, "Die braune Armee-Fraktion", in *SonntagsZeitung*, 7 October 2012, available at http://www.sonntagszeitung.ch/fokus/artikel-detailseite/?newsid=231625, last accessed on 21 November 2014.

[15] This was subordinated to the specialised Service for Combating Racism within the Federal Department of Home Affairs, but it continues to serve exclusively the interests of the Swiss armed forces and it works closely with the latter's human resources.

[16] The legal basis is a directive: RS 121.1 Ordonnance sur le Service de renseignement de la Confédération of 4 December 2009, which defines extremism in Article 4 as follows: "extrémisme violent: menées déployées par les organisations dont les membres rejettent la démocratie, les droits de l'homme ou l'Etat de droit et qui, pour atteindre leurs buts, commettent des actes de violence, les préconisent ou les soutiennent" (https://www.legal-tools.org/doc/665a4b/).

[17] Département fédéral de la défense, "Jugements dans le cas d'Isone", 16 March 2007 (https://www.legal-tools.org/doc/27f69f/); see also Decision TM 2 2006 28 of 15 and 16 March 2007, held in Yverdon-les-Bains.

[18] On the basis of former Article 171c (1) sub-para. 4 of the Swiss Military Code (Racial Discrimination):

The military prosecutor also asked for a demotion for two of them, but the Tribunal held that since no effective discrimination against non-white members of the group had occurred and none of the accused belonged to extremist movements, this sanction was to be restricted to more severe cases.

In this specific case, it may be argued that the main self-interest of the Swiss armed forces lay in ensuring the removal of negative elements from its elite corps, thus safeguarding its good image as well as the identification of its members with it as a form of 'corporate identity'. This is particularly important in a conscription system, where motivation and identification with the employer are key factors for success. The author, who was a member of the former Federal Extra-Parliamentary Commission for Admission to the Civil Service, recalls that the candidates, in supporting their request for reincorporation into the civil service, often criticised the 'working environment', rather than exposing a real conflict of conscience between their moral values and those of the military as an institution. In a conscription system in particular, where the citizen-soldiers are extracted from their normal environment for several weeks a year and transferred into a new context, among comrades with different backgrounds, attitudes and values, it is extremely important for the military to ensure that the risk of exposure to serious crimes is close to zero, or at least that any misconduct is duly reported to the competent judicial

---

Celui qui publiquement, aura incité à la haine ou à la discrimination envers une personne ou un groupe de personnes en raison de leur appartenance raciale, ethnique ou religieuse, celui qui, publiquement, aura propagé une idéologie visant à rabaisser ou à dénigrer de façon systématique les membres d'une race, d'une ethnie ou d'une religion, celui qui dans le même dessein, aura organisé ou encouragé des actions de propagande ou y aura pris part, celui qui aura publiquement, par la parole, l'écriture, l'image, le geste, par des voies de fait ou de toute autre manière, abaissé ou discriminé d'une façon qui porte atteinte à la dignité humaine une personne ou un groupe de personnes en raison de leur race, de leur appartenance ethnique ou de leur religion ou qui, pour la même raison, niera, minimisera grossièrement ou cherchera à justifier un génocide ou d'autres crimes contre l'humanité, celui qui aura refusé à une personne ou à un groupe de personnes, en raison de leur appartenance raciale, ethnique ou religieuse, une prestation destinée à l'usage public, sera puni de l'emprisonnement ou de l'amende.

L'infraction sera punie disciplinairement si elle est de peu de gravité.

---

authorities. Failure to do so may jeopardise the identification of the other members with the institution and the creation of a corporate spirit and of a corporate identity.

14.2.1.2. Mission Accomplishment

Allegations of misconduct can undermine an otherwise successful mission.[19] It is naturally in the armed forces' self-interest to prevent all kinds of serious crimes, including war crimes and other core crimes. This applies in particular to PSOs, where 'ordinary crimes' such as human trafficking may lead to the loss of credibility, and thus support, on the part of the local population.

Incidents of sexual exploitation and abuse have been reported in Bosnia and Herzegovina, Kosovo, Cambodia, Timor-Leste, West Africa and the Democratic Republic of Congo.[20] In such cases it is essential to hold the perpetrators accountable via transparent procedures.[21] In 2004, NATO adopted a zero-tolerance policy on combating trafficking in human beings, based on the belief that trafficking is not only a serious abuse of human rights but it is furthermore conduct that has "the potential to weaken and destabilize fragile governments and runs counter to the goals of NATO-led efforts especially in South Eastern Europe".[22] The policy thus clearly states that this kind of misconduct by NATO personnel runs counter to a NATO military mission.[23]

Evidence in this regard is provided by the fate of Canada's Airborne Regiment following to its deployment in Somalia in 1993 and reports about the torturing to death of a Somali teenager, Shidane Arone.[24]

---

[19] David B. Hodgkinson, Sandra L. Hodgkinson, Diana C. Noone and Gregory P. Noone, "Human Rights Training to Law Enforcement Agents: A Key to PSO Success", in Roberta Arnold (ed.), *Law Enforcement in the Framework of Peace Support Operations*, Martinus Nijhoff, Leiden, 2008, p. 338.

[20] *Ibid.*, p. 329.

[21] *Ibid.*, p. 332.

[22] See NATO, "Policy on Combating Trafficking in Human Beings", 29 June 2004, para. 1, available at http://www.nato.int/docu/comm/2004/06-istanbul/docu-traffic.htm, last accessed on 21 November 2014.

[23] On this topic see Roberta Arnold, "The NATO Policy on Human Trafficking: Obligation to Prevent, Obligation to Repress", in Arnold, 2008, p. 357, see *supra* note 19.

[24] The boy had been caught by a Canadian snatch patrol on 16 March 1993 in an abandoned US compound. Since the Americans had left materiel and garbage around their bases, the order was to prevent infiltrators from stealing. The previous evening, platoon commanders had received authorisation by Major Tony Seward to "abuse" infiltrators resisting capture.

The government appointed the Somalia Commission of Inquiry, according to whom the teenager died following prolonged and severe pain and suffering inflicted by the Canadian peacekeepers.[25] The conclusion was as follows:

> Systems broke down and organizational discipline crumbled. Such systemic or institutional faults cannot be divorced from leadership responsibility, and the leadership errors in the Somalia mission were manifold and fundamental: [...].
>
> *Our soldiers searched, often in vain, for leadership and inspiration* [...]
>
> We can only hope that Somalia represents the nadir of the fortunes of the Canadian Forces. There seems to be little room to slide lower. One thing is certain, however: left uncorrected, the problems that surfaced in the desert in Somalia and in the boardrooms at National Defence Headquarters will continue to spawn military ignominy. *The victim will be Canada and its international reputation.*[26]

As Timothy McCormack observed:

> The level of national shame associated with the behaviour of Canadian troops in Somalia was such that the Canadian National Defence Forces took the unprecedented step of disbanding the Canadian Airborne Regiment – a unit of the Canadian Forces with a proud deployment history.[27]

Arone was found hiding in a portable toilet and taken to a bunker, where his feet and hands were tied with a riot baton and where he was questioned about his intentions. The soldiers had discussed Seward's order and, after questioning Arone, the sergeant on duty left the bunker and told them "I do not care what you do, just do not kill the guy". Medical reports indicated that Arone was found with burns over his genitals and that he had been anally raped with a riot baton and a metal rod. A number of at least 17 soldiers had apparently gone through the bunker that night, and seen Arone at different stages of the beating, some of them contributing to it. See Clyde H. Farnsworth, "Torture by Army Peacekeepers in Somalia Shocks Canada", in *New York Times*, 27 November 1994, available at http://www.nytimes.com/1994/11/27/world/torture-by-army-peacekeepers-in-somalia-shocks-canada.html, last accessed on 21 November 2014.

25. Sandra Whitworth, *Men, Militarism and U.N. Peacekeeping: A Gendered Analysis*, Lynne Rienne, Boulder, 2004, pp. 91–92.

26. Department of National Defence and the Canadian Forces, "Report of the Somalia Commission of Inquiry", Executive Summary, 2 July 1997 (emphasis added).

27. Timothy McCormack, "Their Atrocities and Our Misdemeanours: The Reticence of States to Try Their 'Own Nationals' for International Crimes", in Mark Lattimer and Philippe Sands (eds.), *Justice for Crimes Against Humanity*, Hart Publishing, Oxford, 2003, p. 138;

Similar allegations affected the Belgian elite paratrooper unit serving in the joint United States/United Nations Operation Restore Hope mission in Somalia in 1993.[28] In 1995, 15 members were put on trial for abuses including torture, killings and the mock execution of children. Two of them, Kurt Coelus and Claude Baert, were identified following the release of a photograph in the Belgian daily *Het Laatste Nieuws*, which showed them swinging a boy over a campfire. The prosecutor demanded one month's imprisonment for Coelus, who had moved to the Belgian Navy, and Baert who had left the army. However, the Brussels Military Court, in June 1997, acquitted them on the basis of lack of conclusive evidence.[29] This judgment, however, was reported negatively in the media, in particular the statements of the Presiding Judge Dirk Moereman, according to whom it could not be established that physical violence had been inflicted and that it was not the court's duty to try the Third Paratroop Battalion or Belgium's actions in Somalia.[30] Therefore, it is not sufficient for the military to ensure referral of these cases to justice, but also to ensure a fair and just trial, as long as this is held by a military justice system. To do otherwise may just worsen, rather than improve, the image of the military.

Admission of failures will, on the contrary, contribute to restoring the credibility of the troops and their sending states. A good example in this regard is the Nuhanović Trial,[31] which was held in the Netherlands following the Dutch battalion's ('Dutchbat') failure to protect the Muslim enclave of Srebrenica, Bosnia and Herzegovina in 1995. In July 2011 the Dutch Court of Appeal held the Netherlands responsible as a state for the killing – by omission – on 13 July 1995 of three Muslims, who had been

---

see also Kate Domansky, "The Canadian Forces in Somalia: An Operational Assessment", in *Canadian Army Journal*, 2012, vol. 14, issue 1, p. 101.

[28] "Photos reveal Belgian paratroopers abuse in Somalia", in CNN, 17 April 1997, available at http://edition.cnn.com/WORLD/9704/17/belgium.somalia/index.html?_s=PM:WORLD, last accessed on 21 November 2014.

[29] Nieck Ammerlaan, "Belgian Soldiers Acquitted in Somalia Trial", in Reuter, 30 June 1997, available at http://www.mosquitonet.com/~prewett/belgiansoldiersacquit.html, last accessed on 21 November 2014; for details, see also McCormack, 2003, p. 138, *supra* note 28.

[30] Ammerlaan, 1997, see *supra* note 29.

[31] Court of Appeal of The Hague, *Mustafic c.s. v. State of The Netherlands*, Judgment, 5 July 2011 (https://www.legal-tools.org/doc/108fc7/); Court of Appeal of The Hague, *Nuhanović v. State of The Netherlands*, Judgment, 5 July 2011 (https://www.legal-tools.org/doc/f734b8/).

forced by the Dutchbat to leave its military compound. The Court held that the Dutchbat should have anticipated the risk of subsequent execution of these men; the Netherlands, as a troop-contributing nation, had to be responsible for this under the principle of state responsibility. Informal discussions in November 2012 between a survivor and the author indicated that although the Netherlands may have had the right to appeal against this decision, this would have had a negative impact at the political and diplomatic levels.

Civil proceedings against the Netherlands and the UN[32] in relation to Srebrenica were then initiated on 4 June 2007 by 10 women from Bosnia and Herzegovina and the association Mothers of Srebrenica.[33] On 10 July 2008, the Hague District Court ruled that it had no jurisdiction to deal with the case, citing the immunity of the UN under Article 105 of the UN Charter. The case went to the Supreme Court, which affirmed the absolute immunity of the UN troops on 13 April 2012. The case was then submitted to the European Court of Human Rights, but was ruled inadmissible.[34]

Misconduct by military personnel may thus have undesired side effects such as state responsibility. In the Netherlands, following a report that blamed the politicians for sending the Dutch UN troops to an impossible mission, the whole Dutch cabinet resigned in 2002.[35] Politics is very sensitive and it is in the military's interest to prevent such incidents, which may lead to the loss of political − and thus financial − support.

There are other examples showing how important it is for the military − and the international organisations they act for − to report incidents of misconduct committed by their peacekeepers. In 2011, allega-

---

[32] See, for details, Guido den Dekker, "Immunity of the United Nations Before the Dutch Courts", The Hague Justice Portal, available at http://www.haguejusticeportal.net/index.php?id=9569, last accessed on 21 November 2014.

[33] The Mothers of Srebrenica represent 6,000 women who lost family members during the Srebrenica massacre in 1995; see Van Diepen Van der Kroef Advocaten, "Writ of Summons: District Court, The Hague", 2007 (https://www.legal-tools.org/doc/ca1e99/).

[34] European Court of Human Rights, *Stichting Mothers of Srebrenica and Others v. The Netherlands*, Application no. 65542/12, Decision, 11 June 2013 (https://www.legal-tools.org/doc/7fe2ad/).

[35] Andrew Osborn and Paul Brown, "Dutch Cabinet Resigns over Srebrenica Massacre", in *The Guardian*, 17 April 2002, available at http://www.theguardian.com/world/2002/apr/17/warcrimes.andrewosborn, last accessed on 21 November 2014.

tions surfaced that during the United Nations Stabilisation Mission in Haiti ('MINUSTAH') peacekeeping troops from Uruguay had sexually abused a local young man, leading the Uruguayan military to take "severe and exemplary measures". According to the *Guardian*:

> The incident is likely to pour more gasoline on the fire of resentment that Haitians have for the UN troops who have occupied their country for more than seven years. There has been a dire pattern of abuses: in December 2007, more than 100 UN soldiers from Sri Lanka were deported under charges of sexual abuse of under-age girls. In 2005, UN troops went on the rampage in Cité Soleil, one of the poorest areas in Port-au-Prince, killing as many as 23 people, including children, according to witnesses. After the raid, the humanitarian group Doctors Without Borders reported: "On that day, we treated 27 people for gunshot wounds. Of them, around 20 were women under the age of 18".[36]

MINUSTAH reacted by stating that an investigation had been ordered by its military police and that the UN has a zero-tolerance policy towards misbehaviour, sexual exploitation or abuse.[37] On 13 March 2012, three MINUSTAH officers of Pakistani nationality were sentenced to one year's detention for another case of raping of a 14-year-old Haitian boy. According to the media, the Haitian government had requested the lifting of immunity for the Pakistani officers and the Senate had passed a resolution requesting that they be tried in Haitian courts. The trial was eventually held in Haiti, following the military justice procedure and national laws of Pakistan. However, as reported by Reuters, "Haitian government authorities were given no advance notice of the military tribunal" and there were allegations that had the Pakistani police officers been tried in a Haitian court they would likely have faced much harsher penalties.[38] Once again, this example shows how important it is, for the good image of peacekeeping troops and their sending state, to not only report offenders but also ensure that the judicial proceedings are fair and transparent.

---

[36] Mark Weisbrot, "Is this Minustah's 'Abu Ghraib Moment' in Haiti?", in *The Guardian*, 3 September 2011, available at http://www.theguardian.com/commentisfree/cifamerica/2011/sep/03/minustah-un-haiti-abuse, last accessed on 21 November 2014.

[37] *Ibid.*

[38] "MINUSTAH Officers Found Guilty of Rape – But Get Just One Year in Prison", in Center for Economic and Policy Research, 13 March 2012, available at http://www.cepr.net/blogs/relief-and-reconstruction-watch/minustah-officers-found-guilty-of-rape-but-get-just-one-year-in-prison, last accessed on 21 November 2014.

Misconduct may also have a severe impact on the success of a *war-fare* mission. In 2012, a video showing two US marines urinating on the dead body of a Taliban member in July 2011, during a counter-insurgency operation in Helmand province, Afghanistan, was circulated right after the US announced that its combat role in Afghanistan would end in late 2014 – a very sensitive time for US-Afghan relations.[39] One month later, following rumours that US troops had incinerated a number of copies of the Qur'an, violent protests broke out, claiming approximately 30 lives, among who were two US troops.[40] The US Defence Secretary Leon Panetta denounced the behaviour as "utterly deplorable",[41] while Hillary Clinton expressed her "total dismay", adding that such conduct

> is absolutely inconsistent with American values, with the standards of behavior that we expect from our military personnel and that you know the vast, vast majority of our military personnel, particularly our marines, hold themselves to.[42]

These episodes show that a single incident of misconduct may have serious political implications for a military or law enforcement mission, especially if left improperly investigated.

14.2.2. Self-Interest of Members of the Armed Forces

Beyond the self-interest of the military as an institution, its members may also have different interests in ensuring the prosecution of suspects of serious crimes, including core international crimes. On the one hand, inter-

---

[39] David Blair, "US Marines Urinating Video Comes at Singularly Sensitive Moment for Afghanistan", in *The Telegraph*, 12 January 2012, available on http://www.telegraph.co.uk/news/worldnews/asia/afghanistan/9010952/US-Marines-urinating-video-comes-at-singularly-sensitive-moment-for-Afghanistan.html, last accessed on 21 November 2014.

[40] "US Marines Recommended for Trial for Urination Video", in BBC News, 24 September 2012, available at http://www.bbc.co.uk/news/world-us-canada-19708371, last accessed on 21 November 2014; Adam Gabbatt, "US Marines Charged Over Urinating on Bodies of Dead Taliban in Afghanistan", in *The Guardian*, 24 September 2012, available at www.theguardian.com/world/2012/sep/24/us-marines-charged-dead-taliban, last accessed on 21 November 2014.

[41] Cited in Blair, 2012, see *supra* note 39.

[42] "Hillary Clinton Says Marine Urination Video 'Inconsistent With American Values'", in *The Telegraph*, 12 January 2012, available at http://www.telegraph.co.uk/news/world news/northamerica/usa/9011420/Hillary-Clinton-says-marine-urination-video-inconsistent-with-American-values.html, last accessed on 21 November 2014.

national law imposes on commanders the obligation to ensure that their subordinates observe the laws and customs of war.[43] Failure to prevent or repress international crimes committed or planned by their subordinates, notwithstanding knowledge thereof, may incur their individual criminal responsibility as superiors. It is therefore in their interest to ensure the primary perpetrators are brought to justice. Moreover, the historic case of General Yamashita[44] proves very well the negative outcomes of undisciplined troops from a tactical perspective.

At the same time, it is also in the interest of ordinary soldiers that the 'few rotten apples' will be reported and expelled from the military, an institution with which they may identify themselves. It is in their further interest that commanders prone to giving unlawful orders are removed, to avoid the dilemma of having to refuse such orders one day. Although refusing unlawful orders is expected in theory, in practice one should consider the realities of war and the fact that refusal may lead to retaliations. Ultimately, it is in their interest to work in a 'safe environment', as shown by the Swiss military case of racial discrimination. The servicemen and women of the armed forces have in fact the right to carry out their profession in an environment where they can rely on the proper conduct of their comrades and superiors.

A good example in this regard is the Sexual Harassment/Assault Response and Prevention (SHARP)[45] programme launched by the US military to address sexual harassment and abuses.[46] As stated in the Army policy on harassment of 31 July 2008:

> As Army leaders it is our duty to provide and maintain an environment of trust and respect for human dignity where workplace harassment, including sexual harassment, will not

---

[43] See, for example, Geneva Convention Relative to the Treatment of Prisoners of War of 12 August 1949, Articles 1 and 4(2). Article 1 imposes on High Contracting Parties the duty to ensure the respect of the treaty in all circumstances, thus requiring them to have a system in which all their representatives, such as commanders, will comply with its provisions; Article 4(2) requires militias to be commanded by a responsible person.

[44] United States Supreme Court, *In re Yamashita*, 327 U.S. 1, Judgment, 4 February 1946.

[45] More information is available at SHARP, http://www.sexualassault.army.mil/index.cfm, last accessed on 23 November 2014.

[46] See "'The Invisible War' Exposes Rape and Sexual Assault in the Military", in The Madeleine Brand Show, 21 June 2012, available at http://www.scpr.org/programs/madeleine-brand/2012/06/21/27065/the-invisible-war-exposes-rape-and-sexual-assault-/, last accessed on 23 November 2014.

---

be tolerated. We must reaffirm a commitment to an environment of mutual respect, dignity and fair treatment.[47]

Military sexual abuse can be a greater menace than combat. As stated by the former California Democratic Representative, Jane Harman, in testimony before a July 2008 House panel investigating the military's handling of sexual assault reports: "A woman who signs up to protect her country is more likely to be raped by a fellow soldier than killed by enemy fire".[48]

Exposure to this kind of misconduct is probably more likely to occur if those suspected of having committed core international crimes – in particular gender-based violence – against third parties are not brought to justice. If a military serviceman commits rape or other gender-based violence qualifying as a war crime or a crime against humanity against civilians, he may as well commit the same conduct against his fellow soldiers. Therefore, prosecution of serious international crimes by the armed forces also serves the interests of the servicemen, regardless of their rank.

14.3. Self-Interest Better Served by a Military Judiciary?

The existence of a military judicial system is a sign of willingness of the military not to let go unpunished serious offenders among its ranks. It can, therefore, contribute to its good image, both internally within the armed forces and externally among the public. It provides an easier access to justice for servicemen willing to report misconduct. In the battlefield, its expedience and the fact that its members are trained military personnel are conducive to relatively quick investigation and conclusion of the case, which in turn contributes to prevention. Members of the military justice authorities, moreover, fulfil the important task of advising military commanders on how to treat cases of misconduct.[49]

---

[47] "Army Policy on Harassment" Department of the Army, Washington, DC, 31 July 2008, available at www.bragg.army.mil/directorates/eeo/Documents/ArmyEEO_PL.pdf, last accessed on 6 March 2015.

[48] See H. Patricia Hynes, "Military Sexual Abuse: a Greater Menace Than Combat", in *Truthout*, 26 January 2012, available at http://truth-out.org/news/item/6299:military-sexual-abuse-a-greater-menace-than-combat, last accessed on 23 November 2014.

[49] "Übertragung der Aufgaben der Militärjustiz an die zivilen Justizbehörden", Bericht des Bundesrates vom 16. September 2011 in Erfüllung des Postulats der Kommission für Rechtsfragen des Ständerats 08.3290 ['Federal Council Report', 16 September 2011], p. 27 (https://www.legal-tools.org/doc/d3c130/).

A military judicial system, however, will only serve the armed forces' interest in prosecuting offenders if several conditions are met, in particular independence, transparency and fairness of the system. Judgments should be made publicly available and trials should not be misused for political purposes or propaganda.

If the work done by the military justice is good, this will automatically have a positive resonance in the public opinion and contribute to the good reputation of the armed forces. In Switzerland, for instance, following the implementation of the ICC Statute and the entry into force on 1 January 2011 of the new Criminal Code and Military Criminal Code,[50] military jurisdiction is maintained over war crimes committed by or against Swiss nationals, and/or within the framework of an armed conflict to which Switzerland is a party.[51] Jurisdiction over war crimes committed by foreigners is delegated to the civilian authorities,[52] primarily out of consideration of resources. The reason behind this mixed approach,[53] which was preferred to a complete handover of all cases to the civilian judicial authorities, was that the military has more know-how and experience with regard to this kind of offence, the nature of which is military. This was also highlighted in the Swiss Federal Council's report on the delegation of the tasks of the Swiss Military Justice of 16 September 2011,[54] which concluded that its continued existence was justified by the fact that it is a specialised judiciary. The report also stressed its procedural advantages, in particular its speediness in conducting preliminary investigations and thus in preventing further occurrences.[55] The report, along with the above-mentioned trial on racial discrimination, show that the military prosecution of war crimes committed by servicemen will contribute to the good reputation, image and the proper functioning of the military.

---

[50] Loi fédérale portant modification de lois fédérales en vue de la mise en œuvre du Statut de Rome de la Cour pénale internationale, FF 2010 3889, 18 June 2010 (https://www.legal-tools.org/doc/dc9068/).

[51] Articles 3 and 5, MCC. See also Message to the Parliament: Botschaft über die Änderung von Bundesgesetzen zur Umsetzung des Römer Statuts des Internationalen Strafgerichtshofs vom 23. April 2008, BBl 2008 3863, p. 3971.

[52] *Ibid.*, Articles 448/449.

[53] Loi fédérale portant modification de lois fédérales en vue de la mise en œuvre du Statut de Rome de la Cour pénale international, Projet, FF 2008 3565 (https://www.legal-tools.org/doc/486cd9/).

[54] Federal Council Report, 2011, see *supra* note 49.

[55] *Ibid.*, p. 2.

14.4. Conclusions

The international criminal law community and the military may have different interests in ensuring the prosecution of military personnel suspected of core international crimes: the former may pursue a sense of justice and belief in the peace-enforcing role of international criminal justice (for example, via the creation of international tribunals such as the ICTY or ICTR); the latter, on the other hand, may be interested in safeguarding its good image and reputation, which are key factors for the success of most military operations, particularly PSOs, and in maintaining the necessary political and financial support. The members of the military, then, have an interest in working in a 'safe environment', where troops are disciplined and thus easier to command and control and where the superiors have a lower risk to incur criminal responsibility for the misconduct of their subordinates. A good climate and working environment also contribute to the identification of the servicemen with the military as an employer, thus facilitating the creation of a corporate spirit and identity which, again, contribute to mission accomplishment.

This chapter also shows that a military judicial system may better serve this self-interest, as long as it is independent, fair and transparent. A system unable to meet these conditions would only be counterproductive.

In sum, notwithstanding the different kinds of self-interest of the international criminal law community and the military in the prosecution of core international crimes, the two may work hand in hand. The self-interest of the armed forces identified in this chapter may provide a good argument to win over the military as a partner in the prosecution of core international crimes. In doing so, however, it is important to monitor the proceedings to ensure that they are conducted pursuant to fair trial standards and not misused for propaganda or political purposes. To use Machiavelli's words, in this sense, the end – justice, may justify the means – the use of self-interest arguments.

15

Troop Discipline, the Rule of Law and Mission Operational Effectiveness in Conflict-Affected States

Róisín Burke*

> After the organization of troops, military discipline is the first matter that presents itself. It is the soul of armies. If it is not established with wisdom and maintained with unshakeable resolution you will have no soldiers. Regiments and armies will only be contemptible, armed mobs, more dangerous to their own country than to the enemy.[1]
>
> *Maurice de Saxe*

The international community has an interest in re-establishing the rule of law in conflict-affected, failing or failed states, given the potential impact of regional instability on international peace and security. Tasks relating to re-establishment of the rule of law, the protection of civilians and the promotion of human rights are increasingly inserted in peace operation mandates and the mandates of other multinational forces. Peacekeeping and other multinational military operations are gradually more multidimensional in nature and require frequent civilian-military engagements. Soldiers are often required to conduct a broad array of tasks which may include disarmament, demobilisation and reintegration of former combatants; economic and social development activities; promotion of human rights; security sector reform; reconstruction and capacity building activities with security sector and governance actors; counter-insurgency operations; addressing sexual and gender-based violence; and even transitional administration. A component of this often includes working with host

* **Róisín Burke** is an Irish Research Council Government of Ireland Postdoctoral Research Fellow, Irish Centre for Human Rights, National University of Ireland Galway, and an Attorney-at-Law, New York State. She is the author of *Sexual Exploitation and Abuse by UN Military Contingents: Moving Beyond the Current Status Quo and Responsibility under International Law*, Brill, 2014.

[1]   Marshal Maurice de Saxe (1696–1750), *My Reveries Upon the Art of War*, first published in 1757, quoted in John Fisher, "Worst Case Scenario", Brief to the Special Advisory Committee on Military Justice and Policing, Office of the Judge Advocate General, Department of National Defence, Ottawa, 1997, p. 4.

state armed forces in relation to security sector reform. This may involve activities aimed at increasing professionalism, knowledge of and adherence to human rights standards and international humanitarian law, and ensuring accountability of host state armed forces. Where the international community or foreign states deploy armed forces to conflict-affected states, these forces must themselves be governed by the rule of law if they are to be effective.

This chapter will reflect on why effective investigation and, where appropriate, prosecution of military personnel alleged to have committed international and other serious crimes in host states are in the interest of armed forces deployed on peace operations or other missions, and their sending states. Such reasons may include ethical and moral values, self-regulation and internal discipline of armed forces, the image of the armed forces and their states, their relationship with host state populations and indeed their home public,[2] erosion of military justice systems,[3] operational effectiveness and legitimacy, and the promotion of the rule of law.[4] This applies both to peacekeeping and other military operations.[5]

---

[2] For instance, Philip Alston highlighted the failure of the US to conduct on-site trials of soldiers committing serious crimes in Afghanistan and to convey any outcomes to local Afghanis. UN Human Rights Council, *Report of the Special Rapporteur on Extrajudicial, Summary and Arbitrary Executions, Philip Alston: Addendum: Mission to the United States of America*, 11th session, Agenda Item 3, UN Doc. A/HRC/11/2/Add.5, 28 May 2009, p. 24, paras. 49–50.

[3] See, for example, Commission on Human Rights, Issue of the Administration of Justice through Military Tribunals, 55th, Provisional Agenda Item 3, E/CN.4/Sub.2/2003/4, 27 June 2003, p. 16–17.

[4] See Franklin D. Rosenblatt, "Non-Deployable: The Court-Martial System in Combat from 2001 to 2009", in *The Army Lawyer*, 2010, vol. 448, pp. 27–28. As stated by Michael Gibson: "In other words, it is necessary to be both principled and pragmatic. In military parlance, states and their armed forces will need to be persuaded that adherence to such principles will be a 'force-multiplier' rather than an 'ivory tower' obstacle to operational effectiveness". Michael Gibson, "International Human Rights Law and the Administration of Justice through Military Tribunals: Preserving Utility while Precluding Impunity", in *Journal of International Law and International Relations*, 2008, vol. 4, no. 1, p. 13.

[5] General Assembly, *Report of the Special Committee on Peacekeeping Operations 2011 Substantive Session*, New York, 22 February – 18 March and 9 May 2011, 65th session, UN Doc. A/65/19, para. 48.

15.1. Instances of Crimes and Troop Discipline

Crimes have been committed in the context of military operations world-wide, be they war crimes, crimes against humanity, murder, detainee mis-treatment, kidnapping, assault, sexual offences both within and outside the military, sexual exploitation, trafficking and smuggling, among others. Such crimes are often perpetrated by state armed forces at home and in the context of many forms of military deployments, including in peace operations, counter-insurgency operations and situations of armed con-flict.

For instance, in recent years, cases involving crimes by US and British troops in Afghanistan and Iraq have been highly publicised and detrimental to state operational objectives. The torture, sexual humiliation and general mistreatment of Abu Ghraib detainees is one of the most prominent cases of serious human rights violations by soldiers in recent times. The incidents have had deleterious effects on the US's public im-age at home, in Iraq and abroad. This, in turn, has had a negative impact on the US war effort in Iraq, not least by alienating the public, but also with images of the degradation and abuse of detainees being manipulated and used as propaganda against the US by insurgents and others. As stat-ed, the support of local populations is of strategic importance in all types of military deployments, including counter-insurgency and peace opera-tions. In a report conducted on abuses in Abu Ghraib it was noted that for young soldiers in particular, "it is important that standards of behaviour be *clear and explicit* throughout all phases of an operation and that *lead-ers at all levels represent and reinforce those standards*".[6]

In March 2006, in the *Mahmoudiyah* case, five US soldiers de-ployed to Iraq were involved in the abhorrent rape and killing of a 14-year-old Iraqi girl. The soldiers spotted the girl at a checkpoint. While drinking, the soldiers planned to enter the girl's home – where they knew only one male family member was present – in order to rape her. They murdered the girl's parents, her six-year old sister and the girl herself, subsequent to gang raping her. The girl's body was then burned in an ef-fort to destroy evidence. The soldiers were sentenced to between five and

---

[6] Paul Bartone, "Lessons of Abu Ghraib: Understanding and Preventing Prisoner Abuse in Military Operations", in *Defence Horizons*, 2008, no. 64, p. 1 (emphasis added), available at http://permanent.access.gpo.gov/LPS105635/LPS105635/www.ndu.edu/CTNSP/docUploaded/DefenseHorizon64.pdf, last accessed on 31 January 2014.

100 years' imprisonment.[7] The incident led to calls for revenge by insurgents and others. Allegedly in retaliation for the rape and killings, insurgents beheaded two US soldiers in the same vicinity and threatened to kill others.[8]

The potential implications crimes have on the armed forces, their image and how they operate, are similarly illustrated in the Somali incident involving the murder of Shidane Abukar Arone, a Somali teenager, by Canadian soldiers on 16 March 1993. The teenager was raped with a baton and then brutally beaten to death while in the Canadian soldiers' custody. The Somalia Inquiry was commissioned by the Canadian government subsequent to this and other abuses of civilians, including children, by members of the Canadian Airborne Regiment while deployed on the UN peace operation in Somalia during the 1990s. The commissioners noted that poor leadership, lack of accountability, problems with the chain of command, poor discipline, inadequate selection process of soldiers deployed, inadequate training and theatre readiness, insufficient planning, lack of transparency and flaws within the military justice system all contributed to the conduct of the soldiers in question. This led to an overhaul of the military justice system and placed the military and its culture under public and government scrutiny – a process lasting for years.[9]

The hyper-masculine culture prevalent in military environments is well recognised and may well contribute to some soldiers engaging in

---

7   "'I didn't think of Iraqis as humans,' says U.S. Soldier who Raped 14-year-old Girl before Killing her and her Family", in *Daily Mail*, 21 December 2010, available at http://www.dailymail.co.uk/news/article-1340207/I-didnt-think-Iraqis-humans-says-U-S-soldier-raped-14-year-old-girl-killing-her-family.html, last accessed on 5 December 2014; Associated Press, "Former US Soldier Found Guilty of Raping and Shooting Iraqi Girl: Steven Dale Green Faces Possible Death Sentence for Fatal Attack on 14-year-old after Killing her Parents and Sister", in *The Guardian*, 8 May 2009.

8   John M. Hackel, "Planning for the 'Strategic Case': A Proposal to Align the Handling of Marine Corps War Crimes Prosecutions with Counterinsurgency Doctrine", in *Naval Law Review*, 2009, vol. 57, pp. 239, 257–58; Julian E. Barnes, "US Sees Possible Links Between Incidents in Iraq", in *Los Angeles Times*, 5 July 2006.

9   Capstick notes, "institutional reform has been focused on the military justice system, 'mechanisms of voice' such as the CF Ombudsman, the Military Police, education and training, and CF command and control procedures". Colonel M.D. Capstick, "Defining the Culture: The Canadian Army in the 21st Century", in *Canadian Military Journal*, 2003, vol. 3, no. 1.

---

sexual harassment, violence or other misconduct.[10] There is a high rate of sexual crimes both within many national militaries and in the context of overseas deployments. Indeed, sexual exploitation and abuse of civilians by UN peacekeepers have proved a problematic issue for the UN for many years. Peacekeepers have been accused of rape, sex trafficking, rape disguised as prostitution, sexual abuse of minors, among other acts of sexual exploitation, violence and abuse.[11] This conduct has physical and psychological consequences for victims, not least the spread of HIV/AIDS.[12] Despite UN efforts aimed at promoting eradication of sexual exploitation and abuse by its peacekeepers they continue to be a problem. Part of the problem is the perception of impunity among peacekeepers and the lack of criminal accountability.[13]

Sexual misconduct by military personnel against other military personnel and civilians at home is also a problematic issue for some militaries. These types of incidents have spurred negative public and media reactions in recent years in, for example, the US and Australia. In the Australian case, *Re Colonel Aird*, Justice McHugh stated that "the prohibition against rape goes to the heart of maintaining discipline and morale in the Defence Force. Rape and other kinds of sexual assault are acts of violence. It is central to a disciplined defence force that its members are not persons who engage in uncontrolled violence".[14] Moreover, he observed that other defence force personnel are likely to be reluctant to serve alongside soldiers perpetrating such acts of abuse.[15]

---

[10] Major General C.W. Orme, *Beyond Compliance: Professionalism, Trust and Capability in the Australian Profession of Arms*, Report of the Australian Defence Force Personal Conduct Review, Australian Government, Department of Defence, 2011, para. 31 (https://www.legal-tools.org/doc/a4486a/); Martin Friedland, *Controlling Misconduct in the Military*, Study Prepared for the Commission of Inquiry into the Deployment of Canadian Forces to Somalia, Minister of Public Works and Government Services Canada, Ottawa, 1997, p. 6 (https://www.legal-tools.org/doc/ed9d6a/).

[11] See generally Róisín Burke, *Sexual Exploitation and Abuse by UN Military Contingents: Moving Beyond the Current Status Quo and Responsibility under International Law*, Brill, Leiden, 2014.

[12] Harley Feldbaum, Kelly Lee and Preeti Patel, "The national security implications of HIV/AIDS", *PLoS Medicine*, 2006, vol. 3, no. 6; Burke, 2014, pp. 6–7, see *supra* note 11.

[13] See Burke, 2014, see *supra* note 11.

[14] *Re Colonel Aird; Ex parte Alpert* (2004) 209 ALR 311, para. 322.

[15] *Ibid.*

The involvement of UN peacekeepers in sex trafficking and patronising brothels where trafficked victims were held in the Balkans in the 1990s has been well publicised. The services of prostitutes fund and thereby incentivise trafficking of women and children.[16] This brought the UN mission as a whole into disrepute, undermining trust in the mission and its credibility with the local populace. Such conduct has been prevalent in many UN operations. Moreover, peacekeepers' patronage of brothels containing trafficking victims empowers or feeds into organised crime in already fragile and conflict-affected regions. These activities often occur alongside UN efforts to re-establish the rule of law.

In 2011, for example, an alleged gang rape of an 18-year-old Haitian boy by Uruguayan marines deployed on the UN operation in Haiti, was videoed on a mobile phone and disseminated widely across the Internet and elsewhere. Four of the five marines involved were convicted of acts of "private violence" which carried a light penalty of between three months and three years' imprisonment.[17] The case, along with other instances of sexual abuse and exploitation by UN peacekeepers, in addition to the outbreak of cholera attributed to the UN in Haiti, has given rise to widespread discontent among the local population.[18] There have been numerous protests across Haiti demanding that peacekeepers and the UN be held to account, and that ultimately the UN operation should leave Haiti. Sexual offences have led to the repatriation of whole contingents, which has obvious operational implications. In the Haitian case, for example, 114 members of a Sri Lankan UN military contingent were repatriated from Haiti in 2007 in response to allegations of sexual exploitation and abuse of minors. It is not apparent that any individuals were subsequently held to account.[19]

---

[16] Geneva Centre for the Democratic Control of Armed Forces, "Peacekeepers and Sexual Violence in Armed Conflict Report", 1 August 2007, p. 175.

[17] Kim Ives, "Haiti: Uruguay Will Withdraw from MINUSTAH, President Says Beginning of End of UN Occupation of Haiti", in *Global Research*, 30 October 2013, available at http://www.globalresearch.ca/haiti-uruguay-will-withdraw-from-minustah-president-says-beginning-of-end-of-un-occupation-of-haiti/5356424, last accessed on 10 December 2014.

[18] Associated Press, "Uruguay will Question Haitian about Alleged Abuse", in *Idaho Press-Tribune*, 11 January 2012, available at http://www.idahopress.com/news/world/uruguay-will-question-haitian-about-alleged-abuse/article_3b81f392-3d88-11e1-9343-001cc4c00fca.html, last accessed on 10 December 2014.

[19] Department of Peacekeeping Operations, United Nations, "Human Trafficking and United Nations Peacekeeping", Policy Paper, March 2004, para. 6, available at http://www.un.org/

15.2. Military Culture and Operational Environment

Military society is a highly complex, idiosyncratic set of multilevel social interactions.[20] It relies to some extent on group cohesion, institutionalism, parochialism, institutional hierarchies, regulation, structure, disciplinary control, bonding and camaraderie.[21] Major General C.W. Orme led a review of the Australian Defence Forces regarding deviations by armed forces personnel from acceptable norms of behaviour – in this case unacceptable sexual behaviour by Australian Defence Force soldiers. It was observed that soldiers often relate to 'insider' and 'outsider' identities. Within the military it posits that there is "a 'tight' culture in which shared identity, clear norms and role requirements, strong sanctions for deviations, and social stratification are exercised in a predominantly male culture".[22] This leads to the creation of 'insiders' and 'outsiders' in cultural and social interactions, wherein insiders dominate and outsiders are marginalised. 'Outsiders' may be women, ethic minorities, the local population where deployed abroad, homosexuals or others.[23] The review notes that in this dynamic "[t]he intersection of flaws in a masculine military culture, together with instances of alcohol-fuelled inhibition, has sometimes led to instances of unacceptable behavior".[24] This is why socialisation of positive norms or standards of conduct is of essence lest individuals succumb to negative group behaviour. As pointed out by a study by the International Committee of the Red Cross ('ICRC'), while individuals may not be killers, in a militarised group environment they may become part of the machinery that is. Greater value may be placed by individual soldiers on their group than others. The ICRC study finds that "when an-

---

womenwatch/news/documents/DPKOHumanTraffickingPolicy03-2004.pdf, last accessed on 10 December 2014; and Committee Against Torture, *Sri Lanka: Concluding Observations of the Committee Against Torture*, UN Doc. CAT/C/LKA/CO/3-4, 25 November 2011, para. 23.

[20] Eugene R. Fidell, Elizabeth L. Hillman and Dwight H. Sullivan (eds.), *Military Justice Cases and Materials: 2010–2011 Supplement*, LexisNexis, p. 6 (https://www.legal-tools.org/doc/dae5fe/).

[21] See also Joseph L. Soeters, Dona J. Winslow and Alise Weibull, "Military Culture", in Giuseppe Caforio (ed.), *Handbook of the Sociology of the Military*, Springer, New York, 2006, p. 237.

[22] Orme, 2011, para. 8, see *supra* note 10.

[23] *Ibid.*

[24] *Ibid.* See also Soeters *et al.*, 2006, p. 253, see *supra* note 21.

---

other group is declared to be an enemy, these tendencies become all the more acute. Thus, it is quite easy for the group to slide into criminal behaviour and perhaps even to end up promoting and encouraging it".[25]

Some have noted that another contributory factor to misconduct in military contexts is that soldiers deployed are predominantly male youths, between the ages of 18 to 25, who may have a greater propensity to engage in risk-taking behaviours.[26] These young soldiers are often deployed in dangerous environments and are given increasingly complex tasks having operational importance on multiple levels, including in rebuilding the rule of law in conflict-affected states. Young soldiers are often required to spend prolonged periods in volatile environments in small groups, while having little contact with family support structures. Members of these groups are sometimes killed while on duty.[27] Some may perceive a need, even at a subconscious level, to engage in ritualised behaviour to feel part of a group seen as the dominant group. Others may have difficulty coping. When such behaviour is negative it may have broader impacts on the group, as was seen in the cases of the Canadian Airborne Regiment in Somalia, Abu Ghraib, sexual abuse and exploitation in the context of UN operations, the mass killing of 24 Iraqi civilians in Haditha in 2006 by US forces,[28] among numerous examples.

Discipline is foremost ensured through social interactions and group dynamics within military environments, and the relationship between soldiers and their superiors. Training, strict orders and regulation of combatants, and effective criminal and disciplinary sanctions for breaches of standards, as pointed to by the ICRC study, are the most effective means of guarding against international humanitarian law violations by soldiers.[29] This is often also the case with respect to other forms of criminal behaviour and rights violations.

---

[25] Daniel Muñoz-Rojas and Jean-Jacques Frésard, "The Roots of Behaviour in War: Understanding and preventing IHL violations", in *International Review of the Red Cross*, 2004, vol. 853, p. 194.

[26] Orme, 2011, see *supra* note 10.

[27] *Ibid.*, para. 63.

[28] Michael Duffy, Tim McGirk and Bobby Ghosh, "The Ghosts of Haditha", in *Time*, 4 June 2006.

[29] Muñoz-Rojas and Frésard, 2004, p. 203, see *supra* note 25.

Lack of morale has been cited by a number of commentators as a contributory factor to lack of discipline. Feeding into this may be inadequate living conditions. This was pointed to by Prince Zeid, the United Nations High Commissioner for Human Rights, in the context of UN peace operations, when he found that lack of recreational facilities contributed to sexual exploitation and abuse by peacekeepers. Living and operational conditions were also likely a factor in Somalia when Canadian troops committed violations against Somali civilians. In an interview conducted by the author with a senior official of an international organisation working in Somalia, the interviewee noted that the lack of facilities, poor living standards and absence of recreational opportunities for African Union troops in Somalia, in addition to a dangerous operational environment, were likely to have contributed to the level of sexual exploitation and abuse by African Union troops of Somali civilians.[30]

15.3. Military Operations, Hearts and Minds

As Don Carrick has noted, "[t]he soldier of the future is likely to be not only on occasion soldier, policeman, 'hearts and minds' ambassador or general diplomat, but sometimes all of them alternately on a single occasion".[31] The protection of civilians is often a major purpose of multinational military operations. When soldiers deployed on peace or other operations commit serious criminal offences, human rights violations or violations of international humanitarian law in mission host states, it undermines efforts to promote rule of law, the protection of civilians and the ability to carry out mission mandates. Failures to hold soldiers to account may have broader implications for the mission's relationship with the local population, in creating perceptions of impunity and embedding distrust.[32] This is also the case where individuals are repatriated home, often never to face trial or to face what might be perceived as sham trials conducted for the

---

[30] Personal interview, August 2014, on file with the author.

[31] Don Carrick, "The Future of Ethics Education in the Military: A Comparative Analysis", in Paul Robinson, Nigel de Lee and Don Carrick (eds.), *Ethics Education in the Military*, Ashgate, Burlington, VT, 2008, p. 191.

[32] For example, civilians in Haiti staged protests requesting the UN to leave in response to allegations of sexual crimes by peacekeepers against minors and lack of transparent and effective investigation and prosecution of such. Associated Press, 2012, see *supra* note 18.

purpose of shielding the soldier.[33] Failures to hold soldiers to account put other military personnel at risk of retaliation. Additionally, there is a risk of repeat offences. This was emphasised by Judge Jeff Blackett in the recent *Blackman* case before British courts involving the murder of an unarmed injured Taliban member by a British Royal Marine.[34] Judge Blackett stated:

> Your actions have put at risk the lives of other British service personnel. You have provided ammunition to the terrorists whose propaganda portrays the British presence in Afghanistan as part of a war on Islam in which civilians are arbitrarily killed. That ammunition will no doubt be used in their programme of radicalisation. That could seriously undermine the reputation of British forces and ultimately the mission in Afghanistan [...] committing this sort of act could well provoke the enemy to act more brutally towards British troops in retribution or reprisal.[35]

Moreover, he stated that:

> Hearts and minds will not be won if British service personnel act with brutality and savagery. If they do not comply with the law they will quickly lose the support and confidence of those they seek to protect, as well as the international community. [...] You treated that Afghan man with contempt and murdered him in cold blood. [...] In one moment you undermined much of the good work done day in and day out by British forces.[36]

Negative media coverage with respect to a state's armed forces may have implications for internal morale of troops and affect their relationship with the public at home. As noted by John M. Hackel, the fact is the media, and indeed others, are more likely to publicise cases of human rights abuses by armed forces that have not been adequately dealt with by

---

[33] Timothy McCormack, "Their Atrocities and Our Misdemeanours: The Reticence of States to Try Their 'Own Nationals' for International Crimes", in Mark Lattimer and Philippe Sands (eds.), *Justice for Crimes Against Humanity*, Hart Publishing, Oxford, 2003, p. 107.

[34] *R v. Sgt Alexander Wayne Blackman*, Court Martial, Case Ref: 2012CM00442, 6 December 2013, Sentencing Remarks by HHJ Jeff Blackett, Judge Advocate General ('Blackman case').

[35] *Ibid.*

[36] *Ibid.*

states than instances promptly investigated and prosecuted.[37] Moreover, the media and others often place greater focus on what has been done badly than positive activities of armed forces in the context of overseas deployments. This has strategic and operational consequences. Soldiers have tended to be prosecuted with greater frequency where the media put significant pressure on states and the armed forces.[38]

In the current information age, access to the media and other information is readily available and easily disseminated both in home states, across the globe, and in areas of military deployment, via the Internet, television, radio and other sources. Moreover, the spread of information and propaganda is now rapid and easily subject to manipulation.[39] This has been apparent, for instance, in relation to US counter-insurgency operations in the context of its war on terror, where serious crimes by US soldiers have been used by insurgents to villainise the US.[40] Insurgents tend to rely on popular support. They often seek to delegitimise and demonise counter-insurgents. In essence, this requires 'winning hearts and minds'. Counter-insurgents, generally represented by states, tend to be held to a higher moral standard than that which applies to insurgents. It is to the strategic advantage of those involved in counter-insurgency efforts, or other types of military operations, to build good relationships with local and international media and encourage them to report positively on their activities.[41]

Commentators have highlighted the frequent complete failure to convey to local populations the progress and results of any investigations into alleged crimes by soldiers, including serious criminal offences, some of which may amount to war crimes. Local populations often have no opportunity to attend courts martial or any other form of hearing, and they often never hear of case outcomes.[42] This creates perceptions of impunity, ambivalence and double standards. This was highlighted, for example, by

---

[37] Hackel, 2009, pp. 255, see *supra* note 8.

[38] *Ibid.*, pp. 254–55.

[39] *Ibid.*, p. 257.

[40] See, generally, Dale Walton, "Victory through Villainization: Atrocity, Global Opinion, and Insurgent Strategic Advantage", in *Civil Wars*, 2012, vol. 14, no. 1, pp. 123–40.

[41] See, generally, US Department of the Army, *Field Manual, Counterinsurgency*, US Department of Army, Washington, DC, 2006.

[42] Rosenblatt, 2010, p. 26, see *supra* note 4.

the Special Rapporteur on extrajudicial, summary and arbitrary executions, Philip Alston, in relation to cases against US soldiers for unlawful killings in Afghanistan and Iraq. Alston notes that in some instances there was a lack of adequate investigations, use of administrative procedures where a criminal prosecution should have ensued, and inadequate or lenient punishments.[43]

Today's reality is that many military operations take place in close proximity to civilian populations. Therefore, it is necessary to promote a good rapport with host state civilians and national authorities. Where crimes by military personnel, in particular against civilians, are overlooked, it is not conducive to building these relationships. Equally, as highlighted by Olivier Bangerter, it is not good for the morale of troops.[44] Militaries, states and international or regional organisations concerned with portraying their military interventions as legitimate and well intentioned should be conscious of these consequences. That stated, where this is less of a concern, reputation may not have a similar impact on compliance.[45]

Moreover, there are broader national considerations. As noted by Christopher Borgen, "[i]nternational law is both the language and the grammar of international relations".[46] Failures by soldiers to adhere to certain international legal standards have implications for states in the realm of international relations. States have an interest in maintaining the moral high ground and fostering good international relations. Additionally, there is a clear link between the reputation of a state and state responsibility for the maintenance of disciplined armed forces. A state's fear of loss

---

[43] UN Human Rights Council, 2009, pp. 24–26, see *supra* note 2.

[44] Olivier Bangerter, "Reasons Why Armed Groups Choose to Respect International Humanitarian Law or Not", in *International Review of the Red Cross,* 2011, vol. 93, pp. 353, 362; and Hugo Slim and Deborah Mancini-Griffoli, *Interpreting Violence: Anti-Civilian Thinking and Practice and How to Argue Against it More Effectively*, Centre for Humanitarian Dialogue, Geneva, 2007, p. 25.

[45] Heike Krieger, "A Turn to Non-State Actors: Inducing Compliance with International Humanitarian Law in War-Torn Areas of Limited Statehood", in *SFB-Governance Working Group Paper*, 2013, no. 62, p. 20 (https://www.legal-tools.org/doc/a76ff9/).

[46] Christopher Borgen, "Hearts and Minds and Law: Legal Compliance and Diplomatic Persuasion", in *South Texas Law Review,* 2009, vol. 50, pp. 769, 771.

of reputation for its armed forces' violations of international law is significant both at international and domestic levels.[47]

15.4. Discipline, Operational Effectiveness and Control

Criminal offences by soldiers have serious operational consequences, some touched on already, including undermining legitimacy of the operations and the trust of local counterparts, and efforts to establish or re-establish security and the rule of law in fragile states. Bangerter aptly points to two primary reasons armed groups see it to their advantage to respect international humanitarian law. The first is their reputation and image. The second is military advantage.[48] States also have obligations to prevent and hold to account soldiers committing human rights or international humanitarian law violations. Discipline can be even more difficult to ensure, but even more essential to control, in multinational deployments. Part of the difficulty could be the diverse and sometimes unclear command and control structures, ambiguous regulations, diversity of tasks and difficult operational environments. States have an interest in the effectiveness of UN peace operations as an instrument of international peace and security.[49] Where there is a failure to act as a disciplined whole, it may result in disrespect from the civilian population, as was the case in Somalia, the Democratic Republic of Congo, Haiti, and numerous other operations.

In the late 19th century, Captain J.F. Daniell posited that

> [t]he great aim and object of all discipline is not only to maintain order and to ensure obedience and submission to authority, but also to produce and establish that cohesion between the individuals composing an army, which is essential if complete success is to be obtained in the operations in which it may happen to be engaged.[50]

---

[47] On reputation and compliance with international law see, for example, Andrew T. Guzman, "Reputation and International Law", in *Georgia Journal of International and Comparative Law*, 2006, vol. 38, p. 379.

[48] Bangerter, 2011, pp. 353–84, see *supra* note 44.

[49] Ganesh Sitaraman, "Credibility and War Powers", in *Harvard Law Review*, 2013/2014, vol. 127, pp. 123, 131.

[50] Captain J.F. Daniell, "'Discipline': Its Importance to an Armed Force, and the Best Means of Promoting and Maintaining It", in *Royal United Service Institution Journal*, 1889/1890, vol. 33, no. 148, p. 335.

He highlighted that disciplinary failures lead to barbarity not only against the enemy but also against inhabitants of host states, leading to discontent and local resistance.[51] Captain M.D. Capstick, paraphrasing one commentator, notes that discipline and obedience within military are premised on three basic elements: 1) understanding by soldiers of the value of discipline; 2) reward for discipline; and 3) sanctions for disciplinary failures.[52] In order to ensure military cohesion and effectiveness, the military maintains a hierarchical structure which requires stringent obedience to superiors.[53] Military commanders play an integral role in maintaining a system of mutual respect, moral behaviour, group cohesion and discipline among subordinates.[54] Failures to hold individuals to account for crimes undermine this.[55] A weak commander can therefore have deleterious consequences for the good behaviour of armed forces. This has been recognised in international criminal law.[56] Article 87(1) of Additional Protocol I to the Geneva Conventions requires military commanders "with respect to members of the armed forces under their command and other persons under their control, to prevent and, where necessary, to suppress and to report to competent authorities breaches of the Conventions and of this Protocol".[57] It also requires commanders to take disciplinary or penal action against those soldiers in breach of international humanitarian law.[58] Effec-

---

[51] *Ibid.*, p. 336.

[52] Capstick, 2003, p. 14, see *supra* note 9.

[53] Edwin R. Micewski, "Military Morals and Societal Values: Military Virtue versus Bureaucratic Reality", in Edwin R. Micewski (ed.), *Civil-Military Aspects of Military Ethics*, Austrian National Defence Academy Vienna, 2003, pp. 22–23.

[54] Capstick, 2003, p. 15, see *supra* note 9; Hans Born and Ian Leigh, *Handbook on Human Rights and Fundamental Rights of Armed Personnel*, OSCE Office for Democratic Institutions and Human Rights (ODIHR), Warsaw, 2008 (https://www.legal-tools.org/doc/d61b95/); Friedland, 1997, p. 6, see *supra* note 10; François Lesieur, "A New Appeal to Canadian Military Justice: Constitutionality of Summary Trials under Charter 11(d)", MA dissertation, University of Ottawa, 2011, p. 15; see, for example, US Department of Defense, *Report to Honorable Wilber M. Brucker, Secretary of the Army by Committee on the Uniform Code of Military Justice, Good Order, and Discipline in the Army* (OCLC 31702839), Washington, DC, pp. 11–14.

[55] Steven Smart, "Setting the Record Straight: The Military Justice System and Sexual Assault", 12 July 2012 (https://www.legal-tools.org/doc/b5b458/).

[56] See also Burke, 2014, pp. 54–55, *supra* note 11.

[57] Article 87, Protocol Additional to the Geneva Conventions of 12 August 1949, and Relating to the Protection of Victims of International Armed Conflicts, opened for signature 12 December 1977, 1125 UNTS 3 (entered into force on 7 December 1978).

[58] *Ibid.*

---

tive investigation and prosecution indicate to other would-be perpetrators
that certain conduct is not tolerable.[59]

Command responsibility was also highlighted as a key element in
the prevention of sexual exploitation and in ensuring troop discipline and
accountability for such.[60] The model memorandum of understanding between the UN and troop-contributing states, a bilateral legal agreement,
requires commanders to ensure proper conduct of troops and to take action where appropriate. Commanders of UN contingents may now be held
responsible at least at some level for failures to do so.[61] In the context of
sexual offences and impunity of military personnel, UN Women has aptly
emphasised that "lower-level commanders" must "receive unambiguous
directives that there are no 'rape cultures', only cultures of impunity, and
that there can be no security without women's security".[62]

Discipline is often used as a means of military socialisation, enabling soldiers to obey orders and carry out their duties effectively. Internal
discipline and self-regulation are perceived by most militaries as essential
to operational effectiveness of armed forces and the profession of arms. It
is, therefore, in the self-interest of the military to ensure good discipline,
adherence to international law and accountability for non-compliance.[63]
According to Michael Gibson, "[o]perational effectiveness means the capacity of the armed forces of a country to effectively achieve the purpose
for which it is created and maintained: to conduct military operations on
the direction of the government of, and in service to the interests of, the

---

[59] Smart, 2012, see *supra* note 55.

[60] *Report of the Special Committee on Peacekeeping Operations*, 64th session, UN Doc.
A/64/19, 22 February–19 March 2010, paras. 48, 52.

[61] See Working Group on Contingent-owned Equipment, Manual on Policies and Procedures
Concerning the Reimbursements and Control of Contingent-Owned Equipment of
Troop/Police Contributors Participating in Peacekeeping Missions, 63rd session, Agenda
Item 132, UN Doc. A/C.5/63/18, 29 January 2009, ch. 9, Article 7*ter*.

[62] UNIFEM, United Nations Department of Peacekeeping Operations and UN Action against
Sexual Violence in Conflict, *Addressing Conflict-Related Sexual Violence: An Analytical
Inventory of Peacekeeping Practice*, UN Development Fund for Women, New York, 2010,
p. 35.

[63] This is an argument frequently utilised by the International Committee of the Red Cross,
See Steven R. Ratner, "Law Promotion Beyond Law Talk: The Red Cross, Persuasion, and
the Laws of War", in *European Journal of International Law*, 2011, vol. 22, no. 2, pp.
459, 478.

state".[64] Part of the overall purposes of military justice is to contribute to morale, discipline, control, respect for the law, respect for others, efficiency, peace and justice within the military, and consequently the overall achievement of the mission purpose.[65] As stipulated by Peter Rowe, discipline is pertinent when conducting extraterritorial operations given that "[t]he degree to which soldiers act as a disciplined body whilst forming part of a multinational force will largely determine the success of the operation in relation to the respect due to the civilian population".[66]

Many militaries across the world see the maintenance of military justice as integral to the functioning of their armed forces. The US *Manual for Courts-Martial* stipulates that "the purpose of military law is to promote justice, to assist in maintaining good order and discipline in the armed forces, to promote efficiency and effectiveness in the military establishment, and to strengthen the national security of the United States".[67] Canada's Bill C-15, Clause 62 (NDA s. 3012.1) provides that sentencing violations of the law by Canadian forces have two fundamental purposes, namely, "a) to promote the operational effectiveness of the Canadian Forces by contributing to the maintenance of discipline, efficiency and morale; and b) to contribute to respect for the law and the maintenance of a just peaceful and safe society".[68] For many militaries it seems that military discipline is perceived as having strategic and operational purposes. Discipline is an integral component of maintaining high standards of military professionalism.[69] Discipline is integral to cohesion, the sharing of values, loyalty to the military institution and the implementation of military directives and orders. Holding soldiers accused of serious crimes effectively to account within this system, and publicising such,

---

[64] Gibson, 2008, p. 10, see *supra* note 4.

[65] *Ibid.*

[66] Peter Rowe, *The Impact of Human Rights Law on Armed Forces*, Cambridge University Press, Cambridge, 2006, p. 225.

[67] United States, Department of Defense, *Manual for Courts-Martial*, US Government Printing Office, Washington, DC, 2008, pp. 1, 3.

[68] An Act to Amend the National Defence Act and to Make Consequential Amendments to Other Acts, Bill C-15, Clause 62 (NDA s. 3012.1), 2012.

[69] See, for example, "The Statement of Canadian Military Ethos", in *Duty With Honour: The Profession of Arms in Canada*, Chief of Defence Staff, Ottawa, 2003, p. 27 (https://www.legal-tools.org/doc/c7b14f/); and Smart, 2012, see *supra* note 55.

may guard against the erosion of military justice systems, which is occurring in many countries. We will return to this below.

Failure to maintain this discipline has broader implications than the
act itself; it undermines the army's ability to quickly consolidate and pursue gains and the aims of given mandates. According to the Queen's Regulations for the British Army, "[d]iscipline, comradeship, leadership, and
self respect form the basis of morale and of military efficiency".[70]

The behaviour of individuals or small groups of individuals can
have serious consequences for militaries and their ability to carry out their
missions while deployed abroad.[71] As already noted, crimes by soldiers
undermine trust and confidence in the armed forces both at home and
abroad.[72] This in itself is an incentive for effective regulation of armed
forces and for holding those who commit crimes adequately to account.
The British government recognised, for instance, the need for effective
action to be taken against soldiers complicit in the killing of Baha Mousa,
an Iraqi civilian, at the hands of British soldiers in Basra, Iraq. This was
partially due to possible negative implications it could have on British
operations in Iraq.[73]

Discipline is also key to control over armed forces. Disciplinary
failures are often demonstrative of inadequate control over military personnel by the army and state. As Rowe explains, militaries are trained in
and given access to weapons and technologies that ordinary civilians are
not, making the exercise of stringent control over forces essential.[74] Serious crimes such as international humanitarian law violations, and even
lesser disciplinary infractions, undermine control over armed forces. Mili-

---

[70] Command of Defence Council, Ministry of Defence, *Queen's Regulations for the Army,
1975*, Her Majesty's Stationery Office, London, 1976, para. 5.201.

[71] Orme, 2011, see *supra* note 10.

[72] See further, Bangerter, 2011, p. 364, see *supra* note 44. In the Dumford case before the US
courts, a soldier was charged with violating an order to engage in "safe sex" and aggravated assault. The individual was HIV-positive. The order had required the soldier to inform
partners prior to sex of the HIV infection. The court stated that this order had a military
objective, namely, not to spread the infection among the civilian population, and ensuring
the health and readiness of other service members, and that violating this order undermined this and discredits the military. *United States v. Dumford*, 30 M.J. 137 (CMA 1990),
137–38.

[73] See Rosenblatt, 2010, pp. 27–28, *supra* note 4.

[74] Rowe, 2006, p. 60, see *supra* note 66.

taries across the world see the maintenance of military justice systems as integral to the functioning of their armed forces, reinforcing the military chain of command, hierarchy, obedience, authority and group values. As noted by the Somalia Inquiry into abuses by Canadian forces in Somalia, with respect to discipline, "the more important usage in the military entails the application of control in order to harness energy and motivation to a collective end".[75] And as McDonald has suggested, "[a]n undisciplined military force is a greater danger to Canada than to any foreign enemy".[76]

Some argue that crimes are committed more frequently by individual soldiers where there is a break down in military discipline and control, enabling unscrupulous individuals to pursue self-interested ends, be they murder, sexual abuse and exploitation, trafficking and so forth.[77]

A number of normative end goals might be served by prosecuting peacekeepers or indeed other military actors, particularly where this is done in the host states. Prosecution can serve a number of values in a general context, including retribution, reconciliation, rehabilitation, deterrence, restoration, incapacitation, and expressivism or deontological purposes. In the context of crimes committed during military operations, peacekeeping or otherwise, perhaps the most significant of these goals are deterrence and the expressive or deontological purposes served by prosecutions. For deterrence to be effective perpetrators of crimes must be genuinely in fear of being held to account.[78] Deterrence operates on two levels, that of the individual and that of the broader community.[79] Deterrence requires a realistic threat of sanction. This is equally the case in a military context.[80]

---

[75] Canadian Department of National Defence, *Report of the Somalia Commission of Inquiry*, Minister of Public Works and Government Services Canada, Ottawa, 1997, vol. 2, "Discipline" ('Report of the Somalia Inquiry').

[76] R.A. McDonald, "The Trail of Discipline: The Historical Roots of Canadian Military Law", in *Canadian Forces JAG Journal*, 1985, vol. 1, pp. 1, 28.

[77] See Mark Osiel, "Obeying Orders: Atrocity, Military Discipline and the Law of War", in *California Law Review*, 1998, vol. 86, no. 5, p. 1030.

[78] Burke, 2014, pp. 227–30, see *supra* note 11.

[79] Robert D. Sloane, "The Expressive Capacity of International Punishment: The Limits of the National Law Analogy and the Potential of International Criminal Law", in *Stanford Journal of International Law*, 2007, vol. 43, pp. 39, 43.

[80] Daniell, 1889/1990, pp. 287, 309, see *supra* note 50.

In the context of military operations, punishment may deter other soldiers from committing offences where impunity is not permitted, and it may also deter members of the community in the host state, whether state security forces or members of the civilian population, from committing similar offences. Deterrence, according to one commentator, in the US Air Force context, "is best applied directly from commanders to individual Airmen". He notes that sending cases to a central prosecutor takes time and causes difficulties in forward deployment of air force personnel when discipline is required most urgently.[81] In recognition of the importance of maintaining discipline, during the second half of the 19th century, sanctions used against British soldiers involved in misconduct were particularly swift and harsh, with numerous soldiers even put to death for their crimes.[82]

Perceptions of impunity for crimes committed by deployed troops are also increasingly leading to calls to limit jurisdictional immunities granted under the terms of status of forces agreements ('SOFA').[83] SOFAs are essentially bilateral agreements between host states and states deploying forces, governing their status. In the context of deployments by international bodies such as the UN, SOFAs are agreed between the host state and the body. Failures, or perceived failures, to effectively hold US soldiers to account for crimes allegedly committed in Iraq, for instance, saw the Iraqi government and the US renegotiating the jurisdictional provisions of the SOFA with the US, so that Iraq might prosecute these soldiers for crimes committed while on its territory.[84] Specifically, the new bilateral agreement provides for primary and secondary jurisdiction depending on the crime committed and where it was committed. In essence, Iraq now has primary jurisdiction over off-duty criminal offences by US service members in Iraq where these constitute grave premeditated felonies. While the Iraqi government may waive this primary right to exercise its jurisdiction, should it not do so safeguards must be put in place to pro-

---

[81]   Smart, 2012, see *supra* note 55.

[82]   Friedland, 1997, p. 67, see *supra* note 10.

[83]   Associated Press, 2012, see *supra* note 18.

[84]   Rosenblatt, 2010, pp. 26, see *supra* note 4.

tect the rights of the accused and accord him with due process standards in line with the US Constitution.[85]

The Statute of the Special Court for Sierra Leone contains quite a unique provision regarding the jurisdictional immunities afforded to UN peacekeepers. While Article 1 grants the troop-contributing state primary jurisdiction over members of its armed forces deployed to the host state, it provides that should that state fail to exercise its jurisdiction, the Special Court for Sierra Leone possibly could. This rationale is in line with the principle of complementarity, where a state proves "unwilling or unable" to instigate genuine judicial processes for crimes committed overseas by state actors. The right to secondary jurisdiction is limited to circumstances wherein a state specially proposes that the Special Court for Sierra Leone exercise its jurisdiction and where the UN Security Council authorises the exercise of such jurisdiction. A parallel limitation is increasing being advocated by academics, legal practitioners, policymakers and others with respect to UN peacekeepers given failures to hold peacekeepers involved in sexual violence, abuse and exploitation against members of the civilian populations of host states to account. The complete lack of transparency in relation to these cases is also problematic. States deploying troops are likely to be very nervous about the erosion of the jurisdictional immunities granted to their soldiers. Therefore, it is in the interests of states to ensure, and be seen to ensure, effective investigations and prosecutions of soldiers committing serious criminal offences while deployed overseas.

15.5. Rule of Law and Security Sector Reform

Militaries are increasingly involved in a broad array of activities, including the protection of civilians, facilitating the delivery of aid, capacity building through mentorship and training of local armed forces, humanitarian intervention, tackling terrorism, assisting with the re-establishment of the rule of law, security sector reform, and generally in state-building and reconstruction processes in conflict-affected or fragile states. State-building and reconstruction activities have been central to UN interven-

---

[85] Agreement Between the United States of America and the Republic of Iraq on the Withdrawal of United States Forces from Iraq and the Organization of their Activities During their Temporary Presence in Iraq, US-Iraq, Article 12, 17 November 2008.

tions since the 1990s.[86] Such interventions may be conducted in the context of regional or international deployments, whether through the UN, NATO, Organisation for Security and Co-operation in Europe, the European Union, the African Union or others. Part of the purpose of these interventions has been to ward off regional instability and protect against widespread human rights abuses. The protection of civilians and rule of law and security-related activities are contained in Security Council resolutions establishing the mandates of most current UN peace operations.[87] Good governance, rule of law and stability operations are also key to counter-insurgency efforts. This is based on the premise that an effective means to prevent widespread human rights abuses, insurgency or terrorism is to (re)establish stable states, security, rule of law and good governance.[88]

Failed or failing states are often perceived as potential breathing grounds for terrorism.[89] External interventions, from the Cold War period on, and capacity building efforts to strengthen governance in weak or failed states have been perceived as necessary to ward off security threats and they are now a key component of many states' foreign policy.[90] Moreover, this is also related to state and international community concerns about promoting human rights, the rule of law, stable environments for investment, good governance, and forms part of broader efforts to

---

[86] See, for example, William B. Wood, "Post-Conflict Intervention Revisited: Relief, Reconstruction, Rehabilitation, and Reform", in *Fletcher Forum of World Affairs*, 2005, vol. 29, no. 1, pp. 119–20.

[87] See United Nations Peacekeeping, "Protection of Civilians", available at www.un.org/en/peacekeeping/issues/civilian.shtml, last accessed on 12 December 2014.

[88] US Department of Army, 2006, see *supra* note 41.

[89] Chester A. Crocker, "Engaging Failing States", in *Foreign Affairs*, 2003, vol. 82, no. 5, p. 32; Frances Fukuyama (ed.), *Nation-Building: Beyond Afghanistan and Iraq*, Johns Hopkins University Press, Baltimore, 2006, p. 2; Charles E. Tucker, "Cabbages and Kings: Bridging the Gap for More Effective Capacity-building", in *University of Pennsylvania Journal of International Law*, 2011, vol. 32, pp. 1329, 1335; President of the United States, *National Security Strategy*, May 2010, pp. 26–27, available at https://www.whitehouse.gov/sites/default/files/rss_viewer/national_security_strategy.pdf, last accessed on 2 November 2014. See also Nora Bensahel, Olger Oliker and Heather Peterson, *Improving Capacity for Stabilization and Reconstruction Operations*, RAND Corporation, Santa Monica, CA, 2009, pp. ix–x, 3–4.

[90] Frances Fukuyama, "National-Building and the Failure of Institutional Memory", in Fukuyama, 2006, pp. 1–2, see *supra* note 89. See also Michèle A. Flournoy, "Nation Building: Lessons Learned and Unlearned", in Fukuyama 2006, pp. 86–87, see *supra* note 89.

---

combat transnational crimes.[91] Crime in failing or failed states may have connections with corrupted political actors or state security forces, those in power, warlords and others.[92] Reform and capacity building of state security forces, including the military, are therefore often linked to state and international community concerns over threats to peace and security that weak governance entails.

Stabilisation activities are often prioritised in interventions in conflict-affected states, and may include disarmament demobilisation and reintegration, rule of law reform activities and security sector reforms ('SSR'). Thereafter, focus may shift to reconstruction activities such as promoting democracy, development of state institutions, capacity building of state institutions, reform of the education system, promoting economic activity, governance, promoting human rights and so forth.[93] In the long run, the two are interdependent.

There is no universally accepted definition of SSR. Sean McFate defines SSR as entailing efforts "to institutionalize a professional security sector that is effective, legitimate, apolitical, and accountable to the citizens it is sworn to protect".[94] While SSR is a distinct area to rule of law reform post-conflict, it nevertheless has significant links to and interdependence with the broader rule of law reform agenda. Akin to SSR, rule of law reform has no universally recognised definition and means different things to different actors, often depending on their objectives. Nevertheless, an often referred to definition was provided by UN Secretary-General, that rule of law

> refers to a principle of governance in which all persons, institutions and entities, public and private, including the State itself, are accountable to laws that are publicly promulgated, equally enforced and independently adjudicated, and which are consistent with international human rights norms and standards.[95]

---

[91] Crocker, 2003, p. 34, see *supra* note 86.

[92] *Ibid.*

[93] Bensahel *et al.*, 2009, pp. ix–x, 3–4, see *supra* note 89.

[94] Sean McFate, "Securing the Future: A Primer on Security Sector Reform in Conflict Countries", Special Report no. 209, United States Institute of Peace, Washington, DC, 2008, p. 2 (https://www.legal-tools.org/doc/7fd458/).

[95] United Nations, Report of the Secretary-General: The Rule of Law and Transitional Justice in Conflict and Post- Conflict Societies, UN Doc. S/2004/616, 23 August 2004.

Militaries often play an integral role in SSR and the re-establishment of the rule of law, and are frequently required to work with various national authorities and counterparts in SSR efforts in the context of humanitarian interventions, reconstruction and stability operations. This is particularly the case in volatile operational environments.[96] These efforts require leading by example. In many conflict-affected States this may require assisting national authorities with rebuilding the security sector from scratch or reforming existing structures and actors. There may be widespread civilian distrust of military and indeed other security sector personnel given that they may have been implicated in human rights abuses during or prior to the conflict. Part of the goal of SSR efforts is to build effective and accountable security sector institutions, which are disciplined and abide by rule of law and respect human rights,[97] so that they can provide security to the state and its civilian population. This often includes vetting, recruiting and training state armed forces and building their capacity to act as a professional army, including through reform and instilling norms of military professionalism, ethos and respect for human rights. Training may also extend to the police and to human rights education.[98] A key element for forces deployed abroad is to lead by example, particularly in the context of mentoring national counterparts. As noted by John Nagl and Paul Yingling, in the context of counter-insurgency, "[i]nsurgencies are defeated not by foreign powers but by indigenous forces".[99]

As noted, SSR and rule of law reform in conflict-affected states is often in the interests of states intervening or the broader international community where the end goal is to stabilise regions. Failures may have impacts on international or transnational crimes, terrorism, conflict and violence relapse, and implications for effective exit strategies for military interventions.[100] Vast amounts of money have gone into SSR programmes both in peacekeeping and other intervention contexts. For instance, in the

---

[96] Bensahel *et al.*, 2009, pp. 6–7, see *supra* note 89.

[97] UN Security Council, Report of the Secretary-General: Securing Peace and Development: The Role of the United Nations in Supporting Security Sector Reform, UN Doc. S/2008/39, 23 January 2008.

[98] See, for example, McFate, 2008, p. 15, see *supra* note 94.

[99] John Nagl and Paul Yingling, "New Rules for New Enemies", in *Armed Forces*, 2006, vol. 144, no. 3, pp. 25–26.

[100] McFate, 2008, pp. 3–4, see *supra* note 94.

context of its 1206 programme the US committed to spending USD 200–300 million a year on developing the capacity of foreign militaries to deal with terrorism and stability operations.[101]

By way of example, peacekeepers are increasingly required to undergo some form of gender training prior to deployment.[102] Moreover, they are frequently providing such training to national counterparts when engaging in SSR and rule of law reform activities in transitional and reconstruction phases. This was largely spurred by Security Council Resolutions on women, peace and security. Part of the aim of such training and capacity building is to transform attitudes that lead to discriminatory practices, in particular against women. This includes tackling gender-based violence and the inclusion of women on an equal basis in reconstruction and state-building endeavours. Activities have included mentoring and other supports by military personnel to national counterparts. These activities provide opportunities to imbue certain values, such as zero-tolerance for sexual violence and respect for international human rights standards. In 2010 guidelines on "Integrating a Gender Perspective into the Work of the United Nations Military in Peacekeeping Operations" were developed.[103] Training has also been provided to military peacekeepers, at least those deployed on UN operations, on the implementation of mandate requirements relating to women, peace and security. During conflict women and girls are often disproportionately affected by sexual violence, wherein rape is used as a tool of war, including by security sector personnel. An "Analytical Inventory of Peacekeeping Practice" to address conflict-related sexual violence was drawn up in 2010 in order to determine the contribution military components of UN operations can make to ending violence against women in the context of UN deployments.[104] Links are made between such efforts and building the trust and confidence of the

---

[101] Named after Section 1206 of the National Defense Authorization Act of 2006. *Ibid*, p. 6.

[102] See also Comfort Lamptey, "Gender Training in United Nations Peace Operations", Gender and Peacekeeping in Africa, Occasional Paper no. 5, p. 11.

[103] United Nations Department of Peacekeeping Operations and Department of Field Support, Guidelines: "Integrating a Gender Perspective into the Work of the United Nations Military in Peacekeeping Operations", Department of Peacekeeping Operations, New York, 2010 (https://www.legal-tools.org/doc/66e0ae/).

[104] UN Women, "Addressing Conflict-Related Sexual Violence: An Analytical Inventory of Peacekeeping Practice", United Nations Entity for Gender Equality and the Empowerment of Women, 2012, p. 32 (https://www.legal-tools.org/doc/64b143/).

local population, thereby contributing to mission operational effectiveness.

Where peacekeepers engage in sexual offences against the civilian
population, or indeed other members of their armed forces, this undermines the influence that gender training and capacity building can have in
conflict-affected states. These principles can have little impact on trans-
forming gender relations, in particular with respect to security sector actors, if those seeking to expose them cannot or will not adhere to them.
For instance, in recent months African Union Mission in Somalia
('AMISOM') peacekeepers have been providing Somali National Army
forces with training on human rights, gender-based violence including
sexual violence, civilian protection, international humanitarian law and
military discipline.[105] These training activities coincided with the 2014
release of a report by Human Rights Watch of widespread sexual abuse
and exploitation by AMISOM troops deployed to Somalia.[106] This has
obvious implications.

In the Democratic Republic of Congo sexual offences are widespread. The international community, often with the support of military
personnel, has made significant efforts to curb such abuses. Where soldiers are instead involved in the commission of sexual offences, as has
been the case with UN peacekeepers in the Democratic Republic of Congo, this undermines these efforts. Impunity is seen as the norm.[107] As
highlighted by Muñoz-Rojas and Frésard,

> [a]uthorities should take action, even for offences which are
> less serious than a war crime, so as to ensure the discipline
> of their troops and avoid entering a spiral of violence in
> which violations may become not only more and more

---

[105] "Ethiopian peacekeepers conduct human rights training for Somalia forces in Baidoa", in
AMISOM News, available at http://amisom-au.org/2014/03/ethiopian-peacekeepers-
conduct-human-rights-training-for-somalia-forces-in-baidoa/, last accessed on 2 November
2014.

[106] Human Rights Watch, "'The Power These Men Have Over Us': Sexual Exploitation and
Abuse by African Union Forces in Somalia", Human Rights Watch Report, September
2014, available at http://www.hrw.org/sites/default/files/reports/somalia0914_ForUp
load.pdf, last accessed on 2 December 2014.

[107] United Nations Department of Peacekeeping Operations, "The Comprehensive Report on
Lessons Learned from United Nations Operation In Somalia (UNOSOM)", Lessons
Learned Unit, New York, 1995, para. 57 ('Comprehensive Report').

serious but also more and more acceptable in the eyes of those who commit them.[108]

Failure to hold individuals to account for sexual offences or other criminal offences may have deleterious consequences for military discipline[109] and undermine efforts to address gender-based violence and discrimination. It creates a perception of impunity not only among peacekeepers but also national counterparts and other locals. Justice needs to be seen to be done and individuals need to be held to account in the host state if perceptions of impunity are to be altered. In terms of training soldiers to respect certain ethics or values, including in the context of capacity building, command or mentorship relationships, as noted by Robinson, "[t]here is little point in teaching individuals a particular form of behavior, if they can see that the in-situation to which they belong in practice rewards and values other behavior".[110]

As noted, the success of counter-insurgency operations and indeed peace operations tends to rely heavily on good civil-military relations, civilian protection and activities targeted at improving the lives of the civilian population. Trust of the local population is beneficial on numerous levels, not least in terms of intelligence gathering and the perceived legitimacy of the operation. Moreover, as Nagl and Yingling note, trust "fosters participation in political processes and ethnic/sectarian reconciliation and encourages risk-taking and investment necessary for economic reconstruction".[111] Failures to foster good civil-military relations may lead to the civilian population supporting insurgents, militia groups or other opponents undermining stabilisation activities such as promotion of the rule of law.[112]

Accountability of soldiers deployed to peace-building and other operations for their criminal conduct or human rights violations may well have a rule of law demonstration effect in host states. Namely, it may have a normative effect in demonstrating that nobody is above the law

---

[108] Muñoz-Rojas and Frésard, 2004, p. 204, see *supra* note 25.

[109] William C. Westmoreland and George S. Prugh, "Judges in Command: The Judicialized Uniform Code of Military Justice in Combat", in *Harvard Journal of Law and Public Policy*, 1980, vol. 3, p. 60.

[110] Paul Robinson, "Ethics Training and Development in the Military", in *Parameters: US Army War College Quarterly*, 2007, vol. 37, no. 1, pp. 23, 34.

[111] Nagl and Yingling, 2006, pp. 25–26, see *supra* note 99.

[112] *Ibid.*

and in expressing condemnation for serious crimes by military personnel
to the local populace, security sector and civilians alike. This may be useful, for instance, in efforts to tackle sexual violence in many countries affected by conflict. Action taken against soldiers committing serious
crimes should be communicated both to local populations and other
peacekeeping personnel. Where actions are not taken, or where such
crimes or misconduct arise in the first place, it undermines efforts to work
with host state authorities and national counterparts. Additionally, it taints
the relationship between actors such as the UN, NATO, the European Union and the African Union and the local population.

Compliance with international standards by militaries is often based
on expectations of reciprocity, namely restraint mirrors restraint, despite
international humanitarian law stipulating otherwise.[113] Soldiers' failures
to comply with international standards, whether international humanitarian law, international human rights law or other norms or values, show that
there is a failure to practise what they themselves preach.[114] Those seeking to defeat insurgents, or to re-establish rule of law and security, must
themselves abide by host state laws, international human rights standards
and the laws of war. Moreover, failure to abide by the law risks reprisals
from other belligerent forces, and risks losing the hearts and minds of the
local population.[115] As some commentators have observed, brutality and
targeting weak foes and civilians bestows further brutality and fosters distrust among civilian populations.[116]

In a peacekeeping context or other interventions, winning the hearts
and minds of the local population may be a central goal. Moreover, failures in this regard may actually result in defeat of purpose, in particular
where establishing security and rule of law and security sector reforms are
the aims.[117] Maintaining high standards and respecting international law,
and holding those violating it to account, generates perceptions of legiti-

---

[113] Security Council, Report of the Secretary-General on the Protection of Civilians in Armed
Conflict, UN Doc. S/2013/689, 22 November 2013, para. 41.

[114] Krieger, 2013, p. 16, see *supra* note 45.

[115] Blackman case, see *supra* note 34.

[116] See John Robb, *Brave New War: The Next Stage of Terrorism and the End of Globaliza-
tion*, John Wiley, New York, 2007, p. 27.

[117] Rowe, 2006, p. 65, see *supra* note 66.

macy in the local populace and by national actors. The latter is of particular importance in a capacity building context.

15.6. Military Ethics and Moral Values

Since well before the Napoleonic Wars, state militaries have perceived themselves as being bound by a normative code or code of conduct, which goes hand in hand with the profession of arms. Such values include integrity, honour, loyalty to superiors, the military and country,[118] initiative, courage, respect for the rule of law and justice, self-discipline, respect for the professional image of the military and peace operations, and respect for human rights and international humanitarian law.[119] These are often contained in military codes of conduct, which may vary from state to state. International humanitarian law and the laws of war already legally regulate soldiers' behaviour during armed conflict. These are to a large extent a codification of norms governing professional and ethical conduct of soldiers.[120] However, these laws may not fully reflect codes of conduct or ethics by which a solider is or may feel bound by.[121] An ethical soldier is often perceived as a more effective soldier.[122] Virtues are often the corollary of expectations of pain or pleasure. Norms of behaviour are adopt-

---

[118] US Department of Army, *Field Manual No. 22-100, Army Leadership B-7*, US Department of the Army, Washington, DC, 1999, pp. 1–17.

[119] Stephen E. Wright, *Airforce Officer's Guide*, 36th ed., Stackpole Books, Mechanicsburg, PA, 2014, p. 4; Orme, 2011, see *supra* note 10; Daniel Lagacé-Roy, "The Profession of Arms and Competing Values: Making Sense", in *Elucidating the Future: Soldiers and their Civil-Military Environment*, Austrian Armed Forces, p. 126, (https://www.legal-tools.org/doc/49e828/); and William Lad Sessions, *Honor for Us: A Philosophical Analysis, Interpretation and Defense*, Continuum, London, 2008, p. 69.

[120] Micewski, 2003, pp. 22, 24, see *supra* note 53.

[121] See, for example, Convention for the Amelioration of the Conditions of the Wounded in Armed Forces in the Field, opened for signature 12 August 1949, 75 UNTS 31 (entered into force 21 October 1950); Convention for the Amelioration of the Conditions of the Wounded, Sick and Shipwrecked Members of the Armed Forces at Sea, opened for signature 12 August 1949, 75 UNTS 85 (entered into force 12 October 1950); Convention Relevant to the Treatment of Prisoners of War, opened for signature 12 August 1949, 75 UNTS 135 (entered into force 12 October 1950); Convention Relevant to the Protection of Civilian Persons in Time of War, opened for signature 12 August 1949, 75 UNTS 287 (entered into force 21 October 1950) ('Geneva Conventions'); and Mark J. Osiel, *Obeying Orders: Atrocity, Military Discipline and the Law of War*, Transaction Publishers, New Brunswick, NJ, 2002, p. 25.

[122] Jessica Wolfendale, "What is the Point of Teaching Ethics in the Military?", in Robinson, de Lee and Carrick, 2008, pp. 161, 166, see *supra* note 31.

---

ed from our role models, and become habitual. This applies equally to the military context.

Loyalty (which is key to functional militaries), team cohesion and camaraderie entails also discipline for the soldier.[123] Integrity involves values such as self-discipline, honesty, candour and conducting oneself in accordance with military regulations, and applicable laws and codes of conduct. Honour is professed as a fundamental value of most states' armed forces.[124] According to Michael Ignatieff, "[a] warrior's honour is a slender hope, but it may be all there is to separate war from savagery. And a corollary hope is that men can be trained to fight with honour. Armies train people to kill, but they also teach restraint and discipline".[125] Rain Liivoja posits that honour arises at two levels, that of the personal level and public level in terms of a collective sense of what is right and what is wrong.[126] Atrocities, or indeed crimes, committed by armed forces bring into disrepute the honour of the defence forces of a country as a whole. This was apparent, for instance, in public reactions in Uruguay, Canada and the US, wherein serious human rights violations or war crimes by armed forces from each of these countries, as mentioned previously, led to public outrage. In terms of the US deployment to Iraq, the intervention was termed illegitimate and abusive by many, even within the US.

The military, like other professions, such as the law and medicine, is governed by a self-regulated code of ethics. In one sense, in the military context, it distinguishes soldiers or warriors who are trained to use arms, inflict violence and kill for a given purpose, from being perceived as murderers or criminals by society and themselves.[127] Ethics are central to the

---

[123] Forrest C. Pogue, "George C. Marshall: Global Commander", in Harry Borowski (ed.), *The Harmon Memorial Lectures in Military History, 1959–1987*, Office of the Air Force History, Colorado, 1988, pp. 177, 190, 191–93.

[124] Richard A. Gabriel, *To Serve with Honor: A Treatise on Military Ethics and the Way of the Soldier*, Greenwood Press, Westport, CT, 1982; Paul Robinson, *Military Honour and the Conduct of War: From Ancient Greece to Iraq*, Routledge, London, 2006.

[125] Michael Ignatieff, *The Warrior's Honour: Ethnic War and the Modern Conscience*, Vintage, London, 1998, p. 157; on the honour of warriors, see Sessions, 2008, p. 62, see *supra* note 119.

[126] Rain Liivoja, "Law and Honor: Normative Pluralism in the Regulation of Military Conduct", in Jan Klabbers and Touko Piiparinen (eds.), *Normative Pluralism and International Law: Exploring Global Governance*, Cambridge University Press, Cambridge, 2013, pp. 143, 146–47.

[127] *Ibid.*, pp. 143, 146; See also, Slim and Mancini-Griffoli, 2007, p. 25, see *supra* note 44.

effective operation of the military and maintaining good relationships with civil society both at home and on deployment abroad, including in the context of peace operations, counter-insurgency operations and others.[128] Ethics generally relate to organisational codes of behaviour, whereas the term morals tends to be used to refer to the individual level.[129]

Historically, the military law of some states proscribed "conduct unbecoming of an officer and a gentleman",[130] generally prohibiting conduct that is considered "disgraceful" or "dishonourable". According to the US Uniform Code of Military Justice ('UCMJ'), this might include "acts of dishonesty, unfair dealing, indecency, indecorum, lawlessness, injustice, or cruelty".[131] A gentleman today is taken to refer to both men and women in this context.[132] Similarly, the UCMJ, like the military codes of many states, prohibits conduct to the "prejudice of good order and discipline" or which brings "discredit upon the armed forces".[133] This could encompass an array of conduct which may or may not be criminalised under sending state law but almost certainly should capture most violations of human rights of civilian populations of the host state, where not already criminalised. On the other hand, these provisions may be used to shield soldiers from more serious criminal charges carrying greater penalties, including specific crimes such as rape, drug trafficking, murder and so on.[134] Similar provisions may be found in the military laws of other states. The Australian Defence Force Discipline Act of 1982, for instance, prohibits conduct "likely to prejudice the discipline of, or bring discredit on, the Defence Force".[135] These provisions highlight in effect two operational consequences, the first being the reputation of the states concerned

---

[128] See, Ratner, 2011, p. 478, see *supra* note 63.

[129] George B. Rowell, "Marine Corps Values-Based Ethics Training: A Recipe to Reduce Misconduct", Strategy Research Project, US Army War College, 2003, p. 2.

[130] This has its roots in medieval codes of military chivalry. See Liivoja, 2013, pp. 152–54, *supra* note 126; and Keithe Nelson, "Conduct Expected of an Officer and a Gentleman: Ambiguity", in *US Air Force JAG Law Review*, 1970, vol. 12, pp. 124–41.

[131] See, for example, Article 133, United States Uniform Code of Military Justice, 10 UCMJ 832.

[132] *Ibid.*

[133] *Ibid.*

[134] Ives, 2013, see *supra* note 17; see also Burke, 2014, pp. 36–37, *supra* note 11.

[135] Australian Defence Force Discipline Act 1982, Section 61. See, similarly, Article 19, British Armed Forces Act 2006; and Canadian National Defence Act 1955, Section 129(1).

and their armed forces, the latter being the maintenance of order and discipline within the military.[136] In counter-insurgency operations in particular, but also in the case of peace operations, maintaining the moral high
ground may assist in securing both local and external co-operation.

In the *Semrau* case, involving the wrongful killing of an unarmed
injured insurgent by a Canadian commander who was mentoring Afghan
counterparts, the court stipulated that breaches of military discipline run
contrary to core values and training, and constitute disgraceful conduct.[137]
The court further stated that central to the profession of arms is the "management of violence" and putting into effect the will of the soldier's state
in line with the state's citizens' values. In the context of sexual misconduct by Australian armed forces, including the dissemination of sexual
pictures and videos portraying women in an abusive and degrading manner, Lieutenant General David Morrison, Chief of Army, condemned the
behaviour, stating that it had "not only brought the Australian Army into
disrepute, but has let down everyone of you and all of you whose past
service has won the respect of our nation".[138] He further stated that degrading and exploiting others in no way enhances military capability or
the traditions of the Australian Army. A similar reflection was made in
the Canadian context when it was stated that a state's armed forces are
integral to and must reflect the values of the society that they serve, be
they with respect to women's rights, sexual orientation or other normative
values.[139]

15.7. Erosion of Military Justice Systems

Across the world many militaries have been subject to separate systems of
military norms, laws and institutions regulating their behaviour. Military
justice systems vary significantly in terms of their jurisdictional scope

---

[136] For and explanation of these provisions, see US Rule for Courts-Martial, RCM. 60.c.(1)-
(3); *Mocicka v Chief of Army* (2003) ADFDAT 1 [13]-[14]; see also Liivoja, 2013, pp.
151–52, see *supra* note 126.

[137] *R. v. Semrau*, 2010 CM 4010 [9]–[10].

[138] "Chief of Army David Morrison tells troops to respect women or 'get out'", in ABC
News, 14 June 2013, available at http://www.abc.net.au/news/2013-06-14/chief-of-army-
fires-broadside-at-army-over-email-allegations/4753208, last accessed on 18 November
2014.

[139] Government of Canada, Department of National Defence, *Military Justice at the Summary
Trial Level*, 2001.

ratione material, *ratione loci*, *ratione tempore* and *ratione personae*. Generally they entail judicial or quasi-judicial mechanisms for dealing with disputes or misconduct of a state's armed forces, who are subject to that state's military laws. The degree of civilian oversight varies from state to state. Civilian courts may also exercise jurisdiction over crimes committed by soldiers at home or while deployed overseas in some states, and indeed certain criminal offences may be reserved for civilian courts.[140] Whether or how a soldier will be tried in military courts for crimes committed at home or abroad depends on the particular state and its laws. Military courts are often composed of military officers. Peter Rowe observes that irrespective of whether the offence is a military or criminal one it is often still considered a matter of military discipline.[141] Military justice systems may permit lesser offences to be tried by military officers in command in the form of summary proceedings, and they may provide for greater or lesser procedural and evidentiary safeguards and requirements.[142] Summary trials are often used in the field in order to deal rapidly with offences, to socialise normative values among troops, and to ensure troop morale and unit cohesion.[143] The types of offences provided for and disciplinary sanctions often differ from law applicable to civilians. This may be due to the disciplinary nature of military laws (that is, the purpose may be to ensure control and discipline rather than to punish crime *per se*).

Soldiers are trained in aggression and the use of weapons. Military justice and discipline are often considered key to restraining aggression, maintaining control over soldiers and to allow for easier movement of troops in frequently volatile operational environments.[144] Many states are therefore strong advocates of their military justice systems and are likely

---

[140] Peter Rowe, "United Nations Peacekeepers and Human Rights Violations: The Role of Military Discipline", in *Harvard International Law Journal*, 2010, vol. 51, pp. 69, 79; and Zsuzsanna Deen-Racsmany, "The Amended UN Model Memorandum of Understanding: A New Incentive for States to Discipline and Prosecute Military Members of National Peacekeeping Contingents?", in *Journal of Conflict and Security Law*, 2011, vol. 16, no. 2, pp. 321–55. See also, UN Secretary-General Report, *Summary Study of the Experience Derived from the Establishment and Operation of the Force*, UN GAOR, 13th session, Agenda item 65, UN Doc. A/3526, 8 February 1957, para. 137.

[141] Rowe, 2006, pp. 79–80, see *supra* note 66.

[142] Gibson, 2008, pp. 6–7, see *supra* note 4.

[143] See, for example, Friedland, 1997, p. 72, *supra* note 10.

[144] *Ibid.*, p. 67.

---

to be resistant to their elimination and to excessive civilian oversight, particularly if this potentially impacts on the effective operation of the armed forces and command and control. Mark Osiel posits that in a world where a strong international criminal court is not likely in the foreseeable future, greater attention should be shifted to "how military law can shape the professional soldier's sense of vocation and his understanding and cultivation of its intrinsic virtues, its 'inner morality'".[145] Retention of control through the military justice system is important given that the acts of soldiers, in particular where such acts violate international humanitarian law, may directly or indirectly incur state responsibility. Under the Geneva Conventions states are required to "search for persons alleged to have committed, or to have ordered to be committed, such *grave breaches* [of the law of war], and shall bring such persons, regardless of their nationality, before its own courts". This includes wilful killing, inhumane treatment and torture.

Military justice systems play an important role in many states with regard to the promotion of the rule of law. However, over recent years concerns about military justice systems have arisen particularly regarding rights violations. This, and in some cases lack of accountability and independence, have led to the dismantling or substantial reform of military justice systems in states across the world. Procedures of military courts are arguably subject to a hierarchal structure, sometimes even requiring decisions be confirmed by a senior officer convening the court martial.[146] Moreover, critics often argue that procedures lack transparency, as they are closed to the public, and they may lack independence and impartiality. Where soldiers are not held adequately to account for crimes by a system and procedures perceived as fair and legitimate this leads to erosion of trust, legitimacy of and confidence in military justice systems. This has resulted in loss of autonomy of military justice systems in many states, requiring greater civilian oversight and regulation.[147] States are increasingly limiting the jurisdictional competences of their military justice sys-

---

[145] Osiel, 1998, p. 959, see *supra* note 77.

[146] Rowe, 2006, p. 82, see *supra* note 66.

[147] See Chris Griggs, "A New Military Justice System for New Zealand", in *New Zealand Armed Forces Law Review*, 2006, vol. 26; and Matthew Groves, "Civilianisation of Australian Military Law", in *University of New South Wales Law Journal*, 2005, vol. 28, no. 2, pp. 364–95.

tems often in direct response to their inadequate handling of soldiers' human rights abuses.[148]

Concerns about military justice systems, for instance, came to the fore in the aftermath of the Abu Ghraib abuses, and in relation to British and US forces in Iraq and Afghanistan, Canadian forces in Somalia, among many other cases.[149] Criticisms have also been levelled against abuses within Latin American military justice systems and the military commissions utilised by the US to try Guantanamo Bay detainees. The latter are a specific type of body not typical of a military court, and are beyond the scope of this chapter.[150]

The increased 'civilianisation' of military justice systems is perceived by many state armed forces as a risk to the maintenance of effective control and as undermining disciplinary structures applicable to their militaries,[151] and the ability to carry out their missions effectively. Mark Friedland alludes to possible linkages between the decline in the use of military justice with respect to Canadian armed forces in the year preceding their deployment to Somalia in the 1990s and human rights abuses perpetrated by Canadian forces while deployed.[152] Moreover, many commentators highlight the weaknesses of civilian justice mechanisms for dealing with offences committed within a military environment, particularly when deployed overseas. As Michael Gibson aptly argues, delays associated with civilian justice systems make them unsuitable for dealing with crimes committed in the context of extraterritorial deployments or peace operations, where delays in disciplinary measures may result in fur-

---

[148] Rowe, 2010, pp. 69, 68, see *supra* note 140; Eugene R. Fidell, "A Worldwide Perspective on Change in Military Justice", in Eugene Fidell and Dwight H. Sullivan (eds.), *Evolving Military Justice*, Naval Institute Press, Annapolis, 2002, p. 209–17.

[149] Victor M. Hansen, "Changes in Modern Military Codes and the Role of the Military Commander: What Should the United States Learn from This Revolution?", in *Tulane Journal of International and Comparative Law*, 2008, vol. 16, pp. 419–20. In the context of abuses perpetrated against civilians by Canadian forces deployed to the UN operation in Somalia during the 1990s, the Somalia Inquiry scrutinised the Canadian military justice system. Forty-five recommendations for reform were made in light of identified weaknesses and for increasing independence and accountability within the system. Report of the Somalia Inquiry, see *supra* note 77.

[150] See Gibson, 2008, pp. 46–47, *supra* note 4.

[151] See, for example, Hansen, 2008, p. 423, *supra* note 149.

[152] Friedland, 1997, see *supra* note 10.

---

ther erosion of discipline among troops.[153] Civilian justice systems are not easily deployable, particularly given jurisdictional and practical difficulties such as security, resource and infrastructural concerns.[154] Problems may also arise in obtaining host state co-operation and in accessing witnesses and evidence. States may be reluctant to bring witnesses or victims to the accused soldier's state given the resources required and fears of refugee status claims.[155] Military justice systems are better adapted to deal with some of these issues and are therefore often considered preferable to civilian courts. They are more easily deployable to mission areas and portable in diverse and often volatile operational environments where infrastructure may be scant, and where civilian justice sector personnel may be unable or unwilling to go.[156] Victor M. Hansen points out that having a military justice system that accompanies soldiers to the field is more likely to encourage soldiers to respect the rule of law.[157] In the context of armed conflict, the need for states to have in place a functioning internal legal system to hold armed forces to account for international humanitarian law violations is highlighted in Article 43(1) of Additional Protocol I to the Geneva Conventions.[158]

In *R. v. Généreux*, the Canadian Supreme Court highlighted a number of important advantages of maintaining a separate system of military justice. First, it pointed out that it allows "the Armed Forces to deal with matters that pertain directly to the discipline, efficiency and morale of the military".[159] It stated that this is important as it enables the military to maintain its armed forces in "a state of readiness" as it can deal more efficiently and effectively with internal disciplinary issues as they arise.[160] This may be of even greater importance in the field where disciplinary matters may need to be dealt with urgently. A further advantage of military justice is that it better enables states to hold individual soldiers to ac-

---

[153] Gibson, 2008, p. 16, see *supra* note 4.

[154] See, for example, Hansen, 2008, p. 425, *supra* note 149.

[155] Burke, 2014, p. 20, see *supra* note 11.

[156] Gibson, 2008, pp. 16–17, see *supra* note 4.

[157] Hansen, 2008, p. 425, see *supra* note 149.

[158] Protocol Additional to the Geneva Conventions of 12 August 1949, and Relating to the Protection of Victims of International Armed Conflicts, opened for signature 12 December 1977, 1125 UNTS 3 (entered into force 7 December 1978).

[159] *R. v. Généreux*, Supreme Court of Canada [1992] 1 S.C.R. 259 at 293.

[160] *Ibid.*

count for both acts and omissions.[161] Omissions may be particularly relevant in the context of command responsibility to train, prevent and take action where allegations of crimes, or violations of international humanitarian law or human rights law, at the hands of armed forces arise. Holding soldiers accused of serious crimes effectively to account within this system, and publicising such, may guard against the erosion of military justice systems.

As noted, despite certain positive attributes of military justice systems, in recent years they have been subject to criticism given fears of lack of independence, impartiality and transparency.[162] On the other hand, the weakening of military justice systems has also been due to concerns that such systems inadequately protect soldiers' right to due process.[163] The hierarchical structures under which cases tend to be processed, some have argued, can lead to interference with case outcomes.[164] It has also been argued that in situations of emergency, in particular, military justice systems have a tendency to reinforce impunity for grave human rights violations, crimes against humanity and war crimes.[165] A working group on arbitrary detention has gone so far as to recommend that military courts should be "incompetent to try military personnel if the victims in-

---

[161] Rowe, 2006, p. 133, see *supra* note 66.

[162] John McKenzie, "A Fair and Public Trial", in Fidell and Sullivan, 2002, p. 230, see *supra* note 148; Commission on Human Rights, *Report on the Mission of the Special Rapporteur on the independence of judges and lawyers to Columbia*, ESCOR, 54th session, Agenda Item 8, UN Doc. E/CN.4/1998/39/Add.2; International Commission of Jurists, *Military Jurisdiction and International Law: Military Courts and Gross Human Rights Violations*, vol. 1, Centre for the Independence of Judges and Lawyers of the International Commission of Jurists, 2004; and Mohammed Ahmed Abu Rannat, *Study of Equality in the Administration of Justice*, UN Doc. E/CN.4/Sub.2/296, 10 June 1969, para. 195.

[163] McKenzie, 2002, see *supra* note 162.

[164] See, for example, Sub-commission on the Promotion and Protection of Human Rights, Issue of the Administration of Justice through Military Tribunals – Report submitted by Mr. Louis Joinet pursuant to Sub-Commission Decision 2001/10, 54th session, Agenda Item 8, UN Doc. E/CN.4/Sub.2/2002/4, 9 July 2002, paras.17–23; and Human Rights Watch, "Egypt: Military Impunity for Violence Against Women: Whitewash in Virginity Tests Trial", Human Rights Watch, 7 April 2012, available at http://www.hrw.org/news/2012/04/07/egypt-military-impunity-violence-against-women, last accessed on 18 November 2014.

[165] Commission on Human Rights, Issue of the Administration of Justice through Military Tribunals, 55th session, Provisional Agenda Item 3, UN Doc. E/CN.4/Sub.2/2003/4, 27 June 2003, para. 8.

---

clude civilians".[166] Principle 9 of the Draft Principles Governing the Administration of Justice through Military Tribunals (2006) provides that military courts should not be permitted to try those military personnel accused of serious human rights violations.[167] The rationale is that the system may encourage potential cover-ups by the military. The best counter-argument is evidence of effective and transparent investigations and prosecutions of soldiers alleged to have committed serious criminal offences whether at home or abroad.[168]

Looking again at sexual offences in the context of UN operations, according to official UN statistics, many troop-contributing states have been reluctant to provide any information on action taken against those accused of sexual exploitation and abuse while deployed on UN operations.[169] Franklin D. Rosenblatt highlights failures of the US court-martial system with respect to offences allegedly committed by US forces in both Afghanistan and Iraq. He notes: "After-action reports from deployed judge advocates show a nearly unanimous recognition that the full-bore application of military justice was impossible in the combat zone".[170] Rosenblatt reports that commanders actively avoided use of the court-marital system by "sending misconduct back to the home station, to granting leniency, to a more frequent use of administrative discharge procedures".[171] He notes that courts martial were not impossible but often considered too burdensome to conduct in volatile operational environments. Civilian justice would be faced, however, with even greater difficulties. Nevertheless, when the military justice system is not effectively put into operation this undermines deterrence, retribution, good order and discipline, and contributes to impunity. Rosenblatt posits that this is problematic given that, "[i]n an era of legally intensive conflicts, this court-martial

---

[166] Cited in *ibid.*, para. 21.

[167] Draft Principles Governing the Administration of Justice Through Military Tribunals, UN Doc. E/CN.4/2006/58, Principle 9, p. 4.

[168] Michael Evans and Frances Gibb, "Accused Troops Will Face More Robust Courts-Martial, Says Prosecution Chief", in *The Times*, 2 January 2009.

[169] For UN statistics on sexual exploitation and abuse allegation and State response rates to requests for information on action taken against alleged perpetrators, see United Nations Conduct and Discipline Unit, "Overview of Statistics" (https://www.legal-tools.org/doc/72e603/).

[170] Rosenblatt, 2010, p. 12, see *supra* note 4.

[171] *Ibid.*

frailty is consequential and bears directly on the success or failure of our national military efforts".[172] Part of the rationale for not holding courts martial where warranted could be their possible negative implications on military units' ability to carry out their duties during trials.[173] In the period from 2001 to 2003, US Army officers in Afghanistan apparently sometimes chose to use administrative discharges instead of holding a court martial in order to reduce caseloads.[174]

Courts martial often do face difficulties such as lack of personnel and resources, travel restrictions and dangerous operational environments.[175] Investigating and prosecuting a case is often costly and time consuming, deviating resources from the military operation itself. Linguistic and cultural barriers may exist with respect to victims and witnesses. Moreover, investigations of crimes may themselves put troops and other personnel in danger where conflict and violence are ongoing in investigation areas. The US Naval Criminal Investigative Service personnel, for instance, came under attack by insurgents while visiting the crime scene at night in the aforementioned *Hamdaniyah* case.[176] That being said, this is not an argument for greater use of civilian justice systems with respect to crimes committed by a state's soldiers, as greater difficulties would likely be faced by civilian justice systems.

In light of this, if states and their militaries perceive the erosion of military justice systems, despite their possible flaws, as a threat to control over their forces and the ability to deal more effectively with disciplinary issues, then these systems need to be strengthened. If discipline is a *raison d'être* of military justice systems, failure to effectively investigate and hold persons to account undermines the purpose of such a system.[177] Lack of discipline in one area may lead to lack of discipline in another. Military forces that have the use of arms and are deployed to volatile environments need to be under an adequate system of control lest atrocities occur. If

---

[172] *Ibid.*

[173] *Ibid.*, p. 16.

[174] Carlton L. Jackson, "Plea-Bargaining in the Military: An Unintended Consequence of the Uniform Code of Military Justice", in *Military Law Review*, 2004, vol. 179, pp. 1, 66–67.

[175] Eric Hanson, "Know Your Ground: The Military Justice Terrain of Afghanistan", in *The Army Lawyer*, 2009, p. 36.

[176] Hackel, 2009, pp. 272–73, 277, see *supra* note 8.

[177] Dan Box, "Military Police Handling Defence Crimes Struggle for Numbers", in *The Australian*, 1 October 2014.

militaries and their states contend that military justice systems are necessary then there is clearly a need to put in place strong, independent, effective, independent and impartial systems, if they are to be considered fair
and legitimate.

15.8. Conclusion

There are strategic and operational consequences for failures to hold soldiers to account for serious crimes committed while deployed overseas,
both at home and abroad. Failures to hold military personnel to account
for serious crimes has numerous deleterious effects, not least in creating a
perception of impunity among military personnel, peacekeepers and local
counterparts. Lack of accountability undermines the legitimacy of military
interventions, state and international organisation reputations, relationships with the host state populations and population at home, and indeed
counter-insurgency activities. Negative media coverage ensues, and
crimes are often used for propaganda purposes. Moreover, these failures
undermine many norms of conduct these types of missions arguably seek
to impart to the local population and national counterparts.

Some states are starting to recognise that holding soldiers to account for crimes committed in the host states and conveying these convictions to host state populations have strategic advantages. They assist with
developing amicable relationships with host state populations and with
securing their broader co-operation. In the Baha Mousa case, for instance,
involving the alleged beating to death of an Iraqi civilian by British soldiers while he was in detention in Iraq, Britain made available Arabic
translations of its public inquiry.[178]

Respect for the rule of law by military forces deployed overseas
garners confidence, trust and perceived legitimacy of operations. This
may be of particular strategic importance in the context of peace operations and counter-insurgency operations. Failures to address grave human
rights violations or war crimes by soldiers may actually feed insurgent
activities, recruitment efforts by insurgents, and indeed support of insurgents by the civilian population in the host state.[179] Moreover, such fail-

---

[178] Rosenblatt, 2010, p. 28, see *supra* note 4; and Evans and Gibb, 2009, see *supra* note 168.
[179] Hackel, 2009, p. 245, see *supra* note 8.

ures put the lives of other soldiers at risk.[180] Serious crimes by US armed forces in Iraq led to an overhaul of in mission training and revision of standard operating procedures ('SOP'). Yet training and SOP revisions can do little in the eyes of the public where atrocities have already occurred and individuals have not be adequately held to account.[181]

As highlighted earlier in this chapter, there has been much criticism of military justice systems, including that they risk rights violations such as the right to fair trial, as well as a lack of impartiality, accountability, transparency and independence.[182] States and their militaries may well have an incentive to maintain their military justice systems and to resist civilianisation, for reasons highlighted, not least of which is to maintain control over their armed forces, which in turn is key to discipline and ease of movement of forces. Therefore, states' military justice systems must be seen as fair, equitable, transparent and independent by society.[183] Some of these advantages of military justice systems are not evident when they fail to act adequately and promptly in investigating and, where appropriate, in prosecuting soldiers alleged to have committed criminal offences while on overseas deployment.

There is also a pedagogical value in ensuring effective investigation and prosecution of armed forces committing serious crimes. Habitual compliance and no tolerance of violations of standards of conduct assist with the process of norm internalisation, whether with codes of professional ethics or conduct, compliance with international humanitarian law, international human rights norms, with international criminal law or other standards. Like negative behaviour in a group, positive behaviour likely goes through a similar process or dynamic. As noted by Heike Krieger, "[i]f there is no room for professional training in order to create a habit of norm-compliance, the logic of consequences, particularly the fear of sanc-

---

[180] See Bing West, *No True Glory: A Frontline Account of the Battle for Fallujah*, Bantam, New York, 2005, pp. 61, 74–88, 93.

[181] Hackel, 2009, pp. 260–61, see *supra* note 8.

[182] See, for example, *R. v. Généreux*, [1992] 1 S.C.R. 259, 260 (Can.); and *Findlay v. United Kingdom*, App. No. 2210/93, 24 Eur. H.R. Rep. 221 (1997).

[183] See, for example, Principles and Guidelines on the Right to a Fair Trial and Legal Assistance in Africa, African Union Doc. DOC/OS(XXX) 247; Draft Principles Governing the Administration of Justice through Military Tribunals, 62nd session, UN Doc. E/CN.4/2006/58, 13 January 2006.

---

tions, may induce individual soldiers and fighters to comply".[184] Failure to effectively investigate and prosecute undermines compliance given the lack of fear of actually been held to account.

For disciplinary measures to have adequate effect in terms of deterrence and norm internalisation, particularly in the context of extraterritorial and multinational deployments, prompt judicial measures should be taken against perpetrators in a location proximate to the crime. If this is done, the local population and other soldiers alike can see that certain conduct will not be tolerated.[185] It may assist in highlighting that this is the conduct of a 'few bad apples', as some have coined them, and not the armed forces at large. Well-disciplined armed forces do not generally commit human rights abuses of civilians or others in host states. As discussed in section 15.6., successful militaries consider themselves bound by certain codes or ethics and moral standards, which are in the interest of operational effectiveness and efficiency.

The difficulty with deterrence is that presumptions of rationale action by soldiers may be thrown into flux in volatile and violent conflict environments where rule of law has been eroded. Yet in such environments significant efforts are invested in re-establishing rule of law and security sector reform supported often by external military actors. In terms of mission operational effectiveness, multinational forces involved in such endeavours must be seen to practice what they preach. This applies equally in the case of states and international organisations such as the United Nations.[186]

---

[184] Krieger, 2013, p. 13, see *supra* note 45.

[185] Payam Akhavan, "Justice in The Hague, Peace in the Former Yugoslavia?", in *Human Rights Quarterly*, 1998, vol. 20, no. 4, pp. 737, 751.

[186] Comprehensive Report, para. 57, see *supra* note 107.

16

Military or Civilian Jurisdiction for International Crimes? An Approach from Self-Interest in Accountability of Armed Forces in International Law

Elizabeth Santalla Vargas*

16.1. Introduction

In the discussion concerning the adequate jurisdictional forum to try core crimes, while there has been quite a large consensus as to the inadequacy of military jurisdictions trying civilians,[1] it is more controversial when the

---

* **Elizabeth Santalla Vargas** received her first law degree from the Catholic Bolivian University and an LL.M. from the University of San Francisco, USA. She has undertaken additional courses at the Grotius Centre for International Legal Studies, Leiden University, the Netherlands; the Geneva Academy of International Humanitarian Law and Human Rights, Switzerland; the Erik Castrén Institute of International Law and Human Rights, University of Helsinki, Finland; the Inter-American Institute of Human Rights, Costa Rica; The Hague Academy of International Law, external session held in Peru; and the University of Rosario, Colombia. She has been an Associate Legal Officer at the International Criminal Tribunal for the former Yugoslavia, a legal adviser at the Implementing Agency in Bolivia of the United Nations High Commissioner for Refugees ('UNHCR'), Visiting Professional at the International Criminal Court ('ICC'), and has been a member of Bolivia's legal team in a case filed before the International Court of Justice. She has consulted, *inter alia*, for the International Committee of the Red Cross, Bolivia's office of the High Commissioner for Human Rights, Bolivia's Ombudsman, Peace and Justice Initiative and the Coalition for the ICC. She currently teaches public international law at the Catholic Bolivian University. The author wishes to thank the editors for their useful comments and insights.

[1] For instance, the Human Rights Committee (1984) in relation to Article 14 of the Covenant on Civil and Political Rights reasoned that "[w]hile the Covenant does not prohibit such category of courts [military or special courts], nevertheless the conditions which it lays down clearly indicate that the trying of civilians by such courts should be very exceptional and take place under conditions which genuinely afford the full guarantees stipulated in Article 14". Human Rights Committee, General Comment 13, Article 14, Twenty-first session, 1984, para. 4. Compilation of General Comments and General Recommendations Adopted by Human Rights Treaty Bodies, UN Doc. HRI/GEN/1/Rev.1 (1994). For an overview of relevant case law and national practice regarding the question of jurisdiction over civilian contractors in military operations acting abroad in relation to the European context, see Stefano Manacorda and Triestino Mariniello, "Military Criminal Justice and Jurisdiction over Civilians: The First Lessons from Strasbourg", in Christine Bakker

---

alleged perpetrator is a member of the military personnel, especially when victims are also from the military. This chapter will analyse this question from the premise that self-interest exists for armed forces in accountability. Mindful of the fact that the jurisdictional reach established by any legal system is inherent to the attribute of sovereignty, this analysis will draw on some fundamental tenets[2] that guide the discussion. Assisted by regional and international case law and practice, this chapter argues that human rights violations should be tried by civilian courts, even if they are committed by military personnel. It is further argued that regarding war crimes, although the choice of jurisdictional forum is more controversial, civilian courts are largely more suitable. In order to guarantee legitimacy and credibility at all times, the impartiality and independence of the court should be carefully scrutinised. Resorting to civilian courts is usually found to better serve military self-interests in such examinations.

16.2. Dichotomy Regarding Jurisdiction in Wartime and Peacetime

The discussion concerning jurisdiction over war crimes and other core crimes finds its roots in the realm of jurisdiction in wartime. However,

---

and Mirko Sossai (eds.), *Multilevel Regulation of Military and Security Contractors: The Interplay between International, European and Domestic Norms*, Hart, Oxford, 2012, pp. 559–81. As a matter of State practice, it is interesting to note that by virtue of the legislative amendments adopted in Swiss legislation, which entered into force on 1 January 2011, military jurisdiction that had exclusive jurisdiction over war crimes had actually been exercised on only two occasions with respect to civilians of foreign nationality (namely the *G* and *Niyonteze* cases). In fact, the latter constituted the first time a domestic jurisdiction exercised universal jurisdiction with respect to war crimes committed in a non-international armed conflict. See Luc Reydams, "International Decisions, *Niyonteze v. Public Prosecutor*", in *American Journal of International Law*, 2002, vol. 96, no. 1, pp. 231–36. It was limited to two instances, namely, when the offences have been committed: (a) by or against members of the Swiss armed forces; or (b) in the context of armed conflict to which Switzerland is or has been a party (Article 25 of the Code of Criminal Procedure in relation to Article 23(1)(g)). See Roberta Arnold, "Applying the Laws of Armed Conflict in Swiss Courts", in Derek Jinks, Jackson N. Maogoto and Solon Solomon (eds.), *Applying International Humanitarian Law in Judicial and Quasi-Judicial Bodies: International and Domestic Aspects*, T.M.C. Asser Press, The Hague, 2014, pp. 318 ff.

2   Henry Wager Halleck, "Military Tribunals and their Jurisdiction", in *American Journal of International Law,* 1911, vol. 5, no. 4, pp. 960−61. Halleck, in relation to historical considerations of military jurisdiction within the confines of a country or territory, referred to the "great principles of natural right, deduced from the laws of war, and recognized in international jurisprudence, which must govern in times of insurrection, rebellion or invasion in the particular theatre of military operations, where the jurisdiction of civil courts is suspended or where their powers are entirely inadequate for the particular contingencies".

---

drawing back in history, no fixed rule can be found as to the nature of the jurisdictional fora in wartime scenarios. While the Roman military tribunals exercised jurisdiction in wartime, either in occupied territories or within the Empire, the scope of their jurisdiction varied over time and accommodated the prevailing circumstances. It was accordingly asserted that

> [t]he general principle to be deduced from law and history of those times was [...] that no crime could be committed with impunity; and that, therefore, where the ordinary civil tribunals could not, or did not take cognizance of wrongs or offences, the military would do so, both within and without the limits of the empire.[3]

The maxim that in wartime the civil authorities yield to the military[4] was generally accepted throughout the Middle Ages until the recognition of civil rights gained ground, leading to an expansion of civilian jurisdiction and consequently the restraint and limitation of military jurisdiction.[5] Alongside this view, in *Palamara-Iribarne v. Chile*, the Inter-American Court of Human Rights ('IACHR') stressed that in peacetime the jurisdiction of military courts or tribunals "has tended to be restricted, if not disappear, whereby, where it has not it should be reduced to the minimum".[6]

---

[3] *Ibid.*, p. 959.

[4] Michael A. Newton, "Continuum Crimes: Military Jurisdiction over Foreign Nationals who Commit International Crimes", in *Military Law Review*, 1996, vol. 153, p. 13. Newton points out that the practice of resorting to military commissions to adjudicate violations of international law dates back to at least 1688.

[5] Halleck, 1911, see *supra* note 2.

[6] Inter-American Court of Human Rights, Case of *Palamara-Iribarne v. Chile*, Judgment (Merits, Reparations and Costs), 22 November 2005, para. 132 ('Palamara-Iribarne v. Chile case'). Such an assertion finds echoes in various jurisdictions that have abolished military jurisdiction in peacetime during the 1980s and 1990s. This is the case, for instance, of the Netherlands (that paved the way for the abolition or limitation of military jurisdiction in the European context), Denmark, Slovenia, Estonia, France, the Czech Republic and Belgium (whose Constitution currently limits military jurisdiction to wartime, Article 157). By the same token, Article 126 of the Constitution of Slovenia of 1991 explicitly states: "Extraordinary courts may not be established. Nor may military courts be established in peacetime". Beyond the European context, see Senegal and Guinea. Article 99 of the Constitution of Guinea of 2010 explicitly allows for constitutional review of a military court's decisions: "The orders of the Constitutional Court are without recourse and impose themselves on the public powers and on all administrative, military and jurisdictional authorities, as well as on any natural or juridical (moral) person". See Federico Andreu-Guzmán, *Military Jurisdiction and International Law: Military Courts and Gross Human Rights Violations*, vol. 1, International Commission of Jurists, Geneva, 2004, pp. 159, 294. One jurisdiction where the jurisdictional distinction between wartime and peacetime has

The concurring opinion of Judge García Ramirez pointed to the fact that those supporting the pertinence of military jurisdiction do so with respect to its application in wartime, provided that it applies, *ratione materiae*, to "matters directly and immediately connected to the military performance, with the arms function, the military discipline".[7] Accordingly, the subject matter encompasses offences of a military nature: the so-called 'function crimes', that is, offences strictly related to the military function. In determining such a nature, a restrictive interpretation is to be applied in assessing the type of conduct that can be deemed to affect juridical military interests, which constitutes a laudable holding or position entrenched in the jurisprudence of the IACHR.[8] In this connection, it is interesting to

---

been less stringent – vesting jurisdiction mainly with civilian jurisdiction – has been the United Kingdom. Andreu-Guzmán's report (p. 348) points to the fact that the establishment of courts martial is allowed, in certain circumstances, in the theatre of operations (naval courts having some specific features). The jurisdiction *ratione materiae* bestowed upon courts martial by virtue of the Armed Forces Act of 2006 does not extend beyond disciplinary and service related offences. Indeed, the Act provides that the term "service offences" is to be understood in accordance with Part 1 which lists various types of conduct that are inextricably related to duties and conduct of a disciplinary and operational nature. Manacorda and Mariniello, 2012, p. 560, see *supra* note 1, highlight the expansion of military jurisdiction in the UK with respect to civilian contractors. Andreu-Guzmán's report also provides a detailed account of the regimes of various countries where the traditional distinction between wartime and peacetime is maintained.

[7] Palamara-Iribarne v. Chile case, Concurring Opinion of Judge Sergio García Ramírez, para. 12, see *supra* note 6. The pertinence of military jurisdiction for adjudicating matters of a disciplinary nature had been earlier stressed in Inter-American Court of Human Rights, Case of *Castillo Petruzzi et al. v. Peru*, Judgment (Merits, Reparations and Costs), 30 May 1999, Series C No. 52, para. 128.

[8] *Ibid.*, paras. 13, 14, 16. Various previous cases endorsed such restrictive interpretation. Indeed, the holding coined in *Castillo Petruzzi et al.* and later in the case of *Durand and Ugarte v. Perú* was followed, for instance, in the cases of *19 Merchants v. Colombia, Las Palmeras v. Colombia, Cantoral Benavides v. Perú* and *Lori Berensson Mejía v. Perú* where the Court recalled that "[u]nder the democratic rule of law, the military criminal jurisdiction should have a very restricted an exceptional scope and be designed to protect special juridical interests associated with the functions assigned by law to the military forces. Hence, it should only try military personnel for committing crimes or misdemeanors that, due to their nature, harm the juridical interests of the military system". Inter-American Court of Human Rights, Case of *Lori Berenson Mejía v. Perú*, Judgment of 25 November 2004, para. 142. With further references as to the jurisprudence of the IACHR upholding a restrictive interpretation of the remit of military jurisdiction (applicable with respect to military personnel and in relation to military offences), see Carlos Lascano, "Inter-American Court of Human Rights and Penal Military Justice", in Stefano Manacorda and Adán Nieto (eds.), *Criminal Law Between War and Peace: Justice and Cooperation in Criminal Matters in International Military Interventions*, Ediciones de la Universidad de Castilla–La Mancha, Ciadad Real, 2009, pp. 281–82.

---

note, as did the Inter-American Commission on Human Rights ('Inter-American Commission') in its thematic report on the right to truth,[9] the explicit reference made by the Inter-American Convention on Forced Disappearance of Persons as to the understanding that acts constituting forced disappearance under no circumstances could be deemed having been committed in the course of military duties. Accordingly, the said provision further states: "Persons alleged to be responsible for the acts constituting the offense of forced disappearance of persons may be tried only in the competent jurisdictions of ordinary law in each state, to the exclusion of all other special jurisdictions, particularly military jurisdictions".[10]

Ensuring impartiality and independence is at the heart of the restriction of the scope of military jurisdiction even in times of war. Indeed, in particular the requirement of impartiality is rendered illusory "since the members of the Army often feel compelled to protect those who fight alongside them in a difficult and dangerous context".[11] Bearing in mind that the qualities of impartiality and independence lie at the core of accountability systems that are well regarded and trusted by public opinion, the purported restriction of military jurisdiction – not only with respect to civilians but also in relation to military personnel when it comes to crimes under international law (including war crimes) – finds further support from the perspective of self-interest in accountability.

It is further interesting to note that the Inter-American Commission has adopted, on various occasions, the underlying rationale that had been advanced by the Constitutional Court of Colombia[12] as to the gravity of

---

[9] Inter-American Commission on Human Rights, *The Right to Truth in the Americas*, OEA/Ser.L/V/II.152, Doc. 2, 13 August 2014, p. 49.

[10] Inter-American Convention on Forced Disappearance of Persons, 9 June 1994, Article 9.

[11] Inter-American Commission on Human Rights, Report No. 2/06, Case 12.130, Miguel Orlando Muñoz Guzmán, Mexico, 28 February 2006, paras. 83–84.

[12] For instance, Inter-American Commission on Human Rights, Third Report on the Situation of Human Rights in Colombia, OEA/Ser.L/V/II.102, Doc. 9 rev. 1, 26 February 1999, ch. V, para. 30. Application filed with the Inter-American Court of Human Rights in Case 12.449, *Teodoro Cabrera García and Rodolfo Montiel Flores v. Mexico*. In *19 Merchants v. Colombia*, the Inter-American Commission, in arguing the violation to the right to a fair trial and judicial protection, relied on a Judgment of the Constitutional Court of Colombia of 1997 which reasoned that "[t]he connection between the criminal act and the activity related to military service is broken when the offence is extremely serious; this is the case of offences against an individual. In those circumstances, the offence must be [submitted] to the civil justice system", Judgment of 5 July 2004, para. 157(g). The position or holding of the Constitutional Court of Colombia was reiterated as part of the precedent ruling against military jurisdiction with respect to crimes against humanity in the case of the *Mapiripán*

---

crimes against humanity precluding any connection of such crimes with activity related to military service and thus falling beyond the reach of military jurisdiction. While not being the dominant criterion for determining the suitability of the jurisdictional forum, the consideration as to the gravity of crimes against humanity bears some connection with the nature of the offence, thus making relevant the analysis as to whether the same rationale applies with respect to war crimes. It may be noted in this connection that no difference in terms of gravity was found to exist in law between crimes against humanity and war crimes by the International Criminal Tribunal for the former Yugoslavia ('ICTY'), where the discussion in international adjudication as to the apparent disparity in the gravity threshold between both categories of core crimes emerged in the context of sentencing. The *Tadić* Sentencing Appeals Judgment held that no distinction could be found "between the seriousness of a crime against humanity and that of a war crime", not only in the statutory framework of the ICTY but also in the realm of customary international law.[13] Judge Shahabuddeen's Separate Opinion stressed the view of not being correct that "as a matter of law, the seriousness is necessarily greater where the same act is charged and proved as a crime against humanity".[14] In so do-

---

Massacre: "[t]he tie between the criminal act and the service related activity is broken when the crime is unusually grave, as in the case of crimes against humanity. Under these circumstances, the case must be allocated to regular courts, given the total contradiction between the crime and the constitutional mandates of the security forces", Case of *Mapiripán Massacre v. Colombia*, Judgment of 15 September 2005, para. 205 (in reference to Judgment C-358 of 5 August 1997 of the Constitutional Court of Colombia). In *Pueblo Bello Massacre*, the Court, in finding that military jurisdiction was not the proper forum in addition of not constituting an effective remedy, the IACHR took into account the aforesaid holding of the Constitutional Court of Colombia; see the Case of *Pueblo Bello Massacre v. Colombia*, Judgment of 31 January 2006, para. 193. It may be noted, for further background, that the Inter-American Commission's Report on *Vélez Restrepo v. Colombia* disregarded the State's argument as to the purported suitability of military jurisdiction for violations of human rights law of not extreme gravity, by stressing that according to the IACHR's jurisprudence, all situations that breach the human rights of civilians fall beyond the remit of military jurisdiction. See Inter-American Commission Report on *Vélez Restrepo v. Colombia*, Report No. 136/10, Case 12.658, *Luis Gonzalo "Richard" Vélez Restrepo and Family, Colombia*, 23 October 2010, para. 155 ('Vélez Restrepo v. Colombia case').

[13] International Criminal Tribunal for the former Yugoslavia, *Prosecutor v. Dŭsko Tadić* ("Tadić case"), Case No. IT-94-1-A and IT-94-1-A *bis*, Judgment in Sentencing Appeals, 26 January 2000, para. 69.

[14] *Ibid.*, p. 41.

---

ing, he concurred with Judge LI's Separate and Dissenting Opinion to the *Erdemović* Judgment on Appeal[15] and with Judge Robinson's Separate Opinion to the *Tadić* Sentencing Judgment in first instance, emphasising the view that crimes against humanity are not necessarily to be regarded as "more serious violations of international humanitarian law than war crimes" .[16] Delving into history, the Separate Opinion further referred to the fact that the trials established after the Second World War did not treat both categories of core crimes as bearing a different threshold of gravity.[17] In fact, it has been asserted that the Judgment of the International Military Tribunal did not draw a difference in terms of gravity between crimes against humanity and war crimes, having rather applied a cumulative charging approach with respect to the same facts.[18] As was pointed by the Trial Chamber in its Judgment in *Kupreskić*, the legal framework of the International Military Tribunal did not provide for different penalties in relation to both categories of crimes.[19] The aforesaid holding in the *Tadić* Sentencing Appeals Judgment was later followed in *Furundžija*,[20] having remained a *jurisprudence constante* of the ICTY[21] and the International Criminal Tribunal for Rwanda ('ICTR')[22] Appeals Chamber that therefore rejected an abstract hierarchical construction of core crimes based upon its inherent gravity.[23]

---

[15] Where Judge LI asserted that "the gravity of a criminal act and consequently the seriousness of its punishment, are determined by the intrinsic nature of the act itself and not by its classification under one category or the other". International Criminal Tribunal for the former Yugoslavia, *Prosecutor v. Dražen Erdemović*, Case No. IT-96-22-A, Judgment, Separate and Dissenting Opinion of Judge Li, 7 October 1997, para. 19.

[16] Tadić case, Separate Opinion of Judge Robinson, 11 November 1999, pp. 9–10, see *supra* note 13.

[17] *Ibid.*, p. 4.

[18] See Andrea Carcano, "Sentencing and the Gravity of the Offence in International Criminal Law", in *International and Comparative Law Quarterly*, 2002, vol. 52, no. 3, p. 595.

[19] International Criminal Tribunal for the former Yugoslavia, *Prosecutor v. Kupreskić et al.*, Case No. IT-95-16-T, Judgment, Trial Chamber, 14 January 2000, para. 674.

[20] International Criminal Tribunal for the former Yugoslavia, *Prosecutor v. Anton Furundžija*, Case No. IT-95-17/1-A, Judgment, 21 July 2000, para. 243.

[21] See, for example, International Criminal Tribunal for the former Yugoslavia, *Prosecutor v. Stakić*, Case No. IT-97-24-A, Judgment, 22 March 2006, para. 375. *Prosecutor v. Kunarać et al.*, Case No. IT-96-23 and IT-96-23-1-A, Judgment, 12 June 2012, para. 171.

[22] See, for example, International Criminal Tribunal for Rwanda ('ICTR'), *Rutaganda v. The Prosecutor*, Case No. ICTR-96-3-A, Judgment, 26 May 2003, para. 590.

[23] See Gideon Boas, James L. Bischoff, Natalie L. Reid and B. Don Taylor III, *International Criminal Law Procedure*, Cambridge University Press, Cambridge, 2011, ch. 10, "Judg-

Although the Inter-American Commission, in its aforementioned thematic report on the right to truth in the Americas, has only recommended the elimination of the use of military jurisdiction for cases involving human rights violations,[24] the underlying reasons advanced in support of such an emphatic recommendation can arguably also be extended to war crimes, as they cannot be regarded as falling within the military function or duties and thus entailing a violation of military criminal law. Indeed, the essence of war crimes is the establishment of penal consequences for conduct going beyond or falling short of what is permitted and prohibited under the laws of armed conflict[25] – obviously distinct from military criminal law. In view of the gravity of such violations, a special regime applies to core crimes, including war crimes – non-applicability of statute of limitations, blanket amnesties, provision of universal jurisdiction, and so forth.[26] Accordingly, it is difficult to reconcile the commission of war crimes with military duties. The fact that war crimes, as opposed to the other core crimes, are more closely related to military operations in armed conflict leads to consideration of whether they could be regarded as falling within military duties.[27] But even if that were considered to be the case, the nature of the offences at stake is not changed. Nor

---

ment and Sentencing", p. 397. Advancing a critical view as to the detrimental effects posed by the lack of a hierarchical conception of core crimes towards the aim of attaining a coherent system of sentencing for international criminal trials, see Pascale Schifflet and Gideon Boas, "Sentencing Coherence in International Criminal Law: The Cases of Biljana Plavšić and Miroslav Bralo", in *Criminal Law Forum*, 2012, vol. 23, nos. 1/3, pp. 135–59.

[24] Inter-American Commission on Human Rights, 2014, p. 114 (recommendation 4), see *supra* note 9.

[25] Antonio Cassese, interpreting the holding in para. 94 of the Appeals Chamber in the Interlocutory Appeal in *Tadić*, stressed that "a war crime is any serious violation of a rule of international humanitarian law entailing the individual criminal responsibility of the person breaching the rule". See Tadić case, Separate Opinion of Judge Cassese, para. 12, *supra* note 13.

[26] Stressing this point, see Elizabeth Santalla Vargas, *Bolivia ante el Derecho Internacional Humanitario: Estudio de Compatibilidad entre el Ordenamiento Jurídico Interno y las Normas del DIH*, CICR and Plural Editores, La Paz, 2006, p. 53. With additional considerations on the jurisdictional forum for adjudicating core crimes, in particular war crimes, see pp. 49–57.

[27] Inter-American Commission on Human Rights, 2014, para. 23, see *supra* note 9, where the Commission rightly notes that "military jurisdiction should apply only in the case of violations of military criminal law alleged to have been committed by members of the military during the performance of specific duties related to the defense and external security of a State".

---

is it changed simply by the fact that the victims of war crimes allegedly committed by members of the armed forces may be civilians or military personnel. In fact, a similar situation unfolds in considering the status of victims of crimes against humanity, a question that has been initially addressed by the ICTY, and that has been proven to be relevant in various other contexts of international criminal law prosecution, including at the International Criminal Court ('ICC').[28] This is so as the emphasis on the construction of the notion of crimes against humanity has been placed in the *chapeau*, that is, a widespread or systematic attack on a civilian population, rather than on the status, if any,[29] of the individual victims of the underlying acts. Neither Article 7 of the ICC Statute nor the Elements of Crimes are specific in this regard, having the latter referred simply to 'persons' while describing the elements of the underlying acts.[30] Without entering into the details of the discussion, suffice it to say that the ICTY has held that there is no requirement nor is it an element of this category of crimes that the individual victims are necessarily civilians,[31] provided that the contextual element in which they occur is triggered by a widespread or systematic attack against a civilian population. The civilian character of the population not being affected by the presence within the group of individuals holding a non-civilian status – the exact number de-

---

[28] For a thorough analysis of the *Martić* Appeals Chamber Judgment and related jurisprudence in other Tribunals, see Joakim Dungel, "Defining Victims of Crimes against Humanity: *Martić* and the International Criminal Court", in *Leiden Journal of International Law*, 2009, vol. 22, no. 4, pp. 727–52.

[29] Newton considers that since "crimes against humanity infringe on fundamental human rights, anyone can be a victim". Newton, 1996, p. 61, see *supra* note 4.

[30] It may be noted that the Elements of Crimes describing in Article 7(1)(b) the elements of the crime of extermination additionally establish that "the conduct constituted, or took place as part of, a mass killing of members of a civilian population" (element 2).

[31] This was recently confirmed by the Appeals Chamber of the ICTY in *Prosecutor v. Popović et al.*, Case No. IT-05-88-A, Judgment, 30 January 2015, paras. 569 and 567, recalling its holding in *Prosecutor v. Milan Martić* ('Martić case'), Case No. IT-95-11-A, Judgment, 8 October 2008, para. 307; *Prosecutor v. Mile Mrkšić and Veselin Šlijvančanin*, Case No. IT-95-13/1-A, Judgment, 5 May 20009, para. 32 (see also paras. 28 and 31). Further confirmation of this jurisprudential line occurred in *Prosecutor v. Šainović et al.*, Case No. IT-05-87-A, Judgment, 23 January 2014, para. 549. See also *Prosecutor v. Dragomir Milošević*, Case No. IT-98-29/1-A, Judgment, 12 November 2009, para. 58. These Appeal Judgments drew upon the previous holding in *Prosecutor v. Dragoljub Kunarac et al.*, Case No. IT-96-23/1-A, Judgment, 12 June 2002, para. 90, cited in *Prosecutor v. Dario Kordić and Mario Čerkez*, Case No. IT-95-14/2-A, Judgment, 17 December 2004, para. 95, as well as in *Prosecutor v. Tihomir Blaškić*, Case No. IT-95-14-A, Judgment, 29 July 2004, para. 105.

---

pending on the circumstances[32] – provided that the population targeted by the attack is predominantly civilian,[33] which implies that not the entire civilian population ought to be the target of the attack.[34] Within this framework, it is at odds to conceive military jurisdiction suitable to adjudicate war crimes committed by members of armed forces where the victims are also military personnel, as opposed to the situation where the victims may be civilians.[35] Such inconsistency is even more apparent if it is accepted that in both cases (war crimes and crimes against humanity) not only the alleged perpetrators but also the victims may be military personnel.

Perhaps further consideration as to whether certain war crimes may be deemed closer to the military function, and so impinge upon more strictly defined military interests, may provide a sounder justification for considering military jurisdiction suitable to adjudicate such offences. But

---

[32] It may be noted that the *Katanga* Judgment of the ICC, while accepting that the presence of non-civilians within the targeted group may not deprive it of its civilian character, considered relevant that a substantial number of civilians were victims of the attack for the predominant civilian nature of the population of the attack be asserted. Such a view seems to explain why an emphasis was placed on the factual analysis as to whether the victims of the crime of murder, as a crime against humanity, had not directly participated in the hostilities. See International Criminal Court, *Prosecutor v. Germain Katanga*, Case No. ICC-01/04-01/07-3436, Judgment pursuant to Article 74 of the Statute, 7 March 2014, paras. 1105 and 856. (The latter, while pointing out that the factual analysis prompted by the case did not require the Chamber to consider the question of persons *hors de combat*, shows the importance for the Chamber to establish that the victims of the charge of murder, who were soldiers, could not be regarded as directly participating in the hostilities when their deaths occurred).

[33] The exact number depending on the circumstances, see, for example, Martić case Appeal Judgment, para. 307, *supra* note 31.

[34] See, for example, *Prosecutor v. Blaškić*, No. IT-95-14-A, Judgment, 19 July 2004, para. 105, citing the *Kunarać* Appeal Judgment, para. 90; *Martić* Appeal Judgment, para. 307, see *supra* note 31, also *Prosecutor v. Naletelić and Martinović*, No. IT-98-34-T, Trial Judgment, 31 March 2013, para. 235; *Prosecutor v. Galić*, No. IT-98-29-A, Judgment, 30 November 2006, para. 136 (citing the Appeal Judgment in *Kordić and Cerkez*, 17 December 2004, para. 50).

[35] Such an approach has been adopted, for instance, by Mexico. The Mexican Military Criminal Code, in its latest amendment of 13 June 2014, vested its military courts with competence over offences not only of a disciplinary nature but also of a common nature provided that the victim is not a civilian and the offence is committed by military personnel in active service or when the commission of the offence is service related (Article 57(I) and (II) (a)). It was further explicitly stated that in any event where joint commission of crimes allegedly committed by military personnel and civilians is at stake, only the former could be tried by military courts (Article 57).

---

even if such a justification were convincingly advanced, practical considerations may arise as to prosecutorial effectiveness where war crimes and crimes against humanity charges arising from the same factual situation fall under different jurisdictional fora.[36]

In the context of international humanitarian law, while the four Geneva Conventions of 1949 establish the *aut dedere aut judicare* obligation of states with respect to grave breaches of the Conventions, no indication or requirement is made as to the type of jurisdictional forum.[37] The only express reference to the jurisdictional forum is made in Article 84[38] of Geneva Convention III in relation to prisoners of war in the light of the principle of non-discrimination, so as to ensure that prisoners of war are tried by the same jurisdiction that is also competent with respect to members of the armed forces of the detaining power. It can be asserted that the type of offences contemplated by the provision concern the regime under detention of prisoners of war. As pointed out by the commentary of the International Committee of the Red Cross ('ICRC') from 1960, it was deemed suitable to conceive military jurisdiction as the rule for adjudicating infringements of military law and regulations to which prisoners of war are subject to during detention pursuant to Article 82 of Geneva Convention III which allows for the application of disciplinary measures.[39] Accordingly, the express reference made in Article 84 to military courts as the suitable forum for trying prisoners of war should be read in the light of the aforesaid principle of non-discrimination – underpinning also the penalties applied (Article 87) – in view of the prevailing factual background at the time of the drafting and adoption of the Geneva Conven-

---

[36] For instance, murder as a war crime and as a crime against humanity, as charged and prosecuted in *Katanga* by the ICC, see *supra* note 32.

[37] Geneva Convention I, Article 49; Geneva Convention II, Article 50; Geneva Convention III, Article 129; and Geneva Convention IV, Article 146.

[38] Article 84 reads:

> A prisoner of war shall be tried only by a military court, unless the existing laws of the Detaining Power expressly permit the civil courts to try a member of the armed forces of the Detaining Power in respect of the particular offence alleged to have been committed by the prisoner of war. In no circumstances whatever shall a prisoner of war be tried by a court of any kind which does not offer the essential guarantees of independence and impartiality as generally recognized, and, in particular, the procedure of which does not afford the accused the rights an means of defence provided for in Article 105.

[39] International Committee of the Red Cross, *Commentary on Geneva Convention III*, 1960.

tions and essentially in connection with offences of a disciplinary nature. Moreover, as stressed in the same provision (Article 84), under no circumstances whatsoever could a prisoner of war be tried by a tribunal or court devoid of independence, impartiality, judicial guarantees and, in particular, the defence rights provided for in Article 105.[40] The ICRC commentary makes clear that judicial guarantees are equally applicable to both civilian and military jurisdictions.[41]

The ICRC commentary further points to the fact that the second paragraph of Article 84 was inserted in attention to some countries where civilian jurisdiction applies to both military personnel and civilians.[42] Under the similar treatment to be afforded to prisoners of war in relation to members of the armed forces of the detaining power required by Article 84, that explicitly allows for the possibility that the detaining power's legislation may vest with jurisdiction civilian courts over members of its armed forces, and the fact that according to contemporary developments in international jurisprudence, particularly of the regional human rights systems that have been confronted with the question as to the proper reach of military jurisdiction, alleged violations of human rights law by members of the armed forces ought to be adjudicated by civilian courts. Accordingly, crimes against humanity allegedly committed by prisoners of war would also fall under such jurisdictional forum. Bearing in mind that crimes against humanity can be also committed in armed conflicts, should the prisoner of war be also allegedly responsible for war crimes, he/she would have to be tried in different jurisdictional forums for crimes allegedly committed in the same situation or even in the same incident. Not only do the principles of indivisibility of trial but also practical considerations ensuing from the rights of the defence, the gathering and assessment of evidence, among others, militate against such possibility. This dilemma would be avoided if the detaining power's legislation vests with jurisdiction its civilian or ordinary courts over all core crimes, including war crimes, also if the alleged perpetrators are members of armed forces. In the event that the offences falling under Article 84 may be deemed to encompass other offences beyond the disciplinary purview, the second part of the provision would allow for such a possibility.

---

[40] Geneva Convention, III, Article 84.

[41] *Commentary on Geneva Convention III*, see *supra* note 39.

[42] *Ibid.*, with reference to the UK.

Another reference to military jurisdiction appears in Article 66 of Geneva Convention IV as part of the regime of occupation. The provision enables military courts for the purpose of adjudicating offences against security regulations adopted by the occupying power pursuant to Article 64. The provision establishes three requirements, namely the regular constitution of military courts, their functioning in the occupied territory and their non-political nature. As pointed out by the ICRC commentary, the latter derives from the Second World War where sometimes the judicial machinery was used with political motivations or as a means of persecution on racial grounds.[43] While the competence of military courts acting in occupied territories may arguably be deemed to be limited to security offences by virtue of the aforesaid provisions,[44] it is nonetheless useful to consider that from a practical standpoint the military mission may be hampered if commanders and soldiers are focused on investigating and adjudicating human rights violations.[45] Practical considerations lead also to consider the danger of resorting to military courts for enforcing international humanitarian law.[46] While the chances are that the deterrence effect of criminal prosecution – albeit mindful of its limitations – could enhance compliance with international humanitarian law in the midst of an ongoing conflict, prosecution of foreign nationals of hostile forces by courts martial of one party to the conflict entails a strong presumption of victor's justice or at least the impression of lack of impartiality and independence.[47] By the same token, when a party to the conflict prosecutes its own armed forces, practical issues arising out of the application of the doctrine of command responsibility and superior orders prompt further reflection as to the suitability of military jurisdictions during armed conflict scenarios. What is more, when war crimes and other core crimes are allegedly

---

[43]   International Committee of the Red Cross, Commentary on Geneva Convention IV, 1958.

[44]   Newton, 1996, p. 91, see *supra* note 4, advancing a different view as to a purported requirement under international law for a commander to undertake prosecution of core crimes during occupation as a means of ensuring civil order.

[45]   Supporting this view with practical examples, see *ibid.*, pp. 9 ff. The ICRC commentary of 1960 on Article 66 acknowledges the fact that military courts may be constituted in occupied territory to deal with "the offences committed by the members of the army of occupation", being thus practically feasible to extend their competence under the regime of occupation. See, ICRC Commentary on Article 66, Part III: Status and Treatment of Protected Persons, Section III: Occupied Territories, point 2(a).

[46]   Newton, 1996, p. 8, see *supra* note 4.

[47]   Arguing to the contrary in support of prosecution of foreign nationals of hostile forces, see *ibid.*, p. 85.

committed by the occupying power in the course of occupation, prosecution by the same state may raise concerns with respect to the impartiality and independence in particular of military tribunals.[48]

From a practical standpoint, tactical and operational concerns also come into play. It has been averred that a potential short-term escalation of hostilities or other operational concerns may in turn conflict with the concern of ensuring investigation and prosecution. Accordingly, turning over suspects to ordinary judicial authorities may help to accomplish the military mission from a tactical and operational perspective.[49]

Under the aforesaid considerations, the dichotomous approach to military jurisdiction in wartime and peacetime renders perfunctory or perhaps becomes a matter of pragmatism in dealing with crimes in the midst of armed conflict (including situations of occupation). In this vein, the arguments advanced in support of the proposition of curtailing military jurisdiction with respect to all core crimes (including war crimes) cannot wholly be deemed applicable to one scenario as opposed to the other.

16.3. The Scope of Military Jurisdiction through the Human Rights Lens

It is widely accepted that military jurisdiction *ratione materiae* is predicated upon 'military offences', offences of a military nature or service-related offences. The intricacies in determining what a military offence is, however, lie at the heart of the discussion, as already noted. The question of whether crimes under international law could ever be equated to military offences has been mainly addressed in the context of state responsibility litigation and the implementation of the ICC Statute. In the former scenario, it can be fairly asserted that the debate has gained the upper

---

[48] The issue has been raised in relation to the Gaza Strip conflict where war crimes have been allegedly committed by the occupying power (Israel). The investigation advanced by the occupying power has been put into question on the basis of, *inter alia*, resort to the so-called military "operational debriefings" which detract from contributing to an effective and impartial investigation mechanism. Furthermore, the internal character within the military structure of such investigations has been deemed to render those investigations unable to fulfil the requirements of independence and impartiality by a UN mission reporting on the investigation undertaken by Israeli legal authorities into the Gaza Strip conflict. With further details, see Farhad Malekian, "Judging International Criminal Justice in the Occupied Territories", in *International Criminal Law Review*, 2012, vol. 12, p. 847.

[49] Newton, 1996, see *supra* note 4.

---

hand in the context of regional state responsibility. In the Inter-American human rights system, the Inter-American Commission has asserted that human rights violations do not constitute military or police offences, thus falling beyond the purview of military jurisdiction. Adjudication of alleged violations of human rights by military courts, not only with respect to civilians but also to military and police forces, was deemed by the Inter-American Commission incompatible with the right to an effective judicial remedy, an independent and impartial court and due process of law.[50] It has accordingly issued specific recommendations to states aiming at the adoption of necessary internal measures "to ensure that *all* cases of human rights violations are submitted to the ordinary courts".[51] It is fair to note that the Human Rights Committee has also pronounced along the same line of reasoning, for instance, while analysing the situation in Colombia observed that the transfer from civilian to military jurisdiction of cases involving human rights violations by military and security forces contributed to the institutionalisation of impunity as the impartiality and independence of those tribunals could be reasonably put into question.[52] A similar pronouncement was made with respect to the establishment of military tribunals in Guatemala asserting jurisdiction over military personnel for serious violations of human rights.[53]

By the same token, the jurisprudence of the IACHR has pronounced on the question of impartiality and independence of military jurisdictions trying members of the armed forces for serious violations of human rights law. In *Palamara-Iribarne v. Chile*, the IACHR, while recalling that military jurisdiction is to be confined to offences where the protected legal value is of a military nature, clarified that those kinds of offences can be only committed when military personnel perform specific duties related to the defence and external security of the state.[54] In a more recent Judg-

---

[50] For instance, in *Masacre de Riofrío* (Colombia), *Carlos Manuel Prada González and Evelio Antonio Bolaño Castro* (Colombia), and *Leonel de Jesús Isaza Echeverry and others* (Colombia), referred to by Andreu-Guzmán, 2004, pp. 142 ff., see *supra* note 6, with additional case law.

[51] For instance, see Inter-American Commission of Human Rights, Report on the Situation of Human Rights in Ecuador, ch. 3 (fourth recommendation), OEA/Ser.L/V/II.96, Doc. 10 rev. 1, 24 April 1997 (emphasis added).

[52] Jo Stigen, *The Relationship between the International Criminal Court and National Jurisdictions: The Principle of Complementarity*, Martinus Nijhoff Publishers, Leiden, 2008, p. 271.

[53] *Ibid.*, p. 308.

[54] Palamara-Iribarne v. Chile case, para. 132, see *supra* note 6.

---

ment, *Vélez Restrepo v. Colombia*, the IACHR noted that its jurisprudential line as to the inadequacy of military jurisdiction over human rights violations was construed in relation to the type of cases referred to its jurisdiction, that were mainly concerned with situations entailing grave human rights violations, and thus could not be interpreted as limiting ordinary jurisdiction to cases of such a nature. This is in line with its earlier case law where it had held that it is not the gravity of the offences but more importantly their nature and the protected legal value that deprive certain offences from falling under military jurisdiction.[55] A sound basis can thus be claimed to be found in the Inter-American system of human rights in support of the proposition that military jurisdiction cannot be regarded a proper forum for adjudicating violations of human rights[56] committed by members of armed forces even if acting in armed conflict scenarios. The extent to which the aforesaid rationale – conflating the nature of the offence and of the protected legal interest – lends itself to an analogy with respect to violations of humanitarian law merits consideration. Indeed, as pointed out by the IACHR, its jurisprudence ought to be read in light of the cases submitted to its jurisdiction and its competence.[57]

In view of such compelling case law and pronouncements, military jurisdictions exercising jurisdiction over military personnel for core crimes (including war crimes), at least in the Inter-American context, take the risk of not only rendering judgments that could eventually be overturned at the international level but also of being perceived as illegitimate or devoid of confidence by public opinion.[58] In such a scenario, the self-interest in accountability of armed forces is better accomplished if jurisdiction over military personnel is exercised by civilian jurisdiction in all

---

[55] Vélez Restrepo v. Colombia case, para. 244, see *supra* note 12.

[56] See also Inter-American Commission of Human Rights, 2014, see *supra* note 9, where the Commission recommends abolishing the use of military jurisdictions for cases involving human rights violations. It further contains references to relevant jurisprudence of the IACHR on the matter.

[57] For further discussion on this point, see Section 16.4.2.

[58] Roberta Arnold points out that civil society has a general negative perception concerning military jurisdiction and its capability of being respectful of fair trial principles and thus favouring civilian jurisdiction that can be subject to public scrutiny. By resorting to the Swiss military jurisdiction, Arnold argues that such a general assumption is devoid of foundation. See Roberta Arnold, "Military Criminal Procedures and Judicial Guarantees: The Example of Switzerland", in *Journal of International Criminal Justice*, 2005, vol. 3, pp. 750, 776–77.

cases entailing core crimes under international law. This proposition is further reinforced if one considers that due process rights and judicial guarantees of military personnel could be better guaranteed by civilian jurisdictions, in which the intricacies inherent to trials conducted by the same comrades of an institutional structure, where hierarchy is firmly anchored as in the military, are less likely to prevail.[59] The idea of a military forum entailing a privilege for the armed forces vanishes, therefore, or at the very least leads one to wonder if it is really so, as the accused is likely to be deprived of a trial conducted by an independent and impartial tribunal. In this connection, it has been further put into question whether the constitutional mission of armed forces – commonly ascribed to the defence of external security of the state – justifies the need of such a special forum.[60] These considerations are further echoed by the test of objective impartiality propounded by the European Court of Human Rights ('ECHR'),[61] which requires that a court or tribunal need not only be vested with apparent or formal impartiality, but must also provide such an impression so as to be perceived as such and exclude any legitimate doubt about its independence and impartiality.[62] Such a test does necessarily

---

[59] The Inter-American Commission has taken into account the rank and discipline in which military jurisdiction operates, for instance, in the individual petition of *Aluisio Cavalcante*; see Annual Report of the Inter-American Commission on Human Rights 2000, OEA/Ser./L/V/II.111, doc. 20 rev., 16 April 2001, Report No. 55/01, *Aluisio Cavalcante et al.*, para. 149. In the context of the European Court of Human Rights, in *AD and Others v. Turkey*, the Court found that the deprivation of liberty (of 21 days) involved in the penalty imposed upon the applicant, a sergeant in the Turkish armed forces, for the offence of military disobedience applied by the military superior, lacked the required independence taking into account the hierarchical structure in which such exercise of authority operated. See Manacorda and Mariniello, 2012, p. 569, *supra* note 1.

[60] On these issues with particular reference to the Peruvian case that draws the jurisdictional distinction between wartime and peacetime, see Yolanda Doig Díaz, "La Justicia Militar a la Luz de las Garantías de la Jurisdicción", in José Hurtado Pozo and Yolanda Doig Díaz, *La Reforma del Derecho Penal Militar*, Pontificia Universidad Católica del Perú and Universidad de Friburgo, Lima, 2002, pp. 39–41.

[61] Manacorda and Mariniello draw attention to the fact that unlike the IACHR, the ECHR has not addressed the question of independence and impartiality of military tribunals in connection with the exercise of jurisdiction over military personnel for alleged violations of human rights, but rather in relation to civilians or servicemen allegedly responsible for the commission of military offences. See Manacorda and Mariniello, 2012, p. 569, *supra* note 1.

[62] See Alicia Gil Gil, "El Derecho a un Juicio Justo como Elemento Normativo del Crimen de Guerra de su Privación y su Definición a través de la Jurisprudencia del Tribunal Europeo de Derechos Humanos", in Kai Ambos, Ezequiel Malarino and Gisela Elsner (eds.), *Sistema Interamericano de Protección de los Derechos Humanos y Derecho Penal Inter-*

---

require a casuistic analysis. In fact, in assessing whether those characteristics exist in a given case, the ECHR has mainly relied on the manner of appointment of the tribunal members, the existence of guarantees and safeguards against outside pressures, and whether the tribunal presents an appearance of independence.[63] While all these elements, in general terms, militate in favour of depriving military jurisdiction over core crimes, the latter is particularly relevant from the self-interest of armed forces in accountability approach, as also reflected in the following section.

16.4. Military Self-Interests in Applying a Reliable Jurisdictional Forum

16.4.1. Minimising Risks of Superior Responsibility

Additional considerations arising from the interpretation and application of superior responsibility, a fundamental principle of international humanitarian law and international criminal law inextricably related to the military function, may lead to answer the question as to the preferable forum for adjudicating core crimes in a similar way. As pointed out by Jo Stigen, the likelihood exists that military jurisdictions (a court martial or another kind of military tribunal) may not involve genuine prosecution.[64] From the perspective of the advocated interest in self-accountability of armed forces, the entrenched component of the superior responsibility of a military commander or superior under international humanitarian law of ensuring investigation and prosecution[65] for alleged violations of humanitarian law committed by subordinates, that under international criminal law entails criminal responsibility ensuing from its breach,[66] is to be fulfilled

---

nacional, vol. 1, Fundación Konrad Adenauer, Montevideo, 2010, p. 438, citing Martínez Cardoz Ruiz and the Case of *Piersack*, Judgment of 1 October of 1982 and the Case of *De Cubber*, Judgment of 29 October 1984. Also, Manacorda and Mariniello, 2012, p. 572, see *supra* note 1.

[63] Manacorda and Mariniello, 2012, p. 572, see *supra* note 1.

[64] Stigen, 2008, p. 206, see *supra* note 52.

[65] As pointed out by Mettraux, the so-called "'duty to punish' is somewhat of a misnomer". Guénaël Mettraux, *The Law of Command Responsibility*, Oxford University Press, Oxford, 2009, p. 250.

[66] In the context of the ICC Statute, Article 28 provides a different *mens rea* for military and civilian superior responsibility, which has triggered both critical as well as supporting views. For the latter see, for example, James Levine, "The Doctrine of Command Respon-

not merely by referring the case to the competent jurisdictional authorities,[67] as prescribed by domestic law, but rather referring to a jurisdictional forum capable of conducting genuine proceedings.

Indeed, from such a pragmatic perspective, a military commander or superior is not interested in discharging his superior responsibility only from a formalistic viewpoint, but in significantly contributing to ensure that criminal accountability is fairly attained. In this vein, depending on the institutional, political and the rule of law situation prevailing in a given country, a civilian jurisdiction may be preferable with a view to guaranteeing proceedings of such kind.

Pursuant to Article 87(1) and (3) of Additional Protocol I to the Geneva Conventions, military commanders are under the obligation "to suppress and report to competent authorities breaches of the Conventions and of [the] Protocol" and "where appropriate, to initiate disciplinary or penal action against violators thereof", respectively. This conventional obligation applies to all those who exercise command responsibility, from "commanders at the highest level to leaders with only a few men under their command" and with respect to all those who fall under their control (not only members of the armed forces). As further explained by the ICRC commentary on Article 87:

> As there is no part of the army which is not subordinated to a military commander at whatever level, this responsibility applies from the highest to the lowest level of the hierarchy, from the Commander-in-Chief down to the common soldier who takes over as head of the platoon to which he belongs at the moment his commander officer has fallen and is no longer capable of fulfilling his task.[68]

Interestingly, the ICRC commentary on Article 87 pointed to the fact that during the course of the discussions prior to the adoption of Ad-

---

sibility and its Application to Superior Civilian Leadership: Does the International Criminal Court have the Correct Standard?", in *Military Law Review*, 2007, vol. 193, pp. 54 ff.

[67] The supervisory duty of ensuring punishment under international humanitarian law has been interpreted by the ICTY and ICTR jurisprudence in the sense of being fulfilled by the transmission of the *noticia criminis* to the competent authorities to trigger investigations. See ICTR, *Bagosora and Nsengiyumva v. The Prosecutor*, Case No. ICTR-98-41-A, Appeals Chamber Judgment, 14 December 2011, para. 510.

[68] ICRC, Commentary on Protocol Additional to the Geneva Conventions of 12 August 1949, and relating to the Protection of Victims of International Armed Conflicts (Protocol I), 1987, para. 3553.

---

ditional Protocol I, some delegations had expressed their concerns with respect to the drafting of paragraph 3, considering that it could give place to inappropriate prosecutions and the unwarranted substitution of judicial functions by military commanders. The commentary, however, made it clear that such worries were unjustified as the purpose of the provision was to ensure that military commanders would fulfil their superior responsibility by adopting the most suitable measures depending on the particular circumstances, which could include drawing up a report in case of a breach and submitting the case to a *judicial authority* with such evidence as it was possible to find.[69]

In interpreting the superiors' duty to punish under international humanitarian law, the jurisprudence of the *ad hoc* tribunals can be read as allowing for the possibility of reporting the *noticia criminis* to civilian jurisdiction (also in relation to military superiors). In *Halilović*, the Appeals Chamber held that the necessary and reasonable measures for fulfilling the duty to punish, that involves the undertaking of genuine investigative measures to the extent it renders feasible in light of the prevailing circumstances, could be met by reporting the incidents and evidence, if so, for prosecution to the competent authorities "if the superior has no power to sanction".[70] It goes without saying that the nature and remit of the competent authorities are dictated by domestic law. In *Strugar*, the Trial Chamber Judgment pointed to the fact that the military tribunals constituted after the Second World War had interpreted the superior's duty to punish as requiring the undertaking of an effective investigation and ensuring that the perpetrators would be brought to justice.[71] The necessary casuistic analysis as to what constitutes in a given case and situation the adoption of necessary and reasonable measures for fulfilling the statutory and customary law obligation of ensuring accountability for the crimes allegedly committed by subordinates[72] was emphasised in *Boškoski and*

---

[69] *Ibid.*, para. 3562.

[70] International Criminal Tribunal for the former Yugoslavia, *Prosecutor v. Halilović*, Case No. IT-01-48-A, Appeals Chamber Judgment, 16 October 2007, para. 182 (confirming the reasoning of the Trial Chamber Judgment with further references to previous case law).

[71] International Criminal Tribunal for the former Yugoslavia, *Prosecutor v. Strugar*, Case No. IT-01-42-T, Trial Chamber Judgment, 31 January 2005, para. 376.

[72] The ICRC Study on Customary International Humanitarian Law includes in Rule 153 the duty to punish the persons responsible when war crimes have been committed by subordinates, applicable in both international and non-international armed conflicts, as a norm of customary international law. See Jean-Marie Henckaerts and Louise Doswald-Beck, *Cus-*

Tarčulovski. In fact, the scenario where the superior, knowing that the competent authorities are not functioning, does not discharge his duty by merely communicating the *noticia criminis* or referring the case to such jurisdictional forum was provided as an example by the Appeals Chamber of the casuistic approach.[73] A comparable scenario may exist where the jurisdictional forum is not capable of conducting genuine proceedings or such capability can be seriously put into question. The quality of jurisdictional proceedings and the perception of its legitimacy ought therefore to be of interest for military superiors.

16.4.2. Fulfilling Requirements of the Complementarity Test

The underlying purpose of complementarity, the cornerstone of the ICC Statute, embodies an old conception related to the duty of states to undertake investigation and prosecution for the most serious offences and violations of international law that can be traced back to Hugo Grotius's ideas.[74] The complementary intervention of the ICC is thus predicated upon the two-pronged test underpinning the admissibility criteria, that is, inability and/or unwillingness of a state to genuinely investigate and/or prosecute. Whether proceedings conducted by a military jurisdiction are capable of fulfilling the test, and thus allowing adjudication by the ICC, is a question that does not have a conclusive or generic answer falling under the necessary casuistic analysis.[75] At the outset, while complementarity

---

tomary *International Humanitarian Law. Vol. I: Rules*, ICRC, Cambridge University Press, Cambridge, 2005, pp. 558–63.

[73] International Criminal Tribunal for the former Yugoslavia, *Prosecutor v. Boškoski and Tarčulovski*, Case No. IT-04-82, Appeals Chamber Judgment, 19 May 2010, para. 234.

[74] Michael Newton, "Comparative Complementarity: Domestic Jurisdiction Consistent with the Rome Statute of the International Criminal Court", in *Military Law Review*, 2001, vol. 167, p. 26 (with further references).

[75] Such an approach was emphasised by the Office of the Prosecutor ('OTP') of the ICC, for instance, in relation to the preliminary examination of the situation in Colombia. See Office of the Prosecutor of the ICC, *Report on Preliminary Examination Activities 2013*, November 2013, para. 138: "Under Article 17 of the Statute, the Office's analysis of national proceedings is case specific, and there is no assumed preference for national proceedings to be conducted in civilian as opposed to military jurisdictions *per se*. The Office will evaluate whether specific national proceedings have been or are being carried out genuinely". The statement is particularly relevant with respect to the situation in Colombia where the military justice reform vested military jurisdiction with competence to adjudicate violations of international humanitarian law other than genocide, crimes against humanity, torture, enforced disappearance, forced displacement, sexual violence and extrajudicial killings when allegedly committed by active members of the military and police forces, ini-

---

does not dictate the type of jurisdictional fora, it is concerned with the effectiveness of domestic proceedings in terms of being capable of complying with due process and fair trial requirements, while entailing genuine proceedings. This allows drawing a parallel with the rule of exhaustion of domestic remedies central to the Inter-American system of human rights, since the rule operates on the basis of evaluating the effectiveness and genuine character of national proceedings. In such analysis the existence of an effective domestic remedy plays a pivotal role. Accordingly, the question of whether military jurisdiction constitutes an effective remedy in a given case is relevant for both the determination of the exhaustion of domestic remedies rule and the admissibility analysis in the context of the ICC,[76] although in practice diverse results may exist in both scenarios.

Under that approach and by virtue of the role of human rights case law under Article 21(3) of the ICC Statute, as part of the sources of applicable law for the ICC, the jurisprudence of the regional courts of human rights may be relevant for the analysis of admissibility.[77] Indeed, the interpretation advanced by such jurisprudence, as pointed out in the preceding section, could provide useful insight in the event that the compatibility of military jurisdiction with the admissibility requirements under the ICC Statute is at stake. The fact that the Inter-American system's jurispru-

---

tially accomplished with an amendment, mainly of Article 221, of the Colombian Constitution of December 2012. As pointed out by the reports of the OTP in the context of the preliminary examination, civil society, international organisations and international non-governmental organisations have put into question the pertinence of expanding the reach of military jurisdiction *vis-à-vis* the alleged lack of independence and impartiality of military courts. Pursuant to Article 221, military tribunals are composed of members of the public forces in active service or under retirement. See *ibid.*, paras. 134–38. Also Office of the Prosecutor of the ICC, *Report on Preliminary Examination Activities 2014*, 2 December 2014, paras. 116–18.

[76] Drawing such a parallel and arguing on its relevance, see Elizabeth Santalla Vargas, "Agotamiento de Recursos Internos y Principio de Complementariedad: ¿Dos Caras de la Misma Moneda?", in Kai Ambos, Ezequiel Malarino and Gisela Elsner (eds.), *Sistema Interamericano de Protección de Derechos Humanos y Derecho Penal Internacional*, vol. 2, Fundación Konrad Adenauer, Montevideo, 2011, pp. 517–41.

[77] In fact, the case law of the ICC has resorted on various occasions to the jurisprudence of the regional systems of protection of human rights on the basis of Article 21(3). See, Gilbert Bitti, "Article 21 of the Statute of the International Criminal Court and the Treatment of Sources of Law in the Jurisprudence of the ICC", in Carsten Stahn and Göran Sluiter (eds.), *The Emerging Practice of the International Criminal Court*, Koninklijke Brill N.V., Leiden, 2009, p. 301.

---

dence and pronouncements, as mentioned, have been confined to the analysis of compatibility of military jurisdiction with respect to violations of human rights law may be explained by the very same competence bestowed upon the system by virtue of the American Convention on Human Rights and the fact that it does not directly contain rules of international humanitarian law, preventing the declaration of international responsibility directly on the basis of this body of international law in cases entailing an armed conflict.[78] Divergent views have emerged between the Inter-American Commission and the IACHR as to their competence for resorting to the law of armed conflict when faced with situations where the factual background amounts to armed conflict scenarios. While the Inter-American Commission has found to be competent for applying international humanitarian law rules in such cases, the IACHR has considered that the law of armed conflict could only be applied for interpreting the American Convention on Human Rights and thus being precluded of directly applying international humanitarian law norms. However, the distinction between interpretation and direct application has become blurred with time or at least not so clear-cut as both fields of international law are intrinsically related.[79]

16.5. Concluding Remarks

From an international law standpoint, the question of the adequate jurisdictional forum (civilian or military) is central to the debate posed by the requirement, under conventional and customary law, of a fair and impartial tribunal or court. In this context, the self-interest in accountability of armed forces is necessarily linked to such understanding, and poses additional considerations moving the discussion beyond the purview of a purely 'legalistic' debate that, informed by the confluence of human

---

[78] Along the same lines, Shana Tabak observes "that institutional and procedural constraints within the human rights system had led to a favouring of HRL over humanitarian law"; see Shana Tabak, "Armed Conflict and the Inter-American Human Rights System: Application or Interpretation of International Humanitarian Law?", in Derek Jinks *et al.*, 2014, p. 221, see *supra* note 1.

[79] Alejandro Aponte draws attention to *Kononov v. Letonia* where the ECHR resorted to international humanitarian law rules in tandem with domestic provisions to analyse whether a breach of Article 7 had occurred. Commentary on the case has regarded such an application compatible with the doctrine of *renvoi*, which is embedded in Article 7. With references and further details on the discussion, see Alejandro Aponte, "El Sistema Interamericano de Derechos Humanos y el Derecho Internacional Humanitario: Una Relación Problemática", in Ambos *et al.*, 2010, pp. 129–33, see *supra* note 62.

---

rights, humanitarian law and international criminal law, arguably supports a general preference of civilian jurisdiction over human rights and international humanitarian law violations. This by no means overrides the necessary casuistic analysis supported by the fact that the operational environment and internal structure of military judicial systems vary greatly from country to country, which may result in material discrepancies as to the quality of military trials. The position advanced in this chapter ascribes, therefore, to an overall international law perspective that considers various relevant factors as a whole when addressing the question of the adequate jurisdictional forum. Such an approach applies equally to both wartime and peacetime scenarios, reducing the relevance of the traditional differentiated treatment when it comes to assessing the proper jurisdictional fora through the lens of the underlying rationale of self-interest in accountability.

Accountability for International Crimes within Insurgent Groups

René Provost*

17.1. Introduction

In Syria, dozens of women and men are held in unofficial 'prisons' run by
some of the armed groups fighting Islamic State or the Syrian government. The detainees are accused of a variety of offences, including war
crimes, and wait to be tried by one of the several competing courts established by different groups. Some courts are presided by former judges and
others by clerics or military leaders. They apply anything from the Unified Arab Code prepared by the Arab League to the judge's own personal
interpretation of the *Sharī'ah*. Trials are quick, and punishment is often
death.[1] In a similar fashion, in the rebel-held part of Ukraine, two men
were accused of sexual assault and tried by the "First People's Court" established by pro-Russian insurgents. On the basis of a public vote in the
town hall at the conclusion of a 'trial', one man was condemned to death
by firing squad, the other to serve on the front line to "redeem his honour
in combat".[2] This mirrors the practice of insurgents in other wars in Sri
Lanka, El Salvador, Nepal, Sierra Leone, Colombia, Rwanda, Congo, Sudan, Kosovo and many other places where irregular tribunals were created.

What are the reasons that push a non-state armed group to establish
a court that ostensibly includes within its jurisdiction the sanction of violations of international humanitarian law? Can it be said of insurgent

---

* **René Provost** is a Full Professor at the Faculty of Law and Centre for Human Rights and
Legal Pluralism, McGill University, Canada. He served as Law Clerk to Justice
L'Heureux-Dubé of the Supreme Court of Canada. He was the President of the Société
québécoise de droit international from 2002 to 2006 and the founding Director of the Centre for Human Rights and Legal Pluralism from 2005 to 2010. He is the author of *International Human Rights and Humanitarian Law* (Cambridge University Press, 2002).

[1] Ivan Watson and Raja Razek, "Rebel Court Fills Void amid Syrian Civil War", CNN, 26
January 2013; BBC, "The Boy Killed for an Off-hand Remark about Muhammad – Sharia
Spreads in Syria", 2 July 2013.

[2] BBC, "Ukraine Conflict: Summary Justice in Rebel East", 3 November 2014.

groups that they have self-interest in ensuring accountability of their members, in a manner that parallels what has been suggested with respect to the armed forces of the state?

Irregular armed groups are typically represented as wholly permeated by illegality, from the very resort to armed force to the involuntary recruitment of fighters to the means and methods of warfare used. They are taken to be truly *outlaws*, and often encompassed under a very broad understanding of 'terrorism'. International law broadly has refrained from declaring as illegal the use of force by or against the state in a national setting, limiting itself to extending to insurgents the same criminal sanctions for breaches of the laws of war as are applicable to governmental armed forces, and posing few limitations on a state's ability to criminalise insurgency under domestic law. At a minimum, it appears clear that the nature of non-state armed groups as a fighting force implies that they often share with official militaries a desire to increase their effectiveness by way of higher discipline and morale that can strengthen the chain of command. In two decisions, the Special Court for Sierra Leone found that accountability mechanisms established by non-state armed groups aimed primarily to maintain internal discipline, and had very little or nothing to do with a wish to sanction international criminal law or to act on the basis of moral, ethical or religious opposition to behaviour that amounts to violations of the laws of war.[3] In one of these decisions, the Special Court found that the sanction of what amounted to violations of international humanitarian law (rape, looting, burning) aimed at winning over the hearts and mind of the local population, whose support was needed to secure zones under Revolutionary United Front ('RUF') control and ensure operational success.[4] The desire to win the public's trust in the non-state armed group and thus provide some political stability is all the more evi-

---

[3] Special Court for Sierra Leone ('SCSL'), *Prosecutor v. Augustine Gbao et al.*, Trial Chamber, Judgment, 2 March 2009, SCSL-04-15-T, para 712 ('Gbao case, Judgment') (http://www.legal-tools.org/doc/7f05b7/). See also SCSL, *Prosecutor v. Alex Tamba Brima et al.*, Trial Chamber, Judgment, 20 June 2007, SCSL-04-16-T, para. 1739 ((http://www.legal-tools.org/doc/87ef08/): "[T]he RUF disciplinary system functioned essentially to allow the leadership to maintain control over all the RUF fighters and impose and maintain order in RUF-held territory. It failed to systematically deter or regularly and effectively punish crimes against civilians or persons *hors de combat*. The disciplinary process was fundamentally a means of keeping control over their own fighters and was not a system to punish for the commission of crimes".

[4] *Gbao* case, Judgment, paras. 707, 712, see *supra* note 3.

---

dent in situations in which an insurgent group controls significant portions of national territory for an extended period of time, such as the Liberation Tigers of Tamil Eelam ('LTTE') in Sri Lanka or the Farabundo Martí National Liberation Front ('FMLN') in El Salvador.[5]

It is therefore apparent that non-state armed groups do hold detainees, that they create institutions to hold these individuals accountable, and that their motivation for doing so overlaps at least to some degree with the reasons that move official armed forces to do the same. What should an insurgent group do when it captures an enemy who has committed serious crimes, and even war crimes or crimes against humanity? How should we legally characterise the actions taken by a non-state armed group that represses violations of the laws and customs of war carried out by some of its own fighters?

There are at least four related but distinct bundles of questions that arise from a consideration of the practice of insurgent courts in the context of an armed conflict. First, are there legal standards that explicitly or implicitly legitimise or prohibit the establishment of courts by an armed non-state actor? Second, if such courts could be lawfully created, what are the conditions required under international law for them to exercise their jurisdiction validly? Third, if an insurgent court is lawfully created and has exercised its jurisdiction in compliance with international law, what recognition is to be accorded to its judgments? And fourth, what does this reflection on the possibility and conditions of insurgent justice tell us about our conception of the rule of law and, more broadly, the concept of law?

These are vast and complex questions that call for a detailed exploration of existing international legal standards spanning international humanitarian law, international criminal law, international human rights law and general public international law. What is more, in order to offer a meaningful critique of the suggestion of insurgent justice, the study must be grounded in a fair appreciation of the reality of the practice of non-state armed groups in this respect, something on which little research has been systematically carried out. As a result, this chapter will not seek to offer answers to all these complex questions, much less to the overall legality of insurgent justice, but rather will attempt to map as comprehen-

---

5   Sandesh Sivakumaran, "Courts of Armed Opposition Groups: Fair Trials or Summary Justice?", in *Journal of International Criminal Justice*, 2009, vol. 7, no. 3, p. 489.

sively as possible the questions that must be explored in each of the four bundle of issues identified in the previous paragraph.

17.2. Legitimacy of Establishing Insurgent Courts

Non-state armed groups can emerge as much in the context of an international armed conflict as in a non-international armed conflict, although they have played a more significant role in the latter type of wars, which in turn have been more prevalent than international conflicts over the last half-century. Despite the thickening regulation of internal wars, bringing about an overall convergence in the rules applicable to the two categories of conflicts, the distinction between international and internal armed conflicts remains the *summa divisio* of international humanitarian law. Given that the documented practice of insurgent courts essentially relates to non-international armed conflicts, my remarks will centre on legal norms that are applicable to this category of conflicts, but with some asides to consider the establishment of courts of non-state armed groups in international armed conflicts when it gives rise to distinct questions.

There is both an asymmetry and a paradox in the structure of international humanitarian law applicable to non-international armed conflicts. The asymmetry refers to the fact that state and non-state parties to the conflicts are by and large bound by the same rules on the conduct of hostilities and on the protection of civilians and other non-combatants. This equality of obligations is translated by the balanced application of international criminal responsibility for war crimes, applied equally to government and insurgent combatants. Despite this, the status of insurgent and government forces under humanitarian law is entirely different, because rebels do not enjoy 'combatant immunity', that is the principle that a soldier cannot be held accountable for participating in an armed conflict in which he or she behaves in a manner consistent with humanitarian law. There is in humanitarian law no concept of 'lawful combatant' that can be applied to rebels in a non-international armed conflict. As a result, no immunity attaches to participation by insurgents in a civil war, even if they behave in a manner that respects international legal standards in every way. This corresponds to a radical asymmetry between the state and insurgents under international humanitarian law.

A critical challenge in asymmetrical wars such as the vast majority of non-international armed conflicts is to initiate any kind of compliance.

The fact that insurgents such as the Taliban in Afghanistan are by and large excluded from the benefit of working within the parameters of humanitarian law means that they have, from the outset, very little incentive to do so. Given that taking up arms against the government is treason punishable with the utmost severity, why would insurgents bother to comply with the law of war? The fact that governments have elected to call these norms 'law' does not in itself present a very strong moral or ethical claim upon rebels fighting to topple one of these governments. Indeed, explaining the process whereby international humanitarian law can impose obligations on rebel groups and individual insurgents has remained a challenge to that regime. The best explanation available is that, under public international law, states may elect to directly create rights and obligations for other actors under their jurisdiction. Although I myself have advanced such an argument in the past, I now view it as persuasive only within a strictly positivist reading of law. The broad failure of insurgents in non-international armed conflicts to comply with the laws of war stands as the strongest indictment of such a view. Instead, it can be argued that international law corresponds to real constraints on states' liberty to do as they please because it emerges from a process in which they are centrally implicated. In other words, international law is a collective project in the construction of which states are continuously involved. As constructivists in international relations have put it, the reality of international law corresponds to the solidity of a community of practice.[6]

As between states, deemed sovereign equals by the most fundamental principle of international law, there is at least a formal symmetry which facilitates interactions and suggests that law is more than a conduit for the exercise of raw power. How does this reading of international law inspired by legal pluralism transpose to international humanitarian law in the context of non-international armed conflicts, marked by radical asymmetry between belligerents? The question is fascinating because law in this context is nearly entirely stripped of all institutions which normally come to cloud the visibility of the impact of legal norms alone, and because it applies to a setting in which resort to raw power is already occurring but unable to bring a resolution to the issues at hand (there is no way

---

[6]   See Emanuel Adler, *Communitarian International Relations; The Epistemic Foundations of International Relations*, Routledge, London, 2005, p. 11. This is brought to bear on international law in a fascinating way by Jutta Brunnée and Stephen J. Toope, *Legitimacy and Legality in International Law: An Interactional Account*, Cambridge University Press, Cambridge, 2010.

to 'force' rebels to comply with the laws of war).[7] How, then, can non-state armed groups be induced into better compliance with international humanitarian law? What does "better compliance" correspond to for such groups?

The paradox of international humanitarian law applicable to internal armed conflicts is that it seems to demand on the one hand what it fails to authorise on the other. Thus, under Common Article 3 of the 1949 Geneva Conventions, the single provision of these Conventions applicable to internal wars, "each party to the conflict" is required to respect a number of minimal humanitarian imperatives. Yet, in the part of the provision that deals with enforcement measures presumably required to implement these obligations, the Conventions limit judicial activity to "regularly constituted courts affording all the judicial guarantees which are recognized as indispensable by civilized peoples". The expression "regularly constituted courts" is commonly understood to cover only courts established according to the laws in force in the country, to the exclusion of any "court" set up by insurgent groups.[8] It is thus as if non-state groups are required to respect the laws but that their efforts in ensuring such respect are not ratified as such and they are deprived of what would ordinarily be a key means of enforcing the law.

The same paradox is partly retained in the 1977 Protocol II to the Geneva Conventions, which further develops international humanitarian law applicable to internal conflicts: on the one hand, in order for this Protocol to be applicable, the insurgent must demonstrate the ability to implement its provisions (Article 1); on the other, the Protocol fails to recognise any legality to an insurgent that actually does implement its provisions *vis-à-vis* its own members.[9] Likewise, international criminal law imposes accountability on rebel leaders on the basis of command respon-

---

[7] I have explored the role of reciprocity more fully in René Provost, "Asymmetrical Reciprocity and Compliance with the Laws of War", in Benjamin Perrin (ed.), *Modern Warfare: Armed Groups, Private Militaries, Humanitarian Organizations, and the Law*, UBC Press, Vancouver, 2012, pp. 30–31, and René Provost, *International Human Rights and Humanitarian Law*, Cambridge University Press, Cambridge, 2002, pp. 121–238.

[8] The issue is debated. See Jonathan Somer, "Jungle Justice: Passing Sentence on the Equality of Belligerents in Non-international Armed Conflict", in *International Review of the Red Cross*, 2007, vol. 89, no. 867, p. 655–90.

[9] Protocol (II) Additional to the Geneva Conventions of 12 August 1949, and Relating to the Protection of Victims of Non-international Armed Conflicts, UNTS no. 17513, vol. 1125, 7 December 1978 (http://www.legal-tools.org/doc/fd14c4/).

---

sibility if they fail to sanction a war crime. If rebel leaders do establish a system of internal courts to sanction war crimes, that may limit their own responsibility but no general legitimacy is thus granted to such a practice under international law. There is an opening in the law as it stands now to develop a legal space in which the practice of insurgent groups in setting up courts can be regulated so that it accords to a degree with the requirements of justice under international law. The 1977 Protocol II does not refer to a "regularly constituted court" as does Common Article 3 of the 1949 Conventions, but rather simply to a "court offering the essential guarantees of independence and impartiality". The omission of the "regularly constituted" nature of courts can be interpreted as removing one explicit block to the legal recognition of tribunals established by insurgents. This in turn begs the question of defining the conditions under which an insurgent court could be afforded a measure of legal recognition, an issue I consider in the next section. That said, to add to the confusion, the 1998 Rome Statute of the International Criminal Court, in its section devoted to war crimes committed in non-international armed conflicts, returns to the Common Article 3 formulation referring to a "regularly constituted court".[10]

While the matter has received comparatively little attention, it is possible that a non-state armed group may be a party to an international armed conflict and, in that context, establish its own judicial institutions. This may correspond to the situation of an interstate armed conflict in which militias or organised resistance movements belonging to one of the parties to the conflict take part in hostilities. Pursuant to Article 4(A)(2) of the 1949 Third Geneva Convention, members of such irregular groups are deemed lawful combatants if, among other conditions, they conduct "their operations in accordance with the laws and customs of war".[11] With the rise of international criminal law in the last two decades, the move towards the criminalisation of all serious violations of treaty and customary international humanitarian law, and the growing rejection of any impunity for war crimes, it is reasonable to assert that an aspect of conducting one's operation in accordance with the laws of war is the penal repression of their breach. Under this light, militias or organised resistance movements

---

[10] Statute of the International Criminal Court, 17 July 1998, in force 1 July 2002, 2187 UNTS 90, Art. 8(2)(c)(iv) ('ICC Statute') (http://www.legal-tools.org/doc/7b9af9/).

[11] Convention (III) Relative to the Treatment of Prisoners of War of August 12, 1949, 21 October 1950, Art. 4 (http://www.legal-tools.org/doc/365095/).

would be required to create insurgent courts. The argument seems all the more unassailable pursuant to the 1977 Additional Protocol I, according to which wars of national liberation against colonial domination, alien occupation, and racist regimes are deemed to be international armed conflicts (Article 1(4)).[12] Under Article 86 of Protocol I, "High Contracting Parties" but also "Parties to the conflict" have a duty to "repress grave breaches" of the Conventions and Protocol and to "suppress all other breaches".[13] "Repress" here has been taken to refer to the criminal sanction of violation, while "suppress" does not preclude criminal sanction but leaves open other options such as disciplinary procedures or civil or administrative measures.[14] That said, Protocol I also lays out procedural guarantees applicable to all sentences and penalties imposed for any penal offence related to the armed conflict, requiring that they be based on "a conviction pronounced by an impartial and regularly constituted court".[15] The reference to a "regularly constituted court" mirrors the requirement found in Common Article 3, in contrast to the more open formulation used in Protocol II. As discussed above, "regularly constituted court" is commonly taken to refer to courts established according to the official law of the state, excluding the possibility of tribunals created by non-state belligerents. It thus appears that the same paradox obtains in international armed conflicts as in non-international armed conflicts, that is international humanitarian law requiring on the one hand (the repression of breaches) what it does not authorise on the other (a non-"regularly constituted court").

The legal paradox may reflect an awkward integration of different policy and political objectives pursued in the adoption of the 1949 Geneva Conventions and 1977 Additional Protocols, but it also corresponds to a concrete and immediate concern in the practice of non-state armed groups in times of armed conflicts: what should a rebel group do if one of its

---

[12] Protocol (I) Additional to the Geneva Conventions of 12 August 1949, and Relating to the Protection of Victims of International Armed Conflicts, UNTS no. 17512, vol. 1125, 8 June 1977, Art. 1 ('Additional Protocol I') (http://www.legal-tools.org/doc/d9328a/).

[13] Ibid., Art. 86.

[14] Yves Sandoz, Christophe Swinarski and Bruno Zimmermann (eds.), Commentary on the Additional Protocols of 8 June 1977 to the Geneva Conventions of 12 August 1949, and Relating to the Protection of Victims of International Armed Conflicts (Protocol I), International Committee of the Red Cross, Geneva, 1987, p. 1011.

[15] Additional Protocol I, Art. 75(4), see supra note 12.

fighters commits a war crime or if it captures an enemy combatant or a civilian responsible for a serious violation of international humanitarian law?

In an *amicus curiae* brief submitted to the International Criminal Court ('ICC'), Amnesty International takes the positions that the accused, Jean-Pierre Bemba, could not rely on mechanisms internal to his Mouvement de Libération du Congo ('MLC') to sanction violations of international law carried out by troops under his command; instead, he should have referred the matter to the state on whose territory the events took place, or to a third state willing to act on the basis of universal jurisdiction, or to an international tribunal.[16] The ICC Pre-Trial Chamber, ruling in a preliminary manner on the confirmation of charges, broadly disagreed with the approach advocated by Amnesty International: it discounted a request made by Bemba to the United Nations Secretary-General to open an international investigation into crimes committed in the region, finding it too little too late. On the other hand, it gave particular weight to "the availability of a functional military system within the MLC through which [the accused] could have punished the crimes committed".[17] While it would be an overstatement to affirm that this amounts to a clear proclamation by the ICC of the legitimacy of insurgent courts, as that question was not directly before the Court, it does suggest that an overly narrow reading of the requirement that a court be "regularly constituted" should not be countenanced. Some caution seems warranted in assessing the significance of this decision, on the basis of its preliminary nature, liable to be revisited by the Court in its decision on the merits of the case. A second reason to be cautious is the peculiar rendering of the crime of passing of sentence or carrying out an execution without a prior decision of a "regularly constituted court, affording all judicial guarantees which are generally recognised as indispensable"[18] in the Elements of Crimes. As first noted by Jonathan Somer, the Elements of Crimes subsume the re-

---

[16] International Criminal Court ('ICC'), *Prosecutor v. Jean-Pierre Bemba Gombo*, Amnesty International, Amicus Curiae Observations on Superior Responsibility submitted pursuant to Rule 103 of the Rules of Procedure and Evidence, 20 April 2009, ICC-01/05-01/08-406, paras. 22–23 ('ICC RPE') (http://www.legal-tools.org/doc/9efb78/).

[17] ICC, *Prosecutor v. Jean-Pierre Bemba Gombo*, Decision Pursuant to Article 61(7)(a) and (b) of the Rome Statute on the Charges of the Prosecutor against Jean-Pierre Bemba Gombo, 15 June 2009, ICC-01/05-01/08, paras. 497, 501 (http://www.legal-tools.org/doc/07965c/).

[18] ICC Statute, Art. 8(2)(c)(iv), see *supra* note 10.

---

quirement that the court be "regularly constituted" into the requirement touching on due process:

> There was no previous judgement pronounced by a court, or the court that rendered judgement was not "regularly constituted", that is, it did not afford the essential guarantees of independence and impartiality, or the court that rendered judgement did not afford all other judicial guarantees generally recognized as indispensable under international law.[19]

This conflation tweaks the relationship between the question of the legitimacy of the establishment of a court by a non-state armed group and the conditions under which it must operate to respect the requirements of international law, a second question to which I turn in the next section.

A final element touching on the legal recognition of courts established by non-state armed groups centres on the possibility that an insurgent group is successful and either takes over as the new government of the state or establishes a new state. According to a widely accepted provision in the United Nations International Law Commission's Articles on State Responsibility, in such circumstances, the conduct of the insurrectional movement is to be attributed to the state.[20] The provision forms part of a codification of the principles of state responsibility, and aims to shield states from responsibility for acts or insurgents, save in the exceptional situation where the insurgency succeeds. No attention is directed at the impact of such an attribution on an act the legitimacy of which turns on the fact that it was carried out by a state. Instead, on the basis of consistent state practice, a blanket approach is adopted whereby all acts of any victorious non-state armed group is imputed to the state, regardless of the legitimacy of the insurgency.[21] Applying this principle to the exercise of jurisdiction by insurgent courts, it suggests that judicial decisions become attributed to the state, which would imply that they are legitimate. Indeed, it would be unexpected for the new government issued from an insurgency to challenge the legality of judicial decisions it took prior to victory.

---

[19] ICC, Elements of Crimes, 9 September 2002, ICC-ASP/1/3 (part II-B), p. 34 (http://www.legal-tools.org/doc/3c0e2d/). See Somer, 2007, p. 674, *supra* note 8.

[20] James Crawford, *The International Law Commission's Articles on State Responsibility: Introduction, Text and Commentaries*, Cambridge University Press, Cambridge, 2002.

[21] *Ibid.*, Art. 10, pp. 116–20.

In conclusion, the question of whether it is at all possible for a non-state armed group to legally establish a tribunal with jurisdiction to administer international criminal responsibility is not answered with any degree of clarity in international law. There has been a discernible evolution in international humanitarian law towards a greater opening to the recognition of this possibility, although the newer norms do not replace but rather complement the older, more restrictive provisions. Further, norms found in other parts of public international law such as those pertaining to state responsibility can offer important contextual elements to the analysis. Indeed, it might be suggested that the "responsibility to protect" carries implication for actors other than states, and that non-state armed groups not only may elect to create tribunals to combat impunity, but are in fact under an obligation to do so.[22]

17.3. Exercise of Jurisdiction by an Insurgent Court

If we accept that a non-state armed group may establish its own court system, or alternatively if we follow the direction given to the question in the ICC Elements of Crimes whereby a court will be regularly constituted if it is impartial and independent, what are the conditions for the valid exercise of jurisdiction by this type of courts? This opens two distinct lines of enquiry: the first relates to the law applicable *to* an irregular tribunal, establishing the requirements that will allow an assessment of whether it operates in a lawful manner; the second line of enquiry relates to the law applicable *by* an irregular tribunal, that is the body of norms that such a court would be called to interpret and apply. Each point is explored in turn.

As with international humanitarian law in general, the law applicable to the operation of an insurgent tribunal will be governed by norms that relate to one or the other of the categories of armed conflicts that have been differentiated under international law. As mentioned in the previous section, the lowest threshold of applicability of humanitarian law corresponds to a non-international armed conflict governed by Common Article 3 of the 1949 Geneva Conventions. Paragraph 1(d) of Common Article 3 requires that a decision be given by a regularly constituted court "affording all the judicial guarantees which are recognised as indispensa-

---

22 On the responsibility to protect, see W. Andy Knight and Frazer Egerton (eds.), *The Routledge Handbook of the Responsibility to Protect*, Routledge, London, 2012.

ble by civilized peoples".[23] The reference is quite vague, with no indication as to what judicial guarantees would be regarded as indispensable by civilised peoples engaged in an internal armed conflict. It must be recalled that, at the time of the adoption of the 1949 Geneva Conventions, no binding human rights treaty touching on due process had yet been adopted. The just concluded trials before the International Military Tribunals sitting in Nuremberg and Tokyo had demonstrated limited concerns for questions of procedure and evidence that might have given expression to a notion that some procedural guarantees are indispensable, even in times of war.[24] The commentary to Common Article 3 published by the International Committee of the Red Cross ('ICRC') in 1952 gives a sense of the limited ambition of this reference:

> Sentences and executions without previous trial are too open to error. "Summary justice" may be effective on account of the fear which it causes – though this has yet to be proved; but it adds too many further innocent victims to all the other innocent victims of the conflict. All civilized nations surround the administration of justice with safeguards aimed at eliminating the possibility of errors. The Convention has rightly proclaimed that it is essential to do this even in time of war. We must be very clear about one point: it is only "summary" justice which it is intended to prohibit.[25]

It is known that Winston Churchill initially favoured the summary execution of the Nazi leadership at the close of the Second World War, and only relented in favour of an international tribunal after President Franklin D. Roosevelt and Joseph Stalin insisted otherwise.[26] This, combined with states' general reluctance to agree to any regulation of internal armed conflict in the 1949 Geneva Conventions, suggests rather minimalistic ambitions regarding procedural guarantees under Common Article 3. Of course, the interpretation to be given to this provision cannot remain

---

[23] The standard is repeated in the ICC Statute, which uses the expression "judicial guarantees which are generally recognised as indispensable" (Art. 8(2)(c)(iv)), dropping the reference to "civilized peoples", see *supra* note 10.

[24] See Antonio Cassese, *Cassese's International Criminal Law*, 3rd ed., Oxford University Press, Oxford, 2013, p. 340.

[25] Jean Pictet (ed.), *Commentary on the Geneva Conventions of 12 August 1949*, vol. 1: *Geneva Convention I*, International Committee of the Red Cross, Geneva, 1952, p. 54.

[26] Ian Cobain, "Britain Favoured Execution over Nuremberg Trials for Nazi Leaders", in *The Guardian*, 25 October 2012.

frozen in time but must evolve in light of the state parties' practice as well as the general context of international law, including due process guarantees in international human rights law, a point I will return to presently.

The thickening regulation of human rights in the three decades that followed the inception of the 1949 Geneva Conventions is reflected in the 1977 Additional Protocol II provision dealing with prosecutions. Article 6(2) of Protocol II requires that any conviction be issued by "a court offering the essential guarantees of independence and impartiality", indicating some minimum standards touching on the judicial appointment process, stability of tenure, and the required stance to be adopted by the judge. The provision then goes on to detail some of the procedural guarantees, including the right to be informed of the particulars of the alleged crime, the requirement of individual as opposed to collective guilt, the principle of *nullum crimen, nulla poena sine lege,* the presumption of innocence, the right to be present at one's trial and prohibition against forced self-incrimination. It is interesting to note that these specific elements are also found in the corresponding provision in the 1977 Additional Protocol I, Article 75, applicable to international armed conflicts (including wars of national liberation). Article 75 not only maintains the more restrictive requirement that the court be "regularly constituted", as discussed earlier, but also that the court respect "the generally recognised principles of regular judicial procedure". These principles are described in language that is identical to Article 6(2) of Protocol II, except that further rights are given which include the right to cross-examine witnesses, the prohibition of double jeopardy and the right to a public judgment. There is thus a significant convergence of standards applicable in international armed conflicts and non-international armed conflicts, leading some to suggest that, at a minimum, Article 6(2) of Protocol II should be taken as giving expression to the due process requirement implied in Common Article 3.[27] This is related to the approach adopted by Justice Stevens in his opinion in *Hamdan v. Rumsfeld,* in which he relies on the content of Article 75 of Protocol I to flesh out the procedural guarantees demanded by Common Article 3.[28]

---

[27] Sivakumaran, 2009, p. 502, see *supra* note 5.

[28] Supreme Court of the United States, *Hamdan v. Rumsfeld*, 548 US 557, 627, 29 June 2006. It is interesting to note that Justice Stevens interprets Common Article 3 in light of Article 75 of Protocol I despite the fact that the United States has not ratified Protocol I.

International human rights law provides a distinct source of norms that can be considered either as directly applicable to insurgent justice or as part of the normative context guiding the interpretation of the 1949 Geneva Conventions and the 1977 Additional Protocols. Treaty and customary international human rights provide a comprehensive code of procedural fairness applicable to judicial decision-making. These have been developed to a considerable degree in the jurisprudence of both human rights tribunals and bodies as well as by international criminal tribunals. The application of these human rights standards to insurgent courts raises a number of important issues, however. The first question is whether non-state armed groups are bound by human rights norms at all. The traditional view holds that human rights create obligations for states only, as they were conceived as a bulwark against abuses originating in state action. Human rights treaties, universal as well as regional, are formulated in ways that strongly support this narrow reading of the ambit of human rights law. Seeing as there is no shortage of violations of human rights at the hands of private actors, the general trend in human rights law has been to try to overcome this obstacle by expanding the scope of state obligation. A significant development of human rights in the last three decades, starting with the landmark decision of the Inter-American Court of Human Rights in *Velasquez-Rodriguez* in 1988, has been the expansion of state obligations to prevent, investigate and punish the denial of human rights at the hand of non-state actors.[29] This is an extremely important evolution of human rights, requiring states to be proactive and reactive in the protection of human rights, but it does not seem to have much of an effect on the issue of insurgent justice. In the context of a non-international armed conflict in which non-state actors are either fighting among themselves or fighting against the government, it appears highly unlikely that the government can do anything to better protect the procedural rights of individuals being tried by rebel tribunals. In some circumstances, a third state may be found to exert "effective control" over the

---

[29] See Andrew Clapham, *Human Rights Obligations of Non-State Actors*, Oxford University Press, Oxford, 2006; Andrew Clapham (ed.), *Human Rights and Non-State Actors*, Edward Elgar, Cheltenham, 2013.

non-state armed group and, as such, be held accountable for the group's violation of human rights.[30]

A second, much more ambitious approach draws inspiration from the German constitutional doctrine of *Drittwirkung* to argue that human rights are directly applicable to purely private acts, even absent any state action.[31] In a large measure, this push is driven by a desire to capture in the human rights net the activities of multinational corporations and terrorists, often operating beyond the effective reach of any national government. Normatively speaking, this is an approach that appears much more suitable to regulate the operation of insurgent tribunals. Indeed, one rationale for the extension of human rights obligations to non-state armed groups is based on its effective exercise of state-like power over a determined territory or population. This matches the conditions of applicability of Protocol II, and there may be a stronger argument that human rights should apply directly to this type of insurgent group. Conversely, the position is harder to defend for non-international armed conflicts to which only Common Article 3 is applicable because there is no necessary control over a part of national territory. This is significant because these lower threshold armed conflicts are precisely those for which international humanitarian law remains most vague as to the conditions under which an insurgent court can be said to respect public international law. Ultimately, it must be acknowledged that the full horizontal application of international human rights standards corresponding to the *Drittwirkung* doctrine remains largely *de lege ferenda*.

Even if non-state armed groups are considered bound directly by international human rights law, a second challenge concerns the extent to which human rights are applicable to situations of armed conflicts. While it is now settled that international human rights law does not simply cease to be applicable when an armed conflict occurs, it is also accepted that the onset of an armed conflict does have an impact on the applicability of human rights. The degree to which human rights remain applicable during an armed conflict has been the subject of enormous doctrinal and judicial

---

[30] See, for example, European Court of Human Rights, *Chiragov and Others v. Armenia*, Grand Chamber, Judgment, Application no. 13216/05, 16 June 2016, para. 186 ('Chiragov case, Judgment') (http://www.legal-tools.org/doc/be0923/).

[31] Clapham, 2006, p. 352, see *supra* note 22. See also Andrew Clapham, "The 'Drittwirkung' of the Convention", in Ronald Macdonald, Franz Matscher and Herbert Petzold (eds.), *The European System for the Protection of Human Rights*, Martinus Nijhoff, Dordrecht, 1993, pp. 163–206.

attention, including the International Court of Justice's characterisation of human rights as *lex generalis* and international humanitarian law as *lex specialis*.[32] Beyond the suitability of formulaic approaches such as this one, it seems warranted to adopt an approach that considers distinct human rights norms on a case-by-case basis to determine if and to what extent they ought to be considered applicable to a situation of armed conflict. While Article 6 of Protocol II and Article 75 of Protocol I were inspired by human rights standards, it is clear that express due process guarantees under international humanitarian law are less comprehensive than their human rights counterparts. This is consistent with the possibility that procedural guarantees be derogated from in times of emergency threatening the life of the nation, of which war is understood to be the archetype.[33] To some extent, the fact that the 1977 Protocols borrowed some but not all due process requirements from human rights law stands as a judgment by the international community of states that the humanitarian law conventions represent those norms that are suitable for application to situations of armed conflict. While customary law and the interpretation of treaties are in constant evolution, perhaps opening some space for the progressive enlargement of due process guarantees applicable in war, it appears likely that the changes will be incremental and limited. The situation seems different for armed conflicts to which only Common Article 3 is applicable, as this regime was created at a time when there were no accepted international human rights in positive law; as a result, a strong argument can be made that Common Article 3 must be seen as significantly transformed by the emergence of international human rights law. In is in this light that Article 6 of Protocol I can be taken as a statement of those basic procedural rights suitable to be applied in a non-international armed conflict and, as such, as a guide to the interpretation of Common Article 3.

Two further points must be made regarding the law applicable to insurgent courts. First, the practice of states in the establishment and op-

---

[32] Provost, 2002, see *supra* note 7; William A. Schabas, "*Lex Specialis?* Belt and Suspenders? The Parallel Operation of Human Rights Law and the Law of Armed Conflict, and the Conundrum of *Jus ad Bellum*", in *Israel Law Review*, 2007, vol. 40, no. 2, p. 592.

[33] Under United Nations General Assembly, International Covenant on Civil and Political Rights, 19 December 1966, Art. 4 (http://www.legal-tools.org/doc/2838f3/), due process guarantees are not listed as non-derogable, although the matter has been the subject of some debate.

eration of courts operating in conflict zones to try authors of serious violations of international law is an important consideration in the interpretation of applicable norms. All laws must be interpreted with due regard to the context of their application. It is understood that armed conflicts, whether international or internal, usually correspond to less than ideal circumstances for carrying out judicial functions, with the possible exception of long-term belligerent occupation. It is thus important to take as points of comparison not due process protection granted by courts operating in normal circumstances, but instead the practice of military tribunals operating under battlefield conditions.[34] For example, the requirement that a court be independent may well be taken to correspond to dramatically different arrangements for a military commission sitting near the battlefield, on the one hand, and for a regular court sitting in peace time, on the other. A study of what states have considered to be indispensable judicial guarantees in this unusual context therefore appears as a necessary component of any analysis of international legal standards applicable to insurgent tribunals.

The second point is to recall that states and non-state armed groups are significantly different types of actors. Indispensable judicial guarantees found to be required under international humanitarian law for a state rendering judgment in an armed conflict are not necessarily applicable, *ipso facto*, to an insurgent group doing the same. The material ability of non-state armed groups to administer justice will more often than not be much more limited than that of states. To this material asymmetry corresponds, under a proper interpretation of international humanitarian law, a normative asymmetry. The common but differentiated responsibilities of states and insurgents to afford due process guarantees lead to related but distinct mapping exercises to determine what must be done to maintain compliance with international law.

The issue of the law applicable *to* insurgent tribunals is complex, with intersecting regimes applied differently to state and non-state actors. A second, distinct issue relates to the law applicable *by* insurgent tribunals. This speaks to the nature of rebel courts as institutions of domestic or international legal orders as well as the legislative competence of non-state armed groups. The process whereby a non-state armed group may create a tribunal and the manner in which it structures and operates it are

---

[34] See, for example, the contributions of Christopher Jenks and Franklin D. Rosenblatt in this volume.

distinct from the choice of substantive law to be applied by an insurgent court. There is wide variation in the type of laws applied by such courts, from an invocation of the laws and customs of war to the application of 'codes' enacted by the insurgent movement itself. Starting with public international law, if we leave aside for now all questions related to the legitimacy of establishing a court and the conditions for its valid operations, there seems to be little basis to object to an insurgent court invoking regimes such as international humanitarian law, international criminal law or international human rights law. The universal foundation of these norms suggests that they are applicable to all situations of armed conflict, and indeed at least humanitarian law and international criminal law are meant to bind equally all sides to a conflict. This is articulated in an express fashion in the applicability provision of Protocol II, Article 1(1), which demands that non-state armed groups control a part of national territory so as "to implement this Protocol". Likewise, the possibility under Article 96(3) of Protocol I that a national liberation movement may issue an undertaking to apply the Geneva Conventions and Protocol I stands as confirmation that international law recognises the power of rebel movements to invoke international law. The establishment of insurgent courts may lead to probe with greater insistence the scope of the normative agency recognised to non-state armed groups under the 1977 Protocols, including the possibility that a rebel group may attach a "reservation" of some kind to its agreement to be bound by the humanitarian treaty. This may be taken as a provocative suggestion, but there is a vibrant practice of reservations by states to the Geneva Conventions and Protocols, and it is not obvious why a non-state actor given the autonomy to consent to be bound by a treaty must do so lock, stock and barrel, in the manner of a contract of adhesion, whereas consent by a state may be modulated by way of a reservation.[35]

Questions may also be asked in relation to treaties that have not been ratified by the state on whose territory an armed conflict is taking place: may an insurgent movement invoke and apply a treaty such as Pro-

---

[35] On reservations, see Claude Pilloud, "Reservations to the Geneva Conventions of 1949", in *International Review of the Red Cross*, 1976, vol. 16, no. 180, p. 107; Claude Pilloud, "Reservations to the Geneva Conventions of 1949 II", in *International Review of the Red Cross*, 1976, vol. 16, no. 181, p. 163; Julie Gaudreau, "Les réserves aux protocoles additionnels aux conventions de Genève pour la protection des victimes de la guerre", in *Revue Internationale de la Croix-Rouge*, 2003, vol. 85, no. 849, p. 143.

tocol II or the ICC Statute if the state itself has refused to ratify them? Could a national liberation movement make a declaration under Article 96(3) of Protocol I if the state that it is fighting has not ratified the Protocol? While it may be thought somewhat perverse to imagine setting roadblocks to prevent a non-state armed group from imposing further legal obligations upon itself, it does resonate with one perspective critical of the function of international law in the world community, often designed with the label 'lawfare'. According to this perspective, law is sometimes deployed as a weapon during an armed conflict, often by a weaker party, as a substitute for traditional means and methods of war.[36] The goal is to use legal shackles to prevent a more powerful belligerent from using all the resources at its disposal. While a standard objection to lawfare is that it aims to uphold norms that are otherwise unimpeachable, this is much less compelling in relation to treaty norms that a state has not assented to by way of ratification. There is of course no suggestion that an insurgent court's decision to invoke a treaty not ratified by the state can have the effect of legally binding the state to that treaty, but it will be difficult to draw a bright line if an insurgent court sits in judgment of a government soldier and considers itself bound by a treaty. This is especially so given the fluid relation, in the practice of international criminal tribunals, between customary and conventional norms in the fields of human rights, humanitarian law and international criminal law.[37]

In recent years, non-state armed groups have engaged a different type of transnational normative activity, by binding themselves to supranational standards that are not tied to state consent or practice. Most significantly, Geneva Call, a non-governmental organisation seeking to engage with insurgent groups to convince them to abandon the use of anti-personnel landmines, has managed to induce more than 50 non-state groups engaged in armed conflicts in Asia and Africa to sign a "deed of commitment" whereby they renounce the use of landmines. Although the work of the organisation found inspiration in the Ottawa Convention on Anti-Personnel Landmines, its activities are not part of that regime, directed at states, and indeed most insurgent groups who signed the deed of commitment operate in the territory of a state that has not ratified the Ottawa Convention. Geneva Call later expanded its activities to include

---

[36] Charles J. Dunlap Jr, "Lawfare Today: A Perspective", in *Yale Journal of International Affairs*, 2008, vol. 3, no. 1, p. 146.

[37] Cassese, 2013, p. 9, see *supra* note 24.

deeds of commitments on the prohibition of child soldiers and of sexual violence.[38] It is not altogether clear whether Geneva Call considers its deed of commitment to be legally binding for the rebels, although the very label and formal signing ceremony unambiguously signal a ritualistic invocation of the force and majesty of the law. I would suggest that in agreeing to live by certain humanitarian norms, whether such agreement is expressed in the formal signing of a deed of commitment or simply in the oral undertaking of a rebel leader, non-state actors are creating international humanitarian law in a fashion that is equally as real and possibly equally as effective as states ratifying an international treaty on the same subject matter. This conclusion would certainly be strengthened by a non-state armed group that would enforce its deed of commitment internally through the jurisdiction of its own tribunal.

In addition to the application of international or transnational legal norms, there is reportedly a significant practice for insurgent tribunals to apply local norms. While it is possible that rebel courts might apply the domestic law of the state on whose territory the conflict is taking place, the fragmented information available on the activities of such courts suggests that this is in fact unusual. Not surprisingly, non-state armed groups engaged in armed hostilities against a government may not be eager to bind themselves to the laws enacted by that very government. Instead, rebel movements often will call on regimes that have no link to the state, such as religious-based norms. Thus, in some conflicts, rebel courts have declared that they are applying *Sharī'ah*. In other cases, the rebel movement will have enacted its own substantive code, to be applied by the movement's courts. In Sri Lanka, for instance, the LTTE in 1994 adopted the Tamil Eelam Penal Code and Civil Code, drafted on the basis of a combination of Sri Lankan, Indian and British law, as explained by the then head of the Tamil Eelam Judicial Division:

> Distinguished Tamil jurists, legal experts and leading lawyers studied the British, Indian and Sri Lankan criminal justice systems before formulating the Tamil Eelam Penal Code. We have identified 439 types of crimes. Some crimes considered liable for punishment in the Sri Lankan Penal Code are treated less harshly in our Code. We are in the process of reviewing provisions in the penal code that permit

---

[38] Geneva Call, *Annual Report 2014: Protecting Civilians in Armed Conflict*, Geneva Call, Geneva, 2014.

capital punishment in the light of the increasing international trend against it. However, until such time anyone sentenced to death can petition the Review Committee seeking pardon.

We are endeavouring to introduce progressive laws relating to women. We brought an amendment to the penal code in connection with abortion. Earlier it was permissible on medical or other reasonable grounds only with the consent of both husband and wife. Under the said amendment a woman can take the decision on her own to abort her pregnancy within five months of conceiving on medical or other reasonable grounds.[39]

There are numerous examples of a similar approach by non-state armed groups in other conflicts from Afghanistan to Colombia. There is little surprise to find that the governments of the states in question deny any legal significance of any kind to such rebel codes. Beyond the blanket acceptance or rejection of the validity of insurgent laws, there are complex arguments that could be advanced to explore the possibility that to the limited agency of non-state armed groups recognised under public international law corresponds a limited law-making competence. For instance, it is quite common for armed insurgent groups to adopt codes of conduct that regulate the behaviour of their own members. The Taliban has adopted successive version of its code, the Layha, claimed to be a reflection of *Sharī'ah* rules on the conduct of war.[40] Given that such groups are required to implement international humanitarian law, it appears logical to acknowledge that this is a legitimate action on their part. If they control a portion of national territory, especially for a prolonged period of time as in Sri Lanka and Colombia, non-state armed groups are under a duty to administer the territory under their control, for which the adoption of various types of regulation may be unavoidable. Again, it seems logical to acknowledge that this is consonant with international law, and that some measure of validity attaches to rebel 'laws'. Could an insurgent group go further and, for example, criminalise the taking up of arms against the rebellion, in a manner that mirrors the state's criminalisation

---

[39] E. Pararajasingham, "Tamil Eelam – A De Facto State: Tamil Eelam Legal System", Tamilnet, 30 October 2003.

[40] Muhammad Munir, "The Layha for the Mujahideen: An Analysis of the Code of Conduct for the Taliban Fighters under Islamic Law", in *International Review of the Red Cross*, 2011, vol. 93, no. 881, p. 81; Olivier Bangerter, "Internal Control Codes of Conduct within Insurgent Armed Groups", Occasional Paper, Small Arms Survey, Graduate Institute of International and Development Studies, Geneva, 2012.

of the same against the government? It seems much more difficult to connect such an attempt to the limited agency that has been recognised to non-state armed groups under international law.[41]

The exercise of jurisdiction by insurgent courts thus raises difficult questions due to the interplay of various regimes both within international humanitarian law and among different fields of public international law. The law applicable to rebel tribunals as well as the law applicable by such bodies are in their entirety challenged by the absolute refusal of the territorial state to concede that there is any validity to such acts. The determination of the legal validity and significance of rebel judicial activity does not, however, rest entirely with the territorial state. While the latter may be in a position to exert greater influence, *de facto*, on the recognition of insurgent justice, other participants will likely be called to weigh in on the matter.

17.4. Legal Recognition of Insurgent Justice

The question of whether or not to grant any degree of recognition to insurgent justice is one that has presented itself to belligerents for a very long time. After the end of the United States Civil War, for example, there were cases in which one of the litigants sought to rely on a decision of the courts that had been established by the Confederate States in replacement of federal courts, raising the issue of whether the legal acts of the Confederate States were to be considered an absolute nullity, or whether some degree of validity ought to be acknowledged for at least some of the judicial decisions of Southern courts.[42] Although there were general statements of the illegitimacy of the Confederate administration and, as a consequence, the invalidity of its legal acts, the US Supreme Court quickly adopted a more nuanced approach, as illustrated in *Horn v. Lockhart* decided in 1873:

> We admit that the acts of the several States in their individu-
> al capacities, and of their different departments of govern-

---

[41] See Somer, 2007, p. 686, see *supra* note 8.

[42] See Warren Moise, *Rebellion in the Temple of Justice: The Federal and State Courts in South Carolina During the War Between the States*, iUniverse, Lincoln, NE, 2003; G. Edward White, "Recovering the Legal History of the Confederacy", in *Washington and Lee Legal Review*, 2011, vol. 68, no. 2, p. 467; N.D. Houghton, "The Validity of the Acts of Unrecognized De Facto Governments in the Courts of Non-Recognizing States", in *Minnesota Law Review*, 1928, vol. 13, p. 216.

ment, executive, judicial, and legislative, during the war, so far as they did not impair or tend to impair the supremacy of the National authority, or the just rights of citizens under the Constitution, are, in general, to be treated as valid and binding. The existence of a state of insurrection and war did not loosen the bonds of society, or do away with civil government, or the regular administration of the laws. Order was to be preserved, police regulations maintained, crime prosecuted, property protected, contracts enforced, marriages celebrated, estates settled, and the transfer and descent of property regulated precisely as in time of peace. No one that we are aware of seriously questions the validity of judicial or legislative acts in the insurrectionary States touching these and kindred subjects, where they were not hostile in their purpose or mode of enforcement to the authority of the National government, and did not impair the rights of citizens under the Constitution.[43]

While the historical reality of courts established by the Confederate States during the Civil War may differ in significant respect from the contemporary reality of insurgent tribunals, the interests at stake in creating judicial institutions as described in *Horn v. Lockhart* are present in many non-international armed conflicts today. When a non-state court system has, over a period of many years, issued thousands of decisions touching on all facets of life, it appears simply unrealistic to claim that all such acts will be wiped clean in one fell swoop. The territorial state as well as third states and international institutions will inevitably be called to devise a

---

[43] United States Supreme Court, *Horn v. Lockhart*, 84 U.S. 570, 580 (1873). See also *Texas v. White*, 74 U.S. 700:

> Exact definitions, within which the acts of a State government, organized in hostility to the Constitution and government of the United States, must be treated as valid or invalid need not be attempted. It may be said, however, that acts necessary to peace and good order among citizens, such, for example, as acts sanctioning and protecting marriage and the domestic relations, governing the course of descents regulating the conveyance and transfer of property, real and personal, and providing remedies for injuries to person and estate, and other similar acts, which would be valid if emanating from a lawful government, must be regarded in general as valid when proceeding from an actual, though unlawful, government, and that acts in furtherance or support of rebellion against the United States, or intended to defeat the just rights of citizens, and other acts of like nature, must, in general, be regarded as invalid and void.

more balanced approach, just as it occurred in the United States in the years following the Civil War.

The US Civil War litigation provides a point or departure in another sense: the US Supreme Court, in its decisions considering the legal validity of Confederate judicial holdings, of course relied on the United States Constitution. It goes without saying that the constitutional order of any country is unlikely to contemplate the possibility of a legitimate competing legal order. As such, the recognition of the validity of insurgent judicial decisions as in *Horn v. Lockhart* will ineluctably be in the nature of carefully bounded exceptions to a general principle of illegality. This highlights the importance of determining the legal frame of reference under which will be assessed the recognition owed to insurgent jurisprudence. For the state on whose territory the armed conflict is taking place, it seems logical that national law will be the primary legal framework, leading to a conclusion that the decisions of insurgent tribunals are not valid, save perhaps in circumstances where they exercised broad jurisdiction over a significant period of time in relation to a portion of the national territory and population. For other states, this may be a relevant legal framework as well, should there be questions of recognition of foreign judgments of either insurgent tribunals or of official courts pronouncing on the validity of the decision of an insurgent court. One can imagine, for instance, an action to claim on a debt that had been adjudicated on by a rebel court, with the claimant seeking to have the rebel court decision enforced as a foreign judgment. Private international law offers limited guidance as to the appropriate stance to take in such a situation, especially if due process requirements were met by the insurgent court. The third state may be placed in the uncomfortable position of have to make a determination of the viability of the rebel judicial system, in a manner that recalls the dilemmas facing states at a time when the practice of recognising governments still obtained.[44]

The recognition to be granted to the operation of an insurgent court is a matter that calls for scrutiny not only under the domestic legal order of the territorial and other states but also under public international law. Insurgent jurisprudence may give rise to at least four issues tied to recognition in the areas of international criminal law and international human rights law.

---

[44] Houghton, 1928, see *supra*, note 42.

A first question concerns the functional immunity of individuals in-volved in the administration of insurgent justice: are judges and lawyers running rebel courts liable to be held criminally accountable for the deten-tion and possibly execution of those tried and convicted by such courts? If it can be demonstrated that, under public international law, non-state armed groups may establish and operate their own courts to administer justice under their own or international legal standards, then it would seem to follow that any state attempting to hold judges and lawyers ac-countable for taking part in the operation of insurgent courts would thus breach international law. Even if such a functional immunity can be shown to be an accepted norm under international law, it would be condi-tional upon compliance with binding legal standards touching on the legit-imate creation and lawful operation of insurgent tribunals, as discussed earlier in this chapter. As such, the granting of functional immunity to officers of a rebel court would act as an incentive for them to ensure that the institution operated in conformity with international law. Conversely, holding judges and lawyers accountable for merely taking part in the functioning of rebel courts suggests that their compliance with interna-tional human rights and international humanitarian law would not dimin-ish their liability. The dilemma here recalls the discussion surrounding the granting of combatant immunity to rebel fighters in non-international armed conflicts which would, it is sometimes argued, act as compliance pull to attract greater respect for international humanitarian law.[45]

A second important facet of the recognition of the operation of in-surgent courts concerns the parties. In the criminal context, a trial against a person brought before a rebel court begs the question of the applicability of the doctrine of double jeopardy. This principle, also referred to as *ne bis in idem*, is contested as a general principle of international law that would proscribe any renewed prosecution of an accused that had already been convicted or acquitted of the same crime.[46] If the doctrine is contest-ed even as it relates to the previous criminal prosecution before the courts of a state, one may surmise that its application to the previous prosecution before the courts of non-state armed groups would be greeted with an

---

[45] Sandesh Sivakumaran, *The Law of Non-International Armed Conflict*, Oxford University Press, Oxford, 2012, p. 514–26.

[46] Gerard Conway, "*Ne Bis in Idem* in International Law", in *International Criminal Law Review*, 2003, vol. 3, no. 3, p. 217; Linda E. Carter, "The Principle of Complementarity and the International Criminal Court: The Role of *Ne Bis in Idem*", in *Santa Clara Journal of International Law*, 2010, vol. 8, no. 1, p. 165.

even greater degree of scepticism. The question does arise in a concrete manner with respect to the ICC, however, because the ICC Statute expressly incorporates the principle of *ne bis in idem* in Article 20(3):

> No person who has been tried by another court for conduct also proscribed under article 6, 7 or 8 shall be tried by the Court with respect to the same conduct unless the proceedings in the other court:
>
> (a) Were for the purpose of shielding the person concerned from criminal responsibility for crimes within the jurisdiction of the Court; or
>
> (b) Otherwise were not conducted independently or impartially in accordance with the norms of due process recognized by international law and were conducted in a manner which, in the circumstances, was inconsistent with an intent to bring the person concerned to justice.[47]

The provision raises a number of questions, but to focus only on those specific to the matter at hand, it bears underlining that the reference in the *chapeau* to "another court" is markedly open-ended. It stands in contrast, for example, with the reference to a previous trial before "a national court" found in the equivalent provision in the Statutes of the International Criminal Tribunal for the former Yugoslavia ('ICTY') and International Criminal Tribunal for Rwanda.[48] Bearing in mind the exacting procedural fairness demanded under sub-section (b), it does open a door to an argument that an insurgent court could be "another court" for the purposes of Article 20, although that possibility does not seem to have been discussed in Rome.[49] A variation of the *ne bis in idem* principle operates not as a bar to jurisdiction, as under the ICC Statute, but rather as a factor to be taken into consideration when determining the appropriate sentence for a crime (*ne bis poena in idem*). If a conduct has been sanctioned by a pre-

---

[47] ICC Statute, Art. 20(3), see *supra* note 10.

[48] See Stefano Manacorda and Giulio Vanacore, "The Right Not to Be Tried Twice for International Crimes: An Overview of the *Ne Bis in Idem* Principle with the Statutes of the ICC and the International Criminal Tribunals", in Triestino Mariniello (ed.), *The International Criminal Court in Search of Its Purpose and Identity*, Routledge, Oxford, 2015, p. 61.

[49] Jan Willms, "Courts of Armed Groups – A Tool for Inducing Higher Compliance with International Humanitarian Law?", in Heike Krieger (ed.), *Inducing Compliance with International Humanitarian Law: Lessons from the African Great Lakes Region*, Cambridge University Press, Cambridge, 2015, p. 149.

vious condemnation, then time served should be factored into the calculation of the appropriate sentence.[50]

Third, the issue of double jeopardy is directly related to the principle of complementarity of the jurisdiction of the ICC. According to this principle, entrenched in Article 17 of the ICC Statute, the Court does not have jurisdiction over a case that has been effectively investigated or prosecuted domestically.[51] This begs the question of whether it is conceivable that a prosecution before an insurgent tribunal could be considered a domestic prosecution sufficient to bar the exercise of jurisdiction by the ICC. In this respect, Article 17 appears on the one hand less congenial to any degree of recognition of insurgent justice when it provides that a case is inadmissible where "The case is being investigated or prosecuted by a state which has jurisdiction over it".[52] Unless one is able to attribute to the state the investigation and prosecution actually carried out by an irregular court, a position that appears quite impossible to defend successfully unless it concerns the activities of a court of a non-state armed group that is under the overall effective control of the state, then insurgent justice would not prevent the complementary jurisdiction of the ICC. On the other hand, Article 17(1)(c) provides as a distinct basis of inadmissibility that "[t]he person concerned has already been tried for conduct which is the subject of the complaint, and a trial by the Court is not permitted under Article 20, paragraph 3".[53] This is, fundamentally, a *renvoi* to the *ne bis in idem* principle as articulated in Article 20. As noted by the ICC Appeals Chamber in the *Gaddafi and Al-Senussi* case, the identical wording of the two provisions indicates that they were meant to have the same meaning.[54] In other words, the issue of complementarity

---

[50] Conway, 2003, p. 226, see *supra* note 46. This is reflected in ICC Statute, Art. 78(2), see *supra* note 10; and ICC RPE, Rule 145(2)(i), see *supra* note 16.

[51] See Sarah M.H. Nouwen, *Complementarity in the Line of Fire: The Catalysing Effect of the International Criminal Court in Uganda and Sudan*, Cambridge University Press, Cambridge, 2013.

[52] ICC Statute, Art. 17(1)(a) and (b), see *supra* note 10.

[53] *Ibid.*, Art. 17(1)(c).

[54] ICC, *Prosecutor v. Saif Al-Islam Gaddafi and Abdullah Al-Senussi*, Appeals Chamber, Judgment on the Appeal of Mr Abdullah Al-Senussi against the Decision of Pre-Trial Chamber I of 11 October 2013 Entitled "Decision on the admissibility of the case against Abdullah Al-Senussi", 24 July 2014, ICC-01/11-01/11-565, para. 222 (http://www.legal-tools.org/doc/ef20c7/). Note that the Chamber here refers more precisely to the similarity between ICC Statute, Art. 17(2)(c) and Art. 20(3)(b), which also share the same language, see *supra* note 10.

---

can be decided on the basis of the application of the *ne bis in idem* doctrine which, as we saw previously, does leave a door open to considering that insurgent courts could be "another court" whose intervention may block admissibility of a case to the ICC.

A fourth issue turning on the possible recognition of the jurisdiction of insurgent tribunals relates to international human rights and state responsibility. In both areas of public international law, recourse to supranational institutions or the endorsement of a claim by the state of nationality is predicated upon the prior exhaustion of local remedies. If a claim originates from a territory under the control of a non-state armed group that has established a functioning system of courts which otherwise comply with international law, must the claim be first presented to the rebel court? Again, situations of long-term control of national territory by an insurgent group, such as occurred in Sri Lanka with the LTTE or in Colombia with the Fuerzas Armadas Revolucionarias de Colombia ('FARC') , suggest that this scenario is far from purely academic. The European Court of Human Rights was confronted with this question in a recent decision, *Chiragov v. Armenia,* concerning the taking of property without compensation by forces linked to Armenia.[55] The takings occurred in the territory of Azerbaijan, and the claimants are nationals of that state as well. The authorities that were said to have interfered with property rights guaranteed under the European Convention on Human Rights were either agents of the state of Armenia or of the so-called Nagorno-Karabakh Republic, an entity that claims statehood but that is not recognised internationally as such. Under these circumstances, the Nagorno-Karabakh Republic can be described as a non-state armed group controlling a portion of Azerbaijani territory for more than two decades. During that time, it is said that the Nagorno-Karabakh Republic adopted over 600 laws, including basic laws establishing a Supreme Court and lower courts.[56] In its defence, Armenia claimed that the petition should be rejected because the claimants had failed to use the courts of the Nagorno-Karabakh Republic to enforce their property rights, adducing some decisions of these courts to illustrate their effectiveness.[57] In its judgment, the European Court of Human Rights found that Armenia had failed to show

---

[55]   Chiragov case, Judgment, see *supra* note 30.

[56]   *Ibid.*, para. 79.

[57]   *Ibid.*, paras. 107–109.

that an effective local remedy existed, on the basis that none of the court decisions adduced as evidence matched the situation of the petition before the European Court.[58] This is a very narrow holding, but it does not close the door to a conclusion that the courts established by the insurgents could in some cases offer an effective local remedy that would have to be exhausted before bringing a case to Strasbourg. Indeed, one might have expected the court to decide on the basis of this more general principle had that been its opinion.

These four issues linked to the recognition to be granted to the exercise of jurisdiction by insurgent tribunals underscore the point that the normative *rayonnement* of such tribunals extends well beyond the territory of the state on which an armed conflict is ongoing. Other participants in the international community, whether states, international institutions or others, will likely be confronted with the need to make a determination of the legal effects of insurgent jurisprudence. This in turn begs the question of what influence such jurisprudence might have on the fabric of public international law itself.

17.5. Who Owns the Rule of Law?

If we step back from the details of the conditions under which non-state armed groups may legitimately establish and operate their own tribunals, and the extent to which there should be recognition by other actors, we can see that this practice raises challenging questions about international humanitarian law and even our conception of the rule of law.

At a first level, insurgent justice represents a claim by non-state armed groups that they are not mere objects of the laws of war and human rights, but that they possess legal agency giving them power to interpret, apply and even develop international law. This is sometimes represented as the idea of the "ownership" of international humanitarian law by insurgent groups.[59] Under a traditional understanding of international law, the norms applicable to the administration of justice in an armed conflict

---

[58] *Ibid.*, paras. 117–118.

[59] Marco Sassoli, "Possible Legal Mechanisms to Improve Compliance by Armed Groups with International Humanitarian Law and International Human Rights Law", Paper at Conference on Curbing Human Rights Violations by Non-State Armed Groups, University of British Columbia, Vancouver, 2003; Sandesh Sivakumaran, "The Ownership of International Humanitarian Law: Non-State Armed Groups and the Formation and Enforcement of IHL Rules", in Perrin, 2012, pp. 87–101, see *supra* note 7.

are found first in treaties, negotiated and agreed upon by states, who can thereafter decide whether or not to bind themselves to conventional rules by way of ratification; second, the norms are found in custom, sublimated from the convergence of the practice of states and their *opinio juris*. According to this vision of the sources of the law applicable to insurgent justice, non-state armed groups have no role to play in the elaboration of such legal standards.[60] Authors such as Lon Fuller and Robert Cover have made the point, using different terms, that the actors whose behaviour we seek to regulate are much more likely to comply with a norm if they were involved in some way in the process of its elaboration.[61] Accordingly, the traditional accounts or treaty and, more significantly, custom that were sketched just above have been challenged in recent analyses of international law, with a view to make space for a diversity of actors in the creation of international law. It is now increasingly accepted that intergovernmental organisations and even non-governmental organisations can contribute by their practice to the emergence of international legal norms. For instance, the Appeals Chamber of the ICTY in the *Tadić* Interlocutory Appeal Decision invoked, among other factors, the practice of the International Committee of the Red Cross, a private entity created under Swiss law but whose particular role is recognised by states in the 1949 Geneva" Conventions and 1977 Protocols.[62] To a degree, there is an irresistible force to the practice of an organisation whose creation is linked to the very emergence of humanitarian law into positive international law, when determining what that law might be. The same irresistibility could be invoked in favour of taking into consideration the practice of non-state armed groups when analysing the customary status of the laws of war applicable to non-international armed conflicts. After all, if these norms are meant to apply to all sides of a civil war, and not only to the government, then is it really defensible to discard the practice of at least half of the belligerents in that context? The risk is that half-a-practice might lead us to

---

[60] This is the position adopted, for example, in the ICRC study, Jean-Marie Henckaerts and Louise Doswald-Beck, *Customary International Humanitarian Law*, vol. 1: *Rules*, Cambridge University Press, Cambridge, 2005.

[61] Lon Luvois Fuller, *The Morality of Law*, rev. ed., Yale University Press, New Haven, 1969; R.M. Cover, "The Supreme Court, 1982 Term – Foreword: Nomos and Narrative", in *Harvard Law Review*, 1983, vol. 97, p. 4.

[62] See Claudie Barrat, *Status of NGOs in International Humanitarian Law*, Martinus Nijhoff, Leiden, 2014.

---

half-a-law, a law that speaks to states but very little to insurgents. One may counter that states are creations of the law and owe their very recognition to public international law, thereby justifying an assumption that they behave in a manner that sustains the existence of the international legal order, even if the particulars of their behaviour cannot be said to always correspond to the specifics of the rules of international law. Non-state armed groups, on the hand, are not born through the operation of the law, but often in reaction against it. To go back to an earlier point, they often are, truly, outlaws: often perhaps, but not always, and not in everything that they do. When insurgents establish courts, they position themselves within a narrative of legality. Just like states, their behaviour may not always conform to the letter of the law, but to create a court is at the very least a practice of legality.[63]

The legal agency of non-state armed groups, as I pointed out earlier, is a reality that has been formally acknowledged by states in the 1949 Geneva Conventions and the 1977 Additional Protocols, in that the behaviour of insurgents can be the trigger for the applicability of international humanitarian law to an armed conflict. This can occur implicitly, by way of the application of humanitarian law by the rebels, or explicitly, by way of the declaration of a national liberation armed group under Article 96(3) of Protocol I or a special agreement between belligerents under Common Article 3 to apply some or all provisions of the 1949 Geneva Conventions. The legal agency of non-state armed groups extends beyond issues of applicability, however, and the establishment of insurgent tribunals highlights another facet of this agency. When an insurgent court invokes and applies conventional or customary international humanitarian law, it performs an act of legal interpretation in the fullest sense of the expression. This does not correspond to a claim that the legal significance that attaches to this interpretive act is equivalent to that of an interpretation by a state or a state-sanctioned court like the ICC, but it is a claim that the interpretation of international law by an insurgent court is not necessarily without any legal significance whatsoever.[64] After all, Article 38(1)(d) of the ICC Statute refers to "judicial decisions" as a subsidiary source of international law, without restricting it to decisions of international tribunals

---

[63] Brunnée and Toope, 2010, p. 69, see *supra* note 6.

[64] I have discussed this at some length in René Provost, "Interpretation in International Law as a Transcultural Project", in Andrea Bianchi, Daniel Peat and Matthew Windsor (eds.), *Interpretation in International Law*, Oxford University Press, Oxford, 2015, pp. 290–308.

or even state tribunals.[65] In addition to the interpretation of treaties and customs, the legal agency of non-state armed groups would suggest that their judicial activities can constitute practice which contributes to the formation of customary law.

The reality of insurgent jurisprudence raises a broader challenge to our very notion of the rule of law. That concept is more often than not formulated in a manner that aligns it with an idealised vision of justice administered by state institutions. For example, for the United Nations, the rule of law

> refers to a principle of governance in which all persons, in-
> stitutions and entities, public and private, including the State
> itself, are accountable to laws that are publicly promulgated,
> equally enforced and independently adjudicated, and which
> are consistent with international human rights norms and
> standards. It requires, as well, measures to ensure adherence
> to the principles of supremacy of law, equality before the
> law, accountability to the law, fairness in the application of
> the law, separation of powers, participation in decision-
> making, legal certainty, avoidance of arbitrariness and pro-
> cedural and legal transparency.[66]

It quite clear that informal legal orders and their institutions are unlikely to fulfil all the criteria of legality corresponding to this vision of the rule of law. What is striking here, as noted by Brian Tamanaha, is not only that this overlooks the fact that in many places the dominant legal order and implementing institutions are not those of the state but rather informal, community or customary ones, but that these are often much preferred by the local population because they are more efficient and better grounded in local culture.[67] In this respect, we can situate the discussion of the significance of insurgent justice within a general proliferation of transnation-

---

[65] See, for example, Aldo Zammit Borda, "A Formal Approach to Article 38 (1)(d) of the ICJ Statute from the Perspective of the International Criminal Courts and Tribunals", in *European Journal of International Law*, 2013, vol. 24, no. 2, p. 649.

[66] United Nations Security Council, Report of the Secretary-General: The Rule of Law and Transitional Justice in Conflict and Post-Conflict Societies, 23 August 2004, UN Doc. S/2004/616, para. 6.

[67] See Brian Z. Tamanaha, "Introduction: A Bifurcated Theory of Law in Hybrid Societies", in Matthias Kötter, Tilman J. Röder, Gunnar Folke Schuppert and Rüdiger Wolfrum (eds.), *Non-state Justice Institutions and the Law: Decision-making at the Interface of Tradition, Religion and the State*, Palgrave Macmillan, London, 2015, p. 1.

al judicial institutions that do not owe their legitimacy to state consent. Whether it be international commercial arbitration, popular tribunals or courts of opinion established by non-governmental organisations, or a papal tribunal established to try bishops in relation to sexual abuses, there are several other sites of normativity in which actors adopt and adapt the judicial model to administer justice in some sense.[68] The *Tribunal de les aigües de Valencia*, in Spain, is an example of one such institution that predates both the emergence of Spain and of the Westphalian state, operating on terms that do not fully align with the contemporary requirements of the rule of law, and yet which continues to function in a manner that has been embraced rather than resisted by the Spanish state.[69] While this may be an especially arresting example, it would not be very difficult to list a number of similar judicial institutions recognised or tolerated within their jurisdiction by states. The point is to challenge a vision of the rule of law that projects a picture of law as necessarily monistic and centralised, even as it relates to formal law as applied in a democratic and peaceful state.[70]

The challenge to the rule of law embodied in the creation of courts by non-state armed groups is not limited to questioning whether states alone define the rule of law, or whether insurgent groups may take ownership not only of international humanitarian law but also of the concept the rule of law itself. The challenge emerges as one to the very possibility that a single category of legal agents may "own" the rule of law. In the literature on the laws of war that relies on the metaphor of ownership, little heed is paid to the features of the concept that underpins it: the very notion of ownership speaks to the possibility of a proprietary right, a right to exercise dominium over something and to exclude others.[71] This is indeed consistent with the vision of the rule of law as monistic and centralised in the hands of the state, evoked above, leading to the possibility that a government may not only delegitimise competing norms and institutions but even withhold permission to merely share legal knowledge, as strikingly

---

[68] A number of these are explored in the other chapters of Kötter *et al.*, *ibid.*

[69] More information on this tribunal, which adjudicates on disputes relating to the use of water around Valencia, can be found on its website: www.tribunaldelasaguas.org.

[70] See Roderick A. Macdonald and David Sandomierski, "Against Nomopolies", in *Northern Ireland Legal Quarterly*, 2006, vol. 57, no. 4, pp. 610, 615.

[71] See, for example, Sivakumaran, 2012, see *supra* note 59; Richard J. Goldstone's contribution to this volume.

illustrated in *Holder v. Humanitarian Law Project*.[72] To conceive of the remedy as one whereby non-state armed groups are invited to take ownership of international humanitarian law and possibly the rule of law is to encourage the framing of competing claims to monistic and centralised visions of law, centred in armed groups rather than in states. Instead of ownership of the law, one could aspire to fellowship in the law, to underscore the necessarily dialogical features of the rule of law. Law, in this vision, is not so much a structure to impose uniformity but rather a vocabulary through which we can mediate our differences.

17.6. Conclusion

The practice by some non-state armed groups of creating their own tribunals thus emerges as a complex, multifaceted question that cannot be answered by the simple invocation of a state monopoly on the administration of justice. From what little is known about insurgent courts that have operated in conflict zones in various parts of the world, it appears that the reasons that move them to do so are varied, leading them to shape and operate these institutions in ways that will often conflict with some elements of applicable public international law.

The variety and complexity relate to each of the four aspects of insurgent justice that have been canvassed in this paper. First, regarding the legitimacy of setting such a tribunal, the evolution in the relevant norms of international humanitarian law was noted, but these clarify the picture only to a limited extent. It will be important, when more is known about the actual structures of rebel courts, to compare them to the equally varied practice of states in the administration of justice in conflict zones. Only then can a reasoned position be developed to cogently describe the conditions of validity of the establishment of an insurgent court under international law.

Second, the law applicable to and by insurgent tribunals suggest the interplay of a number of distinct legal regimes, echoing broader concerns about the fragmentation of international law and lingering uncertainties about the intersection of national and international laws. The law applicable to rebel courts includes the various strands of treaty and customary

---

[72] United States Supreme Court, *Holder v. Humanitarian Law Project*, 561 US 1 (2010), upholding a statute barring instruction in international humanitarian law to Kurdish Workers' Party insurgents in Turkey.

international humanitarian law applicable to non-international and international armed conflicts, international human rights law inasmuch as it remains applicable to situations of war and international criminal law. The law applicable by insurgent tribunals can include conventional and customary norms, in a manner not necessarily derivative of the consent of the state on whose territory the conflict is occurring, transnational norms adhered to by a non-state armed group, the municipal law of the territorial state, and "legislation" enacted by the insurgents themselves. Needless to point out that there is no clear hierarchy among these various legal orders, and that even the invocation of the *jus cogens* nature of some of the international norms does not necessarily bring about greater clarity.

Third, insurgent justice raises a number of issues for a range of international agents, and not only for the state against which a non-state armed group is fighting. For the territorial state, although there sometimes are blanket statements as to the absolute legal invalidity of all acts of rebel courts, it will often not be possible or plausible to discard in a generalised fashion everything that these courts have done. All will depend on the duration and extent of the exercise of jurisdiction by rebel tribunals. In addition to the territorial state, other states may be confronted with the need to make a determination of the validity of legal acts of insurgent groups, including decisions of their courts. Here again, the application of private international law by the courts of many states have been marked by caution, not infrequently resulting in the recognition of the effective administration of a territory by an entity that is not the recognised state. This can play out in civil as well as in criminal matters. Likewise, international institutions may be faced with the same dilemma, including whether a prosecution before a rebel court could block the complementary jurisdiction of the ICC, or whether a petitioner must turn to insurgent courts in order to exhaust local remedies before seizing an international human rights body.

Fourth, and finally, all these complex issues raise foundational questions regarding the nature of the rule of law in the international community. Much has been made in the last several years of the rise of actors other than states as recognised legal persons, marking what some have described as a tectonic shift of the international legal order away from a state-centric one in favour of a polycentric one. Perhaps unexpectedly, the practice by non-state armed groups of establishing their own tribunals captures this evolution and begs the question of what its limits might be.

INDEX

A

Abe, Shinzo, 179
absence without leave, 22
Abu Ghraib, 279, 331, 349, 357, 362, 388
Abū Zahra, Sheikh Muhammad, 141, 145, 152
abuse of alcohol, 22
accountability
  failure in, 195
  gap, 13
  good image, 342
  individual, 219
  Japan's lack of will to acknowledge, 207
  judicial proceedings, 110
  lack of, 393
  mechanisms, 422
  preparedness, 111
  processes, 111
  public, 322
  sexual violence, 171
  within insurgent groups, 421
ad hoc tribunals, vii, 35, 39, 112, 217, 416
adjustability, 218
Afghanistan, 24, 83, 90, 261, 273, 277, 284, 293, 350, 357, 425, 441
  US–Afghan relations, 350
African Court of Human and People's Rights, 254
African Union, 244, 252, 363, 375, 381
  Mission in Somalia, 379
  UN/African Union hybrid tribunal, 249
after-action reports, 391
after-action reviews, 298
aggression, 254, 257, 386
AIDS, 359
Al Qaim, 335
al-Adnani, Abu Muhammad, 55
al-Bashir, Omar Hassan, 58, 216
al-Gaddafi, Muammar, 340

Algeria, 327
Alien Tort Claims Act, 187
Allah, 145, 148, 154, 161
al-Nusrah Front, 55
al-Qaʻida, 150, 262, 267, 273, 282
al-Qaraḍāwī, Sheikh Yusūf, 149
al-Qayyim, Imam ibn, 148
al-Sādāt, Anwar, 150
al-Shaybānī, Muḥammad ibn al-Ḥasan, 142, 152
al-Sistani, Ali, 52
Alston, Philip, 322, 366
al-Walīd, Khālid ibn, 164
Ambos, Kai, 233
American Convention on Human Rights, 419
amnesty, 203, 230, 234, 244, 256, 404
Amnesty International, 429
Angkatan Bersenjata Republik Indonesia, 113
Anglosphere, 3
Arab League, 421
Arab peninsula, 144
armed conflict
  humanisation, 19
Armenia, 435, 448
Arms Trade Treaty, 50
Army Trial Defense Services, 308
Arnold, Roberta, 339
Articles of War, 263
articulation process, 3, 42
Asian Women's Fund, 178, 208
assault, 193, 261, 270, 279, 351, 357, 421
asymmetry, 111, 424, 437
atomic bomb, 211
Australia, 137, 359
  Australian Defence Force, 361
  Defence Force, 384
aut dedere aut judicare, 407
authority, 372
  command, 22

H

hadith, 144, 152, 164
Hague Convention No. IV of 1907, 180, 191, 275
Hague, William, 240
Hain, Peter, 98
Haines, David, 162
Haiti, 349, 360, 367
Halleck, Henry W., 37, 61
Harman, Jane, 352
Hashimoto, Ryutaro, 179
hearts and minds, 9, 15
Helmand, 350
hierarchy, 361, 372, 390
high-tech environment, 27
Hillman, Elizabeth L., 61
Himmler, Heinrich, 102

Ḥ

ḥirābah, 160

H

Hirohito, 187
historical evolution, 11
historical lessons, 15
HIV, 359, 371
Holocaust, 117
Holt, Joseph, 80
holy war, 146, 151
honour, 63, 162, 182, 383, 421
Hood, Gavin, 253
hors de combat, 406, 422
Houlder, Bruce, 85
House of Lords
  In re Pinochet, 121
Human Rights Watch, 379
human trafficking, 345, 357, 359, 372
humanitarian interventions, 377
Huntington, Samuel P., 66
Hussein, Saddam, 4

I

immunity, 188, 316, 373, 445
  combatant, 424
impartial international justice, 95
impartiality, 33, 387

imperialism, 103
implementation, international humanitarian law, 43
impunity, 10, 144, 321, 363, 380, 390, 411, 427
incentive, 5, 12, 51, 86, 114, 166, 215, 221, 236, 371, 394, 425, 445
inclusion, 378
indecency, 384
independence, 10, 26, 32, 230, 246, 256, 427, 433
  judicial, 216
India, 215, 218, 440
indigence, 318
indivisibility of trial, 408
Indonesia, 178, 192, 203
Indonesian Armed Forces, 107–15
Indonesia-Timor Leste Commission of Truth and Friendship, 11, 108, 112
information age, 365
inhumane treatment, 387
injustice, 384
innovative approach, 1
instability, 355, 375
institutionalism, 361
insurgent groups, 421
  courts established by, 421
  jurisdiction of courts established by, 431
insurgent justice, 423
  legality of, 423
  recognition of, 423
inter arma silent leges, 126
Inter-American Commission, 401, 419
Inter-American Court of Human Rights
  19 Merchants v. Colombia, 401
  Castillo Petruzzi et al. v. Peru, 400
  Lori Berenson Mejía v. Perú, 400
  Mapiripán Massacre v. Colombia, 402
  Palamara-Iribarne v. Chile, 399, 411
  Pueblo Bello Massacre v. Colombia, 402
  Teodoro Cabrera García and Rodolfo Montiel Flores v. Mexico, 401
  Velasquez-Rodriguez v. Honduras, 434
  Vélez Restrepo v. Colombia, 402, 412
international armed conflict, 37, 266, 424
International Center for Transitional Justice, 235

Supreme Court, 192
Tokyo District Court, 189
Tokyo High Court, 190
US–Japan relations, 188
War Ministry, 185
Yamaguchi District Court, 190
Japutra, Kiki Anastasia, 171
Jefferson, Thomas, 67, 321
Jenks, Christopher, 261
jihād, 143, 146, 154, 168
jingoism, 95
Johnson, Lyndon B., 83
Jørgensen, Nina H.B., 186
judicial capacity, 12
jurisdiction
    civilian, 7, 412, 419
    exclusive, 68
    human rights, 412
    military, 7, 401, 412, 419
    over civilians, 29
    ratione materiae, 400, 410
    universal, 4, 11, 38, 117, 120, 248,
        404, 429
jurisprudence, international, 408
jus ad bellum, 160
jus cogens, 182, 187, 214, 455
jus in bello, xiii, 156, 160
justice
    alternative transitional, 111

K

Kabila, Joseph, 253
Kabul, 310
Kagame, Paul, 253
Kaldor, Mary, 38
Kandahar, 261
Kenya, 12, 91, 230, 238, 253, 258
kevod ha-briyyot, 123
Kfar Kassem, 125
kidnapping, 357
Kishi, Nobusuke, 197
Kitāb al-Siyar al-Kabir, 142, 152, 159
knowledge communities, 7
knowledge product, 2
knowledge-resource, 3
Koichi, Kato, 176
Korea, 182, 188, 197, 200
Kosovo, 345, 421
Krieger, Heike, 366, 394

Kuwait, 300

L

lack of interest, 213
larceny, 270
law enforcement professionals, 306
lawlessness, xi, 59, 80, 384
leadership, 18, 371
Lebanon, 3
legal firms, 96
legal pluralism, 425
legal positivism, 425
leniency, 294
lex generalis, 436
lex specialis, 436
Liberation Tigers of Tamil Eelam, 56,
    423, 440, 448
Liberia, 49
Libya, 12, 52, 58, 230, 239, 340
    National Transitional Council, 52
Lieber Code, 36, 79, 182
Lieber, Francis, 36, 62
Lincoln, Abraham, 80
linguistic barrier, 392
live testimony, 302
local population, 10, 25, 48, 327, 330,
    345, 357, 365, 380, 452
Lord's Resistance Army, 241, 256
loyalty, 25, 108, 383
Lund, Terje, 27

M

MacArthur, Douglas, 200
Machiavelli, Niccolò, 354
Maged, Adel, 141
Mahony, Christopher, 229
maltreatment of persons, 278
management of violence, 385
Mao Zedong, 48
Martens Clause, 182
martyrdom, 150
Mau Mau rebellion, 91
Mazel, Marlene, 117
McClellan, George B., 61
Medina, Ernest, 63
Melos, v
mens rea, 277
mentorship, 374, 380

O

N

P

Rosenblatt, Franklin D., 293
Rowe, Peter, 386
rule of law, 15, 23, 74, 87, 92, 100, 118,
   131, 328, 341, 355, 374, 423, 449
Russia, 180, 250, 421
Rwanda, 3, 31, 55, 421

S

San Francisco Peace Treaty, 188, 191
sanctions, 115, 143, 274, 283, 321, 328,
   361, 368, 373, 386, 395, 421
Saxe, Maurice de, 355
Schaack, Beth Van, 284
Schweizerische Volkspartei, 341
Scott, Winfield, 72
Second World War, 12, 24, 38, 51, 55, 68,
   118, 171, 181, 196, 201, 263, 403, 409,
   416, 432
sectarianism, 95
security risks, 15
security sector reform, 355, 374, 376
self-awareness, 3
self-defence, 154
self-development, 11
self-development and prevention, 16
self-examination, 85
self-interest
   long-term, 23
   negative, 6
   positive, 6
   realist, 6
self-regulation, 6, 369
self-respect, 17
self-scrutiny, 215
Service Prosecuting Authority, 11
Setsuzo, Kinbara, 184
sexual
   abuse, 174, 342, 345, 352, 359, 362,
     372, 379, 453
   crimes, 359
   slavery, 181, 186, 193, 199, 208
Sexual Harassment/Assault Response and
   Prevention programme, 351
sexually transmitted diseases, 184
Shakespeare, William, 25
shame, 12, 99, 175, 209, 218, 221, 346
Shanghai Incident, 171
Sharī'ah, 12, 141–69, 163, 166, 421, 440

jus ad bellum, 144
jus in bello, 156
  just war, 145
Sherman, William Tecumseh, 79
Sierra Leone, 3, 49, 56, 421
sishankamrata, 113
Sixth Amendment, 333
Skelton, William B., 67
Slavery Convention, 182
sleep deprivation, 320
smuggling, 357
Society for a Switzerland without an
  Army, 342
socio-cultural impact, 16
Soeharto, Haji Mohamed, 113
Somalia, 340, 345, 358, 363, 367, 379
  Commission of Inquiry, 346
SONG Tianying, 1, 43
sovereignty, 222, 398
Soviet Union, 110, 197, 201
Spain, 453
Spanish Civil War, 56
Special Court for Sierra Leone, 39, 95,
  241, 248, 339, 374, 422
  Prosecutor v. Brima, 422
  Prosecutor v. Gbao, 422
Spycatcher, 98
Srebrenica, vii, 18, 53, 55, 347, 348
Sri Lanka, 49, 56, 349, 360, 421, 423,
  440, 448
stabilisation, 376
Stalin, Joseph, 432
standard operating procedures, 394
Stanford conference, 3, 14
Stanford Prison experiment, 101
Stanford University, 1
State-building, 374, 378
status of forces agreements, 28, 323, 373
statute of limitations, 189, 191, 404
stick, 4, 85
Sudan, 49, 58, 216, 249, 421
sufficient degree of specificity, 238
summary punishment, 30
summary trials, 386
Sunna, 142, 157, 167
Sūrat al-'Anfāl, 145
Switzerland
   Army Special Forces, 340
   Criminal Code, 353

TOAEP TEAM

OTHER VOLUMES IN THE PUBLICATION SERIES

Morten Bergsmo, Mads Harlem and Nobuo Hayashi (editors):
Importing Core International Crimes into National Law
Torkel Opsahl Academic EPublisher
Oslo, 2010
FICHL Publication Series No. 1 (Second Edition, 2010)
ISBN: 978-82-93081-00-5

Nobuo Hayashi (editor):
National Military Manuals on the Law of Armed Conflict
Torkel Opsahl Academic EPublisher
Oslo, 2010
FICHL Publication Series No. 2 (Second Edition, 2010)
ISBN: 978-82-93081-02-9

Morten Bergsmo, Kjetil Helvig, Ilia Utmelidze and Gorana Žagovec:
The Backlog of Core International Crimes Case Files in Bosnia and Herzegovina
Torkel Opsahl Academic EPublisher
Oslo, 2010
FICHL Publication Series No. 3 (Second Edition, 2010)
ISBN: 978-82-93081-04-3

Morten Bergsmo (editor):
Criteria for Prioritizing and Selecting Core International Crimes Cases
Torkel Opsahl Academic EPublisher
Oslo, 2010
FICHL Publication Series No. 4 (Second Edition, 2010)
ISBN: 978-82-93081-06-7

Morten Bergsmo and Pablo Kalmanovitz (editors):
Law in Peace Negotiations
Torkel Opsahl Academic EPublisher
Oslo, 2010
FICHL Publication Series No. 5 (Second Edition, 2010)
ISBN: 978-82-93081-08-1

Morten Bergsmo, César Rodríguez Garavito, Pablo Kalmanovitz and Maria Paula Saffon (editors):
Distributive Justice in Transitions
Torkel Opsahl Academic EPublisher
Oslo, 2010
FICHL Publication Series No. 6 (2010)
ISBN: 978-82-93081-12-8

Morten Bergsmo, César Rodriguez-Garavito, Pablo Kalmanovitz and Maria Paula Saffon (editors):
Justicia Distributiva en Sociedades en Transición
Torkel Opsahl Academic EPublisher
Oslo, 2012
FICHL Publication Series No. 6 (2012)
ISBN: 978-82-93081-10-4

Morten Bergsmo (editor):
Complementarity and the Exercise of Universal Jurisdiction for Core International Crimes
Torkel Opsahl Academic EPublisher
Oslo, 2010
FICHL Publication Series No. 7 (2010)
ISBN: 978-82-93081-14-2

Morten Bergsmo (editor):
Active Complementarity: Legal Information Transfer
Torkel Opsahl Academic EPublisher
Oslo, 2011
FICHL Publication Series No. 8 (2011)
ISBN print: 978-82-93081-56-2
ISBN e-book: 978-82-93081-55-5

Morten Bergsmo (editor):
Abbreviated Criminal Procedures for Core International Crimes
Torkel Opsahl Academic EPublisher
Brussels, 2017
FICHL Publication Series No. 9 (2018)
ISBN print: 978-82-93081-20-3
ISBN e-book: 978-82-8348-104-4

Sam Muller, Stavros Zouridis, Morly Frishman and Laura Kistemaker (editors):
The Law of the Future and the Future of Law
Torkel Opsahl Academic EPublisher
Oslo, 2010
FICHL Publication Series No. 11 (2011)
ISBN: 978-82-93081-27-2

Morten Bergsmo, Alf Butenschøn Skre and Elisabeth J. Wood (editors):
Understanding and Proving International Sex Crimes
Torkel Opsahl Academic EPublisher
Beijing, 2012
FICHL Publication Series No. 12 (2012)
ISBN: 978-82-93081-29-6

Morten Bergsmo (editor):
Thematic Prosecution of International Sex Crimes
Torkel Opsahl Academic EPublisher
Beijing, 2012
FICHL Publication Series No. 13 (2012)
ISBN: 978-82-93081-31-9

Terje Einarsen:
The Concept of Universal Crimes in International Law
Torkel Opsahl Academic EPublisher
Oslo, 2012
FICHL Publication Series No. 14 (2012)
ISBN: 978-82-93081-33-3

莫滕·伯格斯默 凌岩(主编):
国家主权与国际刑法
Torkel Opsahl Academic EPublisher
Beijing, 2012
FICHL Publication Series No. 15 (2012)
ISBN: 978-82-93081-58-6

Morten Bergsmo and LING Yan (editors):
State Sovereignty and International Criminal Law
Torkel Opsahl Academic EPublisher
Beijing, 2012
FICHL Publication Series No. 15 (2012)
ISBN: 978-82-93081-35-7

Morten Bergsmo and CHEAH Wui Ling (editors):
Old Evidence and Core International Crimes
Torkel Opsahl Academic EPublisher
Beijing, 2012
FICHL Publication Series No. 16 (2012)
ISBN: 978-82-93081-60-9

YI Ping:
戦争と平和の間---発足期日本国際法学における「正しい戦争」の観念とその帰結
Torkel Opsahl Academic EPublisher
Beijing, 2013
FICHL Publication Series No. 17 (2013)
ISBN: 978-82-93081-66-1

Morten Bergsmo and SONG Tianying (editors):
On the Proposed Crimes Against Humanity Convention
Torkel Opsahl Academic EPublisher
Brussels, 2014
FICHL Publication Series No. 18 (2014)
ISBN: 978-82-93081-96-8

Morten Bergsmo (editor):
Quality Control in Fact-Finding
Torkel Opsahl Academic EPublisher
Florence, 2013
FICHL Publication Series No. 19 (2013)
ISBN: 978-82-93081-78-4

Morten Bergsmo, CHEAH Wui Ling and YI Ping (editors):
Historical Origins of International Criminal Law: Volume 1
Torkel Opsahl Academic EPublisher
Brussels, 2014
FICHL Publication Series No. 20 (2014)
ISBN: 978-82-93081-11-1

Morten Bergsmo, CHEAH Wui Ling and YI Ping (editors):
Historical Origins of International Criminal Law: Volume 2
Torkel Opsahl Academic EPublisher
Brussels, 2014
FICHL Publication Series No. 21 (2014)
ISBN: 978-82-93081-13-5

Morten Bergsmo, CHEAH Wui Ling, SONG Tianying and YI Ping (editors):
Historical Origins of International Criminal Law: Volume 3

Torkel Opsahl Academic EPublisher
Brussels, 2015
FICHL Publication Series No. 22 (2015)
ISBN print: 978-82-8348-015-3
ISBN e-book: 978-82-8348-014-6

Morten Bergsmo, CHEAH Wui Ling, SONG Tianying and YI Ping (editors):
Historical Origins of International Criminal Law: Volume 4
Torkel Opsahl Academic EPublisher
Brussels, 2015
FICHL Publication Series No. 23 (2015)
ISBN print: 978-82-8348-017-7
ISBN e-book: 978-82-8348-016-0

Morten Bergsmo, Klaus Rackwitz and SONG Tianying (editors):
Historical Origins of International Criminal Law: Volume 5
Torkel Opsahl Academic EPublisher
Brussels, 2017
FICHL Publication Series No. 24 (2017)
ISBN print: 978-82-8348-106-8
ISBN e-book: 978-82-8348-107-5

Morten Bergsmo and SONG Tianying (editors):
Military Self-Interest in Accountability for Core International Crimes
First Edition
Torkel Opsahl Academic EPublisher
Brussels, 2015
FICHL Publication Series No. 25 (2015)
ISBN print: 978-82-93081-61-6
ISBN e-book: 978-82-93081-81-4

Wolfgang Kaleck:
Double Standards: International Criminal Law and the West
Torkel Opsahl Academic EPublisher
Brussels, 2015
FICHL Publication Series No. 26 (2015)
ISBN print: 978-82-93081-67-8
ISBN e-book: 978-82-93081-83-8

LIU Daqun and ZHANG Binxin (editors):
Historical War Crimes Trials in Asia
Torkel Opsahl Academic EPublisher
Brussels, 2016
FICHL Publication Series No. 27 (2015)
ISBN print: 978-82-8348-055-9
ISBN e-book: 978-82-8348-056-6

Mark Klamberg (editor):
Commentary on the Law of the International Criminal Court
Torkel Opsahl Academic EPublisher
Brussels, 2017
FICHL Publication Series No. 29 (2017)
ISBN print: 978-82-8348-100-6
ISBN e-book: 978-82-8348-101-3

All volumes are freely available online at http://www.toaep.org/ps/. For printed copies, see http://toaep.org/about/distribution/. For reviews of earlier books in this Series in academic journals and yearbooks, see http://toaep.org/reviews/.